The Lessons of Modern War

Volume II

The Lessons of Modern War

Volume II: The Iran-Iraq War

Anthony H. Cordesman
and Abraham R. Wagner

Westview Press
BOULDER AND SAN FRANCISCO

Mansell Publishing Limited
LONDON

Much of the research presented in this volume was supported by the Defense
Advanced Research Projects Agency (DARPA). The views expressed are, of
course, those of the authors and are not intended to reflect any position of
DARPA or the U.S. Department of Defense. The authors are deeply indebted to
Dr. Craig Fields and Dr. Anthony Tether of DARPA for their continued support
and insight.

Published in 1990 in the United States of America by Westview
Press, Inc., 5500 Central Avenue, Boulder, Colorado 80301

Published in 1990 in Great Britain by Mansell Publishing Limited,
A Cassell Imprint, Artillery House, Artillery Row, London SW1P 1RT, England

Reprinted in February 1991

Library of Congress Cataloging-in-Publication Data
Cordesman, Anthony H.
  The lessons of modern war.
  Includes bibliographical references.
  Contents: v. 1. The Arab-Israeli conflicts, 1973–
1989—v. 2. The Iran-Iraq war.
  1. Military art and science—History—20th century.
2. Military history, Modern—20th century. 3. Middle
East—History, Military. I. Wagner, Abraham R.
II. Title.
U42.C59 1990   355.4'8   89-16631
ISBN 0-8133-0954-9 (v. 1)
ISBN 0-8133-0955-7 (v. 2)
ISBN 0-8133-0956-5 (v. 3)

British Library Cataloguing in Publication Data
Cordesman, Anthony H.
  The lessons of modern war.
  Vol. 2, The Iran-Iraq war
  1. Warfare
  I. Title II. Wagner, Abraham R.
  355'.02
  ISBN 0-7201-2044-6

Printed and bound in the United States of America

The paper used in this publication meets the requirements
of the American National Standard for Permanence of Paper
for Printed Library Materials Z39.48–1984.

10   9   8   7   6   5   4   3

To Rachel and Harry

CONTENTS

TABLES AND FIGURES

Figures

PREFACE

This is the second volume in a series of three volumes that the authors have written with the assistance of Raymond J. Picquet, W. Andrew Terril, and Carol K. Wagner and with the support of the Royal United Services Institute. These volumes cover five major wars: the Arab-Israeli conflict of October 1973, the Israeli invasion of Lebanon in 1982, the Iran-Iraq War, the Soviet invasion of Afghanistan, and the Falklands conflict with Argentina. Volume I covers the lessons of the Arab-Israeli arms race between 1973 and 1989 and of the Arab-Israeli conflicts of 1973 and 1982. Volume II in this series covers the Iran-Iraq War. Volume III covers the Falklands and Afghan conflicts and provides the general conclusions of the study.

Each of the three volumes is written as an independent work, but the analysis of the wars in question is standardized as much as possible. The analysis of major conflicts is divided into sections that analyze the forces involved, the history of the conflict, key aspects of the operational art of war, and the impact of major types of forces and weapons.

The analysis in each volume focuses on military events and lessons and treats the politics of each conflict only to the extent necessary to understand the grand strategy, strategy, and tactics of the conflict. Where possible, key events and data are described in a way that will allow the reader to draw his or her own conclusions. A deliberate effort has been made to avoid oversimplifying the complex nature of modern war.

The sources and methods used in each volume are described at its end, and a research bibliography is provided for each conflict. Frequent use is made of tables and charts to allow comparisons of forces, portray force shifts over time, and show the key performance features of major weapons. In most cases, the data are shown as provided in the original source rather than standardized or altered to eliminate minor conflicts. This is done to allow the reader to see the original data on which the analyses are based.

Anthony H. Cordesman

ACRONYMS

AA	anti-aircraft
AC&W	air control and warning
ACDA	Arms Control and Disarmament Agency
ADIZ	air defense interception zone
AEW	airborne early warning
AFV	armored fighting vehicle
AIFV	armored infantry fighting vehicle
ALINDIEN	French Indian Ocean Command
AMCM	airborne mine countermeasures
APC	armored personnel carrier
ARM	anti-radiation missile
ASW	anti-submarine warfare
ATGM	anti-tank guided missile
AWACS	airborne warning and air control system
BM	battlefield management
BPD	barrels per day
BVR	beyond visual range
C^{3}I	command, control, communications, and intelligence
CAP	combat air patrol
CAS	combined antenna system
CEP	circular error of probability
CIA	Central Intelligence Agency
CIC	combat information center
CIWS	close-in weapons system
CJTFME	Commander, Joint Task Force Middle East
COMAIR	commercial aircraft
COMINT	communications intelligence
CPA	closest point of approach
CPMIEC	China Precision Machinery for Import and Export Corporation
CS	O-chlorobenzyl malononitrile
DWT	dead weight ton
ECM	electronic countermeasure
ELINT	electronic intelligence
ESM	electronic support measures

ESSM	electronic systems support measures
EW	early warning
FAC	fast attack craft; forward air controllers
FEBA	forward edge of the battle area
FGA	fighter ground attack
FLIR	forward-looking infrared
FRG	Federal Republic of Germany
GCC	Gulf Cooperation Council
GCI	ground-controlled intercept
GDP	gross domestic product
HE	high explosive
HUMINT	human intelligence
IAD	international air distress
IAEA	International Atomic Energy Agency
ICI	Imperial Chemical Industries
ICP	Iraqi Communist Party
IDS	identification supervisor
IEA	International Energy Agency
IFF	identification of friend and foe
IR	infrared
IRBM	intermediate-range ballistic missile
IRC	Islamic Revolutionary Council
IRGC	Iranian Revolutionary Guards Corps
IRP	Islamic Republican Party
JCSS	Jaffe Center for Strategic Studies
KDP	Kurdish Democratic Party
KDPI	Kurdish Democratic Party of Iran
KWU	Kraftwerke Union
LCU	landing craft-utility
LNG	liquid natural gas
LPG	liquefied propane gas
LSD	landing-ship dock
LSL	landing-ship logistic
LST	landing ship-tank
MAD	military air distress
MCMV	mine countermeasure vessel
MMBD	millions of barrels per day
MRL	multiple rocket launcher
MSB	minesweeping boat
MSC	mineship-coastal
MSO	minesweeper
NLA	National Liberation Army
NM	nautical mile

NMPH	nautical miles per hour
NPT	Non-Proliferation Treaty
NSC	National Security Council
NSPG	National Security Planning Group
NSSD	National Security Study Directive
NTDS	Navy Tactical Data System
OAFV	other armored fighting vehicle
OBA	oxygen breathing apparatus
OECD	Organization for Economic Cooperation and Development
OPEC	Organization of Petroleum Exporting Countries
PACOM	U.S. Pacific Command
PBR	patrol boat-riverine
PDRY	People's Democratic Republic of Yemen
PFLP	Popular Front for the Liberation of Palestine
PGMs	precision-guided munitions
PHOTINT	photo intelligence
PKK	Turkish Kurdish Worker's Party
PLO	Palestine Liberation Organization
POL	petroleum, oil, and lubricants
POW	prisoner of war
PRC	People's Republic of China
PUK	Patriotic Union of Kurdistan
RCC	Revolutionary Command Council
RPG	rocket-propelled grenade
RPV	remotely piloted vehicle
SAM	surface-to-air missile
SAR	search and reconnaissance
SCIRI	Supreme Council of the Islamic Revolution in Iraq
SDC	Supreme Defense Council
SEAL	U.S. Navy commandos
SHORADS	short-range air defense systems
SIGINT	signals intelligence
SLAR	side-looking airborne radar
SNIE	Special National Intelligence Estimate
STIR	separate track and illumination radar
TAO	Tactical Action Officer
TEL	transport-erector-launcher
UAE	United Arab Emirates
UNIMOG	United Nations Iran-Iraq Military Observer Group
USAF	U.S. Air Force
USCENTCOM	U.S. Central Command
VLCC	very large cargo carrier

| VSTOL | vertical and short takeoff and landing |
| WEU | Western European Union |

1

INTRODUCTION

The Iran-Iraq War lasted for nearly nine years. It involved Iran and Iraq in some of the largest-scale fighting in the history of the Third World and involved virtually all of the major powers, either in the political struggles surrounding the conflict or in actual fighting in the Gulf. While it was primarily a land conflict, it also involved extensive naval fighting, strategic bombing, the use of surface-to-surface missiles, chemical warfare, terrorism, and the use of proxy forces.

At this writing, Iran and Iraq have agreed to a cease-fire and have been negotiating for a peace settlement for nearly a year. There still, however, is no way to predict whether both nations will agree to a meaningful settlement or how long the cease-fire and any following peace settlement will last. The Iran-Iraq War threatens to be one of those structural conflicts which is the result of forces that lead to one war after another and to "cold war" in the periods between the fighting.

As might be expected from a conflict with the scale and complexity of the Iran-Iraq War, the conflict provides many insights and lessons regarding strategy, tactics, command and control, operations, intelligence, and technology. It has involved the use of a wide range of advanced Western and Soviet weapons. Further, the war escalated to involve Western naval forces, long-range surface-to-surface missiles, and the extensive use of poison gas. More than any other war in recent times, it provides a warning of the cost of the proliferation of new weapons and military technologies.

The Cost and Intensity of the Conflict

The true cost of the Iran-Iraq War is almost impossible to estimate. It cannot be measured in terms of present losses but, rather, in terms of the impact of the conflict on the future political and economic development of Iran, Iraq, and the neighboring nations that have had to invest in arms instead of their peoples and economies. It is clear, however, that the Iran-Iraq War ranks with Vietnam and Korea as one of the longest and bloodiest conflicts since World War II and has been one of the grimmest wars of attrition in modern times.

The Iran-Iraq War has not had the same devastating impact on the populations of Iraq or Iran as the Afghan conflict has. As the Arab-Israeli conflicts have shown, there is no fixed correlation between large numbers of high-technology weapons and military and civilian casualties. In fact, it is unlikely that the Iran-Iraq War has resulted in more than half the number of people killed in Pol Pot's attempt to consolidate power in Cambodia. Nevertheless, the results of the Iran-Iraq War have been tragic for both societies.

While no accurate estimates exist of the human and economic cost of the war, it is certain that it has produced hundreds of thousands killed, as many as a million wounded, and over 80,000 prisoners of war.[1] As Table 1.1 shows, the Iran-Iraq War has produced anywhere from 500,000 to 1 million dead. It has produced from one million to over 2 million wounded. It also has produced some 2.5 million refugees and has cost two heavily populated developing nations at least 200 billion dollars (Figure 1.1).

Other estimates of the financial cost of the war are even higher. One estimate of the cost of the war to Iran during 1980–1985 put the price as $108.2 billion for the oil sector (of which $23.4 billion was foregone revenue), $30.3 billion non-oil gross domestic product (GDP) loss, $23.4 billion for military expenditures, $76.5 billion in fixed-capital loss formation, and $25.9 billion for destruction of facilities.[2] A similar estimate of the cost of the war to Iraq reached $120.8 billion for the oil sector (of which $23.4 billion was foregone revenue), $64 billion nonoil GDP loss, $33 billion for military expenditures, $43.4 billion in fixed-capital loss formation, and $8.2 billion for destruction of facilities.[3]

The Strategic Implications of the Conflict

The Iran-Iraq War has also been one of the most strategically important conflicts in modern times. Unlike most Third World conflicts, the Iran-Iraq War has threatened the economic well being of virtually every other nation in the world. As Table 1.2 and Figure 1.2 show, the war has directly affected nations whose oil reserves are larger than those of some continents. It has also affected the destiny of a region with more than 50 percent of the world's proven oil reserves. The flow of Gulf oil is critical to the stability of the economies of every Western state and every oil-importing state in the Third World.

TABLE 1.1 Estimates of the Cost of the Iran-Iraq War: 1980–1988[1]

	Iran	Iraq
A. *Human Costs* (Number of Lives)		
Casualties	1,050,000–1,930,000	550,000–1,040,000
Wounded	600,000–1,200,000	400,000–700,000
Killed	450,000–730,000	150,000–340,000
Refugees	2,000,000	400,000
Prisoners of War	45,000	70,000
B. *Economic Costs* (Marginal Cost in $ Billions)		
Arms Purchases	7	25
Oil Revenue	10	55
Pipelines	—	3
Transportation	1	9
War-Risk Insurance	1	—
Petroleum-Product Imports	5	—
Compensation to Families	10	4
Military Salaries	10	10
Repairs to War-Damaged Facilities	5	3
Non-Oil GDP	20	50
Total	$69	$159

[1]Does not include opportunity cost of failing to fund economic development and normal economic operations. Costs of the Iranian revolution and Iraqi operations against native Kurds are excluded. Estimates of direct marginal cost of the war exclude cost of damage to economic facilities and infrastructure not repaired. Tehran assessed damages suffered by Iran at $309 billion for the first five years of war, of which $160 billion was damage to the oil sector. Baghdad has not issued estimates of war costs, but damage sustained by Iraq was significantly less than that sustained by Iran.

SOURCE: Modified by the authors from an unclassified CIA working estimate of April 15, 1988.

The Iran-Iraq War has presented the constant risk that Iran or Iraq could emerge from the war as the dominant power in the Gulf and that the balance between Iran, Iraq, and the weaker southern Gulf states could be shifted to the point where a single power could dominate the region. At the same time, the success or failure of Iran's Islamic fundamentalism in defeating Iraq's secular socialism has had broad

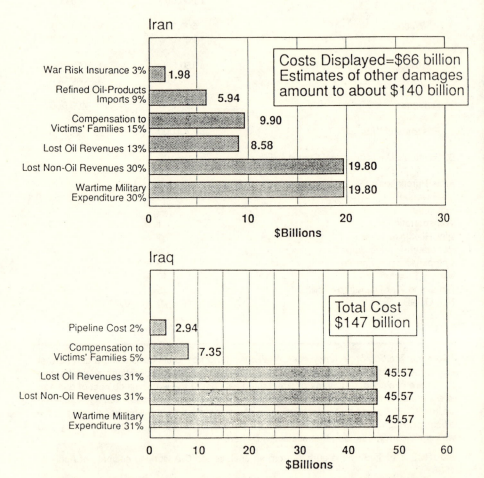

FIGURE 1.1 Estimated Total Cost of the Gulf War for Iran and Iraq: 1980–1988. Derived from work done by Abdullah Toucan.

implications for the future of Islam and the entire Middle East. At various periods in the conflict, the risk of an Iranian victory has threatened to trigger a wave of shifts from secular to religious rule and new patterns of hostility between Islam and both East and West.

The Internationalization of the Conflict

The Iran-Iraq War has had a far broader international character than most Third World conflicts. Within days of the war's beginning, outside nations began to take sides. Both Iran and Iraq also struggled for financial alliances and source of arms. Both were able to win large-scale external support and to obtain extensive supplies of imported arms. Iran's financial support was largely indirect.

Iran relied largely on its own finances, and its external reserves collapsed from $14.6 billion in 1979 to $6 billion in 1986–87. Nevertheless, Syria played a critical role in supporting Iran. Syria closed a key Iraqi pipeline to the Mediterranean early in the war and thus seriously weakened Iraq's financial position. Syria also supported Iran with measures such as sending its fighter aircraft over Iraq in order to divert the Iraqi Air Force away from the front. Syria helped Iranian and Kurdish agents blow up part of Iraq's oil pipeline through Turkey and divert its flow into the Ceyhan River. While the pipeline was repaired within a week, the action cost Iraq $6 million for each day it was out of operation. Syria also continued to funnel support to the Kurds in Iraq until the cease-fire in 1988.

While many states sold arms to Iran, states as diverse as Israel, Libya, the People's Democratic Republic of Yemen (PDRY), Syria, and Algeria provided aid or concessional arms sales as well. Libya helped spark the missile war between Iraq and Iran by sending Scud missiles to Iran via Syria, and nations like the People's Republic of China (PRC) and North Korea entered the world arena as major arms sellers by becoming major suppliers to Iran.

Iraq, in contrast, had massive direct financial assistance from its neighbors. Saudi Arabia and Kuwait provided $25 to $50 billion in financial grants and loans. France extended over $5 billion in loans to finance military equipment. The U.S. aided with credits, while Iraq put increasing pressure on its allies to halt any resupply of Iran. Egypt and Jordan provided weapons and supplies at critical moments in the war, and the USSR played a critical role when it resumed massive arms transfers to Iraq.

Volunteers from the military forces of other Arab nations supported Iraq in limited numbers. The Iraqi Army used cash incentives to recruit volunteers from other Arab countries to serve as Iraqi soldiers, and Iran

TABLE 1.2 World Oil Reserves

	Estimated Proved Reserves	
Region and Country	Billions of Barrels	Percent of World Total
Gulf [a]	396.18	56.7
Bahrain	.17	.02
Neutral Zone	(5.4)	.8
Iran	48.5	6.9
Iraq	44.5 (65.0)[b]	6.4
Kuwait[c]	92.7	13.3
Oman	3.5	.5
Qatar	3.35	.5
UAE	32.49	4.6
Abu Dhabi	(30.5)	—
Dubai	(1.44)	—
Ras al Khaimah	(0.1)	—
Sharjah	(0.45)	—
Saudi Arabia[d]	171.7	24.6
Other Middle East	2.2	.3
Israel	.75	.1
Syria	1.45	.2
Total Middle East	398.38	57.0
Africa [a]	55.54	7.9
Algeria	9.0	1.3
Angola	1.8	.3
Egypt	3.2	.5
Libya	21.1	3.0
Nigeria	16.65	2.4
Western Hemisphere [a]	117.69	16.8
U.S.	27.3	3.9
Mexico	48.6	7.0
Canada	7.075	1.0
Venezuela	25.845	3.7
Western Europe [a]	24.425	3.5
Britain	13.59	1.9
Norway	8.3	1.2
Asia-Pacific [a]	18.5299	2.7
Australia	1.5	.2
Brunei	1.4	.2
India	3.0	.42
Indonesia	8.65	1.2
Malaysia	3.5	.5
Total Non-Communist	614.567	88.0

(continues)

TABLE 1.2 *(continued)*

Region and Country	Estimated Proved Reserves	
	Billions of Barrels	Percent of World Total
Communist	84.1	12.0
USSR	63.0	9.0
China	19.1	2.7
Other	2.0	.2
Total World	698.667	100.0

[a]Breakdown by individual countries includes only major exporting or reserve-holding countries.

[b]The current official estimate is 44.1 billion, which has not been revised because of the Iran-Iraq War, but most U.S. officials now estimate Iraqi proved reserves at 65 billion or more.

[c]Kuwait's reserves are probably in excess of 100 billion, and Saudi Arabia is near 200 billion. The reserves for Kuwait and Saudi Arabia include half of the Neutral Zone.

[d]Neither Kuwait nor Saudi Arabia provide up-to-date estimates of proven reserves.

SOURCE: Adapted from *Oil and Gas Journal*, December 1984 and December 1985. U.S. Department of Energy shows a slightly higher percentage of total reserves in the Middle East. See DOE/EIA-0219(84), pp. 79–81, and *Annual Energy Review, 1986*, Washington, D.C., GPO, 1986.

received a limited number of Shi'ite volunteers from Lebanon and some of the Gulf states.[4]

The war also took on a new international character during its final phase when the West and the USSR entered the Gulf in an effort to secure the flow of oil through the Gulf. This eventually led to major naval clashes between the U.S. and Iran and a broad Western naval effort to secure the shipping routes of the southern Gulf states. At the same time, the United Nations played a powerful role in the events that led to a cease-fire. What began as the struggle between two political leaders and two conflicting ideologies ended as an international conflict that was only contained through a global effort to terminate the war.

This complex mix of forces not only makes the Iran-Iraq War exceptionally important, it means the war provides an exceptionally wide range of lessons. It not only provides important lessons about land and air conflict, it shows how ideology can radically influence the course of conflict in the Third World. It provides many lessons about technology transfer and about the role of power projection by the West. Finally, it provides an important warning about the potential impact of missile conflicts and conflicts involving weapons of mass destruction.

8

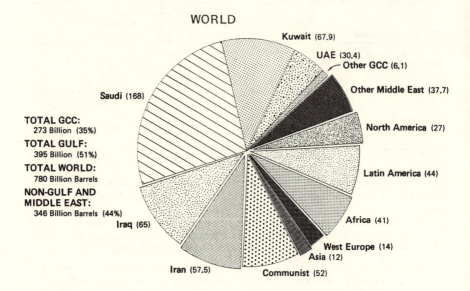

WORLD

Kuwait (67.9)
UAE (30.4)
Other GCC (6.1)
Other Middle East (37.7)
North America (27)
Latin America (44)
Africa (41)
West Europe (14)
Asia (12)
Communist (52)
Iran (57.5)
Iraq (65)
Saudi (168)

TOTAL GCC:
273 Billion (35%)
TOTAL GULF:
395 Billion (51%)
TOTAL WORLD:
780 Billion Barrels
NON-GULF AND MIDDLE EAST:
346 Billion Barrels (44%)

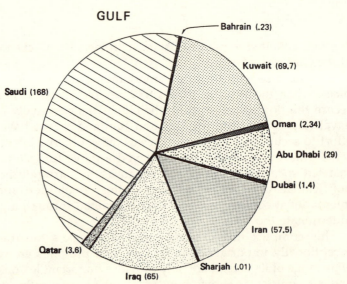

GULF

Bahrain (.23)
Kuwait (69.7)
Oman (2.34)
Abu Dhabi (29)
Dubai (1.4)
Iran (57.5)
Sharjah (.01)
Iraq (65)
Qatar (3.6)
Saudi (168)

FIGURE 1.2 Proved World and Gulf Oil Reserves in 1984 (in billions of barrels). Adapted from ARAMCO, BP, CRS, and MEED statistics.

Notes

1. An April 1986 estimate of the number of POWs was 60,000 Iraqi and 17,000 Iranian. *Washington Times*, April 26, 1986. Estimates of those killed sometimes exceed one million, but a November estimate of 250,000 Iranian and 100,000 Iraqi dead seems more likely to be correct. *Time*, November 24, 1986, p. 41.

2. Japanese Institute of Middle East Economies, as cited in *MidEast Markets*, February 22, 1988.

3. Ibid.

4. Cited in "Not Our War," *The Economist*, June 5, 1982, p. 58. Kuwait and Saudi Arabia also provided massive financial support to Iraq, and various Kurdish factions coordinated their actions with the Iraqis or Iranians, while others fought them; see "A War Without End," *Newsweek*, August 15, 1983, p. 33.

2

THE CONDITIONS THAT SHAPED
THE IRAN-IRAQ WAR

The Conditions That Shaped the Conflict

Unlike many modern wars, the Iran-Iraq War was shaped by a wide variety of historical and military factors that helped to cause the conflict and shape its course once it began. Some of these factors were the result of long-standing historical tensions between the two cultures and nations. Others were the result of the personal worldview and character of the two autocrats heading each state. Still others were the result of the economic, manpower, and military trends that occurred in the period just before the war and which often helped shape the entire course of the conflict.

It is difficult to draw specific lessons from many of these conditions except to note that an understanding of the factors that cause a war is as critical to understanding the outcome of that war as the military decisions and technology which are brought to bear in actual conflict. At the same time, the conditions that shaped the Iran-Iraq War do provide a number of important insights as to how the risk of war needs to be appraised, as to the difficulties in assessing how foreign leaders make their decisions, and as to how one should assess the effectiveness of Third World military forces, particularly under conditions of revolutionary change.

The Prelude to Iraq's Invasion of Iran

There are complex historical, cultural, and strategic causes for any conflict. This is particularly true of the Iran-Iraq War, where both nations involve cultures and power blocs that have been rivals for centuries and which have squabbled over their borders and access to the Gulf ever since their emergence as modern states. At the same time, this long history of conflict and tension between Iran and Iraq, and of their political and cultural rivalry, does not really explain why the Iran-Iraq War took place and why it escalated beyond yet another series of border clashes or political confrontations.

It is unlikely that a major war would ever have taken place if historical, cultural, and strategic causes were really the issue. The Iran-Iraq War is primarily the result of a conflict between the goals and ambitions of Saddam Hussein and Iraq's Ba'athist leadership elite and the Ayatollah Khomeini and Iran's new religious leadership elite. It is a grim warning of how quickly long-standing tensions in the Third World can be transformed from low-level conflicts into much more intense wars of major strategic impact.

The Rivalry Between Arab and Persian

The historical rivalry between Arab and Persian has had great propaganda value to both sides since the start of the conflict but does relatively little to explain its causes. Most of the extreme rhetoric on each side regarding Arab nationalism versus Persian nationalism arose after the Shah's departure from power. It is true that many historical conflicts have occurred between Arab and Persian since the rise of Islam and the Battle of Qadisiyah and that similar conflicts between plateau dweller and river-basin dweller can be traced back to the prehistory of the region. At the same time, there have been many periods of peace, and each culture has had other enemies and has shared many common bonds—including a common religion and many common economic interests.

Something approaching a separate "Arabistan" did exist in southwest Iran between roughly 1690 and 1923. A local emir, Ali Bin Nasir al-Khabi established a Kabide Emirate that controlled Ahwaz in the north, the Shatt al-Arab and the waterways to the Gulf, and Hindian in the east. This emirate managed to play the Persians off against the Ottomans for nearly two hundred years and collected tolls from all the ships moving up from the Gulf to the Ottoman port city at Basra. At this point in time, the Shatt al-Arab—the "Arab River" that flows from the junction of the Tigris and Euphrates rivers to the Gulf—had relatively little trade impact, and the Kabides seem to have deliberately avoided provoking the Turks into military action.

The Abides came into rising conflict with the British forces in the Gulf, however, and tension rose when the Abide Emirate established its own port on the Shatt al-Arab at Khorramshahr (Muhammarah) in 1813. This tension exploded into war in 1823 when Persia invaded the Abide Emirate, destroyed most of its military forces, conquered the Emirate, and seized Khorramshahr. To all intents and purposes, the Abide Emirate and Arabistan then became part of Persia.

The Ottomans waited for over a decade and then invaded the area in 1837. They fought a major battle with Persia and seized virtually all of the Abide Emirate and incorporated it into the Turkish Wilayat of Basra. Turkey's main motive seems to have been to secure its access to the Gulf, but Britain and Russia forced Turkey to withdraw from the east bank of the Shatt in an effort to maintain their own influence over Persia and to strengthen British trade influence in the northern Gulf.

As a result of British and Turkish pressure, a mixed boundary commission was established in 1843, and this led to the second Treaty of Erzerum in 1847. This treaty stabilized most of the land frontier, allowed for international navigation of the Shatt al-Arab, gave Turkey control of most of the Shatt to the east bank, and gave Iran control of Khorramshahr and Abadan Island. The treaty left the Abide Emirate in existence, but it was firmly under Persian influence and had only limited British protection.

A series of boundary commissions, protocols, and treaties followed between 1911 and 1923 that affected the border area, but none of these efforts were really concerned with the Abide Emirates, which had become little more than a regional fiction as far back as the 1850s. When the Treaty of Lausanne established Iraq as a state in 1923, it paid no attention to the issue of Arabistan at all. The entire area was assumed to be part of Persia.

The British had no interest in the area at the time for several reasons. They were far more interested in obtaining unchallenged control over the oil areas around Mosul, and they were actively encouraging the commander of the Iranian Cossack Brigade, Reza Shah, to consolidate his power in Persia and allow Britain to maintain its control over the oil concessions in that country. Reza Shah had seized power in 1921 and eliminated his rivals in 1923. During 1923–1924, he ruthlessly suppressed Persia's various ethnic minorities. In 1924, he put down all Arab resistance in Arabistan and changed the name to Khuzistan. He then proceeded to methodically crush any signs of Arab nationalism, suppress Arabic as a language, resettle the population to reduce what was then a strong Arab majority, and to exploit the province for his own ends.

There was only limited cultural tension in the area at the time the most recent Shah fell from power.[1] Iran had had half a century to "Persianize" the area and a strong incentive to do so. Khuzistan included considerably more territory than the original Abide Emirate, including the province where oil was discovered in 1908. It was hardly surprising that successive Iranian governments encouraged Persian migration into the area and ruthlessly suppressed Arab nationalism and attempts at Arab autonomy.

While this treatment of Iran's Arabs left some bitterness, too much time had elapsed and too many changes had occurred by the time of the Shah's fall to leave Arab separatism a driving political force.[2] The Persianization of Khuzistan had also had considerable success. Khuzistan had become the center of Iran's oil industry and wealth and had nearly 80 percent of its oil installations. Almost all of the oil company personnel, officials, security forces, and technically skilled workers were Persian or Farsi speakers. According to Iranian estimates, only 40 percent of the province had Arab roots. In fact, even a fairly narrow geographic definition of Khuzistan based on the old Abide Emirate would probably have left the Arab population in the minority or as only a bare majority. There had also long been considerable intermarriage between Arab and non-Arab, many Persians were working in Arab states in the Gulf, and the Arab minority in Iran had lost much of its cultural identity.

More broadly, Arab ethnic influence had relatively little impact on Iran as a whole. Any estimates of the ethnic divisions in Iran are highly uncertain, but at the time the war began, about half of Iran's 45 million-plus population was Persian speaking. The rest consisted largely of non-Arab minorities. Anywhere from 6 to 13 million people were Azerbaijani or Turk, 4 million were Kurd, and 1.5 million were Baluchi. Only about 1 million of Iran's citizens seem to have retained a significant degree of identity as Arabs.[3]

Some radical Arab nationalist movements did exist in Khuzistan in 1978 and still claimed the province should be a separate nation called Arabistan. These movements were weak, however, and many were funded by Iraqi intelligence or were affiliated with outside extremist groups like the Popular Front for the Liberation of Palestine (PFLP).[4]

The bulk of the Arab demonstrations that did occur in the Khuzistan during the early years of the revolution called for a limited degree of regional autonomy, a greater share of revenues, the teaching of Arabic as the primary language, and higher priority for Arabs in local jobs, but they did not call for separatism. While some large demonstrations took place in Khorramshahr and Abadan in April, May, and June 1979, they scarcely threatened Iranian control. In fact, Arab separatists where one of the least threatening ethnic movements Khomeini faced during the consolidation of his rule over Iran.

If anything, the Arab separatists probably had more impact on the perceptions of Iraq's leaders than on the political situation in Iran. Saddam Hussein and his Ba'ath colleagues seem to convince themselves that there was a serious Arab separatist movement that would rise up and join a "liberating" Iraqi army and create a separatist state in one of Iran's richest oil-production areas. In fact, one of the major miscalculations that Iraq made in invading Iran was to assume that it could win enough local support to rapidly occupy this area and either partition Iran or use Iran's resulting loss of oil revenue to help bring down the Khomeini government. This miscalculation also seems to have led Iraq to assume that the Arab minority would help reduce the size of the invasion force necessary to seize Khuzistan and the amount of preparation and support it would need.

The Religious Tension Between Iran and Iraq

Religious tension between Iraq and Iran became a major issue largely as a result of Khomeini's rise to power. Both Iran and Iraq are Moslem states in which the Shi'ite sect is dominant. At the time Khomeini came to power, Iran was as much as 90 percent Shi'ite and Iraq was 50 percent Shi'ite.[5] While most of Iraq's Ba'athist leaders were Sunni, there was relatively little effort to control Shi'ite religious activity in Iraq, and most of it was targeted against a relatively few outspoken opponents of the regime. The average Shi'ite cleric did relatively well under the Ba'ath regime. The Iraqi Shi'ite clergy were certainly not strong supporters of the Ba'ath, but they also were not stronger supporters of any of the Iranian Ayatollahs. They also disagreed with the Iranian Shi'ite clergy over a number of religious practices, had somewhat different cultural and ethnic traditions, and disagreed over the status and importance of many of the Shi'ite shrines.

Neither the Iranian nor the Iraqi government had a recent tradition of religious rule, and both Iran and Iraq had extensive secret police networks that permeated all religious activity. At the same time, neither state attempted to suppress religion per se. Each used a mixture of "sticks," in the form of censorship and arrest, and "carrots," in the form of salaries and subsidies for religious schools, shrines, and mosques, to try to control their respective clergies.

Both the Iraqi Ba'ath Party and the Shah, however, did support rival radical or anti-regime Shi'ite movements in the opposing country during the 1960s and early 1970s. They offered leading opposition clerics in the other country both funds and a sanctuary in exile. Khomeini, for example, was allowed to settle in the Shi'ite shrine of Najaf in 1965 after the Shah expelled him for his increasingly vitriolic attacks on the Shah's religious and constitutional legitimacy.[6]

This situation changed when the Shah and Ba'ath Party reached a general settlement of their differences in the Algiers Accord of 1975. Both sides agreed to stop all subversive activity directed from their soil against the other state.[7] Iraq generally lived up to this agreement.

For example, Iraq placed Khomeini under house arrest in late 1978, at the Shah's request. It expelled him from Iraq on October 6, 1978, allowing him to fly to Paris after Kuwait refused him entry.[8] Finally, the Iraqi government hosted a tour by the Shah's sister of Iraq's religious shrines only a few weeks later

At the time the Shah fell, the anti-regime Shi'ite clergy in Iran and Iraq were pursuing their national political objectives in relative isolation, and the primary religious tensions in each country were those resulting from the conflict between the secular ruling elites that were attempting the radical reform of each country and the more conservative elements of their respective Shi'ite clergy.

Khomeini's rise to power, however, quickly created a different concept in Iran of the role the Shi'ite religion should play in all Islamic states. As early as February 1979, Khomeini was exchanging messages with former colleagues in Iraq. Between February and June, Khomeini began to appeal to the Iraqis to overthrow the Ba'athist regime as anti-Islamic, and between June and July 1979, this triggered a bloody effort by Saddam Hussein to suppress all anti-Ba'athist Shi'ite elements. Hussein used the Iraqi Army to fire on Shi'ite demonstrations, conducted a number of executions, and arrested several thousand Shi'ites.[9] He also countered by greatly increasing the funding of the Arab separatists in Iran and began the first major Iraqi arms shipments to such movements.[10]

Ironically, both Khomeini and the Ba'athist regime then miscalculated the nature of Shi'ite feeling in Iraq. Khomeini seems to have felt that the Iraqi Shi'ites in southern Iraq would eventually rise up and welcome his forces if they could drive out the Iraqi government forces. Saddam Hussein and those around him seem to have felt the threat of a fundamentalist Shi'ite movement in Iraq was stronger than it really was, and this made them more willing to take military chances in invading Iran. In practice, however, the vast majority of Iraq's Shi'ite population proved to be loyal and more interested in nationalism than religion

The Border and Waterway Conflicts Between Iran and Iraq

The importance of the geographic issues dividing the the two states is equally easy to exaggerate. There were two continuing border controversies between modern Iraq and Iran. The first was over the control of the Shatt al-Arab, the major waterway connecting the Gulf with Iraq's port of Basra and Iran's ports of Khorramshahr and Abadan. The second was the control of key defensive points along the land border and particularly the land approaches to Iraq's capital of Baghdad and its key oil facilities at Kirkuk.

These two issues had strategic importance for Iraq because it had only 58 kilometers of sea coast, its only major port at Basra was less than 30 kilometers by road from Iran, and its capital of Baghdad was only a little over 100 kilometers from the border and had few natural defenses. Iraq lacked both secure access to the Gulf and strategic depth as a protection from Iran.

The issues were also the heritage of a long history of similar controversies between Turkey and Persia in the period before World War I. In regard to the Shatt al-Arab dispute, the Ottoman Turks generally had the advantage over Persia and controlled the entire "Arab River" to the Persian bank.[11] Neither state agreed to established land borders during the nineteenth century, however, and attempts to demarcate the border in the mid- and late 1800s had little success.

The feuding over the border took on considerably more importance in 1908, after the discovery of oil in Iran. Iran's only modern port was then at Khorramshahr, and free access to the Shatt al-Arab became critical to Iran's ability to export and its economic development. This led to new boundary meetings between Turkey and Iran in 1911, but no agreement was reached until Britain and Russia intervened. This led to the Constantinople Protocol of 1913, which gave Iran the right of navigation and gave Turkey control over most of the disputed territory, the Shatt al-Arab to the Iranian bank, and the islands in the Shatt except for three islands, including Abadan and the port of Khorramshahr, and the waters above and below the confluence of the Karun River.[12]

The Protocol became the de facto settlement of the boundary disputes for some years, but it had an unusually uncertain status. It was never signed by the Ottoman Empire and virtually all the parties involved in reaching it had changed radically by the mid-1920s. The Soviet Union was largely excluded from international negotiations after the Soviet revolution of 1918. The Ottoman Empire finally collapsed in 1922, and Britain had already created modern Iraq as part of the Treaty of Sevres in August 1920. Reza Shah rose to power in Iran in 1921–1923, and this meant new governments had come into existence along both sides of the border.

The Treaty of Lausanne redefined the Iran-Iraq border in 1923, but it did not clarify the status of the Constantinople Protocols of 1913. This led to new border and boundary disputes between 1929 and 1934 and, finally, to the referral of the issue to the League of Nations. Iran then argued that the border should run down the middle of the Shatt, and both sides should have freedom of navigation and the right to freely move warships. Iraq argued it had sovereign rights to the entire waterway, customs jurisdiction over all traffic, and the right to control the movement of all warships.

While the two nations could not initially agree on a settlement, a coup in Iraq in 1936 created a weaker Iraqi government, one that was more willing to negotiate. As a result, a treaty was signed in 1937 which stabilized most of the land border between the two countries and which largely agreed to the Constantinople Protocol of 1913. The agreement put the border in the Shatt along the line of the Thalweg. It gave Iran control of the island of Abadan and of the Shatt al-Arab to the middle of the channel for five miles around Khorramshahr. The treaty also allowed for free navigation of all merchant ships from any nation and allowed Iranian ships to anchor at Iran's main port without being subject to Iraqi customs duties. Finally, it established a joint commission to handle the dredging of the Shatt al-Arab, tools, and other issues and called for a Convention on Navigation and Conservancy, although the latter convention was never agreed to and led to more disputes in the years that followed.

Both Iraq and Iran continued to quibble over the border and control of the Shatt al-Arab from 1937 to the late 1950s, but the issues involved were of negligible practical importance until a coup d'etat overthrew the Hashemite Dynasty in Iraq in July 1958. Iraq's new rulers then made new claims to Khuzistan and attempted to unilaterally extend Iraq's territorial limit in the Gulf to 12 miles. They even demanded Iran cede its sheltered anchorages at Khorramshahr and Iran's main refinery complex at Abadan. In 1960, Iraq added to the dispute by first claiming sovereignty over Abadan. In 1961, it demanded that only Iraqi pilots could navigate ships up the waterway.

The Shah responded by sending Iranian warships into the Shatt and by ceasing to use Iraqi pilots or pay Iraqi tolls. Both sides deployed troops into the border area during this period, although Iraq's demands produced more sound than fury and no serious military clashes occurred. The only real impact on the control of the Shatt was that Iran eventually accepted renewed Iraqi control of piloting up and down the waterway, although Iran made no other concessions to the new Iraqi regime.

These claims and incidents did, however, lead Iran to try to find strategic solutions to its problems. They were one of the major reasons Iran built its massive new crude oil export facilities at Kharg Island, which opened in 1965. This new oil port freed Iran from dependence on the Shatt, although it still left Iran heavily dependent on Khorramshahr and exports from the refinery at Abadan. This became particularly important in June 1967, when Iraq tried to use its control over the waterway to force Iran not to export oil to Israel and the West.

They also were a reason that the Shah reached an accommodation with the USSR in the early 1960s and began to reorient his forces from the defense of the north to a defense of the border with Iraq. In March 1965, the Shah established a new 3rd Army Corps at Shiraz and began a major land and air buildup, including new casernes and air bases to the rear of the border area.

The announcement of British withdrawal from the Gulf in 1968 also changed the strategic situation significantly. Iraq revived its nationalist ambitions. The U.S. turned to the Shah as its new "pillar" in the Gulf, and the Shah rapidly began to create the largest navy in the Gulf, a major new seaport at Bandar Abbas at the mouth of the Gulf, and new ports and rail or road links to the Gulf at Bandar e-Shahpur (now Bandar-e-Khomeini), Ganaveh, and Bushehr. This freed Iran's rapidly growing naval power from dependence on the Shatt.

This renewal of tension took tangible form in 1969, shortly after the Ba'ath Party again seized power in Iraq. Iraq's new government renewed its claim to all waters of the Shatt al-Arab on April 19, 1969. This led Iran to denounce the 1937 treaty, and on April 22, an Iranian ship entered the Shatt with a military escort and refused to pay tolls to Iraq. This confrontation reflected the growing political tensions between the Iraqi government and that of the Shah, and both sides then supported coup and assassination attempts in the opposing country.

On November 30, 1971—the day before the British left the Gulf—the Shah seized three strategic islands in the lower Gulf which were owned by the United Arab Emirates (UAE). These included Abu Musa and the Greater and Lower Tunbs. This seizure led Iraq to sever diplomatic relations with Iran.

There were reports of scattered shooting incidents on the border in 1972, and Iraq expelled some 74,000 Iranians from Iraq and increased its financial support to the opponents of the Shah. Iran retaliated by starting a massive covert action program in coordination with the CIA to aid Kurdish insurgents in northern Iraq. This effort proved to be extremely successful, largely because of the inability of the Ba'athist regime to make intelligent compromises with the Kurds. The resulting battles seriously hurt Iraq financially and militarily but scarcely crippled it. It was the outbreak of the October War in 1973, however, that virtually forced Iraq to secure its eastern flank. The day the October War broke out, Iraq proposed resuming diplomatic relations with Iran, and relations were resumed on October 15, 1973.

This resumption of diplomatic relations did not bring peace to the Iranian and Iraqi border. Instead, a new series of border incidents occurred in February 1974, and both sides deployed substantial numbers of troops. The Shah seized a number of strategic heights and positions in the still-disputed parts of the land border in the Mehran region in February, and serious local fighting took place near the Konjam Dam on February 19 and March 6, 1974.

The Shah's key lever against Iraq, however, lay in the fact that he had begun to provide money and arms to anti-regime Kurdish factions in the early 1960s and had steadily stepped up his support in the early 1970s. With the support of both Israel and the U.S. Central Intelligence Agency (CIA), he had turned the Kurds from a nuisance into a major threat to the Iraqi regime, and it became clear to the Iraqi government that the Shah had the full support of both President Richard Nixon and his National Security Advisor Henry Kissinger in this effort.

During early 1974, Iran again stepped up its support for the Kurds and used its growing U.S.-supplied air force to demonstrate its air superiority over the border. By May 1974, Iraq reached the point where the Shah's support of the Kurds forced it to compromise. Both nations set up a mixed boundary commission. When Iraq delayed reaching an agreement, the Shah used his support for the Kurds to pressure Saddam Hussein to agree directly to a favorable settlement. This settlement took the form of the Algiers Accord, which was announced at the end of an Organization of Petroleum Exporting Countries (OPEC) meeting in Algiers on March 6, 1975, and which was signed by both the Shah and Saddam Hussein of Iraq.[13]

The Algiers Accord was followed by a treaty in June and by a land boundary-demarcation effort and navigation commission that were completed in December 1975. The result made the Thalweg the border along the entire length of the Shatt. This gave Iran half of the Shatt al-Arab and effectively turned the Shatt into an international waterway. In this sense, the Algiers Accord was a victory for the Shah. However, the Accord also generally adopted the land boundaries of the Protocol of 1913. It promised Iraq some 240 square miles of disputed territory, some of the land Iran had seized in the Mehran region, and token improvements in the land border to give it some additional terrain barriers to help compensate for its lack of strategic depth. In this sense, it was a victory for Iraq.

Even in retrospect, it is difficult to argue with the resulting settlement. While Iran never turned over all of the promised points along the border, and Iraq unquestionably had suffered a political defeat, the Algiers Accord did provide a reasonable basis for developing the ports and navigation channels in the Shatt al-Arab. It also provided terms for a settlement of the land boundary dispute that

favored Iraq and, in theory, meant an end to the constant efforts each
regime made to exploit the ethnic tensions in the other state.

It is also important to understand that the military issues that had
been important in the 1960s and early 1970s were also of steadily
diminishing importance by the late 1970s. Two major trends affected
the importance of the Shatt al-Arab and the border area.

The first trend was that each side was steadily reducing its
economic dependence on the Shatt al-Arab. Iraq had created a new
road through Turkey and Jordan to reduce its dependence on Gulf ports,
a new port and naval base at Umm Qasr, another port at al-Faw, and
offshore oil loading terminals in the Gulf. Iraq had also created new
pipelines to reduce its dependence on Gulf ports. By the late 1970s, two
pipelines were in operation. The first was a 1,000-kilometer pipeline
through Turkey which ended in Yumurtalik on the Mediterranean.
This pipeline was finished in 1977 and had a capacity of 650,000 to
750,000 barrels per day (BPD).[14] The second pipeline was a strategic
pipeline through Syria which ran to the port of Baniyas and could
carry 700,000 to 850,000 BPD.[15] These developments reduced each side's
vulnerability to low-level incidents and unilateral political action by
the other.

The second trend was that the massive growth of each side's air
power, artillery, and armor after Britain's announcement of its
withdrawal from the Gulf in 1968 made the control of given border
positions and the dividing line along the Shatt al-Arab less
important. Each side now had major strategic hostages to the other
nation's growing armed forces, and each had the power to close the
Shatt at any time.

In the case of Iran, Khorramshahr and Abadan were still of critical
economic importance, in spite of Iran's new ports and oil-export
facilities at Kharg Island. Regardless of the outcome of any of the
arguments over the boundary line in the Shatt al-Arab, the port and
the refinery would remain within artillery range of Iraq. Both could
easily be cut off if Iraq shelled shipping or mined the waterway. In the
case of Iraq, its main port of Basra, its new oil port at al-Faw, and its
new naval base at Umm Qasr were equally vulnerable to Iranian
military action.

Iraq and Iran's refineries and oil facilities away from the border
area and their oil-loading terminals further out in the Gulf were also
becoming steadily more vulnerable to the other side's air power. Iran's
oil terminal at Kharg was within range of Iraq's new fighters and
bombers. Iraq's new pipelines to Turkey and Syria could provide a
maximum sustained shipment capability of 1.5 millions of barrels per
day (MMBD), but Iraq was exporting 3.2 MMBD.[16] More than half of

Iraq's oil had to move through its deep-water loading points in the Gulf, and loading points for the supertankers in the Gulf had to be placed south of Iran and east of the dividing line in the Shatt al-Arab in order to find waters deep enough for the tankers to load.[17]

As for the land boundary dispute, it was now confined largely to a 200-square kilometer region which was bounded to the north by Khanaqin and Qasr e-Shirin and to the south by Basra and Mehran. The disputed territory varied in width from 3 to 16 kilometers and involved the control of heights in the area where the Iranian plateau drops to Iraq's river plain. From Iraq's perspective, control of these heights offered a potential geographic barrier to block any Iranian invasion of Baghdad. From the Shah's perspective, there were ample defensive positions for Iran on the other side of the disputed area but retaining it gave him continued leverage over Iraq.

What both sides had to consider, however, was that Iraq still had significant terrain defenses near the border, regardless of control of the disputed areas. Iraq could freely operate its armor in the river plain against an Iran which had far longer lines of communication and which had to channel any attacking forces through a limited number of passes and routes. This increasingly made armor and air power, not control of the highest ridge lines and passes in the mountain barriers, the critical factor in securing the border. This became particularly true in the mid- and late 1970s, as the Shah built up a massive heliborne attack force and acquired the capability to outflank the terrain barriers at the border by air.

In short, these changing geographic and military facts of life scarcely made a war for control of the Shatt al-Arab or the border area a strategically sound idea. These facts also made it clear that both sides could not protect themselves by diverting ships away from the Shatt, and they made it clear that Iraq could not acquire any significant strategic depth, or protection from Iran, by squabbling over adjustments to its land borders. Iraq's main cities were too close to Iran, and modern aircraft and armor could rapidly overcome the kind of geographic barriers that had previously been in contention. Further, Iraq could not secure its borders without reaching a full settlement with the Kurds, and the Ba'ath leadership proved unable to do so. The Shah continued to do a far better job of accommodating and coopting his Kurdish population and retained the option of renewing the Kurdish conflict in Iraq virtually at will.

The Struggle for Regional Influence

If there was any significant issue between Iraq and Iran before the Shah's fall, it was the struggle for regional influence and dominance between the Shah of Iran and Saddam Hussein and the Ba'ath Party elite in Iraq. By the late 1970s, however, Iraq had been forced to accept the fact that it was second best. The Shah's access to U.S. and Western arms after 1969 gave him an immense qualitative advantage over the arms Iraq could obtain from the USSR and France. Further, Iran devoted far more of its resources to arms imports than Iraq.

If one compares the total flow of arms imports by each side between the Algiers Accord in 1975 and the beginning of 1980, Iran imported $15.5 billion worth of arms and Iraq imported $8.1 billion worth of arms.[18] Many of Iran's arms were the most modern Western systems available. The bulk of Iraq's arms were Soviet-bloc systems that were inferior to their Western counterparts when they were first deployed and which were then often a generation old.

Regardless of the public rhetoric of both sides, and particularly of that of Iraq's Ba'ath Party after Khomeini came to power, both sides understood these strategic facts of life as long as the Shah remained in power. Iraqi and Iranian military and intelligence officers were well aware of the trends in the military balance and each side's relative geographic and political vulnerability.

The Iraqis were acutely aware not only of their own military limitations but also of the potential ability of Iran to exploit the Kurdish issue. Further, Iraq's Ba'athist leadership had serious problems with Iraq's Communist Party, became embroiled in a feud with Syria's Ba'athist elite, and came to realize that its only major way of countering Iran would be to establish more stable relations with the Arab states in the southern Gulf. In 1978, a direct Iraqi challenge of Iran's regional power seemed as unthinkable as the rapid fall of the Shah.

It was the Iranian revolution that fundamentally changed the conditions under which Iraq and Iran conducted their rivalry. The fall of the Shah created a new political system in Iran that was messianic in character. It was led by a man who felt he had divine inspiration to create a broader Islamic revolution and who had good personal reasons to regard the Ba'ath regime in Iraq as being as much a betrayal of Islam as the Shah's regime had been in Iran. The Ayatollah Khomeini's sudden rise to power created a regime in Iran that was far more of a political threat to Iraq than the Shah had ever been.

While Iraq attempted to reach a modus vivendi with Khomeini, it rapidly became apparent that he was ideologically committed to overthrowing the Ba'ath Party and creating an Islamic Iraq that was dominated by Shi'ite clergy loyal to Khomeini's ideology. Khomeini's rise to power did not produce any massive popular support in Iraq, but it was unquestionably threatening. Further, it raised the prospect that

Khomeini might move from relatively low-level political action to much more aggressive subversion and even military action.

At the same time, the initial course of the Iranian revolution created near chaos in many Iranian military units and cut Iran off from the U.S. and the West. During the year after the Shah fell, many parts of Iran were in near civil war, Iran became involved in a massive confrontation with the U.S. and was cut off from its primary source of arms, and a murderous power struggle broke out between the religious revolutionaries under Khomeini and Marxist radical movements.

This internal disarray in Iran made Khomeini seem far more vulnerable than he really was and led Saddam Hussein to feel he now had his first real opportunity to transform Iraq into the dominant power in the region, and even in the Arab world. Egypt's near isolation from the other Arab states as the result of the Camp David Accords and Syria's limited financial resources must have seemed to be an unusually good opportunity to make Iraq the leader of the Arab states.[19]

It is difficult to put the views and motivations of such different leadership elites into perspective because their public rhetoric was so extreme and because both sides made so many charges and counter-charges with so little regard for the truth. Nevertheless, it is clear that Khomeini and Saddam Hussein systematically attempted to exploit what they felt to be their opponent's vulnerabilities and engaged in efforts of subversion and in border incidents that steadily increased the tension on both sides.

The Clashes That Led to War

The issue of which side is most to blame for the war is one that may well be impossible to determine. By the time the war began, Iran and Iraq were led by two competing autocrats who saw their struggle from totally different perspectives. Khomeini unquestionably saw the struggle primarily in ideological and religious terms. He and his supporters saw Islamic revolution both as the primary means of overthrowing Saddam Hussein and the Ba'ath and as a preface to a broader revolution that would eventually dominate the Islamic world.

Saddam Hussein, in turn, saw an opportunity to build on Iraq's emergence as a leader of the hard-line movement against Israel and of the Baghdad conferences of 1978 and 1979, to become the key leader of the Arab world. He also saw the revolution in Iran as one that severely weakened Iran. He saw both the opportunity to dominate the Gulf region and the struggle with Iran as being events which could be resolved in military terms.

Khomeini's ambitions seem to have been absolute in the sense he sought to create a fundamentally different regime in Iraq and a different kind of Iraqi state. Saddam Hussein's ambitions may have been more limited in that he sought military advantages for Iraq that would have made it the dominant state in the region but did not make Khomeini's overthrow and a complete change in Iran's government a major objective.

Both leaders seem to have operated from a fundamentally egocentric and distorted perspective, which was reinforced by the fact that they obtained virtually all their information through colleagues who were equally ideologically committed to a given view of the situation or who had to simulate such commitment to survive. Neither had access to objective intelligence or paid great attention to the views of the other side except to reinforce their own preconceptions.

The irony behind these different perspectives is that they also had a number of things in common, particularly at the beginning of the war. Both sides severely overestimated the vulnerability of the opposing side and the extent to which key segments of the population in the opposing state would or would not support its leadership. Both sides pictured themselves as leading national movements with broad popular support, but both sides were led by small and relative isolated elites that were continuously forced to deal with armed internal-opposition movements and to take Draconian measures to suppress them. Both sides obtained the support of other states and movements which provided that support only because it helped protect their own security or offered other advantages. Both sides saw the other as the cause of a fundamentally illegitimate struggle in which the other side had deep moral and ethical guilt for the war.

Both sides also began the war with certain key limitations. Both sides had highly politicized armed forces. They never could fully trust their armed forces or allow them to either become fully professional or conduct the details of their military operations. Further, the ruling elite of both sides lacked members with real military professionalism and failed to admit such members throughout the war. Both began the war with intelligence services which could not provide accurate data on any issue because of their political character, and both failed to solve their problem throughout the conflict.

Both sides began the war without any real understanding or analysis of the risk and cost of large-scale conflict and allowed the war to become institutionalized without really considering the meaning of that institutionalization. Finally, both sides began the war with leadership elites that were unprepared to deal with the leadership elites of other nations, particularly the leadership elites of the U.S. and USSR. While Iraq was able to improve its diplomatic situation with far more skill than Iran, it still failed to understand key aspects of Western opinion—such as Western reaction to the use of chemical weapons—at the time the war was suspended by a cease-fire.

It may be argued that most wars grow out of similar failures on the part of each side's leadership elites to objectively understand both the political realities they face and the true cost of war. This may, in fact, be one of the most consistent lessons of war, at least in terms of grand strategy. At the same time, it is equally important to note that the war started, continued, and escalated at least in part because the diplomatic and intelligence services of outside powers failed to understand both the process that led to the conflict and the different character of Iran and Iraq's leadership elite. This also is an important lesson of war. Outside powers tend to deal with conflicts in reactive terms and to become caught up in them without ever understanding the true character of the leadership of the combatants. Strategic warning and understanding are the exception, not the rule. In most cases, the West cannot count on either and must plan its diplomatic and military actions accordingly.

As for the details of the events that led to large-scale fighting, many may remain controversial. The war only occurred after a long series of political and military clashes that began in 1979 and increased steadily in intensity and tempo throughout 1980. It is difficult to provide any clear date for the the start of these clashes, but they began shortly after Khomeini first came to power. In February 1979, however, a leading Iraqi Shi'ite cleric in Najaf, the Ayatollah Muhammed Baqar al-Sadr, congratulated Khomeini on his success and noted that "other tyrants" would see their day of reckoning. At roughly this point, Iran began a propaganda effort calling for the overthrow of "non-Muslim" Ba'ath rule, and Tehran radio began to refer to the Ayatollah al-Sadr as the "Khomeini of Iraq." Pro-Khomeini groups planted bombs in public areas and buildings, and the leading anti-Ba'ath Shi'ite group—Al Dawaa—began to organize active opposition to the government.

Iraq had initially greeted Khomeini's rise to power with great caution and had sought to restore much the same relationship with Iran that Iraq had established with the Shah. As it became clear that this relationship could not be restored, however, Iraq reached out to the opposition factions in Iran and increased its financial support to the Arab nationalist factions, or rebels, in Khuzistan. Iraq had already begun a major crackdown on opposition elements in 1978. It had actively moved to suppress Kurdish nationalists and had executed 21 Communists in May 1978.

Early in 1979, Iraq began to include Shi'ite elements in these purges, although it had previously treated such factions as being so ineffective that it did not regard them as threats. These crackdowns took on new intensity when minor riots took place at the two key Shi'ite holy cities of Najaf and Karbala. The Iraqi government conducted bloody crackdowns on pro-Iranian Shi'ite groups like Al Daawa. Some 97 members of these groups—including a significant number of Iraqi military officers—were executed in March 1979.

Meanwhile, Iran experienced internal security problems of its own. Iran had been forced into a major military campaign to suppress the Kurds and Azerbaijanis in April 1979. In May 1979, Iranian Arabs in Khuzistan began to demonstrate for independence or autonomy and clashed with Iranian troops in Khorramshahr. At the same time that Khomeini was calling for Shi'ite uprisings in Iraq, he was dealing with near civil war in Iran. During much of the summer and early fall, Iran was also actively involved in a war for control of the Kurdish sections of its own territory while providing arms and money to the Kurdish rebel factions in Iraq.

The end result was that the Kurds became pawns in the struggle between Iran and Iraq for the rest of the war. While Iran's Kurds had originally joined Khomeini in calling for the Shah's fall, Khomeini rapidly made it clear that he opposed any form of ethnic separatism or autonomy. As a result, the Kurdish Democratic Party of Iran (KDPI), led by a left-wing radical named Abdul Rahman Ghassemlou, began to organize military forces and occupied many of the Kurdish areas along the Iraqi border in northwest Iran. His forces, called the Pesh Merga, were able to occupy much of the countryside that had been abandoned by the regular army and were even able to occupy the city of Mahabad.

By late 1979, the Iranian Army had only two light formations in the area, and Iran's new Revolutionary Guards only had the strength to take some of the main towns and control the roads by day. The Iranian government could not take permanent control of Mahabad, and Iraq almost certainly began to provide Ghassemlou with funds and arms.

The situation in Iraq was equally complicated. When the Shah ended support of Iraq's Kurds in 1975, the rebel coalition called the Kurdish Democratic Party (KDP) collapsed. These forces were led by Mufstafa Barzani and his sons Massoud and Idris. Many Iraqi Kurds fled into Iran. Most settled in refugee camps and towns in the area, and the elder Barzani eventually died in exile in the U.S. Massoud and Idris, however, kept the KDP going. Syria also sponsored another faction of the KPD led by Jalal Talabani, which was called the Patriotic Union of Kurdistan (PUK).

The PUK originally sided with the KDPI against Khomeini.

Khomeini responded by offering the faction of the KDP led by the Barzanis funds and arms to resume their attack on Iraq in return for their support against the KDPI and PUK forces fighting in Iran. While the Barzanis and the KDP did not prove particularly effective in fighting against Iran's Kurds, they did develop the capability to conduct military operations in Iraq. In contrast, the PUK increasingly flirted with the idea of some kind of deal with Iraq, which steadily increased its support of the KDPI.

The first serious military clashes between Iran and Iraq seem to have begun In June 1979. Three Iraqi aircraft attacked several Iranian villages in the northern border area, which were believed to house Kurdish rebels. Iran responded by working with the Ayatollah al-Sadr to encourage pro-Khomeini riots in the Shia districts of Baghdad and in southern Iraq. This led the Ba'ath leadership to use the Iraqi Army to suppress the riots and to arrest up to 3,000 people.

The Iraqi government placed the Ayatollah al-Sadr under arrest on June 11 after it discovered that al-Sadr was planning to visit Khomeini in Iran. Tehran Radio responded by calling upon Shi'ites to replace the "gangsters and tyrants" of Baghdad. While new protests in Najaf and Karbala led the Iraqi government to limit its public action against the Ayatollah al-Sadr to house arrest, these same protests led to harsh action by the Iraqi security services, which put the protests down with military force. The protests also seem to have convinced the government that al-Sadr could not be allowed to survive. Al-Sadr seems to have been quietly executed the moment public attention diminished. Further, the Ba'ath seems to have purged Abd al-Hussein al-Mashhadi, the Shi'ite Secretary General of the Revolutionary Command Council (RCC), and up to 50 senior Shi'ite members, by the end of June.[20]

The struggle between Iran and Iraq was largely covert during most of the remainder of 1979, but it scarcely decreased in intensity. On July 17, 1979, Saddam Hussein quietly replaced Ahmed Hassan Bakr as President of Iraq and Chairman of the Ba'ath Party RCC, and Bakr left the country for "reasons of health."

Saddam Hussein seems to have taken power as President, at least in part because he felt Bakr was too weak in dealing with subversive elements. Days later, Saddam Hussein announced the discovery of what he claimed was a plot by the Ayatollah al-Sadr to exhort Shi'ite leaders to rise up and create a Khomeini-like revolution in Iraq. The arrests related to this "July Plot" rapidly turned into a purge of the Ba'ath as well, and 68 people—including a number of senior Ba'ath Party officials and military officers—were soon announced to have been arrested as part of a Shi'ite–al Daawa conspiracy. The actual number of arrests ran well over 100, and on August 8, 1979, Saddam Hussein publicly executed 22 of those he had arrested earlier.

Saddam Hussein continued to arrest, and sometimes execute, hostile Shi'ite leaders during the rest of the year. He also cracked down on Kurdish opposition elements and ruthlessly continued the purge of the Iraqi Communist Party (ICP) that he had begun in May 1978. This reached the point where the ICP formally ended its participation in the so-called National Progressive Front that had included the Ba'ath, the Kurdish Democratic Party, and the ICP. While the Soviet Union attempted to ease the treatment of the members of the ICP the Ba'ath arrested, a number of its members were executed.

Meanwhile, Iran shifted toward a steadily more radical and extreme form of Khomeini's revolution. The regular armed forces underwent a long series of purges and changes in command. The Islamic Revolutionary Guards Corps, which had emerged out of several small militias on June 16, 1979, fought a series of small civil wars for control of Iran's ethnic minorities and began to actively train forces to export the revolution. Students seized the U.S. Embassy in Tehran on November 4, 1979, and Khomeini began to issue broadcasts that called for a regrouping of the regular armed forces as the protectors of Islam.

While Khomeini and his colleagues were clearly preoccupied with the the problem of consolidating power in Iran—and began to face a new challenge from Marxist movements like the Fedayeen e-Khalq and Mujahideen e-Khalq, in addition to the earlier threat of ethnic separatism—they sent an increasing number of agents or "messengers" into Iraq in an attempt to encourage Iraq's Shi'ites to have an Islamic uprising of their own.

Iraq reacted by steadily increasing its internal security measures. In December 1979, Saddam Hussein called for the annulment of the Algiers Accord, and Iraq may have gone further. For example, Tehran Radio charged on December 14, 1979, that Iraq had entered Iranian territory but had been forced to withdraw. Saddam Hussein also held Iraq's first elections for its National Assembly since 1958. The elections were held on June 20, 1980, and a carefully selected group of 250 men, including large numbers of carefully chosen Shi'ites, gave Saddam Hussein a new degree of "legitimacy."

The Iranian government became increasingly concerned during this period with the fact Iraq was sheltering Iranian exiles and encouraging a coup d'etat in Iran. Iran's new President Abdul Hassan Bani-Sadr claimed that Iraq was actively sponsoring the Shah's last prime minister, Shapur Bakhtiar, and his last military commander, General Gholamali Oveissi, and had established some 20 training camps with a total of 45,000 men, with another 25,000 men in Bahrain and Oman.[21]

There was some truth to these claims, but these figures seem to have included virtually every opponent of the regime that had fled to other Gulf countries. While senior Iraqi officials admitted that Iraq had supported Bakhtiar and Oveissi in attempts to overthrow Khomeini, they stated that there were at most several thousand active supporters in Iraq and that Bakhtiar and Oveissi relied almost solely on the prospect of military coups and uprisings within Iran.[22]

By early 1980, both nations were sending arms to rebel groups in the opposing country and were conducting limited guerrilla training. Little of this conflict was public, however, until Al Dawaa made an unsuccessful hand-grenade attack on the life of Tariq Aziz, the Iraqi foreign minister, on April 1, 1980. Al Dawaa immediately took public credit for the attack and claimed that it was in part a reprisal for the fact that the Ba'ath had executed nearly 40 of its members the previous month.[23] Saddam Hussein retaliated by making membership in Al Dawaa punishable by death. Three days later, Khomeini made a broadcast that openly called for the Iraqi armed forces to overthrow Saddam Hussein.

Iraq replied by bombing Qasr e-Shirin on April 9. Iraq began to deport large numbers of Iraqi citizens of Iranian birth to Iran and quietly executed the Ayatollah al-Sadr—who had previously declared the Ba'ath regime was un-Islamic and that relations within it were religiously forbidden—and his sister Amina bint al-Huda. Khomeini declared three days of mourning, called for an uprising by the Iraqi military forces, and increased Iran's paramilitary training of Iraqi Shi'ites.

Iraq, in turn, arrested large numbers of Shi'ites in the key religious areas of Najaf, Karbala, and al-Thawa and expelled large numbers of Shi'ites as "Iranians," although many had only the most tenuous connection to Iran. Saddam Hussein also threatened that he would conduct, "any kind of battle to defend (Iraq's) sovereignty and honor."

Both nations severed diplomatic relations in June 1980. Iranian radio began constant broadcasts calling for the overthrow of the Ba'ath and attacking Saddam Hussein. Iraq allowed Khomeini's opponents—like Shapur Bakhtiar and General Oviessi—to broadcast attacks on Khomeini. Iraq also supported attempts to create anti-Khomeini coups inside Iran. The most notable of these coup attempts was sponsored by Bakhtiar and occurred in July 1980. It was called the Nojeh Coup and led to the arrest of some 500 army and air force personnel during July 21–29, long jail terms for at least 200 of them, and the execution of 50.[24] The failure of this coup may well have been a major reason that Iraq decided on overt invasion.

The tension between the two countries rose steadily during the rest of

July and August. In July, Saddam Hussein demanded that Iran return the land it had seized from Iraq under the Shah and that it regain control of the entire Shatt al-Arab. While Khomeini and the rest of Iran's leadership were deeply involved with the struggle to consolidate power in northern Iran, they also continued to step up their own propaganda attacks and efforts to obtain support from Iraq's Shi'ites, Kurds, and military forces. This may explain why Iraq suddenly elected a 50-man Kurdish Legislative Council on September 19, 1980.

A major new outbreak of fighting took place on September 2–4, when a new series of border clashes began near Qasr e-Shirin. Both Iran and Iraq have claimed that the war began in response to the other side's expansion of this clash. Iran has charged that Iraq provoked the clash as an excuse for its invasion of Iran. Iraq has charged that Iran attacked across the border near Qasr e-Shirin, Nasrabad, and Kalantari on September 4, 1980, and shelled the Iraqi border towns of Khanagir, Mendali, Zubatya, and Naft-Khana.

What is clear is that on September 6, Iraq reacted to these border clashes by threatening to seize some 350 square kilometers of Iranian territory in the area from Qasr e-Shirin to the Musain on the grounds that this territory should have been transferred to Iraq under the 1975 Algiers Accord. When Iran refused to cede the territory, Baghdad acted on its threats. Iraqi Radio announced on September 10 that it had seized some 80 square kilometers of the disputed territory in the Qasr e-Shirin area and had taken additional disputed territory near the villages of Saif Said and Zain al-Qaws. On September 14, Iraq announced that it had taken some 140 more square kilometers near Musain and the villages of Diyaal and Haila-Khadir.

Similar border clashes continued during the following week, and sporadic artillery fire occurred across the Shatt al-Arab. Iraq abrogated the 1975 Algiers Accord on September 17. It declared Iran had refused to abide by the Accord and that the Shatt al-Arab was "totally Iraqi and totally Arab." When Iran refused Iraqi demands that its ships take on Iraqi pilots, heavy fighting broke out along the waterway. Iran admitted losing two F-4 fighters in combat on September 19, and President Bani-Sadr decreed a general mobilization on September 20.

The Causes of Iraq's Decision to Invade

It is important to note that large-scale war still was not inevitable. Up to this point, the clashes between Iran and Iraq were no more severe than the clashes in the late 1960s and early 1970s. While both regimes were hostile and were actively working to undermine the other, there was nothing inevitable about committing all their forces to a border struggle or letting a war become an end in itself. Both sides were certainly vulnerable to internal political forces, but neither state had showed it could win major support from any faction in the other state or had the ability to cause a major political upheaval or coup. While both sides could point to the other's actions as cause for war, there was nothing inevitable about a large-scale conflict.

It rapidly became apparent, however, that Saddam Hussein had taken the decision to go beyond border clashes. Iraq's troop movements in early and mid-September showed that it had been preparing for a large-scale invasion for at least several weeks and more probably for several months. Within a matter of days after the clashes on September 14, Iraq launched its invasion, and the two nations became involved in a conflict that was to last nearly a decade and involve millions of men on both sides.

The Question of Iraqi Objectives

There is no way to determine Iraq's precise intentions and goals in invading Iran. It is virtually certain, however, that Saddam Hussein and his colleagues acted to achieve some mix of the following eight objectives:

- Securing the Ba'ath regime from Khomeini's declared intent of overthrowing it and from his efforts at subversion.
- Securing Iraq's borders from military incidents and obtaining the defense positions in the border area that the Shah had promised to transfer as part of the Algiers Accord, including the 200–300 square kilometers of territory around Qasr e-Shirin and Mehran that would help shield Baghdad from an Iranian invasion.
- Revoking the Algiers Accord and giving Iraq full control over all the waters of the Shatt al-Arab.
- Destroying Iranian military power while Iran was still weakened by its purges of its regular military forces and in the process of creating new revolutionary forces, while it was cut off from Western technical support and resupply, and while its manpower, training, logistics, and maintenance systems were in a state of near chaos.
- Creating conditions which would overthrow Khomeini and create a more friendly and secular regime in Iran.
- Conquering or liberating Iran's key oil province of Khuzistan and placing it under Iraqi or Arab rule. This would simultaneously

secure Iraq's access to the Gulf and deprive Iran of the economic assets needed to recover its status as a major Gulf power.

• Becoming so powerful that Iraq would be the dominant power in the Gulf, that no southern Gulf state would risk Iraqi hostility, and would force the Ba'ath Party in Syria to accept Iraq's preeminence.

• Taking advantage of its victory, and Egypt's isolation as a result of its peace treaty with Israel, to become the dominant power in the Arab world.

It is important to note that the fact Iraq invaded Iran is not prima facie evidence of aggressive intent or guilt for the war. The creation of a contingency capability to invade Iran cannot, under the circumstances, be regarded as a premeditated effort to either invade or dominate Iran. Given the conditions involved, such preparations were a prudent measure. Further, Iraq's preparation for its invasion and the initial execution of its attack often proved so inadequate that it is at least credible that Iraq was reacting to the border clashes in September by rapidly executing a plan that was never fully analyzed or prepared for.

While the idea of a defensive invasion may seem a contradiction in terms, it is scarcely historically unusual. Israel, for example, preempted its Arab neighbors in 1967 under conditions where it can scarcely be called an aggressor. It is also important to note that Saddam Hussein publicly accepted the first UN call for a cease-fire (UN Resolution 479) as early as September 28, 1980, and proposed a cease-fire of his own when Iran rejected the UN proposal.

It is also possible that Saddam Hussein cloaked the reason for this war in terms of very broad and ambitious rhetoric but expected to end the war quickly and to make only limited gains. He may have been willing to settle for a peace that would have overcome any taint of defeat that still lingered from the Algiers Accord of 1975, that gave the disputed area along the land boundary to Iraq, which returned control of the Shatt al-Arab to Iraq, which resulted in an end to political and religious pressure from Khomeini, and which enhanced Iraq's status in the Arab world by returning the islands the Shah had seized in the Gulf to Oman and the UAE.[25]

It does, however, seem probable that Iraq's leadership acted with at least some hope of overthrowing the Khomeini regime and/or weakening Iran to the point that Iraq would emerge as the dominant military power in the Gulf. Iraq was actively involved in supporting various coup attempts in Iran, both those supported by ex–Prime Minister Bakhtiar and those supported by various parts of the Iranian military. Iraq was actively encouraging Arab separatism in Khuzistan. It invaded Iran at a time when Iran was isolated in the world community by its seizure of the U.S. Embassy in Tehran and was fighting a variety of ethnic dissidents and two violently hostile Marxist movements. It also invaded at a point where Iran's military forces were in a state of chaos.

While Iraq made many defensive claims in launching its invasion, and soon stated it had limited objectives, this could easily have been political window dressing for a far more ambitious attack. Baghdad Radio certainly encouraged the idea of an Arab uprising in Khuzistan and the Iraqi Ministry of Information circulated books and pamphlets talking about the liberation of Khuzistan. Iraq also backed Bakhtiar in his plans to create a government in exile.

Finally, it is also all too possible that Saddam Hussein led Iraq into war on the basis of a confused and ill-defined mix of all these different goals and objectives. Anyone who has dealt with the senior leadership of the Ba'ath becomes aware of the fact that emotion and ideology are real, and not simulated, forces in shaping its behavior. Setting clear grand-strategic objectives for military action is unusual in any culture at any period in history, and Iraq's fundamentally distorted worldview scarcely equipped it to make highly sophisticated and controlled judgments. One of the basic lessons of war is that nations that see war in terms of rational actors and bargaining are neither able to predict war nor understand it once it occurs. Seeing Iraq in such terms may well be exceptionally unrealistic.

The Question of Iranian Objectives

The question of Iranian objectives is equally difficult to understand. Like many of the detailed diplomatic and military actions of the leaders of the French and Russian revolutions or the American declaration of war in 1812, Iran's new leadership unquestionably did a great deal to provide reasons for a war. It seems likely that Iran's leadership really did expect some kind of major uprising in Iraq and did everything possible to encourage it, including committing the kind of acts of covert subversion that must be treated as acts of war.

At the same time, however, Iran scarcely was ready to launch any large-scale conflict of its own. From the beginning of 1979 to the day that Iraq invaded, Khomeini's new revolutionary elite was engaged in a struggle for control of the Shah's armed forces, which it generally resolved by weakening the capability of the Iranian Army, Navy, and Air Force. Khomeini triggered an initial wave of desertions when on January 17, 1979, he called upon Iranian servicemen still loyal to the Shah to join the revolution. He purged and executed members of the general officer corps beginning in February 1979, and over 550 senior officers (many generals) had left the military or had been killed by the end of March.

Disagreements over the use of the regular armed forces against Iran's Kurds led to additional purges at the high-command level, and these were reinforced when the regular armed forces were used to fire on Arab demonstrators in Arabistan in April and May. These events also helped lead to the rise of revolutionary forces as a substitute for the regular armed forces and to the creation of a new 6,000-man Islamic Revolutionary Guards Corps (Pasdaran e-Inqilal e-Islami) on June 16, 1979. At the same time, the Islamic Republican Party (IRP) created its own military action arm called the Party of God (Hizbollah).

The debates over the role of regular and revolutionary forces in suppressing the Kurds and Arab separatists and in providing security for the revolution led to constant changes in high command throughout the rest of 1979. At the same time, the new revolutionary government cut the conscription period in half, thereby allowing some 40–60 percent of the Shah's military manpower to leave the armed forces through a mix of desertions, purges, resignations, and reassignments to revolutionary forces. Khomeini's new government also cancelled most of its military orders when it came to power and attempted to sell its 80 F-14 aircraft and Phoenix missiles back to the U.S.

The situation grew even worse after Iranian students seized the U.S. Embassy in Tehran on November 4, 1979, and took its occupants hostage. While the U.S. had arranged for a spare-parts shipment in October, the Iranians failed to take delivery, and the U.S. then suspended all spare-parts deliveries and imposed an embargo. All remaining U.S. technicians also left the country. Britain, which had been Iran's second largest Western supplier, also cut off most military deliveries.

Virtually all advanced training and maintenance activities came to a near halt, combined arms and joint exercises halted or degenerated to nearly farcical levels, and something like 30 percent of Iran's land-force equipment, 50–60 percent of its aircraft, and 60 percent of its helicopters were not operational when the war began. Repeated purges and reviews led to the loss of anywhere from 25–50 percent of the majors and field-grade officers in the Iranian Army and Air Force by February 1980, and thousands of skilled technicians and junior officers left the services.

When Iran acquired a new commander-in-chief when it elected Abdul Hassan Bani-Sadr President on February 3, 1980, this immediately added a struggle for political power between Khomeini's secular and religious supporters to the other convulsions in the Iranian military. Senior command shake-ups continued during June, and the

July 1980 coup attempt led to purges and executions which were still going on when the war started.

There was no agreement in Iran as to what—if anything—should replace the regular armed forces. The leftist movements—like the Tudeh, Mujahideen e-Khalq, and Mujahideen e-Fedayeen—opposed any regular forces. Leaders like Prime Minister Mohammad Ali Rajai wanted revolutionary popular forces which depended on mass mobilization and guerrilla warfare rather than regular forces and technology. Khomeini and President Bani-Sadr seem to have been more cautious, but their detailed goals and intentions were still totally unclear.

Khomeini had authorized attempts to reintroduce an effective conscription program before the war began, but these were still far from operational. The Iranian mobilization system—which had never been particularly well thought out—had become largely inoperable. The new Pasdaran or Revolutionary Guards only totaled about 30,000 men in lightly armed, organized units and were concentrating on internal security missions. The untrained volunteers, consisting largely of the Baseej and other volunteers, may have constituted an "army of 20 million" in speeches, but they had little military meaning in September 1980.

While Bani-Sadr was nominally commander-in-chief, there is no evidence that any true high command was still functional within the Iranian regular forces, and the new revolutionary forces lacked any coherent command or direction. Bani-Sadr and Rajai could not agree on the need for spare parts, how to reestablish and manage conscription, or even the need to man skilled positions like military maintenance and logistics. Leaders like Hashemi Rafsanjani and other senior members of the new Islamic Revolutionary Council (IRC) and Islamic Republican Party (IRP) openly stated that they would rather lose much of the country than see a secular government under Bani-Sadr restore professional military forces. In fact, the IRP was still committed to this position to the extent that it helped sabotage the agreement in 1981 that the U.S. would resume some shipments as a result of the accord reached in Algiers to settle the U.S.-Iranian hostage crisis.

Iran's lack of preparation for war is indicated by the fact that it did not even have a higher command operational in the border area at the point where the war began. There were no major combat units located at the border along the 450-mile front where Iraq invaded, and no Iranian regular artillery or armored battalions or attack helicopter units were located near the areas where Iraq claimed Iran fired across the border. Any Iranian artillery fire, therefore, had to be limited in volume and independent of any early intention to begin military operations. There were no major Iranian formations in the most critical area of the border, near Khorramshahr and Abadan. The nearest Iranian division had to move forward from Ahwaz, some 50–60 miles away. In fact, even Iraqi communiques indicate that Iraq did not encounter a single brigade-sized or large unit during the first two days of its invasion.

This does not absolve Iran of guilt for the war, but it does show that the bulk of the blame for any military escalation during September must be laid on Iraq, and that Iran was far from ready to go beyond subversion when the war began. For all the various Iraqi and Iranian claims relating to the incidents before the war, it is clear that it was Iraq that was preparing and deploying its forces for a major invasion of Iran and that Iran was not even prepared for an effective defense.[26]

Notes

1. The principal Arab tribe in the region was the Bani Kab. This tribe occasionally controlled both banks of the Shatt al-Arab, but control normally fluctuated between the Persians and Turks, with the Bani Kab shifting loyalty to the side that offered them the most or dividing their loyalty according to the interest of different tribal factions. Between 1920 and 1925, the local Sheik of the eastern faction of the Bani Kab attempted to capitalize on the various political upheavals in the region to create a separate emirate. He and his son were seized by the Shah's agents on April 25, 1925. The Arab population of the region then was forcibly Persianized, leading to a series of small tribal revolts between 1925 and 1946.

The rise of Nasser and Arab nationalism in the mid-1950s led to the birth of a "people's liberation" movement among the Arabs in Khuzistan and then an Arabistan Liberation Front (which was funded by Egypt and then Iraq). After the mid-1950s, Iran's treatment of those who asserted their Arab identity, or who it regarded as Arabs, was often discriminatory, as was true of the treatment of all non-Persians. This, however, was typical of the region. The Savak, Iran's secret police, did not conduct a particularly stringent effort to suppress Arab nationalism efforts in the area after the late 1960s, although it did conduct some arrests and executions of activists between 1970 and 1975. The first major outburst of Arab activity after that period occurred in April 1980 when Iranian forces, under the commander of the Iranian Navy, General Ahmad Madani, disarmed Arab activists and ordered a series of arrests that led to scattered fighting, some 300–500 dead, 200–300 wounded, and 400–700 arrests. By this time, however, Iraq was actively using the PFLP and other front groups to channel arms and money to the Arabistan Liberation Front and was providing military training in Iraq.

2. For an Iraqi or pan-Arab view of these issues, see Nicola Firzli and Nassim Khoury's *The Iran-Iraq Conflict*, Editions du Monde Arabe, 1981 (no location of publication listed). Distributed by the Iraqi Ministry of Information, pp. 48–49.

3. See Nikki R. Keddie, "The Minorities Question in Iran," in Shirin Tahir-Kheli and Shaheen Ayubi, *The Iran-Iraq War: New Weapons and Old Conflicts*, New York, Praeger, 1983, pp. 85–108, especially pp. 91–98, and Ervand Abrahamian, "Communism and Communalism in Iran," *International Journal of Middle East Studies*, vol. 4, October 1970, p. 293. Abrahamian estimates Iran's ethnic divisions in the late 1960s as 19 percent Azari (Turkic), 7 percent other Turkic, 7 percent Kurd, 3 percent Arab, 2 percent Baluchi, 1 percent Armenian and Assyrian, and 2 percent other. He estimates native Persian speakers as 45 percent, with 8 percent Mazandaranis and 6 percent Bakhtiaris and Lurs as marginal linguistic minorities. The figures issued by the CIA in 1971 in the annual *World Factbook* show a higher Persian speaking estimate, but the CIA analysts involved feel this estimate was too high.

4. Iraqi intelligence used the PFLP, as well as other "cutouts," to fund and train such movements.

5. Central Intelligence Agency (CIA), *World Factbook, 1981*, Washington, D.C., GPO, 1981, pp. 92–94.

6. Khomeini spent roughly a year in Turkey between expulsion from Iran and entry to Iraq. For a good description of Khomeini's role in Iran and Iraq during the 1960s and 1970s, see Dilip Hiro, *Iran Under the Ayatollahs*, New York, Routledge and Kegan Paul, 1985, pp. 42–81.

7. This agreement backfired in part against the Shah. Later talks allowed 130,000 Shi'ites from Iran to visit the key shrines in Iraq each year, and this allowed Khomeini to increase his contacts with Iranian Shi'ites by circulating large numbers of cassettes and prerecorded sermons and messages.

8. Khomeini did not preach openly against the Ba'ath regime during his stay in Iraq. He was carefully watched by the Iraqi secret police because the anti-Ba'athist Al Daawa al Islamiya (Islamic Call) movement had been founded in Najaf in the late 1960s. Khomeini did, however, establish close ties with Iraqi Shi'ite leaders, like the Ayatollah Muhammed Baqar al-Sadr, who were definitely anti-regime. Reports that Iraq somehow had something to do with the unexplained death of Khomeini's son, Mustapha, in late October 1977 seem totally spurious. Islam does not allow autopsies, and the cause of his death has never been established. The only charges made at the time, however, were that he was poisoned by the Savak. The facts are unclear, but the Savak may have done this in retaliation for an attempt on the life of the Shah's twin sister, Princess Ashraf, on September 13, 1977.

9. One of the rumors surrounding President Ahmed Hassan Bakr's resignation in July 1979 is that he split with Saddam Hussein over the latter's ruthlessness in suppressing the Shi'ites.

10. Hiro, op. cit., pp. 164–170.

11. Both Iraq and Iran had long-standing arguments over their boundaries dating back well before the treaties between the Persian and Ottoman empires. During the 17th and 18th centuries, control of the border area went to the strongest nation or to the strongest tribe when both were weak.

12. For an excellent description of the issues involved and their history, see Daniel Pipes, "A Border Adrift: Origins of the Conflict," in Tahir-Kheli and Ayubi, op. cit., pp. 3–26.

13. Keith McLachlan and George Joffe, *The Gulf War*, London, Economist Intelligence Unit, 1984, pp. 10–19.

14. About 630 kilometers of the line are in Turkey. It ends at Iskandarun Bay and is about 10 kilometers from Dortyol and less that 25 kilometers from the U.S. base at Incirlik.

15. More than half of the line to Syria is in Syria. It was the subject of major disputes long before the Iran-Iraq War began. Syria halted shipments during December 1966 to March 1967 and unilaterally nationalized the portion in Syria in 1972 and doubled transit fees in 1973. Shipments halted between April 1976 and February 1979 because of fights over transit fees and the Lebanese Civil War. Production then averaged only 300,000 to 500,000 BPD, and Syria kept 80,000–100,000 BPD for use at its refinery in Homs. Syria finally shut off Iraqi shipments on April 10, 1982, when it made a deal with Iran.

16. For a good discussion of Iraq's views of this vulnerability, see Christine Moss Helms, *Iraq: Eastern Flank of the Arab World*, Washington, D.C., Brookings, 1984, pp. 45–54.

17. The Gulf waters off the coast of Iraq are less than 18 meters (or 60 feet) deep.

18. Arms Control and Disarmament Agency (ACDA), *World Military Expenditures and Arms Transfers* (WMEAT), 1986, Washington, D.C., GPO, 1987, pp. 120–121.

19. See the discussion of Egypt in Firzli and Khoury, op. cit., and the various writings of Tariq Aziz and Saddam Hussein, as distributed by the Iraqi Ministry of Information during 1978 to 1980.

20. The evidence is uncertain, but Iraqi security forces seem to have uncovered a plot by the Ayatollah al-Sadr to flee to Iran in May 1979. The Ayatollah and a number of his followers seem to have been ready to organize a movement in exile to create a Shi'ite movement to overthrow the Ba'ath. See Hiro, op. cit., pp. 164–173; Edgar O'Ballance, *The Gulf War*, London, Brassey's, 1988, pp. 26–27; and Shahram Chubin and Charles Tripp, *Iran and Iraq at War*, Boulder, Westview, 1988, pp. 24–28.

21. O'Ballance, op. cit., pp. 26–27.

22. Based on interviews in Baghdad in 1984.

23. Al Dawaa claimed there had been a total of 79 political executions in Iraq during March.

24. See Nikola B. Schahgaldian, *The Iranian Military Under the Islamic Republic*, Santa Monica, Rand R-3473-USDP, 1987, pp. 22–24.

25. Experts dispute the extent to which Oman and the UAE prepared at the start of the war to support an Iraqi invasion of the Tunb Islands in the Straits of Hormuz and the Aba Musas. It is important to note that the Shah did not seize the islands in the Straits of Hormuz when the British left; they had been in Iranian hands for years. Similarly, it is far from clear that any element of the UAE had the slightest desire to become involved in a war over any of the islands in the Gulf. Nevertheless, some authorities on the Gulf feel that Oman and Abu Dhabi did agree to allow such Iraqi action and were stopped from granting such support only after quiet British intervention. Unconfirmed reports also exist that Bahrain, Kuwait, Qatar, and Saudi Arabia agreed to

provide Iraq with the financial and material support it needed to conduct the war just two days before Iraq invaded Iran. There is no question that Saddam Hussein did inform several leaders in the Gulf in July and August that Iraq planned to invade Iran (the author was told this by some of the leaders involved), but it is far from clear that Iraq got a "blank check" from any southern Gulf state.

26. Senior officials in several southern Gulf countries have indicated that Iraq began to "consult" on its intention to attack Iran in May 1980, and senior Saudi sources stated in early 1981 that President Hussein of Iraq clearly announced his intention to invade Iran during his visit to Saudi Arabia in early August.

3

VARIOUS FACTORS AFFECTING
THE COURSE OF THE WAR

The historical factors that shaped the initial course of the Iran-Iraq War have already been described. There were, however, a number of other strategic and military factors that played a powerful role in shaping the course of the fighting once the war began. These factors include the strengths and weaknesses of each side, the relative economic power of Iran and Iraq, each nation's ability to buy arms, each nation's ability to mobilize their respective manpower, and the initial structure and capability of their forces.

The Strengths and Weaknesses of Each Side

Iran and Iraq began the war with a very different mix of advantages and disadvantages. These advantages and disadvantages shaped each nation's approach to war, led each side to take a different approach to tactics and technology, and helped shape its management of the war.

Iran's Mix of Advantages and Disadvantages

In spite of its political and military instability, Iran began the war with a number of significant advantages. These advantages included:

- Strategic depth: Iran's main cities and most-critical oil facilities were a considerable distance from the Iran-Iraq border area.
- The existence of a large prerevolutionary military structure which still had a significant numbers of troops, first-line U.S. and other weapons systems, and large stockpiles of supplies. While the efficiency of this military machine was severely damaged during the convulsions following the Shah's fall, the stockpiled weapons and trained cadres were decisive in Iran's initial ability to defend.[1]

- The existence of a rising force of armed and semitrained militiamen who had been assembled before the war as Baseej, Hizbollah, and Revolutionary Guards. These forces existed to safeguard the revolution, both as members of Khomeini's local defense and security force and as the "Army of Twenty Million," which was originally formed to meet a possible U.S. invasion following the seizure of American hostages.
- A revolutionary fervor which helped to maintain the morale of Iranian troops because of a perceived threat to the survival and expansion of the Islamic Revolution.
- Possession of some of the most advanced conventional technology which the U.S. was capable of providing. This was the result of a 1972 decision by President Nixon to provide Iran with weapons that would enable it to serve as the "policeman" of the Gulf.[2]
- Large cash reserves and continuing oil revenues.

At the same time, the Iranian military (and especially the Army) faced a number of disadvantages at the outset of the war. These disadvantages included:

- Estrangement from the U.S., Iran's principal supplier of weapons, support, and spare parts, and from virtually all the other nations in the Gulf area and in much of the Arab world. Iran's revolutionary ideology and attacks on the superpowers and more moderate and conservative Arab states isolated it from other nations and drove these nations to support Iraq both before and during the conflict.
- Constant ideological and political interference in the management of the regular forces, including the creation of a whole new class of religious commissars. Once the war began, this was followed by religious and political intervention at every level, from grand strategy to tactics and supply, often forcing the wrong tactics and strategy on Iranian forces.
- Continuing rivalry at every level between the regular armed forces, the emerging Pasdaran, and the various rivals for power around Khomeini. This feuding affected every aspect of Iranian operations from late 1980 onwards.
- A shortage of officers and NCOs because of at least two major purges which had eliminated at least 12,000 personnel (10,000 of whom were from the army) by the beginning of the war. These purges led to a fragmented and dysfunctional command structure in the army, although the navy and air force command structures remained relatively intact.[3]

- A weak logistics system which denied Iran the ability to use much of its stocks. Iran had created the shell of a computerized logistics system but never the software to retrieve stored items. Iranian forces had to rely on squads which individually hunted down key stocks and had no central system for ordering, allocating, and distributing its stocks.
- Prewar dependence on foreign technical support personnel in many critical areas, such as maintenance, technical advice, training, and tactical and procurement planning. Most of this technical support left Iran following the Shah's fall, and much of the remainder had left when Iran seized the U.S. Embassy.
- A decline in proficiency in regard to a variety of military skills. This decline has been particularly important since 1981 when the Iranian military school and training system collapsed and was replaced by ideological and infantry training.
- A large number of desertions. These reached about 60 percent of the Shah's army by July 1980, although the Khomeini regime was able to recover much of this manpower once the war began.[4]
- Continuing internal security problems with various ethnic minorities and Marxist groups like the People's Mujahideen.

Iraq: Advantages and Disadvantages

The Iraqis had a different set of advantages and disadvantages. Iraq's main advantages included:

- Far greater political and military stability during the period before the war. Iraq's leadership was united under a single active autocrat, and its military forces were firmly under his control. While there were some divisions within the armed forces because of the existence of a Ba'ath controlled Popular Army, and both the intelligence service and the Ba'ath maintained a second channel of political control over the armed forces, the Iraqi military never experienced anything remotely approaching the degree of disruption that affected the Iranian military.
- Friendly relations with neighboring states, which began to develop in the mid-1970s when Iraq largely halted its attempts to overthrow the regimes of its wealthy conservative neighbors and opened trade ties with Western Europe. Iraq was able to sustain these relations throughout the course of the war.
- Continuing access to a diversified supply of modern weapons, with most advanced weapons systems being French- or Soviet-made. While multiple sources of supply can create significant problems in terms of standardization and training, they also are a

substitute for limited, but less reliable, sources of supply. Iraq used France to obtain arms during the period the USSR flirted with Iran and afterwards in playing both nations off against each other to obtain key arms and technologies.[5] Iraq also got weapons and spare parts from Italy, Bulgaria, and Poland, and Egypt sold Iraq about $1 billion in hardware following the initial stages of the war.[6]

- Iraq had never placed as high reliance on foreign technical support as Iran. It could not operate or maintain its equipment as well as Iran did before the Shah's fall and the expulsion of Western technicians, but it had a relatively effective national logistics, combat, and service support system and could operate its forces, major equipment, and support systems on its own. While its individual weapons were less capable than those of Iran, they also were easier to maintain and operate.
- Large financial reserves and excellent credit at the beginning of the war.
- A relatively mature revolution with steadily rising living standards, well-planned economic developments, and improving conditions for potentially disaffected Shi'ite and Kurdish groups, mixed with a far more secular history and social structure than Iran.
- Financial backing from the Gulf Cooperation Council (GCC) states and limited military backing from Egypt and Jordan.[7]

Like Iran, however, Iraq faced major disadvantages. These not only helped ensure that its initial offensive against Iran did not succeed, they severely limited the effectiveness of its defense against Iran's counteroffensives.

- Iraq's leaders suffered from a combination of strategic illusions and impossible ambitions. They saw Iran as weak and divided. They accepted pan-Arab myths regarding the willingness of the Arab population of southwestern Iran to shift its allegiance to Iraq, and they saw the war as a quick means of asserting leadership over the Gulf and the Arab world.
- Iraq lacked strategic depth; its oil exports were dependent on access to a narrow stretch of the Gulf and pipelines through Syria and Turkey that were subject to political interdiction and sabotage.
- Iraq had a heavily politicized military which had been subjected to repeated prewar purging. This purging was designed to ensure the rise of officers who were loyal to the Ba'ath and

then to Saddam Hussein. The Iraqis had only sent limited numbers of their officers to receive training abroad because the most likely source of this training was the Soviet Union. It was feared that officers trained there might become subversives.[8] The net result was that the Iraqi officer and NCO corps had little real readiness for offensive combat. This politicization of the officer corps forced new reassignments and purges during the early years of the war to improve the effectiveness of Iraqi forces. As many as 300 generals and other high-ranking officers were reported to have been relieved by the government as of mid-1982 because of dereliction of duty and incompetence, and 15 generals seem to have been shot. Saddam Hussein may also have hoped to deflect blame for the war's disasters and prevent a major coup attempt by disgruntled officers.[9]

- Many senior officers were Sunni Muslims from Mosul and Takrit, while the majority of troops were Shi'ite. These divisions did not weaken the willingness of Iraqi forces to fight, but they put religion, regionalism, and politics before military professionalism in shaping the selection and operations of Iraq's command structure.
- Iraq's forces lacked an adequate training and technical base. Iraq had many first line weapons systems, but few advanced command, control, communications, and intelligence (C^3I) targeting, munitions, training, and support systems.
- When the war began, Iraq was in the process of shifting from reliance on Soviet arms to a mix of Western and Soviet arms. The USSR had transferred weapons but not training and technology. France and other European suppliers had not had any major impact in terms of Iraqi training, tactics, and support. Iraq had virtually no Navy, and its Air Force lacked any real concept of operations or training for large-scale war.
- Iraq had an unsophisticated and highly politicized intelligence system which was almost solely reliant on high ideological human intelligence (HUMINT) resources. Iraq had minimal signals intelligence (SIGINT) capabilities and minimal skills in using reconnaissance aircraft and photo intelligence (PHOTINT). Iraqi intelligence did as much to provide political and military misinformation as information.
- There was a lack of sophisticated and integrated C^3I IBM capability. Iraq's air control and warning (AC&W) system was technically weak, and its surface-to-air missile (SAM) forces lacked effective warning, battle management, and C^3 capability.
- There was considerable initial tension with the USSR, which

dated back to Iraq's struggle with the Kurds and Iraqi Communist Party, compounded by a strong Soviet interest in improved ties with Iran.

• Serious tension existed between Iraq's Sunni-dominated Ba'ath government, its Shi'ite majority and Kurdish minority, and increasing military activity by Kurdish liberation groups from 1984 onwards.

The Impact of Economics

Iran and Iraq's relative ability to mobilize their economy and oil wealth was a major factor shaping the entire course of the war. The detailed military economics of the Iran-Iraq War are shown in Table 3.1. These data are often highly uncertain, but it seems clear that the disorder following the Iranian revolution gave Iraq great economic advantages and that Iraq's access to friendly states was often decisive in giving it the resources to continue fighting once the war began.

The relative trends in Iraqi and Iranian military expenditures during 1973 to 1988, in constant 1984 dollars, are a particularly important indicator. It is clear from these figures that Iraq was able to shift from a 3:1 inferiority in total defense spending relative to Iran in 1973–1974—the period just before the Algiers Accord—to a significant superiority by the time of the Shah's fall.

It is also clear that Iraq was able to maintain this superiority during the course of the rest of the war. This superiority, however, was due far more to Iraq's access to support from its neighbors in the southern Gulf than to any planning on Iraq's part. As the oil production figures in Table 3.1 show, Iraq proved highly vulnerable to Iran's attack on its oil export facilities in the Gulf and then to Syria's willingness to cut off Iraqi oil exports through Syria.

It seems likely from the history of the war during 1980–1983 that if Iraq had not had access to massive external aid and Iran's military forces and economy had not been crippled by the revolution and Iran's willingness to alienate the Soviet Union and the West, Iran would probably have won the war. Iraq's ability to survive was as dependent upon Kuwait, Saudi Arabia, and other friendly states as on its military forces, and its ability to achieve superior military strength at the front was dependent upon some $35 to $45 billion in cash aid and loans.

The CIA estimates which shape the data in Table 3.1 may understate the scale of Iranian military spending and total Iranian military manpower once the war began. Some working estimates by private experts indicate that Iran spent far more of its resources on the

TABLE 3.1 Iranian and Iraqi Military Efforts: 1973–1988

| Year | Military Manpower (1,000s)[a] | | Military Expenditures | | | | Arms Imports | | | |
| | | | Current $M | | Constant '84 $M | | Current $M | | Constant '84 $M | |
	Iraq	Iran	Iraq	Iran	Iraq	Iran	Iraq	Iran	Iraq	Iran
1973	105	285	1486	3112	—	—	625	525	—	—
1974	110	310	3037	8955	—	—	625	1000	—	—
1975	155	385	3286	13440	5969	24410	750	1200	—	—
1976	190	420	3876	14720	6621	25140	1000	2000	—	—
1977	140	350	4736	11910	7583	19060	1900	2600	3028	4143
1978	362	350	6145	14460	9168	21610	2400	2200	3552	3256
1979	444	415	6967	9058	9553	12420	3000	1500	4100	2050
1980	430	305	12160	7725	15280	9708	2500	410	3118	511
1981	392	260	15100	8519	17320	9768	4300	1000	4955	1152
1982	404	240	15380	9593	16750	10330	6400	1600	6900	1725
1983	434	240	15160	8376	15730	8688	6800	925	7025	956
1984	788	335	15920	11690	15920	11690	9500	2400	9500	2400
1985	788	345	(12866)	(14091)	—	—	4000	1700	3860	1645
1986	(845)	(705)	(11579)	(6110)	—	—	4900	1800	4614	1695
1987	(1000)	(654)	(13990)	(5900)	—	—	—	—	—	—
1988	(1000)	(605)	—	(8960)	—	—	—	—	—	—

Year	Military Spending as % of GNP		Military Spending as % of CGE		Arms Imports as % of Total Exports		Average Annual Oil Exports in MMBD	
	Iraq	Iran	Iraq	Iran	Iraq	Iran	Iraq	Iran
1973	25.5	8.3	57.7	30.2	69.9	15.4	2.02	5.86
1974	21.6	13.8	45.1	33.9	26.3	18.4	1.97	6.02
1975	17.4	17.6	29.8	31.9	17.8	11.6	2.26	5.35
1976	17.2	15.6	37.5	37.1	28.8	15.5	2.42	5.89
1977	18.1	11.9	40.6	26.5	48.7	17.8	2.35	5.67
1978	19.2	16.6	28.0	37.4	57.0	16.2	2.56	5.24
1979	14.9	8.2	24.9	25.1	41.8	15.4	3.48	3.17
1980	22.5	6.6	26.9	19.7	17.9	3.3	2.51	1.67
1981	45.1	6.8	43.9	20.7	20.7	8.0	0.99	1.38
1982	44.8	6.7	50.8	21.7	29.7	13.4	0.97	2.28
1983	44.3	5.2	NA	18.6	55.9	5.0	0.92	2.49
1984	42.5	7.2	NA	29.9	85.8	15.6	1.20	2.19
1985	—	—	—	—	37.9	14.6	1.44	2.26
1986	—	—	—	—	52.7	17.4	1.73	1.93
1987	—	—	—	—	—	—	2.08	2.45
1988	—	—	—	—	—	—	2.50	2.20

aFigures for Iran do not include Revolutionary Guards.

SOURCES: Many of the data are adjusted by the author. Economic and manpower data for 1973–1986 are taken from ACDA, *World Military Expenditures and Arms Transfers: 1987*, Washington, GPO, 1988, pp. 62–63 and 105. Note that major fluctuations are made in the entire series of CIA estimates used in each edition of the ACDA document and that the figures shown are highly uncertain. The figures shown in parentheses come from the annual edition of the IISS Military Balance (London: International Institute for Strategic Studies) and are in current dollars when applicable. The oil production estimates were furnished separately by the CIA. They include total production rather than exports. Gas production is excluded.

war than Iraq did. Even so, the CIA figures seem to be broadly correct in indicating that Iran had considerable difficulty in mobilizing its economy and government spending both during the critical period before the war and then during the years that followed.

It also is clear from virtually all the data available on the economics of the war that the conflict rapidly strained both nations to their limits. This strain was compounded by both the "oil war" each side conducted against the other side's ability to export and by the crash in world oil prices in early 1985. While both Iran and Iraq still had the financial resources to continue fighting, both sides faced a growing strain on their economy, and both sides increasingly had to give up more butter for guns.

The importance of economics in any enduring conflict is another critical lesson of the war, as is the vulnerability of Iran and Iraq to strikes on their economy and strategic exports. The war has set a precedent for economic warfare that many other Third World states are likely to follow, both to try to defeat their opponent and to force external action or support for their cause.

The Impact of Arms Imports and Technology Transfer

Iraq was consistently able to benefit from superior access to arms imports and superior technology transfer both just before and during the war. However, if one looks at the five-year period between 1974 and 1978, one finds that Iran imported a total of roughly $8.7 billion dollars, of which nearly $6.7 billion came from the U.S. Virtually all of the rest came from high-technology exporters, and only about $500 million came from nations who export relatively low-technology systems. In contrast, Iraq imported a total of roughly $5.3 billion dollars worth of arms, of which less than $800 million came from from high-technology exporters.[10]

These trends reversed rapidly, however, after the fall of the Shah. In the mid-1970s, the Shah was spending 50 percent to 100 percent more on arms imports per year than Iraq. By 1978, Iraq had achieved near equity, and in 1979, Iraq was spending twice as much on arms imports as Iran. Iraq had a greater than 5:1 lead in 1980 and 1981, in spite of the fact the USSR suspended most of its arms shipments to Iraq. Iraq was also able to obtain more than half its arms from sources outside the Soviet-bloc and nearly one-third from relatively high-technology suppliers in Western Europe. This Iraqi lead in spending and access to high-technology arms continued throughout the war, although its advantage was greater during the first three years of the war than during the period from 1986 to 1988.

TABLE 3.2 Iranian and Iraqi Access to Foreign Supplies of Arms: 1980–1987
(New Arms Sales Agreements in $Current Millions)

Supplier	Iraq			Iran		
	1980– 1983	1984– 1987	1980– 1987	1980– 1983	1984– 1987	1980– 1987
USSR	8,820	11,450	20,270	615	5	620
China	1,610	2,575	4,185	225	1,590	1,815
Other Communist	2,980	2,690	5,670	1,330	2,565	3,895
Total Communist	13,410	16,715	30,125	2,170	4,160	6,330
European Non-Communist	5,710	4,580	10,290	590	2,995	3,585
U.S.*	0	0	0	0	0*	0*
Other Non-Communist	1,195	1,915	3,110	1,120	775	1,895
Total Non-Communist	6,905	6,495	13,400	1,710	3,770	5,480
GRAND TOTAL	20,315	23,210	43,525	3,880	7,930	11,810
Iraq as % of Iran	524%	293%	369%	—	—	—
Iran as % of Iraq	—	—	—	19%	34%	27%

*Does not include covert U.S. arms sales.

SOURCE: Adapted from Richard F. Grimmett, "Trends in Conventional Arms Transfers to the Third World by Major Supplier," Congressional Research Service, Report Number 888-352, May 9, 1988.

The detailed patterns in the total flow of arms to Iran and Iraq are shown in Table 3.2. Other estimates by the CIA and Congressional Research Service reflect the following trends:[11]

- During 1980–1987, Iraq and Iran collectively spent over $64 billion on new arms agreements, or more than one-fifth of all the arms transfers to the Third World.

- The Soviet Union alone accounted for 29 percent of all arms agreements with Iran and Iraq, the PRC accounted for 12 percent, all other non-Communist states accounted for 16 percent, European non-Communist states accounted for 31 percent, and all other non-Communist states accounted for 11 percent.
- During 1980–1987, the USSR made 37 percent of all new arms agreements with Iraq, versus 10 percent for China, and 12 percent for other Communist countries. European non-Communist states made 30 percent of the new agreements, and the other non-Communist states made 12 percent. European non-Communist sales agreements were dominated by France. Other Communist-country sales came from Eastern Europe, and, initially, North Korea.
- During 1980–1987, the PRC made 21 percent of all new arms agreements with Iran, versus 2 percent for the USSR and 31 percent for other Communist countries. European non-Communist countries made 33 percent of these agreements, and all other non-Communist countries made 31 percent. European non-Communist sales agreements were from a wide mix of states. Other Communist-country sales came largely from North Korea.
- During 1980–1987, Iraq and Iran collectively received over $55.3 billion in new arms deliveries, or roughly one-fifth of all the arms transfers to the Third World.
- The Soviet Union alone accounted for 38 percent of all arms deliveries to Iran and Iraq, and the PRC accounted for 11 percent. All other Communist states accounted for 17 percent, European non-Communist states accounted for 25 percent, and all other non-Communist states accounted for 9 percent.
- During 1980-1987, the USSR made 47 percent of all new arms deliveries to Iraq, versus 10 percent for China, and 13 percent for other Communist countries. European non-Communist states made 7 percent of new deliveries. European non-Communist deliveries were dominated by France. Other Communist-country sales came from Eastern Europe, and, initially, North Korea.
- During 1980–1987, the PRC made 15 percent of all new arms deliveries to Iran, versus 5 percent for the USSR and 33 percent for other Communist countries. European non-Communist countries made 30 percent of these deliveries, and all other non-Communist countries made 16 percent. European non-Communist deliveries were from a wide mix of states. Other Communist-country sales came largely from North Korea.
- The patterns in sales versus agreements reflect Iran's shift to the PRC as a major supplier and the fact that European states are

much slower in making major deliveries—largely because of lower production capacity—than Communist states.

- The Soviet Union was consistently Iraq's largest arms supplier. It sold some $20.3 billion worth of arms to Iraq after the war began and $11.5 billion worth during 1984–1987. It has been closely matched by its East European allies. They sold $10.4 billion worth of arms during 1980–1983 and $4.7 billion worth during 1984–1987. These patterns are interesting because they show that East Europe provided massive arms supplies to Iraq during a period that the USSR was publicly claiming to be reducing supply. Further, these sales patterns do not reflect major Iraqi problems in obtaining Soviet-bloc arms during the period Iraq was having the most difficulty in maintaining its oil revenues.

- Iraq got $20.3 billion worth of deliveries from the USSR during 1980–1987, with $8.8 billion worth during 1980–1983 and $11.5 billion worth during 1984–1987. In spite of a major increase in PRC arms transfers to Iran, the PRC delivered $1.6 billion worth of arms to Iraq during 1980–1983 and $2.6 billion worth during 1984–1987. West European countries delivered $5.7 billion worth of arms to Iraq during 1980–1983 and $4.6 billion worth during 1984–1987.

- The PRC gradually emerged as Iran's largest arms supplier, although North Korea has been a strong rival and both Western and Eastern Europe have made major sales. The PRC made $3.04 billion worth of all new arms sales agreements to Iran during 1980–1987. It made $505 million worth of all new arms sales agreements to Iran during 1980–1983 but $2,535 million worth of all new arms sales agreements to Iran during 1984–1987. The PRC made 15 percent of all new arms deliveries to Iran during 1980–1987. It made 6 percent of all new arms deliveries to Iran during 1980–1983 but 20 percent of all new arms deliveries to Iran during 1984–1987.

- The Soviet Union made $615 million worth of arms delivers to Iran during 1980–1983 but only $5 million worth during 1984–1987. Nevertheless, Eastern Europe sold $3.3 billion dollars worth of arms to Iran during 1984–1987.

- Western Europe has profited from sales to both sides. It sold $3.6 billion worth of arms to Iran during 1980–1987 and $10.3 billion worth to Iraq. The patterns in sales to Iran are particularly interesting because virtually all of the sellers were denying such sales took place. Western Europe delivered $590 million worth of arms to Iran during 1980–1983 but $2,995 million worth during 1984–1987.

These sales patterns reflect the lesson that the competition for world arms sales and rivalries between major arms exporters are a key factor sustaining modern wars. These sales patterns also show that applying the term "low-level conflict" to every war in the the Third World is inherently ridiculous. The volume of arms shipments to Iran and Iraq, before and during the war, shows it has been an intense conflict by any standard.

It is important to stress, however, that technology transfer was as important as the imbalance in the total value of arms shipments. Table 3.3 provides further data on the arms transfers to both sides and shows that Iran alienated both its Western and Soviet-bloc arms suppliers, while Iraq was able to buy arms from France and the USSR with comparative freedom. The Iranians also largely rejected or alienated Western and Soviet-bloc sources of aid in training and technology transfer, while Iraq was able to gain access to such support.

The data in Tables 3.2 and 3.3 also understate Iran's problems in making effective arms purchases because Iran was forced to buy from far more diverse sources than these tables can itemize, and to buy many of its critical supplies and munitions for its Western-supplied equipment on the equivalent of the black market. This kind of purchasing often led to gross inefficiencies, outright fraud, long delays, and shortages in key parts and munitions. The need Third World countries have for a reliable source of arms imports, as well as for continued supplies of spare parts and munitions, is another critical lesson of the war.

Even Iraq generally did a poor job of absorbing advanced military technology and using it effectively. The reasons for this failure have been discussed earlier, but the primary factor was the politicization of the military and military decision making. Iraq was educationally advanced enough to have done a far better job of absorbing arms and technology than its politics and government permitted.

This brings up a point of major importance in evaluating Third World military forces. Sheer numbers and the size of the order of battle are rarely relevant measures of military power. It is generally necessary to evaluate each major weapons technology on a case-by-case basis and often unit-by-unit.

In some cases, technology transfer can be remarkably successful and may be coupled to an adaptation to local conditions that can make Third World forces more effective than those of the West. In other cases, politicization, buying arms for prestige or glitter, a tendency to ignore service and sustainability requirements, serious problems in education and training, and weaknesses throughout the command and control system can deprive a force of most of its effectiveness. The

TABLE 3.3 Iranian and Iraqi Access to Foreign Supplies of Arms: 1982–1986
($Current Millions)

Supplier Nation	Sales to Iraq	Sales to Iran
U.S.	0	10
France	4,500	40
U.K.	70	80
FRG	625	0
USSR	15,300	240
Poland	525	20
Czechoslovakia	410	30
China	3,300	1,200
Other	7,010	6,785
Total	31,740	8,405

SOURCE: Arms Control and Disarmament Agency, *World Military Expenditures and Arms Transfers, 1987*, Washington, D.C., GPO, 1988, p.129.

ability to understand this situation on a country-by-country basis is critical to appraising the true military strength of both potential threats and friendly forces.

Both the Iraqis and Iranians felt that they had far more effective support in technology transfer and training from the West than they received from the Soviet-bloc nations, North Korea, the People's Republic of China, and other Third World arms suppliers. In most cases, the Western effort at superior training, at ensuring serviceability, and in providing the munitions and supplies for sustainability proved to be a comparatively cheap force multiplier. This too is a major lesson of the war.

The Impact of Manpower and Demographics

The struggle each side went through to mobilize its manpower is as important as the struggle each side went through to mobilize its economy and to obtain arms. Once again, Iraq won this struggle, both in the period immediately before the war and during the conflict. It again did so largely because of the chaos in Iran's military manpower caused by the Iranian revolution.

By every normal demographic standard, Iran should have had an immense advantage over Iraq. If one adjusts for current population growth rates and uses CIA estimates, one gets the manpower data shown in Table 3.4. There are considerable uncertainties in these estimates, and Iraq was better able to substitute imports and foreign

TABLE 3.4 Iranian and Iraqi Military Manpower

Category	In 1980 Iran (millions)	In 1980 Iraq (millions)	In 1980 Iran × Iraq	In Early 1988 Iran (millions)	In Early 1988 Iraq (millions)	In Early 1988 Iran × Iraq
Total Population	39.1	13.6	2.9	50.4	17.0	3.0
Annual Growth Rate	2.9%	3.5%	.82%	3.3%	3.6%	.91%
Ethnic Divisions						
Persian	63	—	—	63	—	—
Other Iranian	13	—	—	13	—	—
Arabs and Other Semitic	1	70.9	—	3	75	—
Kurds	3	18.3	—	3	15–20	
Assyrians	—	2.4	—	—	—	—
Turkic/Turkoman	18	2.4	—	18	—	—
Turkoman, Assyrian, and Other	—	—	—	—	5–10	—
Other	—	7.7	—	—	—	—
Religion						
Shi'ite	95	50	—	93	60–65	—
Sunni	2	40	—	5	32–37	—
Christian	—	8	—	—	—	—
Other	3	2	—	2	3	—
Work Force						
Native	12.0	3.1	3.9	14.9	4.4	3.5
Foreign	(?)	(?)	—	([a])	1.0	—
Total	12.0	(3.1)	3.9	14.9	5.4	2.9
Military Manpower						
Males Ages 15–49	8.6	3.0	2.9	11.5	3.8	3.0
Militarily Fit	5.1	1.7	3.0	6.8	2.2	2.1
Annual Total Reaching Military Age (Age 21)	0.383	0.146	2.6	0.54	0.18	2.7

[a]Data on Afghan workers are not available.

SOURCES: Projected by the authors from the Central Intelligence Agency, *The World Factbook, 1981,* pp. 92–94, and *1987,* pp. 117–118, Washington, D.C., GPO, 1980 and 1986.

labor for its own military manpower and work force, and this helped it overcome Iran's advantage in total population. Nevertheless, the Iran-Iraq War is a lesson in the fact that it is military organization and not total population that counts.

Iraq started the war with a decisive advantage because of the disarray in Iran's forces. It lost this advantage in 1981–1984 because of the revolutionary and nationalist fervor that allowed Iran to rapidly increase its manpower. After some false starts, however, Iraq built up a steadily expanding, permanent professional army. This eventually allowed Iraq to build up a standing force of nearly one million men and to recapture its advantage over Iran.

Iran relied heavily on a rapid temporary mobilization of manpower, with short periods of training, to meet its manpower needs and then let much of this manpower go back to civilian life. Even during 1981–1984, Iraq often had more manpower on the front than Iran and virtually always had more trained manpower. Iran also lacked the mix of combined arms, the logistic and supply systems, and wealth to use its manpower numbers effectively. Iran was forced to rely on training and equipping most of its manpower for light infantry roles. Even when Iran did call up masses of volunteers for particular offensives, these call-ups were often at least partial failures because of internal political battles within the government over how mobilization should be accomplished and who should control the recruiting and training base.

As a result, Iran had severe difficulties in using such volunteers to do more than score short-term gains near the front. A successful offensive requires mobility and firepower, and Iran needed far more armor, artillery, air defenses, and logistical support than it possessed to exploit its potential lead in manpower with full effectiveness. Iran also took high casualties among its combat-trained Revolutionary Guards forces, while other Pasdaran cadres tend to have become institutionalized in urban and rural security roles or in Iran's new emerging power elite. Poor medical care sometimes increased the death-to-wound ratio, while erratic mobilization campaigns rotated volunteer manpower in and out of service that needed more training and experience to become properly effective. This limited Iran's ability to absorb popular reserves and use them effectively.

A combination of age and political upheaval meant that Iran continued to lose the trained personnel that served under the Shah in the regular armed forces. Recruiting for the regular forces was erratic from 1978 onwards, and the regular forces never rebuilt their training base. Further, the bulk of Iran's regular forces were kept in the border area that guarded the traditional invasion route. They had little refresher training, and most were not heavily committed to battle since 1984.

This mix of manpower, equipment, and economic problems helps to explain why Iran proved unable to launch more than one or two major offensive thrusts at a time, in spite of the fact that Iran's best strategy for exploiting its superiority in manpower would be to attack simultaneously on several fronts. Such a simultaneous attack strategy might have denied Iraq the ability to reinforce its defenses against any given thrust by drawing on manpower in other parts of the front and to match a single major Iranian thrust with an equivalent mix of Iraqi manpower and technology.

Iraq also had manpower problems. It began the war with only limited mobilization. It then managed to mobilize a large part of its male population by stripping its domestic labor force to the bone but only at cost of forced call-ups and, often, forced recruiting sweeps in its major cities. Iraq did provide better training—and better equipment, support, living conditions, and medical services—for its troops than Iran. Yet, Iraq also had to use much of its manpower to secure its Kurdish regions and was forced to commit significant military manpower to this diversionary effort. Iraq also continued to substitute ideology for effective training and leadership until very late in the war, and this deprived its manpower of much of its potential military effectiveness.

Shifts in the Structure and Capability of Iranian and Iraqi Forces

The broad trends in Iran and Iraq's military forces in the period between the Algiers Accord of 1975 and the start of the Iran-Iraq War are shown in Table 3.5. These trends clearly reflect the size of the arms race on each side during the five-year period between the Algiers Accord of 1975 and the beginning of the war. They also show that Iran tended to emphasize force quality, while Iraq invested in force quantity, both because of its limited access to advanced Western arms during the period before 1978 and because of its effort to achieve at least numerical parity with Iran.

It is important to note, however, that any estimates of the forces each side could make combat effective at the time the war began are very uncertain. It is equally important to note that both sides began the war with major limitations on their ability to use their forces effectively.

Some of these limitations are roughly comparable and provide important lessons as to why intelligence on Third World forces cannot

TABLE 3.5 The Trends in Iranian and Iraqi Military Forces: 1974–1980

Force Category	1974/75		1979/80	
	Iran	Iraq	Iran	Iraq
Total Active Military Manpower Suitable for Combat	238,000	112,500	240,000	535,000
Land Forces				
Regular Army Manpower				
Active	175,000	100,000	150,000	200,000
Reserve	300,000	250,000	400,000	256,000
Revolutionary Guards/			30,000	—
Baseej/Popular Army	—	—	75,000	650,000
Hizbollah (Home Guard)	—	—	?	—
Arab Volunteers	—	—	—	6,000?
Gendarmerie	70,000	—	?	—
National Guard	—	10,000	—	—
Security Forces	—	5,000	—	—
Division Equivalents (Divisions/Brigades)				
Armored	3/—	2/—	3/1	12+3
Mechanized	—	—	—	4
Infantry and Mountain	2/2	3/1	3/1	4
Special Forces/Airborne	—/2	—/2	—/2	—
Pasdaran/People's Militia	—	—	—	—
Major Combat Equipment				
Main Battle Tanks	1,160:	1,390:	1,735:	2,750:
	400 M-47	1,300 T-54/55/62	400 M-47/48	50 T-72
	460 M-60A1	90 T-34	460 M-60A1	100 AMX-30
	300 Chieftain		875 Chieftain	2,500 T-54/55/62
				100 T-34
Other Armored Fighting Vehicles	2,000	1,300	1,075	2,500
Major Artillery	664	700	1,000+	1,040
Air Forces				
Air Force Manpower	50,000	10,500	70,000	38,000
Combat Aircraft	216:	218:	445:	332:
	32 F-4D	8 Tu-16	188 F-4D/E	12 Tu-22
	64 F-4E	60 Su-7	166 F-5E/F	10 Il-28
	100 F-5A	20 Hunter	77 F-14A	80 MiG-23B
	4 RF-4E	100 MiG-21	14 RF-4E	40 Su-7B
	16 RF-5A	30 MiG-17		60 Su-20
				115 MiG-21
				15 Hunter

(continues)

TABLE 3.5 *(continued)*

Force Category	1974/75 Iran	1974/75 Iraq	1979/80 Iran	1979/80 Iraq
Attack Helicopters	0	0	205 AH-1S	41 Mi-24
Total Helicopters[a]	264	101	744	260
Surface-to-Air Missile				
Forces	1 Hawk	SA-2, SA-3	Hawk	SA-2, SA-3
	Bn[b]	SA-6	5 Rapier Sqns	25 SA-6
			25 Tigercat	
Navy				
Navy Manpower	13,000	2,000	20,000	4,250
Destroyers	3	0	3	0
Frigates	4	0	4	1
Corvettes/Submarine Chasers	4	3	4	0
Missile Patrol Craft	0	3	9	12
Major Other Patrol Craft	7	0	7	—
Mine Warfare Vessels	6	2	5	5
Hovercraft	10	0	14	0
Landing Craft and Ships	4-7	6	4	17
Maritime Patrol Aircraft	0	0	6 P-3F	0

[a]Includes Army helicopters.
[b]Includes some Rapier and Tigercats.

SOURCES: Adapted by the authors from the 1974/1975 and 1980/1981 editions of the IISS *Military Balance* (London: International Institute for Strategic Studies).

be limited to data like force strength and orders of battle and must carefully examine a range of qualitative and political factors that are often of far greater practical military importance.

- *Neither side had an effective high-command structure.* The Shah had constantly overruled his high command, arbitrarily dismissed commanders who disagreed with his orders and force expansion plans, and had surrounded himself with political survivors that often pandered to his authority. The fall of the Shah had disrupted even this fragile basis for command and control, and the revolution had produced a rapid succession of senior commanders and major purges throughout the top of the Iranian officer corps. At the time the war began, a struggle for power had already begun between the new secular leaders, like Bani-Sadr, and the new religious leaders, like Rafsanjani, that was to dominate Iran's high command for the first year of the war, and a similar struggle had broken out between the regular forces and the emerging Revolutionary Guards.

Iraq had undergone similar purges, and its high command had undergone such purges each year from 1977 to the beginning of the war. The high-command structure had effectively become Saddam Hussein and his political supporters, none of whom had practical military experience and training, and was staffed by a military high command whose survival was dependent on its support of, and responsiveness to, Saddam Hussein. Much of the high command was chosen more for loyalty than competence, and no real planning or command staff existed in an operational sense. The Iraqi high command administrated and provided intelligence rather than commanded.

- *Intelligence on both sides was highly ideological and decoupled from objective observation, reporting, and analysis.* The political struggles between Iran and Iraq, and the highly political character of each regime, created intelligence branches that spent more time on internal security than external intelligence functions. Little attention was paid to modern technical intelligence or to military intelligence functions like reconnaissance and target acquisition. The diverse intelligence branches of each side competed to show their loyalty, and they responded to the preconceptions and ideological beliefs of the leaders of their states rather than examine the military situation, the true nature of the support and opposition to the regime of the opposing state, and the host of details necessary to effectively plan and conduct modern war.
- *Neither side had any clear grand strategy or understanding of the risk and cost of war.* While Khomeini and Saddam Hussein believed in very different things, both regimes had a belief structure that led them to take victory largely for granted. They did not articulate a clear and detailed set of objectives in starting their campaigns against each other or determine a clear strategy for reaching those objectives. Neither regime seems to have had any idea of how costly a war could be or of the true nature of its political, economic, and military vulnerability. The price of this lack of knowledge of the cost of war was to become brutally apparent during the first weeks of the conflict.
- *Neither side had any clear concept of operations.* Even before the Shah fell, Iran had built up its forces without creating a clear concept for how it would employ them in war. Ironically, Iran did have a fairly clear set of well-exercised plans for naval combat against a Western/Soviet-style force, but it had no clear plans for

attacking Iraq's naval forces. Iran was converting to a force structure that mixed highly mobile armored forces with attack helicopters, but it had acquired equipment it still lacked the training, plans, and operation exercise experience to use, particularly without massive amounts of Western support and advice. It had effective individual squadrons but nothing approaching an effective air staff that could plan large-scale attack operations or which could effectively organize a regional air defense.

Iraq was still organized largely along Soviet lines, although it is important to stress that it was not trained along Soviet lines and did not exercise in the manner of Soviet forces. Iraq had no concept of naval operations and was in the midst of acquiring new Western ships it had bought for technical reasons and which it would have had to integrate into a concept of operation which would have been developed after their delivery. Iraq's land forces were organized largely for defense and "stovepiped," in the sense they lacked effective training and organization to cooperate with each other. They emphasized mass and firepower rather than maneuver and exploitation, and their only practical experience was that of hammering away at largely undefended Kurdish villages. Iraqi airpower had little operational effectiveness. Even the best squadrons were really collections of good individual pilots that lacked realistic combat training and an effective concept of operations at the squadron, much less the force, level. There was no real concept of offensive operations except for the outline of ideas borrowed from other forces, and air defense consisted of large numbers of air and land-based elements that were not integrated into anything approaching an effective overall concept of operations.

- *Neither side had a balanced and integrated force structure or a clear concept of combined arms and combined operations.* Iran's forces were split between regular and revolutionary forces. While Iran had held some combined arms and combined operations exercises, these were largely set-piece executions of U.S.-planned exercises, and Iran was largely incapable of conducting such operations on its own even before most of the key personnel involved were purged or fled the revolution. Iran's regular infantry and armor could cooperate defensively before the revolution but lacked offensive training and exercise experience. Artillery cooperation with armor and infantry was poor. Air operations were largely compartmented away from land operations and were more oriented toward area air defense than the support of land operations. Fighter air defense and surface-to-air missile defense were very poorly coordinated and awaited the completion of an air C^3I/battlefield management (BM) system that was not operational before the revolution, and only limited progress took place during the war.

Iraq's forces were being organized into two basic groups: the Regular forces and a Ba'ath-dominated Popular Army that was to remain corrupt, politicized, and often incompetent through the entire war and even after the cease-fire. Iraq's stovepiping created virtually all of the separation between branches of the land forces and air forces that has just been described for Iran, with the added complications that the elite Republican Guards were used more as a security force than as combat forces and that armor was poorly coordinated with infantry. Iraq's equivalent of Iran's religious "commissars" consisted of Ba'ath Party supervisors and informers and two competing intelligence services. These encouraged the separation between the branches of the land forces and air forces, and a natural tendency developed to refer every decision upwards and to refuse to take decisions on anything approaching a timely basis at the appropriate level of command.

- *Lack of consistency within the order of battle and within a given service.* Both sides had units within radically different levels of individual proficiency, and this made it very difficult to organize a large group of forces to perform effectively. In the case of Iran, the Shah had often attempted modernization through something approaching a rule of terror. Commanders were rapidly and arbitrarily demoted for failing to meet the Shah's expectations. This reached the point where one of the senior U.S. advisors attempting to train and organize Iran to use its attack helicopters had the equivalent of a nervous breakdown, and where the Iranian command was so frightened of the Shah that when he demanded that all armored divisions be brought up to the proficiency of the best division, they faked the improvement by transferring officers and technicians from the best division into the worst.

At the same time, the constant turbulence within given units from the Shah's flood of arms orders—many of which were placed in spite of the direct opposition of senior commanders who felt they could not be absorbed at anything like the rate the Shah demanded—meant that even the best-equipped units were often poorly trained and could not operate without Western contractor support. The revolution then made a bad situation far worse.

Iraq's near compartmentation of its combat units meant that virtually every force element had different levels of proficiency, and these problems were compounded by a lack of anything approaching standardized unit equipment and training. Iraq also suffered from the same turbulence in terms of constant rapid equipment changes as Iran did and from the kind of rapid force expansion that meant that trained and skilled officers, NCOs, and technicians lacked stability in their units, rotated too rapidly to create effective units, and were diluted among far too large a force structure.

These problems shaped much of the behavior of Iranian and Iraqi military forces throughout the war. It is extraordinarily difficult to change the basic organization and competence of military forces while they are engaged in combat. At the same time, Iran and Iraq faced very different pressures during the course of the war to change.

Iran's forces were so disorganized at the start of the war that they had to innovate simply to mobilize and deploy. This meant that they were initially more flexible in responding to the military conditions they had to face and evolved a mix of regular and "revolutionary" war that served them well during the period where they first had to defend and then expel Iraq from Iranian territory.

However, this same success in innovation then turned into a liability. It is clear that Iran's religious leadership came to feel that Iran's success during the first two to three years of the war validated their ideological approach to a war that stressed revolutionary forces and popular warfare. Iran's ability to drive Iraq out of its territory and to successfully conduct offensives against Iraq gave Iran's leadership little reason to correct the weaknesses that resulted from its revolutionary approach to war. In the long run, this led Iran's leadership to make miscalculations that crippled its ability execute the war and to make effective judgments about the situation it faced.

If Iraq began badly, Iraq had the advantage of a more secular ideology, one which was determined by a single autocrat who led and managed the state, rather than acted as a spiritual leader. Saddam Hussein and his supporters rapidly learned they faced a very different reality than the one they believed in when they started the war. When Iran successfully went on the offensive, Iraq's leaders were forced to make a steady series of corrections to the problems in their command structure, intelligence, concept of operations, training, and a host of other aspects of their war-fighting capability that allowed them to survive and eventually gave them victory. This process of growing realism, innovation, and adaptation was scarcely quick or efficient, but in the long run, it gave Iraq a significant edge over Iran.

Trends in Iranian Forces

The key difference between Iran and Iraq before the war was that the Iranian revolution cost Iran much of its military forces and the ability to make use of the Shah's massive arms buildup during the two years before the war began. It is also important to note that Iran's forces had only token military experience and that that experience was limited to supporting Oman in suppressing its poorly armed Dhofar rebels under conditions where the British and Omanis did most of the fighting.

In early 1979, and before the Shah began to encounter massive political opposition, Iran had about 415,000 men under arms, although only about one-third of this force had anything approaching realistic military training. The Iranian army had about 285,000 men, including some 300,000 active reserves, but most of this force lacked the training needed to operate modern weapons in any kind of offensive combat. Only 1 of its 3 armored divisions and 2 of its 3 infantry divisions were effectively organized for modern combat.[12] Iran had about 10 division equivalents in its force structure, including its reserve brigades, but many of these units existed only as cadre formations and had little military effectiveness.

The Iranian Army had a total of some 1,735 main battle tanks, including 875 Chieftains, 400 M-47/M-48s, and 460 M-60A1s. The 875 Chieftains had recurrent reliability and service problems and were undercooled and under-engined for the terrain and climate. The M-47s and M-48s were often not properly maintained. The Iranian Army also had about 250 Scorpion light tanks and 825 armored infantry fighting vehicles (AIFVs), including some 500 Soviet-made BTR-50, BTR-60, and BTR-152s and 325 M-113 armored personnel carriers (APCs).

The army had roughly 700 major artillery pieces, depending on what calibers were counted and whether the total included weapons in reserve or storage. These included 75-mm pack howitzers, 330 M-101 105-mm towed weapons, and Soviet D-20 130-mm towed guns, 112 M-114 towed 155-mm howitzers, 14 M-115 203-mm towed howitzers, 440 self-propelled M-109 155-mm howitzers, 38 M-107 self-propelled 175-mm guns, and 14 M-110 203-mm self-propelled howitzers. Iran also had 72 BM-21 122-mm multiple rocket launchers (MRLs). It had large stocks of TOW, Dragon, SS-11, SS-12, and ENTAC anti-tank guided missiles.

The Iranian Army's land-based air defense weapons strength consisted of some 1,800 anti-aircraft guns, including 100 ZSU-23-4 radar-guided 23-mm self-propelled guns, 20-mm guns, M-1939 37-mm guns, 40-mm guns, and 85-mm cannon. Its major surface-to-air missile strength included Hawk surface-to-air missiles.

The Iranian Air Force had a strength of roughly 100,000 men. It had 447 combat aircraft, including 10 fighter-ground attack squadrons with 190 F-4D/Es and 8 fighter-ground attack squadrons with 166 F-5E/Fs. It had 4 interceptor squadrons with a total of roughly 77 F-14As and 1 reconnaissance squadron with 14 RF-4Es. Iran had modern ordnance for all these aircraft, including Maverick air-to-surface missiles and the latest air-to-air missiles, such as the long-range all-weather Phoenix missile.

The Iranian Army Aviation Command added about 70 fixed-wing light reconnaissance and support aircraft to this force, plus well over 200 armed helicopters, including 205 AH-1Js and some of its 285 Bell 214As. It had 50 AB-205As, 20 AB-206A, and 90 CH-47C transport helicopters. Iran's transport aircraft included 2 tanker/transport squadrons, with 13 B-707s and 9 B-747s, and 4 transport squadrons with 54 C-130E/Hs. It had some 84 helicopters and 25 small utility jets and turboprops. It also had 5 Rapier squadrons and 25 Tigercat surface-to-air missile launchers for air-base defense.

Iran's 30,000-man Navy had moderate effectiveness. Iran had 1 ex-U.S. Tang submarine. It had 3 destroyers with Standard surface-to-surface missiles, 4 Saram-class frigates with Seakiller and Seacat missiles, and 4 ex-U.S. PF-103 corvettes. It had 6 large Kaman-class missile patrol boats with Harpoon missiles and 7 large patrol boats without missile systems. It had 5 small mine vessels, 1 landing-ship logistic (LSL), 1 landing craft utility (LCU), 8 SRN-6 and 6 BH-7 Hovercrafts, and 3 support ships. It had modern naval bases at Bandar Abbas, Bushehr, Kharg Island, Khorramshahr, Shah Bahar, and Bandar Pahlavi. Iran also had a 74,000-man gendarmerie with Cessna 195/310 aircraft, 32 AB-205/206 helicopters, and 32 patrol craft.

The Shah's military forces, however, were scarcely the ones Iran went to war with. As has been discussed earlier, Iran repeatedly purged its senior command and officer corps beginning in February 1979 and often added the problem of terror in terms of executions and arbitrary arrests. At the same time, the revolution caused major problems at every level. Khomeini called for large-scale desertions in late January 1979, and most conscripts did desert. The Army dropped from roughly 260,000–285,000 men to 90,000–150,000. The Air Force dropped from about 90,000–100,000 to 60,000–65,000, and the Navy from 25,000–28,000 to 20,000–23,000. The gendarmerie and other paramilitary forces virtually collapsed and dropped from around 74,000 men to roughly one-third of their original strength.[13]

By February 1979, this had reached the point where the new

Khomeini government had to appeal for personnel to return and had to create a new "Islamic" officer corps. At the same time, however, the new Islamic commanders selected by the government found themselves with little authority and presiding over a hollow force. Further, the new Minister of Defense and commander of the Navy, General Ahmad Madani, was forced to cut the Iranian defense budget by another third, reduce the conscription period to 12 months, and allow conscripts to serve in their home provinces—a concession that ensured that Iran's units in the forward area could not get even a proper proportion of the limited number of conscripts that actually showed up under the new system.[14]

It seems likely that Iran would have let its military capabilities decline even further if the various separatist movements in Iran had not become increasingly more violent once they saw that the revolution was very definitely Persian-dominated. However, the Kurds began to challenge the new government as early as March 1979. This led to the almost immediate use of the Army and to new shake-ups in the command of the regular land forces as the result of the fact the army fired on the Kurds. These military problems became much more serious in April and May 1979 when Iranian troops had to be used against Arab separatists in Khuzistan.

The government's response was to blame the regular armed forces for both an excessive use of force and an inability to deal with popular uprisings. Largely as the result of the efforts of Ibrahim Yazdi and Sadiq Ghotbzadeh, Khomeini's ruling Islamic Revolutionary Council decided to merge the small revolutionary militias that were being set up by various supporters of Khomeini into a popular army. This decision was taken after some debate over how to create such an army during May and June 1979 and over who should be in charge and the role the Islamic clergy should play in the leadership of the new force. The result was a decree of June 16, 1979, that set up the Pasdaran e-Inqilal e-Islami, or Revolutionary Guards, as a body that was under Khomeini's direct political control and which had religious as well as civil leadership. Khomeini also agreed to establish the Hizbollah as a separate force under the Islamic Revolutionary Party and to use the popular volunteers or Baseej as a recruiting base for the Pasdaran and as a substitute for conscription, which further hurt the intake to the regular forces.

The Air Force also continued to experience continuing command shake-ups at every level, as well as the loss or purging of more of its critical personnel. Moreover, it began to suffer badly from logistic and support problems. The computerized logistic system that the U.S. was helping the Shah's government to set up had only reached the point where stocks were computer-coded and logged, and the computers were installed. Most of the software necessary to operate the system was not in place when the Shah fell, and critical types of spare parts were still awaiting delivery. (Advanced combat fighters have over 20,000 critical parts per aircraft.)

By August 1979, most of Iran's combat aircraft were no longer operational, and all 80 of its F-14 aircraft had been sabotaged to make it impossible for them to use their Phoenix long-range air-to-air missiles. Most of Iran's helicopter force was inoperable, and plans already existed to cannibalize half of the force for spare parts. The situation was also only marginally better in the case of the ground forces. Only about one-third of Iran's Chieftain tanks were operational and no more than 60–70 percent of its M-60s. Iran had had to cancel plans for a tank repair base at Dorud, and its armored warfare parts and ammunition factory near Isfahan was being converted to civil production. Months before the seizure of the U.S. Embassy in Tehran on November, 4, 1979, the Iranian Air Force and Army were experiencing critical spare-parts problems.

Commanders continued to come and go, and the military forces continued to lose key personnel, between June and September 1979. It was only after Iran seized the U.S. Embassy that the Khomeini government began to mobilize. It then focused on the threat of an American invasion rather than on the threat from Iraq. While Khomeini had called earlier for the regular armed forces to be reorganized as the "protectors of Islam," it was the embassy crisis that led his government to authorize rebuilding the army to its pre-revolutionary strength and raising the Pasdaran from roughly 6,000 to 26,000 men.

On December 10, 1979, Khomeini went much further and called for Iran's youth to be organized into an "Army of 20 Million." As has been discussed earlier, however, none of these measures halted the purges in the armed forces, and at least another 7,500 personnel were purged during January and February 1980. The Khomeini government had begun to face active plotting within the military as well as the armed opposition of initially prorevolutionary leftist movements like the Mujahideen e-Khalq and Fedayeen e-Khalq. This simultaneously discredited the regular military while creating an even greater demand for loyal revolutionary forces.

All of these trends continued during the first five months of 1980, and the June-July 1980 coup attempt by members of the armed forces made this situation even worse. Iranian Prime Minister Rajaur expressed the view that a popular army based on martyrdom and zeal was better than a victorious army, and the government greatly stepped up the introduction of religious commissars into the armed forces. The regular Iranian armed forces reached the point where they had lost 30–50 percent of the officers that were serving at the time the Shah fell. The Iranian Army had lost up to 60 percent of its prerevolutionary manpower.

In spite of various government statements, no serious effort was made to rebuild the regular forces until September 20, 1980, when Bani-Sadr called for general mobilization. This did lead to the rapid mobilization of some 200,000 men, but they were split between almost immediate transfer to the Pasdaran forces already fighting at the front and regular and Pasdaran units which required trained manpower. In spite of large-scale pardons and reactivations, and even the hiring of more politically suspect officers as "consultants," Iran was almost totally unready to deal with this new flow of personnel. Most conscripts and other ranks had been poorly trained under the Shah, and the Iranian training base had collapsed.

The continuing split between the advocates of rebuilding the regular forces and the Mullahs and others advocating popular forces, also led to the decision that the Pasdaran should rapidly be built up to the same size as the regular forces. The Pasdaran not only rapidly expanded to some 150,000 men, it was given authority over the Kurdish areas and built up a separate command of roughly 30,000 men in northeastern Iran. Further, while Khomeini did make President Bani-Sadr the head of a seven-man Supreme Defense Council on October 13, 1988, three of the seven members were Mullahs, and the Mullahs and their supporters retained control over Iran's military procurement efforts and the manpower intake to Iran's rapidly expanding armed forces.

While Bani-Sadr did succeed in revitalizing some of the command structure of the regular forces, the Mullahs continued to maintain their own separate chain of command through the various religious commissars in the forces and often exercised a command authority which overrode that of the regular commanders. This created a constant struggle for power between Bani-Sadr and the Mullahs and constant divisions within the military that were only resolved when Khomeini finally removed Bani-Sadr from any command rule on June 11, 1980.

Trends in Iraqi Forces

In contrast to Iran, Iraq steadily strengthened its military relations with the West during the late 1970s while preserving its ties to the USSR. As a result, it was able to buy virtually any major weapons it sought from the Soviet bloc or Western Europe during the last few years before the Iran-Iraq War, as well as obtain a constant flow of replacements, critical spares, and munitions to support its logistic pipeline.

Iraq did, however, experience additional military problems that affected its capability at the start of the war. The Ba'ath never fully trusted the armed forces after they seized power from the party following Brigadier Abdul Karim Kassim's "free-officer" coup against the monarchy on July 15, 1958. Many senior members of the Ba'ath assumed military rank to ensure control of the armed forces, including Saddam Hussein, who was made into a general after receiving an honorary degree from Iraq's military college in 1970.

The military was subjected to a long series of limited purges during the decade before the war, although scarcely the kind of dramatic cuts common in Iran after the revolution.[15] These included officers suspected of sympathy to the Kurds, alignment with the Iraqi Communist Party, and officers which seemed to be too closely aligned to Shi'ite factions. At the same time, military forces were often treated as political symbols. For example, an Iraqi brigade was sent to support the PLO against Jordan in 1969, although Iraq had no ability to support it in combat. During the October 1973 War, Iraq deployed an armored division to aid Syria on the Golan without adequate support, air defense, transport assets, or an effective high command. Syria then committed the unit to combat under circumstances where it was little more than a sacrifice pawn, and it took heavy casualties.

Iraq's long war against the Kurds also did little to prepare it for war against anyone else. Only about 20–30 percent of Iraq's Kurds ever took part in the movement for an independent Kurdistan, but Iraq still found it could not fight a guerrilla war against the Kurds and win. Its tactics became oriented around destroying the villages and population that the Kurdish guerrillas depended upon to survive. Rather than strike quickly and surgically at enemy military forces, Iraq came to depend on slow massive assaults on villages and population centers where artillery barrages would clear the advance, Iraqi forces would surround an area, artillery would largely destroy a population center, and troops would advance on the devastated result—and then largely only if the remaining Kurds were not capable of more than minimal resistance.

While Iraq had about 225,000 men and women under arms by late 1980, at least two-thirds of this force had limited military training. Its army had about 190,000 men, plus some 250,000 active reserves, but most of this force lacked the training needed to operate modern weapons in any kind of offensive combat. Its forces were heavily committed to securing the Kurdish areas in the northeast, and only 1 of its 4 armored divisions and 2 of its 6 mechanized and infantry divisions were effectively organized for modern combat.[16] Iraq had 13 to 17 division equivalents in its force structure, including its Popular Army and reserve brigades, but many of these units existed only as cadre formations and had little military effectiveness.

Iraq's political and paramilitary forces were particularly ineffective. The Popular Army was a Ba'ath militia that was founded in 1970, which had been greatly expanded after 1975 when the Ba'ath Party leadership became convinced it still faced opposition in the regular armed forces. The Popular Army theoretically provided military training to every male party member between 18 and 45 and had a nominal strength of 250,000 trained men when the war began, but very few members of the Popular Army were in active units and many had only limited training.

Iraq did have a Vanguard Force which had trained some 285,000 youths between the ages of 9 and 16, but this training had far stronger political elements than military ones. In contrast, Iraq did have some good formations including two special forces brigades and a Presidential Guard force with one-to-two armored and one commando brigade.

In late 1980, the Iraqi Army had some 2,700 main battle tanks. Up to 2,500 of these are Soviet-supplied T-54, T-55, and T-62s; up to 100 were T-72s, about 100 were T-34s, and up to 100 were French AMX-30s. The Army also had about 100 PT-76 amphibious tanks and 2,500 armored infantry fighting vehicles (AIFVs) including some 200 Soviet-made BMP armored fighting vehicles (AFVs). The rest were largely BTR-50, BTR-60, BTR-152, OT-62, and VCR armored personnel carriers (APCs).

The army had roughly 800 major artillery pieces, the actual number depending on what calibers were counted and whether the total included weapons in reserve or storage. These included a wide mix of Soviet-bloc towed weapons and multiple rocket launchers and 26 Soviet FROG-7 and 12 Scud B free-rocket and guided-missile launchers. Iraq had large stocks of Milan, SS-11, AT-2, and AT-3 anti-tank guided missiles.

The Iraqi Army's land-based air defense weapons strength consisted of some 1,200 anti-aircraft guns, including ZSU-23-4 23-mm self-propelled guns, M-1939 37-mm guns, ZSU-57-2 self-propelled 57-mm guns, and 85-mm, 100-mm, and 130-mm cannon. Its surface-to-air missile strength included SA-2 launchers, SA-3 launchers, and 25 SA-6 launchers.

The Iraqi Air Force had a strength of roughly 38,000 men, including some 10,000 air defense personnel. It had air bases at Basra, H-3, Habbaniyah, Kirkuk, Mosul, Rashid, Shaiba, and thirteen additional military air strips. These bases were due to be sheltered, but this sheltering was only partially complete when the war began.

Estimates differ, but the Iraqi Air Force seems to have had 332 combat aircraft, including 2 bomber squadrons with 7–12 Tu-22 Blinders and 8–10 Il-28s. The Tu-22 bomber units had limited proficiency, and the Il-28s were little more than obsolete sitting ducks. Iraq had 12 fighter-ground attack squadrons: 4 squadrons with 80 MiG-23Bs, 4 with 60 Su-20s, 3 with 40 Su-Bs, and 1 with 10 Hunters.[17] Only a few of the MiG-23 and Su-20 squadrons had a high level of operational capability. It had 5 interceptor squadrons with a total of roughly 115 MiG-21s. Iraq, however, was only able to deploy about 60 aircraft out of these interceptor forces per day, they had poor air-to-air combat training and very limited export versions of Soviet radars, and they were restricted to an air-to-air missile inventory which consisted largely of obsolescent Soviet-made AA-2s.

The Iraqi Army Air Corps added around 70 armed helicopters to this combat air strength, including 41 Mi-24 Hinds with AT-2 Swatter, some SA-342 Gazelles, and Mi-4s. Iraq's transport aircraft included 2 squadrons with 9 AN-2s, 8 AN-12s, 8 AN-24s, 2 AN-26s, 12 IL-76s, 2 Tu-124s, 13 IL-14s, and 2 DH Herons. The Iraqi Air Force had large reserves of training aircraft, including MiG-15s, MiG-21s, and MiG-23Us.

Iraq's 4,250-man Navy had little effectiveness. Ironically, Iraq had allowed its navy to run down before the war because it was awaiting the arrival of new frigates and corvettes, which were under construction in Italy. At the start of the war, it only had one training frigate, eight fast attack craft (FAC) armed with Styx SSMs, four FAC armed with torpedoes, three large and eight coastal patrol boats, two Polnochy-class landing craft, and some inshore patrol vessels. Iraq's only naval bases were small facilities at Basra and Umm Qasr, which only had a small channel, plus docking capability and a radar at Faw.

The Terrain

The final factors that need to be considered in understanding the conditions that existed at the start of the war and which helped shape its course are geography and terrain. Both these factors played a critical role in determining the conditions that shaped the war. The key features shaping their impact were (a) Iraq's lack of strategic depth (Tehran is 700 km from the border, while Baghdad is only 100 km), (b) Iraq's lack of secure access to the Gulf, (c) the water barriers of the Tigris-Euphrates rivers, and (d) the mountains near the border to the north. These terrain conditions are shown in Figure 3.1.

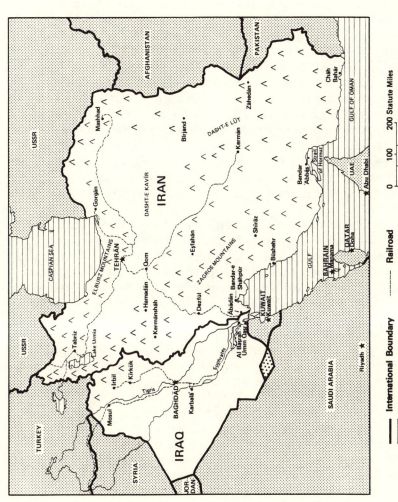

FIGURE 3.1 Map of Iran and Iraq. *Source:* U.S. Defense Mapping Agency.

The Iran-Iraq border is roughly 1,300 kilometers long. It begins just south of the point where Iran ceases to share a common border with Turkey and at a latitude of approximately 37 degrees north. There are roads that move across the border area in the north, but it is mountainous and easily defensible. More trafficable areas for military operations stretch from Qasr e-Shirin, an Iranian border town northeast of Baghdad, to as far south as Basra, an Iraqi port city located near the opening of the Shatt al-Arab.

In the north, the mountain areas are steep and bleak, with minimal vegetation and tree cover. Some peaks rise to around 2,700 meters and most of the land is over 1,000 meters in height. The region is largely Kurdish and is warm in summer but cold during the rest of the year, and the peaks and high plateaus are covered with snow in the winter. The direction of the mountain ridges is southeast to northwest and the ridge lines roughly parallel the border. This creates serious logistic problems, and fighting has to take place on a ridge-by-ridge basis, and road lines of communication are often limited and vulnerable to sabotage or ambush. Infantry can often easily outflank or bypass armor and vehicles.

Altitude was a factor in the north for both operational and climatic reasons. Both Iran and Iraq had serious problems in maintaining good helicopter performance at high altitudes, and combat in the mountains in the north imposed a heavy service burden on land vehicles. In many cases, it forced both sides to rely on infantry or heliborne troops, and during several months of the year, the cold and snow made sustained combat impossible.

During Iraq's invasion and during most of the war, the major fighting concentrated along the central and southern border sectors, although significant fighting began in the north in 1984. Vehicular traffic in the central and southern border area is inhibited by both mountain and water barriers. Vehicular traffic is fair-to-good in southwestern Iran (Khuzistan) for as far north as Dezful. Vehicular traffic, as well as foot mobility for large military formations, becomes extremely difficult farther north and in the Zagros Mountains.

The central sector covers the area roughly parallel to Baghdad. The border follows a broadly curving salient that thrusts into Iraq and largely follows the separation between a river plain and the Iranian plateau. The Iranian side of the border consists of the Zagros Mountains, which reach heights of up to 1,700 meters although most are below 1,000 meters. Much of the border is disputed, including the area around Mehran and Qasr e-Shirin. Iran is vulnerable to an attack from the west in the vicinity of Qasr e-Shirin. A successful attack in this area establishes a strong strategic position along the historic invasion route, Khanaquin and Kermanshah, leading toward Tehran. Baghdad, however, is vulnerable to armored operations via several passes through the Zagros Mountains. The flat plain on the Iraqi side, however, offers infantry little cover and requires an Iranian force to use both armor and mobile supply lines to be effective.

There are extensive rivers and marshes on either side of the southern-central border area. The major rivers include the Euphrates, Tigris, Karun, and Shatt al-Arab. There are many marshes, including the Hawizeh Marshes. Precipitation can render the ground virtually impassable to military vehicles. The strategic hills around the Baghdad-Basra Highway in southeastern Iraq are shielded by several marshes. There is also a belt of marshland along the Tigris River, which flows within Iraqi territory. These marshes vary sharply in depth according to the time of year. Some are wet all year round, but many only flood during the rainy season. They tend to be filled with tall reeds and provide extensive natural cover. In contrast, the terrain outside the river plain and marshes is barren and flat, and many of the seasonally flooded areas turn into totally dry and exposed earth that is ideal for armored operations.

Flooding was equally important in the far south, in the region from roughly Dezful to the Shatt al-Arab. The area around Basra and Abadan is still prone to natural flooding. On the coastal plains, military movement is slowed considerably with the onset of the winter rains in November, although it is possible to fight comparatively easily until major flooding begins in mid-April, when the thaws in the mountains in Kurdistan raise the level of all the rivers in the area. Roads only become passable in the late spring, after the flooding caused by melting mountain snows has subsided. Movement can remain hampered until June or July, when rising temperatures become a major factor in inhibiting combat.

Iraq and Iran built dikes that in the southern sector turned parts of the terrain into massive water barriers. Iraq made particularly extensive use of such barriers once it was forced onto the defensive. Iraq diverted the Tigris and Euphrates to the east and north of Basra and created massive lakes and swamps. It then diverted the waters from these lakes to feed canals that flowed down the eastern shore of the Shatt al-Arab and toward the Karun River and Khorramshahr. These created water barriers to help defend Basra.

In the far south, toward the Shatt al-Arab, the coastline is low and swampy during much of the year and was often ill-suited for anything but amphibious or infantry combat. Rivers present a major problem even when no marsh area is present. The rivers have steep banks, and when the levels fall, the shore has a sharply rising angle that infantry sometimes must climb with ladders. Alternatively, a sudden rise in river level can make its bank muddy and impassible for up to several hundred meters on both sides. The coastal terrain around Abadan Island and Faw is also surrounded by a salt marsh whose level varies with the season and sometimes with the tide. Iraq only has about a 50-mile coastline on the Gulf. This coast is low, and during the flood season, it is swampy and best suited to amphibious combat.

Temperatures in the southern and central sectors during May to September can range well over 100°F, and the area is virtually a no-man's land during much of the year. These environmental conditions are unsuitable for armored warfare during part of the year and make any kind of war brutally unpleasant during much of the year. Temperatures in closed vehicles can exceed 130°F, and temperature and water problems can deprive infantry units of much of their effectiveness within a day of exposure on open terrain.[18]

Notes

1. See Alvin J. Cottrell, "Iran's Armed Forces Under the Pahlavi Dynasty," in *Iran Under the Pahlavis*, George Lenczowski, ed., Stanford, Hoover Institution Press, 1978.

2. R. K. Ramazani, *The United States and Iran*, New York, Praeger, 1982, p. 44.

3. The one professional group that seems to have suffered somewhat less than the others was that of the less technical senior NCOs. This group was mostly anti-monarchist due to the Shah's policy of educating these people while refusing to grant them privileges commensurate with those enjoyed by commissioned officers. The data on Iranian military purges are complex and uncertain, but Nikola B. Schahgaldian provides an excellent analysis in *The Iranian Military Under the Islamic Republic*, Santa Monica, RAND R-3473-USDP, March 1987.

4. IISS, *The Military Balance*, 1979–1980, London, International Institute for Strategic Studies, 1979, p. 39.

5. During the beginning of the war, Saddam Hussein went so far as to blame the superiority of Iran's American weapons for Iraq's slow advance; see "Iraq Covets Opponents' Weaponry," *Middle East Economic Digest*, October 27, 1980.

6. "The Avengers of Karbala," *The Economist*, July 17, 1982, p. 29.

7. Jordan supplied volunteers, food, medicine, and trained troops for the use of Western technology, served as a supply route, and provided its air bases as refuge for the Iraqi Air Force and civil air fleet. Iraq, however, often failed to pay its bills to Jordan after 1983. Wallace A. Terrill, Jr., "Saddam's Closest Ally: Jordan and the Gulf War," *Journal of South Asian and Middle Eastern Studies*, Winter 1986, vol. IX, no. 2.

8. Daniel Southerland, "Iraq-Iran War: Neither Seems Able to Win, But Have Both Lost Enough to Negotiate?" *Christian Science Monitor*, November 5, 1980, p. 1.

9. Thomas W. Miller, "Will Saddam Outlast the Iran-Iraq War?" *Middle East Insight*, April/May 1984, p. 33.

10. ACDA, *World Military Expenditures and Arms Transfers, 1969–1978*, Washington, D.C., GPO, p. 160.

11. This analysis draws heavily on Richard F. Grimmett, "Trends in Conventional Arms Transfers to the Third World by Major Supplier," Congressional Research Service, Report Number 88-352, May 9, 1988.

12. The armored or mechanized divisions all differed in structure. A nominal armored division had two armored and one mechanized brigade.

13. Many of these estimates are based upon Schahgaldian, op. cit.; Edgar O'Ballance, *The Gulf War*, London, Brassey's, 1988, pp. 20–24; Sepehr Zabih, *The Iranian Military in Revolution and War*, London, Routledge, 1988; and Shahram Chubin and Charles Tripp, *Iran and Iraq at War*, Boulder, Westview, 1988, pp. 21, 33–35.

14. Madani was also governor of Khuzistan and could devote only a limited amount of time to the problems the regular services then faced.

15. These purges included the assassination of some officers in exile, including General Hardan al-Takriti.

16. The armored or mechanized divisions all differed in structure.

17. This estimate is based largely on the IISS, *Military Balance, 1980–1981*, London, International Institute for Strategic Studies, 1981), pp. 40–42.

18. Water use often exceeds two gallons per day per man.

4

PHASE ONE:
IRAQ INVADES IRAN, 1980

The history of the Iran-Iraq War had many dimensions, although the key dimension throughout the war was the land conflict. Both Iran and Iraq were locked into a relatively static land battle along their border area during most of the war, although this land battle was punctuated by periods of intense offensive combat. These battles were largely a battle of attrition. Both sides occasionally attempted maneuver warfare but usually with limited success. It was only in the spring of 1988 that Iraq showed the ability to conduct effective combined arms and maneuver warfare. The Iran-Iraq War is a classic case study in the problems of technology transfer to Third World armies and in the difficulty of converting from relatively static and attrition-oriented land forces to forces which are capable of fully utilizing modern weapons to carry out every aspect of combined-arms warfare.

The war did, however, provide important insights into other aspects of war. Iraq gradually developed a relatively effective mix of air and missile power, while Iran saw much of its air power decline into virtual impotence. Iran supported terrorism, coup attempts, and uprisings in Bahrain, Kuwait, and Saudi Arabia. Both Iraq and Iran conducted a "tanker war" against shipping, and significant engagements occurred between Iranian and U.S. naval forces. A major "war of the cities" helped shape the outcome of the conflict, as did the use of chemical weapons.

The complex interactions among all of these types of warfare do, however, make the lessons of the Iran-Iraq War exceptionally difficult to summarize. There were significant shifts in the nature of the fighting, in the nature of the forces engaged, and in the number of nations engaged. Many of the key lessons of the war relating to strategy, tactics, conflict management, and escalation management changed with time. As a result, many of the key lessons of the Iran-Iraq War can only be understood in historical terms.

The Major Phases of the Conflict

The Iran-Iraq War had several major phases, including Iraq's invasion of Iran, Iran's attempt to conquer Iraq, and foreign intervention in the conflict. There is no way to divide the main phase of war into precise periods, but the key shifts in the fighting may be summarized as follows:

- Iraq's invasion of Iran and its attempt to become the dominant power in the Gulf (1980);
- Iran's liberation of its territory (1981–1982);
- Iran's initial attempt to conquer Iraq (1982–1984);
- a stalemate and bitter war of attrition in which Iran sought to overthrow the regime of Saddam Hussein, and Iraq tried to force Iran to make peace (1984–1985);
- renewed Iranian "final offensives" against southern Iraq (1986–1987);
- expansion of the tanker war in the Gulf to include Western navies, while the land and air war of attrition continues (1987–1988); and
- major Iraqi victories on land, the collapse of Iran's military forces, Iranian agreement to a cease-fire, and uncertain peace negotiations (1988–1989).

Phase One: The Iraqi Invasion

The first phase of the war includes the period that began when Iraq shifted from limited military action to outright invasion and attempted to consolidate control over part of Iran and/or reach a cease-fire on favorable terms while it still occupied Iranian soil. This period ended when Iraq was forced onto the defensive, and Iran began to successfully counterattack. More than anything else, this initial period of the war is a case study in the cost of treating military forces primarily as political symbols and tools for internal security purposes and then attempting to use them as real-world military forces. At the same time, it is a lesson in how seriously leadership elites can miscalculate in initiating a conflict and in the factors that can drive Third World states into patterns of conflict they rapidly find they have little ability to control.

Iraq's Invasion Plan

Even in retrospect, it is difficult to understand many of the motives behind the way in which Iraq planned and executed its invasion of

Iran. Even if one ignores all of the political and strategic factors discussed in the previous chapter, the Iraqi attack provides an important lesson in just how unrealistic and incompetent a Third World state can be in launching a major war. Both the initial air attack and land invasion were so badly planned and executed that they cost Iraq virtually all of the initial advantages it obtained from surprise, superior forces, and the disorganization of Iran's military forces.[1]

Part of the problem was unquestionably the lack of an effective Iraqi planning staff and high command and the overall lack of Iraqi military professionalism discussed in the previous chapter. One authority has indicated that Iraq was actually forced to draw heavily on a exercise organized by British instructors at the Baghdad War College in 1941, and which tested Iraq's ability to seize Abadan, Dezful, and Khorramshahr within a week to ten days.[2]

Yet, Iraq made many other mistakes which went far beyond problems in strategy and in the initial planning of its attack. These tactical mistakes may be summarized as follows.

- Iraq does not seem to have ever really analyzed the impact of launching an attack on a state in midrevolution. It seems to have simply assumed that its attack would divide Iran rather than unite it because of the basis of the power of the elites and ethnic leaders that existed before the revolution. Even some of the most senior Iraqi leaders admitted during interviews later in the war that they had never considered that the net effect of their attack would be to create a massive uprising of support for Khomeini.[3]
- In broader terms, Iraq lacked an effective intelligence system. This failure is symptomatic of problems which provide important lessons for all nations. Some intelligence failures are inevitable. No reliable methodology exists for estimating the combat effectiveness, adaptability, or will of enemy forces which have never been tried in combat. It is easy to make estimates of such capabilities, but it is virtually impossible to back them up with meaningful intelligence indicators and methods of analysis. These problems are particularly severe when estimates must be made about the forces of developing nations, forces in political transition, and forces acquiring new tactics and technologies.

  The problems in intelligence also increase in cases like the assessment of Iran, when reliable human intelligence (HUMINT) is not available in great detail and when there is little recent training, exercise, or combat performance data to draw on. Order-of-battle intelligence, technical intelligence, and data on manning and stock levels are important but only in the context of adequate HUMINT and readiness intelligence. Finally, no intelligence estimate can be adequate which lacks a reliable basis for understanding how enemy and allied forces will be commanded in war and the probable political and military behavior of both their ordinary troops and high command.

- Iraq planned for a short war; Iran captured documents from Iraqi prisoners of war that called for Iraq to take Khorramshahr, Abadan, Ahwaz, Dezful, Masjid e-Suleiman, and some of the key oil centers in Khuzistan in 10 to 14 days.[4] Yet, the Iraqis never seem to have understood the importance of speed and maneuver in achieving these objectives. The Iraqi high command seems to have grossly underestimated the speed with which Iran could organize effective resistance and failed to understand the urgency of acting on surprise and on maneuver around the early resistance it encountered.
- Iraq's land and air operations were planned in virtual isolation from each other. Once Iraq's initial air operation failed, the Air Force retreated out of the conflict for several months, often leaving the ground forces to fight on their own.
- Iraq either did not analyze its own vulnerabilities or it assumed Iran was incapable of taking advantage of them. Although Iraq planned massive artillery fire across the Shatt at Iran's cities and oil facilities, it does not seem to have considered the risk that Iran would fire at equally vulnerable Iraqi facilities. In particular, it ignored the vulnerability of its ports and oil facilities at Basra and Faw and of its own oil-loading platforms in the Gulf at Khor al-Amaya and Mina al-Bakr.
- Iraq sought to minimize day-to-day casualties without ever understanding that delays designed to reduce casualties on any given day could sharply raise casualties in the future. Iraq failed to be properly aggressive when time was critical and committed too few forces early in a battle or conflict. Until the last year of the war, it failed to achieve concentration of force and, far too often, sent too few forces and sent them too late.
- Iraq did not have an effective concept of operations for land warfare. It did not have a realistic concept of maneuver based on the actual capabilities of its forces. It began the war with only a mechanistic concept of combined operations and began the war without any capability for warfare in urban and built-up areas and with limited ability to combine armor, infantry, and artillery. It lacked both a concept of defense in-depth and an

understanding of the need for aggressive area defense, as distinguished from defending a single line or a few key points and lines of communication.

- Iraq had no real concept of air power. Its planning and operations had no real cohesion or effectiveness above the individual unit level. At best, it went by the book, and someone else's book at that. It did not understand the need for large-scale exercises and to test its plans in practice. It was equally unprepared for both air offense and air defense.

- Iraq did not provide effective leadership at any level. Although Iraq's top leadership deliberately created many of Iraq's military problems through systematic politicization of the armed forces, that same leadership seems to have totally ignored the military cost of its own actions. Every level of command tended to refer all decisions upwards. The entire burden of command eventually rested on Saddam Hussein and his immediate staff in Baghdad, a burden of command they lacked both the communications and the expertise to bear effectively. There was no momentum of command. Operations tended to halt while awaiting orders rather than go on until it was necessary to make an adjustment or change.

- The command-and-control system was incapable of transmitting the true tactical situation. Senior Iraqi officers later noted that they often got more timely information from the media than they did from their own commanders at the front.

- Iraq relied on slow-moving, mass artillery fire when armor could easily have seized a given objective. Iraq also often failed to support its armor with infantry when this was necessary. Iraq was unprepared for urban and popular warfare.

- Iraq allowed its forces to be channeled into roads and other fixed lines of communication. Iraq also never seems to have understood the need to fully secure its flanks and the rear areas in the territory it captured.

- Iraq did not conduct aggressive land or air reconnaissance. It allowed Iran to deploy and achieve tactical surprise under conditions where it should easily have been able to acquire adequate intelligence.

- Iraq did not properly secure its sources of resupply. It did not inform Moscow of its actions, and the USSR promptly cut off most supplies. This forced Iraq to turn to other Arab states, the PRC, and North Korea under crisis conditions.

- Iraq had no real contingency plans for a long war and was forced to improvise a mobilization plan once the war began. At least for the first few years, it never seems to have considered the risk of a truly prolonged conflict.

- Many key weapons and munitions had never been realistically tested before the war. For example, much of Iraq's artillery failed to be effective because of simple fusing errors. Most of Iraq's surface-to-air missile units failed to operate effectively except at medium-to-high altitudes.

Iraq's Air Attack on Iran

The Iraqi air force began its attack war by attempting to copy Israel's successes of 1967 against Egypt, Jordan, and Syria. Iraq seems to have acted on the fact that only about 18 percent to 50 percent of Iran's combat aircraft were operational in any form, and its command structure was in a state of chaos. Iraq ignored the fact that the Arab-Israeli war of 1973 had shown in great detail that even the best air force could not destroy an air force on its bases if the target was a well-sheltered and dispersed force.

Iraq also ignored the practical limits of its attack aircraft. While Iran had a modern attack force of 188 F-4D/Es and 166 F-5E/Fs when the Shah fell, Iraq had a far inferior attack force when it struck at Iran. It had 12 Tu-22s optimized as nuclear-strike bombers, 10 obsolete IL-28 bombers, 80 export versions of the MiG-23, 40 short-range Su-7Bs, 60 export versions of the Su-20, and 15 obsolete Hunters. This gave Iraq an effective modern attack force for long-range tactical missions of about 120 MiG-23s and Su-20(22)s.

Iraq started the war with the pilot and support capability to generate a maximum of 80–90 sorties a day from such aircraft for a period of no more than 3 days. It would have taken hundreds of sorties more per day for Iraq to have achieved its initial objectives with the aircraft then available in its forces, and then it would still only have been able to crater Iranian runways and hit vulnerable facilities, not destroy sheltered aircraft.

Iraq proved this on the first day of the war. It did commit virtually all of its combat-ready fighters and bombers to its surprise air attack on September 22. Iraqi aircraft struck six Iranian air bases and four Iranian army bases. Iraq claimed to have caused heavy damage to the air bases and airports at Mehrabad, Kermanshah, Sanandaj, and Al-Ahwaz, and the Army bases at Hamadan, Tehran, Isfahan, Dezful, Shiraz, and Tabriz. In fact, however, Iraq's first major attack on Iran was its first major failure of the war.

Iraq's attack against Mehrabad exemplified Iraq's problems. Iraq's bombing runs scattered ordnance over so wide an area that the Iranians on the ground later found it difficult to determine the original targets.

Efforts to close the base by cratering the runways were a dismal failure. The bombs designed to crater the runways had little effect, even in the few cases where they hit the runway. They skipped over the hardened surface, causing only small, easily repairable craters. Many of the bombs failed to explode, possibly because of fusing and arming problems. Long rows of transport aircraft, which could not be sheltered like Iran's fighters, were left untouched. Only one B-707 and an F-4 undergoing repairs suffered any damage.

Iraqi commanders committed less than 20 percent of the sorties necessary to achieve the effects they sought and did not provide for meaningful reconnaissance and follow-up attacks. While Iraq launched follow-up air raids against four Iranian airfields on September 23 and six on September 24—hitting Tabriz and Dezful twice, and Shahroki, Kermanshah, Ahwaz, and Sanandaj—the raids only damaged Dezful to the point where they had more than a minimal effect in halting Iranian air operations, and Dezful was repaired relatively rapidly.

Admittedly, the Iraqi raids attacked an extremely difficult set of targets. Iran's air bases were well-designed. Shelters and command facilities were well-dispersed. While runways could be hit, they were very well built, and a limited number of shallow runway craters were easy to repair.

In spite of more than a year of revolutionary turmoil, Iran's Air Force had a very different force posture from the posture of Arab air forces in 1967. Most of the aircraft on the Iranian air bases were sheltered or dispersed. While Iraq did hit some exposed transport aircraft and a few combat aircraft, it did not do any serious damage to the Iranian Air Force.

The Iraqi air attacks on Iran's army bases were equally ineffective. The army bases were large, dispersed targets with well-bunkered munitions. There were no high-value targets where a limited number of hits would have had a devastating effect, and the location of the Iraqi air strikes indicated that the pilots had never been assigned specific areas of the base to attack. It would have taken wave after wave of attack sorties to kill or disable a significant amount of armor and heavy weapons or even to produce high casualties. Iraq flew less than a tenth of the sorties needed against any major Iranian army target. It confused smoke and damaging buildings—many of which had few occupants—with producing massive damage.

The problems inevitable in attacking with insufficient force to achieve the objective were compounded by the fact that Iraqi pilots and aircraft generally lacked the attack training and experience to achieve anything like the lethality of Western or Israeli forces, even in those cases where Iranian aircraft were openly exposed to attack. Pilots lacked the training to accurately hit small tactical targets in high-speed passes and had to attack with little mission prebriefing and reconnaissance data. They also had to fly Soviet fighters whose avionics did little to assist the pilot in making his attack and using conventional ordnance which often lacked the special fusing needed to attack the hard targets involved.

Later discussions with senior officers of the Iraqi Air Force confirm this explanation of why Iraq was unsuccessful in its air attacks on September 22 and why it was unsuccessful in so many other attacks during the course of the war. Several senior Iraqi officers stated separately that the Iraqi pilots flying the attack missions had little practical training, aside from limited range training with dummy munitions and the bombing of Kurdish villages. The avionics on their aircraft were relatively primitive export versions of Soviet technology and had circular error of probabilities (CEPs) which often exceed 200–500 meters. There were no technical personnel experienced with the details of weapons effects. There were no operations research facilities. There were no technical crews with experience in arming or fusing air munitions for demanding missions. There were no photo interpreters and commanders experienced in damage assessment, and the USSR failed to provide more than minimal technical support and aid in any of these areas.[5]

Iraq also entered the war with a highly politicized Air Force command structure that had little real operational experience in attacking anything other than undefended targets like Kurdish villages. This may explain why the high command of the Iraqi Air Force lacked any realistic concept of the amount of air power needed to achieve a given objective, or "mass." The Iraqi high command simply did not, or could not, do its homework. It failed to work out a realistic picture of the number of attacks necessary to destroy a given objective or of the forces it would have to commit over time. Iraq flew few low-level reconnaissance missions before its initial air attacks on Iran and failed to conduct detailed mission planning or provide detailed mission briefings to its squadron commanders. At the unit level, it failed to provide detailed photos of the target area or to properly identify high-priority targets when it did brief, by using maps or photos. It did not realistically allocate the proper number of sorties to a given target, even at the unit level, and often failed to select munitions which could do suitable damage.

Iraq had no real experience with armed reconnaissance. After the initial attacks, most sorties had to be approved at relatively high echelons of command and took hours or even days to schedule. Mission pre-briefs were poor to nonexistent. There were few trained forward air controllers (FACs), and most units lacked any at all. Many of the individual pilots sent out on attack missions had little experience in delivering munitions, and the majority had only flown a handful of sorties—if any—using the attack payloads they were being asked to use in combat.

Further, once it executed its attack missions, the Iraqi command systematically lied to itself about the results. It failed to fly enough damage-assessment or reconnaissance missions to get a realistic picture of what it had accomplished. It accepted wildly exaggerated pilot damage claims and often added to these claims at higher echelons of command. These claims reinforced the Air Force's initial tendency to underestimate the number of sorties required to achieve a given objective, and false claims of success were so heavily institutionalized at every level of operations and command that the Air Force could do little to learn from experience.

As for the Iranian Air Force, it not only emerged from Iraq's attacks virtually intact, it rapidly went on the counteroffensive. While it had suffered badly from various purges during the course of the revolution, it was able to mobilize enough pilots to take advantage of the fact it had acquired much better aircraft, munitions, and training from the U.S. than Iraq had from the USSR. As a result, Iran was able to fly some 100 sorties against Iraq on September 23, 1980.

While these Iranian sorties were not particularly effective, and Iran's sortie-generation capability rapidly dropped to less than 50 per day, the attacks still came as a considerable shock to Iraq. The Iranians were also able to win most air-to-air duels during the early period of the war, and while they could only fly limited numbers, they occasionally proved highly successful in delivering low-altitude air attacks against Iraqi targets. Similarly, Iran was initially able to make good use of the helicopters purchased by the Shah to fly transport and attack missions.

The Iraqi Air Force then virtually abandoned the skies. Iraqi sortie rates dropped to a minimum except when Saddam Hussein sought to achieve some major strategic effect or reprisal against Iran. Some Iraqi aircraft were dispersed to countries in the southern Gulf, and others were flown to bases in western Iraq. While Iraqi aircraft and pilots were individually inferior to those of Iran, it is important to note that they conducted this retreat from the skies in spite of the fact they had a 3:1 to 4:1 superiority in operational strength over Iran.

Iraq's Land Invasion of Iran

The initial performance of Iraq's Army was somewhat better than that of its Air Force, but Iraq still scored only limited strategic successes when it should have been able to achieve far more. When the war began, Iraq had five full divisions in the north, two more guarding the central front opposite Baghdad, and five more in the south. The five divisions in the south included three armored and two mechanized divisions. These Iraqi forces underwent substantial redeployment after the war began. Iran, in contrast, had only four of its nine understrength divisions along the 1,300-kilometer border. (For the deployment of the forces of both Iraq and Iran, see Figure 4.1.)

Iraqi land forces attacked at four points along a 700-kilometer front the same day that Iraq launched its air strikes against Iran. The Iraqi Army sent about half of its combat-ready manpower and most of its 12 fully manned divisions across the Iranian border. By the first day of the war, Iraqi ground troops had penetrated about 15 kilometers into Iran, captured Qasr e-Shirin, and reached the outskirts of Sumar, Zahab, and Charmel. Other Iraqi troops and artillery were approaching Abadan and Khorramshahr.

In the north, one Iraqi mechanized or armored division, one mountain division, and supporting elements, advanced from positions in the Kurdish part of Iraq, just west of the Iranian border town of Qasr e-Shirin, toward Gilan e-Gahreb and Kermanshah.[6] The Iraqi forces attacking through Qasr e-Shirin rapidly took the small border city, pushed Iran's forces back, and advanced as deep as 45 kilometers into Iran. Iraq's forces then spent six days reaching the villages along the main route to Tehran at the edge of the mountains about 10 miles northeast of Qasr e-Shirin. They spent seven days taking Gilan e-Gahreb, and eleven days taking Sumar.

The advancing Iraqi forces made heavy use of artillery and used anti-tank guided missiles to attack hard points and road blocks. They conquered roughly 120 square kilometers of Iranian territory and met with little more than minor resistance from a mix of Pasdaran and gendarmerie infantry forces until Iranian regular artillery forces arrived in support. They did not encounter any opposition from Iranian armor and armed helicopters and at most faced a few Iranian attack sorties per day.

This thrust seems to have been largely defensive and directed at blocking any counterattack by the Iranian armored division at Kermanshah. If so, it succeeded in guarding the main route to Baghdad from Tehran and the main route near the frontier which connects southwards to Gilan e-Gahreb and Ilam. It also gave Iraq access to routes to several Iranian towns near the border, including Naft e-Shah, Sumar, and Mehran. Nevertheless, it left the Iranian division at Kermanshah intact and gave Iranian forces ample time to regroup.[7]

In the center, an Iraqi armored division and additional supporting

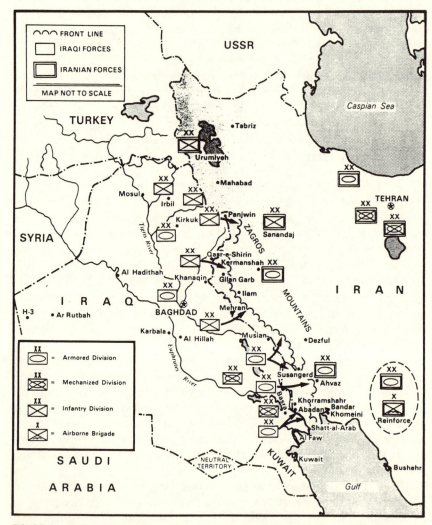

FIGURE 4.1   Iranian-Iraqi Deployments During the Iraqi Invasion. Adapted from material provided by the U.S. Army War College and the CIA.

forces advanced toward Mehran, with one wing of the attacking forces moving north toward Ilam and another to the south.[8] These forces rapidly took Mehran, a town near the border at the edge of the mountains, and thrust toward Ilam. The Mehran area was already heavily depopulated because insufficient water existed to provide for the normal amount of irrigation.

While the Iraqi forces did encounter some successful attacks by Iranians using Cobra attack helicopters and pop-up tactics, this resistance was far too weak to have any major effect. Iraqi forces succeeded in spreading out along a 50-kilometer front, from north to south, in the central sector of the front. The Iraqis then destroyed most of the villages in the area and their dam and irrigation system and expelled most of the Iranians. This thrust shielded Iraq against any Iranian attempt to penetrate into its road system near the border at Kut and shielded the southeastern approaches to Baghdad.

The Iraqi Army's main offensive thrust was in the south. Three armored and two mechanized divisions attacked along a broad front from Musain to Khorramshahr. Two armored divisions, with a mechanized division in support, attacked Dezful and Ahwaz. Another armored division, with a mechanized division in the rear, thrust toward Abadan and Khorramshahr. These forces were supported by special forces units and at least one independent brigade and sought to conquer the entire Abadan Island. The Iraqi infantry and armored forces in this southern attack included six of Iraq's nine most effective brigades. The attack not only thrust toward the Arab population of Khuzistan, it led it toward Iran's main refinery and oil facilities.

The armored division that led the northern part of this attack was stripped of its infantry to increase its speed of movement and attacked as separate brigade-sized elements. It soon took much of the territory around Musain and Bustan and slowly moved across the Kharkeh River, which was fordable at this time of year. It then moved toward Shush. Part of this Iraqi attacking force was in a position to move toward the main Iranian air base and command center at Dezful, but it never did so.

Other elements of the main Iraqi attack in the south thrust across the frontier south of Qalat Salih, through Hoveyzeh, and entered Susangerd on September 28. Susangerd was undefended, and the Iraqi force moved on toward Dezful and Ahwaz without securing its rear or leaving a garrison in Susangerd. To the south, Iraqi armored forces crossed the Karun River and entered the outskirts of Ahwaz and Khorramshahr. Ahwaz was the main administrative center for Iran's oil industry and the location of one of Iran's armored divisions. The remaining Iraqi armored division crossed the Tigris at Kharkiya and reached Khorramshahr on September 28. Iraqi artillery had begun to heavily shell the Iranian refinery complex at Abadan on the first day of the war, and Iraqi Army forces now threatened to seize all of the major cities in southwestern Iran.[9]

Iran's Initial Failure to Organize Effective Opposition

If Iraq had been more aggressive and had been better prepared to attack Khorramshahr and Abadan, it might well have succeeded in taking all of these Iranian cities and possibly much of Khuzistan. The Iranian forces near the border were poorly prepared to resist the Iraqi thrust into southern Iran, although small elements of the Iranian Air Force immediately began to attack the advancing Iraqi fighters and struck at Basra and Wasit.

On September 22, 1980, Iran's regular army deployments in the entire border area consisted of (a) one infantry division posted near Urumiyeh in the far north, (b) an infantry division at Sandaj, reinforced by Pasdaran and covering the threat from Iran's Kurds, (c) an armored division farther south in Kermanshah with a brigade at Qasr e-Shirin, and (d) an armored division at Ahwaz tasked with the defense of Khorramshahr and Abadan, and which shielded the Iranian air base at Dezful. Iran did, however, deploy most of a battalion to Mehran just before the war began. One more Iranian armored division, and an airborne division, were in reserve. When Iran did begin to move the rest of its divisions forward in October, there were so many transportation problems that it took six weeks to get an infantry division from Mashad to a position near Khuzistan.[10]

These Iranian divisions had a substantially larger authorized manpower and equipment strength than Iraqi divisions, and Iran would have had a relatively strong defense force if its divisions and support forces had been at anything like their full authorized strength under the Shah. As has been described in the previous chapter, however, the regular Iranian Army had suffered at least a 30 percent desertion rate since the fall of the Shah. Many enlisted men, NCOs, and officers had deserted, and Iran had purged at least 12,000 men from its regular military. Most combat units had only 30–50 percent manning.[11]

As for the rest of the Iranian Army, roughly 140,000 Iranian military personnel had deserted during the course of the revolution, cutting the strength of the regular armed forces from 260,000 to between 110,000 and 150,000. The U.S. Embassy hostage crisis had cut Iran off from its main source of weapons, spare parts, and logistical assistance. In addition, many elements of the Iranian armed forces were occupied in dealing with Kurdish insurgents or stationed along the Soviet border.

Many of the support functions in Iranian forces had virtually disintegrated. Other support and logistic functions were under the control of different, and sometimes competing, revolutionary organizations. Iranian logistics were in a near state of chaos, and there was little central control of assets.[12] The Iranian Army had lost so many critical technical personnel that a number of specialized combat and support elements could barely function. As a result, the regular Iranian Army could only provide a poorly coordinated defense during the first weeks of the war. Most Iranian units rapidly encountered serious technical, repair, or support problems and lost the ability to use much of their armor, heavy artillery, or attack helicopters after the first few weeks of combat.

Iran's new revolutionary forces in western Iran also were scarcely ready for war. Although Iran's President, Bani-Sadr, had called for the full mobilization of all forces and military reservists on September 20, and Iran had announced it was deploying the regular army to the border and mobilizing 150,000 popular reserves on September 21, few of these forces were even in motion when the Iraqi Army entered Iran. Iran was still in the early stages of transforming its Pasdaran, or Revolutionary Guards, into a serious alternative to the Army. This meant Iran had to react to the Iraqi invasion by mobilizing massive numbers of new popular volunteers into a highly diverse and disorganized mix of regular, revolutionary, and rapidly mobilized units.[13]

This left much of the initial defense of much of Iran's territory in the central and southern border areas to Iran's paramilitary forces, a few scattered regular-army brigades, and only 12,000–30,000 men in the Pasdaran. The Pasdaran forces, however, were better deployed and organized to deal with domestic opposition than the threat from Iraq and had relatively young officers and NCOs. Their military experience consisted largely of training as conscripts in the Shah's army or low-level fighting against Khomeini's opponents or hostile ethnic groups like the Kurds. The Pasdaran forces and rapidly mobilized volunteers were just beginning to convert to heavy weaponry, and many elements had to fight largely with light-infantry weapons and with "Molotov cocktails."

Iraq's Failure to Exploit Its Initial Success

It is not surprising, therefore, that Iran did so little to resist Iraq's regular forces during the period from September 22 to September 28. At the same time, Iraq failed to exploit its initial successes in the land fighting and halted for nearly five days following its initial penetration into Iran. The precise reasons for this Iraqi pause are unclear. Iraq has since claimed that it paused because its objectives were limited, and it was seeking a peace settlement. It is far more likely, however, that Iraq's attack paused because of sheer disarray at the command level.

Some of the Iraqi combat elements that invaded the south penetrated into key cities and objectives and had to withdraw because other units fell behind and did not provide proper support. The Iraqi Army lost concentration, cohesion, and momentum as it advanced, and combat and service-support elements did not thrust forward aggressively. Iraqi commanders exhibited little understanding of the critical importance of speed, maneuver, and of the need to exploit the shock value of armor. They rarely risked bypassing an objective or opposing forces. Some combat elements halted when they met relatively light opposition, and Iraq showed little ability to maneuver its armor or use its air power.

Iraq may have simply expected Iran's forces and revolution to collapse. Iraqi planners were fully aware of the weaknesses in the Iranian Army. Several Iranian generals were then in Iraq and may have told Saddam Hussein that the Khomeini regime was far more fragile than it really was. In any case, Iraq's pauses gave Iran time to call up and deploy massive numbers of revolutionary reserves and gave its regular and revolutionary forces time to deploy forward, to establish defensive lines, and to dig in.

These Iraqi behavior patterns are scarcely unique to the Third World. At the same time, these patterns reflect problems which are much more severe in Third World countries, and they provide an important lesson about both the vulnerability of Third World states and their probable actions as allies.

The Oil War Begins

An equally important development took place during the first few days of the war whose full strategic implications became clear only much later. When the war began, oil prices were at a near record high. Iraq was exporting about 3.0 to 3.4 MMBD, and Iran was exporting about 1.4 to 1.6 MMBD. Both nations depended on oil for most of their export earnings and, indeed, for their economic survival. (See Table 4.1.)

All oil exports from both countries ceased, however, on the first day of the war. While exports resumed a few weeks later, they remained at significantly lower levels throughout the war. Regardless of what Iraq's original intentions may have been, the war immediately escalated all along the Shatt al-Arab. The Iraqis seem to have started this escalation with artillery attacks on the oil facilities at Abadan,

TABLE 4.1 Average Daily Oil Production in Thousands of Barrels per Day

	Iran	*Iraq*
1978 (Peak)	5.2	2.6
1980	1.7	2.5
1981	1.4	1.0
1982	2.3	1.0
1983	2.5	0.9
1984	2.2	1.2
1985, 1st Quarter	2.1	1.3
1986, 2nd Quarter	2.3	1.3

SOURCES: CIA estimates in various editions of its periodical report *Economic and Energy Indicators.*

and virtually all of the more than 150 oil storage tanks at Abadan were destroyed or burning by the second day of the war.

Both sides then launched a limited number of air raids against the other's oil facilities, although with little initial effect. Iraq launched its first strike on Iran's oil terminal at Kharg Island on September 24, 1980. The Iraqi attacks had some strategic impact on Iran. The tank farms and some of the oil-exporting facilities at Kharg Island were damaged in the first weeks of fighting, along with some of Iran's smaller refineries, but Iraq used insufficient air strength to inflict decisive damage and failed to repeat and follow up its attacks. Most Iranian facilities were quickly repaired, and Iran rapidly strengthened its anti-aircraft defenses.

Both combatants continued to make sporadic efforts to use air power to destroy the other side's economic installations, particularly its oil production and export facilities. However, Iran's first air raids against Iraq's oil fields and facilities involved very limited numbers of sorties and had as much impact as Iran's air attacks against Iraq. Some storage tanks burned, some facilities were closed, and Iraqi production dropped, but the overall impact on Iraq's oil-exporting capacity was negligible. Iran did launch larger air raids against Iraq's oil facilities at Kirkuk and Sulaimaniyeh on October 7, but these, too, did little real damage.

Iraq retaliated with its first air attacks on Iranian shipping, but most of these attacks took place around the port of Bandar-e-Khomeini, which was at the head of the Gulf and close to the war zone. Iraq's air strikes did not affect Iran's crude oil shipments which came from ports lower in the Gulf. Iraq did destroy some oil tanks in Tehran on October 16, but it did not launch its first major air strike against Kharg Island until December 24.

Other forms of combat damage to the oil facilities on each side proved to be far more serious. Iran started a blockade of the Shatt al-Arab and Basra on the first day of the war and used artillery fire to shut down the Iraqi oil-loading facility at al-Faw. Some 62 ships and tankers were rapidly trapped or sunk in the Shatt, and the waterway was extensively mined. Six more ships were trapped in the Khor Abdullah, and Iranian aircraft sank several of these ships to help block the channel on October 6, 1980.[14]

Iran then used artillery, naval gunfire, and naval commando raids to attack Faw and to seize the Iraqi oil-loading points in the Gulf at Mina al-Bakr and Khor al-Amaya. It launched these attacks during September 23 and 24 and again on September 29. As a result, Iran succeeded in destroying both of Iraq's oil-loading points in the Gulf and much of Faw's ability to function. Iranian artillery fire also damaged some of the petrochemical facilities around Basra, and the Basra refinery was forced to close.

The strategic importance of this damage was not clear at the time. Iraq had immense hard-currency reserves when the war began, could export through pipelines to Syria and Turkey, and seems to have felt it would be able to resume exporting through the Gulf in a matter of weeks or months. Iran, in contrast, seemed to be far more vulnerable. Its refinery at Abadan fed much of its domestic market, and other supply disruptions and air attacks reduced the output of its refineries at Shiraz, Tehran, and Kermanshah to less than half their normal capacity. Iran began to experience serious fuel-supply problems during October, which is the beginning of winter in parts of Iran.

In actual practice, however, Iran proved to be less vulnerable than Iraq. Iran retained the option of redirecting its crude oil exports through pipelines far to the east of the battlefield. In contrast, many of Iraq's critical facilities were in the forward area. As a result, a relatively limited amount of Iranian air strikes and artillery fire destroyed or shut down enough of Iraq's refinery and gas production to force Iraq to introduce rationing by October. Iranian air raids led Iraq to temporarily stop pumping from the Kirkuk field on October 13, 1980, and Iran forced Iraq to make major power cuts in December, when Iranian air strikes damaged the Iraqi power plants at Harthya and Nasirya.

The Battle of Khorramshahr:
Iraq's Invasion Slows to a Crawl

Iraq had another painful shock during October. Iraq may have expected Iran to begin to sue for peace the moment Iraq achieved its initial gains. If so, it was badly mistaken. Iran immediately made it clear that it had no intention of suing for peace, and Khomeini and his supporters stated they were ready for a prolonged war that would result in Saddam Hussein's overthrow. These words soon proved to be more than rhetoric. The Battle of Khorramshahr, however, showed that the Khomeini government was not only able to survive Iran's initial defeats, but that Iran could put up serious resistance to Iraqi forces.

While an Iraqi armored division reached the outskirts of Khorramshahr within a matter of days, it then waited while Iraqi artillery was used in an attempt to soften up the city. This artillery fire did little other than arouse the populace and create added barriers to the movement of Iraqi forces. When Iraqi armored forces finally entered the city of 70,000 people on September 28, they encountered Iranian forces equipped with rocket launchers and Molotov cocktails that were willing to fight street by street through the city.[15]

The Iranian forces only seem to have consisted of about 2,000 regular army forces and several thousand Pasdaran. Nevertheless, Iraq rapidly found that it could not send tanks unescorted into the city and that it had to send in infantry support.[16] This new attempt to attack Khorramshahr failed because neither the Iraqi armored or infantry forces involved had any real training in urban warfare. They moved far too cautiously in maneuvering through the less-defended parts of the city and repeatedly became the victims of Iranian ambushes. Neither Iraqi armor nor infantry conducted aggressive reconnaissance, and both tended to wait until massive firepower could be brought to bear. Iraq was forced to slowly secure the perimeter of the city with the armored division it had initially committed to the attack and then rush a special forces brigade and Republican Guard brigade through a quickly improvised course in urban warfare.

This process took several weeks, and Iraq lost as many as 2,000 killed and 6,000 wounded as it committed its forces piecemeal to a battle that required a coherent mass attack.[17] Iranian regular army and Pasdaran units had time to reinforce the city. Both groups of Iranian forces also fought Iraqi troops with great determination, although there were reports that Pasdaran and Hizbollah elements shot regular army troops that attempted to retreat.

Even though Iraq first claimed to have fully secured Khorramshahr on October 13, 1979, Iranian patrols continued to move through the city. Iraq only really gained real control over most of the city on October 24. The end result of this battle was that Iraq and Iran suffered 8,000–12,000 killed and seriously wounded, and Iraq lost roughly 100 armored vehicles. Much of of Khorramshahr was destroyed, and Iraq found that it took nearly a month for its forces to secure a city that was initially defended by the equivalent of a few poorly equipped Iranian infantry battalions.

The battle for Khorramshahr also stalled the Iraqi assault on the much larger city of Abadan, and the refinery complex in Abadan Island, for nearly two critical weeks. While Iraq shelled Abadan from September 22 onwards, using positions across the Shatt al-Arab, Iraqi forces did not begin to surround the city and island until October 10. This delay proved critical because Iran was able to reinforce a city located on a natural island which was separated from Khorramshahr by the Karun River and which had the the Shatt al-Arab on its west and the Bahmanshir River, a tributary of the Karun, on its east. By the time Iraq attacked, there were as many as 10,000 regular troops in the city, including a mechanized brigade, a mechanized battalion, a naval unit, an armored unit with 50 tanks, and up to 5,000 Pasdaran.[18] There also were massive saltwater marshes to the southeast. This made it almost impossible for Iraq to secure the island against reinforcement once it became involved in a prolonged battle.

Iraq began its attack on Abadan by sending a mechanized division far enough to the north of Khorramshahr so that it could cross the Karun River, come down the road on the east bank of the Karun, and cut off Abadan from Ahwaz and the road to Bandar e-Mashahr and Bandar-e-Khomeini. The key to this Iraqi movement was a difficult river crossing that demonstrated that Iraq's military engineers could be highly effective, even if its combat arms were not.

Iraq tried to achieve surprise during its river crossing and to minimize casualties by only working on the bridging operation at night and by only allowing military movements to take place at night. This meant Iraqi engineers had to conceal their operations during the daytime. They also had to cope with the fact that the Karun River had high muddy banks, and the approaches to the bridge required considerable work. Even so, Iraqi engineers put a pontoon bridge across the river on the second night, and the entire Iraqi division had completed its crossing on the fourth night. While Iraq's insistence on night operations did delay the completion of the crossing until October 14, the wisdom of this delay is indicated by the fact that the bridge was later destroyed by Iranian aircraft and helicopters.

The Iraqi force secured the northern road to Ahwaz on the 15th, after a brief skirmish with advancing Iranian armored forces. Iran lost roughly a battalion's worth of armor when an Iraqi ambush forced the Iranian unit to move into the mud off the road, and it bogged down and the equipment had to be abandoned. The rest of the Iraqi mechanized division moved southwards along the east bank of the Karun River without significant opposition and surrounded all of Abadan Island but its southern end by October 16.[19] The Iraqi force could not fully secure the island because the salt marsh at its southern end is untrafficable by military vehicles and can be reached only by boat.

Once this operation was completed, Iraqi forces fought their way across the bridges to Abadan along three different routes. They only succeeded, however, in securing the western and central bridges. Iranian forces continued to block all access across the eastern bridge. The Iraqis did not fully secure the eastern bank of the Bahmanshir River and the road to Khosrowabad and, therefore, had to be reinforced and resupplied by sea.[20] By now Iran had had nearly a month to deploy its forces to Abadan and had built up a considerable garrison and large supplies of light weapons and ammunition.

Abadan was a city of nearly 300,000 and was even more difficult to attack than Khorramshahr. As a result, Iraq had to fight its way south and east through the city street by street. While Iraqi forces slowly reached the edge of the tank farm along the Shatt at the southern end of the city, Iraq seems to to have refused to take the losses necessary to fully secure all the city and the island. Iraqi forces never occupied the southeastern end of the city or the village of Torreh ye-Bakhkhak. Although Iraq sporadically claimed to have secured Abadan, the Iranian garrison remained, and both Iranian small craft and helicopters were able to move to and from the island at night with relative freedom.

By mid-October, Iran had also begun to organize an effective command structure, and its Supreme Command Council began to have some effectiveness in coordinating its forces. While this did not suppress the deep divisions within Iran's forces, and particularly between the regular forces and Pasdaran, it did improve their performance all along the front. Iraq never took any other key cities or targets in Iran. It is also important to note that Baghdad failed to get significant support from Khuzistan's Arab population. Iraq captured nearly a third of Khuzistan province during the first two months of fighting, but it never gathered any meaningful popular support. Iraq's efforts to encourage Arab separatism with movements like the Al Ahwaz National Popular Front had no meaningful impact on the war during any part of the Iraqi invasion of Khuzistan.[21]

As for the fighting on the rest of the battlefield, the three Iraqi armored forces which originally invaded the south remained virtually in place during Iraq's capture of Khorramshahr and the siege of Abadan. These forces did not conduct any significant offensive operations during the rest of September and all of October and only began to move forward in early November. By this time, however, the

Iranian buildup had gone far beyond simply rushing in infantry and helicopter gunships. Substantial amounts of artillery had arrived during early October, and armor had followed. Shush and Dezful now had substantial garrisons and artillery forces, and Iran had built up a lightly fortified defense line along the western bank of the Kharkeh River. Substantial Pasdaran forces had also entered Susangerd, which Iraqi forces had taken but not garrisoned, and were supported by substantial amounts of artillery.

While Iraqi forces probably still had something like a 3:1 to 5:1 advantage in most heavy weapons, they now faced parity or superiority in manpower. They also remained road- and vehicle-bound and continued to move slowly and to try to use artillery assaults as a substitute for maneuver. The end result was that Iraqi armor proceeded up the dry riverbed of the Kharkeh River, but halted south of Shush.

Iraq was never able to retake Susangerd, which thrust between the northern and southern part of the Iraqi advance. The forces Iraq used to attack Susangerd on November 13 and 21, 1980, had a superiority of between 6:1 and 7:1, but they never were able to break though Iran's initial defensive lines. The Iraqi forces halted after the attack on November 21, dug in, and then did little more than shell the city.

Iraq was even less successful when it tried to advance to the south. Iraqi armored forces attempted to move south from Hamidiyeh toward Ahwaz, but Iran then flooded the area, which consisted of low fields that had once been irrigated by an ancient canal. The end result was that part of the Iraqi forced drowned, and some 150 armored vehicles were left mired in the mud.[22]

By late November, Iraq had been halted on all fronts. The seasonal rains then began and continued until February. Many of the areas that Iraqi armor had been able to use days before the rains arrived became totally untrafficable. Iranian infantry forces were able to take effective control of many of the new wetlands because the Iraqi Army remained road-bound and did little patrolling. Iraqi engineers did build some excellent all-weather roads from Basra to the front near Ahwaz and connecting roads to the north and south. Iraq, however, made little attempt to fortify its positions, secure its rear areas, or create defense in depth.

The only major offensive action Iraq was to take during the rest of 1980 came on December 24, a day on which Iraq also launched its first major air raid against Kharg Island. Iraq sent an infantry division from the area around Panjwin in northern Kurdistan toward the Iranian town of Marivan. This attack seems to have been designed to achieve several different objectives: to help secure the Kurdish area of Iraq and the Darbandikhan Reservoir, to control the Marivan Valley, to block any attack forward by the Iranian infantry division stationed at Sanandaj, and to aid the anti-Iranian Kurds in the Kurdish Democratic Party of Iran (KDPI), or Pesh Merga, which were still actively fighting Khomeini and which controlled a substantial part of the Kurdish area of Iran.

The Marivan area had little strategic importance to Iran, and there were no significant Iranian forces in the area. As a result, Iraqi forces quickly took a roughly 300-square kilometer area, although they only secured the initial line of heights in the Zagros Mountains east of Marivan. Iraq backed up its advance on January 15, 1981, by sending an Iraqi mountain division east from Halabjah, a small border garrison between Qasr e-Shirin and Panjwin, to seize the Iranian town of Nowdesheh. This winter attack hit a small garrison of Pasdaran and regular forces without warning and was successful in giving Iraq control of the town and the heights above the Baghdad-Tehran Highway and the road nets in the area. It helped secure Kirkuk and the Darbandikhan Reservoir and gave Iraq a position directly contiguous to the areas held by the KDPI.

Iraq gave the KDPI, which was still led by Abdul Rahman Ghassemlou, a base and training and supply center in Sunn, an Iraqi town near Halabjah. This allowed the KDPI to build up its forces to around 7,000 to 10,000 regulars and win the support of roughly twice that number of part-time guerrillas. This proved to be of considerable importance during the following year. The KDPI—in combination with some factions of Jalal Talabani's Patriotic Union of Kurdestan (PUK), and anti-Khomeini Kurdish Marxists—were able to score significant gains beginning in the spring of 1981. They were able to take a number of Kurdish towns, including Bukan, Mahabad, Saqqez, Sanandaj, and Urumayeh.

Iraq's limited success in the north, however, did more for the anti-Iranian Kurds than Iraq. In fact, by the end of 1980, the Iraqi Army had established a pattern that it could not change until 1988. It generally failed to maneuver effectively, conduct effective offensive combined-arms operations, counterattack and patrol aggressively, and to conduct active reconnaissance and intelligence operations. Iraqi forces made heavy use of artillery bombardments and slow and careful tank movements. Iraqi forces did not try to find weaknesses in Iran's defense and thrust through them. They instead relied on surrounding and besieging major Iranian cities like Khuzistan, Abadan, Ahwaz, Khorramshahr, and Dezful. Iraqi forces found it difficult to spearhead offensive operations unless they achieved virtually complete surprise, and they found it equally difficult to commit their reserves. They moved too slowly, too little, and too late.

While the Iranian Army also had many weaknesses, it was clear after the first few days of Iraq's invasion that the Iranian revolution now had massive popular support. The moment Iraq's initial offensive momentum failed, Iraq faced a mobilized nation with revolutionary fervor and which was willing to take incredible losses. This was to give Iran a degree of military leverage which went far beyond its numbers of weapons and soldiers.

The Air Fighting During the Rest of 1980

The war in the air and at sea had surprisingly little impact on the conflict during 1980. Both the Iranian and the Iraqi Air Forces flew occasional attack sorties, and these often produced significant effects against highly vulnerable targets like tank farms and refineries. Both Air Forces, however, had serious problems in conducting large-scale operations.

The Iraqi Air Force had dispersed many of its aircraft to other Arab countries after the initial Iranian counterraids on September 23, 1980. It brought these aircraft back a week to ten days later but then generally kept its air units out of the battle. Iraqi officers indicate there were several reasons for this limited activity. The first reason was that Iraqi pilots lacked the avionics, training, and air-to-air munitions to win air-combat encounters with Iranian pilots. They also had little air-to-air combat training under simulated combat conditions, and most of the training they did have was in fair weather and at relatively high altitudes. The second was that Iraq feared Iranian reprisals for any strategic bombing. The third was the lack of tactical target opportunities that justified risking scarce pilots and aircraft, and the fourth was that Saddam Hussein ordered that the Air Force be kept in reserve as an ultimate defense for Iraqi land forces and territory.

Some of these reasons seem valid. The initial air-combat encounters during the first days of the war scarcely threatened the survival of the Iraqi Air Force—Iran lacked both the numbers and battle-management capability to deploy an effective air screen—but Iran did consistently win the few dogfights that did occur and forced the Iraqi pilots to break away and flee the combat. There were relatively few hits per dogfight encounter or missile fired, but Iran also won most of the encounters that resulted in a hit or kill. By and large, both sides found it difficult to force an air-to-air encounter to the killing point and shot far more often than they hit.

Iraq also could not correct the basic problems in its ability to fly attack missions that had hurt it during the first days of the war. It had not learned to mass air power or that a repeated cycle of reconnaissance-strike-damage assessment was necessary to kill rear-area and interdiction targets. It tended to launch a few sporadic sorties and to try to use claims as a substitute for actual damage. The few strategic bombing attacks Iraq did carry out at this time—like its attacks on Iran's refineries and storage tanks in October 1980—produced more smoke than long-term damage.

Iraqi fighters also found it extremely difficult to find meaningful targets for close air support. Iran's land forces were largely irregular formations deployed in dug-in or urban areas and which generally only moved at night. It was difficult to find a target where an attack fighter could score a meaningful kill, and minor losses of infantry and support vehicles were not worth risking airplanes.

Iran's success during the first days of the war, and its ability to fly over 100 sorties on the second day of the war, gave Iraq an exaggerated picture of Iranian air capabilities that was to last for some time. Iraq concluded that it was as vulnerable to urban and key-facility attacks as Iran and potentially more vulnerable to attacks on its air bases because of its lack of strategic depth. Iraqi planners were also surprised by the virtual ineffectiveness of their Soviet-made radar net and surface-to-air missiles against low-altitude Iranian attacks.

The USSR made some of these problems worse by refusing to support Iraq's attack on Iran, withdrawing some of its advisors, and refusing to offer Iraq any technical solutions to the problems in either the Iraqi Air Force or Iraq's land-based air defenses. Iraq not only could not improve its air power, it could not improve its command-and-control net or obtain more SA-6s—the only major Soviet system it had with a low-altitude kill capability. Iraq had begun the war with only about 25 SA-6 fire units.

This suddenly forced Iraq to try to find its own substitutes for effective area defense. Iraq deployed anti-aircraft (AA) guns, provided earth mounds and sand bags for key facilities, and bought short-range surface-to-air missiles for the point defense of key economic and military targets. These measures were somewhat successful, although Iranian F-4s continued to overfly Baghdad as a threat of what Iran could do in an intensive air war, bombed Iraq's nuclear reactor at Tuwaitha on September 10, 1988, and even struck at one of Iraq's most western air bases deep in Iraqi territory.[23]

Iraq never succeeded in creating an effective national area air-defense capability that could operate below medium altitude during the rest of the war, and it was Iran's rapid loss of operational air strength—not Iraq's air defense —that ultimately protected Iraq. In fact, if Iran had retained its ability to use the Shah's air power, it might well have been able to do enough damage to Iraq's oil facilities to cripple Iraq, in spite of the massive economic aid it later got from Kuwait and Saudi Arabia.

Iran, on the other hand, lost most of its operational air strength by late 1980. It still had sufficient pilots, but its remaining ground crews could not operate effectively without U.S. technicians and support. The F-4 and F-14 proved to be particularly difficult to keep fully operational. While Iran did not need to use the F-14 extensively, it did have to use the F-4. The F-4, however, presented maintenance problems even in U.S. hands. It needed some 35 man-hours of maintenance per flight hour, and the Iranian Air Force simply could not handle the resulting burden.

The collapse of Iran's logistic system created a situation where it could not assemble all of the spare parts it needed to maintain readiness without cannibalizing (or "vulturizing") its aircraft, and this created a vicious cycle where more and more aircraft had to be stripped of a few key parts to keep the others flying. Iran's lack of access to Western parts made this situation steadily worse, as did later purges of the Iranian Air Force. Its operational air strength dropped to a peak level of less than 100, with less than one sortie per day of sustained capability, and Iran never was able to rise above this level until the end of the war.

As for combat helicopters, Iraq began the war with limited strength, and more emphasis on transport missions than attack missions. It tended to use attack and armed helicopters more as flying artillery or cavalry than in close-support attacks. Unlike the Iranians, who used the deep penetration, earth-hugging, and pop-up techniques the U.S. had pioneered in Vietnam, the Iraqis tended to stay near their own lines, come in like fighters, and fire from a distance. Iraq also made too much use of helicopters for mobility. It failed to garrison or occupy areas where troop presence was critical for physical security and to establish control over the area. Iraq could, however, keep most of its helicopters flying. If it never really used its helicopters as effectively as it should have, it could at least deploy between 60 and 70 percent of its helicopter strength on any given day.

Iran had very different problems in using its helicopters. Its force of nearly 800 helicopters had 205 AH-1J attack helicopters, which were organized to act as a "force multiplier" which was supposed to have an armor kill capability equal to that of up to two armored divisions. The Iranian Army was also supposed to have air mobile forces capable of extensive offensive operations. In fact, however, the Shah's helicopter forces had very limited overall effectiveness even before his fall.

Iran did retain a number of skilled American-trained pilots and ground crews, and these often were very effective in operating in small numbers during the first years of the war. Even under the Shah, however, Iranian helicopter forces had never been able to operate in large-scale formations except in set-piece demonstrations with massive Western support. Iran's helicopter force also generally required even more maintenance and resupply of parts than its fighters during the period before the Shah's fall, and these forces had rapidly degenerated in readiness and sustainability once the U.S. withdrew its technical support and cut off resupply. The Iranian Army was soon forced into the same cycle of cannibalization or vulturization in using its helicopters as the Iranian Air Force had been in using its fighters, and the army helicopter force was never able to recover from its initial problems and operational liabilities.

This experience provides us with several lessons about air power in Third World countries which may be obvious, but which seem to be consistently ignored in practice.

- Command organization, battle-management capability, command and control, and targeting and damage-assessment capability are as important as air strength and technology.
- Dependence on foreign support and resupply can be crippling unless that support and supply are absolutely assured.
- Air power is only as real as training and exercise experience allow and as the ability of a given country to adapt its tactics, technology, and command systems to local conditions permit. No air force can be effective that has not thoroughly exercised and tested its operational concepts.
- Peacetime air forces and air-defense forces tend to grossly overestimate both their killing power and defense capabilities.
- It is far more difficult to create an effective fighter and surface-to-air missile defense system than is generally realized, both for technical and battle-management reasons.

The Naval Fighting During 1980

Little use was made of seapower after the closing of the Shatt al-Arab and Iraq's loss of its oil-export terminals in the Gulf. In spite of the revolution, Iran could still deploy most of its ships and at least three of its P-3F Orion maritime patrol aircraft. Iran proved this during its naval attacks on Iraqi gun boats in the Shatt and on Faw during the first few days of the war and again when it conducted an amphibious raid on Faw on September 28, 1980.

By the end of September, Iranian ships and aircraft dominated the upper Gulf and Iraqi waters. All shipping to Iraq halted, and the southern Gulf states had not begun to provide aid to Iraq or extensive transshipment facilities. Iran already had enough troubles with the West because of the Iranian hostage crisis and had little reason to attack non-Iraqi shipping as a means of putting pressure on other states.

Iraq began the war without any detectable naval strategy and lacked any serious surface-warfare capability. Its new Western-made ships were still under construction, and its obsolescent Soviet-made missile patrol boats were technically inferior to Iran's Western-made missile ships and had poor readiness and operational training. In fact, Iraq was so conscious of its naval inferiority that it sought assistance from two Western navies during 1978 and 1979 in an attempt to improve the training and readiness of its naval forces. The Iraqi Navy rapidly retreated to Umm Qasr, Basra, and the Khor Abdullah waterway during the first days of the war and never sent significant forces into the Gulf until the 1988 cease-fire.

The Iranian Navy did, however, play an important role in supplying Abadan Island and in evacuating casualties. It also exercised its rights to interrogate and search ships that might be carrying military cargos or contraband to Iraq. Iran also created an exclusion zone in the Gulf on October 1, 1980, that roughly paralleled its offshore oil rights. This zone effectively blockaded Iraq.

As for the use of air power in naval combat, Iran did bomb several ships early in the war but then had no further incentive to do so. Iraqi aircraft did strike sporadically at Iran's western ports but never in sufficient strength to have great effect. Iraq could not use its Air Force as a substitute for ships because it had not organized, trained, or equipped its Air Force for naval warfare. It lacked any maritime patrol aircraft and had no aircraft equipped with air-to-ship missiles. While it could probably have used rockets and iron bombs against Iran's combat ships, these had relatively modern air defenses. Its lack of a maritime patrol aircraft also meant that it could not provide effective naval surveillance and targeting, and at this point in the war, Iraq seems to have been unwilling to take the chance of attacking naval targets that did not fly Iranian flags.

The Role of External Powers

Both Iraq and Iran began the war in a state of near alienation from their respective major military suppliers. Iran suffered most from this alienation because it had virtually severed all relations with the U.S. over the Iranian hostage crisis, and the U.S. cut off all technical support and resupply.

The U.S also reacted strongly to the risk the war presented to the

West's oil supplies and to some initial Iranian threats to block the Straits of Hormuz in retaliation for Arab and Western aid to Iraq in launching its invasion. At Saudi Arabia's request, the U.S deployed an airborne warning and air control systems (AWACS) force called ELF-1 to Dhahran Air Force Base on September 30, 1980. It sent four E-3As, two KC-135 tankers, and 300 support personnel. This force allowed Saudi Arabia and the U.S. to obtain long-range air defense and maritime surveillance, and a major command and data display center was sent up in an underground bunker at Dhahran. This deployment later became the nucleus of all the U.S. air surveillance capability in the region and remained in Saudi Arabia during the entire length of the war.

While President Bani-Sadr attempted to defuse some of the tensions with the U.S. by declaring that Iran would not blockade or mine the Straits of Hormuz, he was not successful. The U.S. deployed a major surface task force to the Gulf area in mid-October. This included 2 aircraft carrier battle groups, some 35 warships, and over 160 combat aircraft. The U.S. also deployed a small Marine assault force on an amphibious assault ship on October 26, 1980. The UK sent a small task force called the Armilla Patrol that included a missile destroyer and strengthened its advisory team with the Omani Navy and at Goat Island in the Straits. The French strengthened their Indian Ocean force and presence at Djibouti, and Australia sent a combat ship as well. The Soviet squadron in the Indian Ocean was reinforced to a peak strength of one ASW carrier, three destroyers/frigates, three submarines, a naval assault ship, and several support ships.

Iraq did little better in dealing with the USSR than Iran did in dealing with the U.S. Iraq had long been at odds with the USSR over the Ba'ath crackdowns on the Iraqi Communist Party and Iraq's growing shift toward military and civil trade with the West. The USSR had also begun to court Iran almost immediately after Khomeini's rise to power and was actively supporting efforts by Iran's Tudeh (Communist) Party to expand its influence in Iran. As a result, the Soviet Union responded to Iraq's invasion by immediately declaring its neutrality and an embargo of all arms shipments and even recalled its shipments to Iraq that were then at sea.

The Soviet Union was careful to allow Eastern Europe to continue to provide Iraq with a limited number of arms and spares via the port of Aqaba in Jordan, but it did not ease its own embargo on arms sales to Iraq. Although the Iraqi Minister of Defense, General Adnan Khairallah and then Tariq Aziz, rushed to Moscow, and King Hussein personally appealed to the USSR for the resumption of arms shipments in early October, the Soviet Union rejected these appeals. While the

USSR did quietly ship some parts, munitions, and other items to Iraq in the months that followed, it did not officially change its arms-supply policy until 1982, when Iraq was forced onto the defensive and Khomeini ruthlessly suppressed the Tudeh Party and expelled a number of Soviet diplomats from Iran.

Other powers, however, took sides more actively. Syria, Libya, and the People's Democratic Republic of Yemen (PDRY) came out in support of Iran, and Algeria tilted in Iran's direction. Israel also began to covertly support Khomeini both out of the fear of an Iraqi victory and out of concern over the treatment of Iranian Jews. North Korea and a number of Western European nations also quietly offered to sell arms to the Iranian government.

Syria and Libya began to supply Iran with Soviet-made SA-7 manportable surface-to-air missiles and Sagger anti-tank guided missiles during the first ten days of the war, and Israel soon provided air supplies, such as parts and tires, for Iran's F-4s. Iran was soon flying its aircraft to Syria and Libya via Greece and Turkey and receiving Israeli shipments via Cyprus. Other arms seem to have arrived over land via Turkey and Pakistan, although Turkey formally embargoed all arms shipments to both Iraq and Iran.

As for Iraq, it received immediate support from virtually all the Gulf states and from Jordan.[24] Both Kuwait and Saudi Arabia agreed almost immediately to increase their oil production and market the increase for Iraq, with the oil to be repaid after the war. Kuwait mobilized its armed forces on October 5, 1980, and began to rigorously enforce new regulations requiring all foreigners to register their religions as a means of identifying (and later expelling) Iranian and other Shi'ite supporters of Khomeini. Jordan went further and offered Iraq volunteers, supplies, and a shipping route through Aqaba.

Iraq also did not face any cutoff of European supplies. France stated that it would continue to ship all the arms ordered as part of Iraq's $1.6 billion arms deal with France, including 60 Mirage fighters, radars, air-to-air and air-to-ground missiles, and anti-tank weapons. It also immediately agreed to expand these orders to include light surface-to-air missiles and to expedite helicopter and artillery deliveries. Other European suppliers also agreed to rush arms deliveries, as did North Korea and a number of other Arab states. While the precise date cannot be determined as to when Iraq first covertly turned to Egypt for arms, in spite of Egypt's peace treaty with Israel, Iraqi officials seem to have visited Egypt no later than November 1980.

These developments rapidly gave the war both a region-wide and international character. So did various early efforts to reach some kind of cease-fire or peace. President Zia of Pakistan led the first peace mission to Iraq and Iran, on behalf of the Islamic Conference, on September 27, 1980. The end result, however, was no more productive than the call of Dr. Kurt Waldheim, the Secretary General of the UN, for a cease-fire on September 23.

As for other peace efforts, the UN Security Council agreed to Resolution 479 calling for a cease-fire on September 28. Secretary General Waldheim called for Iraq and Iran to allow the ships trapped in the Shatt to escape on October 10, and the Security Council requested that Dr. Waldheim send an envoy to both sides on November 4, 1980. The other Gulf states attempted their own peace initiatives, as did Algeria, the Palestine Liberation Organization (PLO) and members of the Arab League. Leonid Breznev called on September 30, and Swedish Prime Minister Olaf Palme visited Tehran and Baghdad in November 1980 and February 1981.[25]

The peace efforts during the first months of the war revealed that Iraq and Iran were more interested in using peace initiatives for self-justification and self-advantage than anything else. Iran made it clear that it was committed to going on with the war unless Iraq agreed to terms that virtually amounted to surrender. These terms included an admission of Iraqi war guilt, Saddam Hussein's removal from power, surrender of Iraqi arms, Kurdish autonomy, and Iranian control over Basra until Iraq paid reparations. Iraq insisted on an agreement that would have ended all Iranian attempts at subversion and political action in Iraq, Iraqi control over the entire Shatt, and Iraqi control over the border area and possibly part of Khuzistan.

Notes

1. The analysis of phase one is based heavily on Anthony H. Cordesman's trips to the region and interviews of Iraqi and Iranian officers and officials, plus his prior writing for the *Armed Forces Journal International* (especially "The Lessons of the Iran-Iraq War," Parts I and II, April and June, 1982) and in the book *The Gulf and the Search for Strategic Stability*, Boulder, Westview, 1984. It also draws heavily upon the work of Colonel W.O. Staudenmaier, U.S. Army Strategic Studies Institute; Edgar O'Ballance, *The Gulf War*, London, Brassey's, 1988; Nikola B. Schahgaldian, *The Iranian Military Under the Islamic Republic*, Santa Monica, Rand R-3473-USDP, 1987; Sepehr Zabih, *The Iranian Military in Revolution and War*, London, Routledge, 1988; Keith McLauchlan and George Joffe, *The Gulf War*, Special Report 176, London, Economist Press, 1984; Keith McLauchlan and George Joffe, *Iran and Iraq: The Next Five Years*, Special Report 1083, London, Economist Press, 1987; and various working papers for the International Institute for Strategic Studies, Royal United Services Institute.

2. O'Ballance, op. cit., p. 48.

3. Based on the authors' interviews in Baghdad, London, and Washington.

4. Zabih, op. cit., pp. 169–170.

5. Based on conversations with Iraqi Air Force officers in Iraq, the U.S., Britain, and France in 1982 and 1984.

6. Reports differ on the size of this force. Some say it was only one division plus a brigade in support.

7. O'Ballance, op. cit., p. 33.

8. Some reports indicate an infantry division.

9. Estimates of the size of the Iraqi forces used differ sharply. These estimates are modified from the IISS, *Strategic Survey, 1980–1981,* London, International Institute for Strategic Studies, 1981, pp. 49–52.

10. Estimates of the size of the Iranian forces in 1980 differ sharply. These estimates are modified from the IISS, op. cit.

11. Claim by then-President Bani-Sadr, FBIS/MEA, *Daily Report,* October 15, 1980, I-12. A Rand expert estimated that by 1986, some 23,000 men had been formally purged from the Army, some 17,000 of which were officers. Schahgaldian, op. cit., p. 26.

12. Views differ over whether the computerized logistic system the Shah had purchased was sabotaged during the revolution or simply never was functional. One American advisor involved stated that the computer hardware existed and that stocks were computer coded, but that the software in the system never functioned.

13. The Pasdaran or Iranian Revolutionary Guard Corps (IRGC) was formally established by Khomeini on May 5, 1979. It grew out of elements that had seized arms in February, and it began to emerge as an effective force in November. Estimates of its strength differ sharply. One estimate puts it at 4,000 in May 1979; 10,000 by December 1979; 25,000 by mid-1980; 50,000 in 1981; 150,000 in 1983; 250,000 by 1985; and 350,000 by 1986. Most likely, its strength exceeded 50,000 to 80,000 men by late 1980, although not in regular formations.

14. Lloyds of London had to write off virtually all 68 ships as losses several years later.

15. The descriptions of Iranian cities are taken from notes during the authors' travels through Iran and from the Hachette guide to the Middle East.

16. Zabih, op. cit., pp. 172–173.

17. Ibid.

18. Ibid.

19. The terrain involved is complex, and the reader may wish to consult Defense Mapping Agency "Map ONC H-6" for the details. The terrain in the region varies sharply according to rainfall and the resulting seasonal flooding. The Iraqi division moved across the border along roads that lead east toward Ahwaz off the main road between Ash Shanin and Duwa and north of the Basra power station. It is possible to drive across the border at this point across relatively firm land and reach the Karun River fairly quickly by going east. The Karun River joins the Shatt al-Arab in the middle of Khorramshahr. The Shatt is roughly 300 meters wide at this point, and there is solid land on both sides, with a salt pan to the west on the Iraqi side. There is a large salt marsh to the east on the Iranian side, which is separated from Abadan Island by the

Bahmanshir River, which splits off the Karun before it enters Khorramshahr and the Shatt.

20. See Zabih, op. cit., pp. 173–175.

21. Iraq did, however, selectively drive non-Arabs out of much of the territory it captured. The Arabs that remained suffered significantly when Iran recaptured the area.

22. O'Ballance, op. cit., p. 41.

23. Views differ sharply over whether Israel played any advisory role in this raid and whether it damaged either the Tamuz I or Tamuz II reactor. The Iraqi air defenses seem to have been totally inactive during this raid, but only two Iranian F-4 aircraft were involved, and it is doubtful they did much damage. Israel successfully destroyed much of the installation some eight months later, on June 7, 1981.

24. Iranian news service reports that Bahrain, Qatar, Saudi Arabia, and the United Arab Emirates (UAE) agreed on September 20, 1980, to provide Iraq with all its military and nonmilitary requirements do not seem to be true. Interviews in the region do indicate that Saddam Hussein may have "consulted" with individual heads of state, but there is no evidence he obtained anything like the blank checks that Iran later claimed.

25. For a more detailed discussion, see RUSI's "The War in the Gulf: International Mediation Efforts," London, Royal United Services Institute, September 1987.

5

PHASE TWO: IRAN REGAINS ITS TERRITORY, 1981–1982

The Situation at the Beginning of 1981

At the beginning of 1981, Iraq still held substantial gains along the Iranian border from a position roughly 40 kilometers north of Qasr e-Shirin to the outskirts of Abadan. While the only major Iranian city it had captured was Khorramshahr, Iraq still held a salient across the Kharkeh River in the direction of Dezful, another broad salient in the direction of Ahwaz, and much of the Iranian territory south of Ahwaz west of the Karun River.[1]

The war also had as yet produced relatively limited casualties. While any estimates are very uncertain, Iraq's killed and wounded were still probably only a little over 10,000, with the loss of some 200–300 armored vehicles and major artillery weapons and some 40–70 aircraft. Iran's losses probably were still less than 15,000, with the loss of roughly the same number of major weapons and aircraft. Iraq had a substantially higher number of POWs and equipment captures than Iran, but the numbers were small enough to have had little impact on the balance on each side.[2]

At least in statistical terms, Iraq could still claim to be the victor. Nevertheless, Iraq's failure to take Abadan and the virtual stalemate in the war after November 1981 left Iraq with few clear alternatives. It was apparent that Khomeini would not settle for a limited war or a limited peace. It was also apparent that the Iraqi invasion had aroused immense popular support for the war, if not the Khomeini regime, and that there was no chance of any popular uprising among the Arabs in Khuzistan. Finally, it was apparent that any major Iraqi advance could simply end in making the situation worse, unless Iraq could penetrate far deeper into Iran's oil centers than seemed likely. Taking another city simply meant more urban warfare, more massive commitments of troops, and more casualties.

This left Iraq with two military alternatives: trying to use strategic bombing to force Iran to end the war and creating sufficiently strong defenses of its conquests to be able to withstand any Iranian counterattacks. In retrospect, Iraq might have been successful if it had fully committed its air power in an attempt to destroy key aspects of Iran's infrastructure, such as its refineries and power plants, or even if it had used its land forces to destroy Iran's regular armored forces and deprive Iran of its capability for massive counterattack and invasion. At a minimum, Iraq should have mobilized and deployed enough manpower to fully occupy the areas in Iran it was trying to control and shifted to area defense and defense in depth.

In practice, however, Saddam Hussein does not seem to have fully understood the military problems Iraq now faced or the dangers inherent in fighting a popular and highly ideological revolution. Iraq adopted a strategy of "guns and butter" in which it kept its forces on Iranian territory, but sought to minimize both the risk of military casualties and any disruption of normal life. This strategy almost certainly reflected the belief or hope that internal events in Iran might still bring down Khomeini. Throughout 1981 and 1982, many senior Iraqi officials continued to believe that each new internal power struggle in Iran meant the end of Khomeini and the beginning of peace. At the same time, Saddam Hussein and his colleagues seem to have feared that they would lose popular support for the war unless they did everything possible to reduce losses and convince the Iraqi people that they could have something approaching a normal life plus rising living standards and continuing economic development.

Iraq's senior decision makers also seem to have been more interested in self-justifying propaganda and internal politics than in creating realistic military options. Iraq was extremely slow to learn from its military mistakes. Rather than attempt to professionalize its army and train it for maneuver and combined-arms operations, Iraq tried to build up the Ba'ath Party-dominated Popular Army from a force of around 75,000 to 100,000 in the period just before the invasion to one of 150,000, with the goal of rapidly expanding it to 275,000 to 325,000.

For all his political skills, Saddam Hussein was never to show any particular military aptitude during any phase of the war and only accepted serious military advice nearly half a decade later and after Iran had scored significant gains. For nearly a year, he concentrated on building up the Popular Army, making major equipment purchases, and providing the military equivalent of bread and circuses.

The early efforts put into the Popular Army were particularly ineffective, and Iraq put much of its effort into creating a force that was even more politicized than the regular forces. Popular Army units were given responsibility not only for rear-area air defense and civil defense, but for providing the combat units to man part of the front. Low-grade Popular Army "brigades" were rapidly created with officers whose own real qualification was party membership and loyalty to the regime.[3] Youth volunteers and women were assigned to paramilitary functions and a host of ceremonial duties, and the Iraqi Women's Organization was given the responsibility for creating a service corps of some 250,000 women for duties ranging from nursing and civil defense to political education.

The Iraqi government also allowed frequent leaves and educational deferments and did little to regroup and retrain its regular forces. Most of Iraq's best regular army units were kept in the forward area, and those units that were allowed to recover in the rear were not properly reorganized or given the retraining they needed. Little change was made in Iraq's command structure to either reward successful commanders or to give lower-ranking officers and commanders more freedom of action.

While Iraq talked about improving the capability its air force, it did little other than attempt to accelerate deliveries of French fighters. Much to the frustration of its foreign friends and advisors, the Air Force refused to act on most of the advice it was given. Instead of intelligent self-criticism, it also tended to blame its weapons and equipment and to adopt a posture of waiting for the delivery of the Mirage F-1s and the more advanced munitions it had on order. Iraq also continued to spend money as if it had never suffered the loss of much of its oil-export capability. It spent billions on both the war and development and spent far more rapidly than it earned.

Iran had problems of its own. It concentrated as much on the internal struggle between the secular and religious supporters of the revolution as it did on the war. The creation of the Iranian Supreme Defense Council (SDC) on October 13, 1980, simply created a new forum to air all the same differences over whether Iran should rely on the pre-revolutionary regular forces or the new revolutionary forces. While Bani-Sadr did manage to recreate some of the Iranian command structure and a combined command in Khuzistan, this tended to deprive him of revolutionary legitimacy because of his growing ties to the Army, and the local Pasdaran commander in Khuzistan, the Hojatolislam Ali Hussein Khameini, became a serious rival both in terms of his impact on regional command decisions and in terms of his overall impact on command as Khomeini's representative on the SDC.

The situation was made worse because the regular forces tended to husband their resources while trying to organize for counteroffensives, while the Pasdaran infantry were constantly at the front of the day-to-day fighting and took most of the casualties. The Pasdaran got virtually all the favorable coverage in the Iranian media, while the Mullahs began to accuse the regular forces of sacrificing the Pasdaran while protecting their own lives. The net result was that President Bani-Sadr increasingly came to rely on his role as commander-in-chief of the regular forces as a basis for power under conditions which cost him both religious and popular support.

While Iran succeeded in mobilizing enough regular and Pasdaran forces during November and December to turn its cities in the southeast into major defense points, to keep fighting in Abadan, and to provide an increasingly cohesive defense of the border area, the revolution turned from punishing the supporters of the Shah to feeding upon itself. By late December, this reached the point where Khomeini began to put serious pressure on Bani-Sadr and the regular forces to carry out some form of counterattack. This evidently led Bani-Sadr to approve the planning of such attacks around December 20, 1980, with the goal of attacking in early January.

Iran's First Counteroffensives Fail

Iran, however, was not ready to launch major counterattacks. Iran's military forces not only were deeply divided between regular and revolutionary forces, they lacked anything approaching the strength necessary to overwhelm a major Iraqi force with sheer numbers. Most of the Pasdaran still had little experience in using combined arms and practically no experience with offensive operations. Although Iran was on the edge of ending its hostage crisis with the U.S., it had no immediate prospects of resupply, and much of its air force, helicopter forces, and heavy armor were already inoperable or had been lost in the war.

Iran's regular forces were still manned by the cadre of the men who had been trained under the Shah, but they had been severely purged. Because of the desertions and upheavals at the time of the Shah's fall, more than half of the manpower of most units had been conscripted since the start of the revolution. Many armored units were not able to operate their equipment effectively, and the regular army had only limited capability to conduct combined-arms operations.

These conditions did not deny Iran any hope of achieving limited tactical victories. Iraq's static deployments and tendency to remain dispersed in small garrisons or strong points, and to remain road bound during actual operations, gave Iran considerable opportunity to concentrate its forces and to achieve superiority in both numbers and tactical position along a limited part of the front. It is a long way, however, from limited counteroffensives and defensive victories to the ability to launch major attacks.

Bani-Sadr and the commanders of the regular forces attempted to deal with these problems by putting enough pressure on Iraq over the entire front to keep it from redeploying its forces, while they concentrated much of Iran's armor along a single axis of attack.[4] Their diversionary attacks, however, did not succeed in pinning down Iraq's forces. They also did not have time to properly train and exercise many of the forces it had to use. While Bani-Sadr later blamed the Mullahs for the failure of his offensive, the Iranian Army simply was not ready.

Even so, Iran attacked at four points along the front in early January 1981. The first thrust began on January 6, near Qasr e-Shirin. Formations of Iranian mountain troops with an effective total strength of roughly one brigade attacked Iraqi forces covering the main highway between Baghdad and Tehran. In a pattern that was to become familiar later in the war, the Iranian troops began their attack at night, successfully infiltrated around the Iraqi positions, and were able to capture some Iraqi units. The battle then rapidly became a battle for each ridge and mountain position, however, and Iraq rushed up reinforcements and artillery. The end result was that Iran advanced about eight kilometers, but did not achieve any significant tactical advantage. Iran also had the equivalent of a battalion taken prisoner.

The second attack took advantage of the fact that Iraqi forces lacked the strength and direction to occupy all the heights around Mehran. Iranian forces again infiltrated into the area and took a limited amount of territory in the foothills above Mehran.

The third attack was more serious and attempted to drive the forces in the Iraqi salient near Ahwaz far enough west of the city and the Karun River to put the city out of artillery range. While Iran used most of a mechanized division in this attack and achieved initial tactical surprise, the terrain did not favor Iran. The Karun flows through the center of the city, the territory to the west of the city is relatively trafficable even in January, and the road net from the west is relatively good. Iraq was driven back several miles, but regrouped its forces and held positions well within artillery range. The Iranian mechanized division took moderate to severe losses.

The fourth attack was the main thrust of the Iranian offensive. It was designed to relieve Abadan. It consisted of an armored thrust from the northeast that was to drive past Susangerd and Ahwaz and drive down the west bank of the Karun River and reach Abadan. At the same time, Abadan's defenders were supposed to drive north, put pressure on the Iraqi forces besieging the city, and, ideally, link up with the

Iranian armored column that was driving south. The force was formed of the Iranian 16th Armored Division at Kermanshah and the 55th Regular Paratroop Brigade.

The Iranian forces used in this fourth thrust were assembled east of the Kharkeh River. They were substantially larger than the Iraqi forces in the area, which consisted largely of one regular armored division. The Iranian units had nearly 300 operational tanks but were short of artillery and mechanized infantry vehicles. They also lacked helicopter support and armored reconnaissance capability. It is unlikely, however, that the Iranian forces involved would have been sufficient under even the best conditions. Iran did not have the kind of 3:1 superiority necessary to assure victory and may not have had even 2:1 superiority. The Iranian plan of attack depended on achieving almost total surprise in order to avoid a meeting engagement, and the distance the Iranian forces had to penetrate was so long that it virtually ensured that Iraq would have time to reinforce before Iranian armor could link up with the Iranian forces in Abadan.

The situation was made even worse because Iran attacked across the plains southeast of the Kharkeh River in an area subject to seasonal flooding and where only surfaced roads were trafficable to armor. This forced the Iranian force to assemble and start its movement in a way that was easily detected by Iraqi helicopters and aircraft, and the Iranian units then moved in a long column, with the armor preceding the airborne unit.[5]

The Iranian movement was slow, and this gave the Iraqi commander in the region time enough to position his armored division along the Iranian line of advance. Each brigade in the Iranian armored division advanced separately, and the first brigade ran into the Iraqi trap on January 6, 1981.[6] At this point, Iran's lack of reconnaissance proved fatal. The Iranian brigade tried to drive through the Iraqi defenses and was hit from the front and both sides. When the Iranian brigade attempted to maneuver, it became trapped in the mud. While some Iranian helicopters did appear in support, they were outnumbered by the Iraqi helicopters and had to operate in the open against Iraqi forces with much better anti-aircraft capability. The result was that the battle rapidly became a killing ground, and Iran lost most of the brigade.

If Iran had halted at this point, its losses would have become acceptable, but Iran did not stop its attack or attempt a different line of advance. Instead, the Iranian commander committed his second brigade against virtually the same Iraqi defenses the next day. By this time, Iraq had been able to reinforce its defense with infantry equipped with anti-tank weapons, while adding artillery and some armor. This time the fighting was even worse. Not only did Iranian forces bog down even more in the mud, combat took place at very short ranges. Iraq was able to commit both its helicopters and some attack fighters, and Iran lost a number of helicopters trying to reply without achieving any military result.

The third Iranian brigade repeated the process on January 8 and did no better. The only difference was that it did succeed in breaking away from combat and retreated out of the Iraqi trap. The Iranian paratroop unit, which had never been committed, was then moved out of the battle and deployed to help defend Susangerd against the risk of a counterattack. As for the Iranian forces in Abadan, they did attempt several breakouts but were defeated each time and suffered substantial losses.

The end result of the Iranian attack near Susangerd was that the regular army lost more of one of its few combat-ready armored divisions and a large amount of irreplaceable armor. While both sides took substantial losses—and Iraq had lost some 80–130 armored vehicles in what was often point-blank fighting—Iraq could recover most of its lost equipment and had access to relatively rapid resupply. Iran had lost between 140 and 215 tanks. To put these loses in perspective, Iran had a total of some 1,735 tanks when the Shah fell and something like 1,000 usable tanks at the start of 1981. The Iranian offensive had cost Iran between 15 percent and 20 percent of its heavy armor, and Iran had no way to replace either its U.S. M-60 or British Chieftain tanks. Iran had also lost at least 100 other armored vehicles, some heavy artillery, and several of its remaining helicopters.[7]

The failure of Iran's first major counteroffensive had several significant effects. The first effect was to encourage Iraq to believe that a relatively static defense of its gains in Iran might work. Iraq had every reason to believe it had scored a major defensive victory. It was clear at the time that both Iraq's leaders and many of its commanders felt that Iran's poor performance had demonstrated that Iraq's defense concepts were sound and that Iran could not attack successfully in the face of superior Iraqi firepower and air power.

The second effect was to undermine the remaining secular authority in Iran. President Bani-Sadr and the regular Iranian forces faced an immediate storm of political attacks from Iran's Mullahs, which were as devastating in their end result as the Iraqi ambush. Prime Minister Rajai's public attacks became so virulent that Khomeini was forced to intervene. While this intervention quieted the Mullah's public comments, it did nothing to reduce their political activity, and this activity increased in scale as it became apparent that Iran's losses had been so great that the regular army had virtually lost its ability to conduct a major spring offensive.

The third result was to further weaken the already damaged political and military credibility of the Iranian regular forces. The Mullahs' criticisms had many valid points. The Iranian attack was a poorly organized charge rather than a balanced attack. Iran's armored forces, which had never performed well in offensive exercises under the Shah, had suffered an additional loss of effectiveness as the result of the revolution. There was no real military excuse for what happened near Susangerd except poor planning and incompetent command. The end result, however, was that the regular forces were treated as something of a second-class force, and Iran ceased giving the proper emphasis to acquiring and training high-technology forces and trying to build upon its past cadre of military professionals. Priority clearly shifted to the Pasdaran. After January 1981, virtually all Iranian military action was either dominated by the Pasdaran or involved joint Pasdaran and regular army operations.

Finally, the triumph of the Mullahs meant that Iran gained little in military terms from returning its American hostages in January 1981. While Iran did get some $480 million dollars worth of military deliveries as a result of the settlement of the hostage crisis, it never got many key spare parts. The Mullahs' continuing hostility to both the U.S. and most European nations meant Iran never found a reliable or reasonably priced source of Western arms, and the priority given to equipping the Pasdaran meant that most regular forces were constantly in short supply of some key part or munition.

The Land Battle from February to September 1981

There was little military action during February 1981. Iraq did, however, briefly resume offensive action in March. Iraq had tried to counterattack the Iranian positions in the salient around Susangerd in January, immediately after it defeated Iran's armored attack, but gave up when it realized that these positions had been reinforced by a paratroop brigade. Iraq made a more serious attempt to capture the city of Susangerd during March 19–20, 1981, but Iraqi forces did not make any real progress against the steadily increasing strength of Iran's defenses. Iraq halted the attack when it met serious resistance and converted it to an artillery barrage. The failure of this Iraqi offensive against Susangerd had little strategic importance by itself, but it did represent the end of Iraq's efforts to win any major objectives in Iran and was the high point of Iraq's conquests. (See Figure 5.1.)

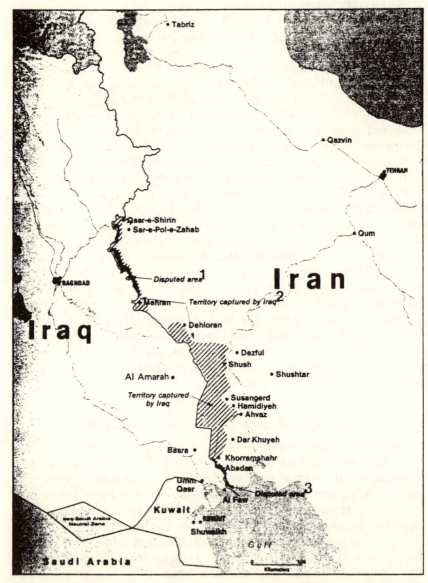

FIGURE 5.1 Maximum Iraqi Gains During the Iran-Iraq War. "1" shows the area Iran ceded to Iraq under the 1975 Algiers Accord but did not turn over. "2" shows the maximum line of Iraqi advance. "3" shows the area claimed by Iraq but ceded to Iran under the 1975 Algiers Accord. Adapted from material provided by the CIA.

During the rest of the spring, both sides did little more than spar across the front lines. Iran scored some minor gains in the Bazi Deraz heights near Qasr e-Shirin in April, and Iraq made minor gains near Dehloran in late May. Iran launched a major artillery barrage against Basra on June 15, which triggered sporadic firing across the front lines by both sides for the rest of the spring. In August, Iran also renewed its shelling of Faw. While Faw was now a desolate ghost town, Iran seems to have been attempting to attack a sheltered Iraqi command post and some radar and radio installations in the area.

The most dramatic action on either side occurred off the battlefield. The Mullah's battle against Bani-Sadr succeeded to the point that he lost much of his command authority in mid-March. Khomeini then formally stripped Bani-Sadr of his status as commander-in-chief on June 11 and ordered his arrest on June 20. Bani-Sadr was forced to go underground and then flee the country, while Khomeini appointed a three-man Presidential Council of Prime Minister Ali Rajai, Majlis Speaker Ali Akbak Hashemi Rafsanjani, and the leader of the IRP, the Ayatollah Mohammed Husseini Beheshti.

Khomeini appointed a new Minister of Defense, a new Chief of Staff, and a new head of the Air Force to ensure that any lingering loyalties to Bani-Sadr would not affect the loyalty of the regular forces. He made the commander of the Pasdaran forces at the front the chief military commander of all forces in the area. It is clear from Khomeini's statements at this time that he sought to keep the Mullahs from interfering in the management of the war and that he hoped to keep the regular forces loyal enough to play a major role in the campaign against Iraq while the Pasdaran, Hizbollah, and Baseej helped him overcome his remaining domestic opposition.

This opposition was still significant. While Khomeini had quickly suppressed unrest in Azerbaijan in January, and the supporters of the Ayatollah Shariet-Madari—perhaps the most senior and respected Shi'ite clergyman in Iran—he faced a much more serious threat from the People's Mujahideen and other radical elements. The Mujahideen and a number of allied movements declared an open attack on Khomeini on June 20, 1981. They launched a series of bombing incidents and assassination attempts directed against senior Khomeini officials, and this led the Khomeini government to ruthlessly hunt down and execute any Mujahideen supporters they could find.

The intensity of this struggle is indicated by the fact that the Iranian government admitted to more than 2,000 executions between June and September 1981 and that outside experts felt the real number was over 3,300. It is also indicated by the fact that an explosion in the headquarters of the IRP killed 74 people on June 28, including

Beheshti, 27 members of the Majlis, and 14 Ministers and Deputy Ministers. Further, Rajai—who had been elected President of Iran on July 28—was killed in another major bombing incident on August 30, along with Mohammed Javad Bahonar, the new Prime Minister. While the Mujahideen were largely eliminated by arrests and some open street battles in September, the situation was so bad that some senior Iranian officials like Rafsanjani were reported to travel with an ambulance.[8]

The fall of Bani-Sadr also triggered a murderous new set of purges in the Air Force when it was discovered that Bani-Sadr had fled the country in an Iranian Air Force B-707 in August. The Mullahs reacted by arresting many of the regular Iranian Air Force officers that Bani-Sadr had freed or allowed to return to the service at the start of the war. Something like half of all of Iran's remaining American-trained pilots and aircrews were purged from the Air Force, and Iranian operational air strength dropped well below 100 aircraft. Virtually all training halted, all missions had to have approval from religious officials, and aircraft were given the minimal fuel needed for the mission. While Iran was able to acquire enough spare parts from various sources to keep some of its aircraft operational, it no longer had any advanced-training capability. The Iranian Air Force suffered for the rest of the war from a lack of parts, advanced munitions, and new aircraft, and the quality of its pilots and aircrews never fully recovered from the effects of this purge.

The Limited Impact of Air Power in 1981

More generally, air power played only a limited role during most of the fighting in 1981. While Iraq and Iran committed fighters and armed helicopters to the battles in January, they did not commit large amounts of either kind of aircraft even during the most critical phase of the battle around Susangerd. Both sides continued to conserve their air power and flew only a few missions whose impact had more of a symbolic or political than military value. Attacks against economic targets were rare and were largely restricted to the southern-border region near the front. Iraq was obviously concerned with avoiding additional air combat losses and did little more than sporadically attack the Iranian refining, petrochemical, and export facilities west of Abadan.

Iran had even more reason to conserve its aircraft. Its operational strength at the beginning of 1981 could not have exceeded 120–150 fighters. Iran's aircraft maintenance problems grew steadily more severe with time, and Iran rarely did more than launch a few strike sorties to act as a deterrent to Iraqi action. Iran's Air Force did manage to strike deep into Iraqi territory on April 4, and destroyed 46 Iraqi warplanes at the Al-Walid air base (Iraq later claimed that Syria had provided air cover for the Iranian attack), but this was a rare exception. The only other major Iranian air activity during the period occurred as a result of what seems to have been intended as a warning to Kuwait to reduce its support of Iraq: Several Iranian F-4s overflew Kuwait on June 13, and Kuwait air defenses fired on the aircraft.

In fact, it was Israel that made the most important use of air power in the region during 1981. Eight Israeli F-16s, escorted by six F-15s, flew a mission of over 1,000 miles and destroyed Iraq's nuclear reactors at Tuwaitha on June 28, 1981. While Israel was obviously attempting to keep Iraq from getting nuclear weapons for Israel's own defensive reasons, it is at least possible that Iraq might have been able to build one or two weapons before the end of the war if it had not been for this attack. As Iraq's later use of chemical weapons showed, Iraq might have been willing to use nuclear weapons against Iran.

The Conditions That Led
to New Iranian Counteroffensives

In some ways, Iraq cannot be blamed for not being fully ready for a new series of Iranian offensives in the fall of 1981. It not only had scored a major defensive victory against some of Iran's best regular army units at Susangerd, it knew that the Iranian Air Force was in severe trouble, and every day brought news of the struggle between the Iranian government and the Mujahideen. In many ways, Khomeini seemed even weaker than at the time of the Iraqi invasion, and many senior Iraqis were firmly convinced during the summer of 1981 that the Iranian government was about to fall.

Iraq also had the edge over Iran in both land weapons and resupply. While the USSR had not resumed major arms shipments, Iraq had been able to obtain virtually any French weapon it wanted. It had obtained several hundred tanks and other armored vehicles from Eastern Europe and some 4,000 tons of munitions from President Anwar Sadat of Egypt. Iraq was still getting arms deliveries from North Korea and the PRC, support from Jordan, munitions from Eastern and Western Europe, and some weapons from Brazil.

Iraq had also used call-ups of its reserves and the recruiting into its Popular Army to increase its active land strength to something approaching 450,000–550,000 men. Iraq had forcibly enlisted Egyptian and Sudanese workers for its armed forces and had encouraged large numbers of others to work in Iraq. This considerably eased its military manpower problems while allowing it to keep its civil economy running.

Iraq's oil exports continued at a level of roughly 500,000 barrels per day (BPD). These exports included the flow of crude oil through Iraq's pipelines to Turkey and Syria and shipments of oil products by truck to Jordan and Syria. While Syria had already shut its pipeline to Baniyas twice in an effort to blackmail Iraq into higher payments, it still shipped some 50,000 BPD. Iraq's pipeline through Turkey only experienced brief interruptions because of minor sabotage. Iraq still had substantial hard-currency reserves from its past exports, and Iraq's leaders remained confident enough to continue funding most of Iraq's highly expensive development plans and even issued a new 1981–1985 Five Year Plan.

The war also had so far produced relatively limited Iraqi casualties. While Western experts admitted they could not make accurate estimates, most felt that Iraq had only lost some 9,000–12,000 killed by the end of August 1981 and some 16,000–23,000 wounded. In contrast, Iran had probably lost 14,000–18,000 dead and some 26,000–31,000 wounded.[9] Iraq had not suffered any loss of territory and the damage to Iraqi economic facilities was very limited and largely confined to the area around Basra and Faw. Virtually all of Khorramshahr and Abadan had been evacuated and non-Arabs had been driven out of the Iraqi occupied territory. There was no visible opposition to Saddam Hussein aside from some very rare bombings, and Iraq continued to expel any Shi'ites it felt had ties to Iran; these now totaled between 40,000 and 50,000.

Ironically, however, the state of political upheaval in Iran seems to have led Iraq to exaggerate Iran's vulnerability almost as much as it had a year earlier. Iran had suffered damage costing close to 100 billion dollars and had to deal with over a million refugees. Even so, Iran was able to export about twice as much oil as Iraq, and its volume of exports recovered steadily during 1981. Iran did have to cut back severely on all development activity and civil spending and introduce some forms of rationing, but it had sufficient funds to establish a major network of arms-purchasing efforts which ranged from an official purchasing office in London to a host of covert and second- and third-party efforts.

North Korea, which had originally aligned itself with Iraq, became a major arms seller to Iran. The PRC began small arms shipments while continuing to sell to Iraq. Many other Asian countries sold U.S. parts and munitions to Iran, including Singapore, South Korea, Taiwan, and Thailand. A wide range of Western European munitions and light-arms manufacturers—including companies in Belgium, Britain, France, the Federal Republic of Germany (FRG), Greece, the Netherlands, Norway, Portugal, Sweden, Switzerland, and Spain—began to sell arms to Iran. In spite of numerous denials, Britain supplied large numbers of parts for Iran's Chieftains, including new engines.

Israel continued covert arms shipments through a dealer network that used third parties in countries as diverse as Cyprus, Denmark, Norway, and the U.S. Syria and Libya moved arms by sea and through Turkey, and Libya supplied considerable amounts of armor, including some 190 Soviet-made tanks. The USSR also shipped some parts to Iran for its Soviet-made armored personnel carriers (APCs).

This mix of arms deals had serious limitations. Iran's purchasing efforts often led to fraud and to the shipment of used or obsolete equipment, arms, and munitions. Many of the Iranian personnel involved became corrupt. Iran could never obtain enough parts of enough kinds at the proper time to restore its U.S.-made and other Western heavy weapons, helicopters, and aircraft to anything like their prewar readiness. Nevertheless, Iran was significantly better equipped in other ways by mid-1981 than it was at the beginning of the year. While it was to experience constant problems in obtaining high-technology equipment and parts for its more sophisticated U.S. and British equipment for the rest of the war, it never again experienced critical shortfalls in artillery, munitions, small arms, manportable surface-to-air missiles and light anti-aircraft weapons, and variants of Soviet tanks and armored vehicles. It also gradually was able to increase its own manufacturing capability and made a substantial amount of its own small arms and munitions by the time the war ended in a cease-fire.

The struggle for power in Iran had also had some indirect military benefits. The fall of Bani-Sadr and the new command arrangements for the regular forces freed the Army and Pasdaran to cooperate far more closely than in the past. The power struggles in Tehran had far less effect at the front, and the regular army was able to set up a regional command that could concentrate on assembling enough forces to be effective and which had both the time to plan and the freedom to choose its moment of attack.

While the Army and Pasdaran continued to argue over whether the Army should have a monopoly of heavy weapons and advanced technology, the Pasdaran at the front increasingly learned to cooperate with local Army commanders and had their own problems with interference by the clergy. As a result, Khomeini approved a system that restricted the religious commissars in each unit to a role of advising and reporting on the loyalty of these units, but which clearly deprived them of command authority.

Iran also was beginning to be able to take advantage of its larger population and potential superiority in manpower. By August 1981, it had mobilized a total of several hundred thousand Revolutionary Guards.[10] The Pasdaran now had enough combat experience to have created a number of well-organized and effective combat units and to develop a good cadre of officers and NCOs, although its forces still included large numbers of young, untrained local volunteers (or Baseej). While Iran's regular forces had suffered significant losses both in combat and because of the revolution, they were still strong enough to both fight on their own and provide the Pasdaran with considerable support.

While the Pasdaran could not yet establish control over all of Iran, they had the power to control its Azerbaijanis and take the offensive against the Kurdish Democratic Party of Iran (KDPI) forces occupying much of Iran's Kurdish areas. A combination of Pasdaran and regular forces launched a major offensive against the KDPI in September 1981. While the KDPI remained in many areas and continued to counterattack, Iranian government forces occupied most of the towns the KDPI had taken, including Mahabad, Piranshahr, Sanandaj, and Urumiyeh.

Equally important, Iran began to conduct a territorial war in the south, while Iraq remained tied down to strong points and major lines of communication. Iraq still held about 14,000 square kilometers of Iranian territory—mostly in Khuzistan—but its forces in Iran were stretched relatively thin and over far too wide an area to occupy the countryside. While Iraq had built up an impressive network of roads, supply dumps, and strong points, its forces tended to remain in their defenses or confine their movement to roads and make extensive use of armor and helicopters.

Iraq still did not build up defenses in depth, and significant gaps existed between the deployments of major Iraqi units. Iraq also failed to correct its command problems. As time went on, Iraq tended to layer new cycles of command approval over the normal chain of command and to micro-manage the war from Baghdad. It also made reconnaissance the exception rather than the rule.

Iran's Counteroffensives Began to Succeed

There was little fighting during July and August, although Iran did makes its first charge on August 12 that Iraq had used poison gas against Iranian troops. This charge may have been correct. Iraq was experimenting with gas warfare at this time and Iranian forces had begun a series of small attacks and patrols all along the Iraqi lines. There is little indication, however, that Iraq made extensive use of poison gas at this time.

It was during this period that Iran began to systematically plan for the relief of Abadan. Iran began to build up considerable regular army and Pasdaran forces in Khuzistan and to the east of the Kharkeh River. Iran also conducted a quiet campaign to convince Iraq that it was considering plans for an attack across the border to cut the road to Basra. This Iranian effort seems to have been successful. Iraq did little to reinforce its forces in Iran and kept its reserves to the rear on Iraqi soil.

On September 2, 1981, Iran launched its second major counter-offensive or "Thamil ul' Aimma" attack. This attack, however, had none of the elements of a reckless cavalry charge that characterized Bani-Sadr's offensive in January. A combined-arms force of some 30,000–40,000 men attacked on a wide front across the Kharkeh River and toward the main road linking Basra to the north.[11] Regular Army forces, supported by Pasdaran Infantry, moved forward with full artillery support and a mix of small tank units supported by other armored vehicles. This force convinced Iraq that it was Basra that was under attack, and it did not reinforce the 50,000–60,000 men it had in the area around Khorramshahr and Abadan.

For reasons that are still unclear, the Iranians were able to quietly move a force of around 15,000 to 20,000 men down the east side of the Karun River without arousing any major Iraqi action. By this time, they had up to 9,000 regular troops and 4,000 to 6,000 Pasdaran in Abadan.[12] The result was that Iran acquired a considerable superiority over the five Iraqi brigades that formed the eastern part of the Iraqi forces besieging Abadan, and which were deployed across the Bahmanshir River. The Iraqi forces do not seem to have properly patrolled or conducted reconnaissance to their north and their rear and did not detect the Iranian movement until Iranian forces actually attacked them on September 26. The Iranian forces in Abadan then joined the attack, and this put all of the Iraqi forces south and east of the Karun River under considerable pressure.

In theory, Iraq had roughly as many troops in the area as Iran, as well as control of the bridges to the northern part of Abadan Island and the east bank of the Bahmanshir River. In practice, Iraqi forces fought hard but did not receive effective reinforcement or artillery and air support, although Iraq had some 150–200 major artillery pieces within range. Iranian forces were also able to infiltrate through the gaps in the Iraqi positions at night and fought far more aggressively at night. The end result was that the Iraqi forces began to take heavy losses and some elements became isolated. This seems to have driven their command into a panic, and what started as a tactical withdrawal became a rout. The Iraqi troops abandoned their armor and heavy equipment and either retreated across the one pontoon brigade in the area or used small boats and rafts.

By September 29, Iraq had been forced back across the Karun River. Iraq had lost 40–100 tanks, some 200 armored vehicles and artillery weapons, and at least several thousand men. Some estimates go up to 8,000 casualties on both sides, but these seem to be far too high, and the true losses may have been only half that number. In any case, Iran had relieved Abadan and fully secured its road network from Ahwaz to Abadan. This removed the Iraqi threat to Bandar e-Mahshahr and Bandar-e-Khomeini, and Iranian forces continued to slowly press forward. While Iraq continued to hold part of Khorramshahr, the city had lost most of its strategic value because Iran rapidly consolidated its position, and Iraq could not counterattack without taking massive casualties.

Iran succeeded in attacking an equal or superior Iraqi force without any major offensive use of tanks, with almost no air support, and with only token support by attack helicopters. It succeeded for several reasons.

- There was a lack of effective Iraqi preparation and quick reaction.
- Iraq was not willing to take the losses necessary to be successful.
- Iranian preparation for the attack had been left largely to regular officers believed to be fully loyal to the regime, and the fighting was done by a combination of well-prepared regular forces stiffened by direct support from Pasdaran units subordinated to the regular army command.
- Iranian forces moved slowly and cohesively. Iran did not expose its forces to counterattack or allow them to move into Iraqi positions which were well-defended enough to become killing grounds.
- Iran adapted combined-arms techniques to fit its circumstances. It emphasized infantry combat. It used artillery barrages to prepare the area and then committed infantry in frontal and flanking assaults. Tanks and artillery then provided fire support as needed. In contrast, Iraqi commanders were vulnerable because they remained relatively static and lacked any central concentration of forces to counterattack.

In short, the Iranian victory at Abadan provides another illustration of the fact that apparent superiority in armor and air power can be meaningless. It also provides an important warning to the West. Even though Western forces would probably be far more effective in using their air power and combined arms than Iraq, they might encounter similar problems because their increased effectiveness would be counterbalanced by the fact they could find it politically impossible to absorb the kind of losses that would result from a similar attack in a low-level conflict.

It is unclear how Iran planned to follow up its success, but an accident then intervened which seems to have disrupted Iranian operations for at least several weeks. On September 30, the major commanders responsible for Iran's victory were killed in a C-130 crash on their way from the front to Tehran. Those killed included the Minister of Defense, Chief of Staff, Army Chief of Staff, and the regional commander of the Pasdaran. While the political and military impact of this accident is difficult to estimate, it did suddenly deprive Iran of the leaders that had shown that the regular forces and Pasdaran could fight effectively as a combined force and under professional military leadership.

In any case, major offensive action halted during October and most of November. Iraq and Iran did conduct a number of minor actions along the front, but these did little more than make minor adjustments in position. Even so, the impact of Iran's success was revealed by the fact that Saddam Hussein proposed a one-month cease-fire in early November to coincide with Ramadan. Iran rejected Hussein's offer and made it clear that it would not compromise with Iraq or end the war as long as Saddam Hussein was in power.

Serious fighting resumed in late November. On November 29, a mixed forced of roughly 10,000–14,000 Pasdaran and regular Iranian troops attacked an Iraqi strong point and logistic center near Bustan in the Susangerd Salient, on the main road west of Susangerd. The attack was called the Tariq al-Quads (or Tarigh ol-Qods) offensive.[13] It was designed to liberate Bustan, capture the Jazzebeh Gorge and cut the Iraqi line, reach the border and the edge of the Hur el-Azim Marshes, and recapture up to 200 square kilometers of Iranian territory. The attack achieved some degree of surprise because the rains had come and the attack occurred at a time when armored movement and any form of reconnaissance was difficult.

The attack was confused, however, because Pasdaran attacked without waiting for either a regular army artillery barrage or support. The end result was a human-wave attack that closed on the Iraqi force and led to hand-to-hand fighting that lasted for over a day. The result was a victory in the sense that Iranian forces took Bustan, and Iraq lost up to 1,000 soldiers killed and 500 prisoners of war. Iran took even heavier casualties than Iraq, however, and Iraqi forces were able to retreat up the road in relatively good order and create a new defense position east of Susangerd.[14] Even so, Saddam Hussein reacted by removing and demoting some of the commanders involved, and Iraq charged that Iran had committed atrocities and had killed several hundred Iraqi prisoners of war (POWs). The battle did not really change the tactical situation, but it may have helped convince some Pasdaran commanders and Mullahs that the Pasdaran could win through direct assault and ideological fervor and did not need complex battle plans and regular army support.

The next Iranian attack came near Qasr e-Shirin and lasted from December 12 to December 16, 1981. It was called the Al Fajr (Rising of the Dawn) attack and was the first of a series of offensives that the central government in Tehran gave a formal name in an attempt to give Iran's attack more public and propaganda impact. This attack was much more orderly than the attack on Bustan and was organized and led by the regular forces. While estimates differ of the strength of the Iranian forces involved, they seem to have been the equivalent of some 10,000 men or three brigades.

The Iranian forces took advantage of bad weather and rain to achieve tactical surprise and hit Iraqi forces that were not alert and which reacted slowly. The battle went on for nearly a week, and Iraq again failed to react quickly and effectively and to counterattack and commit artillery and air power in a timely manner. The end result was that Iran retook about 100 square miles of the land around Qasr e-Shirin.

Other Developments During 1981

There was virtually no significant naval and strategic-bombing activity during 1981. Sea power had virtually no impact on the war at all. The Iraqi Navy remained in port, and the only Iraqi naval development was to reach a formal agreement for the Italian ships it had informally agreed to order before the war began. The contract, however, implied that Iraq would not receive the ships until the fighting was over. The Iranian Navy did conduct patrols and interrogated ships it felt might be carrying contraband. It seized a Kuwaiti survey ship and a Danish freighter it thought was carrying arms to Iraq, but Iran let both ships go. Iran was careful to avoid provoking either its southern Gulf neighbors or the West. It had become highly dependent on transshipment from the United Arab

Emirates (UAE) and was dependent on both oil exports and two-to-four billion dollars worth of food imports through the Gulf for its survival.

Neither side had any great incentive to launch air attacks against civilian and economic targets. Both sides felt their respective air capabilities were too weak to prevent reprisals, and Iraq almost certainly felt that if it kept such action to a minimum, it would find it easier to deal with Iran if Khomeini fell. Iran did, however, follow up its first military incursion into Kuwait air space in June 1981 with an actual attack. On October 1, three Iranian F-4s bombed the Kuwaiti oil installation at Umm al-Aish, and Kuwait recalled its ambassador from Iran. The Iranian attack was part of a broader pattern of Iranian political activity in the Gulf. That same month, Iran seems to have directed the first major uprising by Iranian pilgrims to the Haj in Saudi Arabia.

Iran also supported a coup attempt in Bahrain. On December 16, 1981, Bahrain announced it had suppressed a Shi'ite coup attempt by a group that included local, Saudi, Iranian, and other Shi'ites. It blamed the Iranian clergyman, Hojatolislam Hadi al Mudoros, for sponsoring the coup and expelled an Iranian diplomat, Hassan Zadeh, for complicity in arms smuggling. While Bahrain probably exaggerated the role of Iran in supporting this coup attempt in order to help disguise its internal political divisions, the Iranian role was real enough to show that Iran may have sought to use subversion to reduce the willingness of the southern Gulf states to support Iraq.[15]

Iran was reacting to several factors in launching these attacks on southern Gulf states. The six southern Gulf states—Bahrain, Kuwait, Oman, Qatar, Saudi Arabia, and the UAE—had created a new organization called the Gulf Cooperation Council on February 4, 1981. This idea had been talked about for years, but it had clearly come into being in large part because of the fear of the member states that the Iran-Iraq War might escalate and because of Iran's attempts to export its revolution. It also had become clear that Kuwait and Saudi Arabia were doing more than simply provide Iraq with political support. Kuwait had gradually become a major transshipment point for Iraq, and both Kuwait and Saudi Arabia had begun to provide Iraq with significant loans.

Iran's actions, however, did more to provoke the southern Gulf states than deter them and followed the pattern Iranian diplomacy and military action set throughout the war. Probably for ideological reasons, Iran never seems to have fully realized the need to secure external allies and to minimize the opposition of other states. It attempted to use its revolution as a means of punishing other states, using intimidation to change those states' behavior. Iran, however, could not make the threat of subversion or military action credible enough to achieve its goals through these means. The end result was to isolate Iran, and Iran suffered severely as a result.

As for other political developments, the U.S., U.K., and Soviet Union kept small naval forces in the Gulf, and the U.S. made active use of the surveillance capabilities of its ELF-1 AWACS force in Saudi Arabia, but external powers did not play any active role except to support a round of peace settlements. Olaf Palme continued to at least keep the option of a UN cease-fire alive and visited Tehran and Baghdad in June, although without any real success. Various bilateral, Arab, and Islamic efforts continued with equally little impact, and Saddam Hussein repeated a series of peace offers. These included a Ramadan cease-fire for July 3 to August 1, 1981, a cease-fire for Murram, and an offer to settle the war in December in return for Iranian recognition of Iraq's rights and borders. Khomeini continued to reject all these offers and to insist on Saddam Hussein's removal from power, reparations, and substantial territorial adjustments and concessions as the price for peace.

Iraqi Counterattacks Fail and New Iranian Offensives Liberate Khuzistan and Khorramshahr

The winter of 1981 brought a temporary halt to Iran's offensives, although Iranian forces continued to put sporadic pressure on Iraqi positions in scattered parts of the front. Iraq did begin to improve its infantry forces and began to select Republican Guard and other regular units for special urban warfare and assault training. By and large, however, it still did not see Iran's offensives as a major threat. In fact, Iraq reacted by launching a series of counterattacks that seemed designed more to restore Iraqi prestige than serve any tactical or strategic purpose.

The first attacks occurred on January 5 and 6, 1982. Iraqi forces attacked the now virtually ruined town of Gilan e-Gahreb, which was located southeast of Qasr e-Shirin and on a road junction south of the main highway from Baghdad to Tehran. The town was only lightly defended and Iraq took the position. Iraq also secured some minor defensive positions in the foothills south of Naft e-Shah.

Iraq launched a more major attack on February 5, 1982. It attempted to recapture Bustan. Iraq conducted an artillery barrage and sent a mixed force of armor and infantry against the city from positions at Sableh southeast of Susangerd. Although Saddam Hussein had given the attack considerable priority, and the battle lasted until February 8, the Pasdaran continued to hold the town, and Iraq was forced to withdraw. Part of the problem was the terrain. Iraq could not use its armor off-road effectively because of mud and flooding. Although Iraq tried night attacks and heavier barrages in a second attack on February 13-15, and again in a third attack in late March, all three attacks failed. This led Saddam Hussein to carry out further purges and demotions of the Iraqi commanders involved.

Iran spent its time building up its forces in the area near Dezful and northeast of Khorramshahr. Once again, Iraq's presentation was slow and methodical and showed considerable care. It became clear that new attacks would begin in the spring. The Iraqis prepared to defend against an Iranian offensive that they correctly predicted would begin during the Iranian holiday of Noroz, but they did not expect the scale of attack that occurred.

By the beginning of February, the Iraqi forces assigned to defend Iraq's positions in Iran had a strength of eight regular divisions plus Popular Army forces and independent support formations. Seven of these divisions and some 65,000–80,000 men were on Iranian soil. The Iraqis had organized these forces into what came to be called the 4th Corps. The key formations were three divisions holding the area around Khorramshahr and the three to four more division equivalents holding the entire front northwest of the Karun River from Khorramshahr to Susangerd.

The Iraqi force defending the area from Dehloran and Shush south toward Ahwaz included two armored and one mechanized division and up to eight independent brigades. A number of Popular Army brigades were sandwiched between the regular Iraqi divisions in the forward area, but Iraq's forces were still about two to three divisions short of the forces necessary to create a cohesive defense of such a broad front. Another Iraqi division, and several brigade equivalents, were in reserve to guard the eastern road from Basra to Baghdad and to secure the logistic centers in the rear.

Iran put its forces for the attack on the Iraqi positions in Khuzistan under the command of General Said Shirazi, the new Chief of Army Staff. He had a total force of between 100,000 and 110,000 men. About one-third of this force consisted of regular Iranian Army troops, and the rest was split between trained and experienced Pasdaran and untrained and poorly armed Baseej. The regular Iranian Army forces included at least two full divisions. The revolutionary forces included ten-to-thirteen Pasdaran brigades, which included large numbers of Baseej.

Iran's Fath ul-Mobin or Fathol-Mobin Offensive
in Northern Khuzistan

Iran launched its Fath ul-Mobin offensive to liberate Khuzistan before dawn on March 22, 1982. It attacked to the west of Shush and Dezful. The objective of the offensive was to prepare the way for a final push to recapture the rest of Khuzistan, to eliminate the threat to Dezful, and to deny Iraq the ability to observe Iranian air movements from radars on the mountains above the town.[16]

Iran attacked when the terrain was trafficable on foot, but still wet enough to limit Iraq armor and vehicles largely to road movement, and attacked over a front nearly 60 kilometers long. Rather than attack at a few points, Iran sent 120,000 to 200,000 regular troops, Revolutionary Guards, and Baseej militia against six points in the Iraqi lines to the areas north and south of the main Iraqi concentrations defending the plain above Khorramshahr.

The Iranian forces which attacked on March 22 were led by the Pasdaran, which struck in two main thrusts to the north and south of the main Iraqi positions and hit at weak points and the gaps between regular Iraqi units in echelons of roughly 1,000 men. The Pasdaran were supported by the Baseej and attacked as waves of combatants, many armed with shoulder-held rocket launchers, which advanced at intervals of 200 to 500 meters. The first waves would often be decimated, but the following waves then often overran the now exhausted Iraqi positions.

After a morning of intense fighting, Iran's mass assaults drained Iraq's forward-deployed ammunition supplies and eventually overpowered the Iraqi defenses in a number of areas. Iran had made Iraq's newly formed Popular Army units a particular target. They were generally easy to identify because of their special unit numbers, and many of the Popular Army forces broke in the face of human wave attacks, leaving the regular Iraqi Army units exposed.

During March 23 to March 28, Iran exploited its initial victory by using the Pasdaran to keep Iraq's forces in place, while its regular army divisions advanced around two of Iraq's divisions in the area. This Iranian tactic was especially effective because Iraq had put too many of its combat forces forward and virtually dug them into dispersed positions. Its armor virtually never counterattacked even the most exposed and unsupported Pasdaran and Iranian regular forces. Iraq did not provide for defense in depth, did not have sufficient forces ready for a counterattack, and held too few reserves too far in the rear.

Saddam Hussein had given orders that no Iraqi units were to withdraw from their forward positions. The Iraqi commanders on the scene lacked the authority to redeploy the forward troops or reserves. The Iraqi regular army failed to properly commit its reserves to halt the resulting Iranian breakthroughs for nearly four critical days and then committed them piecemeal in brigade strength rather than in a coherent counterattack.

This Iraqi failure to properly commit its reserves was partly the result of insufficient forces, the need to keep forces in defense, and the fact that the road system west of the Karun River and the electrified railway between Khorramshahr and Ahwaz did not permit easy or rapid movement. It also, however, was the result of the fact that Saddam Hussein and the senior command in Baghdad only allowed the withdrawal of forward units and the commitment of the reserves after Iraq had already begun to suffer from serious Iranian breakthroughs.

The end result was that Iraq reinforced with too little and too late. Iraqi forces also had to shift from fighting in prepared defensive positions to fighting in "meeting engagements" in which Iraq's dependence on major lines of communication gave Iran the ability to predict Iraqi movements, exploit the rest of the terrain, and achieve superior concentration of force.

Iran made mistakes of its own. The Pasdaran either did not wait for the regular artillery support that was planned or did not receive it. Iran only used tanks as direct-fire artillery, and Pasdaran units often pursued local success rather than drove forward around the north and south of the Iraqi formations. Nevertheless, Iraq moved so slowly that the advancing Iranian forces were able to envelop nearly half of the Iraqi 4th Corps.

Both sides used fighters and helicopter gunships but with little real effectiveness. While Iranian aircraft did attempt to attack Iraq's lines of supply and stockpiles, the number of sorties involved was so low that the Iranian aircraft probably had more effect on morale by showing Iran was still in the sky than it did on the battle. Iraq flew up to 150 fighter sorties per day, but committed its sorties too late to be effective in most tactical situations and often against the wrong targets. Iraq also tended to use its armed helicopters more as flying artillery than as an instrument of maneuver, and they too had little tactical effect.

The location of Iran's offensive in northern Khuzistan is shown in Figure 5.2, as well as that of Iran's other efforts to regain its territory in 1982. This time, however, Iran's offensive resulted in more than a point on the map changing hands. In roughly a week, the Iranian line had advanced roughly 40 kilometers from positions east of the Kharkeh River around Dezful to the Iranian side of the Hawizeh Marshes and within less than 15 kilometers of the Iraqi border in

FIGURE 5.2   Iran Recovers Khuzistan. Adapted
from material provided by the CIA and in *Armed
Forces Journal International*, May 1983, p. 38.

some areas. By April 3, Iranian communiques boasted that Iranian
forces were consolidating their victories in the Ein Kosh (Duflak)
region and Neshard, west of Dezful. The communiques stated that Iran
was pursuing Iraq forces near Saleh Abad, Sunar, Gilan e-Gahreb, and
Pol e-Sar e-Zahab.

Both sides suffered heavy casualties in this battle. The Iranians destroyed major elements of at least one Iraqi mechanized division, one
armored division, and large numbers of Popular Army units.[17] Iran lost

well over 5,000 dead and over 7,000 wounded. Total Iraqi casualties and POWs may have reached more than 14,000 to 15,000. Iraq lost something on the order of 400 to 500 major armored vehicles and some 200 artillery weapons. Iraq also lost a substantial portion of its munitions and supplies, although large reserves still existed in the rear.[18]

Western journalists reported that many of the Iraqi POWs simply surrendered, in spite of orders to "fight to the death," and that few showed signs of combat stress or battle fatigue. Many of the Iraqi POWs, however, came from the new Popular Army forces rather than the regular army. The Iraqi Army was not defeated because of any major disaffection for the Ba'ath regime or because of any lack of Iraqi courage and patriotism. When Iraq removed many of the inexperienced political leaders from command positions in the Popular Army as a result of its defeat and stiffened the units with experienced officers, these problems largely disappeared.

Some sources indicate that Saddam Hussein gave his commanders more freedom of action as a result of Iraq's defeats, and the regular forces were purged of some of its less effective officers and commanders. Unfortunately, if such changes did occur, they had only a very limited effect. Saddam Hussein retained central authority over virtually every major and tactical decision. Iraq also failed to begin to make broader military reforms. Nearly four more years were to elapse before Iraq's leadership was to fully accept the need to retrain and restructure Iraq's military forces and to properly emphasize professionalism in the form of counterattack capability, improved maneuver capability, and increased autonomy for field commanders.

Syria Deprives Iraq of Much of Its Oil-Exporting Capability

While Iran took several weeks to shift from its effort to free the Karun River plain to an offensive designed to liberate Khorramshahr and the rest of southern Iran, it soon scored a victory of another kind. As has been discussed earlier, the destruction of Iraq's oil facilities in the Gulf had left it dependent on two pipelines to the West. The first pipeline, through Turkey, was sabotaged occasionally but was relatively secure. The second pipeline went through an increasingly hostile Syria. (See Figure 5.3.)

During March 1982, Iran carried out a political offensive that was as successful as its military one. Iran negotiated a complex 10-year agreement with Syria that bartered Syrian agricultural products for oil. The agreement gave Syria 174,000 BPD of oil to operate its refineries. A significant amount of this oil was free and the rest was provided at subsidized prices. The end result was that Syria quietly accumulated 1.5 million barrels worth of Iraqi oil at the Syrian

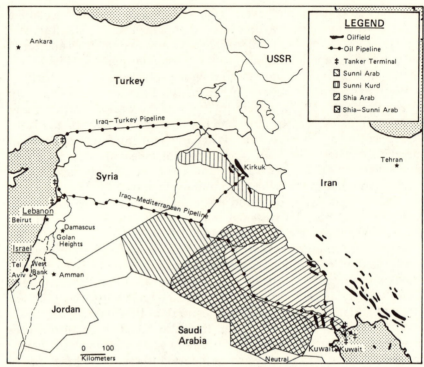

FIGURE 5.3   Iraq's Vulnerable Oil Routes. *Source:* U.S. Defense Mapping Agency.

terminal of Baniyas. It then closed its borders with Iraq on April 8, 1982, on the grounds that Iraq had been supporting the Syrian Muslim Brotherhood. Damascus cut off the flow of Iraqi oil exports to the terminal at Baniyas on April 10 and seized all the Iraqi oil in storage.

The Syrian cutoff deprived Iraq of the use of a pipeline with up to 300,000 BPD capacity. Coupled to the loss of its Gulf terminals at the start of the war, this reduced Iraqi oil exports from several million barrels a day at the start of the war, and 900,000 BPD before the Syrian cutoff, to about 600,000 barrels per day. Iraq became totally dependent on its one remaining pipeline through Turkey.

Although the Turkish pipeline had a maximum capacity of some 900,000 BPD, it was operating at less than maximum capacity at the time of the Syrian cutoff. Kurdish and Iranian agents also sabotaged the Turkish pipeline during 1982 and diverted its flow into the Ceyhan River. While the pipeline was back in operation within a week, Iraq was unable to increase its exports to anything close to 1 MMBD for some time. As a result, Syria's action reduced Iraq's expected export earnings by some $5 billion annually. Iraq had already had to cancel its new five-year development plan early in 1982 because of the cost of the war. This new loss of revenue meant that Iraq's oil earnings no longer even covered the monthly cost of the war, which was in excess of $1 billion a month.

In contrast, Iran brought its exports up to around 2 MMBD and had revenues of nearly $2 billion a month. It also had been able to repair all of its refineries except the one at Abadan and no longer had to ration petrol or heating oil. The war and revolution had halted Iranian economic development and much of Iran's economic activity, there was growing inflation, and many goods could only be readily obtained on the black market. Nevertheless, Iran was more than able to finance the war.

Fortunately for Iraq, its Arab allies provided more support in response. More Egyptian and Sudanese "volunteers" were recruited for the Iraqi Army from the hundreds of thousands of Egyptian and Sudanese workers in Iraq. Egypt agreed to sell Iraq $1.5 billion worth of war materials, small arms, ammunition, and Egyptian-made anti-tank rockets in late March. Jordan offered to send troops to the front. More importantly, Kuwait and Saudi Arabia began to provide Iraq with massive financial aid to compensate for its loss of oil revenue and declining reserves of foreign exchange and began to sell up to 300,000 barrels per day of some of their oil for Iraq on the basis it would be repaid through exchanges after the war. As a result, Iraq began to receive flows of outside aid which reached a total of around $35.0 billion by early 1988.

Iran's Quds or Bait al-Muqdas (Jerusalem) Offensive Liberates Khorramshahr[19]

Iraq's reaction to its defeats at Abadan and its loss of most of northern Khuzistan was to attempt to fortify Khorramshahr and to create sufficiently strong defenses of the routes to Khorramshahr to ensure that it could not be flanked and cut off from the West.[20] This defense was a matter of considerable urgency. Iraq was shielded in part from the effects of its losses in northern Khuzistan by the fact the border area consisted largely of the Hawizeh Marshes, which extended north of Susangerd in Iran and to the edge of Al Amarah and Al Halfayah in Iraq. The terrain leading toward Basra, however, was relatively dry, and while the Shatt al-Arab and a number of other water barriers and smaller marshes provide natural defenses, Iraq was still vulnerable to the loss of its territory northeast of the Shatt if it lost Khorramshahr.

Iraq deployed the equivalent of roughly eight divisions and 70,000–90,000 men for the forward defense of the area, although many of the

Iraqi formations involved had suffered as a result of its defeat in Khuzistan. Roughly three of these divisions were deployed to Khorramshahr and the access route to the Iraq border and the Shatt al-Arab. While Iraq had built up a number of roads in the area, this force depended on a single major road and military bridge across the Shatt.

The Khorramshahr area was fortified with arcs of earth barriers with bunkers, observation points, and fire posts. Fire zones were created by leveling buildings and vegetation. Barbed wire and minefields provided further reinforcements, and artillery fire points and large supply depots were created in the rear. Another defensive wall was built in the city with the Shatt to its back, and fire zones were leveled near the bridges to the south to prevent any attack from Abadan.

Two armored divisions, one mechanized division, and some eight Popular Army brigades defended the rest of Iraq's remaining positions on Iranian soil. These extended along the Karun River east of the electric railway from Khorramshahr to Ahwaz to roughly Isgah e-Ahu, and then turned northwest toward the border along a line passing through points near Huzgan and Jarayeh.

Iraq's strategy remained one of static warfare. Iraq concentrated on fixed defense positions. It dug in all its forces, including much of its armor and artillery. This deprived Iraq's armor of its ability to maneuver and concentrate and meant that Iraqi forces had to defend against frontal assaults. Iraq also still lacked the force numbers to hold the amount of territory in its remaining positions north of Khorramshahr, particularly because only its regular forces were generally effective in combat. It meant that Iran could continue to attack Iraq's defenses piecemeal without Iraq attempting major counterattacks or maneuver.

Further, Khorramshahr was allowed to become a strategic objective for political reasons and was given far more value than it deserved in military terms. While the city was a natural defense point, it also was relatively isolated from Iraqi territory, and Iraq could not fully clear the approaches to the city. Creating a citadel again deprived its armor of any major advantage in terms of maneuver and counterattack and forced Iraq to disperse its forces around a relatively large perimeter. Like all fortresses, the use of a ring defense also created a potential trap. While such defenses made it difficult for Iranian forces to get in, they also made it difficult for Iraqi forces to get out.

As for Iran, it now had well over 150,000 men in the area surrounding Iraq's positions at Khorramshahr and in southern Khuzistan. Its forces included several regular army divisions, large numbers of Pasdaran and

Baseej, and large amounts of regular army artillery and support equipment. The Iranian force remained under the titular command of the Army chief of staff. Although the Pasdaran and regular forces remained divided in many ways, Iran had the advantage of the momentum of revolutionary fervor and two victories and was fighting for the liberation of its territory.

Iran attacked in three major thrusts. The first was to the north along the access routes to the Iraqi-held town of Hoveyzeh, about 12 miles west of Susangerd. The second was against the former Iranian fortress garrison of Haim, and the major rail and road net from Khorramshahr to Ahwaz. The third thrust came later and was directed against Khorramshahr itself.

The first thrust began early on the morning of April 30. Like most Iranian attacks, Iranian forces closed on the Iraqi positions at night to limit the threat from airpower and artillery. Pasdaran forces thrust west from Shush toward the northern part of the Iraqi positions and the Baghdad-Basra road. The Pasdaran force totaled 35,000–40,000 and attacked an Iraqi armored division which had Popular Army support.

The Iraqi force fought well, and if it had maneuvered, it might have been able to defeat the attack. Instead, the Iraqi forces remained dug-in and on the defensive. As a result, Iran's human-wave attacks led to very heavy Iranian casualties but still allowed Iran to eventually penetrate and overrun the Iraqi forces. According to some reports, Iranian airborne troops also were dropped behind the Iraqi forces along the Karun River that same afternoon to create disruption in the rear. It is not clear whether this attack occurred or what effect it had.[21]

On May 1, 1982, another Pasdaran formation attacked westwards across the Karun River at a point near the place where Iraqi forces going the opposite direction had crossed in 1980 during Iraq's attempt to surround Abadan. Once again, Iraq was slow to react and the Iranian forces rapidly secured their crossing. They erected a series of pontoon brigades across the Karun, and Iran was able to move the equivalent of several divisions across the river.

Iraqi forces failed to counterattack until May 3 and 4, and these counterattacks failed. Iran was able to launch another major series of attacks on May 6. Bitter fighting then took place around Hoveyzeh and Hamid. The Iraqi forces, however, lacked sufficient force to counterattack successfully and tended to counterattack up too narrow an axis of advance. After several days of fierce fighting, Iran took Hamid and forced Iraq to abandon Joyfer. Iran then retook Hoveyzeh (Howeyziyeh) in the north. Iraqi forces began to collapse on a broad front as their attempts to use firepower alone to counter the Iranian attacks failed to stop repeated human waves of Iranian attackers. Iran also made an unusually effective use of helicopters during this battle and even launched some diversionary helicopter attacks on the Iraqi town of Fuka and an Iraqi command post at the border town of Chalamcheh (Shalamcheh).

Within a week, Iran had regained a 30-kilometer-wide slice of its territory from Istgah e-Husseiniya in the north to a point about ten miles north of Khorramshahr. The Iranian advance also left the remaining Iraqi forces in the area with Iranian forces to the east and marshes to the west, while the Iranian drive south threatened to cut them off from Khorramshahr.

On May 9, Iran launched the last phase of the battle. Iranian forces cut the road through Hamid, which was on a raised dike and which was the key to defending the area. As a result, Saddam Hussein ordered his troops to retreat south on May 10 to positions ten to fifteen kilometers north of Khorramshahr. The retreating Iraqi formations were now down to the equivalent of about five to seven brigades, however, and had taken heavy losses. They also had to retreat too quickly to move many of their dug-in tanks, artillery weapons, supplies and support equipment; as a result, they lost as many as 100 tanks, some 150 other armored vehicles of all types, and 50–100 major artillery weapons. Thus, the Iraqi forces were deprived of much of their effectiveness by the time they reached their new positions.

Iran spent the next ten days deploying its forces to attack the Iraqi position at Khorramshahr, while Iraq spent the time frantically attempting to improve the fortifications in the city. By this time, however, Khorramshahr had become more of a trap for Iraq than a fortress. Iraqi troops often fought well, but they lacked the reserves and depth to fully secure the city from being surrounded by Iran. This created a situation where Iran could trap up to two Iraqi division equivalents in the city or force them to ferry across the Shatt and abandon much of their supplies and equipment.

It took more than ten days of hard fighting, but on May 21, a Pasdaran division overran one of the Iraqi divisions defending the one major Iraqi supply road into Khorramshahr. The Iraqi division collapsed under the pressure of Iran's human-wave attacks and abandoned much of its equipment. The other Iraqi forces lacked the strength and will to counterattack effectively, and Iran was able to cut off Khorramshahr from Iraq.

Iran's final push to recover Khorramshahr began on the morning of May 22. Roughly 70,000 Iranians moved against the 35,000 Iraqi troops, some 15,000–22,000 of which were now trapped in the city. The Iraqi forces outside the city had taken so many losses that they now remained relatively static and could not counterattack effectively from the west. The Iraqi forces in Khorramshahr lacked the strength to hold their entire defensive perimeter against a force of roughly eight Pasdaran brigade equivalents.

While the Iraqi forces in Khorramshahr initially inflicted extremely heavy casualties on the Pasdaran, the Pasdaran were able to saturate and overrun the Iraqi defensive positions. Once the Pasdaran broke through Iraq's defensive lines, they immediately presented severe problems for the Iraqi defenders. The Iraqi troops were forced out of their defensive strong points and had to fight street by street. While there were Iraqi artillery fire points in the city and substantial amounts of artillery across the Shatt al-Arab to the west, it was difficult to bring this fire to bear in an urban area with any effectiveness.

Iraq did commit up to 100 sorties per day, but usually too late to have maximum tactical effect and in individual concentrations that were too small against any given target to be highly effective. The Iranian targets generally consisted of infantry, and any given Iraqi sortie could only achieve a limited number of kills under the best conditions. Iraqi pilots had no night-warfare capability. They could not find significant targets most of the time and could not deliver their weapons at the moment Iranian forces closed with Iraqi troops. Iran also flew some fighter and helicopter sorties, but in relatively limited numbers. No significant air-to-air combat took place, although both Iraq and Iran seem to have lost fighters in such encounters.

While the Iraqi forces did manage to regroup behind their defensive wall inside the city on May 23, they already had taken substantial losses and had lost many of their weapons and equipment. Further, the moment the Pasdaran were able to breach any part of the defensive wall, the Iraqis were forced to fight on an equal basis against much larger and far more fanatic Pasdaran infantry. The end result was that the Iraqi forces involved began to collapse. While sporadic fighting continued until May 24, and roughly 30–40 percent of the Iraqi troops were able to retreat across the Shatt al-Arab by abandoning their equipment, Iran took nearly 12,000 prisoners. For once, Iran may have been correct when it said it had destroyed two Iraqi mechanized brigades and two border brigades.[22]

Iran also scored some additional successes in dealing with its Kurdish insurgents in the north. After scattered fighting throughout the winter, regular army forces and Pasdaran forces launched a major offensive against the KDPI in April. This broke up the KDPI's own efforts at an offensive, but the fighting remained inconclusive.

Ghassemlou launched an unsuccessful offensive in June, and Iranian forces slowly drove the KDPI forces back.

Iran's final major offensive action of 1982 was less successful. It occurred on May 28, when Iranian forces attacked Iraqi forces in the north in the sector from Qasr e-Shirin to Sumar, in an attempt to open up an attack route that would allow Iran to recapture its lost territory in that region. Reinforced Pasdaran forces attempted to attack strongly held Iraqi positions in the mountains. The attack was conducted with little surprise as a frontal assault against strongly held Iraq positions and was repulsed. Iran launched a smaller attack in the area on August 8, with a single unsupported attacking wave of Pasdaran, but this attack was quickly halted with the loss of much of the Pasdaran force.

The End of Phase Two of the War

Iran's recapture of Khorramshahr effectively brought an end to both the 1981–1982 campaign season and the phase of the war in which Iran concentrated primarily on recapturing its lost territory. While Iran was to fight many other battles in the border area that began against Iraqi positions that were still on Iranian soil, these offensives were almost all a preliminary phase in what was intended to be an invasion.

This change in the war was clear in both military and political terms. Iraq's small defensive successes in the north in May 1982 did little to compensate it for its massive losses elsewhere. Almost from the beginning to the end of Iran's spring 1982 offensives, Iraq had attempted to defend in a way which either required far more forces than Iraq had available, or which deprived Iraq of the advantages of its superiority in armor and artillery the moment its major defensive lines were penetrated.

From March 22 to May 24—a period of almost exactly two months— Iraq gave up some 5,500 square kilometers of captured territory, suffered as many as 30,000 to 50,000 killed and wounded, and lost up to 25,000 prisoners. Iraq also lost up to 200 hundred tanks, as many as 300–400 other armored vehicles, several hundred artillery weapons, and vast amounts of supplies. While Iraq might have been driven out of most of its gains in Iran in any case, it paid an immense price for its lack of military professionalism, its ability to conduct effective maneuver warfare, and its cumbersome and politicized structure of command and control.

Saddam Hussein was also forced to admit his attempt to force Iran to peace by holding Iranian territory had failed. On June 9, 1982, he ordered all Iraqi forces to observe a unilateral cease-fire. On June 10, he ordered all Iraqi forces to withdraw from Iranian territory, supposedly to reinforce the PLO and Syrian forces in Lebanon against the Israeli invasion that had begun on June 6.

Iraq desperately sought help in new efforts at peace negotiations. Iran, however, rejected new peace efforts by the Islamic Conference Organization and Olaf Palme of the UN in March, an Algerian peace effort in May, a Gulf Cooperation Council (GCC) peace initiative in early June, a new UN cease-fire attempt in mid-June, and private Soviet and Egyptian peace initiatives.[23] Khomeini personally made it clear that he would only agree to a settlement that involved Saddam Hussein's ouster.

The most that Saddam Hussein could do was to change his explanation of Iraq's withdrawal on June 20 to a statement that he was withdrawing from Iranian territory to remove any reason for prolonging the war. Saddam Hussein also acted on his statement that Iraq would make withdrawals. During the month between June 20 and July 20, Iraq gave up most of its forward positions in Iran, although it kept some 500 square kilometers of Iranian territory shielding the approaches to Baghdad, as well as other key defense positions along the border.

Neither Saddam Hussein's statements nor Iraq's withdrawals from some of its positions in Iran did anything to move the situation toward peace. Iran expressed its willingness to negotiate, but various Iranian leaders issued terms which included restoration of the 1975 treaty borders, removal of Saddam Hussein from power, repatriation of over 100,000 Iraqis expelled by Baghdad, the payment of over $100 billion in war reparations, acceptance of war guilt by Iraq, and a new regime in Iraq.

Iran's victories and demands had put Saddam Hussein in a very different position from the leader of the Arab world that he had hoped to become when he invaded Iran. He was now forced to turn to virtually every moderate Arab state for support. He also was finally forced to abandon his plans to host the summit meeting of non-aligned nations in September 1982. Iraq had poured nearly half a billion dollars into the construction of hotels, meeting halls, monuments, and new roads in order to be ready to host this meeting, which was to make Saddam Hussein chairman of the movement for three years. Its cancellation must have been as bitter a blow as having to become a virtual supplicant in seeking aid from the southern Gulf states and Egypt.

Saddam Hussein also seems to have faced unrest within the government and Iraqi armed forces. On June 23, 1982, Saddam Hussein dismissed his Revolutionary Command Council and reappointed a smaller one of nine, rather than the original seventeen members. The

Ba'ath Party Council was cut in size, and Saddam Hussein also purged part of the Cabinet and senior officer corps. He shot twelve of his generals for their performance in battle and then his Minister of Health for suggesting he should temporarily step down from power. This move helped suppress the opposition within the Ba'ath regime and helped secure the Ba'ath government against internal threats.

At the same time, the Ba'ath regime was careful to court people. It kept up the supply of consumer goods and services and the payments to those who had lost a father or son in the war. It began to actively court the Shi'ites in the south and put even more emphasis on Iraqi nationalism and Arab consciousness in its propaganda. Funds suddenly were poured into development projects in the south and to the shrines at Najaf and Karbala.

Equally important, Iraq began to regroup its forces for defense. It began to establish strong defensive lines along the entire border area that was now threatened by Iran, with major defenses along the entire Basra-to-Baghdad road, from Basra to Al Amarah, and west of the Hawizeh Marshes. Work began on creating water barriers to help defend the south, and Iraq urgently sought military supplies from throughout the Arab world.

As for Iran, it had achieved a major victory and had captured enough Iraqi equipment to begin organizing and training some new armored units to use such equipment near Shiraz. Iran also, however, had suffered over 110,000 casualties, with up to 60,000 dead. Some estimates even put Iran's dead at 90,000. A state of civil war still existed between Khomeini's supporters and the Mujahideen, and Tehran was still the scene of a constant cycle of bombing attempts and executions. Khomeini's supporters began to arrest senior members of the Tudeh Party in June, as any form of Marxism came to be seen as a potential threat against the revolution.

This civil fighting affected Iran's military capabilities at the front as well. While Khomeini again called for unity within the armed forces on April 18, 1982, and seems to have sought improved relations between the Pasdaran and the regular forces, the situation actually grew worse. Iran's former Foreign Minister Sadiq Ghotbzadeh was arrested on April 9 for plotting the assassination of Khomeini. Shortly after Khomeini's unity speech, he made a televised confession that implicated the regular armed forces in his "plot." While it is impossible to determine how real Ghotbzadeh's confession was, the government announced in mid-August that at least 70 officers in the regular forces had been shot for supporting him.[24] The government also announced another coup attempt by Colonel Azar Dakham on June 27.

These internal developments discredited the regular forces in spite of Iran's recent victories against Iraq. Further, both the media and the Mullahs gave most of the credit to the Pasdaran and Baseej and to the value of martyrdom and human-wave attacks. Iran began to conduct its military operations under conditions where it was harder and harder for military professionals to take the lead in planning and operations. Primary attention was given to building up the Pasdaran, and the government paid less and less attention to the need for armor and mechanized forces.

The Situation Outside Iraq and Iran

Although Iran's new successes caused considerable concern throughout the southern Gulf and the Arab world, the West still showed relatively little concern with the fighting. The U.S. and Britain did become concerned with the potential risk that Iran might now attack Iraq and even conquer it but did little more than show new concern about the flow of arms to Iran. Most Western analysts still did not view the situation with sufficient concern to see the change in the fighting as presenting new strategic problems for the West.

Part of the reason for this attitude was that there was little strategic bombing and little action at sea. Iraq did launch air raids against Kharg Island and Shiraz on May 20, but these were flown as single sets of attacks and did only limited damage. They seem to have been intended largely as an effort to push Iran toward a cease-fire and had little effect on either Iranian or outside perceptions. There was virtually no activity at sea until June 1982, when Iraq began to conduct sporadic air strikes against Iranian ships going to Bandar-e-Khomeini and seems to have put new mines in the Iranian waters in the Gulf around the channels to Abadan, the Khor e-Musa, and the Khor e-Ghazlan.

Activity in the rest of the Gulf was also relatively quiet, although both Bahrain and Kuwait had new indicators of Iranian support for militant Shi'ite radicals in those two countries. The new Gulf Cooperation Council, which had agreed to form a joint military command in late March, did little more than make its brief attempt to help both sides reach a cease-fire. There was no major new Western or Soviet military activity.

Notes

1. The analysis of phase two is based heavily on Anthony H. Cordesman's trips to the region and interviews of Iraqi and Iranian officers and officials, plus his prior writing for the *Armed Forces Journal International* (especially "The Lessons of the Iran-Iraq War," Parts I and II, April and June, 1982) and in the

book *The Gulf and the Search for Strategic Stability*, Boulder, Westview, 1984. It also draws heavily upon the work of Colonel W.O. Staudenmaier, U.S. Army Strategic Studies Institute; Edgar O'Ballance, *The Gulf War*, London, Brassey's, 1988; Nikola B. Schahgaldian, *The Iranian Military Under the Islamic Republic*, Santa Monica, Rand R-3473-USDP, 1987; Sepehr Zabih, *The Iranian Military in Revolution and War*, London, Routledge, 1988; Keith McLauchlan and George Joffe, *The Gulf War*, Special Report 176, London, Economist Press, 1984; Keith McLauchlan and George Joffe, *Iran and Iraq: The Next Five Years*, Special Report 1083, London, Economist Press, 1987; and various working papers for the International Institute for Strategic Studies, Royal United Services Institute.

2. Iraq claimed only 4,500 Iranian killed and 11,500 wounded at the beginning of 1981. Iraq also, however, made ridiculous claims to have cost Iran more than 400 combat aircraft, 500 tanks, and 18 major combat ships. As for Iran, it is interesting to note that it claimed 25,000 Iraqi casualties and the destruction of over 4,000 tanks and other armored weapons and over 500 artillery weapons. Iran won the "war of lies" in 1980, if little else.

3. Many of these brigades had the strength of only one or two battalions.

4. Zabih, op. cit., p. 172.

5. For a detailed description, see O'Ballance, op. cit., pp. 61–64.

6. Some sources indicate that the Iranian force was cut off from the rear when the Iraqi Air Force cut the bridges behind it. It is unclear that the Iraqi Air Force had any such impact. See Zabih, op. cit., 172–173.

7. Authors' estimate based on the total strengths shown in the IISS *Military Balance*, London, International Institute for Strategic Studies.

8. One of the grimmer jokes in Teheran at the time was that Rafsanjani had the wrong vehicle behind him and really needed to be followed by a hearse.

9. Red Cross figures in January 1982 showed that there were about 28,400 Iraqi POWs and 5,300 Iranian POWs.

10. This estimate may be high. Some sources indicate only about 120,000.

11. Up to two-thirds of the total force may have consisted of revolutionary forces. See Zabih, op. cit., pp. 174–175.

12. The reader should be aware that any such estimates are even more uncertain than most of the statistics available on the war.

13. Zabih, op. cit., p. 176.

14. Iranian sources claimed that Iraq lost 100 tanks, 70 APCs, 19 artillery pieces, 70 anti-aircraft guns, and large quantities of ammunition—including many boxes indicating they had come from Saudi Arabia. They claimed that between 80,000 and 100,000 Iranian troops (two-thirds of which were Pasdaran and Baseej) were involved against a force of six Iraqi brigades. Casualty rates are put as high as 30 percent. See Zabih, op. cit., pp. 174–175.

15. *Guardian*, December 17, 1981, and *Financial Times*, January 5, 1982.

16. See Zabih, op. cit., p. 177.

17. Some sources cite the Iraqi 10th Armored Division, the 11th Special Mission Brigade, the 96th Infantry Brigade, and the 60th Armored Brigade. It is unclear that these unit designations are correct.

18. Iran claimed that it captured 150 tanks, 670 other armored vehicles, 150

152-mm artillery weapons, and 165 182-mm artillery weapons. It claimed that there were 75,000 Iraqi casualties and 15,450 prisoners of war, of which 200 were officers and 4 were generals. It claimed to have recaptured 1,500 square miles of territory. See Zabih, op. cit., p. 177.

19. Also called the Beytol-Moghaddas offensive.

20. Khomeini renamed Khorramshahr as Khuninshahr, or the "city of blood," in honor of Iran's losses during this phase of the war.

21. For a detailed description, see O'Ballance, op. cit., pp. 82–84.

22. Iran claimed the total operation gave Iran some 19,000 Iraqi POWs, 105 tanks, 56 armored vehicles, large numbers of small arms, and stocks of some 300,000 mines and 11,000 "bombs." See Zabih, op. cit., pp. 178–179, and O'Ballance, op. cit., p. 85.

23. The Algerian peace initiative ended on May 3, 1982, when the Algerian Foreign Minister's aircraft crashed while flying from Turkey to Iran. Iranians have suggested Iraq was responsible. Others have suggested some anti-peace faction in Iran. The facts remain unclear.

24. Ghotbzadeh was executed on September 10, 1982. The Ayatollah Shariet-Madari was implicated in the plot and died while still under house arrest on April 3, 1986.

6

PHASE THREE: IRAN INVADES IRAQ, JUNE 1982–MARCH 1984

Iran's First Major Offensives Against Iraq[1]

It is unclear how serious a debate Khomeini and his supporters really conducted over their decision to invade Iraq.[2] Some reports emerged in 1988, at the time that Iran had already suffered major defeats, that Khomeini and others around him had originally stated that they would not go on fighting once Iran's territory was liberated. This seems doubtful. While Khomeini had made some statements earlier in the war, indicating that Iran would not invade Iraq, these were generally linked to the idea that Saddam Hussein would be removed from power and that some form of uprising would take place within Iraq that would change the character of its regime. Further, Khomeini clearly described his revolution in terms that implied that it would eventually have control of the main Shi'ite shrines in Iraq and that this would be a major step in the liberation of Jerusalem.

By June 1982, Iran's victories had also reached a scale where the temptation to attack Iraq must have been virtually irresistible. Iran had smashed through Iraq's defenses in Khuzistan. It had defeated, and in some cases broken, some of Iraq's best regular units. Iraqi airpower had failed to have a decisive impact on any battle, and it was clear that Iraq had begun to face financial problems because of its loss of oil exports. There were minor indicators of unrest in the Shi'ite cities in southern Iraq, and Iraq seemed to lack any clear defense against Iran's revolutionary fervor.

June and July 1982 were also scarcely a time in which any voice around Khomeini could have felt secure in advocating moderation. The near civil war in the capital and repeated coup attempts reinforced the tendency to encourage military action. This, in fact, was increasingly reflected in the statements of both senior Iranian politicians and military officers. Between late June and early July, both Khomeini and virtually every major spokesman for the Iranian government began to hint at the fact Iran would soon invade Iraq.

The State of Iranian and Iraqi Forces
at the Beginning of Iran's Invasion of Iraq

These hints soon became reality. The third phase of the war started when Iran deployed the equivalent of more than five divisions in an attempt to capture Basra. (See Figure 6.1.) By this point in the war, Iranian divisions had between 12,000 and 15,000 men each, depending on the amount of Pasdaran and Baseej that made up the "shock" or assault troops in each unit. They had both armor and artillery, but they essentially were heavy infantry forces designed to use frontal assaults and human-wave attacks to overcome any opposition.

The Iranian formations were structured to allow their commanders to commit large amounts of infantry troops in repeated attack echelons or waves and were designed to use the same tactics that Iran had been successful with in retaking Khuzistan and Khorramshahr. These formations did, however, have a number of major disadvantages. First, they could not maneuver quickly or effectively, particularly once forces were committed to battle. Command and control was difficult. The Pasdaran elements leading an attack tended to be semi-autonomous, and the coordination between infantry and artillery was usually poor. While the practice of moving up directly against Iraq's defensive lines early in the battle, and at night where possible, made it more difficult for Iraq to use its airpower and artillery, it also made it difficult for Iran to provide air support or use artillery at the breakthrough point except in preparation for the infantry assault.

Iranian organization and assault tactics also depended heavily on success. Once the waves of Pasdaran and Baseej began to advance, they were largely beyond the tactical control of the high command.[3] The unit commanders also were ideologically committed to achieving their objective or "martyrdom," often to the point where they had no alternative plan. It was difficult to recall forces once they were committed and if they were not trained to conduct a successful retreat. There often was no clear role that Iranian armor could play except to provide fire support for the infantry. Iranian armor could occasionally flank an Iraqi force but could not maneuver in depth against Iraqi opposition without infantry support, and the bulk of Iran's infantry lacked the equipment and skill to operate as a mechanized force.

Further, Iran's tactics presented major problems in supply and in exploiting a breakthrough. Infantry forces generally carried their supplies, and only a rudimentary system existed to resupply the

A. The Main Thrusts

B. The Drive on Baghdad in September–October

C. The Scene of the November Offensive

FIGURE 6.1 Iran's Offensives of 1982. Adapted from material provided by the CIA and in *Armed Forces Journal International,* May 1983, p. 40.

attacking echelons once they advanced. This system worked on the basis of supply push as long as the Iranian units were not forced to retreat or alter their plan but often broke down if they were forced to regroup or they advanced too quickly. There also was no echelon of mechanized assault infantry and armor to follow up after the Pasdaran broke the Iraqi defense line and to quickly exploit initial success.

These problems were not critical to Iran as long as it could both afford to expend large amounts of manpower and equipment and achieve a high ratio of concentration of force and local superiority to Iraq. The favorable force-to-space ratio in Khuzistan and Iraq's static defensive tactics had given Iran these advantages in liberating its own territory. So had the fact that the Iraqi troops in Iran were fighting for an objective that was relatively abstract, while the Iranian troops were fighting for their homeland. While no one can quantify the ideological and morale aspects of war, there is no question that Iranian troops had fought during 1981 and 1982 with a willingness to die that often frightened or awed their Iraqi opponents.

Iraq now, however, was fighting for its own soil, although it continued to hold defensive terrain on Iranian soil near Qasr e-Shirin, Naft e-Shah, Sumar, Mandali, Mehran, and Musain. As was the case with the USSR in World War II, the war had ceased to be Saddam Hussein's war and had become a national conflict which every Iraqi soldier could now understand. For all its losses, Iraq also still had a major advantage in air power of nearly 4:1, a superiority in operational armor and artillery of nearly 3:1, and superior infantry arms and area munitions. Iraq also was now fighting in defense of positions with excellent lines of communication and which allowed far faster resupply and reinforcement. Iraq also had roughly the same force strength in its Third Army around Basra that Iran had in its attacking forces: about 70,000 to 90,000 men.

Iraq had purged the Popular Army units of their worst commanders and had learned to subordinate them to the regular forces rather than commit them to the front lines in places where they furnished natural points of vulnerability for Iran to attack. It also had learned from its experience in Khuzistan and around Khorramshahr. Iraq had turned the entire front south of the Hawizeh Marshes into a fortress.

A line of massive earth berms was set up along the border area east of Iraq's main north-south roads. A large number of lateral roads reached to the forward lines with smaller north-south roads immediately behind the berms. There was a cleared "fire zone" in front of the berm, and the berms had observation points and fire points all along their top. They were defended by dug-in tanks and large numbers of anti-aircraft machine guns and cannon which could be used to "hose" attacking Iranian infantry. Iraq made extensive use of mortars, minefields, and barbed wire. Where possible, Iraq also began to divert water into the area to create further defensive barriers.

Major artillery complexes existed to the rear of each berm, which had the range to reinforce each other in an emergency. Central supply depots and hospitals existed in echelons to the rear, and all positions were overstocked to allow supplies to be fed into the front on a supply-push basis and to prevent positions from running out of ammunition. The defenses immediately around Basra and some of the other urban areas in the south were also set up in rings or semicircles. While Iraq did not establish a broad system of defense in depth at this time, Basra had such defenses by mid-1982.

This structure also simplified Iraq's command-and-control problem as long as Iraq understood where Iran would begin its main attack and as long as Iran attacked fully manned large-scale Iraq defenses. Iraqi commanders could use artillery against presurveyed points. Fighters and helicopters had a well-defined fire zone. The barrier defenses gave Iraq time to move reinforcements north and south, and Iranian forces were too far from their rear areas and lines of communication to quickly exploit any tactical breakthrough.

In short, many of the conditions that had led to Iranian success in the previous months no longer really applied. It is also important to note that both sides were largely incapable of modern maneuver warfare. Relatively small movements and increases in distance meant considerable disorganization and supply-and-command problems.

Iran's Operation Ramadan Against Basra

The first major Iranian attempt to conquer Iraq was called Operation Ramadan al-Mubarak (Ramazanol-Mobarak). It began during the month of Ramadan on the night of July 13–14, 1982. Elements of four divisions, led by the Pasdaran, assaulted the Iraqi border defenses near Shalamcheh, with the obvious goal of cutting the main roads north from Basra and isolating the city. The Iranian attack was relatively well prepared. It began at night and attacked across the wetlands north of the Hawizeh Marshes. The Iranian forces quickly penetrated past Iraq's screening defenses at the border and thrust up against Iraq's main defense line to the rear. In the process, they advanced a little less than 20 kilometers in a relatively narrow thrust of less than 10 kilometers in depth.

The Iranian forces then, however, came up against Iraq's main defense line. The result was that Iran had to repeatedly attempt to break directly through a position where Iraq had good defenses and a massive superiority in overall firepower, particularly artillery firepower. While both sides took heavy losses, the Iranians lost three to four times as many men as the Iraqis. The Iranian offensive also quickly bogged down. This allowed the Iraqi armor to flank the Iranian force from both sides. While the Iraqi maneuver lacked speed and elegance, it was highly effective. The Iranian force was caught in a three-sided trap and driven back to a place near their starting point.

The battle then became a battle of attrition versus firepower. This was a battle that Iraq was well-equipped to win. Its superior artillery and armored strength could be used against Iranian forces which had lost much of their cohesion and which moved and reacted slowly. Iraqi fighters and helicopters did not produce major casualties, but they did present open movement and major resupply. There are also indications that Iraq began to use artillery to fire O-Chlorobenzyl-malononitrile (CS) "tear gas," or incapacitating gas, during this period. This use of gas seems to have been effective in breaking up at least some Iranian assaults and may have contributed to Iraq's later decision to use poison gas.

While Iraq suffered serious damage to at least two armored brigades, Iran lost major elements of both an armored and infantry division. Iran also lost a significant amount of artillery and armor, as well as men. Iran almost certainly should then have paused and rethought its attack. Instead, it quickly regrouped and began a similar attack from a position near Zaid on the Iraqi border about 15 kilometers further south on July 21.

This Iranian attack again came at night but involved two thrusts, rather than one. It was somewhat more successful and broke through part of Iraq's defense line; Iran again failed to secure its flanks and lacked the armor to defend against Iraq's slow moving counterattack. Iran was driven back with only minimal gains and lost well over 10,000 killed to around 3,000 killed for Iraq.

In spite of its losses and the fact that Iran did not receive any significant sign of popular support from Iraq's Shi'ites, Iran tried a third time on August 1, 1982. By this time, however, Iran's forces had taken major manpower and equipment losses and had lost most of the momentum they had possessed when the attacks began. Iran's new thrust took place against Iraqi positions between Zaid and Mashwa and collapsed within days. By this time, Iran had lost between 20,000 and 30,000 killed and critically wounded and about 20–25 percent of its equipment.[4]

These losses were so great that they meant that Operation Ramadan cost Iran more manpower than Iraq had lost at Khorramshahr, that Iran lost a great deal of its trained and experienced manpower, and that Iran suffered serious equipment losses. In fact, these losses forced Iran to halt major attacks for the rest of the summer. They also led to new reports about feuding between the regular army commanders and the Mullahs and to reports of Iranian problems in recruiting volunteers.

Nevertheless, some elements in the Iran leadership seem to have viewed Operation Ramadan as a victory in the sense that it had begun to force Iraq into a battle of attrition that they felt Iraq could not sustain. Operation Ramadan also established a pattern of massive Iranian offensives that continued through the beginning of 1988.

The problem was that limited tactical success never meant strategic success. Iran had created forces that could be a very real threat to Iraq and could make token gains on Iraqi territory. Iran's basic strategy, however, was roughly equivalent to trying to use a hammer to destroy an anvil. Iran eventually broke its forces on this anvil by hammering away at Iraqi defenses, scoring largely symbolic gains, and then pausing for months while it recovered its offensive capabilities. These repeated attacks also depleted Iran's cadre of leaders, skilled manpower, and equipment. They deprived it of the tools it needed to take advantage of its superior manpower, and they undercut popular support for the war, military morale, and Iran's recruiting base.

It is also important to note that Operation Ramadan seems to have reflected a major shift in the belief structure of the autocrats leading Iran and Iraq. Iraq's successes in early 1982 seem to have convinced Khomeini that revolutionary forces could eventually be successful using tactics that emphasize sacrifice and martyrdom. This view was almost certainly reinforced by his religious convictions and constant problems with the loyalty of the regular Iranian military forces. While some of those around Khomeini may not have fully shared his belief structure, and leaders as diverse as Ayatollah Hossein Ali Montazari and Rafsanjani clearly showed more caution in given instances, it seems likely that both they and many Pasdaran commanders and officials shared enough of this belief structure to make it extremely difficult for Iran to make major changes in the way it fought or the way it organized its forces.

As a result, Iran failed to give the proper emphasis to military professionalism, even in recruiting, training, and organizing its Pasdaran. It relied on revolutionary fervor and ideological pressure to support its recruiting until virtually the end of the war and never properly exploited its far larger population and manpower pool. It never brought an end to the feuding and lack of coordination between the Pasdaran and regular forces, and it continued to reward loyalty and belief, rather than professionalism. In many ways, the very adaptations of military organization and tactics that allowed Iran to succeed in early 1982 limited its success for the rest of the war.

In contrast, many of the problems in Saddam Hussein's approach to war that had cost Iraq so dearly during its invasion of Iran were far less serious once Iraq went on the defensive. While Iraq's static approach to war was to prolong the war for at least several years—and cost it dearly at Majnoon, Faw, and the later battles around Basra—it was increasingly able to exploit its superior access to arms deliveries. It also was able to exploit its advantage in firepower with far greater success.

While neither side ever developed a political leader that exhibited any great aptitude for war, it must be said to Saddam Hussein's credit that he understood the supply and technical issues in war better than his Iranian opponents. Iraq continued to improve its defenses and fortifications throughout the war. It built up immense stocks of weapons and supplies and consistently sought to improve their technical quality. Iraq steadily increased its road net, the numbers of its vehicles and tank transporters, and its ability to rapidly redeploy and supply its forces. While Iraq had only limited success until the last year of the war, it also constantly tried to improve the training of its armor, infantry, artillery, and airpower. Iraq's secular leadership not only aided its ability to develop and improve its forces, it ultimately was substantially more pragmatic in adapting to changing conditions than the religious leadership of Iran.

At the same time, Iraq's defensive victory had several additional strategic effects. It demonstrated that Saddam Hussein had the popular support and military capability to continue the war. It showed that Iraq's Shi'ites were no more ready to support Iran than Iran's Arabs had been to support Iraq. It showed the rest of the world that Iran did intend to try to conquer Iraq and that Saddam Hussein and his regime were worth supporting. This later proved critical in terms of Arab aid and in terms of Western and Soviet efforts to ensure that Khomeini would not conquer Iraq and dominate the Gulf. It helped lead the USSR to tilt back to Iraq, partly because of Iran's increasingly anti-Soviet attitude and persecution of the Tudeh. It helped lead France to provide more equipment and support, and it helped lead the U.S. to conduct a much more concerted effort to block arms transfers to Iran, called "Operation Staunch."

Iran's Fall Offensives of 1982

Iran's next offensive came against its own Kurds rather than Iraq. The Kurds in the Kurdish Democratic Party of Iran (KDPI) were now the only major ethnic group still at war with the Khomeini government, and it was clear that they were increasingly becoming a tool for Iraq. Iran reinforced its forces near Urumiyeh, and in September, Iranian regular army forces and Pasdaran launched a major attack on the KDPI. This offensive turned into a guerrilla battle that lasted until the weather forced a near halt to the fighting in November. The attacking Iranian forces pushed the KDPI forces back and took a number of towns and roads but left the Pesh Merga in control of the mountains along the border.

Iran's next offensive against Iraq came on October 1, 1982. It was called the Muslim Ibn Aguil (Moslem Ibne Aqhil) offensive and was intended to improve Iran's position near the border approaches to Baghdad by conquering some strategic heights in Iran overlooking the Iraqi town of Mandali, about 65 miles from Baghdad. The attack took place in the area around Naft e-Shah. This area, like that around Qasr e-Shirin, is one of the few parts of the border in the north where there is a large plain on the Iranian side, and a good road net leads from Iran toward the plains to the north of Baghdad. If this area is taken, an attacking force can drive southwest toward Mandali and Baghdad or north toward As Sa Diyah and Kirkuk.

There were roughly 40,000 men in the Iranian attack force, including Pasdaran brigades, and a regular army armored brigade. This force took time to assemble. Iraq detected it several days in advance and built up the forces available to the Iraqi 2nd Army in the area. The Pasdaran countered this by attacking on a broad front and were able to infiltrate close to the Iraqi positions they planned to attack by taking advantage of the cover provided by the relatively rough terrain.

The Pasdaran forces scored some initial successes and forced the Iraqi forces slowly back along the road from Sumar to Mandali. The Iraqi forces retreated slowly, however, and took advantage of the fact the Pasdaran had to expose themselves in order to use human-wave attacks. Iraq also seems to have again used some form of gas to help break up the Iranian assaults. The Iraqi forces also regrouped after each Pasdaran attack and counterattacked. The Iranian forces continued to press forward until October 6 but took heavy casualties and scored only token gains. At most, Iran gained about 50 square kilometers of the mountainous territory on the Iraqi side of the border above the Mandali plains.

Iran then launched another attack near Basra. This was called the Muharram al Harram (Moharram ol-Harram) offensive and began on November 1. It was intended to recapture the Iranian territory near the border that Iraq still held and to position Iran's forces to cut the

Baghdad-Basra road between Kut and the area northeast of Al Amarah.

This time Iraq seems to have had little warning, and the terrain did not permit rapid Iraqi reinforcement. The Pasdaran echelons also attacked at night. After about a week of fairly intense fighting, most of which was infantry combat, the Iranians crossed the Doverichj River and pushed to the Iraqi border near Beid. They gained about 350 square miles, of which about 190 were in Iraqi territory. Iran claimed to have taken some 3,500 prisoners of war, roughly 140 tanks and other armored vehicles, and 40 artillery weapons.[5]

Iran attacked again to the north near Mandali on November 7, and sporadic fighting took place near the border around Musain. The fighting continued for about ten days. Iran made limited gains but did not achieve any decisive results. The rains then set in and largely halted offensive action, although small patrol actions continued along much of the front, and artillery exchanges were common.

This pause in the fighting tended to favor Iraq. It continued to work on its network of defenses and extended them all along its border area as rapidly as possible. The Iraqi bunkers and fortifications became steadily more sophisticated. Many had recreation rooms, education rooms, small clinics, and even an occasional barbershop. The Iraqi regime also made sure that the forward positions were well supplied with both equipment and facilities, such as telephones and television.

As time went on, the Iraqi positions were defended by steadily greater numbers of mines and obstacles. The amount of supporting artillery increased, and more tanks were dug in to provide a direct-fire kill capability. While Iran also built barrier defenses, they never came close to the sophistication of the Iraqi defenses and never reflected anything like the same concern for the welfare and morale of individual soldiers.[6]

The domestic conditions in Iraq also continued to be somewhat better than those in Iran, although both regimes were highly repressive. In Iran, a massive hunt for the Mujahideen continued throughout the summer and fall of 1982. Although the Iranian government claimed to have suppressed the Mujahideen by late July—and some 5,000–6,000 people had been killed or executed during the fighting—bombings and explosions continued into December. The local revolutionary committees that were organized through Iran also began to put more and more pressure on Iran's citizens to conform to Islamic standards and to be at least publicly loyal to the revolution. They put increasing pressure on young men to volunteer to go to the front and began to raise money directly for the war.

At the same time, Khomeini expanded his crackdown on the Tudeh

Party. In August, the Iranian media began to publicly attack the Tudeh as anti-revolutionary, and mass arrests began in November. The Pasdaran continued to ruthlessly suppress any ethnic dissidents, and Pasdaran forces were brought into Tehran and Tabriz to help protect the regime.

On a more mundane level, the casualties from the war were now serious enough to affect many Iranian families. While the regime attempted to glorify martyrdom and even set up a fountain of red colored water it called a "fountain of blood," it was obvious that many of Iran's ordinary citizens had no desire to lose their sons. The cost of the war also forced Iran to cut imports, and a major black market built up that lasted throughout the war. Inflation became a serious problem, and so did corruption. By mid-1983, it had become obvious that the Khomeini regime was at least as corrupt in actual practice as the regime of the Shah.

Iraq too suffered from repression. The regime continued to try to court the Kurds and Shi'ites with high-level government posts and by funding ethnic and religious projects. At the same time, the secret police ruthlessly suppressed any active political opposition. Living standards in Iraq, however, were now much higher than in Iran, and consumer goods and services were cheaper and more readily available. The Iraqi government also continued to provide significant compensation to the families of those who had died in the war, although the quality of what was provided dropped and some special awards—like cars for the families of dead officers—often failed to be delivered.

The Impact of Arms Sales and New Developments in Iraq's Air Power

Iraq continued to have a distinct edge in terms of arms imports and resupply. Iraq was able to import some $3.7 billion worth of arms in 1981 and $4.3 billion worth of arms in 1982. Iran only imported $1.0 billion worth of arms in 1981 and $1.5 billion worth of arms in 1982.[7] This meant Iraq was getting more than three times as many arms as Iran, and Iraq was able to get far more in terms of supply and technology per dollar. Khomeini's crackdown on the Tudeh also ended the Soviet flirtation with Iran at an ideal time for Iraq. From September onwards, the USSR began to provide Iraq with all its back orders and with virtually all the new arms Iraq could pay for. This gave Iraq access to Soviet T-72 tanks, replacement fighters, new surface-to-air missiles, and more artillery.[8]

Equally importantly, France provided nearly 40 percent of its arms exports in 1982 to Iraq. Iraq's Mirage F-1 forces became operational and

Iraq soon used these fighters and French Magic 1 air-to-air missiles. This allowed Iraq to take advantage of the steady decline in Iran's operational air strength because of Iran's lack of spare parts and technical support. This gave Iraq increasing success in air-to-air combat. At the same time, the Mirage F-1 provided far better avionics for air-to-ground missions than any of Iraq's export versions of Soviet fighters. Iraq also acquired a new capability to attack Iranian shipping when France provided it with the ability to fire AM-39 Exocet missiles from its Super Frelon helicopters. These helicopters had relatively short range and could not reach most of Iran's oil traffic, but they set an important precedent in providing an air-launched weapons system that Iraq could use to attack without warning and with relatively little risk of intercept.

Iraq resumed its strategic bombing attacks on Iran in response to Iran's summer offensives. It claimed that it began these new air and missile strikes as a response to Iranian air strikes on Baghdad on July 21, but their goal was obviously broader. Iraq had begun to try to use its growing advantage in air power to push Iran toward a cease-fire or peace settlement, an effort which was to become steadily more important with time.

Iraq began this new strategic bombing campaign by launching a series of fighter, bomber, and FROG 7 strikes against Iranian cities. This raised the total number of FROGs that Iraq had fired at Dezful and Ahwaz since October 1980 to 64 missiles. Iraq then declared, on August 12, the northern Gulf to be a military exclusion zone and launched air strikes at Kharg Island on August 18, August 25, and September 17. Iraq also used helicopter-launched Exocet missiles against shipping in Iranian waters in the northern Gulf.

Iraq also launched its first Scud Bs against Iran during 1982. It began to launch these missiles against Dezful on October 27, killing 21 civilians and wounding several dozen others. Iraq fired two more Scuds and two more FROG-7s against Dezful on December 18, and Iran claimed that these caused 349 casualties. Iraq then went on to strike at Masjid e-Suleiman and Ramhourz. Iraq launched a total of 33 more Scuds in 1983, 25 in 1984, and 82 in 1985, plus two FROGs in 1984. These missiles did little more than kill and wound the civilians that happened to be in the area where the missiles hit, although they added a new terror weapon to Iraq's inventory.[9]

Iraq continued its air offensive against civilian and economic targets in Iran during December and January. On January 18, it launched what seems to have been intended as a major attack. Iraq claimed to have flown 66 bombing sorties. The real number was substantially larger, and Iraq sent in attack aircraft without adequate fighter escort and training in evading ground-based air defenses, and in some cases, Iraq seems to have sent aircraft out with insufficient maintenance and on missions at ranges where they ran out of fuel.

This mix of missile and air attacks was relatively large in scale by Iraq's standards, but they were poorly planned and targeted. The missiles lacked the targeting systems and accuracy to achieve any serious military effect. As for the bombing missions, Iraq still flew far too few sorties against any one target to be effective and still failed to follow up its strikes when it did achieve damage. As a result, Iraq's air effort did not achieve any significant strategic effect.

The Iranian Air Force replied to the Iraqi attacks during January 25 to 30 and showed it could still successfully penetrate Iraqi air space at low altitudes and hit many targets. The Iranian aircraft, however, rarely attacked with more than two or four aircraft per target, and Iraq's low-altitude air defenses and fighters also inflicted significant losses. The end result was something of a stalemate in the strategic bombing effort. While Iraq's air performance was improving as the result of Indian, Jordanian, and Egyptian advice, and Iraq now had considerable Soviet and French technical support, it still attacked as a scattered group of units rather than as a cohesive air force. Iran, in contrast, was still strong enough to deter Iraq by flying its own bombing missions but was too weak to achieve any real results. Further, every new loss of aircraft cut further into Iran's operational strength. According to some estimates, Iraq lost as many as 80 combat aircraft during January, and Iran lost 55.[10]

At this point in the war, Iraq had roughly 330 operational combat aircraft and large numbers of armed helicopters. These included 7–9 Tu-22 bombers and 5–8 IL-28 bombers. Iraq's air-attack forces include four squadrons with 70 MiG-23BMs, six squadrons with 70 Su-7s and Su-17(20)s, and one squadron with 12 obsolete Hunter attack aircraft. Iraq's air-defense forces included five squadrons with 14 MiG-25s, 40 MiG-19/F-6s, 70 MiG-21/F-7s, and over 30 new French Mirage F-1EQ and F-1BQs. Iraq had eight MiG-25 high-altitude reconnaissance aircraft.

These air-strength levels varied sharply according to the status of losses and resupply at any given time, but Iraq could normally fly 150–200 combat sorties per day. Iraq's armed helicopter strength is difficult to estimate because many armed helicopters were modifications, rather than designed as attack helicopters. Iraq did, however, have 13–41 operational Mi-24 attack helicopters, 6–47 Alouette IIIs armed with guns and AS-12 ASMs, and 15–50 Gazelles armed with HOT anti-tank guided missiles. Iraq obtained delivery of 11 Super Frelons equipped to fire AM-39 air-to-ship missiles.[11]

Iran's air strength is much harder to estimate. Its operational strength at the beginning of 1983 may have been anywhere from 70 to 120 operational aircraft, although it now seems likely that it began the year with over 100 operational aircraft and reached a low of 70–80 by mid-1983. Anywhere from 12 to 35 of its F-4D/Es may have been serviceable, 40–65 of its F-5E/Fs, 5 to 15 of its F-14As, and 3 to 5 of its 14 RF-4Es. Its operational combat helicopter holdings were well below 100 AH-1Js, 150 Bell 214As, 30 AB-205As and 206As, and 70 CH-47s.

Iran's operational strength also had a very different meaning from that of Iraq. Iran could peak its strength to levels close to 100 aircraft for one day and 30–50 aircraft for a week, but this meant rapidly losing operational capability for a month or more. Iran's need to vulturize its aircraft often presented serious problems. While Iran lied throughout the war about its progress in obtaining spares and manufacturing them in country, it never solved its spare parts and supply problems. Many of its aircraft had to be stripped to supply a critical part, and if the aircraft using the remaining part or parts were lost, Iran might have to spend days or weeks finding a replacement somewhere on the world arms market.[12] Throughout the war, the Iranian Air Force served as a lesson that it is not equipment inventory that counts in war but operational strength and sustainability.

The Iranian Air Force also was never able to establish its reliability as a "revolutionary" force. Defections of both Iranian military and civil aircraft took place in late 1982 and at sporadic intervals throughout 1983. Khomeini again changed the commander of the Iranian Air Force in April, and a minor coup attempt in May was blamed on Air Force personnel. Unlike the regular Iranian Army, the Air Force could not recruit and train revolutionary leaders and remained under extremely tight surveillance and political suspicion. Arrests continued, as did the practice of holding the family of pilots and aircrew hostage and restricting fuel to prevent defections. So many officers, pilots, and skilled personnel were imprisoned or lost that Iran lost far more aircraft to accidents and poor maintenance than combat.

Continuing Iranian Attempts to Invade Iraq Early in 1983

Iran began the land fighting in 1983 by launching its first Wal (Val)-Fajr offensive.[13] This offensive began in the Musain area, west of Dezful, on February 7, 1983. (See Figure 6.2.) The attack came to the north of the Hawizeh Marshes and drove across relatively dry and flat terrain toward Amara. The Iranians had five to six formations that were called divisions but which were the size of reinforced brigades. The bulk of the Iranian forces were Pasdaran units with

160

A. Location Relative to the Offensives of 1982

B. Main Offensive Thrust

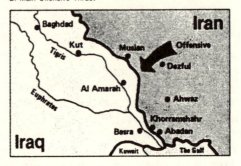

C. Scene of the Fighting

FIGURE 6.2 The First Iranian Offensive of 1983. Adapted from material provided by the CIA and in *Armed Forces Journal International*, May 1983, p. 43.

limited mechanized support, but there was one armored division or brigade. The total Iranian force was between 40,000 and 50,000 men. The Iraqi force in the area consisted of the 4th Army with the equivalent of about seven Iraqi divisions and 50,000 to 55,000 men.

The Iranian forces attacked at night, having deployed at a time when rain prevented major air and helicopter operations. The Iranian attack was divided into sequential thrusts of about two divisions each. Iran evidently sought to decoy Iraq into using all its reserves to attack the first thrust, while it then launched the second to cut the Basra-Baghdad road. In practice, however, the Iraqi commander kept his forces behind the main Iraqi defensive line. This line was one of the best built-up positions on the front north of Basra, and the Iraqi's turned it into a killing ground for the advancing echelons of Pasdaran infantry, which did not penetrate Iraq's main defenses.

As the morning went on, Iraq was also able to make extensive use of armed helicopters and attack aircraft, including its new Mirage F-1s. The Iranian forces were often exposed enough for the Iraqi air attacks to be unusually effective. Iraq was able to use aircraft and helicopter gunships in battlefield support missions with more effectiveness against targets advancing against a static front on its own territory and where it had time to both erect large defensive barriers and to concentrate its superior armor and firepower to counterattack and push Iran back. Iraq claimed to fly well over 150 sorties per day, and these claims seem to have been justified. It also launched a limited number of attacks against Iranian cities in reprisal for the Iranian offensive by hitting targets in Ahwaz, Dezful, and Khorramshahr.

In spite of heavy losses, Iran repeated its human-wave attacks that afternoon and again on February 8. The next day, Iran committed the 92nd Armored Division to an attack in an area where Iraq had only limited manpower. Although this division seems to have had less than two full brigades of tanks, it punched through the Iraqi defense positions, but it then advanced into the open plain without infantry support. The end result was that the division was counterattacked by Iraq armor, and the forward elements were surrounded by Iraqi infantry. Iran lost at least one brigade element, while another surrendered.

The fighting ended around February 10, and Iran gained little other than a strip of a few kilometers along the less-defended part of the border area that was to the east of the main Iraqi defenses. The total casualties on both sides ranged anywhere from 10,000 to 15,000. As many as half of the casualties were killed, with Iran losing about three times as many men as Iraq.

Iraq launched a counteroffensive near Shahrani in the central sector in late March 1983 but made no gains. Iran then launched another attack in the Musain area. The attack took place on April 10 and lasted until April 17. It was intended to recapture the heights in a 30-kilometer stretch along the front north of Fuka. It scored some gains near the border area, and Iran took roughly 400 Iraqi prisoners of war, but the offensive also cost both sides some 4,000–7,000 casualties.[14]

Iraq launched a number of new FROG, Scud, and air strikes on Iranian civilian targets in May and attempted again to call for a cease-fire on the ground that this would protect civilians. It also unsuccessfully sought a truce for the month of Ramadan. While Iran had clearly taken serious losses of personnel, including experienced officers and NCOs, and of equipment, the Iranian government was still committed to pressing ahead with its invasion of Iraq.

Each side's relative ability to import arms, however, was becoming a steadily more critical issue. The dollar value of arms-import trends affecting the Gulf war at this point in the conflict are shown in Figure 6.3 and Table 6.1. It is important to note that Iraq had an effective monopoly in being able to buy the most modern military technology and modern weapons systems. Although Iraq had now lost more than 100 jet fighters and over 2,000 tanks and armored personnel carriers, its continuing arms purchases allowed it to increase its total number of major weapons and its stockpiles in spite of these losses.

Iran managed to get some arms and military supplies through Syria, Libya, and Israel, and it increasingly turned to states outside the region, such as the PRC and North Korea. Nevertheless, Iran's combat losses and its lack of spare parts had gradually reduced Iran's operational air strength from over 400 operational aircraft at the time of the Shah's fall to as low as 70 by mid-1983. Iran could not support high sortie rates for these aircraft and was forced to limit their use to defensive purposes and to protecting key points, such as airfields, refineries, important cities, and economic installations. Even then, Iran could only provide limited coverage and was unable to provide air cover for its troops or meaningful air support.

Iran did, however, retain two major advantages in other areas: superior oil earnings and a far greater capacity to sustain casualties. Iran retained its religious and revolutionary fervor. It used this fervor to expand the naval and air branches of the Pasdaran it had started in 1982. More importantly, it used it to further build up its land forces along the border and then deploy its forces over a wider area.

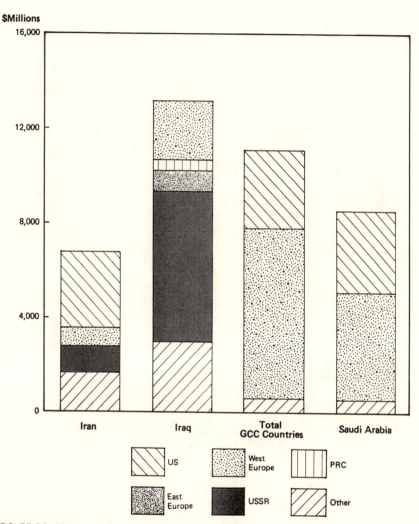

FIGURE 6.3 Major Arms Sales to the Gulf States: 1979–1983. Adapted from U.S. Arms Control and Disarmament Agency data.

TABLE 6.1 The Impact of Arms Imports on the Iran-Iraq War

A. Near Term Annual Trends in Gulf Arms Imports (in current $millions)

IMPORTING NATION	1972	1974	1976	1978	1980	1982	1984
Iran	525	1,000	2,000	2,200	400	1,300	1,600
Iraq	140	625	1,000	1,600	1,600	4,300	3,800
Iran-Iraq Total	665	1,625	3,000	3,800	2,000	5,600	5,400
Saudi Arabia	100	340	440	1,300	1,800	2,600	2,700
Kuwait	5	10	80	300	40	130	100
Bahrain	—	—	—	—	80	40	80
Qatar	—	—	5	20	90	250	200
UAE	10	50	100	50	170	40	220
Oman	5	10	10	270	100	100	120
GCC Total	120	410	635	1,940	2,280	3,160	3,420
TOTAL	780	2,035	3,635	5,740	4,280	8,760	8,820

B. Gulf Arms Imports by Importing Country (in Current $millions): 1979–1983

Importing Nation	TOTAL	Seller Nation										
		USSR	US	France	UK	FRG	Italy	Czech	Poland	Romania	China	Others
Iran	5,365	975	1,200	20	140	5	150	–	40	5	230	2,600
Iraq	17,620	7,200	–	3,800	280	140	410	40	850	400	1,500	3,000
Sub-Total	22,985	8,175	1,200	3,820	420	145	560	40	890	405	1,730	5,600
Saudi Arabia	12,125	–	5,100	2,500	1,900	525	200	–	–	–	–	1,900
Kuwait	450	30	180	–	50	70	110	–	–	–	–	10
Bahrain	120	–	10	40	–	40	10	–	–	–	–	20
Qatar	765	–	10	440	310	–	–	–	–	–	–	5
UAE	620	–	20	350	90	110	30	–	–	–	–	20
Oman	565	–	80	20	430	–	10	–	–	–	5	20
GCC Total	14,645	30	5,400	3,350	2,780	745	360	–	–	–	5	1,975
TOTAL	37,630	8,205	6,600	7,170	3,200	890	920	40	890	405	1,740	7,575

SOURCE: Data provided by the U.S. Arms Control and Disarmament Agency.

Further Iranian Attacks on the Kurds
and the Wal-Fajr 2 Offensive

Iran seems to have had the goal of overstretching Iraq's limited manpower resources and of exploiting Baghdad's political vulnerability to casualties through a war of attrition. Iran launched a new offensive on July 23, 1983, in the Piranshahr area of the northern sector of the front and along a 30-kilometer stretch between two Kurdish towns called Sardasht and Piranshahr. This attack was called the Wal-Fajr 2 offensive and was linked to an earlier offensive in mid-March against the pro-Iraqi and anti-Khomeini KDPI forces led by Abdul Rahman Ghassemlou. During this offensive, Iranian regular and Pasdaran forces had attacked the KDPI forces with a local superiority of over 4:1 in manpower and vastly superior firepower. They drove the remaining KDPI forces out of their positions near Baqqez, Bukhan, and Mahabad and consolidated many of the gains Iran had made against the KDPI the previous fall.

The Iranian forces that now attacked Iraq as part of Wal-Fajr 2 included about two divisions, plus independent Pasdaran forces and Kurdish Democratic Party (KDP) forces of about a battalion in size. The Iranian forces infiltrated the Iraqi and anti-Iranian Kurdish positions in the Ruwandez Valley and then overran them with human-wave assaults. The Pasdaran attacked through rough terrain which had considerable natural cover. They also seem to have had considerable intelligence and scouting assistance from the KDP. After about five days of fighting, and at least one major Iraqi counterattack, the Iranians were able to advance about ten miles forward into Iraq. This advance also took place even though the Iraqis seem to have made use of mustard gas against some of the KDP forces. Iran captured the Iraqi 1st Corps garrison of Haj Omran, the main heights and artillery positions in the area, some 43 Kurdish villages, a major headquarters of the KDPI, and much of the KDPI's equipment.

The territory Iran took was not of great significance, but Wal-Fajr 2 marked the end of much of the anti-Khomeini Kurdish resistance in Iran. It gave Khomeini an excuse to declare the existence of a government in exile on Iraqi soil. More importantly, it gave Iran far better ability to use anti-Iraqi Kurds against Saddam Hussein and to attack areas dominated by Kurdish factions hostile to Iraq.[15] These anti-Iraqi factions consisted primarily of the KDP factions led by the Barzanis, but the Patriotic Union of Kurdistan (PUK) forces under Talabani had largely ceased to support the KDPI. As a result, a large part of the anti-Iraqi Kurd groups were now actively engaged in campaigns against both Iraq and Turkey.[16]

In fact, the PUK was so successful in the areas along Iraq's border with Turkey that Turkey had to restructure much of its 2nd Army to guard the Iraqi-Turkish pipeline and the road along it. While the pipeline continued to be defended by pro-government Kurds, the Turks now had to station Army forces in the area and to force the evacuation of Kurdish villages. Turkey also reached a joint security agreement with Iraq in late April.

This agreement effectively allowed Turkey to compensate for Iraq's lack of manpower in the north by pursuing PUK forces onto Iraqi territory. It also led to major Turkish raids against the PUK in May, August, and September. These raids were effective enough to eventually force Talabani to begin negotiations with Baghdad for a compromise agreement where he would give up the search for independence for increased Kurdish autonomy. Talabani signed a cease-fire with the Iraqi government in December.

The Wal-Fajr 3 Offensive near Mehran

Iran launched its Wal Fajr-3 offensive on July 30 in the area near Mehran. This offensive was intended to clear the heights above Mehran. Iraq had evacuated the town in late June but had kept the heights surrounding the roads between Dehloran and Mehran and between Ilam and Mehran. The attack began against the forces of the Iraqi 2nd Corps in the area along the Dehloran-Mehran Road and drove forward into the border area near the Badra Dam and Doraji in Iraq. This time the Iranian attack was able to take advantage of rough terrain on the edge of the Iranian plateau, which offered the Pasdaran considerably better protection and concealment than the open plains to the south.

Iraq had ample warning of the attack, and Iraqi armor and aircraft attempted to counterattack the Iranian forces as they assembled for the offensive. Iran had some 35,000 men in the area, however, and were already in good defensive positions. The Iraqi spoiling attack failed and left the Iraqi forces off balance when the Iranian offensive began.

Wal 3-Fajr then became a fight for each successive defensive position, and the resulting fighting lasted until August 10. According to some reports, Iraq used helicopters and fighter-bombers to deliver mustard gas against the Iranian forces. A French source indicates that the initial attacks failed because they were delivered without adequate attention to the wind conditions and because the heavy gas tended to flow down the side of the heights and away from the Iranian positions.

Iraq also succeeded in reinforcing its forces during this period, but it could not counterattack successfully. Iraq lacked the kind of open fire zones that had allowed it to be successful in the south, and its air power and artillery fire were considerably less effective. The battle produced a total of between 10,000 and 17,000 casualties.[17]

While Iran did not score a major victory, it pushed forward about eight to ten kilometers and took control of more than 100 square kilometers in the eastern heights above Mehran. The battle also demonstrated that the Pasdaran could continue to make at least limited gains if they picked the right terrain, and Iraq had taken nearly as many casualties as Iran.

At the same time, however, the Wal-Fajr 3 attack showed that while Iran was steadily modifying its tactics in using human-wave attacks, it could not change the fundamental problems it faced in exploiting any initial success unless Iraqi commanders made serious mistakes. Iran tried to avoid massive, direct human-wave assaults against well-defended Iraqi positions and shifted to smaller attacks at a number of different weak points along the border. Iran lacked the strength and command-and-control capability, however, to launch more than one major assault at a time. Iran's attacks also usually developed slowly. This meant they provided Iraq with considerable warning and that they moved at a pace, and with a concentration of force, that gave Iraq ample time to react. Even when Iran scored initial offensive successes, it still could not exploit them against well-prepared Iraqi positions, and Iraq now had such defenses in most strategically vital areas.

Iran also had increasing problems in equipping its ground forces. While estimates differ sharply, Iran now had about 300,000 full-time regulars, including reserves and conscripts. It had roughly the same number of Pasdaran and Baseej. This gave it a total force of three corps. Depending upon the source, these were organized into as many as 21 divisions, 12 armored and mechanized units, and a number of airborne and special forces elements of up to brigade size. The regular army had about 8 divisions out of this total.

Estimates of Iran's equipment holdings are equally uncertain, but they seem to have included 700 to 1,000 operational main battle tanks: roughly 190–340 Soviet and North Korean T-54, T-55, and T-72, 200 Chieftain, and up to 300 M-47/48/60 tanks. Iran had anywhere from 500 to 1,000 operational other armored vehicles, including a growing number of BMP armored fighting vehicles. It had about 1,000 major artillery pieces. Even by regional standards, this was only about one-third the major equipment needed for a force of 600,000 men.[18] While Iran had begun to receive major arms deliveries from North Korea and had captured considerable equipment from Iraq, its equipment losses were often as high as its manpower losses. Iranian ground forces also continued to lack the logistic support, air cover, and mobile artillery to exploit their occasional penetrations of Iraq's forward defenses.

Iraq, in contrast, had at least 475,000 to 575,000 men, or near parity with Iran in manpower. The regular army had four major corps and about 15 division equivalents, including six armored, four mechanized, and six regular mountain and infantry divisions. Iraq also steadily improved its Republican Guard brigades since early 1981 and corrected a number of the deficiencies in the Popular Army, which now contributed 15 additional brigades. Iraq had around 2,500 operational main battle tanks, 3,000 other armored fighting vehicles, including large numbers of BMPs, and 1,100–1,500 artillery weapons.[19]

Iraq also continued to receive a steady flow of arms and munitions. It saturated its forces with anti-aircraft guns to provide high volumes of fire against Iranian infantry, deployed large numbers of Western anti-tank guided missiles like HOT and Milan, and continued to build up both its Soviet-made land-based air defenses and its strength of French Rolands. Unlike Iran, Iraq's land forces also had massive modern support and training facilities. Iraq continued to lead in improving its already sophisticated fixed defenses and was able to set up vast supply dumps in virtually every part of the front.

It is doubtful that Khomeini or most of those around him understood these trends in the balance or would have cared if they had. Even when Iran was defeated in achieving its major objective, it usually took some territory. Iranian forces often seemed to be on the edge of a breakthrough, even during the worst tactical reversals. Even though Iraq's forces showed relatively good morale, and its Shi'ites remained loyal, it seems likely that Iran's leadership felt their ability to launch large-scale Pasdaran and Baseej infantry assaults was still a way that Iran could eventually shatter Iraq's defenses by exploiting what they perceived to be Iraq's weakening economy, internal divisions, and inferior ability to take casualties.

Iran's losses during the first six months of 1983 did, however, lead Khomeini to reduce the ability of the Mullahs and religious commissars to interfere with operations at the front. Khomeini also made continuing efforts and public statements to reassure the regular forces that they had the same importance as the Pasdaran. Nevertheless, Khomeini had mixed success. The Mullahs and the leaders of the Revolutionary Guards in Tehran continued to exaggerate Iraq's vulnerability in much the same way that Saddam Hussein and his colleagues had exaggerated Iran's vulnerability earlier in the war.

The Mullahs and more radical leaders of the Pasdaran and Baseej had sufficient power to prevent Iran from developing both a cohesive command structure and concept of operations and continued to try to substitute ideological fervor for strategy, tactics, and training. Iraq, in contrast, continued to respond by exploiting its superior ability to import arms and military technology. It continued to obtain the external financing it needed to survive, and it built up an improved capability to reduce or cripple Iran's ability to export through the Gulf.

The War in the Gulf Resumes

The Wal-Fajr 3 attack had another major strategic effect on the war. The conditions that had led to a near cease-fire in the Gulf since late 1980 had ended. Iraq's leaders decided to expand the war by attacking the shipping and tanker traffic moving to and from Iran. Iraq had several objectives in mind in starting what later came to be called the "War of the Tankers." Iraq's leadership realized that Iran was having problems in funding its arms imports and critical civil imports like food. Striking at tankers and offshore oil facilities seemed to be an ideal way of striking at Iran's economic lifeblood without risking the kind of reprisals that might occur from attacks on Iranian cities.

Iraq also felt that it was now far less vulnerable to Iranian attack on its oil exports. Both Iran and Iraq had sought to create export capacity through Turkey shortly after the war began, and Iraq began to actively consider plans to link its pipeline system to the Saudi lines going to the new Saudi port on the Red Sea and to expand its pipeline to a refinery near Amman in Jordan to reach the Jordanian port of Aqaba. Iran, however, could not find the money to fund a new pipeline through Turkey, and Iraq could offer Turkey substantial construction and transit fees to expand the capacity of its existing pipeline to over one million barrels a day.

Turkey and Iraq signed an agreement to carry out such an expansion in February 1983, with a scheduled completion date in 1984. Iraq also obtained Saudi agreement to provide an additional 1 MMBD link to the Saudi system, plus Saudi and Kuwaiti agreement to market up to 350,000 barrels per day of their oil, for Iraq, as part of a loan that was later to be repaid in oil. While the pipeline link to Aqaba fell through when the U.S. would not guarantee its security against Israeli attacks, Iraq was still able to plan on the basis it would be able to export at least as much oil as Iran at some point in the next few years.

Finally, Iraq concluded that it could not mobilize world opinion in favor of peace unless it could broaden the war. Some Iraqi spokesmen were publicly accusing the superpowers of encouraging the war to weaken both Iraq and Iran at this time, but it seems likely that the leadership in both countries had more sophisticated goals in mind. Broadening the war meant bringing in both the southern Gulf states and Western oil-importing states into the periphery of the war. It was also clear that Iran might well overreact and take a relatively xenophobic stand. Iraq not only proved to be right in this calculation, it eventually found Iran's inability to deal with other states to be as great a strategic vulnerability as Iraq's dependence on oil-exporting facilities in the Gulf had been at the start of the war.[20]

Iraq's Threats to Halt Iran's Oil Traffic

Tariq Aziz warned on July 1 that Iraq would attack economic targets in Iran if Iran did not halt its attacks on Iraq. This warning came after many previous threats that Iraq would use new weapons in the oil war, but this time the threats had substance. Iraq had already received Exocet air-to-ship missiles from France but could only launch them using short-range helicopters which could not cover targets east of Bandar-e-Khomeini. It lacked a delivery system with the range to attack naval targets as far away as Iranian oil ports. In January 1983, however, France had agreed to supply Iraq with five Super Etendard jet fighters. While the Super Etendard aircraft were still limited in range to a radius of about 360–380 nautical miles and could not reach naval targets in the lower Gulf, they had more than enough range to enable Iraq to threaten Iran's oil exports by attacking tankers in the waters near Iran's main export facility at Kharg Island. (See Figure 6.4.)

Iraq declared a formal "exclusion zone" on August 12, 1983. Iraq then warned foreign shipping to stay clear of all Iranian waters in the upper Gulf on August 15, including the waters around Kharg Island from which Iran was then exporting up to 2 MMBD. This forced Iran to respond on August 19 with a declaration that it would protect foreign shipping, institute an escort policy for foreign ships, and deploy ships with surface-to-air missiles at Kharg.

Iraq did little initially to actually attack ships, but it began to make exaggerated claims of air strikes that were clearly designed to deter foreign ships from loading at Kharg. These claims and threats, however, had no immediate effect upon the Iranian leadership or most of the world's tanker fleets, although Iran did to try to persuade France not to transfer the Super Etendard aircraft.

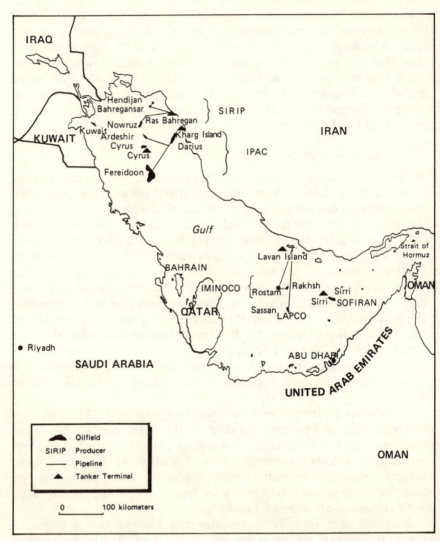

FIGURE 6.4 Iran's Vulnerable Loading Points in the Oil War. *Source:* U.S. Defense Mapping Agency.

The Limitations of Threats and Limited Escalation

The Super Etendards were delivered in late September 1983, in spite of Iranian protests. Iraq confirmed the fact they had arrived on October 9. As might have been expected, however, the deployment of the Super Etendards did no more to alter Iranian behavior in Iraq's favor than previous Iranian threats. Like most forms of limited escalation, the Super Etendards did as much to keep the conflict going as they did to terminate it.

The reasons for this failure provide some important insights into the problems inherent in the use of limited escalation in modern war. The first reason Iraq failed to have its desired impact on Iran was insufficiency of force. Iraq made its threats months before it actually could use the aircraft, which were not actually put into operation until March 1984. It then could not find and damage enough tankers to convince Iran that its threats were credible. In fact, from the introduction of the Super Etendards to the point where Iraq finally made extensive use of missiles and poison gas, Iraq never used sufficient force in any of its efforts at escalation to make the transition from harassment to achieving a significant strategic effect.

Second, Saddam Hussein and his colleagues confused the use of new forms of force, and/or the new technology, with the level of force that could confront an enemy state with a situation where prolonging the conflict at a similar or higher level of force was so much worse than agreeing on a peace or cease-fire that it would actually change national behavior. Mere novelty is not enough.

Third, Iraq ignored the level of commitment to the war that was already evident in Iran's words and actions. Limited escalation and graduated response usually fail to achieve their objective once states have become committed to full-scale conflict unless it is apparent that such limited increases in force can and will lead to far more decisive uses of force.

Fourth, Iraq failed to be realistic about the probable effectiveness of its own actions. Iraq exaggerated the effect of its attacks on Iran. It also assumed that Iran would view the attacks from the same perspective as Iraq and see the process of escalation with Iraq's logic. Like most states under similar circumstances, however, Iran saw the limited impact of such attacks as being as much a sign of Iraqi weakness as a sign of strength. The shock effect of new forms of attack was quickly dissipated when these attacks took place in limited numbers and produced limited damage.

This kind of response to limited escalation has been typical of inter-state conflicts since the first bombings of civilian targets in World War

I, and it is important to note that the U.S. made similar mistakes in its "Rolling Thunder" campaign in Vietnam as the USSR did in attacking the Afghan population in the latter years of its war in Afghanistan. It is a grim warning that (a) escalation must be high enough to achieve a decisive tactical or strategic effect, (b) the enemy must have no alternative that is even approximately as attractive as continuing the war on its own terms, and (c) it is the enemy's attitudes and frame of reference that determine the success of the new form of attack and not those of the side that is escalating.

The Impact of Iraq's Threats in Broadening the War

Iraq did eventually prove to be correct, however, in thinking that it could use the tanker war to broaden the war to include the southern Gulf states and superpowers. Further, Iraq was correct in believing that it could step up the "tanker war" with only pro forma protests from the USSR and the West. While oil prices still remained relatively high, the oil supply already significantly exceeded demand. Iran had alienated the Soviet Union, and key Western states had strong strategic and financial reasons to back Iraq. The U.S. feared the impact of an Iranian victory on the stability of northern and southern Gulf states far more than it feared the impact of Iraq's action on the flow of oil, and Iran was extraordinarily unpopular in U.S. official circles.

France had similarly favorable strategic interests in the survival of a secular regime in Iraq and strong financial incentives as well. French military sales to Iraq had reached $5.6 billion since September 1980, plus $4.7 billion in civilian and commercial contracts. At least $7 billion of this total was in the form of French loans and credits which would be at risk if the present regime were to be replaced by one strongly under Iranian influence.

This left Iran with little other response than to make its own threats to widen the war to include the southern Gulf and to close the Straits of Hormuz. Rafsanjani even went so far as to outline alternatives, such as using anti-ship missiles, the 120-mm guns on the Iranian islands in the Straits, mines, and sinking blockade ships. Iran then moved some small detachments of Pasdaran to Larak, Hengin, and Sirri Islands in the Straits. It also built up its artillery and anti-aircraft installations on Qesham and Greater Tumb Islands and established an expanded presence on Farsi Island.

The U.S. responded by strengthening its naval forces in the Gulf region and warned that Washington would not allow Iran to close the Gulf. France agreed to speed up its arms deliveries, and the USSR continued to increase its support of Iraq.

U.S. planners concluded that they could halt any Iranian effort to close the Straits or halt the export of oil in a matter of days. U.S. planners based this conclusion on four main factors: First, Iran had little operational air power; second, most U.S.-supplied Iranian surface-to-air and anti-ship missiles now had limited effectiveness; third, any Iranian artillery positions near the Straits could be quickly suppressed; and fourth, the Straits were too wide and deep and had currents too strong to be easily closed. As later events showed, however, these calculations did not take account of the transfer of new missiles by other countries, the creation of a large naval guerrilla-warfare capability, and the vulnerability of Gulf shipping to a much broader pattern of mine warfare and anti-shipping attacks throughout the Gulf.

The Wal-Fajr 4 Offensive Takes Place near Panjwin

Iran quickly demonstrated that it had no intention to halt its land offensives in response to the tanker war. Iranian forces crossed into Iraq in the Marivan area in mid-September, and Iran launched its fourth major offensive of 1983 near Panjwin on October 19. This offensive occurred in the Iranian part of Kurdistan, to the east of Sulaimaniyeh and along a 130-kilometer area between Marivan and Sardahst. The offensive involved two to three Iranian divisions (some Iraqi reports refer to 21st and 24th armored divisions and elements of the Pasdaran), plus forces from the KDP and other anti-Iraqi groups.

The offensive was directed at two mountain passes which the Iraqis were using to supply Ghassemlou's Kurdish Democratic Party (KDP), the Iraqi positions in the Panjwin Valley, and the Iraqi garrison towns of Panjwin and Garmak in Iraqi Kurdistan. These positions were about 144 kilometers from the Kirkuk oil fields and 48 kilometers from Sulaimaniyeh.

Iran claimed it was trying to put its own border towns of Baneh and Marivan out of Iraqi artillery range and that it was striking at counter-revolutionaries supporting Iraq, who seemed to have been Iranian Kurds. Iraq claimed that attacks were directed at its Kirkuk fields and at isolating its Kurdish areas. Iraq launched new missile attacks on Iranian cities in the south—Dezful and Masjid e-Suleiman—and claimed to have mined the shipping routes to Bandar-e-Khomeini. Iraq also seems to have experimented with mustard gas-attacks on October 2 and October 25, using both its Mi-8 helicopters and Soviet attack fighters to deliver bombs, although the validity of these claims is unclear.[21]

While the full details of the fighting remain obscure, a number of trends clearly emerged that later proved to be important. Iran, as usual, infiltrated its forces into forward positions and attacked at night. This time, however, Iran attacked with more than a dozen primary and secondary thrusts along a broad enough front to prevent Iraq from rapidly concentrating its defenses. It took good advantage of the mountain terrain and made use of its infantry to launch well-targeted assaults against Iraqi positions.

Iran's initial success showed that the proper use of volunteers to charge machine guns or walk over mine fields still made sound military sense if it was directed at achievable, well-defined, and practical goals, kept within careful limits, the resulting penetrations were properly exploited, and the fighting had a well-chosen and meaningful objective. While Iraq counterattacked and flew up to 122 fighter and attack-helicopter sorties per day, it could not halt the Iranian advance. Iran was able to use human-wave assaults to advance steadily up the Panjwin Valley for nearly 15 kilometers between October 19 and 24, and it took five more camps operated by the KDPI.

The Iranians launched a second wave of attacks on October 25 and forced the Iraqis to retreat to positions outside Panjwin. By October 31, Iran had retaken about 80–110 square kilometers of Iranian soil. Iran claimed to have destroyed large elements of the Iraqi 49th Armored Brigade and other elements of the Iraqi 1st Corps.[22] Iran claimed to have killed 2,800 Iraqis, while Iraq claimed to have killed 5,000 Iranians.

On November 4, Iran launched its third wave of attacks. It infiltrated the mountains and hillsides immediately above Panjwin and attempted to take the town. Iraq, however, was already rushing reinforcements into the area and deployed elements of its elite Republican Guards to Panjwin. Iran took heavy casualties in attempting to seize the town and the fighting died down by November 9. While Iran launched a new attack to consolidate its gains in the mountains on the Iraqi side of the border on November 19, the Iraqi 1st Corps was able to create new defensive positions.

Iran still failed to properly control the exploitation of its initial successes. Rather than continue to infiltrate and advance on a broad axis and wear the Iraqis down in a series of carefully calculated blows, Iran kept trying for dramatic and rapid breakthroughs against heavily defended areas. As a result, Iran suffered serious casualties. While the total number of killed in Wal-Fajr 4 did not reach anything like the 15,000 level claimed by Iraq, it may well have approached 7,000 to 10,000. It also seems fairly clear that Iraq did use mustard gas to help defeat at least some of the Iranian assaults and that this time its use of gas was effective. Iran later claimed up to several thousand casualties as the result of these gas attacks.

By the end of November, the net impact of more than a month of fighting was that Iran had pushed forward 20 to 25 kilometers into Iraq's mountains and conquered about 130–200 square kilometers of Iraqi territory. Iran had moved to within a mile of Panjwin and gained control of the Chilere salient. This put Iranian forces within 120–130 kilometers of Iraq's pipeline to Turkey, which originates near the city of Kirkuk. Iran also captured or destroyed 400 tanks and other armored vehicles, 20 artillery weapons, 20 AA gun and surface-to-air missile (SAM) batteries, large amounts of ammunition, 33,000 mine detectors, and 1,800 POWs.

The attack did not, however, result in a major defeat of Iraqi forces. Iran's gains still did not give it a good territorial springboard for a future attack and breakthrough, although they had further reduced the tenuous ability of the KDPI to conduct any kind of military operations in the Kurdish parts of Iran. Iran also did little to demonstrate it could counter Iraq's advantage in armor and air power once its forces had penetrated far beyond its starting point and cost Iran significant amounts of its own equipment.

All in all, 1983 was not a good year for Iran. In human terms, its offensives had brought the cost of the war to about 245,000 killed (65,000 Iraqis and up to 180,000 Iranians), with three to five times as many wounded, and some 50,000 Iraqis and 8,000 Iranians taken prisoner. It was also during these battles that the first major Iraqi use of chemical weapons was reported, and Iran began to launch major protests to the UN.[23]

Iran's offensives also continued to fail in two critical areas where Iran had to be successful if it was to defeat Iraq. Iran's first failure was that it did not carry out the the kind of mass national mobilization that would give it a decisive advantage in trained manpower. This failure to mobilize a decisive advantage in manpower numbers and to keep Iran's manpower at the front long enough to turn it into a trained force seems to have stemmed from several causes: (a) divisions within the Iranian armed forces, particularly between the regular forces inherited from the Shah and the new revolutionary forces, (b) the cost of such mobilization to the Iranian economy, (c) an ideological belief in the efficacy of revolutionary war and single "final offensives" on the part of the leadership elite, (d) a lack of sufficient supplies of weapons and military equipment, and (e) the fear that such mobilization would have to be forced upon the people and then would either have to totally successful in defeating Iraq or threaten popular support for the revolution.

Iran's second failure was that it still gave Iraq far too much time and ability to concentrate its forces. Attacking at several points on a broad front increased Iraq's difficulties, but it presented far fewer difficulties than a simultaneous attack on multiple fronts. This Iranian failure to launch simultaneous major offensives on several fronts was a natural result of Iran's failure to carry out mass mobilization. It was also the result of Iran's lack of supplies and logistics organization, its problems in organizing any activity on this scale in the midst of a divided revolution, the problems inherent in coordinating Pasdaran and regular army efforts, and Iran's lack of modern equipment.

Iraq, in contrast, steadily improved its use of fortified defensive positions during 1983 and exhibited a slowly growing capability to handle limited counterattacks, trade space for time, and regroup after an attack. Iraq's forces remained overcautious and rarely exploited Iran's mistakes with major counterattacks or pressed such attacks home. Iraq also had the benefit of an organization whose leadership and manpower were far more stable than that of Iran and which could benefit from experience, a steadily growing advantage of superior access to heavy weapons, and superior strength in operational aircraft and helicopters.

Iraq was not, however, able to make more effective use of its air and missile power to attack civil, economic, and naval targets. When the new wave of Iranian offensives continued through October, and Iran launched several follow-up attacks in November, Iraq retaliated by mining the port of Bandar-e-Khomeini and attacking Dezful, Masjid e-Suleiman and Behbehan with Scud B surface-to-surface missiles. Iran did not slow its attacks, however, and attempted to reply in kind. When Iraq's elite Presidential Guard was committed to the battles around Panjwin on November 5, 1983, Iranian artillery hit at civilian targets in Basra the next day. Both Iraq and Iran issued propaganda that claimed their respective attacks had a major impact on the morale of their opponent. In fact, the attacks did little more than stiffen public support for continuing the war and strengthened the opposing regime.

The Wal-Fajr 5, Wal-Fajr 6, and Operation Kheiber Offensives of 1984

Iran attempted to correct one of the major failings in its offensive tactics when it launched a new series of attacks in early 1984. It shifted from an emphasis on using favorable terrain and broad front attacks in the north to multiple attacks in the central and southern parts of the front. In February 1984, Iran launched four thrusts against Iraq. While there was only one major line of advance, these thrusts did create a more serious problem for Iraq in concentrating its forces than Iran's previous offensives.

The first Iranian thrust was a limited offensive by Iranian-supported PUK forces on February 12 in the area near Nowdesheh. The PUK made limited gains, but the attack tied up a significant amount of Iraqi forces and allowed Iran to pin down a significant number of Iraqi troops at very little cost. It also showed that the "Kurdish balance" had shifted, and it was pro-Iranian Kurds that were to be on the offensive until the cease-fire in 1988. The Iraqi-supported KDPI movement had lost virtually all of its ability to operate in Iran, had lost some 27,000 dead, and was now little more than an support element of the Iraqi forces on the northern front.

The main three Iranian thrusts came in the south. Iran had built up forces variously estimated at from 250,000 to 350,000 men, with a total of 25–33 divisions and brigades. These forces were deployed along a broad front covering Dehloran, Mehran, and the Hawizeh Marshes. This gave Iran the option of striking at a wide range of points along the Baghdad-Basra Road or of cutting off Basra from the north.

Iran started the offensive by launching two limited Wal-Fajr attacks, which acted as something of a diversion, and then a major new offensive called Operation Kheiber. The first Wal-Fajr attack began along a 50-kilometer front between Dehloran and Mehran and to the east of Al Kut. This attack was launched from positions near Mehran on the night of February 15–16 and was called Wal-Fajr 5.

Wal-Fajr 5 was directed at the positions of the Iraqi 2nd Corp, which had something on the order of nine divisions and about 100,000 men. The attack was intended to either cut the Basra-Baghdad Road or attack Baqubah on a key road from Tehran to Baghdad. Like Basra, Baqubah was a heavily fortified city defended by arcs of earthen berms and bunkers and with extensive artillery fire points and supply depots in the rear. The Iranian forces participating in Wal-Fajr 5 consisted largely of Pasdaran and Baseej and took some Iraqi villages and a number of positions in the hills above the plains along the Basra-Baghdad Highway.

The second Wal-Fajr attack was called Wal-Fajr 6 and began near Dehloran on February 21. Iranian forces attacked the Iraqi-held heights near the Basra-Baghdad Road near Ali al-Gharbi. Neither Wal-Fajr 5 or Wal-Fajr 6 scored more than limited gains, but their main purpose was to try to force Iraq to redeploy its forces from the south.

The fourth Iranian thrust was called Operation Kheiber. This attack had far more serious goals than either Wal-Fajr 5 or Wal-Fajr 6. It was intended to achieve a major strategic surprise by driving through the Hawizeh (Hur el-Howeyzeh) Marshes.[24] As has been touched upon earlier, the Hawizeh Marshes form a natural barrier along the Iranian-Iraqi border from Al Amarah in the north to a point just north of Basra in the south, where there are dry sand plains on the Iranian side. The marshes are fed by the watershed of both the Tigris and Karun rivers and begin just east of Susangerd in Iran in the east and extend all the way to Nasiryah in Iraq in the west. The eastern road from Basra to Baghdad runs through a built-up area to the west of the Tigris. The area has a maximum width of about 20 kilometers but sometimes appears to be surrounded by water on either side of the road. The marshes have water levels of one to three meters in February and thick clumps of reeds, which are often two meters high.

The Hawizeh Marshes did give Iraq a major barrier to Iranian movement, but they also were often impassable to Iraqi armor and artillery. At this point in the war, Iraq had also paid more attention to flooding the marshes and creating improved water barriers than to establishing a continuous line of fortifications to defend the rear of the marsh area, where an Iranian attack seemed unlikely. Iraq had placed its defenses just east of the Basra-to-Baghdad Road, and Iranian infantry could move forward with only limited opposition and fear of armored and artillery counterattacks. Although the area was originally inhabited by marsh Arabs, Iraq also did relatively little to patrol it or secure it. It carried out only limited reconnaissance and had relatively poor intelligence coverage of what went on in the wetlands. Finally, the defense of the area was divided, with the Iraqi 4th Corps covering the area north of Qurnah (also Qarneh, Qurna, or Al-Quornah) and the 3rd Corps covering the area to the south.

Iran deployed a strike force near the marshes of 50,000 to 150,000 men, with up to another 100,000 men in reserve for rapid deployment. Although the main Iranian attack did not develop until February 22, Iran began its preparations much earlier. On February 14, Iran launched a probing attack near the Arvand River. By February 16, Iran expanded its attacks into a major helicopter and water-borne assault which used rubber boats and small craft (the Fatima al-Zahra attack). These attacks overran the Iraqi marsh villages of Al Baydha and Sakhra. Iran then launched its main attack in an attempt to cut the Baghdad-Basra Road. It launched three major amphibious thrusts using barges and small craft: These were directed at Beida, the Majnoon Islands, and the main defense points of the Iraqi third Corps at Ghuzail.

The attack on Beida was initially successful. Beida was a marsh village which was only lightly defended by the 3rd Corps. The Pasdaran rapidly took the village and began to dig in. They took two other undefended villages called Sabkha and Ajrada. These villages were connected by tracks on earth mounds and made the Iranian advance relatively easy. In fact, some scattered elements of Iranian troops may actually have reached the Basra-Baghdad Road.

The success of the Iranian attack, however, depended on building up a major Iranian bridgehead by boat before Iraqi forces could counterattack with artillery and armor. The Pasdaran and Baseej forces in the attack also lacked artillery and modern anti-tank weapons. The Iranian attacks in Wal-Fajr 5 and 6 did little to divert the Iraqi 3rd Corps, and the Iraqi forces counterattacked relatively quickly. The Iranian forces lacked the strength and heavy weapons to put up a real defense, and the Iranian small craft attempting to reinforce the area became ideal targets for Iraq's armed helicopters. By February 25, three successive Iraqi counterattacks had overrun the Iranian forces. The fighting was grim. Iraqi tanks ran over some Pasdaran infantry, and Iraq electrocuted others by diverting power lines into the marshes. The Iraqi Ministry of Information later showed films showing thousands of exposed Iranian dead.

The Iranian attacks on Ghuzail further to the south attempted to use amphibious forces, which infiltrated by night to overwhelm the Iraqi position before its defense could be organized. The Iranian attacks did score some initial successes, but the Ghuzail area had good barrier and firepower defenses. Iran then claimed, on February 23, to have taken the city of Qurna, at the junction of the Tigris and Euphrates rivers. An Iraqi television broadcast from Qurna showed that Iran was lying, however, and that many of Iran's attacking troops had been killed at the edges of various water barriers or near Iraq's entrenched forward-defense positions.

After Iran's initial successes on the first night of the battle, the fighting had become a battle of attrition, with wave after wave of advancing Pasdaran attempting to overcome a massive Iraqi superiority in firepower and position through sheer numbers. There was little cover in front of the main Iraqi defenses; Iraqi firepower inflicted terrible casualties on Iran, and Iraqi fighters and helicopters often found Pasdaran concentrations in open positions. Iraq also made good use of flooding to complicate the problems Iran faced in advancing through a mix of wetlands and the drier territory in the area. The Iranian forces could not advance their forces quickly enough to prevent Iraq from being able to reinforce their positions in the time between attacks.

As a result, the battle became a killing ground for the Iraqi troops and began to reach a bloody climax on February 29. An Iranian force of over 20,000 men advanced over open ground in broad daylight and into an Iraqi position that could concentrate massive firepower against Iran's flanks as well as against its center. Iraq also seems to have used artillery and helicopters to deliver mustard gas and to have inflicted several thousand casualties with this weapon. By March 1, Iran had exhausted its ability to keep attacking, and Iraqi forces counterattacked the next day against Iranian forces that had now run out of supply and which were exposed on a dried salt flat. Iran suffered five to seven times more casualties than Iraq and lost between 12,000 and 20,000 men.[25]

The only success Operation Kheiber produced for Iran occurred as the result of a limited attack through the Hawizeh Marshes that began on February 22, when Iranian troops advancing by boat found that an Iraqi oil drilling complex called the Majnoon Islands was virtually undefended. These "islands" consisted of two main networks of sand mounds that enclosed areas in the marshes east of Qurna. Iraq had built up the islands to help develop a major oil field, which some sources credited as having several billion barrels of oil and up to 20 percent of Iraq's oil reserves. There were over 50 producing wells in the area, which Iraq had capped before the fighting began.

Both the Iraqi 3rd and 4th Corps were occupied in defending the main defenses east of the Basra-Baghdad Road, and Iran was able to dig in unopposed. Iran built sheltered bunkers, and by February 25, Iran reinforced its positions to about 15,000–20,000 men. Iranian engineers established a pontoon bridge to the Iranian dry lands southeast of Hamid, and Iran was able to bring artillery into the area.

The Iraqis had to wait until they could consolidate their defense of the Basra-Baghdad Road to counterattack, and this took until March 6. Iraq then found it had to fight its way meter-by-meter through wetlands where it could not deploy armor or artillery except along a single road. Even after bitter fighting, the extensive use of mustard gas, and what may have been Iraq's first experimental use of a nerve gas called Tabun, Iraq could only fully recover the southern island.

This gave Iran a kind of victory. Iraq had to defend the southern part of the Majnoons like a fortress under siege. It had to set up continuous lighting, fire posts at every point along the perimeter, and make new attempts to use the diversion of power lines into the marshes to make the waters impossible to infiltrate.[26] The fact that Iran still held the northern complex of the Majnoon Islands also allowed the speaker of the Majlis, Ali Akbak Rafsanjani, to claim that "we have now more than enough in terms of proven oil reserves to take care of the cost of reparation for the enormous damages we have suffered at the hands of the enemy."[27]

The overall impact of Operation Kheiber, however, was that Iran took losses that were so high that they forced Iran to stop launching major offensives until March 1985.[28] Iraq had lost 6,000 dead and 10,000 to 12,000 wounded. Iran's Pasdaran and Baseej had suffered a total of up to 20,000 killed, including noncombat related losses and missing in action, and 20,000–30,000 wounded. Iran's regular forces had lost 6,000 men out of a total of 40,000. Iran had also lost far more equipment than Iraq.

Even so, between 250,000 and 330,000 Iranian troops were kept at the front and in a position to attack until later that summer when part of the force was allowed to return home. Iran also replaced its pontoon bridge to Majnoon with a nine-mile-long earthen causeway by May 7. Iraq had no choice other than to launch new efforts to correct every possible weakness in its forward defenses and to reinforce every critical defense point around a city or major objective.

Iran's Leaders and the Impact of the Fighting in Operation Kheiber

Although there are many reports and rumors, it is unclear how Iran's political leadership really judged the outcome of Operation Kheiber. Iranian broadcasts and speeches following the offensive continued to insist that the war could only end with Saddam Hussein's ouster, but they provided mixed signals as to whether Iran would launch major new offensives. It seems likely from the rumors surrounding the meetings of the Iranian Supreme Defense Council that followed Operation Kheiber that some Iranian planners questioned whether Iran could succeed using tactics that cost it so much manpower and which had so little ability to sustain deep breakthroughs or hold on to major gains. This helps explain why the Wal-Fajr attacks halted for the rest of 1984 and why the Iranian Supreme Defense Council began to debate a new series of attack options.[29]

- The first of these options included a major offensive against Kirkuk and Iraq's pipeline system in the north. The problem with this option was that it meant fighting through very defensible mountainous and rough terrain, trying to occupy most of the Kurdish areas in Iraq, and facing the risk of Turkish economic or military counteraction.
- The second option included attacking Baghdad via Qasr e-Shirin or Mandali, but Iran lacked both the armor and air capability to sustain such a thrust and would have to expose its forces to an offensive across open plains that were an almost ideal killing ground for Iraqi forces.

- The third option was to try to reinforce the "success" of Operation Kheiber and launch another attack across, or bypassing the edges of, the Hawizeh Marshes.
- The fourth option was another frontal assault on Basra. This option offered the potential ability to seize much of the Shi'ite part of Iraq and to reduce Iraq's access to the southern Gulf but meant a direct attack on what was now a massive fortress.
- The final option was to bypass Basra to the south, attack the weakly defended al-Faw Peninsula, and try to cut Iraq off from Kuwait by driving to the Iraqi naval port at Umm Qasr. This offered the potential ability to force the southern Gulf states to halt their support of Iraq or risk an Iranian invasion of Kuwait. It also, however, was the option most likely to lead to Western intervention in the war.

The Iranian Supreme Defense Council eventually chose the option of repeating Operation Kheiber. At the same time, it seems to have begun to actively examine the option of attacking Al Fao and Umm Qasr. It also gave the planners in the Pasdaran and Iran's regular forces the time necessary to prepare their troops and obtain some hope of achieving success.

It still seems, however, that a significant number of Iran's war leaders fundamentally failed to understand the reasons for the failure and success of previous revolutionary conflicts like those in China and Vietnam. In spite of the fact that Iran now had at least some North Korean advisors, there was little overt recognition of the amount of effort that the PRC and North Vietnam had put on developing trained forces and cadres and on providing their troops with cohesive leadership and with adequate combat experience and preparation before an attack.

Iran's leaders seem to have interpreted each of Iraq's defensive successes as being so marginal that even a minor change in the size or dedication of the Iranian forces involved could have reversed the outcome. They also seem to have grossly overestimated Iraq's vulnerability to losses and attrition, particularly since Iran was suffering almost three times as many losses of men and equipment while having only parity in total deployed manpower and less than half of Iraq's equipment.

Above all, many top Iranian leaders, including Khomeini, must have continued to stress ideology over the practical details of making a revolutionary force work. There was a strong tendency in Iran to sloganize popular warfare and to ignore the actual experience at the front, even though an increasing number of senior Iranian officials had actually served in the Pasdaran. Iran still was willing to throw thousands of Baseej into combat, almost straight from their cities and villages. It provided them with little military equipment and resupply capability and gave its volunteers few instructions other than to advance to their primary objective and obtain supplies from the newly liberated Iraqi Shi'ites.

Chemical and Economic Warfare

This phase of the war was also affected by the use of chemical weapons and changes in the economic aspects of the conflict. Iran made a steadily growing number of charges that Iraq had made use of chemical warfare. Iran later charged that Iraq had used chemical weapons to kill 1,200 Iranians and injured 5,000 between May 1981 and the end of March 1984, and many of these charges were certainly valid. Iraq almost certainly used mustard gas, and possibly a nerve agent called Tabun, in the battles near Hur ul-Hoveyzeh on February 25, in the Shatt e-ali area on February 26, in the Talayeh area on March 2 and 3, in the Majnoon Islands on March 9, and in the Jofeyr-Al Ba'iza and Kawther regions on March 17.[30] Iran's tactics made Iraq's use of mustard gas particularly effective, since Iranian forces moved slowly and on foot. Mustard gas achieves its maximum effect as a persistent poison.[31]

It is important to understand, however, that the reason for Iraq's defensive victories in 1983–1984 was the combination of *both* Iraqi superiority in firepower, armor, and air power *and* of Iran's failure to properly plan and manage its infantry attacks. Even if all Iranian claims are assumed to be valid, Iraq's use of a gas would still account for only three to five percent of Iran's casualties. Further, Iran helped defeat itself by consistently exposing its manpower in direct human-wave assaults on heavily held Iraqi positions in broad daylight, without major artillery and air support, and without effective battle management.

By the spring of 1984, the balance of economic warfare had also changed significantly and had ceased to favor Iran. Iran produced an average of about 2.43 MMBD in 1983 and exported about 1.71 MMBD, with annual earnings of about $12.3 billion. In 1984, a combination of demand, price, and military factors cut Iran's production to an annual average of about 2.18 MMBD, with exports of about 1.36 MMBD and annual earnings of around $10.9 billion.[32] Iraq was still suffering severely from the loss of its oil-exporting capability, and its revenues had dropped from $21.3 billion in 1979 and $26.1 billion in 1980, to $10.4 billion in 1981, $9.7 billion in 1982, and

$9.65 billion in 1983. Its revenues had climbed back to $11.24 billion in 1984.[33]

Although its economic situation was anything but easy, Iraq was on the way to solving many of the economic problems that had resulted from the near cutoff in its oil exports and from rapidly drawing down its foreign reserves to try to simultaneously fund guns, butter, and development during the first two years of the war. By March 1984, Iraq was able to use the expansion of its pipeline through Turkey to increase its exports from a monthly average of 800,000 BPD to an average of 1.2 million. Iraq was also completing contracts to establish a new pipeline link through Saudi Arabia. While Iraq could not make use of this pipeline link until late 1985, the fact it was now under construction was a powerful factor in influencing Iraq's foreign creditors to refinance Iraq's debt and to make new loans. Iran never again was able to threaten Iraq's export capability or ability to finance the war.

Notes

1. The analysis of phase three is based heavily on Anthony H. Cordesman's trips to the region and interviews of Iraqi and Iranian officers and officials, plus his prior writing for the *Armed Forces Journal International* (especially "The Lessons of the Iran-Iraq War," Parts I and II, April and June, 1982) and in the book *The Gulf and the Search for Strategic Stability*, Boulder, Westview, 1984. It also draws heavily upon the work of Colonel W.O. Staudenmaier, U.S. Army Strategic Studies Institute; Edgar O'Ballance, *The Gulf War*, London, Brassey's, 1988; Nikola B. Schahgaldian, *The Iranian Military Under the Islamic Republic*, Santa Monica, Rand R-3473-USDP, 1987; Sepehr Zabih, *The Iranian Military in Revolution and War*, London, Routledge, 1988; Keith McLauchlan and George Joffe, *The Gulf War*, Special Report 176, London, Economist Press, 1984; Keith McLauchlan and George Joffe, *Iran and Iraq: The Next Five Years*, Special Report 1083, London, Economist Press, 1987; and various working papers for the International Institute for Strategic Studies, Royal United Services Institute.

2. Virtually every Iranian leader has at some point been called a hawk or a moderate. It is almost certainly true that the Iranian military commanders generally counseled far more caution and restraint than the Mullahs and that the regular officers put far more emphasis on military professionalism. It is also probably true that the major civil leaders and ministers—such as President Khameini, Prime Minister Mousavi, Majlis Speaker Rafsanjani, and Foreign Minister Velayati—were far less willing to risk the stability of Iran, and the future of the revolution within Iran, than Khomeini and the more radical Mullahs. Nevertheless, these debates were probably over tactics and timing, rather than the ultimate objective, until at least 1987.

3. By this time, the Baseej were drawn from ages 12 to 72, although the majority tended to be relatively young. They were usually recruited by young Mullahs who stressed the fact that martyrdom against heresy (Kfor) would

grant them both glory and entrance to paradise. The Pasdaran or Sepah gave them brief training for between 10 and 28 days. In theory, the Foundation of Martyrs (Bonyde Shaheed) looked after the families of those killed, and they had special treatment in terms of food rationing, the allocation of housing and property taken away from those loyal to the Shah or other opposition movements, and being sent on pilgrimage.

4. Iran treated the battle publicly as a victory. It claimed to have captured 101 tanks, including 12 Soviet T-72s, and 1,110 prisoners of war. See Zabih, op. cit., p. 181.

5. Ibid.

6. Anthony H. Cordesman visited several Iraqi positions on a number of occasions during the war. The comments on Iran are based upon discussions with Iranian soldiers in the west and visits to captured Iranian positions in 1988.

7. ACDA, *World Military Expenditures and Arms Transfers, 1985,* Washington, D.C., GPO, 1985, pp. 108–109.

8. According to Edgar O'Ballance, the USSR agreed to begin reshipment of arms in return for the release of 180 Iraqi Communists in May. (See O'Ballance, op. cit., p. 103.)

9. Iraq began the war with a Scud regiment with nine launchers. The regiment was not trained well enough to operate the missiles, however, and it took Iraq over a year to deploy a combat-ready unit. See Steven Zaloga, "Ballistic Missiles in the Third World," *International Defense Review,* 11/1988, pp. 1423–1427.

10. O'Ballance, op. cit., pp. 123–124.

11. Estimates are based upon the IISS, *Military Balance, 1983–1984,* London, International Institute for Strategic Studies, 1983, pp. 55–56. The lower number in the range of strengths for each helicopter type is the minimum believed to be armed and operational at the beginning of 1983.

12. Estimates are based upon the IISS, op. cit., pp. 54–55.

13. Wal-Fajr means "behold the dawn" and is a reference to the Koran. Some sources feel the first Wal-Fajr offensive began on April 16, 1983.

14. Some sources feel this was the first Wal-Fajr offensive. See Zabih, op. cit., p. 184.

15. This declaration, and various Al Daawa bombings, led to ruthless Iraqi efforts to hunt down and eliminate any remaining opposition. Shahram Chubin and Charles Trip, *Iran and Iraq at War,* Boulder, Westview, 1988, pp. 101–103.

16. Iran had now gathered the various Shi'ite and Kurdish movements and other anti-Saddam Hussein groups in Iraq that it supported under an umbrella organization called the Supreme Council of the Islamic Revolution in Iraq (SCIRI).

17. Iran claimed to have taken some 600 POWs, 41 tanks, nearly 300 artillery weapons, and 13,000 light arms. Experts sharply disagree over the number of casualties and wounded on each side in all of the Wal-Fajr battles, as well as on the number of POWs and equipment losses.

18. Estimates are based upon the IISS, op. cit., pp. 54–55.

19. Ibid., pp. 55–56.

20. These comments are based on conversations during this period with senior Iraqi officials.

21. O'Ballance, op. cit., p. 149.

22. As usual, claims are impossible to verify and the data are uncertain. See Zabih, op. cit., p. 186.

23. Iran claimed Iraq used chemical weapons in the Panjwin area on November 7, 9, and 19, 1983. A number of earlier claims have already been mentioned. Iran claimed Iraq was using gas during an attack near Shalamcheh as early as late 1980. It reported its first gas casualty during fighting near Hoveyzeh in early 1981 and its first killed (4 dead) after fighting near Musain on October 27, 1982. Iran began to claim it suffered large casualties (318) from mustard gas and arsenic agents during the fighting in mid-August. It was only during the Wal-Fajr 4 offensive, however, that gas warfare became a major issue and received widespread world attention. It also was the battle that first seems to have led Iran to buy chemical defense equipment, and Britain announced it had sold Iran 10,000 protective kits on December 22, 1983.

24. Some sources refer to this attack as Wal-Fajr 6 and call both diversionary attacks Wal-Fjar 5. This identification of the battle is based on O'Ballance, op. cit., p. 143, which seems to be the best available description of the land fighting through 1986.

25. *Guardian and Times,* March 2 and 3, 1984; *Observer* and *Sunday Times,* March 4, 1984.

26. *Times,* February 25, 1984; *Times* and *Guardian,* March 7, 1984; *Telegraph,* March 12 and 26, 1986; Zabih, op. cit., pp. 186–188.

27. *Jamhuriye Islam* (Tehran), May 8, 1984, and *Le Monde,* February 18 and March 30, 1984.

28. Iran had acquired a total of about 350 square kilometers of Iraqi territory, but most had only limited strategic value.

29. See *Le Monde,* February 18 and March 30, 1984, and Zabih, op. cit., pp. 189–190. Chubin and Tripp credit the regular forces for winning the leadership's agreement to this pause in a debate with the supporters of the Pasdaran. Chubin and Tripp, op. cit., p. 84.

30. The U.S. charged in December 1983 that West German firms had given Iraq the ability to manufacture Tabun and that the rapidly expanding Iraqi chemical corps had used it in 1983. The U.S. had stated that Iraq now had major chemical warfare plants at Samara, south of Baghdad, at Akachat, and at a number of other locations. The U.S. suspended the shipment of possible chemical feedstock to Iraq in March 1984, and the West German government tightened its controls of the export of chemical-weapons equipment and technology in August.

31. For an excellent and objective technical discussion, see J. P. Robinson, "Chemical and Biological Warfare: Developments in 1984," *World Armaments and Disarmaments, SIPRI Yearbook, 1985,* Solna, Sweden, 1985, pp. 178–188 and 206–217. Also see Pearce Wright, "Why Troops Still Have to Fear Mustard Gas," Science Report, *Times,* March 6, 1984. Part of the confusion may have stemmed from the effects of mustard gas. Mustard gas, or

Lewisite, often initially appears to be little more than a mild irritant because it acts as a vesicant or skin-blistering agent. It sometimes takes hours before the lungs begin to blister and the skin deforms. Limited exposure produces very uncertain symptoms.

32. Such estimates are controversial. These are taken from the Wharton Econometrics, the Petroleum Finance Company, and work by John M. Roberts, a senior advisor to the Middle East Institute.

33. These estimates are also controversial and were taken from the same sources as in note 32 in this chapter: Wharton Econometrics, the Petroleum Finance Company, and work done by John M. Roberts, a senior advisor, Middle East Institute.

7

PHASE FOUR: THE WAR OF ATTRITION AND THE WAR IN THE GULF, APRIL 1984 TO 1986

The Beginning of the War of Attrition[1]

Iran did not halt its offensives in March 1984, but the cost of its battles had been so high that Iran did not launch another all-out offensive against Iraq until the Faw campaign of 1986 and did not seek to conduct a final offensive against Iraq until the Battle of Basra in 1987. During the next two years, Iran conducted a war of attrition, punctuated by a few major offensives. Iraq, in return, escalated its tanker war and attempted to weaken Iran by attacking its major source of income. At the same time, Iraq increasingly sought to use outside fear of an Iranian conquest of Iraq and Kuwait as a lever to obtain foreign support.

The war put steadily increasing pressure on both regimes throughout this period as casualties and costs mounted. Both regimes, however, now had the ability to control their internal opposition. The main factor that shaped the course of the war continued to be the war on the ground, and this was shaped by the extent to which Iran could exploit its superior manpower and revolutionary fervor versus the extent to which Iraq could exploit its superior ability to obtain arms.

By and large, it was Iraq that took the lead. Iran was able to obtain about $3.9 billion worth of arms during 1983–1985, but Iraq obtained about $18.1 billion worth, or well over four times as much. Iraq's superior access to Western and Soviet arms also made a dollar of Iraqi expenditure on arms worth at least 50 percent more than an Iranian dollar, and the true Iraqi advantage was probably over 5:1.[2]

Iran never succeeded in properly exploiting its potential advantage in manpower. In mid-1984, Iran had about 555,000 men of all kinds under arms, with the ability to surge about 200,000 more. This added up to about 755,000 men; but the division into regular forces, Pasdaran, and

Baseej, the constant political turbulence, and the failure to retain and train much of Iran's battle-experienced manpower, deprived Iran's manpower pool of much of its effectiveness. In contrast, Iraq built up standing forces of around 675,000 to 750,000 men. In spite of its secular regime and a population less than one-third that of Iran, Iraq was usually able to deploy a larger and more experienced pool of manpower than Iran.[3]

The overall trends in Iraqi and Iranian forces are shown in Table 7.1. While the detailed numbers are uncertain, they show that Iraq was building up a major advantage in land-weapons strength and airpower.

The Air War and the Tanker War

While Wal-Fajr 5 and 6 and Operation Kheiber created a near stalemate on the land, they did nothing to halt the escalation of the air war and tanker war. On February 1, Iraq threatened that it would strike at key Iranian cites like Abadan, Ahwaz, Dezful, Ilam, and Kermanshah and called for their evacuation. On February 3, Iran threatened to retaliate against Basra, Kanaqin, and Mandali. Iraq struck heavily at civilian and economic targets during the Iranian land offensives in February, however, and fired Scud missiles at Dezful on February 11. Iran shelled Basra in response, and Iranian fighters hit Kanaqin and Mandali, Basra, and then Babubah and Musain. While Iran could only launch a few sorties per air raid, it was clear that Iraq still lacked adequate air defenses against low-flying aircraft.

Iraq tired to initiate a cease-fire on civilian targets that was to go into effect on February 18, 1984, but Iran rejected the offer. As a result, Iraq seems to have tried to avoid any attacks on its population centers by shifting to attacks on oil targets. The tanker war had already been going on during January and early February, but Iraq had been making far more claims than were credible, and many of its claims seem to have been directed more at achieving a propaganda impact on its own population and friendly states than a military impact on Iran.[4] In late February, however, Iraq threatened to attack any ship putting in to Bushehr and Bandar-e-Khomeini. Iraqi aircraft struck at Kharg Island on February 27, and Iraq then again threatened that it would blockade Iranian oil exports and strike at any ship near Kharg.

Iraq then gave its threats teeth. Although the exact figures remain uncertain, Iraq seems to have used its regular fighters to hit seven ships in the Gulf between February 25 and March 1. On March 27, 1984, Iraq finally launched the first of a long series of Super Etendard and Exocet strikes and hit two small Indian and Turkish tankers southwest of Kharg. The next day, Iraq formally announced that it had used an

TABLE 7.1 The Trends in Iranian and Iraqi Military Forces: 1979–1985

Force Category	1979/1980		1984/1985	
	Iran	Iraq	Iran	Iraq
Total Active Military				
Manpower Suitable				
for Combat	240,000	535,000	555,000	675,000
Land Forces				
Regular Army Manpower				
Active	150,000	200,000	250,000	600,000
Reserve	400,000	256,000	350,000	75,000
Revolutionary Guards	30,000	—	250,000	—
Baseej/Popular Army [a]	75,000	650,000	200,000	650,000
Hizbollah (Home Guard)[a]	—?	—	2,500,000	—
Arab Volunteers	—	6,000?	—	10,000
Gendarmerie	?	—	—	—
National Guard	10,000	—	—	—
Security Forces	—	5,000	5,000+	4,800
Division Equivalents				
(Divisions/Brigades)	9	23	21–24	22–26
Armored	3/1	12+3	3	6/2
Mechanized	—	4	4	5
Infantry and Mountain	3/1	4	3	5
Special Forces/Airborne	—/2	—	2	1/1
Pasdaran/People's Militia	—		9–13	—/9
Major Combat Equipment				
Main Battle Tanks	1,735:	2,750:	1,050:	4,820:
	400 M-47/48	50 T-72	200 M-47/M-48	4,500 T-54/ 55/62/72
	460 M-60A1	100 AMX-30	200 M-60A1	260 T-59
	875 Chieftain	2,500 T-54/55/62	300 Chieftain	60 M-77
		100 T-34	100 T-72	
			150 T-54/T-55/ -59/T-62	
Other Armored				
Fighting Vehicles	1,075	2,500	1,240	3,200
Major Artillery	1,000+	1,040	1,000	3,000
Air Forces				
Air Force Manpower	70,000	38,000	35,000	38,000
Operational Combat Aircraft	445	332	95	580
	188 F-4D/E	12 Tu-22	35 F-4D/E	7 Tu-22
	166 F-5E/F	10 Il-28	50 F-5E/F	8 Tu-16
	77 F-14A	80 MiG-23B	10 F-14A	45 Mirage F-1EQ/BQ

(continues)

TABLE 7.1 *(continued)*

Force Category	1979/1980		1984/1985	
	Iran	Iraq	Iran	Iraq
Operational Combat Aircraft (continued)	14 RF-4E	40 Su-7B	3 RF-4E	100 MiG-23BM
		60 Su-20		95 Su-7
		115 MiG-21		80 Su-20
		15 Hunter		5 Super Etendard
				25 MiG-25
				5 MiG-25R
				150 MiG-21
				40 MiG-19
				11 Hunter
Attack Helicopters	205 AH-1S	41 Mi-24	80-90 AH1S	150
Total Helicopters[b]	744	260	390	380
Surface-to-Air Missile Forces	Hawk	SA-2, SA-3.	Hawk	SA-2, SA-3
	5 Rapier Sqns	25 SA-6	5 Rapier Sqns	SA-6, SA-9,
	25 Tigercat		25 Tigercat	30 Roland
Navy				
Navy Manpower	20,000	4,250	20,000	4,500
Operational Ships				
Destroyers	3	0	1	0
Frigates	4	1	3	0
Corvettes/Submarine Chasers	4	0	2	0
Missile Patrol Craft	9	12	6	10
Major Other Patrol Craft	7	5	2–3	2
Mine Warfare Vessels	5	5	1	5
Hovercraft	14	0	17	0
Landing Craft and Ships	4	17	5	11
Maritime Patrol Aircraft	6 P-3F	0	2 PF-3	0

[a]Total manpower pool. Active strength far lower or none.
[b]Includes Army helicopters.

SOURCES: Adapted by the authors from the 1979–1980 and 1984–1985 editions of the IISS *Military Balance* (London: International Institute for Strategic Studies).

Exocet missile to hit a Greek vessel. These initial Iraqi attacks followed an interesting pattern.

The Super Etendards generally flew at medium to high altitudes with a Mirage F-1 fighter escort. They covered an area from the Shatt to positions south and slightly east of Kharg Island and generally fired their missiles at a range of 30 kilometers without ever inspecting their targets. While Iraq did have some 200 Exocets at this time, it is unclear why it did not use conventional bombs—which often would have been far more lethal against commercial ships—and why it failed to overfly its targets and confirm their value. Iraq often seemed to be protecting its Super Etendards at the cost of using them effectively.

The timing of Iraq's first use of the Super Etendards is also interesting because it coincides with its use of poison gas and the failure of its attempt to retake Majnoon. It also, however, may have had something to do with the fact that the Iranian National Oil Company was negotiating with Japanese traders for the renewal of a contract for 200,000 BPD of crude. Iran was trying to increase production to try to recoup some of the costs of the fighting and was exporting from Kharg Island at the exceptionally high rate of three million BPD.

Iran used its dwindling air assets to respond in kind.[5] Iranian fighters hit a Saudi tanker on May 7 and Kuwaiti tankers near Bahrain on May 13 and 14, 1984. These were the first major Iranian attacks on foreign commercial shipping since the start of the war, although Iran rarely acknowledged responsibility for these or subsequent attacks.[6] Another tanker was hit in Saudi waters on May 16, near Jubail, and provoked the Saudi government to create its own air defense zone and start flying air cover over the area with the support of the AWACS aircraft in the U.S. ELF-1 detachment based in Dhahran.

Within five weeks, both sides had hit a total of eleven ships, ten of which were oil tankers. The rise in the tanker war, however, still had only a limited initial international and economic impact. The U.S. did warn Iran against any efforts to close the Straits. The U.S. also had a carrier battle group in the area, led by the USS *Midway*, but it did not take military action. While Iraq got a great deal of press play when it first used the Super Etendards and was able to hit more targets than Iran, neither side could inflict enough damage to cut off a major part of the other side's exports on a sustained basis or to affect world oil supplies in the face of a growing world oil glut and full stockpiles of oil in the major importing countries. (See Table 7.2.)

Oil prices showed little movement, even in the usually sensitive spot market. Insurance rates rose, but Iran quickly offered compensatory price discounts. While Iranian exports fell by up to 50 percent for a few days as customers diversified their supplies, they quickly recovered. It rapidly became clear that five Iraqi fighters with Exocets might be able to harass Iran's exports but could scarcely halt them. Iraq's attempts to bring Iran to peace negotiations also failed, in spite of a five-day suspension of attacks between May 19 and 24, 1984.

TABLE 7.2 Iranian and Iraqi Oil Production: Average Daily Production in Millions of Barrels per Day

	Iran	Iraq
1978 (peak)	5.2	2.6
1980	1.7	2.5
1981	1.4	1.0
1982	2.3	1.0
1983	2.5	0.9
1984	2.2	1.2
1985 (Monthly Low/High)	2.3 (1.9–2.6)	1.4 (1.3–1.7)
1986 (Monthly Low/High)	1.9 (1.5–2.2)	1.7 (1.6–1.8)
1987 (Monthly Low/High)	(1.7–2.7)	(1.7–2.6)
1988 (January)	2.1	2.4

SOURCES: CIA estimates in various editions of its internal periodical *Economic and Energy Indicators*.

Iraq launched new air strikes in the southern Gulf in early June. The Iraqis sank a Turkish tanker off Kharg Island on June 3. This led the Iranian Air Force to start patrolling over the southern Gulf, and the U.S. and Saudi Arabia then took steps to limit such escalation to the upper Gulf. Saudi Arabia set up an air defense interception zone (ADIZ) known as the "Fahd Line," which went far beyond Saudi territorial limits and covered all of the Saudi oil zone to the middle of the Gulf. Saudi Arabia announced that Saudi F-15s, guided by U.S. E-3A AWACs and refueled by USAF KC-10 tankers, would engage any aircraft threatening Gulf shipping in the ADIZ.

Saudi jet fighters proved that this ADIZ was effective on June 5 by downing an Iranian jet flying over Saudi waters. The Saudi F-15s, assisted by the U.S. AWACS, shot down the Iranian aircraft before it could perform any significant maneuvers. Iran immediately ceased any further incursions into Saudi territory. Iran lacked the air assets, technology, and training to compete with the rapidly improving Saudi Air Force, which was equipped with F-15s. It never again seriously challenged Saudi air-defense capabilities.[7]

Iran faced similar problems in conducting attacks on Iraq. When Iran launched a new artillery barrage on Basra on June 5, Iraq made no attempt to reach another cease-fire on civilian targets. It replied with a raid on Baaneh the same day, and followed with raids on Dezful, Masjid e-Suleiman, and Nahavand the next morning. Iran then struck. A Kuwaiti tanker was hit near Qatar, probably by an Iranian aircraft. This attack on the tanker was the first in the southern Gulf and led to considerable concern about the broadening of the war. Nevertheless, it was Iran that had to accept a cease-fire. On June 11, the day after the Kuwaiti tanker was hit, both Iran and Iraq accepted another U.N.-initiated halt to attacks on each other's towns and cities.

On June 15, the speaker of Iran's Majlis, Rafsanjani, proposed extending this truce to oil facilities and Gulf shipping as well. Iran's exports from Kharg were still averaging 1.6 million BPD, however, and Iraq made it clear that any such truce must allow it to repair or replace its own export facilities in the Gulf in compensation. Iran made no response to this proposal, but it set a pattern that was to last until the war ended. Iran would never accept a partial cease-fire in the Gulf that deprived it of a major strategic advantage over Iraq, and Iran constantly sought a partial cease-fire that would allow the fighting on land to continue while protecting Iran's oil exports.

Iraq hit several more ships in the Gulf and struck at the Iranian oil-export facilities at Kharg Island on June 24, 1984. The Iranians later confirmed that their loading facilities at the western or Sea Island side of Kharg were damaged in this raid, but it rapidly became clear that Iraq was not ready to take the air losses necessary to destroy Kharg's ability to load tankers. Iraq, instead, escalated the war against shipping. Between June 23 and July 25, the Iraqis launched at least four additional series of attacks against shipping.

Iraq's air strategy followed a similar pattern during the rest of 1984.[8] Iraq alternated strikes on Iranian cities and attacks on shipping to Iran with calls for cease-fires and peace talks. Iraq, however, lacked the combination of sensors, air, and missile power to inflict major damage on Iran's civil and economic centers and to sustain a blockage of Iran's export facilities.

This failure to achieve strategic results stemmed partly from a lack of technology: Iraq's aircraft lacked adequate range and endurance; its anti-shipping missiles were not sufficiently lethal to score quick, decisive ship kills; and it had no maritime patrol aircraft. It also stemmed from a lack of adequate military organization and leadership. Iraq still failed to commit its air power in sufficient numbers to achieve the proper mass to destroy enough of a given target and did not follow up its attacks on a sustained basis. Finally, Iraq failed to properly exploit each successive improvement in its capability to strike at tankers or Iran's oil facilities with sufficient intensity to have a major strategic or political effect. Iraq's attacks always came in brief bursts and with a flood of rhetoric which greatly exaggerated the military reality.

Once again, Iraq made the kind of mistakes which are typical of recent attempts to manage escalation. Attackers often assume that relatively limited levels of military escalation can be decisive in their effect and can change the political and military calculations of their opponent because of the potential for further escalation. In practice, efforts to achieve military or political goals through limited escalation, backed by implied threats, virtually always fail to have their desired effect. The opponent almost inevitably misunderstands signals which have so limited an effect or reacts only to the size of the escalation and not to the implied threat. Limited or gradual escalation has often ended in doing little more than increasing an opponent's hostility.

Iraq generally made the mistake of giving Iran ample time to recover after each new major round of its attacks. Iraq sometimes pursued this path because of new rounds of cease-fires or peace initiatives. Iran used these new peace initiatives, however, to reduce the level of Iraqi attacks on its cities and shipping traffic and then reiterated its demands for Saddam Hussein's ouster and for billions of dollars worth of reparations.

Iran also found ways to respond to put counterpressure on Iraq, even though Iran now had far less air power. Iran used artillery barrages against targets like Basra and a few air raids to deter Iraq from hitting Iranian civilian targets. Iran also made occasional threats to broaden the war to include the rest of the Gulf, although at this point Iran was taking the risk of provoking Western action into careful account. It then conducted occasional air attacks on Gulf shipping, used its Navy to harass cargo ships moving to southern Gulf ports, and/or exploited a mix of threats, subversion, and terrorism. These Iranian actions had at least some effect in persuading the southern Gulf states to try to get Iraq to limit its attacks on Iranian shipping.

More broadly, many other nations have found that there are sharp limits to any effort to use fighter-bombers to force major changes in an enemy's behavior.[9] Attempts to use limited amounts of air power as a substitute for victory on the ground have rarely had any success except against the most unsophisticated or uncommitted opponent. While attacks by a limited number of fighters and bombers may produce initial panic or disruption, the economic, political, and military structure of the nations that have been subjected to such air attacks has proved far more resilient than the advocates of strategic bombing estimated in launching such attacks. Supposedly critical vulnerabilities generally prove to be easily repairable or subject to substitution, particularly when the country under attack is given time to recover. The net effect of such attacks has generally been to unite a nation in hostility rather than to intimidate it.

Iran's Shift Toward Initiating a War of Attrition

Iran's land strategy during the rest of 1984 shifted from frontal assault to attrition. It occasionally maneuvered its forces in what seemed to be preparation for a new major offensive but only made limited attacks which were clearly designed to gain key terrain advantages near the front. The reasons for this shift are relatively easy to understand. Iran's casualties in the 1984 offensives must have approached 30,000 to 50,000 dead. While Iran's leaders did not move toward peace, such losses demonstrated to Iran's religious leaders and revolutionary commanders that Iran's ground forces could not continue to attack in the same manner without far better training, leadership, and organization.

Iran's military leadership also seems to have realized that it had made Iran's defeats much worse by attempting to hold on too long to initial territorial gains that had no strategic meaning and by committing untrained volunteer manpower with inadequate leadership and equipment to attacks with no goal short of total victory. Iran's understanding of these lessons was reflected by changes in Iran's forces.

Iran scarcely reacted by developing professional forces and could not react by acquiring the armor, stocks, mechanized mobility, air support, and air cover it needed. Iran did, however, increase its efforts to obtain new heavy-combat equipment and organized its popular and infantry forces to conduct more orderly and better-structured mass attacks. Iran paid more attention to logistics and support and created an impressive network of military roads and logistic storage areas, especially in the south. Iran did make limited improvements in the training of its volunteers, especially NCOs and junior officers. More importantly, it began to train its forces for new methods of attack and conducted extensive mountain and amphibious-warfare training.

At the high-command level, Iran also at least made an effort to plan its assaults more carefully and to limit its attacks to areas where it could infiltrate at night or take advantage of terrain and achieve limited gains. This kind of attack still gave the Iraqis serious problems. In spite of all of Iraq's efforts, Iran could often seize a limited amount of territory and confront Iraq with the alternative of either ceding the loss or counterattacking and taking casualties for relatively unimportant objectives.

Iraq's Overconfidence

Iraq countered these Iranian moves by continuing to build up its now massive superiority in firepower and its mix of fixed defenses, water barriers, cross-reinforcement capability, and logistics stocks. The failure of Iran's spring 1984 offensive, however, convinced Iraq that Iranian forces lacked the ability to make significant breakthroughs as long as Iraq could preserve its superiority in mass firepower and military technology and that static defensive warfare within fixed positions would minimize Iraqi casualties. Iraq became overconfident and came to believe that static defense on the land, and limited attacks in the air, could force Iran to accept some form of peace settlement.

Iraq did launch a few limited counterattacks during the rest of 1984, but most of these attacks were far more limited than Iraq claimed, and few had any real impact on Iran. Iraq still lacked the skill to fully exploit its superior firepower and mobility and take offensive action. It also failed to properly improve its infantry assault, infiltration, and counterinfiltration tactics. Iraq sat behind its defenses and failed to improve its capability to fight and patrol in mountain areas and in the marshes and wetlands in the south. Iraq's fear of losses and its over-confidence in technology helped paralyze a critical part of its military development, and Iraq failed to find any tactical solution to its lack of strategic depth.

There was some excuse for this failure. Iraq faced the strategic and tactical problem that its land forces could not succeed in defeating Iran simply by staying in place, but as long as Iran's people supported the war, Iraq could not force Iran to peace by taking limited amounts of Iranian territory. Even so, the problem Iraq faced in dealing with a war of attrition was scarcely all that unusual in military history, and it had a clear solution. It was increasingly clear that unless Iran collapsed, Iraq's only hope of defeating Iran on the ground was to inflict such massive casualties on Iranian troops that the resulting losses would undercut popular support for continuing the war.

As for the air war, it is important to note that Iraq's superiority in numbers was somewhat misleading. Iraq lacked many of the elements necessary to make its overall force effective. Iraq did not have the range/payload, sortie-generation capability, maritime patrol, sensor and target acquisition aircraft, and air defense fighter look-down/shoot-down and loiter capabilities to target and strike effectively at the volume of shipping that was moving through Iranian waters.

Iraq also found it still had problems in using its Exocets effectively. The Super Etendard aircraft did not have the range and loiter capability to properly cover the area around Kharg Island. Many of the missiles did not hit their targets,[10] and the Exocet's warhead proved to be too small to do catastrophic damage to large tankers. This deprived Iraq's missile attacks of much of the shock value they might have had if entire ships and crews had been lost. These problems led Iraq to order additional Mirage F-1s, equipped with extended-range fuel tanks and capable of launching both Exocets and laser-guided weapons.[11]

Iraq also failed to improve the effectiveness of its sporadic air and missile strikes against Iranian cities during the rest of 1984. Iraq lacked the combination of aircraft and missile numbers and range and payload to conduct the successful mass attacks against the Iranian population. At the same time, Iraq failed to concentrate on clearly defined sets of vulnerable economic targets, such as power plants and oil refineries. Iraq made the mistake of attacking a wide range of targets sporadically and never pursued any given mix of targets long or intensely enough to deliver unacceptable damage or to prevent relatively rapid recovery. The situation was somewhat different, however, when it came to close support. Iraq began to employ cluster bombs in close air support missions and steadily improved its sortie rates and mission effectiveness in support of its ground forces.[12]

Iran's More Controlled Offensives in 1985

Iran launched nine land attacks in 1985, and Iraq launched three counterattacks.[13] The Iranian attacks, however, usually had limited objectives and were more controlled than Iran's final offensives of 1984. Iran also was more careful in planning and training for its major attacks. Iran deliberately struck at a wide range of areas, particularly in the north and south where the terrain and water barriers made it difficult for Iraq to obtain tactical warning or make use of its defensive barriers and superior firepower. Iran also kept up considerable pressure on the Baghdad-Basra Highway and new fighting took place in the Hawizeh Marshes, but it did not produce the massive levels of casualties common in early 1984.

The land fighting began with some small and inconclusive Iraqi offensives which took place at Qasr e-Shirin on January 31 and Majnoon on February 28. Iraq did not score any gains, and it suffered a significant political reversal elsewhere. It tried on February 13 to reach an amnesty agreement that was largely intended to halt fighting with the Kurds. Both the Barzanis and Jalal Talabani's Patriotic Union of Kurdistan (PUK) rejected this offer. This meant that Iraq was becoming increasingly vulnerable to Iranian pressure on its Kurdish areas in the north.

The land fighting did not become serious until March and came after a long series of artillery exchanges during late February and early March, which were targeted against civilian and oil targets and killed up to 400 civilians.[14] Iran then launched a major new offensive called Operation Badr. This Iranian offensive was designed to seize Basra or cut it off from the rest of Iraq. Iran prepared for it for months. It repeated some aspects of Operation Kheiber in 1984, but the offensive was more limited in scope and was better planned and controlled.

Iran seems to have chosen the Hawizeh Marshes as the site of its first major offensive of 1985 for several reasons. It hoped to achieve tactical surprise by repeating an attack in an unexpected area. It had learned that Iraq did not aggressively patrol the Marshes and that Iranian troops could successfully infiltrate large amounts of troops into the small islands in the Marshes.

Iran had acquired growing experience in marsh warfare during the previous year. It had built up excellent lines of communications into the marshes and acquired large numbers of small craft. Iranian troops patrolled the marsh area aggressively. It took advantage of reeds that often reach 10 feet in height and forced Iraqi troops to stay in their fixed defenses on shore. The Hawizeh Marshes also made it difficult for Iraq to take advantage of its superiority in airpower, armor, and artillery until Iranian troops hit the dry land near the Basra-Baghdad Road. Armored vehicles could not move through the Marshes or their edges in the wet season, and Iraq had no way to acquire meaningful targets as long as Iranian forces were dispersed.[15]

Iran had a total of some 75,000 to 100,000 troops available in this part of the front, but only some of these forces seem to have been prepared to participate in Operation Badr. Iran assembled an attack force of 45,000 to 65,000 men, organized in formations that were the equivalent of something approaching 7 to 8 divisions, including 4 to 5 divisions of Revolutionary Guards and Baseej volunteers. These forces were a mix of regular army and Pasdaran, and the Pasdaran were better trained and equipped than in 1984. Virtually all the forces now had assault rifles and ample supplies of ammunition, and many of the troops had RPGs and large supplies of rockets. Iran established a chain of pontoon bridges through the marshes and developed floats, boats, and rafts carrying PRC 105-mm and U.S. 106-mm recoilless rifles and mortars. Iranian forces were equipped with German-made gas masks, protective capes, and Dutchpine kits as an antidote to nerve gas.

The Iraqi forces, in turn, consisted of the equivalent of ten divisions of 4th Corps troops, with two of these divisions deployed to guard the Basra-Baghdad Road and railway and the approaches through the Hawizeh Marshes. By this time, Iraq also had formidable land defenses. It had an extensive chain of bunkers, earth mounds and observation points, mine fields, barbed wire, and obstacles to prevent landings. Iraq had established the capability to use flooding to create additional water barriers once the Iranian forces landed and now kept some mobile brigades in the rear to provide for defense in depth, although both the terrain and Iraqi planning limited the preparation of defensive barriers to one main defense line in many areas.

Iran seems to have tried to distract the attention of Iraq's leadership by launching a massive artillery barrage against Basra on March 10–11 and by conducting its first air raid on Baghdad in months, which Iraq replied to with an air raid on Tehran. The actual Iranian land assault began well before midnight on March 11. Three major groups of Iranian forces hit a 10-kilometer front between Qurnah and Uzayer.

The Iranian forces came out of the Hawizeh Marshes at the southern end of the 4th Corps defense zone and achieved enough tactical surprise and concentration of force to immediately break through the initial Iraqi defenses and seize some positions on the dry land near the road. Iran had to employ human-wave tactics from the start, however, and immediately began to take heavy casualties. Even so, Iranian forces advanced about 10 kilometers on the first day and a total of 14 kilometers on the second. On March 14, the equivalent of a Pasdaran brigade reached the Tigris, and on the night of March 14–15, Iran was able to put two to three pontoon bridges across the Tigris. The next day, Pasdaran forces actually reached the Basra-Baghdad Road.

The problem with this Iranian advance was that there was no clear way to sustain it. Iran could not move forward large amounts of armor and artillery, rapidly widen its breakthrough, and keep Iraqi forces off balance. It also experienced growing support and logistic problems with each kilometer it advanced, and its forces became steadily better targets as they emerged out of the wetlands and onto dry land.

By this time, Iraq had fully identified the main thrust of the Iranian offensive and had forces equivalent to 20–25 brigades ready to counterattack. While Iraq never approached the point where it was on the edge of a major defeat, it fully committed their elite Republican Guard Division. Iraq also fully committed its air force for the time— flying as many as 150 to 250 sorties per day—and deployed massive artillery reinforcements. By the time the defensive battle was over, Iraq had a force of roughly five divisions and 60,000 men actively engaged on a single sector of the front.

By March 15, all of Iraq's forces were in a position to attack a relatively narrow Iranian thrust simultaneously from the north, south, and west. Iraq also was able to counterattack with virtual air supremacy, and its armed helicopters could operate well into the rear of Iran's positions with no opposition other than machine guns and a few SA-7s. Iraq's helicopters destroyed a number of Iran's boats and bridges, and Iraq made the rear area difficult to traffic by flooding many of its former defense positions. As a result, the Iranian defense began collapsing early on March 17, and by the end of the next day, Iraq had recaptured all of its positions. Both sides took very heavy casualties before Iran was driven back. Iraq lost 2,500 to 5,000 men and several thousand POWs, and Iran lost 8,000 to 12,000.[16]

For reasons that are difficult to explain, Iran then launched a new phase of its attack and struck against the Iraqi positions near Majnoon. This attack took place nearly a week after it should have begun, if its intent was to divert Iraqi forces or take advantage of the broader Iranian attack through the Hawizeh Marshes.

Iran had steadily improved its two access roads to Majnoon during the course of late 1984 and early 1985 and now had two major causeways to the northern island. It had deployed 15,000 to 20,000 men, or two division equivalents, in Majnoon. These forces were ready to attack Iraqi forces in the Majnoon and the northern sector of the Iraqi 3rd Corps by late February and should have been used at the same time as the rest of the forces in Operation Badr.

Iran seems to have waited to use these troops, however, because it hoped that Iraq would cut its forces in Majnoon and the 3rd Corps to deal with the attack further north.[17] In fact, this diversion of Iraq's strength never took place. As a result, Iraq was fully prepared when the Iranian forces finally attacked Majnoon on March 19 and again on March 21. By the time Iran halted its attacks on March 23, it had lost up to 3,000–5,000 more men without taking an inch, and Iraq had suffered only very limited casualties.[18]

Iraq also inflicted at least several thousand more casualties using Tabun and mustard gas. While Iran's forces now had better protection against chemical weapons, they were still vulnerable to mustard gas, particularly when they were forced to remain in the gassed area for any length of time. While Iraq still lacked extensive supplies of Tabun and found it difficult to use gas to attack any target close to its own troops, mustard gas proved effective when Iraqi fighters, helicopters, and artillery could find exposed Iranian forces in a rear area.[19]

This helps explain why there was little additional fighting for several months. Iran did launch another assault in the northern Hawizeh Marshes on June 14, but this at best scored limited gains before the Iranian forces withdrew. Similar raids took place near Qasr e-Shirin on June 19 and in Majnoon on June 28. Iran seems to have tried to keep up the pressure on Iraq without risking major losses while it tried to increase its pressure on the Iraqi positions in Majnoon by surrounding them and inching forward through the wetlands. Iraq responded by steadily improving its defensive positions.

The overall impact of Operation Badr on the leadership of Iraq and Iran seems to have been somewhat similar to the impact of Operation Kheiber in that it tended to reassure each side that its respective tactics were correct. Iran's leadership almost certainly received more warnings from the regular army about the limitations of human-wave tactics, but its initial successes encouraged it to believe that it could overcome the effect of Iraq's lead in weapons and technology if it struck at the proper point, exploited revolutionary fervor, and pressed the attack home. While Iran did not treat the offensive's failure as a victory, it does seem to have seriously believed that it was still successful in terms of attrition and pushing Iraq to the position where it no longer could continue the war. Iran also seems to have become convinced that Iraq was vulnerable to any attack where Iran could use night attacks, mountain warfare, and/or water barriers to deny Iraq the ability to use its armor, artillery, and airpower effectively.

Iraq, in turn, concluded that its basic strategy and tactics were correct and that it could still rely on technology, limited counter-offensives, and fixed defenses. Iraq continued to fight relatively passively. It failed to give the proper emphasis to increasing its infantry and assault capability and concentrated on increasing its reliance on technology.

As for the internal situation in each country, neither state faced a major internal threat. The war may not have been anywhere near as popular as either set of leaders claimed, but it did seem inevitable. The various anti–Saddam Hussein groups in Iraq had little practical influence and little power to threaten the regime, although there were occasional bombs and assassination attempts. The People's Mujahideen of Iran, or Mujahideen e-Khalq, continued to explode bombs, but their leader, Massoud Rajavi, remained in Paris. While there were a few anti-war demonstrations, they had little more effect than the protests of the Freedom Party led by ex-Prime Minister Barzargan. Iran was able to hold new elections and Khameini was re-elected on August 16. The new cabinet was sworn in on October 23 and continued to support Khomeini and the war. The only major development was that

Khomeini and the Assembly of Experts made the Ayatollah Hossein Ali Montazari the official successor to Khomeini on November 23.[20]

The Air and Tanker Wars in 1985

Iraq's concentration on technology was reflected in new strikes against urban and oil targets. Between January 1 and March 31, Iraq claimed to have hit roughly 30 ships, while Iran hit seven. According to some estimates, this brought the total strikes in the tanker war since March 1984 to 65 Iraqi and 25 Iranian attacks. Iranian ships also began to patrol more aggressively in the Gulf, inspecting occasional freighters and making new threats to halt any traffic being transshipped to Iraq. Iraq responded with naval artillery fire against the offshore wells and facilities in Iran's Cyrus oil field.

Iraq also launched a series of relatively large-scale air and missile strikes against Iranian cities. It carried out as many as 158 air strikes over a three-day period in March. It hit nearly 30 towns and cities and struck as deep as Tehran. Iran responded to these strikes on March 12 and 14 by launching its first Scud B strikes against Iraqi cities, using what seem to have been Libyan-supplied missiles, although they may have come from Syria. Other deliveries came later from the PRC and/or North Korea.[21] The Scuds were fired by the Khatam ol-Anbya Missile Force, attached to the air element of the Revolutionary Guards.

The Scud's range exceeded 300 kilometers and allowed Iran to strike against Baghdad. The missile only had a 1,000 kilogram warhead, however, and its accuracy was not predictable within less than 1–2 kilometers. Even after Iran fired enough missiles to be able to compensate for various bias errors in the the targeting and guidance system, it rarely hit meaningful targets.

Iran launched a total of 14 Scuds in 1985, 8 in 1986, and 17 in 1987. Most of these missiles were launched against Iraqi cities, and Iran had an advantage over Iraq in that it could reach Iraq's major cities from the front, while Iraq could not reach key targets like Tehran and Qom. Even so, most of the missiles Iran launched against Baghdad tended to strike in the southwest suburbs of Baghdad rather than the Ministry of Defense, which seemed to be Iran's main target. While Iran did score some accidental hits on civilian targets, most missiles hit vacant lots or buildings with only a few people and did little more than knock out windows and make a loud bang. Iran did continue its attacks well into May, however, and eventually launched enough missiles to kill several hundred people.

Both sides continued their attacks on civil targets until yet another limited cease-fire was declared on June 30. By this time, Iran and Iraq had been exchanging missiles for air raids against civilian targets for more than a month, and the cease-fire on civilian targets of June 1984 was little more than a memory. The political and strategic effect of the missile casualties Iran inflicted on Iraq was as limited, however, as the civilian casualties that Iraqi bombing inflicted on Iran.

Each side's strikes at population centers still failed to have the desired political or economic impact of forcing the opposing side to end the war. The attacks were too scattered in time, lacked concentration of force, and did not produce major effects in any given civilian target. In fact, once the initial shock of new rounds of attacks wore off, public opinion seems to have accepted each new round in the "war of the cities" as yet another reason to hate the opposing side and continue the war.

Iraq, for example, conducted its fiftieth air raid on Tehran by mid-June, but the net effect of such raids was at best to make Iranians camp outside Tehran at night and then return to live and work in the city during the day. Although Iran had launched its twelfth Scud attack on Baghdad by mid-June, it did so little real damage that life proceeded virtually as normal. This reaction became even more clear when attempts at a new UN-sponsored civilian bombing moratorium failed. Even a major series of Iraqi air strikes on eight Iranian cities in August, which lasted for nearly ten days, ended in business as usual in spite of several hundred more casualties.[22]

Iraq was learning, however, that it could now conduct such raids with far less fear of losing aircraft to Iranian fighters. Iraqi pilots began to make extensive use of Matra 530 air-to-air missiles in addition to the Magic 1. Iraq limited its use of Soviet fighters largely to bombing and close air support roles and increasingly relied on its Mirage F-1s for both air-to-air combat and deep strikes. By mid-1985, Iraq claimed to have shot down 12 to 14 F-14 fighters. While these claims were sharply exaggerated, Iraq found that its new French air-to-air missiles allowed it to achieve much higher kill ratios that the export versions of Soviet missiles, such as the AA-2 Atoll. Iran also was unable to put up much of a fighter screen to defend either its cities or oil targets. Iranian fighters rarely engaged Iraqi aircraft, even when they attacked Tehran, Tabriz, Isfahan, and other cites.

The Fighting on the Ground During the Rest of 1985

The fighting on the ground still involved serious clashes involving thousands of men, but it did not lead to massive offensives. Iranian forces scored limited gains in the wetlands north of Fakken on July 3 and 13. Iran also conducted small operations near Sumar on July 26 and near Mandali on July 30. A more serious battle took place near Sumar on September 25, and Iran launched a limited ground offensive and made some gains in the north in the Neimak region of Bakhtaran province.[23]

In the north, Iran continued to outbid and outplay Iraq in gaining the support of the Kurds. Iran had shown in previous years that it had the manpower and ethnic unity to mercilessly put down any Kurdish resistance. At the same time, its victories in the north put it in a position to give the Barzani faction of Iraq's Kurds considerable military support. The Barzani-led Kurdish Democratic Party (KDP) was able to steadily increase its raids throughout 1985 and early 1986, and the rival Patriotic Union of Kurdistan (PUK) finally decided not to reach a new autonomy agreement with Baghdad.

Iran succeeded in further undermining the Kurdish Democratic Party of Iran (KDPI) throughout the course of early 1985, and Iraq provided it with little support. The end result was that Ghassemlou, the leader of the KDPI, seems to have broken with Iraq in April and to have turned to Iran for terms. This led the KDPI to be expelled from the anti-Khomeini coalition in Paris headed by Massoud Rajavi, the leader of the People's Mujahideen. It also allowed Iran to increasingly work with the Barzanis and Jalal Talabani of the PUK to launch operations against Iraq. This led to new fighting during the summer and fall of 1985.

During July, constant guerrilla and low-level infantry fighting took place in the Kurdish border area of Iraq between a mix of Pasdaran and anti-Iraqi Kurds and Iraqi troops backed by pro-Iraqi Kurdish scouts and home guards. Iran seems to have had the edge in this fighting, although it had little strategic effect. The pro-Iranian forces eased their pressure on Iraq in August but only in preparation for a more serious attack on the Ruwandez Valley.

This attack began on September 8 and lasted for more than a week. Iran took up to 200 square kilometers, although its gains had little more than limited tactical value. Iran also captured part of a 240-square mile area in Iraqi Kurdistan, west of the Iranian town of Piranshahr, about 550 kilometers north of Tehran. Both sides lost at least 2,000 men during this fighting in the course of one 10-hour encounter, and Iraq and Iran may have lost as many as 2,500 men in a day.[24] It was becoming increasingly clear that Iran now dominated the battle for the Kurds and could exploit its alliances to achieve limited gains of Iraqi territory.

At the same time, Turkey made it increasingly clear that it would secure the portion of the pipelines on Turkish territory and help Iraq in suppressing the Kurds near the border area. Turkish forces continued to actively seek out and destroy Kurdish rebel groups in Turkey and actively hunted down such groups in Iraq as part of the Turkish-Iraqi "hot pursuit" agreement reached in 1985. Strong Turkish threats to cut Turkish trade with Iran kept Iran from exploiting Kurdish separatism in the areas near Iraq's northern oil fields and pipeline to Turkey. The Turkish Third Army also deployed some 12,000–20,000 men in the border area. When Iraq withdrew some of its troops in northern Iraq to reinforce the southern front in late 1985, it issued arms to the Christian villages near Kirkuk.

Similar skirmishing occurred on other fronts. Iran constantly kept up its pressure on Iraqi positions guarding the western edge of the Hawizeh Marshes. The low-level fighting that occurred on the southern front during the periods when no formal offensive action took place killed about 100 men a day, with most of the fighting occurring in the marsh areas. Similar fighting and losses occurred on the northern sector of the front.

Even minor clashes and battles could produce significant losses, and one of Iran's small July attacks may have produced over 2,000 Iranian casualties in a single day. The net result was that Iran did not score any major gains during 1985, but it did gain about 150 to 220 square kilometers in the central and northern sectors by the time most of the land fighting halted in November.

The key tactical result of all of this scattered land fighting, at least in terms of its impact on shaping what happened in 1986, was that Iran continued to dominate the struggle for control of the marsh areas and the wetlands in the south. This was particularly true in the Hawizeh Marshes. Iraq tried to deal with this by improving its fields of fire and warning. It cut down the reeds in the marsh area near its positions to remove the cover available to Iranian forces. It built watch towers, with night vision devices and acoustic sensors, to try to provide warning of Iranian action. Iraq, however, followed passive strategy and largely conceded the wetlands to Iran. At the same time, the Iranians also increased their patrols off the Iraqi shore of the Shatt. As a result, Iran improved its ability to launch amphibious and wetlands attacks to both the north and south of Basra.

Iraq Again Escalates the Air War

As for the oil war, Iraq relied largely on strikes against tankers until August. It continued to use its Exocets. While Iran was now attempting to use decoy balloons, chaff, and special paint, Iraq also improved its tactics. It launched the Exocet at lower altitudes and flew closer to its targets. France helped Iraq make these improvements in its tactics, and France provided U.S.-made inertial navigation systems on its Super Etendards to improve their accuracy.[25]

The Iraqi attacks were not able to interdict tanker traffic to Iran, however, and produced a relatively limited number of kills relative to total tanker movements. They also followed a pattern in which Iraq tended to fly its peak sortie numbers on Sunday. This seems to have reflected a pause on Friday (the weekly holiday and day of worship), extensive service and preparation activity on Saturday, and then a slow loss of operational capability during the week. Nevertheless, commercial tankers showed they were not interested in taking any chances and many refused to come to Kharg Island.

Iran also created an effective tanker shuttle. It leased six tankers and started to shuttle oil on its own vessels between Kharg and Sirri Island, which was well over 800 kilometers further away from Iraq. Iran felt that Iraq's Exocet attacks were largely limited to the area south and immediately east of Kharg Island and that Sirri would be beyond the range of Iraqi attack aircraft. The shuttle was also structured to allow Iran to conduct a convoy operation, with the tankers moving close to the coast with Iranian ships providing escorts, and Iranian fighters and surface-to-air missiles providing some area defense coverage. Iran still lost some of the tankers to Iraqi Exocets, but the "Sirri Shuttle" was effective enough to lead Iraq to change its bombing tactics.

Up to the time the shuttle began in the spring and summer of 1985, Iraq had tended to avoid strikes on Kharg Island. Iraq did launch an air raid on Kharg Island on May 30, but this attack was more a symbolic gesture than an attempt to achieve serious results. The new Iraqi air strikes did little more than start new fires in the island's sixty-square-mile tank farm. The new strike was the first successful strike on Kharg since June 1984, and Iraq did not repeat this attack for several months.

In mid-August, however, Iraq began a far more serious set of attacks on Kharg Island whose timing strongly indicates they were a response to the new Sirri Shuttle. These air raids began on August 14. While the new attacks did not damage Iran's newly repaired Sea Island terminal, they did seriously damage the main offshore loading point of "T-Jetty." They were followed by another major attack on August 25, and may have temporarily cut Kharg's export capacity by about 30 percent.

In order to achieve these results, Iraq had made significant changes in its aircraft, tactics, and training. Indian and French experts had steadily improved Iraq's training and planning. Iraq had taken deliveries of new versions of the Mirage F-1, which could launch the Exocet missile, carried additional fuel tanks, and could be refueled over Iraq before they struck at Iran. These measures greatly extended the operational range of the Iraqi F-1s and the range at which Iraq could launch Exocet attacks; eventually, as a result, Iraq returned the Super Etendards it had borrowed from France, although one Super Etendard seems to have been lost in an accident or in combat.

This Iraqi experience with the need to improve its fighter performance reflects a general lesson of modern war. As is the case in the other wars under study, every improvement in fighter range-payload and in navigation and munitions delivery avionics proved to be important. Although Kharg Island is only about 225 kilometers south of the Iraqi coast, it was still close to the range limit of fully loaded Iraqi fighters of the type that Iraq had at the start of the war.

As for tactics, it is important to note that Iraq faced a major challenge. Nearly 90 percent of Iran's wartime oil exports had to be exported from Kharg Island, and this made it a key target. The facilities on Kharg, however, were very difficult for Iraq to destroy without advanced long-range attack aircraft or bombers. Kharg Island is comparatively large (32 kilometers miles wide by 60 kilometers long). All of the main pipelines and oil facilities on Kharg are well dispersed, redundant, and well buried or sheltered. Oil flows to Kharg from the mainland through buried and underwater pipelines. Iranian oil also flows under natural pressure, and oil production in Iran does not require the large vulnerable surface facilities like desalinization plants and gas-oil separators common in the southern Gulf.[26]

As a result, the loading facilities on Kharg Island became the main air target for fighter bombers. These facilities include the T-Jetty on the island's eastern side and the much smaller J-Jetty or Sea Island loading facility on the western side. These targets are comparatively small, however, and Iran defended them with surface-to-air missiles and anti-aircraft (AA) guns. Iraq could only successfully destroy them by committing large numbers of aircraft and hitting jetties with considerable accuracy. This meant that direct attacks on Kharg meant Iraq had to risk considerable fighter losses.

Iraq counted this vulnerability with French help in countermeasures and in changing its attack runs to reduce their vulnerability to ground-based air defenses. At the same time, France may also have given Iraq a limited stand-off capability. The precise munitions Iraq used in its attacks after mid-August 1985 are unclear. By now, however, Iraq seems to have acquired French AS-30 laser-guided bombs, Thompson CSF Atlis laser designators, Soviet X29L laser-guided missiles with 12–15 kilometer ranges, other laser-guided bombs, Armatt missiles, and three types of cluster bombs. It is clear that from August on, Iraq's strikes were more accurate than in previous attacks. Iraqi reports claimed Iraq succeeded by using "some 100,000 pounds of bombs," but Iraq never launched enough aircraft to remotely approach such a payload delivery capability.

Foreign reports differ on whether the Iraqis attacked on August 14 using two or four waves of aircraft, but some of these reports indicated that the first wave used French ECM and anti-radiation missiles to suppress the Hawk and Shilka surface-to-air missiles.[27] These same reports indicate that the succeeding waves of Iraqi aircraft launched stand-off missiles at ranges of 6 to 8 kilometers. Iraqi fighters also seem to have fired Brandt 68-mm rockets.[28] Other factors that indicate Iraq used AS-30 missiles in its attacks on oil facilities are the accuracy with which Iraqi aircraft hit the western jetties and control facility and the size of the explosions. The AS-30 has a 240-kilogram warhead, flies at less than 100 meters above the surface, and is much more effective against hard targets than unguided rockets. The AS-30 and its associated Atlas laser designator pods are known to have been delivered to Iraq no later than November 1985, and Iraqi pilots are known to have trained in France during this period.[29]

Iraqi fighters went on to hit Kharg with a total of four large-scale raids between mid-August and the beginning of September. Iran responded by stepping up its naval harassment of Gulf shipping. By early September 1985, a total of more than 130 ships had been attacked by both sides since the renewal of the new tanker war in March. Iran also made new threats to attack ships going to southern Gulf ports.

Iraq ignored these threats and kept up its attacks on Kharg Island. By September 12, Iraq had launched its ninth major attack on Kharg since mid-August, and on September 19, it launched another major raid that cut export production by up to 50 percent. This raid was so serious that it led President Khameini to make yet another threat to close the Straits. Iraq again ignored such threats and kept up its raids.

Each Iraqi attack, however, became progressively more difficult. Iran steadily reorganized and strengthened its air defenses on the Island and shot down several Iraqi Mirage F-1s. Iraq evidently benefited from virtual surprise during its first mass attacks on Kharg in 1985. It flew at extremely low altitudes and suddenly popped up to attack Iranian air defenses.[30] After this time, Iran countered by strengthening its SHORAD defenses to force Iraqi fighters to fly at higher altitudes and learned to identify the flight profiles of the fighters illuminating targets on Kharg. Iran may also have begun to use radar reflectors and/or decoys to discourage AM-30 attacks on ships at Kharg, and it claimed to have made modifications to its oil facilities to reduce their radar return.[31]

Nevertheless, Iraq seems to have scored new successes in damaging the loading terminals at Kharg on September 27 and October 3. By early November, some sources indicate Iraq had reduced Iran's shipments via its tanker shuttle to Sirri by 30 to 50 percent and that Iran was forced to draw down on its limited strategic reserve (about 15 million barrels in tanks on Sirri) to supplement the 250,000 additional barrels it could ship from its southern fields at Lavan. By mid-November, Iraq had hit Kharg at least 37 different times.[32] By the end of December 1985, some reports indicate that Iraq had conducted nearly 60 major air strikes against Kharg.

These Iraqi strikes had a considerable political effect. Iran announced it would open its new loading facilities at Ganaveh and would soon issue contracts for a pipeline at Jask. Iran even went so far as to indicate it planned to abandon Kharg for the war's duration, although such plans proved to be far more ambitious than real.[33]

The military and economic impact of Iraq's strikes is far more uncertain. Iraq took serious losses of skilled pilots and of Mirage aircraft. Iran's aggressive discounting and chartering of more shuttle tankers allowed it to keep its average monthly oil exports relatively high in spite of the damage it suffered, and Iran both continued to improve its short-range air defenses and its ability to repair any damage to the jetties. Iraq found it difficult to sustain significant damage at an acceptable loss rate.

Part of the problem Iraq faced lay in the number of loading points involved. Kharg was designed for a maximum loading capacity of 6.5 MMBD and had actually loaded a maximum of 6 MMBD before the war. The global oil glut had already reduced Iran's daily output, and Iran had facilities for 14 small- to medium-sized tankers on the east side of the island and for 20 tankers on the west side, including three super-tankers. A well-sheltered, computerized switching facility allowed Iran to avoid oil spills and rapidly shift from one loading point to another. The loading-points targets were also relatively easy to repair, and this made it very difficult for Iraq to achieve enough damage to really halt Iranian exports.[34]

This helps explain why the statistics on the overall impact of the oil war do not reflect a major loss of annual oil exports or earnings. Work by Wharton Econometrics, the Petroleum Finance Company, and John Roberts of the Middle East Institute shows that Iranian exports actually rose from 1.36 MMBD in 1984 to 1.8 MMBD in 1985 and dropped to 1.5 MMBD in 1986. Iranian oil revenues were $10.9 billion in 1984, $12.95 billion in 1985, and then dropped to $6.81 billion in 1986, largely as the result of the crash in world oil prices. In short, the flow of Iranian exports was far more affected by the growing world oil glut than by Iraqi bombing.

Both sides continued the tanker war during late 1985, although both followed very different patterns. Iran was not yet ready to attack third-country shipping in the Gulf or to try to put direct military pressure on Saudi Arabia or Kuwait. It concentrated largely on search ships moving through the Straits and harassing shipping moving to and from Iraq's main allies to the Gulf. The Iranian Navy stepped up its search of ships moving through the Gulf in September. It intercepted nearly 300 cargo ships during the month of October and kept these levels up during the rest of the early winter. It also had its first encounter with a Western warship since early in the war when a French frigate prevented an Iranian gunboat from searching a French cargo vessel.[35]

Iraq, in contrast, concentrated on doing physical damage to shipping in Iranian waters. By the end of 1985, Iraq's use of Exocet helped it to raise the number of ships hit, damaged, or attacked to nearly 200 since the first major air attacks on ships in the Gulf began in May 1981. Over 150 of these attacks had occurred since March 1985.[36]

In spite of its problems in sustaining any serious damage to Kharg, Iraq was confident enough to declare that 1985 was the "year of the pilot." It claimed to have flown 20,011 missions against Iran, 77 destructive raids against Kharg Island, and to have scored 124 effective hits on "hostile" maritime targets. An Iraqi military spokesman also claimed that Iran had lost 38,303 dead.[37] Iraq also was actively benefiting from a rise in its own oil exports. Its average annual daily production rose from 1.0 MMBD in 1983 to 1.209 MMBD in 1984 and 1.433 MMBD in 1985. In spite of cuts in the price of oil, oil revenues rose from $9.65 billion in 1983 to $11.24 billion in 1984 and $12.95 in 1985. Iraq now claimed to be exporting 1.0 MMBD through its Turkish pipeline and 200,000 BPD of oil and product by road. It also began to export up to another 500,000 BPD in September, when it opened a connection to the Saudi pipeline to the Red Sea port of Yanbu.

As for Iran, it still avoided any major provocation in the Gulf. It did, however, put new pressure on the southern Gulf states. In December, Iranian-sponsored terrorists conducted a series of car-bombings against the U.S. Embassy and other targets in Kuwait. These attacks were aimed at forcing Kuwait to halt its aid to Iraq. Iraq then responded by launching air and missile attacks against five Iranian towns. This led to a series of sporadic missile and artillery exchanges against area targets but did not produce any significant results.

Notes

1. The analysis of phase four is based heavily on Anthony H. Cordesman's trips to the region and interviews of Iraqi and Iranian officers and officials, plus

his prior writing for the *Armed Forces Journal International* and in the book *The Gulf and the Search for Strategic Stability*, Boulder, Westview, 1984. It also draws heavily upon the work of Edgar O'Ballance, *The Gulf War*, London, Brassey's, 1988; Nikola B. Schahgaldian, *The Iranian Military Under the Islamic Republic*, Santa Monica, Rand R-3473-USDP, 1987; Sepehr Zabih, *The Iranian Military in Revolution and War*, London, Routledge, 1988; Keith McLauchlan and George Joffe, *Iran and Iraq: The Next Five Years*, Special Report 1083, London, Economist Press, 1987; and various working papers for the International Institute for Strategic Studies, Royal United Services Institute.

2. ACDA, *World Military Expenditures and Arms Transfers, 1986*, Washington, D.C., GPO, 1986, pp. 120–121.

3. The authors' estimate is based on the IISS, *Military Balance, 1984–1985*, London, International Institute for Strategic Studies, pp. 61–63.

4. Iraq claimed to have hit more than 10 Iranian ships. It is unlikely that it hit more than one or two.

5. There is at least one report that Iran planned to seize Goat Island in the Straits of Hormuz from Oman in mid-February and was discouraged only by an American warning. This report is very uncertain. See O'Ballance, op. cit., p. 156.

6. See Jim Bussert, "Iran-Iraq War Turns Strategic," *Defense Electronics*, September 1984, pp. 134–136.

7. Ironically, Saudi Arabia's brilliant chief of operations was shunted aside for allowing the intercept and kill of the Iranian F-4. Saudi Arabia was trying to avoid any steps that could broaden the war.

8. Douglas Martin, "Iranian Jets Damage Japanese Tanker," *New York Times*, July 6, 1984, p. 3.

9. Note, for example, the U.S. during many phases of the war in Vietnam and the USSR during many phases of the war in Afghanistan.

10. See Nick Cook, "Iraq-Iran—The Air War," *International Defense Review*, November 1984, pp. 1605–1606.

11. Estimates of Iraqi Mirage F-1 holdings differ sharply. One French journalist estimated in October 1985 that Iraq had taken delivery on as many as 87 regular Mirage F-1s by October 1, 1985, and was in the process of taking delivery on 24 more Mirage F-1s with extended range and the ability to use lasers for optically guided smart bombs. This same journalist indicated that Iraq had ordered 24 additional such Mirages and had taken roughly four months of training and technical effort to learn how to use smart bombs before launching its August 1985 attacks on Kharg Island. The IISS estimated in the 1986/1987 edition of its *Military Balance* that Iraq had 20 Mirage F-1EQs in the interceptor role, 23 Mirage F-1EQ-200s in the attack role, and 20 Mirage F-1EQ5s with Exocet in the interdiction role. U.S. sources note that Thompson CSF has copied the laser illuminator and laser-guided smart bomb technology that the U.S. first employed in Vietnam and that Iraq is now using this technology with one fighter illuminating the target and the other launching the laser-guided bomb. This attack method is highly effective only because Iran lacks effective medium- to long-range air defense missiles and fighter cover.

12. These cluster bombs were Chilean copies of U.S. bombs, which were made using stolen U.S. plans.

13. These attacks included such Iranian attacks as Operation Badr across the Hawizeh Marshes on March 11–23, an attack north of the Hawizeh Marshes on June 14, an attack near Qasr e-Shirin on June 19, fighting around Mandali and Merivan on June 20, an attack around Fuka on July 3, an attack near Sumar on July 26, an attack in the Ruwansddiz Valley on September 8, an attack on Mehran on September 16, and an attack near Sumar on September 25. Iraq attacked Qasr e-Shirin on January 31 and Majnoon on February 28 and June 28.

14. O'Ballance, op. cit., pp. 160–161.

15. According to some sources, the regular army challenged Rafsanjani and the Mullahs over the wisdom of this attack because they felt that Iranian forces could not successfully exploit any initial successes and would become trapped in having to use human waves to penetrate Iraqi defenses once they crossed the Hawizeh Marshes. It is unclear that such reports are correct. See O'Ballance, op. cit., pp. 161–162.

16. *Economist*, March 30, 1985, p. 47; *Jane's Defence Weekly*, March 30, 1985, p. 532. Other sources report Iranian losses of 30,000 and Iraqi losses of 10,000: *Washington Post*, February 11, 1986.

17. O' Ballance blames Rafsanjani for the delay. See O'Ballance, op. cit., pp. 165–166.

18. According to some Iranian sources, this brought the total number of Iranians killed during the war to around 650,000, with 490,000 seriously wounded, although Iran was later to claim that it had only about 150,000 dead during the entire war.

19. These figures are based on supposed Iranian government documents circulated by the People's Mujahideen, and their reliability is uncertain.

20. The People's Mujahideen claimed in mid-August that Khomeini had now executed at least 50,000 and imprisoned 140,000.

21. It is more likely that the missiles were Libyan. Libya had delivered 50 Scud missiles to Iran. Steven Zaloga, "Ballistic Missiles in the Third World," *International Defense Review*, 11/88, pp. 1423–1437.

22. See Zaloga, op. cit., pp. 1423–1437. Also see *The Middle East*, May 1985, pp. 16–18; *Washington Post*, May 27 and July 21, 1985; *New York Times*, May 29 and June 13, 1985; and *Economist*, June 22, 1985, p. 35.

23. *New York Times*, September 10, 1985; *Chicago Tribune* and *Christian Science Monitor*, September 9 and 11, 1985.

24. Ibid.

25. O'Ballance, op. cit., p. 171.

26. *New York Times*, *Baltimore Sun*, and *Wall Street Journal*, August 16 and 17, 1985.

27. The validity of these reports is unclear. The IHawk radars on Kharg seem to have been inoperable during this period, and Iran was badly short of missiles. Some Swedish optically guided laser homing missiles may have been present on the island, but they would not have been affected by ECM.

28. See Gwynne Dyer, "The Gulf: Too Late for a Crises," *Washington Times*, November 6, 1985.

29. See Kenneth Timmerman, "Mirage over Kharg," *Defense and Armaments*, No. 44, October 1985, pp. 53–58.

30. According to some Western sources, this tactic allowed Iraqi planes to directly overfly Iran's surface-to-air missiles for optimal ECM effectiveness and to fire their anti-radiation missiles (ARMs) against targets with fully active radars. These sources claim Iran then rapidly improved its ECM techniques to counter Iraq's ECM (the Hawk is a very difficult system to jam) and adopted radar emission tactics that made Iraq's ARM strikes more difficult. It is uncertain whether these claims are accurate or whether Iran simply redeployed some of its surface-to-air missiles to cover the jetties better and move in new defenses from outside the island.

31. *New York Times*, September 10, 12, and 21, 1985.

32. One has to be careful about accepting such claims. CIA data show little variation in Iranian production during these months. Iran's average monthly production is estimated to have been 2.2 MMBD to 2.6 MMBD from July to January 1986. There is little evidence of more than seasonal fluctuation in Iranian oil exports over any given month.

33. *Chicago Tribune*, December 30, 1985; *New York Times*, December 30, 1985.

34. *Chicago Tribune* and *New York Times*, September 3, 1985; *Washington Times*, September 4, 1985.

35. An interesting sidelight on the Iranian Navy at this time is that Iran failed to take delivery on a new landing ship being built in Britain, called the Lavan, only because the Iranian officer sent to take delivery defected. This ship could carry up to 280 troops and tanks and vehicles, and Britain then refused to deliver the ship to a new Iranian crew. This ship might have been very useful during the Iranian assault on Faw. O'Ballance, op. cit., p. 172.

36. *Los Angeles Times* and *Washington Post*, September 7, 1985.

37. Ibid.

8

PHASE FIVE: IRAN'S "FINAL OFFENSIVES," 1986–1987

Iran Prepares for New "Final Offensives"

Iran's failure to launch new "final offensives" during most of 1984 and 1985 was deceptive. Iran had taken serious losses during 1984 and its spring offensive of 1985, but it had scarcely given up its ambitions to topple Saddam Hussein's regime. Iranian planners continued to try to find some way to strike across or around the Hawizeh Marshes and developed detailed plans to attack Iraq in the south and to capture the Faw Peninsula and Umm Qasr.

The problems Iran faced were formidable. Iran still could mobilize a maximum of little more than a million men. Its regular army had a strength of roughly 305,000 and the Pasdaran a strength of about 350,000. Iran had roughly 1,000 operational main battle tanks, about 1,400 other armored vehicles, and between 600 and 800 artillery weapons. Its Air Force still had some 35,000 men, but only about 60 to 80 operational aircraft.

In contrast, Iraq's regular army and Popular Army had a strength of roughly 800,000, including some 230,000 active reserves. Except for those periods Iran rapidly mobilized the Baseej, Iraq had the advantage in manpower. Iraq also had roughly 4,500 operational main battle tanks, 4,000 other armored vehicles, and over 5,000 artillery weapons. Iraq's Air Force had some 40,000 men, including air defense personnel, and about 500 operational combat aircraft.[1]

This Iraqi strength was reflected in the fact that it was Iraq that launched the first major offensive of 1986. Iraq spent weeks preparing its supply depots near Majnoon and improving its access to the Islands. It then lowered the water level and built up a massive reserve of engineering equipment to support an attack on the Iranian-held northern island. On January 6, which was Iraqi Army Day, two brigades of the

Iraqi Third Corps attacked the Iranian positions on the northern island. The Iranian positions were not particularly sophisticated and were designed more for offensive forces than a strong defense. By January 8, Iraq had pushed Iran out of the southern half of the island.

This Iraqi success did not, however, either halt or delay Iran's plans to attack. Iran's leadership continued to believe that if it could put sufficient strain on Iraq's forces and regime, it could force Iraq's defenses to collapse. Some leaders, like Khomeini, may also have believed in some form of divine intervention.[2] As a result, Iran had built up a powerful attack force in southern Iran during the latter half of 1985. Iran also made major improvements in its amphibious assault capabilities.[3] Iran had also bought large numbers of small boats, bridging equipment, and pontoons during 1985 and had begun major amphibious training exercises in the Caspian Sea. It carried out extensive engineering efforts south of Abadan and built a new military road system on earth mounds through the marshes and flooded areas along the Shatt.

Iran began to use women for rear-area military tasks for the first time in October 1985 in order to free men for assignments at the front. It also drew up provisions for sending civil servants to the front, with up to 10 percent of them serving at full pay.[4] It called up at least 50,000 new volunteers in December 1985 and January 1986, and some estimates went as high as 300,000. Iran bought more chemical defense equipment, and indications began to appear in late 1985 that Syria was providing Iran with aid in developing its own chemical warfare agents.[5]

When Iran mobilized, it deployed its forces to the south. These deployments included nearly two-thirds of its elite Pasdaran Corps, including the Karbala 25th division, Najaf-Ashraf 8th Division, Ashoura Division, and Special Martyr's Brigade, and nearly half of the regular army, including the Bakhtaran 81st Division, Mazandaran 30th Division, and the Khorassan 77th Division. These deployments created a total force of nearly 200,000 troops and the equivalent of some 20 to 25 divisions. A significant number of these Iranian forces were deployed between Ahwaz and Dezful and in the Hoor-al-Azim and Hur el-Hawizeh regions.[6]

During early 1986, Iran deployed its new amphibious lift along the Shatt al-Arab south of Abadan and stockpiled large amounts of small craft and pontoon bridging equipment. Iran also deployed amphibious commando units of roughly 1,000 men. These units were specially trained for amphibious assaults and fighting in wetlands and had an effective command structure similar to that of airborne or special-forces units. These deployments gave Iran greatly enhanced capability to strike across the Shatt al-Arab.[7]

Wal-Fajr 8: Iran Takes Faw

By early February, Iran was ready to launch its new series of offensives. While Iran's exact objectives in launching these offensives are unclear, the main strategic goals seem to have been to seize and retain the Faw Peninsula and block Iraqi access to the Gulf, to carry out a follow-on attack to seize Basra from the north, to disrupt oil production in southern Iraq, to disrupt Iraqi access to Kuwait, and to support a Shi'ite uprising or anti-government operations in southern Iraq.[8]

On February 9, Iran launched the first phase of a two-pronged attack against the Iraqi 3rd Corps and 7th Corps. Iran attempted to split Iraq's forces by attacking at both the northern and southern ends of the southern front. The Iranian forces in the northern prong of the offensive launched three separate thrusts. These thrusts were pressed home as though they were actual offensives, although their real purpose seems to have been largely diversionary.

One thrust occurred near Qurnah at the junction of the Iraqi 3rd and 4th Corps. It ran head on into well-prepared Iraqi defenses, and although Iran launched human-wave attacks for nearly three days, Iraqi firepower drove the Iranian forces back with heavy losses of manpower and equipment. The second thrust was a small armored attack across relatively dry ground south of Qurnah, and this led to a shooting match between Iranian and Iraqi forces at close range. Iraq had superior numbers and better-trained forces, and Iran again suffered heavy losses and around 4,000 casualties. The third thrust occurred on February 14 when Iranian forces attempted to recapture the northern island of Majnoon and were contained in their existing position after suffering heavy losses.

The outcome of the Iranian attacks in the south was different.[9] Iran used the cover of night and poor weather on the night of February 10–11 to launch a major two-pronged amphibious assault on Faw. One part of this assault, supported by frogmen, attacked an island group in the Shatt called Umm al-Rasas, just south of Khorramshahr. Iranian forces quickly took the virtually undefended main island and moved on toward the Basra-Faw Road. The Iranian advance then began to encounter heavy Iraqi opposition, however, and Iranian forces lacked the armor and artillery strength to hold or counterattack. Iraqi forces retook Umm al-Rasas on February 12, and the Iranian division fell back across the Shatt.

It was the second attack that made major gains. These forces struck at the Faw Peninsula in the area near Siba. Although the Shatt was

280-meters wide at this point, and the Iranian forces had to make their crossing at night and in the middle of a driving rain, the Iranian landings were successful. Iran did not succeed in rapidly putting a pontoon bridge across the Shatt near Siba, but it did use boats to land nearly a division's worth of troops at six different points, and Iranian troops began to move forward along a broad front on the coast of the Faw Peninsula.[10]

The Iraqi high command was fooled into thinking Iran's attacks to the north were the main thrust of the offensive. They had most of their reserves in the area around Qurnah and were slow to react. the Iraqi senior commanders in the region were preoccupied with a major Iranian artillery barrage of Basra, and once they understood that Iran was attacking, they seem to have felt the main Iranian thrust was directed at Iraq's positions immediately south of the city.

The Iraqi defenses covering Faw were also relatively poorly prepared. Iraqi planners do not seem to have fully considered the possibility of an Iranian amphibious assault in this area before the Iranian landings and seem to have ignored Faw's potential strategic importance.[11] While the port of al-Faw was largely abandoned, and the long marsh-ringed Faw Peninsula was isolated from Basra and Iraq's main lines of communication, a successful Iranian thrust still offered Iran the ability to cut Iraq off from the Gulf. It also put Iran into a position to both attack Basra from the south and Iraq's main lines of communication to Kuwait.

The local Iraqi forces near Iran's main landing points were limited in number, and the city itself had only about 1,000 Iraqi reservists to defend it. These local forces could not cope with either Iran's multiple landings or Iran's ability to rapidly move over water barriers and surround the town. Iranian forces penetrated deep into Iraqi positions during the initial hours of the attack. The Iraqi troops in Faw held out until February 14, but some of the Iraqi units outside Faw panicked and abandoned their fixed defenses and much of their heavy equipment. While estimates disagree, Iraq seems to have suffered about 4,000 casualties during the initial fighting for Faw, versus 2,500 for Iran, and Iran took some 1,500 Iraqis as prisoners of war.[12]

Further, Iraq could not use its air power effectively during the critical initial phase of the battle. Although Iraq later claimed to have flown up to 355 fighter and 134 combat helicopter sorties per day during the Iranian assault on Faw, the heavy rain over the battle area during the first day of combat made it difficult to fly effective attack sorties. Adequate flying weather did not occur until February 14, and even then the weather was erratic. Iraq took serious fighter losses without being able to find suitable targets. Iran's infantry had learned to disperse, dig in and take cover, and move heavy equipment and supplies in small amounts or at night. Iraq lost 15 to 30 aircraft during the first week of Wal-Fajr 8 and found few exposed targets. This scarcely justified the loss of airplanes which were each worth nearly twenty million dollars.[13]

Iraqi air attacks were also ineffective in destroying communications on the long causeway along the shore of the Shatt al-Arab, from Khorramshahr and Abadan City to the Iranian launch point on the southern tip of Abadan Island. Most movements took place at night. The weather was poor during the day, Iraqi efforts to bomb the causeway were quickly repaired, and Iraqi aircraft failed to do consistent enough damage to any of the bridges across the canals, or *khors*, that cut through the main causeway to inhibit Iranian movements.

As a result of these developments, Iraq was not ready to counterattack during the first few days of the attack, and this allowed Iran to reinforce its troops in Faw to a total of nearly 20,000 men. The Iraqi high command held back its reserves far too long because of its fear of an Iranian attack on Basra and of the Iranian attacks farther north.[14] Once the Iraqi high command did rush forces from the Basra and Qurnah fronts, its initial counterattacks on February 13 and 14 were poorly organized. Iraq did not have elite infantry trained to fight on foot in the assault role. When Iraq did commit elite units, like its 10,000-man Republican Guard Brigades, these were not ready for infantry assaults, close fighting, or movement through the wet lands and marshes. Iraq's superiority in artillery and armor also proved to have little effect against well dug-in troops.

At the height of Iran's success, Iran threatened to break out of the Faw Peninsula and attack Umm Qasr. Iranian troops reached the Khor Abdallah waterway opposite Kuwait, and there were even reports that Iranian forces had surrounded the Iraqi navy base at Umm Qasr, which was only 16 kilometers from Faw. Iran also captured Iraq's main air control and warning center covering the Gulf, which was located north of al-Faw.[15] This resulted in near panic in Kuwait and Saudi Arabia.[16] The resulting fear of an Iraqi defeat led to constant consultation among nearby Arab states, as well as a special Arab Foreign Ministers meeting.

By February 14, the fighting had reached the point where Iran had lost some 8,000 to 10,000 casualties, and Iraq had lost 3,000 to 5,000. Iraq, however, was now deploying its reserves and steadily improving its defenses. Iran also had begun to reach the limit of the forces it could deploy and support. It held Faw and positions near Siba in the north and the Mamlha salt beds in the west but was not strong enough to take on the Iraqi forces in open terrain.[17] Iraq was now able to contain Iran, but it experienced problems when it tried to launch major counter-offensives.

Iraq began its counterattacks with three reinforced brigade groups operating as separate columns. These groups rapidly grew to divisional strength. One column moved southward on the road along the bank of the Shatt al-Arab. It was halted at positions south of Umm Qasr. The second, or central, column moved south along a new road built the previous year in order to allow rapid Iraqi movement without coming under observation or fire from across the Shatt. This road, however, cut through terrain which is soft desert in the dry season and a sea of mud in the wet season. The Iraqi attack was road-bound and could not advance against Iranian forces equipped with large amounts of artillery and light anti-tank weapons. The third column moved along the road on the northern shore of the Khor Abdullah. It too had to fight in open territory and under conditions where its forces could not move off the main road.

Iraq's forces took unacceptable casualties whenever they attacked Iranian forces under these conditions. Iranian troops still fought with fervor and had extensive stocks of weapons. Although Iraqi forces attempted to drive south for nearly a week, they could only make limited gains. While estimates are uncertain, Iraq seems to have lost at least 5,000 dead or critically wounded during these counterattacks. The weather also did not allow Iraq to make optimal use of its superiority in fighters, armed helicopters, and artillery until February 22. By this time, Iranian forces were fully dug-in, and Iran had had more than 10 nights to move men, equipment, and supplies across the Shatt, possibly using a pontoon bridge that was disassembled during the day.

Nevertheless, Iraq then tried to push Iran out of Faw by using sheer brute force. It assigned its best combat commanders to each of the three columns and then used artillery barrages and short infantry rushes to advance from one defensive position to another. Iraq had now fully deployed its superiority in air power, firepower, and armor. Improving weather helped Iraq to make more effective use of multiple rocket launchers (MRLs) for area fire and reduced its use of largely ineffective tube artillery weapons, which could not deliver the required mass of fire within a sufficiently short time period. Iraq expended massive amounts of ammunition against scattered infantry targets in the process. It used up some 200 tank barrels. It fired up to 600 rounds per artillery weapon per day—usually without clear targets. In fact, Iraq used up so much of its artillery ammunition, it had to scour the world for emergency purchases of new ammunition stocks.[18]

Both sides committed many of their key assets to the battle. Iraq continued to lose major amounts of armor and suffered significant fighter losses to ground-based air defenses. Iran claimed to have shot down roughly seven Iraqi fighters a day, while Iraq claimed to have shot down several of Iran's remaining F-4s. Even so, the Iraqi Air Force kept up a sortie rate of several hundred sorties per day, and Iraq claimed to have flown 18,648 sorties over Faw between February 9 and March 31.[19]

Iraqi pilots began to press home their attacks at unusually low altitudes as the weather improved and took the losses inevitable in flying more effective attack sorties.[20] They also began to deliver comparatively large amounts of mustard gas and at least some Tabun. While these fighter attacks had limited killing impact, they did force the Iranians to dig in and largely paralyzed rear-area activity and daytime infantry attacks during fair weather daylight hours. Mustard gas was particularly effective because the Iranian forces were not properly trained in the use of chemical defense gear, and the Baseej received only negligible training and protection equipment.

Iraq was able to score some gains from this effort, but they were scarcely worth the cost. Iraq found that it was paying a high price for its lack of infantry assault and infiltration capability. Even though Iraq committed major further reinforcements from its Third Corps area after February 21, Iraq still could not fight or maneuver effectively. Iraq also continued to take heavy losses when it counterattacked. It lost nearly two battalions in one such attack on February 23–24. Iraq's clumsy attempt to launch a small amphibious flanking attack on March 9–10 may have cost it several additional battalions, and Iraq lost the equivalent of another brigade trying a three-pronged counterattack against dug-in Iranian troops.[21] Many of the limited gains Iraq did make during the day were lost at night, when Iran could make use of its superior ability to fight on foot.

Iraq's 28th and 704th brigades took particularly severe casualties while attempting to advance on Faw in March, and Iraq was forced to organize special trains to carry its wounded.[22] Iraq went to such extremes as forced blood donations, trying to mass recruit the staff of some leading tourist hotels, and forcing empty taxis going north from Basra to carry corpses inside the vehicle and on their roof racks.

Although Iraq launched another counterattack on March 11, Iraqi troops were only able to advance about 7 kilometers over the course of three weeks. By the time Iraq recaptured most of the Mamlha salt beds, the fighting had taken its toll, and both sides had reach a point of near exhaustion. This point of exhaustion finally seems to have been reached on March 20, when an Iranian attempt to improve its position sputtered out, and Iraq then failed to take advantage of the drier terrain to launch new counterattacks.[23] By this time, some 20,000 Iranians and 25,000–32,000 Iraqis were locked into positions only a few hundred meters apart, and neither side had the energy to risk new offensives. Iran had suffered some 27,000–30,000 casualties and Iraq had lost 5,000–8,000.

The Iraqi counterattack on Faw also led to more use of artillery to deliver gas weapons. For example, Iraq tried to use both bombs and artillery gas to support its offensive on February 24. It succeeded in affecting up to 1,800 Iranian troops, but it also gassed some of its own forces.[24] As a result, Iraq gained little from its initial attempts to use gas warfare to support offensive operations. Its still-developing Chemical Corps still could not develop effective area concentrations of gas in most target areas. Weather and water effects robbed Iraqi nerve agents, cyanide agents, and mustard gas of much of their impact. While up to 8,500 Iranian soldiers were affected by gas during the Wal-Fajr 8 and 9 offensive, only 700 seem to have been killed or seriously wounded—an uncertain return in casualties for the size of the Iraqi effort and worldwide criticism of Iraq's use of poison gas.[25]

Wal-Fajr 9: The Continuing Struggle in the Kurdish North

Iran began another offensive while its main forces were still involved in the attack on Faw. This offensive was called Wal-Fajr 9 and took place against the Kurdish area of Iraq, near the northern border and about 270 kilometers north of Baghdad, 95 kilometers northwest of Kirkuk, and 22 kilometers from Sulaimaniyeh. It involved a mix of roughly two divisions worth of Iranian Pasdaran and Baseej and Kurdish forces from the Barzani and KDP factions. It was designed to take advantage of the fact that Iraq lacked the forces to cover the entire north with extensive defensives, and it tried to take some of the valleys in the border area that opened into Iraq.

Wal-Fajr 9 began on February 15 as a comparatively limited attack, and Iranian troops rapidly took some of the ground and villages in the Sulaimaniyeh Valley. They then moved toward Chwarta and took some of the key ridges in the valley about 20 kilometers from Sulaimaniyeh. On February 24–25, Iran launched an attack of up to eight brigades in strength.[26] This Iranian attack seems to have been directed at seizing the high ground above the Sulaimaniyeh-Chwarta Road and took place in areas with mountains over 6,600 feet and involved about 300 square kilometers of Iraqi territory.

Although most Iraqi villages in the area had already been

abandoned, Iran surrounded the town of Chwarta. Iraq then began to withdraw forces from the area to help deal with the struggle for Faw, and Iran took the small garrison town of Sitak on March 2, the day after some 2,500 Iraqi troops had been removed from the area.[27] Although Iraq then began to use chemical weapons, Iranian forces got close enough to Sulaimaniyeh on March 3 to shell it for the first time in the war.

At this point, Iraq seems to have returned forces to the north, and Iran ceased to make major gains. It is clear, however, that Iran was obtaining more support from Kurdish dissidents and from the Barzani faction and the KDP, than it had ever obtained from Iraq's Shi'ites. This became even more clear in May, when Iraqi troops failed to sweep the area between Dahok and Badinan free of Kurdish forces. Barzani and KDP troops were able to start raiding near the Iraqi-Turkish pipeline and seized the small garrison town of Mangesh in the vicinity of Mosul as its supply dump. They held on to the town in spite of a counterattack on May 19 by a regular mountain brigade, a small Republican Guard detachment, and Jash (pro-Iraqi Kurdish) forces. While the Iranian and Kurdish attacks had limited strategic value, their success did tie down significant numbers of Iraqi troops, including the entire Iraqi 11th Division, and reinforced the political impact of Iran's gains in Faw. It was also clear that only the presence of some 30,000 Turkish troops in the area ensured the security of Iraq's oil pipeline to Turkey.[28]

A Stalemate in the South and New Air Strikes

By early April, a pattern of fighting was established in Faw that was to last until early 1988. Iran retained about 200 square kilometers of the Faw Peninsula and managed to keep pontoon bridges operating across the Shatt al-Arab. Iran used this bridge, powered floating bridges, and small craft to supply the bridgehead. Iran also maintained an active force of 20,000–25,000 men in the Faw Peninsula. Iran did not succeed in bringing many heavy weapons into Faw, but it brought artillery forward elsewhere along the front and started to shell Iraq's main air base near Basra at Shuabia.

Iraq, however, was now fully able to contain Iran in the south. It had reestablished solid defensive positions all along the perimeter of Iran's positions in Faw, and, unlike the Iranian positions, Iraq's position had several main defensive lines fed by three major roads and with rear areas filled with supplies, air-defense units, and artillery fire points. Iraq had built up extensive ammunition stocks and had a massive superiority in firepower of something like 5:1 to 7:1. Iraq also gained a much better idea of where Iranian targets were located, as the front stabilized into fixed positions. This improved the accuracy of Iraqi fire and helped force Iran's forces to stay dug in and concentrate on holding their existing gains.[29]

At the same time, Iraq's previous losses discouraged Iraq from launching more counterattacks on Faw, in spite of the fact that changes in the weather continued to dry out the terrain in Faw and gave Iraq a steadily improving capability to use its armor. Iraq could not face the sheer cost in casualties, and it also could not take the risk of tying up so many of its forces in such a counteroffensive.

Iran continued to keep 300,000–400,000 men along the 1,100-kilometer front in positions where they were constantly ready for another attack, and Iran had the edge in terms of strategic position. In the north, Kurdish rebel groups expanded the areas under their control, and Iranian troops remained within ten miles of Sulaimaniyeh. In the center, Iranian troops were in the Meimak Hills about 70 miles from Baghdad. Major concentrations of Iranian troops were still in position to attack across the Hawizeh Marshes to reach the Baghdad-Basra Highway, and Iran remained in Faw with the equivalent of two full divisions. Iran could concentrate its forces at any point and take advantage of Iraq's lack of strategic depth, while Iraq had no major objective in Iran that its forces could credibly seize.

Iran also kept up its military pressure on shipping and the southern Gulf. The Iranian Navy had searched its first West German ship on January 9, its first U.S. ship on January 12, and its first British ship on January 13. It carried out several helicopter attacks on shipping, beginning with an attack on a Turkish tanker on March 3. Iran also kept up its terrorist pressure on Kuwait, and it may have released some mines in the Gulf as a harassing gesture.[30] Iran's leadership made a new and harsher series of threats against Kuwait and Saudi Arabia and pointedly reminded Kuwait that Iraq's loss of Faw had left Kuwait far more exposed to Iranian military action.[31]

Iran also stated on January 7 that it would open three new oil terminals on its southern coast outside the range of Iraqi fighters. These terminals were to be opened in February and March and to be located at Bandar Lengeh in the Straits, on Qesham Island in the Straits, and on Jask outside the straits. These terminals were to be fed by Iran's shuttle of leased tankers. Iran also stated that it would create a new pumping station at Ganaveh, about 40 kilometers from Kharg.[32] In practice, however, Iran generally found it easier to transfer oil to tankers from a floating terminal off the coast of Larak, which opened in June 1986 and which was to become a major target for long-range Iraqi air raids.

It is scarcely surprising, therefore, that Iraq kept up its emphasis on strategic bombing. It hit targets like the Qotar Bridge, a key link between Iran and Turkey, on March 13. On May 7, the Iraqi Air Force launched a major raid on Tehran. This raid left Iran's biggest oil refinery in flames and damaged one of its processing units, although it missed both catalytic crackers in the 254,000 BPD facility. Iraq hit the Yarchin arms factory on May 23 and carried out occasional strikes against targets like trains and other civilian targets. Iraq succeeded in destroying the satellite dish at Assadabad in raids on June 9 and July 2, which knocked out much of Iran's overseas telephone and telex links for nearly two weeks.[33]

The Iraqi Air Force also kept up its attacks on the Iranian tanker shuttle to Sirri. The chief of Iraq's Navy, Rear Admiral Abed Mohammed Abdullah, claimed in July 1986 that Iraq had destroyed 58 Iranian tankers, 85 other merchant ships, and 40 supply ships since the beginning of the war in September 1980.[34]

The Battle for Mehran and Karbala-1

Iraq did launch one major counterattack against Iran in 1986. While Saddam Hussein seems to have felt he could tolerate the situation in Faw and Kurdistan, he seems to have become increasingly concerned about the need to find some way of showing that Iraq could win an offensive victory and about the need to secure the attack routes to Baghdad. As a result, Iraq prepared a major offensive to recapture the town of Mehran, which was on one of the key invasion routes from Iran to Baghdad.

Iraq deployed about two division equivalents of the Iraqi 2nd Corps, totaling about 25,000 men, around Mehran on May 10. Mehran was a relatively easy target. It was a virtually abandoned town, about one-third of a mile inside the border, and about 160 kilometers east of Baghdad. It also was located in an area defended by only 5,000 low-grade Iranian troops. As a result, it offered Iraq a relatively easy victory and the ability to conquer Iranian territory with none of the risks inherent in counterattacking Faw.

The Iraqi forces attacked Mehran on May 14. By May 17, Iraqi forces took Mehran, the heights above Mehran, and five neighboring villages in Iran. They fought their way through the initial hills in the border area and inflicted heavy casualties on the poorly prepared Iranian troops. Iraq made effective use of its multiple rocket launchers and was able to drive Iranian troops out of virtually all the lower ground.

This success gave Iraq a significant symbolic victory, although the

Kurds in the KDP scored minor victories against Iraq at Mangesh and Dahok in northern Iraq. Iraq also scored another minor victory at Fuka in the south and then noisily vowed to stay in Mehran until the end of the war. Iraq did not, however, succeed in taking the high ground and mountains, ranging up to 1,500 meters, to the east of Mehran.[35] According to some reports, this was because Saddam Hussein rejected plans by General Tawfiq, the 2nd Corps Commander, to advance toward Dehloran and secure the surrounding heights, and because the Iraqi attack force was armor heavy and lacked the infantry to fight in mountainous terrain.[36]

Iran responded immediately with a new set of threats about a final offensive, and there even indications that it might attack on May 19, which was the anniversary of the death of the Prophet's nephew, Ali.[37] In practice, however, Iran secretly prepared for a counteroffensive to retake Mehran. The Iraqis had made the mistake of trying to hold the area in spite of the fact they were exposed to attacks from the heights on several sides.

Iran built up a force based on the 10th Infantry Division that was equivalent to four to five Pasdaran brigades and which had a large number of companies with experience in mountain warfare. This force was named after the Caravan of Karbala, and it was at this point that the Karbala offensives began to replace the Wal-Fajr offensives.

The Iranian forces began to attack Iraqi positions in the heights on June 20 and rapidly demonstrated that Iran retained the edge in mountain warfare. Iran used at least some poison gas and also took advantage of the fact that Iraqi forces did not aggressively patrol more than 20 kilometers outside Mehran and had stopped below the first ridge in the nearby Poshtkuh Mountains. As a result, Iranian forces rapidly overran the positions of the Iraqi forces defending Mehran, killing one brigade commander and causing 1,200–2,000 Iraqi casualties.

Once again, command-and-control problems inhibited the Iraqi Air Force. The command to provide full-scale air support came far too late, and Iraq flew only 33 helicopter sorties during the critical phase of the Iranian assault, versus a capacity of over 500, and only 100 air-support missions, versus a capacity of over 300.

By the 3rd of July, Iraq was forced to admit that Iran had liberated Mehran. Iran not only took back the five heights Iraq had captured, it took four new minor hill positions in Iraqi territory and advanced 12–40 kilometers further to the west. While it is unclear whether U.S. arms shipments played any direct role in this victory, it is important to note that the TOW anti-tank weapon was well suited for striking bunkers and weapons located in mountain cover and for stopping any Iraqi armored counterattacks.[38]

Iraq Shifts Back to the Air and Tanker Wars

Iraq tried to respond to its defeat at Mehran with an attack on Iranian positions at Majnoon, but the attack quickly failed and forced Iraq to turn to air power.[39] Iraq launched a new wave of bombing directed at area targets in Iran after a three-month lull. Between July 20 and 30, Iraq hit at targets as diverse as a sugar factory, military camps, an oil refinery, and urban targets in Arak, Marivan, and Sanandaj. The raid on Arak on July 27 resulted in the death of at least 70 civilians.[40]

Iraq also extended the range of its air strikes against Iran's oil targets. On August 12, Iraqi fighters raided the Iranian facilities at Sirri Island for the first time and hit three tankers loading at the terminal. This attack had special importance because Iran was now transshipping virtually all of its oil exports from Kharg. Sirri was also about 640 kilometers from Iraq and only 240 kilometers from the Straits of Hormuz. The attack showed that Iran faced far more serious difficulties in finding a secure way to export its oil than it had previously believed.

The full details of Iraq's attack on Sirri are unclear. Iraq sent four Mirage F-1s, but it is unclear whether they fired Exocet air-to-ship missiles, electro-optical guided missiles, or laser-guided bombs. Iraq may have used converted Antonov tankers to refuel the Mirages or even have staged out of a friendly Gulf country. Other sources indicate, however, that Iraq simply took the risk of flying at very high altitudes, knowing that if its fighters had to engage in air-to-air combat they would probably use too much fuel to return.

In any case, the attack on Sirri confronted Iran with major problems in transshipping its oil. Iran had already learned that it did not have easy alternatives to using Sirri. Iraqi fighters had first overflown Sirri on June 24, and this had led Iran to shift its transshipment activity to Larak. The Iranian effort to set up an alternative 1.5 MMBD terminal called Wal-Fajr II at Larak Island, about 130 miles east of Sirri, presented major difficulties, however, because of weather during the monsoon season and porting problems. As a result, the five mother tankers or transfer ships at Larak had moved back to Sirri.[41] The Iraqi strike now forced Iran to relocate three major transfer ships back to Larak and to move its tanker-transfer loading site to a position about 15 miles northeast of Sirri, which placed its tankers closer to its coastal air defenses. It also forced Iran to make further major oil discounts in order to attract the tanker traffic it needed to its transfer terminals.

Iraq followed up its strike on Sirri with repeated raids against the key oil-shipping facilities on the mainland, against Kharg, and against Iran's refineries. By late August, Iraq had flown 120 sorties against Kharg alone in the preceding twelve months. Iran also formally declared on September 3 that all Iranian oil facilities were now within its Naval Exclusion Zone.

Iran had to raise its shuttle tanker fleet from 11 to 20 ships. Iran even chartered the world's largest tanker—the 564,739 ton *Seawise Giant*—to try to provide a stable loading platform at Larak. These charters cost Iran some $60 million annually, excluding rising insurance premiums, the cost of replacing combat losses, and $20,000 per day per tanker in operating costs. Nevertheless, Iraq's air strikes continued to be effective. Iran's average daily exports dropped from around 1.6 MMBD to 1.1 MMBD and reached daily lows of as little as 800,000 BPD.[42] Iraq also flew an unusually aggressive number of sorties against Iranian forces at the front, averaging 45–75 sorties per day.

Iran replied by firing its first missile at Iraq in thirteen months, evidently targeting the Iraqi refinery at Dowra.[43] It also began to fire a missile of its own manufacture against Iraq, called the Oghab. Iran had been developing this missile since the first Iraqi FROG attacks on Dezful in 1980. It was 4,820 mm long, 230 mm in diameter, and weighed 360 kilograms. It had a range of roughly 40 kilometers and a warhead weighing 70 kilograms, and it was evidently derived from the Chinese Type-82 field rocket. Iran fired a total of 19 Oghabs in 1986, 81 in 1987, and 104 in 1988. These missiles, however, had relatively little effect. Iran lacked any beyond visual range (BVR) targeting capability, the Oghabs could not reach Iraq's key cities, and their warhead was too small to have high lethality.[44]

Iran again used the annual pilgrimage to Mecca to have its pilgrims cause unrest in Saudi Arabia and launched a conspicuous attack on a tanker loading at the Fateh oil field terminal in United Arab Emirates (UAE) waters south of Sirri.[45] This brought the annual total number of attacks on Gulf shipping up to 59, versus 46 in all of 1985 and 40 in 1984.[46] Iran, however, lacked the mix of air and sea power which it needed to retaliate effectively against the shipping that aided Iraq.

Iran did send daily patrols by its P-3 Orion and C-130 Hercules aircraft from Lavan Island to try to plot tanker movements. It also retained a limited capability to strike with its remaining F-4s, which could fire Maverick missiles. Tankers and other ships were generally safe, however, and particularly if they could transit between anchorages around Dubai and anchorages west of Qatar at night.

The Iranians did not acquire even a limited capability to conduct night anti-ship attacks until June 1986 when they obtained delivery of night-vision goggles for their helicopter pilots and subsystems to allow their AB-212 helicopters to fire short-range wire-guided AS-12 missiles. While they hit a Greek freighter off Dubai in August and the U.K.-registered tanker *Pawnee* on September 25, 1986, the helicopters had limited range and endurance. This was true even though Iranian helicopters operated from forward areas in the Gulf, like the offshore oil platform at Rustam and the Iranian-held island of Abu Musa near Dubai.[47] These strikes raised the total number of attacks on Gulf shipping to 144 since the tanker war resumed in March 1984. They also led Iran to start examining tanker protection systems, such as systems firing canisters of aluminum chaff, reflecting nets to be draped around tankers, and painting crew quarters with dull nonreflecting paint to weaken radar detection.[48]

Shifts in Iranian Forces and Arms Imports

It was obvious from these events that Iran would have to win on the ground, if it was to win at all. Iran continued, however, to have manpower problems. Even so, Iran was only able to reach temporary peak manning levels of 1,250,000 men, and it normally had well under 1,000,000. This manpower was not particularly well organized. It remained divided into about 650,000 full-time active forces and some 400,000 to 550,000 mobilized and reserve forces that served for different periods of time. Iran's active regular army consisted of about 300,000 to 350,000 men, but its divisions were now down to forces of around 10,000 men, or roughly half the size of the division "slices" that existed under the Shah. The Pasdaran numbered about 350,000 men, and its divisions were generally smaller than those of the regular army. It also had large numbers of irregular divisions that were as small as 1,000 men. The Pasdaran were organized under a separate ministry, but even they lacked unity. Iran activated separate air and naval branches of the Pasdaran in May, and this created another new manpower management problem.

Unlike the regular army, the Pasdaran still played a role in internal security as well as at the front. They carried their arms home on leave; the regular army was not allowed to. As a result, Iraq continued to be able to maintain parity in total manpower and had the advantage of being able to create a far less turbulent and more professional force.

The Faw offensive did not materially change Iran's manpower structure, but it forced Iran into major new recruiting efforts which indicated that Iran was beginning to reach the point where it could no longer rely on revolutionary fervor and nationalism to provide either manpower or motivation. Whole new Baseej brigades had been called up during the campaign from each of Iran's largest cities to provide a rapid flow of volunteers, and the percentage of the Baseej that each district could send to the front had been doubled from 10 percent to 20 percent.

In April, Khomeini issued a Fataw stating that another final offensive would follow the Faw offensive and that the war must end by the next Noroz, or Iranian New Year, which was to occur on March 21, 1987. The government called for 500 new volunteer battalions of 1,000 men each after Khomeini issued his Fataw in April.

Iran talked about mobilizing all classes and all regions, and it decentralized the mobilization process and gave 90 provincial councils the responsibility for meeting its new manpower goals.[49] The Pasdaran and Baseej were given new powers to call up those who had served in the past, and civil ministries again were required to contribute manpower.

Stiff new changes were also made to the conscription law. All conscriptees had to spend at least a year on the front and could no longer bargain for safe assignments in the rear. The punishment for failing to report for the draft was also extended to include six months additional service. Baseej began to be drafted for the first time in July. On September 3, it was announced that the universities would be closed, and the 30,000 teachers would be subject to the draft.[50] All of these changes, however, did little more than allow Iran to maintain the manpower strength it had had at the beginning of the Faw offensive.

In contrast, Iraq now had a relatively professional army of full-time regulars, regular reserves, and experienced popular army forces of over 780,000 men. It also had some 680,000 Popular Army forces for home defense. While Iraq had had to stiffen its terms of conscription and call up more students and civil servants, it continued to have near parity in manpower and had a force that was considerably more professional, more coherent, and less turbulent than that of Iran.

Iraq also was able to obtain virtually all the arms it needed, while Iran continued to have mixed success in solving its arms-supply problems. While Iran did obtain a growing number of Western arms and was then getting covert shipments of arms from the U.S., it could not obtain enough arms and parts to bring its U.S.- and European-supplied arms to the level of readiness desirable for major combat operations.[51]

This hurt Iran, but scarcely meant that it could not continue fighting. Iran was able to obtain some $4 billion worth of arms from North Korea and $230 million from the PRC between 1980 and 1985. Iran signed a new agreement for $1.6 billion worth of PRC-designed fighters, tanks, and anti-ship missiles.[52] Iran also got delivery of Chinese-made SA-2 surface-to-air missiles and Chinese SS-N-2, or "Silkworm," naval surface-to-surface missiles.[53] Total arms deliveries from the PRC between March and August 1986 rose to $300 million. The deliveries included such key items as T-59 tanks, anti-ship missiles, and possibly more Scud B missiles. Shipments from other sources, including Greece, provided more spare parts for Iran's U.S.-made F-4 and F-5 aircraft, including vitally needed F-4 engines.[54] Iran got some 20 Contraves Skyguard anti-aircraft (AA) fire-control systems from Switzerland.[55] Further, Iran obtained more arms from Czechoslovakia and probably from Romania and Bulgaria as well.[56]

Nevertheless, Iran could not get enough high-technology arms from such sources to convert from Western- to Soviet- and PRC-supplied arms or to give Iran confidence that it could strengthen its air defenses and sustain any breakthrough it made in some final offensive attack on Iraq. The PRC deliveries also came slowly and often at rates that indicated they were being delayed until payment was received. Equally important, Iranian foreign exchange reserves continued to sink, and its foreign exchange earnings were barely enough to fund its most essential military and civil imports, and could not meet its loan payments to critical foreign lenders like Japan.[57]

The Karbala-2 and Karbala-3 Offensives

The end result of Iran's new efforts to build up its offensive capabilities began to become apparent in August and September, although there were growing rumors of severe splits within Iran's leadership. New rumors surfaced of rivalry between Khameini and Rafsanjani and over differences between the regular forces, that advocated a careful strategy based on professional military advice, and the Pasdaran and Baseej, which advocated an emphasis on human-wave tactics, battles of attrition, and revolutionary fervor.

Regardless of how real these divisions in Iran's top leadership may have been, they did not stop Iran from preparing to attack. On August 29, Rafsanjani stated that 650,000 volunteers were massed for the final attack. In September, Iran issued reports that it had sent 350,000 new troops to join the Revolutionary Guards at the front for the final offensive and announced the arrival of its 500 new battalions of volunteers. At the same time, Iran attempted to exploit any internal divisions within Iraq. It made a token release of Iraqi POWs, and Iranian officials made speeches indicating the fact that a new government in Baghdad might not have to pay reparations in the event of an Iranian victory.[58]

Iran launched a series of land attacks to recover the key heights in the Haj Omran area on August 31, which it called the Karbala-2 Offensive. While the data on the details of this attack are unusually uncertain, Iran seems to have begun the attack with elements of the 28th Kurdistan and 64th Rezaiyeh divisions of the regular army. These units struck at night at elements of about five brigades of the Iraqi 5th Corps.

Both sides made the usual conflicting claims regarding gains and losses during these attacks, but Iranian forces seem to have rapidly taken the Kordeman Heights overlooking Kurdistan. Iraq flew over 100 sorties per day in support of its defensive actions, and it became clear that some of the local fighting was intense. By September 3, Iran was able to take Mount Marmand and score other gains in the mountainous area of the Haj Omran Basin near Kurdistan.

At this point, Pasdaran and Baseej forces seem to have been ordered into the battle, without adequate coordination, because Rafsanjani sought to give them some of the credit for the battle.[59] Iraqi reinforcements from the 5th Corps, 404th Special Force Battalion, and 102nd Presidential Guards Battalion seem to have counterattacked and to have taken advantage of the disruption of the Iranian offensive. They drove the Iranians out of most of their gains. Iran obtained little more than some minor villages and road bridges and an improved position in some strategic heights near the roads in the border area.

There may have been similar coordination problems in Iran's Karbala-3 Offensive. This offensive began on September 1, when ground elements of the Aviation Corps seized the Al Amayah oil platform from a limited number of Iraqi defenders and destroyed an Iraqi radar facility on the platform that Iraq was using to locate Iranian shipping targets in the Gulf. The Iranians hoped to establish a position where they could use artillery fire to hit Umm Qasr and the Albakr oil terminal from the south. On September 2, however, the Iranian Guards' commander seems to have ordered up to 2,000 Pasdaran to move by small craft from Ras ol-Bisheh to the Al Amayah and Al Bakr oil platforms in the Gulf. In the process, they were hit by Iraqi aircraft, helicopter gunships, and artillery. Only about 130 men out of 2,000 made it to Al Amayah. Iraqi paratroopers than landed on the platform and recaptured it.[60]

The most that Iran could do in the Gulf was to step up its search-and-seizure operation. Iran increased its naval intercepts of shipping through the Gulf to 15–20 inspections a day, briefly detained a Soviet cargo vessel, the *Pytor Yemtsov*, and hit a British ship with a helicopter-fired missile on September 23.

More Iraqi Air Raids and Minor Fighting on the Land

Iraq still concentrated on the air war and continued to fly long-range air attack missions. Iraq hit the Iranian refinery at Tabriz on August 10, 1986, and then attacked the Iranian oil-loading points at Lavan on September 7. Iraq then launched a highly successful series of raids on Kharg Island on September 16.[61] These raids forced Iran to put still more reliance on Larak Island and made significant temporary cuts in its average oil exports.

The Iraqi air force also continued to hit ammunition dumps and other Iranian military targets along the border and struck at border towns like Marivan, Mosk, and Rabat. While Iran launched another Scud missile at Baghdad and fired three more Scuds at Baghdad in November, it could do relatively little in the air. Aside from a limited number of attack and air-defense sorties and a few successful kills of Iraqi aircraft, Iran had to sit back and accept the Iraqi air strikes. The war remained a struggle between Iraq's ability to use its air power to weaken Iran's economy and Iran's ability to use its ground forces to invade Iraq.

Iraq still suffered from the same problems that had affected its ability to use air power throughout the war. It still lacked enough air power to have a decisive effect, and it still failed to use the air power it did have systematically and effectively. Even though Iraq scored important gains in its attacks against Iran's oil-export facilities and forced Iran to make large-scale expenditures and heavily discount its oil, Iraq failed to attack with the consistency and strength needed to sharply reduce Iran's average monthly oil exports. Iraq also failed to consistently attack Iran's most vulnerable targets—its refineries and electric power plants—and its raids did not have a major impact on Iran's civil economy. Iraq also tended to target too many of its raids for political effect, and this seems to explain why it often struck at low-value urban targets when it had far more to gain from striking at economic targets and facilities.

Iraq does seem to have understood enough of these problems to continue to build up its land power. Senior Iraqi officials like foreign minister Tariq Aziz continued to warn that the Iranian final offensive might come at any time and that Iran might attack in more than one sector and attempt to exhaust Iraqi reserves. In spite of Iraq's financial problems, total Iraqi Army manning rose to around 820,000 men, and Iraq succeeded in filling out all seven of its corps along the 1,100-kilometer front with Iran.

By this time, the Iraq Army had some 46 major combat units. While

Iraq called these units divisions, by Western standards they were only manned and equipped to the size of reinforced brigades.[62] More importantly, Iraq built up its elite Presidential Guard from six "brigades" to 16 to 17 mechanized "brigades" totaling about 25,000 men which were equipped with armor, including some T-72 tanks. This gave Iraq a growing "shock force" that was trained for counteroffensive and offensive action and gradually led Iraq to change its emphasis of relatively static defense warfare. Iraq also, however, continued to strengthen its forward defenses. It added more barriers, minefields, and barbed wire and increased the number of dug-in tanks. It increased the amount of artillery in each defense zone and put more emphasis on preregistered target coordinates and immediate response with mass fire.[63]

No major land fighting occurred between the end of Karbala-3 and late December, but Iran did not halt all ground action after the Karbala-2 and -3 offensives. It took some of the key heights above Mehran on the night of September 16 and occupied other heights in the border area around Badra, Zurbatiya, and Varmahraz.[64] Khomeini also held a meeting with his senior commanders on September 16, and rumors began to circulate that Iran would launch its all-out offensive on September 22, the day which Iran used to date the beginning of the war in 1980.

During late September and October, Iran continued to conduct small land actions that nibbled away at Iraq's positions and morale. It kept up sporadic artillery barrages against Basra and sponsored a series of combined Iranian and Kurdish special forces and commando raids on key targets like the major refinery at the Kirkuk oil field and the Iraqi military bases at Koi Sanjaq and Altun Kopru, although these commando raids had comparatively little initial success.

Iraq, in turn, continued strikes at Iran's oil targets. It hit at Iran's gas compression facilities, the refinery at Shiraz, industrial centers in Isfahan, the Rustam and Sasan offshore oil fields, and at the oil pumping stations at the Marun and Ahwaz oil fields. Iraq continued to strike at tankers and even hit a newly acquired Iranian shuttle tanker before it could reach Larak. This tanker had just been converted for oil transloading at the drydock in Dubai and had some $500,000 in defense equipment. This included nonreflective paint, radar reflectors at either end of the vessel, chaff launchers, and an electronic decoy system.[65]

Iraq launched exceptionally successful raids on Kharg on September 29 and October 6, 1986, the latter strike temporarily closing the last two functional terminals in all of Kharg's fourteen tanker berths.[66] The new Iraqi air offensive temporarily cut Iranian oil shipments to about 800,000 BPD—or about half of Iraq's normal export level—and delayed shuttle shipments to the point where 25–30 long-haul tankers were normally waiting off Larak to load. The raids also forced Iran to try to rush full operational capability for the two mooring buoys it had bought in 1985 so that it could provide a survivable capability to load its shuttle tankers without sending them to Kharg. Finally, Iraqi raids on Iran's refineries forced Iran to start importing about 100,000 BPD in refined product and led to still further increases in tanker insurance premiums. Once again, Iran had to increase petrol rationing.[67]

The Iran-Contra Arms Scandal

It was at this time that the internal struggle for power between Montazari and Rafsanjani helped lead to the exposure of the covert U.S. shipments to Iran. This tragi-comic fiasco had begun in 1985 and eventually caused a major scandal in U.S. domestic politics and created political forces that helped thrust the U.S. into a major naval intervention in the Gulf. While the history of this scandal scarcely provides an important lesson in war, it does provide an important lesson in how not to handle terrorism and foreign relations and important background to the events of 1987 and 1988.

The history of the covert U.S. arms sales to Iran can be traced back to 1980 and the U.S. effort to win the freedom of the hostages Iran had taken when it seized the U.S. Embassy in Tehran. The main cause, however, was the effort of various officials of the Israeli government to try to reestablish U.S. ties to Iran as a counterbalance to what they perceived as a U.S. tilt toward Iraq. The U.S. had gradually been improving relations with Iraq since Iran had gone on the offensive in 1983. It had attempted to shut off deliveries of arms to Iran in what it called Operation Staunch, and this caused some concern in Israel that the war might end with a strong and hostile Iraq that would be a considerable strategic threat to Israel.

As a result, a series of exchanges began between several Israeli officials and U.S. consultants outside the government that have still not been fully explained. These exchanges helped persuade the senior officials of the U.S. and the Director of the Central Intelligence Agency that it might be possible to rebuild American political ties with moderates in the Iranian government and to also find a way to free several Americans who were held hostage by pro-Iranian Shi'ite factions in Lebanon.

This effort took place in spite of a major reappraisal of U.S. policy toward Iran that had begun in late 1984. The National Security Council (NSC) had issued a National Security Study Directive (NSSD), and the resulting study had concluded that there were no new options for rebuilding U.S. ties to Iran. Nevertheless, senior members of the National Security Council staff who were dealing with the Contra issue, and which had close ties to some of the Israelis who were providing arms to countries in Central America, sought independent advice from the CIA. In May 1985, this resulted in a five-page memo from the CIA National Intelligence Officer on the Middle East that argued the U.S. should permit allies to sell arms to Iran to counterbalance Soviet efforts to gain influence in Iran.[68]

Two members of the National Security Council staff—Howard Teicher and Donald Fortier—used this paper, indirect inputs from Iranian middlemen, Israeli arguments, and the views of private consultants—to prepare a draft National Security Decision Directive (NSDD) arguing that the U.S. should take short- and long-term initiatives to reestablish relations with Iran to counterbalance what they felt was growing Soviet influence in Iran. These options included providing limited shipments of U.S. arms to Iran in an effort to open up lines of communication to the more moderate factions and to deal with the hostage problem.

The background to this CIA paper and NSC action is complex, and some aspects remain uncertain in spite of extensive Congressional hearings and other investigations. In brief, however, the U.S. had long realized that Israel was making low-level shipments of arms to Iran. The U.S. rejected quiet Israeli arguments that these shipments were of strategic value to the West and made some objections to these shipments. At the same time, U.S. officials tolerated them, in part because of its hope that this might moderate Iran's conduct in sponsoring radical groups in Lebanon and in part because it felt that keeping any line of communication open to Iran's leadership might be useful.[69]

Israel had resumed its efforts to persuade the U.S. to join it in such initiatives and capitalized on the seizure of William Buckley, the CIA station chief in Beirut, on March 16, 1984. This provided what some NSC staff members regarded as further evidence that U.S. counterterrorism efforts could not suppress the activities of pro-Iranian groups in Lebanon or win the release of the U.S. citizens they had captured.

Michael Ledeen, a consultant to the NSC, also visited Israel on May 4–5, 1985, and talked to senior Israeli officials, including Prime Minister Shimon Peres and senior members of Israeli intelligence, about Iran. It is still unclear whether Ledeen did this as the result of prior contacts with Israeli officials or contacts with European intelligence officers and whether he acted at the formal request of National Security Advisor Robert McFarlane. In any case, Ledeen briefed McFarlane in mid-May 1985, and McFarlane tasked the intelligence community with producing a Special National Intelligence Estimate (SNIE) on Iran on May 20, 1985.

These actions, however, ran in direct contradiction to the policies of the U.S. State Department, which still supported Operation Staunch and the effort to halt all arms shipments to Iran. Though Secretary of State George Shultz formally objected to Ledeen's activities on June 5, 1985, and McFarlane advised Shultz on June 14 that he had instructed Ledeen to discourage any arms sale initiative, the work on the NSDD still proceeded.

Shultz's objection might have halted the entire arms deal, but a TWA airliner, Flight 847, was hijacked on June 14, 1985. This reopened the entire issue of how the U.S. should deal with terrorism. While President Reagan gave a speech calling Iran part of a "confederation of terrorist states" and "a new international version of Murder Incorporated," the NSC staff concluded that there was little punitive action the U.S. could take.[70]

This led to new discussions of what Israel could do to help the U.S. and of alternative ways to win the freedom of the hostages in Lebanon. It also brought the Iranian policy issue to the attention of President's Chief of Staff, Donald Regan. The whole issue of how Iran should be treated then steadily became one which was handled at the political level, as distinguished from the foreign policy level, and gradually became entangled in the issue of how the Administration could keep supplying arms to the Contras in spite of Congressional prohibitions of such aid.

McFarlane responded by transmitting the draft NSDD, recommending both arms sales and intelligence transfers to Iran, to Secretary of State George Shultz and Secretary of Defense Caspar Weinberger on June 17, 1987.[71] Both Secretaries quickly rejected the NSC argument in writing. Shultz stated on June 29 that it was "perverse" and contrary to American interests, and Weinberger stated on June 16 that it was "almost too ridiculous to comment upon."[72]

Once again, the whole idea of trying to build a new approach to U.S. relations to Iran might have been killed, except for the problem of freeing the U.S. hostages in Lebanon. It was increasingly clear that Iran was the only outside power which could exert any control over the fate of the hostages. The fate of the American hostages, and the fear that leaving them in captivity might hurt the President and the Republican Party, began to take steadily greater precedence over strategic considerations. This trend was reinforced by each hostage incident, particularly after Syria informed the U.S. in late 1985 that Buckley had been tortured and killed.

Meanwhile, Israel continued to take strong initiatives to support a

U.S. initiative toward Iran. David Kimche, Director General of Israel's Foreign Ministry, had supported the idea of a U.S. initiative toward Iran since the early fall of 1984. On July 3, 1985, Kimche visited the White House and again asked McFarlane for U.S. support, stating that he was acting on the instructions of Shimon Peres. Another "private emissary" from Israel visited McFarlane on July 13. The next day McFarlane sent Shultz another cable supporting the Iran initiative and indicating that it might help the seven U.S. hostages in Lebanon. This led Shultz to reply that the U.S. should show interest without formally supporting any action and that McFarlane should take the initiative.

It was at this point (July 13–17) that McFarlane visited President Reagan, who had just had an operation, in the hospital. As a result, McFarlane felt he had the President's approval to make covert contacts with Iran. These contacts were simultaneously being supported by two private arms dealers, a Saudi named Adnan Khashoggi and an Iranian named Manucher Ghorbanifar—sometimes described as an advisor to Iran's Prime Minister. Further, an Israeli arms dealer, Al Schwimmer, was introduced to McFarlane by Ledeen at the suggestion of David Kimche.

This ultimately led Ledeen to meet in Israel in late July with Kimche, Ghorbanifar, Schwimmer, and another Israeli, Yaacov Nimrodi—an ex-Israeli military attache to Iran.[73] This eventually produced a new NSC proposal to establish contacts with Iran and to trade the sale of U.S. TOW anti-tank and Hawk anti-air missiles for the U.S. hostages.

These developments led to a meeting in the White House on August 6, 1985, where President Reagan presided. Although the details are unclear, it is clear that the key issue was whether to trade arms for hostages, and that CIA Director William Casey and Donald Regan supported the arms initiative and that Secretaries Shultz and Weinberger opposed it. The meeting does not seem to have reached a formal outcome, but the practical result was that Israel felt it obtained authority from the NSC on August 30 to sell 508 TOW missiles to Iran, which the U.S. would replace.

The first 100 missiles arrived in Iran on August 30, 1985, and the remaining 400 on September 14, 1985.[74] This arms transfer helped lead to the release of one U.S. hostage—Reverend Benjamin Weir—on September 14, but it did not lead to the much larger release of U.S. hostages that the White House officials expected. In fact, Iran established a pattern that it was to repeat throughout 1986, when the U.S. shipped arms directly to Iran. Iran released one hostage but kept the others to retain its leverage over the United States.

Iran repeated exactly this same pattern when it responded to later arms shipments by persuading its Lebanese supporters to release Reverend Lawrence Jenco on July 26, 1986, and David P. Jacobsen on November 2, 1986. On each occasion, the pro-Iranian groups in Lebanon carried out only one-third to one-half the releases the U.S. expected. Further, Iran seems to have encouraged such groups to take new hostages in compensation. By the time the covert U.S. arms deals became public in early November 1986, pro-Iranian groups had as many U.S. hostages as they did before the arms deal.[75]

The exact reason why Iranian sources leaked the existence of the covert arms sales to the Lebanese press has never been determined, but the leak seems to have occurred as the result of a complex internal political battle between Rafsanjani and Montazari. It came when *As Shiraa*, a pro-Syrian magazine in Lebanon, announced McFarlane's visit to Tehran in its November 4, 1986 issue.[76] Its editor, Hassan Sabra, later stated that the source of his story was Montazari's office.[77] Rafsanjani officially confirmed the story on November 5, 1986, and again on November 24 and December 5.[78]

The broad outlines of the U.S. transactions with Iran became public by the end of the first week of November, and one leak after another then led to the disclosure that the U.S. had shipped at least 2,008 TOW missiles and 235 Hawk assemblies. It also became clear that Israel had provided much larger shipments of U.S. parts and arms than had previously been believed.[79] This disclosure had a powerful impact on U.S. relations with the Gulf countries and the Arab world. It discredited much of the U.S. effort to improve its relations with Iraq, gave the impression that the U.S. had abandoned its efforts to reduce the flow of arms to Iran, and gave many of the southern Gulf states the impression that they could no longer trust the U.S.

The legacy of the covert sales effort is a powerful lesson in terms of the care and professionalism required in managing covert operations. The arms sales were the project of a small group of amateurs in the National Security Council that ignored both the area experts on the region and the professionals in the State Department and Department of Defense. Their covert sales effort undoubtedly encouraged Iran to continue the war, while doing nothing to reduce the problem of hostage taking.

At the same time, the backlash from the disclosure of their program discredited Operation Staunch and created powerful pressures on the U.S. to reassert its power in the Gulf and prove it could be a reliable friend to the southern Gulf states. Rather than improve relations between the U.S. and Iran, the covert sales contributed a great deal to U.S. military intervention in the Gulf under conditions that led both countries to a state of near war. Virtually none of the funds raised through the sales to Iran ever reached the Contras. Further, it later became clear that rather than dealing with Iranian moderates, the Iranians had created a coalition of as many factions as possible—including the most radical—and then failed to keep the effort covert because it could not co-opt all the factions and power struggles necessary to create broad support.[80] All in all, the entire project can only be described as a miserable fiasco.

The Increasing Impact of Iraqi Air Power

The U.S. arms transfers, however, had only a limited effect on the fighting. Iraq kept up the air war while Iran prepared for new major land offensives. On November 25–26, Iraq launched another major series of air raids. Roughly 54 Iraqi fighters attacked six military targets. These included a Hawk unit near Dezful, an army base, an air base, the Andimeshk railway station, and Larak.

The Iraqi Mirage F-1EQ5 fighters that hit Larak had to fly a mission of 1,560 miles. While two Iraqi fighters ran out of fuel during the raid and had to land in Saudi Arabia, the raid on Larak took Iran by surprise. Several ships were hit, and the raid was considered a significant strategic success. The raid raised the number of tankers struck in 1986 to 90 and demonstrated that Iran could not protect its oil-export facilities unless it could also rebuild its air defenses.[81]

The extent to which Iraq actually upgraded its refueling capability is uncertain, but the Larak raid demonstrated that the Iraqi Air Force now had greater range than ever before. Reports again surfaced that Iraq had modified 10 Soviet AN-12 Cub transports for use as tankers. These carried a palletized air-to-air refueling system that trailed a drogue from the rear ramp. Iraq also had the ability to use a "buddy-buddy" refueling system developed by the French Air Force which allowed one Mirage F-1 fighter to refuel another from a 2,300 liter centerline tank on the "mother" fighter. These refueling systems were difficult to operate and were unsuitable for mass long-distance raids, but they may have helped bring Larak within Iraqi fighter range and give the Iraqi Mirages the nearly 1,400-km range Iraq needed for such strikes.

Iraq also kept up its strikes on Kharg. On November 27, it announced its 250th strike on Kharg Island and claimed there was not a single jetty still operating. It also continued to strike at the Iranian refineries in Tehran, Isfahan, and Tabriz, and at hydroelectric facilities and power plants. Iraq claimed it was able to reduce the Sirri Island ferry fleet to only five ships.[82] Iraq made better use of its laser-guided bombs and had improved its evasion tactics and flew larger numbers of combat sorties. On the same day Iraq first struck Larak, it flew a total of 164 combat missions, including many over the front, where it often used its Soviet-made Sukhoi Su-20s and MiG-21s as well as its Mirages.[83]

In spite of all its various arms deals, there was little Iran could do in response to improve its air-to-air combat capability. By the winter of 1986, Iran seems to have been reduced to as few as 40 fully operational fighters capable of air-defense missions and a total of 80–100 aircraft capable of some kind of operations. It no longer was able to operate the avionics on its P-3C maritime reconnaissance aircraft. Some sources indicated Iran had only seven operational F-14s, none with functioning radars.[84] A defecting Iranian Air Force Colonel also claimed that Iran's F-5 force was at 10–15 fighters and the F-4 force was down to 20. He claimed that Iran now had no operational RF-4 reconnaissance aircraft, had lost three C-130s because of a lack of spare parts, and could only operate about 10 percent of its 17 B-707s, 7 B-747s, and remaining C-130s.[85]

Iran did manage, however, to improve some of its land-based air defenses. It claimed that its surface-to-air missile forces and ground-based air defenses shot down as many as 10 Iraqi fighters in November and that 9 out of 10 of its surface-to-air missiles scored kills.[86] These claims were almost certainly exaggerated, but Iraq did lose at least 5–12 fighters during the fall and early winter, and this was enough to start considerable speculation that the covert U.S. arms shipments allowed Iran to make its Hawk defenses more effective.

This suspicion was gradually confirmed in December when it became clear that Iran had operational mobile missile sites on Kharg Island and that these were presenting increasingly serious problems for attacking Iraqi aircraft. Iraq also later claimed that its losses to the Hawks were forcing it to sharply reduce its attacks on the island, although many of its losses may actually have occurred to guns and light Swedish-made RBS-70 missiles.[87]

Iran also compensated for its lack of air power with its surface-to-surface missiles. It continued sporadic Scud strikes against Baghdad, one of which killed 48 Iraqis and wounded 52 when it hit a crowded apartment complex.[88] Further, Iran continued its pressure in other ways. In late November, Iran bombed Dahook in the southern Gulf and may have conducted a demonstrative raid on the Abu Boosk (Abul Bukush) offshore oil field about 100 miles north of Abu Dhabi— although some sources indicate this was an accidental raid by Iraq.[89] Iran also issued a new set of threats against the GCC states that Iran would remember their actions if they continued to back Iraq. These threats were particularly hostile to Saudi Arabia, which Iran claimed had aided Iraq in a strike on Larak.

Meanwhile, the tanker war continued its grim process. While Iran had previously limited its fighter and helicopter attacks on ships to daylight hours, it began to conduct experimental night attacks in September. On October 17, 1986, Iran also began night attacks with its Saram-class surface ships. It hit the *Five Brooks*, a tanker, with what later turned out to be Sea Killer missiles. The ship was only five miles off the coast of Oman and suffered five dead and 13 missing. Iran then hit two more ships—the *Sham* and *August Star*—i n November.

By early December, some 50 seamen had died in attacks on tankers in 1986, versus 50 in all of the preceding 5 years. Insurance rates continued to rise, and nearly a ship a week was being lost. According to Lloyd's, there had been 97 attacks on cargo ships and tankers during the first 9 months of 1986, with 17 total losses. This compared with Lloyd's estimates of 259 attacks during the entire war up to that time.

Iraq kept up its air strikes on Iran's cities and economic facilities during December, but Iran's improving Hawk and other surface-to-air defenses on Kharg Island seem to have led Iraq to limit its attacks on the island. Further, Iraqi air losses seem to have been cumulatively significant enough to lead Iraq to be more cautious about committing its aircraft to other defended targets, and Iraqi raids were spread out to cover a wider range of targets.

Iran replied by bombarding Basra on the 8th and followed up with artillery attacks along a 50-mile front that included the logistic areas of the Iraqi III, IV, VI, and VII corps.[90] In spite of these Iranian barrages, Iraq continued to fly daily MiG-21 and Su-20 attacks against Iranian cities and oil targets and used its Mirages with laser-guided bombs to hit high-value economic targets. On December 13, Iraq hit a power plant and anti-aircraft system in Tehran—its first attack on Iran's capital in seven months.[91] Similar raids against Iranian towns and cities continued into late December, killing a number of civilians, although Iraq generally claimed its aircraft were hitting at major economic or military targets.[92]

All of these attacks showed that Iraq was willing to pursue the war in the air, although the strategic effect of the strikes continued to be diluted by Iraq's failure to concentrate enough air power to attack any one of three major objectives effectively. It seems likely that if Iraq had concentrated on attacking Iran's refineries, its power plants, or its shipping facilities and tankers in the Gulf, it would have had much more effect than by sporadically attacking one set of targets and then going on to another.

Iran's Karbala-4 Offensive

Although Iran had done little on the ground between the end of September and late December, it had made repeated threats to resume its major offensives. It also had claimed in mid-October that pro-Iranian Kurds and the Pasdaran had bombarded Kirkuk, a claim that had so little substance that it seems explainable only in terms of Iran's internal politics. The winter rains came in mid-November without incident.

In fact, a steadily more serious debate seems to have gone on within the Iranian leadership over how to prosecute the war, although it is almost impossible to figure out exactly what happened. According to some Iranian sources, this debate took place between the more experienced combat leaders of the regular army and Pasdaran, who favored a careful and well-planned series of small attacks and who were backed by figures like Khameini, and the Pasdaran and senior Mullahs, like Rafsanjani, who favored new human-wave assaults whose success depended on revolutionary fervor and Iraq's vulnerability to some form of military collapse.

Other sources feel that a split occurred between the commanders of the regular forces, like General Said Shirazi, and the commanders of the Pasdaran, like Mohsen Rezai. According to these reports, the regular forces advocated a carefully planned envelopment of Basra from positions in Faw and Howeyzeh, while the Pasdaran favored more direct assaults across the Shatt and more human-wave attacks. Still other sources feel that the exposure of the arms deals with the U.S. forced leaders like Rafsanjani to take a much harder line and to show they favored major new offensives.[93]

In any case, Iran seems to have first planned to renew its attacks as early as August and then to have planned to renew them in November. Some signs of these developments occurred in November, when Iran claimed it had now trained one million women Baseej since September 1980 and had 90 military training camps for women. Iran stated that nearly 1,000 women had earned a combat instructor's rating and that women were trained to use RPGs and machine guns. Iran claimed five divisions of women volunteers marched past the Majlis building in Tehran on November 30th.[94]

Rafsanjani held a major military rally on December 3. He spoke to some 100,000 Pasdaran and Baseej troops and some 2,000 Mullahs, and it was clear that Iran was preparing for some kind of attack. Iran announced that 100,000 new Baseej troops were leaving for the Gulf front. This deployment followed a pattern set in previous years when volunteer troops were called up after the rains began in late October and early November and when the initial call-up necessary to deploy them in the winter had less impact on Iran's economy. In theory, the timing of the call-up allowed the new Baseej troops to receive three months of training in small arms and combat techniques; they then served a three- to six-month tour of duty. The Baseej were then given the option of reenlisting or returning home.[95]

Regardless of any debates within the leadership, Iran did not wait for its new call-ups to receive any significant training. It launched a new offensive on the night of December 23–24 called Karbala-4. The timing of this attack may have had something to with Iran's efforts to intimidate the Islamic Summit Congress that was to meet in Kuwait at the end of December. According to at least one source, it was rushed ahead for this purpose, although it originally was to be part of a much larger offensive that included a broad encirclement of Basra.[96]

The attack was one of the few to be led by a Pasdaran commander, and the Iranian forces thrust across the Shatt al-Arab on a 25-mile wide front. The new offensive extended from Abu al Khasib, south of Basra, to the island of Umm al-Rasas near Abadan. It was directed against the positions of Iraqi 3rd Corps forces in the area east of Basra and the Iraqi 7th Corps in the area near the Faw Peninsula. These were some of Iraq's best-defended positions.

Sources differ sharply over the scale of the attack, which Iran later tried to minimize. It would seem, however, that the attack began with an assault force of up to 15,000 men that secured the islands of Umm al-Rasas, Umm Babi, Qate (Qatiyeh), and Sohial (Sahiniyeh). These islands form a kind of strategic bridge across the Shatt, which is a slow-moving river about 480 meters wide at this point. The attack was led by a first wave of commandos and frogmen, and they rapidly took the weakly defended island of Umm al-Rasas and its nearby islands or sandbanks in much the same way as they had the previous February.

Iran then launched a daylight attack on the Iraqi positions on Iraqi soil defending the Shatt road. This attack was led by elements of the so-called "Division of the Prophet Mohammed," which was the name Iran had given its efforts to mobilize 100,000 more popular volunteers in a 500-battalion force. While the attacking force did include significant numbers of experienced troops, it relied primarily on less-experienced volunteers. Up to 60,000 Pasdaran and Baseej had crossed the Shatt al-Arab to Umm al-Rasas and the Iraqi side of the Shatt.

When the Pasdaran and Baseej assault force tried to move up the Shatt road toward Basra, they could only be given minimal support from Iran's regular forces, largely in the form of artillery fire from across the Shatt. Most of Iran's regular troops were in other locations opposite Basra or were concentrated in positions in the central front and opposite Baghdad. The assault force also exhibited little of the systematic preparation characteristic of the attack on Faw. The Iranians had to attack well-prepared Iraqi defenses in the rear of Umm al-Rasas, and they attacked head-on through barbed wire and mine fields and against the kind of firepower that turned the area into an ideal killing ground for Iraq.

The assault force was also committed in ill-coordinated human-wave formations. The Iranians made no real attempt at using complex infiltration tactics, aside from using the cover of night at the beginning of the attack. Once the Iranian commanders had committed their forces, they continued to launch direct mass-infantry assaults against fully prepared Iraqi positions. In fact, the Karbala-4 offensive may have been the worst planned and executed major Iranian offensive since Bani-Sadr's ill-fated offensives early in the war. It had much of the character of the hopeless mass-infantry assaults that Britain, France, and Germany had launched against well-entrenched defenses in World War I.

Roughly a day and a half of fighting showed just how much Iran could still suffer when it made the mistake of a head-on attack against well-prepared Iraqi positions. Iraq not only could kill with direct fire weapons and artillery, the bulk of Iran's troops were exposed to armed helicopters and aircraft, and much of the amphibious lift Iran had deployed was sunk during the battle. Iran was thrown back across the Shatt, and while experts disagree over the size of the attack, most agree that Iran lost at least 9,000–12,000 dead and wounded. Iraq claimed there were 100 Iranians killed for every Iraqi and that there was a total of 60,000 to 90,000 casualties and 10,000 dead.[97] Iraq may have suffered casualties of up to 1,000–2,000 dead and wounded in return, but Iran's claims that there were 9,500 to 14,000 Iraqi killed and wounded were clearly absurd.[98]

Iran's Final Offensive Against Basra

Iran's reversals in Karbala-4 did not stop its efforts to defeat Iraq with new offensives. Only several weeks after Karbala-4, Iran launched two new offensives: The first offensive was called Karbala-5 and was directed against Basra. The second offensive was called Karbala-6 and was directed against the area north of Baghdad between Qasr e-Shirin and Sumar.

Karbala-5 was by far the most important of these two offensives. It also was far better planned and executed than Iran's rapidly organized December offensive. Iran had been examining plans for a major attack on Basra since 1985. During the summer and fall of 1986, Iran had held exercises in the marshlands near the Caspian port of Anzali to test some of the concepts it could use to strike across the water barriers in front of Basra. These exercises involved combined-arms exercises by the equivalent of several Iranian divisions and involved some of the most serious Iranian efforts at organizing an offensive since the period following Iran's reversals in the spring of 1984.[99]

By early January, Iran had deployed roughly 200,000 troops in the southern front, roughly the same number as their Iraqi opponents. The pool of forces actually used in the attack, however, did not exceed 120,000–140,000, and most of these were Pasdaran and Baseej. There were roughly 60,000 men in the initial strike force concentrated to move rapidly into the forward Iranian positions near Salamcheh, the border crossing point about 20 kilometers from Basra. Another 60,000 Iranian troops were deployed in immediate reserve and a pool of up to 80,000 more men in a rear-area reserve. About 70 percent of the total manpower consisted of Pasdaran and Baseej and about 30 percent of regular forces.[100]

The tactical objective of Karbala-5 was to strike across the border near Basra and then drive around and through the water barriers in the area. The strike force was then supposed to penetrate Basra's massive land defenses and cut Basra and Faw off from the rest of Iraq. Iran's precise strategic and political objectives in executing Karbala-5 can only be guessed at, but at a maximum, they could have included seizing Basra and creating an alternative pro-Khomeini capital in the south, destroying the Iraqi army in the south and bringing down the Ba'ath government, and moving north to take Karbala and Najaf. At a minimum, they were to weaken the Iraqi army through sheer attrition, lay siege to Basra, and provide a further lesson about vulnerability to the southern Gulf states.

Iran faced serious difficulties in achieving any of these objectives. Iraq had built up formidable land defenses and water barriers around Basra. This massive effort in defensive engineering had begun in 1981 and had been constantly improved in the years that followed. Iraq created a long water barrier nearly a kilometer wide along the north-south stretch of the border opposite Basra, just near the corner where it suddenly turns 90° to the east. It used earthen barriers to keep the marsh area along the border from draining.

Beginning in 1982, Iraq had slowly created a large man-made lake across the Shatt al-Arab from Basra called Fish Lake, which was located at the point where the Iraqi 3rd and 7th Corps joined. Fish Lake was filled with sensors, underwater obstacles, barbed wire, and areas which could be electrified with the output from power lines. Iraq was able to move to defensive positions in the lake along a causeway that began near Salamcheh, and a number of other small earthen berms existed in the lake. These major water barriers were reinforced by smaller canals and water barriers wherever possible. Roughly 200 square kilometers of water barriers helped defend the areas nearest the border, and the Shatt al-Arab created another major barrier just behind them.

Iraq supported its water barriers with the virtual fortification of Basra, and these fortifications had five to six separate defensive rings when the Iranian attack began. Iraq also built strong earthworks and defensive positions along the border north of the Shatt, although it relied heavily on the water barriers and marshes in the area to help provide a defensive buffer against Iran, and it did not establish fall-back defenses in depth near the border. Iraq did have good forward defenses on the southern side of the Shatt to the east of Abu al Khasib, which is a refinery complex not far from the corner in the border and about 10 kilometers from Basra.[101]

These defenses might have been even more effective if Iran had not achieved some degree of tactical surprise. The exact reasons for this surprise are unclear. Iraq detected Iran's preparation for the Karbala-5 offensive but does not seem to have anticipated its precise direction or timing. Iraq had strong forces in the area, including four divisions and five Republican Guard brigades.[102] Iraq should have been able to put up an equally strong defense from the start, but a number of its key defensive units were out of position at the time the attack began. Two of Iraq's divisions were kept on the western side of the Shatt to defend Basra, and Iraq and did not have enough of its forces defending its forward positions.[103]

Iraq also does not seem to have learned all the lessons it should have from its experiences in marsh warfare in 1985 or from its loss of the Faw Peninsula early in 1986. Iraqi reserves were not fully ready to move when the Iranian assault began and then moved too slowly. Seasonal factors also favored Iran: The water in the marshy area near Basra was not at its peak, but was high enough to allow powered boats to move freely. In contrast, any Iraqi armored movement was difficult.

As a result, Iran achieved some significant early successes. On January 9, 1987, Iranian forces struck in a line toward Khusk at two points northeast of Fish Lake and at another point to the southeast in the general direction of Shalamcheh. These Iranian forces were supposed to surround Fish Lake, eliminate the Iraqi forces covering Basra on the eastern shore of the Shatt, and link up at some point near Abolhazib.[104]

Iran committed up to 50,000 troops to this initial wave of attacks, and Iranian troops started their advance at about 1:00 A.M. at night. Iran was now experienced enough to take full advantage of such night attacks, and the season again favored Iran because the nights were long, and there was considerable cloud cover.[105] As usual, Iran used waves of Baseej volunteers to attack Iraqi positions; the Baseej were followed by the Revolutionary Guards.

The Pasdaran and regular army troops involved in the attack were unusually well armed and equipped and had been briefed with well-defined tactical objectives. Their initial battle management was good, and the leaders of the assault included large cadres of experienced officers, NCOs, and troops. The Baseej forces included a significant element of young volunteers of 14–15 years of age who had little training and volunteered for periods as short as 45 days. These Baseej forces, however, often did little more than take the initial shock of the assault. More experienced Guards forces then moved forward against the remaining Iraqi troops.

During the first day of the attack, Iran's forces rapidly took the small border town of Duayji. In spite of Iraq's use of massive amounts of firepower, air power, and poison gas to halt the breakthrough, Iranian forces then went on to capture other more significant positions near the border. Iran may also have made its first use of poison gas against Iraq, although this could have been either captured Iraqi shells or mistakes by Iraq's Chemical Corps. In any case, Iran took Salamcheh, about 30 kilometers south of Basra, and the first two Iraqi defensive lines near Khusk, about 40 miles to north.[106] This gave Iran a secure bridgehead across the Iranian border, and Iranian forces then moved up the eastern side of the Shatt al-Arab about 20 kilometers south of the outer suburbs of Basra.

Iraq's attempts to counterattack on January 10 were not successful. Iraq tried to use amphibious armored vehicles, but these vehicles lacked mobility in wetlands and mud, and Iraq was unable to maneuver effectively in the face of Iranian infantry armed with light anti-armor weapons. Iran held on to a six-kilometer strip of land between Fish Lake and the Shatt and then made further progress to the southeast. Some of Iran's initial assault forces also penetrated two of the major defense lines around Basra. Both sides made increasingly strident claims about each other's losses. By January 11, Iran claimed to have killed or wound 14,000 Iraqis. Iraq claimed to have destroyed 11 Pasdaran divisions and four additional brigades totaling some 60,000 men.

The seriousness of the fighting is also indicated by the fact that on January 13, the Ministry for the Revolutionary Guards called upon all citizens to register for service in the "Division of the Prophet Mohammed." Efforts were made to obtain new volunteers at mosques, factories, and offices. The prior mobilization had evidently produced only about 200,000 of the 500,000 men that the government sought for the Pasdaran. Iraq, in turn, called on January 21 for volunteers from the ages of 14 to 35, although Saddam Hussein had earlier denounced Iran's use of boys under 18 as "immoral." Iraq required university students and lecturers under 35 to enroll as officer candidates.[107]

The course of the battle began to turn on which side could deploy the most reinforcements. Iraq committed new Republican Guard forces on January 12, and Iraq's defenses then began to hold. While Iraq's troop losses were severe, they also were far less serious than those of Iran. Iraq still had most of its major equipment and artillery intact and was able to use it with growing effectiveness. This increasing effectiveness was partly a matter of better organization and larger forces and partly a matter of terrain. As Iranian troops moved forward onto dry land and assaulted Basra's main defenses, they increasingly suffered from a relative lack of firepower and from a lack of the mobility they needed to sustain an advance through the Iraqi positions. Iranian forces began to have serious problems with supplies and in moving sufficient ammunition forward.

Iraq also was able to fully commit its air power after January 13, and this time Iraq did not hold its aircraft back. Iraq claimed to have flown over 500 missions in support of Iraqi ground forces on January 14 and 15 alone. Iraq also claimed to have killed an Iranian F-14 in air-to-air combat on January 15, and to have destroyed 218 Iranian vehicles and 21 boats.[108]

Iran responded by committing up to 50,000 more troops to the battle. These reinforcements allowed Iran to make limited gains, and on January 17, Iran also launched a small naval assault at targets near the eastern shore of the Shatt. By January 18, Iran had captured the islands of Bovarin, Duwijah, Umm Tuvalal, and Fayaz in the Shatt. The main Iranian forces attacking from the north and south could not, however, link up as they had originally planned.

In spite of its reinforcements, Iran soon took so many additional casualties that it again lost forward momentum. By January 16, the U.S. estimated that the fighting had led to roughly 40,000 Iranian and 10,000 Iraqi casualties.[109] The evidence of such casualty levels was all too tangible. Iran suffered an exceptionally high ratio of killed to wounded, and many of the dead were left on the battlefield. On the worst days, the Iraqi mortuaries near Basra processed well over 1,000 bodies.[110]

The best Iran could do between January 16 and January 19 was to edge forward in a few positions near Basra and begin to lay siege to the city by shelling its civil areas and firing more missiles. A new wave of Pasdaran infantry attacks took place on January 19 and 26. These attacks put Iranian troops only about 14–15 kilometers miles east of Basra and about 3 kilometers from Iraq's main defenses at Abu Khasib, but they did not add significantly to the 60 square kilometers of ground that Iran had already captured. Iran continued to advance by meters instead of kilometers, when it advanced at all.[111]

Iraq suffered continuing manpower losses in the process of these Iranian attacks, however, and took serious additional tank and air losses.[112] Even Iraq eventually admitted that it lost some 50 fighters, or roughly 10 percent of its operational force, during January and February. Iraq also experienced continuing technical problems in using its artillery and air power effectively. Iraq's shells and conventional fragmentation bombs lost much of their effectiveness because the soft or marshy terrain absorbed much of the force of the explosion and offered a relatively high degree of shelter. As a result, Iranian forces were often able to infiltrate at night, dig in, and survive massive Iraqi artillery attacks on their positions.

The Iranian pressure on Basra was severe enough to force Iraq to commit more elite reserves from its Presidential Guard and to redeploy 7th Corps forces to strengthen the defenses around Basra. The exact size of the new forces Iraq committed is unclear, but it is clear the 7th Corps forces—which normally were responsible for defending the area east and northeast of Basra—had to aid the 3rd Corps, the forces responsible for defending the area east and southeast of Basra.

According to some reports, the fighting also exposed problems in Iraq's high command. Saddam Hussein seems to have distanced himself from immediate responsibility for the fighting and only rarely visited the front, a marked contrast to some previous battles. General Abdul Jawad Thanoon, Iraq's Chief of Staff, seems to have fallen into disfavor, along with Major General Talia Khalil Douri, the commander of the 3rd Corps. A number of officers in the 3rd and 7th Corps were relieved from duty and several may have been shot.[113] Quite aside from these firings and executions, Iraq lost significant numbers of officers, NCOs, and trained personnel. It expended tens of millions of dollars worth of ammunition a week, and by late January, Iraq had lost as many as 500–1,500 major armored vehicles.[114]

The fighting on the land was particularly brutal between January 29 and 31. Iran launched a new night attack on January 29 and cut through the third ring of Iraq's defenses and reached the west bank of the Jasmin River. These gains, however, had little practical value. Iran suffered massive additional numbers of killed and wounded in the process, and its new attack bogged down. In fact, Iranian losses were so severe that Iraq again gained the initiative. On January 31, Iraq launched several counterattacks and freed around 20 square kilometers in the area around Fish Lake.

By early February, casualty estimates rose to 17,000 Iranian dead and 35,000–45,000 wounded and 6,000 Iraqi dead and 12,000–15,000 wounded. Bad as these estimates of Iranian losses may seem, they may still have been too low. Iran had now committed well over 100,000 men to actual combat and may well have lost over 20,000 to 30,000 killed.[115] Iran did, however, claim to have taken 1,750 prisoners of war, including 2 generals, 10 colonels, and about 145 other officers.

In any case, Iran now lacked the strength to provide more massive reinforcements. By February 11, 1987, the seventh anniversary of the Iranian revolution, Iran's leadership seems to have realized that the chances of a major breakthrough at Basra were slim. Rafsanjani and others began to refer to the "world's strongest defense line" and to having achieved a victory by destroying much of the Iraqi army.[116]

The battle, however, was scarcely over. Khomeini emerged on February 12, from three months of near silence, to declare that the war was a "holy crusade" and would go on until "victory." He also reminded his audience that he had called for final victory by the beginning of the Iranian new year on March 21. Iran claimed it was building up a new force of another "100,000 volunteers" for a Division of Vali Asr (Mahdi).[117] At least 30,000 Iranian troops still held positions near Fish Lake, and Iran committed still more popular volunteers into the front.

Intense fighting continued through the middle of February, and Iraqi troops did not always perform well. A few of Iraq's secondary positions were virtually abandoned, along with large stocks of equipment and munitions, although Iraqi forces generally inflicted very high casualties for what ultimately were minor losses of territory.[118] Iran only made limited further progress on the ground. While Iran occupied positions in a wide arc only 10 kilometers from Basra, it could not move out of the narrow strip between the Shatt al-Arab and Fish lake, and many of its troops were concentrated in a narrow area about five kilometers long and one kilometer wide. By the third week of February, Iran's total territorial gains consisted of about 100 square kilometers of marsh, flooded terrain, and date palms, most of which had been reduced to stumps in the course of the fighting.

Iran replied by moving some of its regular army units south from the Sumar front and raised some speculation that it was redeploying its armor and heavy artillery for an all-out strike at Basra. Iran did launch a two-pronged assault on February 22–23, but this assault involved only a few infantry divisions. It attacked the Iraqi positions east of Basra and along the road from Shalamcheh to Basra. The new assault was called the "Ya Zahra" attack. It scored some limited gains and caused some 2,000 casualties in Iraq's 98th, 705th, and 437th infantry brigades.

Once again, however, the Iranian attack failed to significantly weaken Iraq's defenses and caused massive new Iranian casualties. For reasons that are still unclear, this failure also marked the official end of Karbala-5. On February 27, the Iranians announced that a new phase in the war had begun. This announcement came at a time when Iran claimed to have caused 56,500 Iraqi casualties, and Iraq claimed 230,000–280,000 Iranian casualties.[119] While both sets of claims were exaggerated, the fighting had been extremely bloody by any standard.

The formal end of the Karbala-5 offensive also did not mean an end to the fighting. Only three days after Iran announced the end of its Karbala-5 offensive, Iranian forces again attacked the Iraqi defenses around Basra. When this attack failed, Iraq responded with a limited counterattack on the Iranian positions around Fish Lake. This counterattack took place on March 1, and the commander of the Iraqi Air Force, Air Marshal Hameed Shaban, and the new commander of Iraq's 3rd Corps, Lt. General Diauldine Jamal, issued claims to have destroyed large numbers of Iranian troops. In reality, Iraq scored only limited gains. It also took losses of 500 to 1,500 casualties and at least 50 tanks and armored vehicles. As at Faw, the Iraqi Army could defend, but it still took heavier losses than the Iranian forces when it tried to counterattack.[120]

The end result was that the battle of Basra turned into a siege in which Iran largely halted infantry assaults, but occasionally attacked and often bombarded the city. Iraq proved it could defend Basra but was unable to drive Iran's forces back. The main impact of the battle was that Iran seems to finally have faced the fact that it could not defeat Iraq by even well-prepared head-on attacks. Several months later, the commander of the Revolutionary Guards, Mohsen Rezaide, referred to the attack on Basra as having, "put the war's decisive stage behind it . . . and (the war) has now entered a stage to determine the future of Iraq. . . . (The coming struggle will be) a series of limited operations and a series of bigger ones. We have plans to organize, train, and arm popular forces inside Iraq. . . . This is the new front."[121] This quote was particularly interesting for its emphasis on smaller attacks all along the front and use of the Kurds, although similar comments had been made after many of Iran's failures to achieve decisive results, particularly after its losses in the spring of 1984.

Basra and the War of the Cities

The struggle for Basra also led Iraq to revive the war of the cities. During January, Iraq conducted over 200 long-range air and surface-to-surface missile strikes against 35 Iranian cities, including Qom, Nahawand (southwest of Tehran), Ramhormoz, Isfahan, and Dezful. By the end of January, Iran claimed that over 3,000 civilians had been killed in a single week.[122] Iraq also carried out some 75 strikes against Iranian economic installations between January 1 and February 14, 1987.

Iran reported that the number of Iranians hurt in Iraqi air raids during January was more than 1,800 killed and 6,200 wounded and that as many as 202 killed and 644 wounded were casualties on any given day. Iran later claimed that a total of 4,000 civilians were killed by all causes between January 1 and February 18 and that there were 12,000 injured.

Iran could do little to retaliate in the air, although one Iranian plane dropped bombs on Basra on February 9. Iran did, however, launch more Scud attacks at Baghdad and Basra, six of which hit Baghdad during the first eleven days of the new offensive. This figure increased to nine Scud strikes by February 5, and massive artillery exchanges against urban targets in the border area took place on both sides.[123]

Iraq also continued to strike at targets in the Gulf, and Iran retaliated by striking at the ships of nation's friendly to Iraq. These strikes were heavily targeted against Kuwait, which lost 15 Kuwaiti-owned or -chartered ships during the four months between the beginning of December and the end of March. The deliberate character of Iran's actions is indicated by the fact it struck a total of twenty ships during this period. These attacks were a major factor behind Kuwait's efforts to reflag its tankers and helped lead to the next phase of the war.

The data on the overall patterns in the strategic bombing efforts of both sides are uncertain. According to one source, however, Iraq carried out 5 attacks on shipping during January 1–15, and Iran carried out none. Iraq carried out 30 urban and economic strikes, and Iran carried out 3. Iraq carried out 2 attacks on shipping during January 15–30, and Iran carried out none. Iraq carried out 18 urban and economic strikes, and Iran carried out 15, 3 with Scud. Iraq carried out 4 attacks on shipping during February 1–15, and Iran carried out none. Iraq carried out 27 urban and economic strikes, and Iran carried out 5, all 5 with Scud. Iraq carried out 5 attacks on shipping during February 16–28, and Iran carried out none. Iraq carried out 8 urban and economic strikes, and Iran carried out none. During all of March, Iraq carried out 8 attacks on shipping, and Iran carried out 1. Iraq carried out 4 urban and economic strikes, and Iran carried out none.[124]

The main cause for the changes in these patterns seems to have been another cease-fire in the war of the cities which occurred on February 18. Iraq announced such a cease-fire on February 18 and claimed it was doing so in response to the wishes of Massoud Rajavi, the leader of the Iranian Mujahideen. In practice, it seems to have worked out some form of quid pro quo in which Iran moderated its land assaults on Basra in return for a halt to Iraqi air strikes on civilian targets.

The war of the cities may, therefore, have given Iraq a limited victory, although this victory came at a considerable cost. On January 22, Iran reported 57 Iraqi planes shot down, and Iraq admitted to 15. By the end of January, Iran claimed to have shot down 69 aircraft, although Iraqi sources claimed the figure was under 38. Iraq seems to have lost 3 more planes on February 14 and 15 over Iranian cities like Gacharan, Isfahan, and Izeh, at least one to a surface-to-air missile.[125]

The primary causes of Iraq's air losses during the war of the cities seem to have been short-range air defenses and a mixture of maintenance problems and pilot error. Iran rarely flew either air defense or attack sorties and normally flew only 4 to 11 sorties a day.[126] Iran had only a limited number of operational medium to heavy surface-to-air missile units, and observers of the Iraqi air raids in Iran reported that Iraq's aircraft were able to overfly Iran's cities and inland oil facilities without little sign of Hawk missile activity. Nevertheless, some Hawk kills seem to have occurred. Iraq claimed to have lost a MiG-25 to a Hawk missile on January 9, two Tupolev bombers on January 14, and a MiG-23 flying at 13,000 feet in the rear of the Iranian front at Basra on January 28, 1987.[127] These Iraqi claims support the conclusion of the Tower Commission that Iran concentrated the Hawk units it had been able to reactivate, as the result of covert U.S. and Israeli arms shipments, in Kharg Island and the rear of its forces attacking Basra.[128]

Karbala-6: New Iranian Attacks to the North

Iran's second major offensive during early 1987 was called Karbala-6 and struck in the area north of Baghdad between Qasr e-Shirin and Sumar. The Iranian forces in the Sumar Basin north of Baghdad totaled roughly 80,000 men, many of whom were regulars. These forces had most of Iran's remaining armor and self-propelled tanks, and U.S. experts estimated that Iran had nearly 1,000 tanks in the region.[129] The

Iranians concentrated up to 60,000 of these men for the assault wave near the abandoned Iraqi village of Naft-Khaneh, about 110 kilometers northeast of Baghdad.

The Iranian forces began their advance on the night of January 13, 1987, only five days after the beginning of Karbala-5. The attack was clearly intended to confront Iraq with the threat of having to defend two fronts at once and to present problems in committing its reserves. Like most of the Karbala attacks, however, the timing was staggered just enough for Iraq to properly characterize one attack before the next was launched.

Iranian forces quickly scored limited gains, and the fighting was intense enough for Iran to claim that it had destroyed 20 Iraqi aircraft and destroyed 400 tanks and other armored vehicles. The execution of the Karbala-6 offensive did not, however, produce the kind of hard-driving or full-scale thrust that might have exploited the fact Iraq had already committed many of its best reserves to Basra, some 375 kilometers to the south. The main phase of the Karbala-6 offensive lasted only five days, and the Iranian assault ultimately failed to put any major pressure on Iraq.

It is unclear whether the limited weight of this attack had any relationship to the fact that most of the Iranian forces involved in the attack in the north were "regular," but the fact is that Iranian forces did not press hard enough to penetrate the major defenses of the Iraqi II Corps, much less threaten Baghdad, some 90 miles to the southwest. They only took some hill positions near the border and about 65–100 square miles of territory, much of which was Iranian land that Iraq had captured in 1980.

The Fatah-4, Karbala-7, Karbala-8, and Karbala-9 Offensives

Iran launched other attacks while it was still attempting to take Basra, or at least claimed to have done so. On February 12, shortly after Khomeini's newest exhortations to attack until final victory, Iran claimed to have carried out a Fatah-4 attack near Haj Omran in the northern sector. Iran claimed that it was attacking in the direction of Arbil. On February 14, Iran stated that the attack had been successful and claimed to have destroyed Iraqi radar installations that were being used to direct bombing missions over Iran. The evidence that any such offensive took place is uncertain, however, and Fatah-4 may have been little more than a propaganda claim designed to give Iran a morale-boosting victory.[130]

Anti-Iraqi Kurds did launch new raids in the far north above Kirkuk during this time, but they too achieved comparatively little. The

Kurdish attacks were not well coordinated, had little practical effect, and did not force Iraq to divert significant amounts of manpower to the region. This was partly due to Turkey, which had steadily cracked down on the Turkish Kurdish Worker's Party, or PKK. The fighting in Turkey had lead to the death of some 180 civilians and 260 rebels between 1984 and 1986, and Turkey had begun to arm its villages against its Kurdish rebels. Turkey also cracked down on the Patriotic Union of Kurdistan (PUK) and Kurdish Democratic Party (KDP) forces in Iraq when they attempted to operate near the border. In November 1986, the Turkish government had revealed that it had conducted two land-incursion and twenty hot-pursuit air raids in Iraq. On March 4, 1987, it bombed Sirac, Era, and Alanish in the Kurdish areas of Iraq, seemingly in support of Iraq's efforts to suppress PUK and KDP operations in the area.[131]

Iran halted its offensive operations for the rest of February and most of March, except for the fighting near Basra. Khomeini's March 21 deadline for victory came without incident, even at the Basra front. It was clear that the Khomeini regime had to make some hard decisions about what to do next. Iran was having growing trouble in mobilizing more manpower and had now taken massive casualties since the start of its first offensive of the year on December 24, 1986. The weather was making Iranian offensives in the southern and central fronts far more difficult because Iraqi armor, artillery, and air power could take advantage of drier ground and clearer skies.

Iran was left with eight military options, each of which involved a different balance of risks:

- attempting to directly overrun the ring of massive and well-manned Iraqi defenses around Basra;
- using the newly captured islands in the Shatt al-Arab as a spring-board to attack across the Shatt in new areas;
- attempting to thrust south of Basra and link up with the Iranian forces at Faw;
- maintaining a slow siege of Basra with artillery and missile fire in an effort to deprive the city of its strategic value and wear down the Iraqi troops with continuing casualties;
- driving toward Baghdad from the Sumar basin southeast across heavily defended Iraqi positions, most of which were well entrenched in rough or mountainous terrain;
- launching a limited or spoiling attack to the far north to try to take advantage of the Kurdish rebel groups hostile to Iraq, threaten Iraq's oil exports, and force Iraq to move troops north;
- using the growing naval guard forces and Iran's new Silkworm

missiles to counter Iraq's attacks on Iranian tankers and to try to persuade the southern Gulf states to reduce their support of Iraq;
* using terrorism and political intimidation to force Kuwait and Saudi Arabia to reduce their support of Iraq.

It is unclear which mix of options Iran's regular military and Pasdaran officers advised, but it is clear which options Iran's Mullahs chose. Iran first attempted to attack to the north, perhaps in part as a diversionary effort. In spite of all its previous losses, Iran then made one last attempt to seize Basra and the south.

On March 4, 1987, Iran launched a new attack called Karbala-7. This offensive took place in the mountainous area in the far north, called the Gerdmand Heights. These heights are in the region near the Haj Omran region. They are west of Piranshahr in Iran and east of the Iraqi town of Rawanduz in Iraqi Kurdistan. The area had been the scene of bitter fighting in 1983 and was important because it allowed Iran to take positions some 18 kilometers inside Iraq which overlooked the main valley road to Rawanduz, to strengthen its ties to the anti-Iraqi Kurdish rebel groups, and to increase its pressure on Kirkuk, some 60 miles to the south of Rawanduz.

Roughly 4,000 Iranian army regulars, Pasdaran troops, troops from the regular 64th Urumiyeh Division, and Kurdish forces from the PUK and KDP, skillfully infiltrated into fixed Iraqi positions some 8,300 feet above sea level which were held by the 96th Brigade of the Iraqi 5th Corps. The Iranians attacked on foot, but used bulldozers and road graders to create a road directly behind the advancing troops that allowed rapid resupply and reinforcement in spite of the terrain. Iraq had the firepower to defend these positions, but the Iraqi defenders were too unprepared or inflexible to use it effectively. The attacking Iranian and Kurdish forces seized the summit within less than 24 hours. They also took other positions they had seized above the Iraqi town of Shuma Mustafa, in spite of repeated Iraqi counterattacks during 5–8 March. By March 9, the Iranians had advanced 20 kilometers in some areas.[132]

The new Iranian gains still left Iraq in a good position to protect Kirkuk and the north, but—in combination with the continuing fighting around Basra—they were of deep concern to Saddam Hussein and the Ba'ath Party. On March 15, 1987, Saddam Hussein held a five-hour meeting with his commanders in Baghdad, including General Adnan Khairallah, the Minister of Defense; Ali Hassab Al Mejid, a senior member of the Ba'ath, and Information Minister, Latif Nasif Jassem. While the contents of this meeting are uncertain, Iraqi sources feel that it involved discussions of the risk of Iraq being slowly defeated by attrition. They also seem to have lead to decisions to further expand the Republic Guards and other elite forces and prepare a large force for counterattacks, escalate the tanker war, and make further use of poison gas. These decisions all reflected a growing Iraqi fear that a war of attrition might eventually lead to defeat.

There was good reason for Iraq to fear further Iranian attacks. On April 6, Iran again launched a major set of human-wave attacks against Iraq's positions around Basra in the area southwest of Fish Lake. This offensive was called Karbala-8, and involved some 30,000–35,000 Iranian troops, most of which were Pasdaran. These forces attacked in a narrow front from the positions Iran had won in the previous fighting for Basra and launched a new series of human-wave attacks across the dual or twin canals which were the main water barrier in the area.

The Iranian attack only lasted about three days and was a blood bath. The Iranian forces attacked well-defended Iraqi positions in head-on attacks, and the Iraqi defenders either had warning or were fully ready. Iran suffered some 8,000 to 10,000 casualties and a very high proportion of dead. Iraq suffered about 2,000 casualties, with a relatively low percentage of killed. The most Iran did was to cross one of the water barriers and advance about a kilometer and a half against a minor Iraqi salient.[133] While it is difficult to be sure of a connection, Khomeini also promoted nine officers to general officer rank during this period, possibly to improve discipline and boost morale.[134]

Even so, Iran did not quit its offensives. Rafsanjani made new threats on April 8 that Iran would achieve victory during the coming year.[135] The next day, Iran launched a new attack in the northern part of the central front. This new Karbala-9 offensive took place on April 9 near Qasr e-Shirin, about 110 miles north of Baghdad. It involved the equivalent of two Iranian divisions and lasted about four days. Like Karbala-7, it was designed to improve Iran's position in the strategic heights in the border area and to force Iraq to keep a substantial part of its forces deployed along the central and northern part of the border. It did not score the same gains as Karbala-7, however, and only made limited progress.[136]

The Karbala-8 and -9 offensives marked the end of the major land fighting in 1987 and in some ways marked the end of Iran's effort to win the war with new "final offensives." They showed that Iran had the potential to win limited tactical victories but lacked the capability to make a major strategic breakthrough unless Iraq made massive mistakes in using its superior firepower and committing its reserves. Iran was to continue to talk about final offensives, but it never again could both mobilize the manpower it needed and commit them to massive human-wave attacks.

The key problem was casualties. By the end of April 1987, both Iraq and Iran were suffering severely, but Iran took about three to six times as many casualties during these two offensives as Iraq. The graveyards near Tehran and Baghdad continued to grow, but Iran was clearly suffering the most.[137] While casualty estimates remain uncertain, Iran may have lost 50,000 killed between late December and April and its total losses since the start of the war may well have exceeded 600,000–700,000 killed and twice that number of wounded. Nearly two million Iranians had been made homeless since the start of the war, and no real economic growth had taken place since 1977.

Even in retrospect it is not clear whether Basra became the turning point in the war or that Iran's offensives of 1987 smashed the Iranian hammer against the Iraqi anvil. Too much depends on the uncertain issue of how they affected Iranian public opinion, morale, and recruiting capabilities. It is clear, however, that Iran took losses that began to severely affect the morale of its forces, their willingness to sacrifice their lives, and the willingness of other Iranians to replace them. Even the Pasdaran began to present problems. They launched their first significant anti-war demonstration in mid-April when a small group appeared on Vali-Ar Avenue to ask for "forgiveness" for Saddam Hussein.[138]

It is equally clear that the rumors in Tehran increasingly blamed the Mullahs for sacrificing lives without any clear point and that Iran began to approach that peculiar level of political and military fatigue that saps a nation's ability to continue a war, at least a war whose goals were offensive in character. Further, the offensives also clearly led to new debates over both the value of the war and the value of human-wave tactics. While it is tempting to see these debates in terms of the regular military versus Rafsanjani and the Mullahs, with Pasdaran combat leaders increasingly divided against the Pasdaran leadership behind the front, there simply is not enough evidence to justify this position. What is clear is that Karbala-8 was in many ways the last time Iran could successfully throw tens of thousands of men into a frontal assault on well-defended Iraqi positions.

As for Iraq, it scarcely had reason to be confident. Estimates of the Iraqi killed and wounded since the first Iranian offensive in December 1986 reached 65,000, of which as many as 8,000–15,000 may have been killed. Basra was nearly half-deserted, and Iraq had acquired a large refugee population. Further, Iraq had no reason as yet to believe it could defeat Iran. While Iraqi ground forces performed better than in previous years, they still could not efficiently counterattack Iranian forces with armor. They also still continued to have problems in making effective use of Iraq's vast superiority in artillery. Iraqi units often wasted their artillery superiority on mass barrages in marsh areas where much of the effect of Iraqi shells was lost because of the use of untargeted fire against dug-in forces and the absorptive capability of the soft ground. Some reports claimed that Iraq had fired as many as one million rounds during the worst day of the fighting and was spending $1 billion a month on the defense of the south.[139]

Iraq's total air losses since the beginning of Karbala-4 were also serious. Iraq lost at least 70 aircraft and possibly as many as 90. Iraq also continued to take air losses of several aircraft per week through both March and April, losses it could not easily absorb because it lacked pilots.[140] Once the peak moment of each offensive was over, Iraq again showed great caution in employing its attack aircraft in close support missions, and Iraqi commanders indicated that they now had to conserve attack helicopters. Iraq often used air tactics such as having its helicopters fire rockets at Iranian forces from points inside the Iraqi lines, and its forces continued to fail to coordinate its ground, air, and helicopter forces efficiently. It still lacked an effective overall command structure, and it consistently committed its technology and firepower piecemeal rather than in a coherent form or in support of some coordinated form of maneuver warfare.

Notes

1. These strength estimates for Iran and Iraq are based on the IISS, *Military Balance, 1986–1987*, London, International Institute for Strategic Studies, pp. 96–98, and working materials provided by the Jaffee Center for Strategic Studies (JCSS).

2. It is almost impossible to be certain of the strategic perceptions of Iran's leadership. Most leaders under Khomeini made at least several statements that can be interpreted as calling for moderation or caution in using human-wave tactics, but these same leaders often expressed extremist views. While some authors trace clear separations between radicals and moderates or changes in attitude regarding the casualties Iran was suffering, the evidence involved is highly ambiguous. It is also important to note that the actors managing a war rarely operate from an objective perspective. For example, virtually every available historical record shows that the British, French, and German civil and military leaders in World War I conducted a massive war of attrition without any objective knowledge of the conditions at the front and on the basis of data and a belief structure that were at least as decoupled from reality as the data and belief structure reflected in the statements of Iran's leadership.

3. *Economist*, November 2, 1985, p. 36; *Washington Times*, November 6, December 9 and 21, 1985; *Wall Street Journal*, November 15, 1985; *New York*

Times, December 13 and 30, 1985; *Chicago Tribune* and *Washington Post,* January 7, 1986.

4. Shahram Chubin and Charles Tripp, *Iran and Iraq at War,* Boulder, Westview, 1988, pp. 75–76.

5. "A New Gulf War Offensive?" *The Middle East,* February, 1986, pp. 10–12; *Washington Times,* October 26, 1986, p. A-9.

6. *Jane's Defence Weekly,* February 8, 1986, p. 177.

7. *Washington Times,* April 3, 1986.

8. Sepehr Zabih, *The Iranian Military in Revolution and War,* London, Routledge, 1988, p. 191.

9. This attack took place on the day of the seventh anniversary of the Iranian Revolution. *Jane's Defence Weekly,* February 13, 1986; *Los Angeles Times,* February 12, 1986; *New York Times,* February 13, 1986.

10. *Washington Post,* February 11, 1986; The *Economist,* February 15, 1986.

11. Faw had exported some 75 percent of Iraq's oil in 1980.

12. *Washington Times,* February 13, 1986; *Los Angeles Times,* February 14, 1986.

13. *Jane's Defence Weekly,* February 19 and March 1, 1985; *Washington Post,* February 14, 1986.

14. U.S. intelligence sources provided a number of newspapers with satellite photo data during this phase of the fighting. For example, the *Washington Post* reported on February 14, 15, and 16, 1986, that satellite photos clearly showed Iraq had failed to mass forces for a counterattack during the first three days of the fighting.

15. *Washington Times* and *Christian Science Monitor,* February 16, 1986.

16. The commander, Major General Shawkat Ata, disappeared after being recalled to Baghdad. *Washington Times,* September 19, 1986, p. D-6.

17. *Washington Post,* February 13, 14, 15, 16, and 17, 1986; *Economist,* February 22 and March 1, 1986.

18. *The Middle East,* April 1986, pp. 7–9; *New York Times,* February 14, 15, and 21, 1986. Iraq bought hundreds of millions of dollars worth of ammunition from South Africa, Egypt, and other sources. It also had to buy barrier equipment on a panic basis to make up for the barbed wire, mines, and other material lost in Faw. The Iraqis did not help things by making a long series of claims about repulsing the attack and successful counterattacks, all of which proved false. For example, Iraq denied losing Faw until February 16. These lies did much to further discredit Iraq's political and military credibility.

19. *Washington Post,* March 4 and 26, 1986; *Washington Times,* March 26, 1986.

20. *Los Angeles Times,* February 20, 1986.

21. *New York Times* and *Washington Times,* February 25, 1986.

22. *Economist,* March 15, 1986; *New York Times,* March 6, 1986; *Washington Post,* March 7 and 9, 1986.

23. The *Washington Post* reported this was confirmed by satellite photography on February 19, 1986.

24. Edgar O'Ballance, *The Gulf War,* London, Brassey's, 1988, p. 179.

25. John Laffin, *War Annual I,* London, Brassey's, 1986, p. 87.

26. The size of the Iranian attack force is controversial, and it is not clear how many Barzani and KDP forces are included in this total.

27. O' Ballance, op. cit., pp. 180–181.

28. *Philadelphia Inquirer, New York Times, Baltimore Sun,* February 25 and 26, 1986; *Washington Times,* February 26 and 27, 1986; *Washington Post,* February 28, 1986; *Washington Times,* March 4, 1986.

29. *Jane's Defence Weekly,* March 29, 1986, p. 561.

30. *Philadelphia Inquirer,* March 3, 1986; *USA Today,* March 13, 1986; *New York Times,* March 15, 1986; *Washington Post,* March 4, 11, and 17, 1986.

31. *Jane's Defence Weekly,* December 13, 1986, p. 1373.

32. O'Ballance, op. cit., p. 183.

33. The Kurdish Democratic Party claimed to have overrun an Iraqi battalion of some 800 men and to have captured Mangesh, a town near Mosul. These claims later proved to be exaggerated. The Iraqis did, however, arrest the local village chief (a Kurd) for refusing to support the Iraqi counteroffensive, and it was clear that the KDP's strength in the area was growing. *The Guardian,* May 19, 1986; *Financial Times,* May 28, 1986; *Washington Post,* August 8, 1986, p. A-15.

34. *Washington Times,* July 2, 1986, p. 5B.

35. *Financial Times,* May 19, 1986.

36. O' Ballance, op. cit., p. 180.

37. The refinery was supplying about 45 percent of Iran's refined product. *Financial Times,* May 8 and 9, 1986; *Times,* May 9, 1986; *Guardian,* May 9, 1986. Also see "Can Iran Hold Its Bridgehead?" *The Middle East,* April 1986, pp. 7–9.

38. The confusion in reporting on the war is typified by the fact that Iran originally claimed to have overrun the 443rd and 705th brigades and then to have captured the deputy commander of the 71st Brigade and to have broken the 71st, 72nd, 93rd, and 113th brigades in the fighting. Iraq in turn claimed to have wiped out a major portion of the 5th, 10th, Lord of the Martyrs, 17th, 25th, 27th, and 41st revolutionary guards divisions and the 2nd Guards or Imam Riza Brigade. Iran claimed to have killed 2,000 Iraqis, and Iraq claimed to have killed or wounded 10,300 Iranians and captured 1,303 between June 30 and July 10, 1986. The real casualties seem to have been about 500 Iraqi killed, 1,500 wounded, and 1,100 taken prisoner. The Iraqi commander on the scene during the defeat, Major General Adin Tawfiq, was recalled to Baghdad and disappeared. *Los Angeles Times,* July 3, 1986, p. I-5; *Washington Times,* July 4, 1986, p. 8A; *Washington Times,* July 9, 1986, p. 7A, and September 19, 1986, p. 6D; *Chicago Tribune,* July 10, 1986, p. I-6.

39. Reports that Iraq attempted to use poison gas at this time seem to be incorrect. Timothy Renton, a British foreign office official speaking at Geneva, did announce, however, that Iraq was expanding its poison gas facilities, and that poison gas attacks had produced up to 10,000 casualties during the course of the war.

40. *New York Times,* July 25, 1986, p. A-5; *Washington Post,* July 30, 1986, p. A–16.

41. *Jane's Defence Weekly,* August 23, 1986, p. 268; *Washington Post,* August 13, 1986.

42. *Washington Times,* August 13, 1986, p. 8C, and August 15, p. 7; *Wall Street Journal,* August 22, 1986, p. 21; *Economist,* August 23, 1986, pp. 33–34.

43. As usual, the missile missed and fell in a suburban area near the refinery. Iran had only received about 20–30 Scud missiles from Syria and Libya and could not sustain a high fire rate. *New York Times,* August 13, 1986, p. A-3.

44. *Jane's Defence Weekly,* February 11, 1989, p. 219; Steven Zaloga, "Ballistic Missiles in the Third World," *International Defense Review,* 11/1988, pp. 1423–1437.

45. *Washington Post,* August 18, 1986, p. A-14.

46. Sources differ sharply according to whether they count confirmed hits or reported strikes and depending on the level of damage they count as serious. Different sources reported in August that 45 to 60 ships had been struck in the Gulf since the beginning of the year and that some 280 ships had been hit since the resumption of the tanker war in 1983.

47. Rupert Pengelly, "Gulf War Intensifies," *International Defense Review,* vol. 20, no. 3, 1987, p. 279.

48. *Washington Post,* August 21, 1986, p. A-22; *Washington Times,* August 25, 1986, p. 8A.

49. These goals were set by the Supreme Council of War Support, which had been formed early in the war and which was only slightly different from the Supreme Defence Council. Chubin and Tripp, op. cit., p. 76.

50. O'Ballance, op. cit., pp. 187–188.

51. The arms shipments in August evidently included some 1,500 TOW missiles. *Washington Post,* December 1, 1986, p. A-1, and December 7, 1986, p. A-25.

52. Iran may have gotten delivery of the first of some 50 J-7 (also called F-7 and MiG-21 variant) fighters. If so, they never appeared in battle.

53. This agreement is thought to have been the formal outcome of an arms offer negotiated by Rafsanjani during a 1985 visit to Peking. *Aviation Week,* November 24, 1986, p. 29; *Economist,* November 22, 1986, pp. 41–42; and *Jane's Defence Weekly,* November 29, 1986, p. 1257.

54. There are some reports that Iran got critical spares for the APQ-120 radars on its F-4s from the U.S. during this period which allowed it to repair the Klystron amplifiers on the radars and use them to illuminate targets with the continuous-wave beam needed to fire the Aim-7E radar-guided air-to-air missile. Other reports indicated that Iran was critically dependent on covert Israeli arms sales to keep its entire F-4 force functioning. One of the major uncertainties affecting the flow of arms to Iran during this period was the flow of parts for Iran's 250 Bell 214A and 40 214C transport helicopters and CH-47 heavy lift helicopters. While both Bell Textron and Boeing refused Iranian efforts to buy parts directly from U.S. companies, some parts seem to have been sold by firms in Israel and Italy. *Washington Post,* August 26, 1986, p. 1; *Wall Street Journal,* September 5, 1986, p. 1; *Aviation Week,* November 17, 1986, pp. 16–17.

55. This I/J band radar is normally used to control the Oerlikon 35-mm AA gun and AIM-7 Sparrow or Selenia Aspide missile.

56. *Washington Times*, October 1, 1986, p. 9A.

57. Uncertain reports issued during this period put Iran's total reserves at about $43.5 billion. *Christian Science Monitor*, August 27, 1986, p. 1; *Philadelphia Inquirer*, August 27, 1986, p. E-1; *Wall Street Journal*, September 4, 1986, p. 3; *Washington Times*, September 4, 1986, p. 5B.

58. Reports of Iranian land strength were issued of 200,000–250,000 Revolutionary Guards and 250,000–400,000 regular army. Iraq's strength was estimated at 700,000–1,000,000. Iran released 200 POWs. It claimed to have released 650 since the start of the war and to have 52,000 still under detention. *Washington Post*, August 27, 1986, p. A-7, and August 31, 1986, p. A-1; *Baltimore Sun*, August 31, 1986, p. 6A.

59. Zabih states that major debates were taking place at this time between the regular forces, supported by figures like President Khameini, and Rafsanjani, who supported the use of the Pasdaran and human-wave tactics. This rivalry is possible, but impossible to confirm. See Zabih, op. cit., pp. 192–194.

60. Ibid.

61. *New York Times*, September 17, 1986, p. A-15.

62. *New York Times*, September 26, 1986, p. A-10, and October 12, 1986, p. 3. *Washington Post*, October 12, 1986, p. A-22.

63. *New York Times*, October 12, 1986, p. 3.

64. O'Ballance, op. cit., p. 189.

65. Defense Analysts, a British consulting firm, had been aiding Iran to protect its tankers. It recommended that Iran use radar-absorbent materials and reflectors to change the radar image of the ship, simple ECM gear to help prevent radar lock-on, and boiler protection systems. Iran modified four of its chartered tankers—*Pegasus 1, Achilles, Free Enterprise*, and *Lady A*—to use this equipment.

Both the *Achilles* and *Free Enterprise* were still hit by Iraqi Exocets. Neither ship suffered serious damage, however, which was unusual given the impact of Exocet hits on other ships.

At least one ship owner also purchased MEL Matilda passive-warning radars so his crews would know they were under attack and could take shelter and trigger their ships' automatic protection systems.

Another group, a consortium of Gulf Agency, Hotforge of Aberdeen, and Special Projects Consultants of Aberdeen, offered similar protection systems for all tankers moving through the Gulf, plus training in maneuver and minimizing secondary damage. This led to some changes in attack tactics. As a result, the Iraqis started firing AS-12 missiles from their Aerospatiale helicopters at the superstructure and hull to affect ship control and the crew, rather than try to sink the ship. The Iranians changed their tactics to fire without overflight to minimize warning and the use of countermeasures. *Jane's Defence Weekly*, October 25, 1986, p. 932; Pengelly, op. cit., p. 279.

66. *Washington Times*, September 30, 1986, p. 8C, October 7, 1986, p. 4D, and October 8, 1986, p. A-21.

67. *Economist*, October 18, 1986, pp. 46–47. *New York Times*, October 19, 1986, p. E-3.

68. Unless otherwise referenced, this and all the following references to the history of U.S. covert arms sales to Iran are based upon the chronology in the unclassified version of the *Report on Preliminary Inquiry* of the Senate Select Committee on Intelligence, January 29, 1987, and the *New York Times* edition of the *Tower Commission Report*, New York, Bantam and Times Books, February 1987.

69. McFarlane later testified that he had asked the CIA if Israel was shipping arms to Iran and that the CIA denied it. His deputy, Admiral John Poindexter, seems to have been fully aware of Israel's interests. *Report on Preliminary Inquiry* of the Senate Select Committee on Intelligence, January 29, 1987, p. 2; *Tower Commission Report*, New York, Bantam and Times Books, 1987, pp. 16–29 and 102–147.

70. *Washington Post*, July 8, 1985, and December 7, 1986, and U.S. Senate Committee on Intelligence, *Report on Preliminary Inquiry*, January 28, 1987, p. 4; *Tower Commission Report*, New York, Bantam and Times Books, 1987, pp. 19–24.

71. *Washington Post*, December 7, 1986, p. A-25.

72. *Report on Preliminary Inquiry* of the Senate Select Committee on Intelligence, January 29, 1987, pp. 1–2; *Tower Commission Report*, New York, Bantam and Times Books, 1987, pp. 23–26.

73. It later became clear that these latter three individuals had been discussing an Iranian initiative since mid-1984.

74. *Report on Preliminary Inquiry* of the Senate Select Committee on Intelligence, January 29, 1987, pp. 4–8; *Tower Commission Report*, New York, Bantam and Times Books, 1987, pp. 28–31.

75. Fred Reed was abducted on September 9, 1986, and Joseph James Cicippio on September 12. Edward Austin Tracy was taken on October 21, 1986. In all three cases, the U.S. State Department identified pro-Iranian radical groups as being responsible. The net result neatly balanced out the total hostage releases. See *Washington Post*, December 7, 1986, p. A-25; *Tower Commission Report*, New York, Bantam and Times Books, 1987, pp. 153–334, for full details.

76. *Washington Post*, December 7, 1986, pp. A-30 to A-31. *As Shirra* announced that an American envoy had visited Tehran and had shipped key tank and radar parts in four C-130 cargo planes from the Philippines. See *Washington Post*, November, 1986, p. A-15; *Newsweek*, November 17, 1986; *Time*, November 17, 1986, pp. 49–52; and *Aviation Week*, November 17, 1986, pp. 16–18. Senate Select Intelligence Committee, *Report on Preliminary Inquiry*, January 29, 1987, p. 38; *Tower Commission Report*, New York, Bantam and Times Books, 1987, pp. 51 and 414–449.

77. The editor of *As Shirra* later declared that the story had been leaked to him by a member of Montazari's staff. He stated that the story was not Syrian-inspired and that that issue of the magazine had been suspended in Syria. *Washington Post*, December 7, 1986; *Baltimore Sun*, December 14, 1986, p. 18A; *Economist*, November 1, 1986, pp. 43–44; *Washington Times*, October 29, 1986, p. 6A; and Barry Rubin, "My Friend Satan," *New Republic*, December 15, 1986, pp. 14–15.

78. *Washington Times*, November 25, 1986, p. 5A, and *Washington Post*, December 6, 1986, p. A-13.

79. It is important to note that the exact motivation for the split in the Iranian leadership that led to the exposure of the U.S. arms sales does not seem to have been along moderate versus radical lines over the arms sales per se. In June 1988, reports surfaced about secret testimony to the Congress by George Cave and George Allen, the CIA agents who had worked most closely on the deal. Cave made it clear that Rafsanjani had developed a broad group of advisors on the deal precisely to avoid being charged with being moderate and that Rafsanjani had deliberately included a mix of conservatives from the bazaar and regular military and radicals from Iranian intelligence and the Revolutionary Guards. According to Cave, Rafsanjani had proposed a U.S.-Iran commission on the normalization of relations in September 1986, shortly before the arms sales became public. The Iranian side of this commission would have included conservatives, radicals, and moderates. *Washington Post*, December 7, 1986, p. A-25, and June 12, 1988, pp. A-4 and A-5.

80. *Washington Post*, June 12, 1988, p. A-4.

81. The aircraft were originally denied permission to land and were given landing rights only after they insisted that the alternative would be to crash over Saudi territory.

82. *Jane's Defence Weekly*, August 16, 1986, p. 232.

83. This helped lead to reports that Iraq was using mercenary pilots from Egypt, France, or Belgium. *Baltimore Sun*, December 16, 1986, p. 6A. These reports were not confirmed at this writing.

84. *Jane's Defence Weekly*, December 12, 1986, pp. 1372–1373.

85. Ibid.

86. *Jane's Defence Weekly*, December 6, 1986, p. 1323.

87. *Wall Street Journal*, March 2, 1987, p. 25.

88. Ibid.

89. *Washington Post*, November 26, 1986, p. A-14; Anthony R. Tucker, "The Gulf Air War," *Armed Forces*, June 1987, pp. 270–278.

90. *Washington Post*, December 7, 1986, p. A-37; December 22, 1986, p. A-20, December 14, 1986, p. A-52; *New York Times*, December 9, p. A-8; *Washington Times*, December 12, 1986, p. 6A.

91. The most recent previous attack had been on May 7, 1986, when Iraqi aircraft seriously damaged the Shahr Ray oil refinery.

92. *Washington Post*, December 22, 1986, p. A-20.

93. Based on the authors' interviews with Iranian exiles and Zabih, op. cit., pp. 194–196.

94. *Jane's Defence Weekly*, December 13, 1986, p. 1372.

95. *Washington Post*, December 4, 1986, p. A-49; *Washington Times*, December 2, 1986, p. 8A.

96. Zabih, op. cit., pp. 195.

97. Speech by Iraqi Minister of Defense Adnan Khairallah, December 27, 1986. The Mujahideen opposition movement claimed Iran had 16,000 dead.

98. *Washington Post*, December 26, 27, and 28, 1986; *Economist*, January 3, 1987, pp. 26–27.

99. Zabih, op. cit., p. 196.

100. *Washington Post*, February 9, 1987, pp. A-13 and A-16; *Economist* January 17, 1987, pp. 36–37; *Newsweek*, February 2, 1987, pp. 30–31.

101. The geography involved is complex, and most maps do not accurately show the changes in water barriers that occurred since the beginning of the war. The extent of wet terrain is also seasonal and is visible only from satellite photography. In general, the Iranians picked a relatively dry period, since the major floods do not hit the area until March. The north-south line that forms the Iran-Iraq border in the south is parallel to a line about one kilometer east of 48.00.00 longitude until it hits the Nahr el Khaiin River at a point called Boundary Pillar 1. It then runs along the Nahr el Khaiin for about eight kilometers until the river flows into the Shatt at a point called Boundary Pillar 2 (30.26.90N, 46.06.62E). The border then generally follows the east bank of the Shatt al-Arab until it reaches the sea at the end of the Faw Peninsula, although it is to the west of a large island in the Shatt variously called Jazireh ye Salbukh or Muhalla Island.

102. O'Ballance, op. cit., pp. 194–195.

103. *Washington Post*, February 9, 1987, pp. A-13 and A-16.

104. According to some reports, the commander of the Iraqi Third Corps, Major General Talia Khalil Douri, was replaced by the head of the Fifth Corps, Lt. General Dhia ul-Din Jamal, for his failure to properly prepare his forces. The Iraqi Army Chief of Staff was also replaced. *Jane's Defence Weekly*, May 9, 1987, pp. 899–900.

105. Iran favored cloud cover because it believed this affected satellite coverage and reduced foreign intelligence support of Iraq.

106. *Washington Post*, January 10, 1987, p. A-16.

107. An October 1986 census in Iran had estimated a population of over 47 million and a growth rate of nearly 4 percent. Iraq's population was less than a third of this total. O'Ballance, op. cit., pp. 198–199.

108. Tucker, op. cit., pp. 270–271.

109. *Washington Post*, January 16, 1987, p. A-19; *Christian Science Monitor*, January 20, 1987, p. 1.

110. *Washington Times*, January 21, 1987, p. 6A.

111. *Washington Post*, January 20, 1987, p. A-1, January 28, 1987, p. A-15; *Christian Science Monitor*, January 20, 1987, p. I-1; *New York Times*, January 21, 1987, p. A-6; *Sunday Times*, January 25, 1987.

112. *New York Times*, January 12, 1987, p. A-1, and January 13, 1987, p. A-12; *Washington Post*, January 13, 1987, p. A-14.

113. *Washington Post*, February 9, 1987, p. A-16.

114. According to some reports, part of these losses were due to wire-guided missiles that may well have been the TOWs that were part of the covert arms shipments to Iran. *Washington Post*, January 27, 1987, p. A-1.

115. Iran admitted to only 2,000 dead and 7,000 wounded.

116. Some reports indicate that the killed on both sides now approached 1 million. To put this figure into perspective, it compares with 2.9 million in Korea, 2.4 million in Vietnam, and 2.2 million in Cambodia. *Washington Post*, January 16, 1987, p. A-1; *New York Times*, January 16, 1987, p. A-9, January 20,

1987, p. A-8, and January 23, 1987, p. A-1; and *Christian Science Monitor*, January 20, 1987, p. 1.

117. *New York Times*, February 11, 1987, p. 10; and *Washington Post*, February 9, 1987, p. A-1.

118. *Wall Street Journal*, January 14, 1987, p. 27; *Washington Post*, January 14, 1987, p. A-19; *New York Times*, January 14, 1987, p. A-6; and *Washington Times*, January 21, 1987, p. 6-A.

119. *Washington Times*, February 28, 1987, p. 5.

120. *Washington Times*, March 2, 1987, p. 7A.

121. *Keyhan*, June 29, 1987, quoted in FBIS, July 7, 1987.

122. *Jomhuriyeh Islami*, Teheran edition, February 3, 1987.

123. This was the nineteenth Iranian missile attack on Baghdad in two years. Rumors surfaced at this time that the USSR had sold Iran some 200 Scuds in an effort to improve relations and in return for two electronic intelligence (ELINT) listening posts in Iran.

124. Based on a working paper by Gary Sick.

125. Tucker, op. cit., pp. 270–271.

126. *Washington Post*, January 27, 1987, p. A-1. U.S. officials later said on a background basis that the Hawk parts had added only 3 percent to Iran's air defenses, and the TOWs knocked out only a few dozen Iraqi tanks. *Washington Times*, January 29, 1987, p. 6A.

127. Tucker, op. cit., pp. 270–271; O'Ballance, op. cit., p. 200.

128. *Wall Street Journal*, March 2, 1987, p. 2.

129. *Washington Post*, February 9, 1987, pp. A-13 and A-16; *Economist*, January 17, 1987, pp. 36–37; *Newsweek*, February 2, 1987, pp. 30–31.

130. O'Ballance, op. cit., p. 200.

131. *Newsweek*, February 2, 1987, p. 31.

132. *Washington Post*, March 15, 1987, p. A-1.

133. One source claims that the Iraqi defenders were warned by Iranians opposing the attack. See O'Ballance, op. cit., p. 203.

134. Chubin and Tripp, op. cit., p. 48.

135. O'Ballance, op. cit., p. 202.

136. *Washington Times*, April 9, 1987, p. 6A, April 10, 1987, p. 6A, April 13, 1987, p. 9B.

137. *Washington Post*, April 22, 1987, p. A-21.

138. *Washington Post*, May 17, 1987, p. A-31.

139. Claims made to the authors by a senior Egyptian defense official in May 1987.

140. *Jane's Defence Weekly*, May 9, 1987, pp. 900–901.

9

PHASE SIX: THE WAR OF ATTRITION CONTINUES AND THE WEST ENTERS THE GULF WAR, MARCH 1987–DECEMBER 1987

The Increasing Importance of the War at Sea

Important as the fighting around Basra was in shaping the future of the land war, developments in the Gulf were leading to a major new phase of the war. January involved more Iraqi and Iranian attacks on Gulf targets than any previous month in the conflict. Iraq struck at Kharg Island, Iran's transloading facilities at Sirri, and Iran's shuttle tankers and oil facilities. These strikes did not make major cuts in Iran's oil exports, but they did force Iran to go on another purchasing mission to Greece, Britain, and Norway to buy 15 more tankers.

Iraqi aircraft continued to strike at tankers and the Iranian oil fields. They hit Iran's Cyrus and Noroz fields in late March and April, as well as the Ardeshir oil field, and they continued attacks on Iranian shipping to Sirri. Nevertheless, Iraq still did not score the kind of successes it had scored against Kharg and Iraq's tanker shuttle the previous year. Iran's exports remained relatively high.

Iran Seeks New Ways to Fight the Tanker War

It was Iran, not Iraq, that was making the most important changes in the tanker war. Iraq's attacks on the shipping in Iranian waters led Iran to go beyond harassing the shipping moving to and from such pro-Iraqi states as Saudi Arabia and Kuwait. Iran shifted to attacks of its own. (See Table 9.1.)

In launching these attacks, Iran faced a number of serious problems. Iran could not afford to commit its limited remaining air power. The Iranian Air Force only had 63 to 90 operational fighters, with some

TABLE 9.1 Patterns in Iraqi and Iranian Attacks on Gulf Shipping: 1984 to June 30, 1987

Date	Iraqi Attacks	Iranian Attacks	Total Attacks	Deaths	Ships Lost
1984	36	18	54	49	32
1985	33	14	47	16	16
1986					
October	1	3	4	—	—
November	9	2	11	—	—
December	5	0	5	—	—
Total 1986	66	41	107	88	30
1987					
January	7	6	13	—	—
February	6	3	9	—	—
March	3	3	6	—	—
April	2	3	5	—	—
January-June	29	29	58	10	4

SOURCES: Adapted from the *Economist*, April 25, 1987, p. 34; and Lloyd's Maritime Information Service.

20–35 F-4Es, 30–45 F-5Es, and 7–12 F-14s. Most of these could only fly limited numbers of sorties and most lacked fully functional avionics. While Iran's F-4E force has recently improved in readiness because of deliveries of spare parts from various unidentified sources, none of its F-14As seemed to be able to use its Phoenix missiles, and only a limited number seem to have had operational radars. While reports kept appearing that Iran had up to 50 PRC and North Korean copies of the MiG-19 and MiG-21 on order, none appeared in combat.

Iran faced equally serious problems in using most of its regular navy. It had lost significant amounts of its trained maintenance personnel in the various purges and upheavals following the revolution. It had suffered serious damage to at least two of its destroyers, two Saram-class frigates, and 1 US PF-103 corvette. It had lost two minesweepers. It had lost two Kaman-class patrol boats, and two more were seriously damaged.

Iran not only could not buy new combat ships to replace these losses, it was experiencing serious difficulties in maintaining the sensors and weapons systems on its remaining ships and had serious shortages of both anti-ship and anti-air missiles. Most of Iran's key radar and electronic systems were no longer operational. This included the Contraves Sea Hunter, SPG-34, and Mark 37, 51, and 61 fire-control systems; the WM-28 tactical and fire-control radars; the Plessey AWS-1 and SPS-6 search radars; and the SPS-37 air-surveillance radars on its larger ships. Iran lacked usable stocks of such key weapons as RIM-66

Standard (anti-aircraft), Sea Cat (anti-aircraft), and RGM-84 Harpoon (anti-ship). Further, most of the missiles delivered before the fall of the Shah now were far older than their maximum reliable storage life, and Iran had no access to Western parts or services.[1]

Iran, however, was still able to operate many of its British-made Saram-class fast attack craft. Further, the Iranian Navy retained up to seven AB-212 helicopters, each with two Sea Killer Mk II or AS-12s. Both systems could be used for sudden attacks against tankers or U.S. warships. The Navy also had two PF-3 Orion maritime patrol aircraft. These lacked operational radars and other sensors but could be used for visual reconnaissance missions. Further, Iran had seven Sikorsky SH-3D ASW helicopters and two RH-53D minelaying helicopters. It had Hercules C-130 and four F-27 Mark 400 Fokker Friendship aircraft for minelaying and patrol missions.

Iran now began to use these remaining regular navy forces to strike at the cargo ships and tankers in the Gulf and often struck at night.[2] In most cases, the missile Iran used seems to have been the Italian-made Sea Killer. The Sea Killer first became operational in 1984 and was sold to Iran before the fall of the Shah. It is a relatively light missile, about 1.01 meters long and 20.6 cm in diameter. It weighs 300 kilograms and has a small 70-kilogram high-explosive semi-armor piercing warhead. It has a maximum air-to-surface range of 25 kilometers and a minimum range of six kilometers. It is a "sea skimmer" which flies at a height of three to four meters. The missile normally rides a radar beam to the target, but it can be radio directed in a heavy jamming environment.[3]

Few of the cargo ships that Iran and Iraq hit during this period were sunk or seriously damaged, but 16 ships were damaged between January 1 and early February, raising the total hit since the war began to 284.[4] On at least one occasion in early March, the Sea Killer also showed that it could do catastrophic damage. It hit the small 998-ton tanker *Sedra* in a vulnerable area and turned the ship into an inferno, killing at least seven crewmen.[5]

As a result, both Soviet and Western naval forces began to take action. The USSR reacted in mid-January by sending a Krivak-class missile frigate to escort four Soviet ships carrying arms to Iraq from the Straits to Kuwait. This was the second Soviet warship to enter the Gulf since 1982—the first had been sent when Iran detained two Soviet ships in September 1986—and was clearly intended as a signal to Iran, Iraq, and the southern Gulf states that the USSR would protect its ships.

The U.S. increased its force in the Indian Ocean to a full carrier group, including the 85,000-ton carrier *Kitty Hawk* and eleven escort ships. The U.S. deployed the carrier task force just east of Masirah, off the coast of Oman. Britain and France increased their ship activity, and the British Armilla or Indian Ocean squadron began to spend roughly 50 percent of its time in the Gulf.[6]

Iran Deploys the Silkworm

The movement of the U.S. carrier group to the Gulf of Oman was in reaction to more than Iranian use of the Sea Killer. The U.S. had found that Iran was deploying a much heavier land-based anti-ship missile near the Straits of Hormuz and detected at least one test firing of the missile at Qesham Island near the Straits of Hormuz in late February.[7]

This new system was part of the family of Chinese missile systems shown in Table 9.2. It was a Chinese version of the Soviet CSS-N-2, or Styx anti-ship missile, which the Chinese had begun to deliver to Iran in the summer of 1986. The PRC designates this system as the Hai Ying HY-2, and it is nicknamed the "Silkworm." It can be deployed in both mobile and fixed sites, and the Iranians chose to use a mix of mobile equipment and fixed concrete bunkers and launch rails. In this form of deployment, the launch sites are presurveyed to provide precise range and sensor locations, and the missile moves on a wheeled or tracked launcher rail. This allows the missiles and the launch vehicles and support vans to be kept in dispersed locations, where they are safer from attack, and then moved to the site when needed.[8] Each fire unit has two or four missile launchers.[9]

The Silkworm missile is made by the China Precision Machinery for Import and Export Corporation (CPMIEC). It is not particularly sophisticated by Western standards and has been on Chinese ships for twenty years. It has only been exported, however, since 1984. It is 6.5 meters long and has a diameter of 75 centimeters. It weighs 2,500–3,000 kilograms and has a 500-kilogram or 1,100-pound warhead. This warhead weight is about seven times the weight of that on the Sea Killer and three times the weight of that on the Exocet. It has a maximum range of 95 kilometers and comes with three different guidance systems: The HY-2 homes in on target by using the tracking radar at the launch site, the HY-2A homes in using passive infrared (IR) to defeat electronic countermeasures, and the HY-2G uses terminal radar homing plus altimeter.

The Silkworm is most effective at ranges under 40 kilometers, but it has an effective range of 70–80 kilometers if a ship or aircraft can designate the target and allow the Silkworm to reach the point where its on-board guidance can home in on the target. China sold Iran such radar designation capability to use on some of its ships and aircraft.

TABLE 9.2 Chinese Missile Systems Affecting the Iran-Iraq War and Arms Exports to the Third World

Model	Speed	Launch Platform	Description
Surface-to-Ship, Ship-to-Ship, Missiles			
FL-1	0.9	Ship	Fei Lung or Flying Dragon. An upgraded Soviet CSS-N-2. Radio-altimeter monopulse active seeker. Improved ECM seeker. Sea Skimmer with 30-meter altitude for cruise and 8-meter altitude for terminal attack. Range is 40 kilometers. Has 500-kg HE warhead. Weight 2.3 metric tons. CATIC.
FL-7/ C-801	1.4	Ship	Surface-launch model of C-801. Compatible with FL-1 fire control system (Square Tie). Minimum software changes. Counter-ECM passive infrared guidance. Sea Skimmer with 50–100 meter altitude for cruise and 8-meter altitude for terminal attack. Range is 32 kilometers. Has 500-kg HE warhead. Weight 1.8 metric tons. CPMIEC.
HY-2A/ Silkworm	0.9	Land	Hai Ying or Sea Eagle. Mobile improved version of HY-2 shore-to-ship missile. Monopulse anti-jamming and passive IR guidance. Range is 20–95 kilometers. Warhead is 500 kilograms. Hit probability greater than 70 percent. CATIC.
HY-2G	0.9	Land	Variant of HY-2A with active seeker. Sea Skimmer with altitude options of 30, 50, or 100 meter flight. CATIC.
HY-4	0.85	Land	Coastal defense missile. Improved variant of the HY-2G. Counter-ECM and passive IR guidance. Range increased to 35–135 kilometers. Weight 2 metric tons with strap-on booster. Cruise altitude of 200–700 meters. CPMIEC.
SY-1	0.85	Land	Shui Yang or Water Eagle. Sea Skimmer missile. Seems to have some technology similar to C-801. Similar in look to HY-1, but mounted on T-63 tank chassis. Uses active seeker guidance. CATIC. Is also submarine-launched variant called SY-2.
YJ-6	1.2	Ship	Has appearance and mission similar to Exocet and Harpoon. Uses counter-ECM and passive IR guidance. Semi-armor piercing warhead with two-stage solid fuel propulsion. CPMIEC.
Air-to-Surface Missiles			
C-601	0.9	Aircraft	May derive in part from Kennel or Styx. Uses monopulse, countermeasure resistant guidance, with terminal seeker. Range up to 160 kilometers from altitude of 9,000 meters. Launch weight 2.44 metric tons. CPMIEC.
HY-4	0.85	Aircraft	Improved HY-2G. Counter-ECM, passive IR seeker. Range up to 135 kilometers. Launch weight 1.74 metric tons. CPMIEC.
YJ-1	1.4	Aircraft	Ying Ji or Hawk Attitude/Strike Eagle. Air-launched version of C-801. Counter-ECM, passive IR seeker. Attack altitude 5–7 meters. Weight 815 kilograms. CPMIEC.

(continues)

TABLE 9.2 *(continued)*

Model	Speed	Launch Platform	Description
Surface-to-Surface Missiles			
C-101	1+	Land	A land-mobile cruise missile with counter-ECM and passive IR guidance. It is 5.6 meters long, 0.54 meters in diameter, and has 2 ramjet engines and 2 solid fuel boosters. Its range is 50 kilometers. Its cruise altitude is 50–100 meters.
HY-3	1+	Land	Longer range version of the C-101. It has counter-ECM and passive infrared guidance. It is 9 meters long, 0.76 meters in diameter, and has 2 ramjet engines and 4 solid fuel boosters.
M-Series	—	Land	Battlefield support missile. Preprogrammed inertial guidance. Solid fuel. Range up to 600 kilometers. Transported and launched from a cross-country vehicle. Preparation time of less than 30 minutes. Reportedly non-nuclear. CPMIEC.
DF-3	—	Land	IRBM designed in 1970. Inertial guidance. Range up to 2,700 kilometers. Sixty deployed. Normally has 2-megaton warhead.

Manufacturer: CATIC=Aero-Technology Import/Export Corporation; CPMIEC=China Precision Machinery Import/Export Corporation.

SOURCES: Adapted from Bradley Hahn, "Chinese Tactical Defense Missiles," *Journal of Defense and Diplomacy*, March 1988, pp. 26–29; IISS, *Military Balance, 1987–1988*, London, IISS, 1987; *Directory of Chinese Military Equipment, 1987–1988*, Worcester, PA, HAI, 1987.

The missile reaches most targets within its range within six minutes of firing. The missile normally climbs to an altitude of 145 meters before dropping to a final approach altitude of about 30 meters. The primary warning a target receives is from radar contact at launch before the missile drops to near sea level and when the missile is completing its final approach and no longer is masked by the curve of the earth. This is at a range of 16–32 kilometers in the case of active radar homing or 10 kilometers in the case of IR, since the IR seeker remains passive until this point. It is large enough to be detected and killed by some surface-to-air missiles, but these require good kill capability against very low-altitude attacks.

While the resulting mix of anti-ship capabilities scarcely gave Iran a powerful strike force by Western standards, the combination of the Sea Killer and Silkworm missiles did give Iran a significant capability to strike at tankers and cargo vessels in the Gulf, a growing capability to sink ships rather than damage them.[10]

This rise in the Iranian missile threat to Gulf shipping created a very different problem for the West from the one created by Iran's naval and air strikes on tankers in Iranian waters. It was arming to strike at third-country ships moving through international waters to ports outside the war zone. This meant Iran planned to threaten or attack international shipping to the southern Gulf states.[11]

The problem American planners faced was not the current level of the tanker war as much as the broader trends and risks that affected the security of Western oil supplies. Even in a period of comparative oil glut, the West faced the problem that the Gulf region provided 63 percent of the West's oil reserves, supplied over 25 percent of all oil moving in world trade, 30 percent of the oil used by OECD European states, and 60 percent of Japan's oil. Even with the expansion of pipelines through Turkey and Saudi Arabia, 17 percent of the West's oil still moved through the Straits of Hormuz.[12]

The mix of potential threats to Kuwait was particularly important. Kuwait had nearly as many proven oil reserves as Iraq and Iran combined. It had more than 100 billion barrels of oil reserves, or 13 percent of the world's proven oil reserves versus roughly 3.9 percent for the U.S. It had overseas investments of over $100 billion (80 percent government and 20 percent private).[13]

Kuwait Seeks to Reflag Its Tankers

On January 13, 1987, Kuwait asked the U.S. Embassy if its tankers could receive U.S. Navy protection if they were "reflagged" to fly the U.S. flag; Kuwait also informed the U.S. it had an offer to have such protection provided to it from the USSR. In making these initiatives to the U.S., Kuwait was more concerned with the need to find outside protection against Iranian land and air threats and attacks as it was with attacks on Kuwaiti flag ships.

Although the tanker war was serious—and ships moving to Kuwait had been the target of 15 of the 19 attacks Iran had conducted on Gulf shipping after September 15, 1986—the tanker war still affected only a small portion of the 168–196 tankers a month that moved through the Gulf. Tanker movements to Kuwait averaged at least one ship per day and often reached a total of as many as 70–80 tankers per month. By early 1987, only seven Kuwaiti-flagged ships had been hit out of some 284 attacks on shipping since the beginning of the tanker war. No Kuwaiti-flagged ship had been included in any of the 34 vessels Iran had attacked between Christmas day on 1985 and September 17, 1986.[14]

Kuwait was coming under a steadily growing series of Iranian political attacks for allowing Iraq to use its port of Shuaiba to ship

Soviet and other arms and war material. Kuwait had also increased the risk of Iranian attacks on its own ships or other ships moving to Kuwait by allowing Iraqi planes to overfly Kuwait so that they could fly down the southern coast of the Gulf and attack Iranian shipping without warning. It also seems to have allowed the Iraqi Navy to send small ships down the Sebiyeh waterway between Kuwait and Bubiyan Island and may have allowed Iraqi helicopters to stage out of Kuwaiti territory.[15]

Four factors catalyzed the Reagan Administration into supporting the reflagging plan. The first was the U.S. discovery that the Soviet Union had agreed to a similar reflagging request and that Kuwait was now proposing that the U.S. and USSR share protection of eleven of its tankers—with the USSR protecting five and the U.S. protecting six. The second was the need to reassert U.S. influence in the region after the fall of the Shah, continuing problems in selling arms to friendly Gulf states, the impact of the U.S. withdrawal from Lebanon, and the Iran-Contra arms scandal. The third factor was the fact Iran had deployed the Silkworm missile and was building up a new branch of the Revolutionary Guards for naval operations. Finally, the Reagan Administration concluded that Iran had not attacked the flag carriers of the major powers earlier in the war, was unlikely to do so now, and lacked the conventional naval and air strength to challenge the U.S. Navy.

In reaching this decision, the Reagan Administration made an error that provides an important lesson to any defense planner. It allowed its interest in supporting a given policy to make it focus on enemy intentions as were perceived at the policy level, to the exclusion of enemy capabilities and a full analysis of enemy intentions at the expert level.

The Administration did not go through the full inter-Agency process in shaping its decision to reflag the Kuwaiti tankers. In fact, the Chairman of the Joint Chiefs, the Secretary of the Navy, and most of the Reagan Administration's leading officials on Gulf affairs were not consulted in detail.[16] The Department of Defense did prepare a contingency plan to strike at the Silkworm missiles, but it did not prepare plans to deploy a force that could deal with all of the threats the U.S. would face in conducting a convoy operation that had to extend from the Gulf of Oman to ports in Kuwait.

Because the Reagan Administration underestimated the risks involved, it also did not pay proper attention to the probable reaction of the U.S. Congress if the reflagging effort should lead to fighting and many of the risks inherent in a rising Iranian threat to the southern Gulf states. It saw the Soviet problem almost solely in terms of the risk the Soviets might gain influence with the GCC states and not in terms of the risk that it might force Iran to improve its relations with the USSR. It ignored Iraq's incentive to try to exploit the reflagging to bring the U.S. into the war against Iran, and it largely ignored Western Europe in its desire to reassert U.S. leadership and demonstrate the importance of a U.S. military presence to the Gulf states.

On March 7, the U.S. informed Kuwait that it would protect all eleven of the tankers Kuwait had originally discussed with the U.S., and Kuwait tentatively accepted this offer on March 10. Kuwait signed a formal reflagging agreement with the U.S. on April 2, 1987. Kuwait still, however, was careful to avoid giving its arrangements with the U.S. any unnecessary publicity. It continued to emphasize the fact it had chartered Soviet tankers.[17] This gave the entire tanker escort activity an "international character" and further defused some of Kuwait's domestic and regional problems in accepting U.S. support.[18]

Like the U.S., Kuwait seems to have underestimated the risks involved in the reflagging effort. It almost certainly felt that Iran would not challenge a combination of U.S. and Soviet guarantees and that it now had an implied U.S. and Soviet guarantee to defend it from Iranian attacks or invasion. It does not seem to have considered the risk that Iran would try to reestablish some kind of relationship with the USSR or that it would challenge the U.S. in much the same way it did during the U.S. hostage crisis and intervention in Lebanon.

During the rest of February and through most of March, Iran continued to pound at Basra. Iran's leaders continued to talk about final offensives, but Iranian forces did nothing more than launch limited attacks in the North and conduct a battle of attrition in the south. Iraq, in turn, continued to fight a relatively static defense on the ground and concentrated on using its air power to pound away at Iran's ground forces, oil targets, and cities.

Iraq kept up its air attacks on the thirteen major cities in western Iran throughout early and mid-February. Iraqi aircraft also continued to strike at Tehran, something they had not done so consistently since the war of the cities in 1985, when Iraq claimed to have bombed Tehran 30 times.

Iran's Air Force could do little to respond. In fact, a defecting Iranian Air Force Officer claimed that only one-third of Iran's remaining 65 F-4s were now really operational and less than a third of its 1,000 helicopter gunships.[19] The most Iran could do was to launch a few more Scud missiles at Baghdad and make futile calls for Iraq's population to evacuate Baghdad. The resulting size of the casualties on each side is indicated by the fact that Iran claimed that Iraq's air attacks had resulted in 3,000 killed and 9,000 wounded and that 35 Iranian towns and cities had been hit since January 9. Iraq reported 11 missile attacks on Baghdad since January 9, plus the Iranian shelling of several towns, but indicated it had suffered only 300 killed and slightly more than 1,000 wounded.[20]

Iran's ground-based air defenses also remained limited. U.S. and Israeli shipments of Hawk parts and missiles probably did reduce Iraqi ability to attack Kharg, Sirri, Larak, and the otherwise vulnerable bridges and supply lines to the rear of Faw and the Iranian positions near Basra. Nevertheless, Iran also scored as many kills with the far less capable variants of the SA-2 it had received from the PRC and with the short-range laser-guided Robot-70 surface-to-air missiles it had bought illegally from Bofors in Sweden.[21] Many of Iran's surface-to-air missile (SAM) sites and radar stations were no longer functioning—if, indeed, they had been functioning at the start of the year.

Nevertheless, the war of the cities came to a temporary end on February 18, 1987—although both sides claimed violations of the cease-fire as early as February 22—and the halt in such attacks continued on into April. The reasons for this halt are somewhat unclear. Iraq claimed at the time that it declared a halt on its anticity attacks because Rajavi had asked Saddam Hussein to halt attacks which were hurting Iran's struggling masses rather than its leadership. The real reason, however, was probably a combination of the fact the Khomeini regime agreed to call off its artillery attacks on Basra and Iraq's cumulative air losses.

Iraq not only halted its attacks on Iranian cities after February 18, it reduced its air support of its ground forces. Even admitted Iraqi losses now amounted to at least 5 percent of Iraq's operational force; if one considers Iranian claims, they were as much as 10–15 percent. More importantly, most of these losses had cost Iraq part of its small cadre of high quality pilots. While the USSR agreed to rapidly replace the lost aircraft, the loss of experienced pilots was becoming critical. Even if one includes a limited number of foreign mercenaries, Iraq only had high quality pilots for 15–25 percent of its aircraft, and only a smaller number were top quality by Western standards.

Iraq could not afford to keep committing irreplaceable pilots and aircraft which cost $15–$25 million each to close support, interdiction, or low pay-off strikes on oil facilities if these meant substantial losses. The average value of the target being destroyed was generally far less than cost of the plane, and the tactical and strategic impact of any damage it did to Iran was usually limited. This meant Iraq was forced to turn to targets where most of its planes could survive or where it felt air strikes were desperately needed or could have major strategic or political impact.

The Battle for Influence in the Gulf

Iran found other ways to strike against Iraq. It increased its pressure on Kuwait to reduce its support of Iran and on Iraq to reduce its attacks on Iranian oil facilities. Pro-Iranian Shi'ites carried out a new series of protests in April. These reached the point where it was clear that Kuwait faced problems with its own Shi'ite citizens and was forced to stop attributing all such incidents to foreign elements. The government admitted that some 25 native Shi'ites were under arrest for terrorism. It also removed at least one Shi'ite Minister from his position and some 200 Shi'ites from sensitive jobs in the oil industry.

The risks Kuwait faced in terms of sabotage were made even more clear on May 22, when a major fire was set at a propane storage tank at the Ahmadi refinery, near the city of Fahaheel. The fire burned for three days and was the second attempt to burn the refinery in two years. The fire was designed to explode six 450,000-barrel propane and butane tanks and threatened to spread to the entire oil installation, and even part of Fahaheel city.

Most importantly, Iran completed the siting of two-to-four full batteries of Silkworm missiles near the Straits of Hormuz. By mid-April, 1987, it had at least 12 Silkworm launchers and 20 missiles on-line, with up to 28 more in reserve or on order. The only problem delaying active deployment of the missiles seemed to be a shortage of critical parts, and even this was controversial.

One of the batteries detected early in the year was relocated from the Island of Qesham (Onqeshim), located on the edge of the Straits to the Iranian naval base at Bandar Abbas, on the northwest shore of the Straits of Hormuz, to provide surface-to-air missile protection. The other battery was located at Kuhestak to the east. While the missiles could just barely cover the 64 kilometer-wide Straits with reasonable accuracy and with their normal payload, they could reach up to 75 kilometers with less accuracy and a lower payload.[22] Iran began to build another battery site on the southern tip of the Faw Peninsula. This site gave Iran the ability to site the missile within firing range of Kuwait City and its port and gave Iran increasing ability to put pressure on Kuwait and its tanker shuttle.[23]

Low-Level Land Warfare in Mid-1987

In spite of its reversals during the Karbala offensives, Iran launched still another offensive in the north in mid-April called Karbala-10. Shortly before this offensive, Iran supported several raids by Kurdish supporters of the Barzanis. It claimed on April 18 that the Pesh Merga and Iranian troops had killed 1,500 Iraqis, overrun 20 Iraqi-held villages, and taken 10 key ridges in Sulaimaniyeh Province.

The Karbala-10 offensive took the form of a three-pronged assault. It was conducted in the mountainous area southwest of Baneh and northeast of Sulaimaniyeh and seems to have been directed at taking the roads and heights between Mawat and Chwarta. While Mawat is nothing but a small village of mud huts, it is one of the main Iraqi defense points near the border and is ringed with bunkers and minefields. Chwarta is a key population center on the the road to Sulaimaniyeh.[24]

The offensive began on April 23, 1987, which was a Thursday night and a time when Iraqi troops tended to be least alert. By the end of April, Iran claimed to have taken 11 Iraqi villages and 310 square kilometers, killed 4,000 Iraqis, and captured 350, including an Iraqi brigade commander. Iraq claimed to have repelled an assault by two Iranian regiments and to have caused 1,500 Iranian casualties and destroyed 66 vehicles.[25]

By the end of May, however, it was clear that Iran had not taken Mawat, Chwarta, or any other key strategic position, although the Iranians did occupy the heights around Mount Sargehelou, above Mawat. This still put Iran about 48 kilometers from Sulaimaniyeh and about 100 kilometers from Kirkuk. The Iranian positions were in 8,000-foot mountains, many of which were still snowcapped at the end of May, and did not represent a significant springboard for new attacks or strategic success.

Iran attacked in an area where months of similar victories would not give it any real strategic advantage. In fact, the terrain was so difficult that it led to speculation that the government was simply keeping up the offensives in the north to show the Iranian people a continued series of "victories" or even that Rafsanjani was keeping up the offensives to show his dedication to the war and maintain political leverage over Montazari.[26] This may have been the case, but the original thrust of the attack was in an area where Iran could continue to exploit Kurdish hostility to Iraq, force Iraq to keep troops in the area, win small victories without losing more casualties than Iraq, and slowly wear down Iraqi resistance. Most probably, the attack simply failed to achieved its purpose.

The Attack on the USS *Stark*

The most important developments during the rest of the spring of 1987 took place in the Gulf. Iran's efforts to deprive Iraq of its ability to dominate the tanker war and the Kuwaiti reflagging effort led to the growing internationalization of the naval conflict in the Gulf. This began with a confrontation between Iran and the USSR, but it soon became dominated by a far more serious process of confrontation between Iran and the U.S. along the routes shown in Figure 9.1.

During April 1987, Iran began to respond more actively to the Soviet agreement to escort the three Soviet tankers which Kuwait had leased from the USSR and made part of its tanker shuttle. Iran warned on April 15 that Soviet leasing of oil tankers to Kuwait could create "a very dangerous situation."[27] Four days later, on April 19, Iran responded to a visit to Kuwait by the Soviet Deputy Foreign Minister, Vladimir Petrovsky, by warning the USSR that the Gulf could become a "second Afghanistan."[28] Rafsanjani issued a similar warning to the U.S. on April 20.[29] The next day, U.S. intelligence experts announced that Iran had deployed its Silkworm missiles on Faw.[30]

This time, however, Iran's threats did not depend on missiles but, rather, on the new naval capabilities Iran had developed for its Revolutionary Guards. As has been touched upon earlier, Iran faced major challenges in competing with Iraq in conducting a tanker war. Unlike Iraq, it had to attack shipping to third countries since there were no Iraqi ships in the Gulf and no ships moving to Iraqi ports. This, in turn, meant it had to risk reprisals from both the southern Gulf and Western navies.

The risk from southern Gulf forces was relatively minor. Iran had suffered some major naval losses, but it was still able to deal with the southern Gulf navies. The UK-built air defense destroyer *Artemiz*, and the U.S.-built destroyers *Babr* and *Palang*, with FRAM II conversions and improved air defenses, were largely inoperable. Iran did, however, have four British-built frigates with Sea Killer anti-ship missiles: *Saram, Zamm, Rustam,* and *Faramarz.* At least four of its original eight Combattante II-class patrol boats were still operational and were equipped with 76-mm and 40-mm guns and Harpoon launchers, although supplies of the Harpoon missiles were evidently very limited.[31] These 154-foot ships could reach speeds of up to 33.7 knots, and had a range of 700 to 2,000 miles, depending upon speed.

Iran also had a wide mix of smaller ships. One 320-ton minesweeper survived, the *Shahrokh*, but this was deployed in the Caspian. There were four landing ship-tanks (LSTs): The *Hengahm, Larak, Lavan,* and *Tonb.* The latter two had been delivered in 1974 by Britain under the pretext they were hospital ships. They carried Agusta-Bell AB-212 helicopters with AS-12 missiles, smaller landing craft, TACAN beacons, and minelaying equipment. Three more 67.5 meter, 2,024-ton

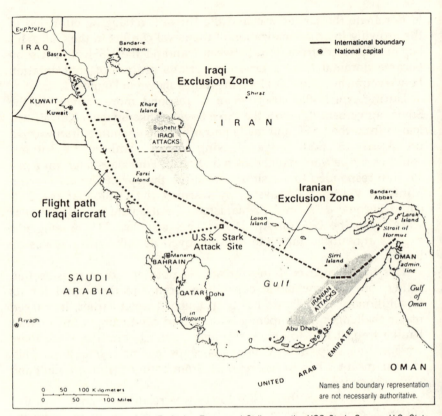

FIGURE 9.1   The Location of the Exclusion Zones and Strikes on the USS *Stark*. Source: U.S. State Department.

landing ships had just entered service, and four 654-meter Dutch-built freight barges were being used as landing ship tankers.

Two small FRG-built 5,000-ton replenishment tankers—the *Bandar Abbas* and *Bushehr*—were modified in 1984 to carry 40-mm guns and a telescopic helicopter hanger. The Navy still had some BH-7 and SRN-6 Hovercraft operational and up to 150 patrol craft, although many of the latter might have been sunk, damaged, or turned over to the naval Guards. Iran had the repair ship *Shahbahar* and floating docks *"400"* (300-ton lift) and *Dolphin* (28,000-ton lift), which it had bought from the FRG in 1985.

This regular navy surface strength was sufficient to keep Iraq from trying to break out of its ports and to challenge the navies in the southern Gulf, but it scarcely allowed Iran to challenge the West. Iran had to find new solutions to using naval power if it was still to play a major role in the tanker war.

Iran's first solution to these problems was to use its support craft to lay mines as an indirect method of combat. The Iranian Navy had stocks of U.S. Mk. 65 and Soviet AMD 500, AMAG-1, and KRAB anti-ship mines, and PRC- and North Korean-made versions of Soviet contact mines.[32] Iran was beginning to manufacture nonmagnetic, acoustic, free-floating, and remote-controlled mines. While Iran only had one surviving minesweeper deployed in the Caspian, it could lay such mines with virtually any small ship, including dhows and small cargo vessels.

Iran's second solution was to create a new naval branch of the Revolutionary Guards under the command of Mohsen Rezai. Iran had begun serious efforts to create such a force over two years earlier. By late 1986, the naval Guards had roughly 20,000 men and were larger than Iran's regular navy.

The naval elements of the Guard were equipped with a wide mix of small craft, including Swedish-built fast interceptor craft and numerous Zodiak rubber dinghies. Many of these boats were very difficult to detect by radar and could carry out high-speed rocket, machine gun, small arms, and 107-mm recoilless rifle attacks. The Swedish fast interceptor craft were built by Boghammer and were 42-feet long. They were purchased in 1985 and could carry a six-man crew and up to 1,000 pounds of weapons for ranges of about 500 nautical miles. They could cruise at 46 knots and could reach speeds up to 69 knots. The Guards were reported to have ordered at least 40 to 50 and to have deployed at least 29.[33]

The naval elements of the Guards were also given dhows equipped with cranes. These boats were hard to identify from the small commercial ships in the area and could carry up to 350 tons worth of mines. They had at least some landing craft and small craft borrowed from the Navy and a North Korean miniature submarine of 6–9 meter length.

The naval Guards forces were based at a number of offshore islands and oil platforms, with key concentrations at Al Farisiyah, Sirri, Halu Island, Abu Musa, the Greater and Lesser Tunbs, and Larak.[34] Guard units publicly trained in suicide boats designed to ram ships with high explosives, and claimed to have other boats it could fill with fast-drying concrete and use to block key ports or shipping channels. They also made it clear they had extensive stocks of Scuba equipment and an underwater combat center at Bandar Abbas.

The Guards also had air and missile capabilities. They were given the 35 to 46 Pilatus PC-7 light training/attack aircraft that Iran had bought from Switzerland and were training with North Korean instructors. They were rumored to be receiving Chinese supplied F-6 and F-7 fighters and to be seeking more advanced fighters from the Soviet bloc. They had a facility at Nowshahr Naval Academy on the Caspian Sea, where some Guards were reported to have had training in suicide attacks using light aircraft as well as small craft. Finally, the Guards had Iran's new HY-2 Silkworm anti-ship missiles.[35]

During the period after the announcement of the U.S. convoy effort, the Revolutionary Guards units continued work on eight hardened sites for the 35–50 Silkworm missiles Iran then had in inventory and created hardened concrete bunkers for the radar sites for the missiles, which were located on Quesham Island and the mainland. They reinforced their naval forces on Farsi Island, Abu Musa, and the Greater (Sughra) and Lesser (Kubra) Tunbs to levels of about 1,000 men, fortified their positions, and deployed helicopters. The Shah had seized these latter islands from the nation of Sharjah in 1971; Abu Musa is about 60 miles west of the Straits and the Tunbs are about 40 miles west.[36] They also began to make more use of Iran's offshore oil platforms as military bases.

This combination of forces gave Iran considerable ability to conduct hit-and-run attacks using mines and small craft and the ability to escalate using its Silkworm missiles and suicide attacks by boats and aircraft. Further, for all its losses, Iran still retained the largest regular surface force in the Gulf.

Iran fully realized that such forces could scarcely win a direct battle with the U.S. or Soviet Navy. Iran was, however, well postured to fight the naval equivalent of guerrilla war and to exploit any political weakness in the willingness of U.S. or other outside naval forces to engage in a long low-level conflict or take casualties. Equally important, Iran had considerable capability to conduct mining and sabotage operations that would be very difficult to trace directly to the Iranian government and could use the Guards under conditions that made it difficult to tell whether they were small units acting on their own or units directly under the control of the government.

As the spring wore on, the Iranian government left little doubt about its intentions to use these options to end Iraq's advantage in the tanker war. On April 27, Hussein a'Lael, the Revolutionary Guards naval commander, announced that Iran now had "full control" of the northern Gulf and had established the "first Iranian Revolutionary Guard Corps (IRGC) naval zone." On April 28, the commander of the Iranian Navy, Commodore Mohammed Hussein Malekzadegan, claimed in a speech over Iranian radio that Iran had boarded 1,200 ships since the war had begun and had seized 30 cargoes. He also warned that Iran would close the Straits of Hormuz if there was any disruption of Iranian exports and imports.[37]

These claims took on a special meaning because of the geography involved. Iraq had been relatively modest in defining its naval war zone, which it set at 29 degrees, 30 minutes, north latitude. This included Kharg Island but did not include a large part of the Gulf's navigable waters. The Iranians, however, claimed both a 12-mile limit from the shore and an exclusion zone that ran along the Gulf at a point roughly 40 miles from the shore.

This zone was so large that it created points at which traffic to Kuwait was confined to a very narrow channel outside the Iranian zone. This was particularly true of the waters south of Farsi Island, where the exclusion zone permitted a main navigation channel only two miles wide, although the actual depth of the Gulf permitted passage over a 60-mile area. The Iranian exclusion zone acted to force tankers into a vulnerable area and create routes that made tanker passage relatively predictable if Iran chose to carry out mining and other attacks outside its declared zone.

In early May, Iran further increased its naval activity. On May 2, 1986, Iranian naval units boarded a total of 14 tankers. The naval Guards attacked the 89,450-ton Indian tanker *B R Ambedkar* off Sharjah. On May 4, Guards units attacked the 31,120-ton *Petrobulk Regent* and on May 5, the Guards attacked the 258,000-ton Japanese tanker *Shuho Maru* about 48 kilometers off the Saudi coast.

Naval Guards units launched many of their attack craft from the Guards base closest to Bahrain and Saudi Arabia. This was the small island of Farsi (Al-Farisiyah), midway between the Iranian coast and northern Saudi Arabia.[38] The naval units in the Guards also used an oil platform near Halul Island, Sirri Island, Abu Musa, and Larak. Their normal pattern of attack was to challenge the tanker at night, establish its identity and destination, and then return several hours later. Such attacks normally used machine guns and rockets, and while these did not do serious damage, it was obvious that that they were often aimed at the crew's quarters.

These shifts in Iranian capability led the U.S. to establish a two-track policy toward Iran. The first track was to use the UN to force a general cease-fire in the war that would lead to a peace settlement based on the 1974 Algiers Accord and a return to prewar borders. The second track was to take military steps to contain the war in the Gulf, limit the growth of Soviet influence, and help push Iran toward accepting a cease-fire.

This U.S. action, and the initial operation of Kuwait's charters from the USSR, led Iran to launch a new series of political attacks on both Kuwait and the tankers. On May 6, Iranian Prime Minister Mir Hossein Mousavi warned Kuwait to stop its search for the "protection of the superpowers." On May 8, 1987, Iran went further: Unmarked Iranian small craft used machine guns and rocket launchers to attack a 6,459-ton Soviet freighter, the *Ivan Korotoyev*, while it was sailing near Iran's Sassan offshore oil field, about 30 miles from Iran's Rustam oil platform.

While it was unclear at the time whether the attack was a deliberate effort by the Iranian government or the effort of some more extreme faction of the Revolutionary Guards, later evidence pointed strongly toward a deliberate attack. During the months that followed, there was no evidence that the naval Guards units acted independently of government policy or even the regular armed forces.

The Iranian Navy used its helicopters, small craft, and P-3 maritime patrol aircraft to track ship movements in the Gulf and help target such Guard activity. The Guard bases on Al-Farisiyah and Abu Musa seemed to be firmly under central government control. Further, the *Ivan Korotoyev* was a cargo vessel which regularly visited the Gulf and was exiting Kuwait on route to the Saudi port of Dammam via Dubai along a route precisely known to Iran. This made it somewhat unlikely that the attack was accidental.[39]

Iraq stepped up its attacks on Iranian ships in return and, on May 13, launched its first major air strikes on Iranian refineries since the start of 1987. The Iraqi fighters struck at the refineries at Isfahan and Tabriz. Iraq sought U.S. and British air charters to help carry new purchases of small craft and outboard motors to Baghdad for use in its rivers and water barriers and the Gulf.[40] While the land war remained relatively quiet, Iraq also responded to a step up in Patriotic Union of Kurdistan (PUK) activity by launching a number of raids on Kurdish camps and villages. It seems to have begun to use mustard gas on Kurdish villages and PUK camps near the border to raze villages and displace their population.[41]

Iran responded by continuing to escalate. Its next step was to mine one of three Soviet tankers that had been leased to Kuwait on May 16. The *Marshal Chuykov* was damaged by a mine in the upper Gulf, not far from the Neutral Zone. While this damage might have been coincidental and could have come from a free floating mine, the combination of location and timing made an accident seem highly unlikely, particularly because Iran rapidly demonstrated it could carry out such attacks with excellent precision.[42] Further, that same day, Iranian radio quoted Chief Justice Abdulkarim Mousavi as saying that Iranian forces might have hesitated in attacking Kuwaiti tankers but would never do so in attacking foreign ships.[43]

These events might well have led to a confrontation between Iran and the USSR, if other events had not acted to change the U.S. role in the Gulf. The attack on the *Marshal Chuykov*, however, was rapidly overshadowed by other events.

At approximately 9:12 on the evening of May 17, an Iraqi Mirage F-1EQ attacked the U.S. radar frigate, the USS *Stark*, about 85 miles northeast of Bahrain and 60 miles south of the Iranian exclusion zone. It fired two Exocet missiles, both of which hit the ship and one of which exploded. This was perhaps the last event that anyone had expected, and while the Iraqi attack was unintentional, it sparked a whole series of debates over the U.S. role in the Gulf, U.S. defense capabilities, and U.S. relations with Saudi Arabia.

The *Stark* was hit with two Exocet missiles. The first missile hit on the port side on the second deck. It did not explode but broke in two parts, spewing some 300 pounds of flammable propellant through a sleeping area where sailors were just settling down and then tore through the barber shop and post office and came to rest against the opposite hull. The second missile was spotted seconds later and detonated. It hit in the same general area in the crew quarters near the ship's Combat Information Center (CIC), ripped a 15-foot hole in the side of the ship, and exploded about five feet into the hull. This blew five men into the water. Thirty-seven American sea men died, and 11 others were seriously wounded. It shut off all power to the CIC, caused serious structural damage, compromised watertight integrity, and cut the main-port water main used for fire fighting.

The Iraqi pilot later claimed that his navigation gear indicated the ship was 5–10 nautical miles inside the Exclusion Zone, not 10–15 nautical miles outside it. Nevertheless, the Iraqi pilot seems to have preserved radio silence and simply fired at the first target confirmed by his radar.[44] All the pilot's actions in flying both to and from his target indicate that he knew his position and knew he was firing outside the Iranian exclusion zone. If he had not known his position, he could not have flown the precise return course he used to get back to base. Finally, the Iraqi pilot only turned on his tracking radar seconds before he fired. This was only justifiable in a combat environment where he faced hostile ships with air defenses, which he did not. The Iraqi pilot made no real attempt to identify his target, even by radar.[45]

In any case, the loss of 37 American lives suddenly transformed the growing U.S. commitment in the Gulf from a low-level political-military activity—which received little public attention in the U.S., and which was handled at the expert level—into a major American political crisis. The attack on the *Stark* immediately led to Congressional investigations, to a heated debate over whether the U.S. presence in the Gulf needed approval under the War Powers Act, and to a debate over whether the U.S. should even have military forces in the area.

The attack sent a signal to every nation in the Gulf that the U.S. might respond to Iranian behavior by withdrawing, just as it had done in Lebanon. This not only encouraged Iran to take a tougher line than it might otherwise have done, it indicated that any nation whose aid to the U.S. became too visible might simply end up as the target of Iranian hostility and associated with a U.S. defeat.

It is impossible to know just how much this encouraged Iranian weakness to try a military test of wills with the U.S, but it seems likely that it at least encouraged Iran to believe that a peripheral strategy of indirect attacks on U.S. ships and forces, the tankers under convoy, or those nations supporting the reflagging effort might lead the Congress and American people to demand that the U.S halt its reflagging effort or even withdraw from the Gulf. Iran had, after all, already achieved two significant limited victories over the U.S. under somewhat similar circumstances. The first was the hostage crisis after Iranian "students" seized the U.S. Embassy in Tehran. The second was U.S. withdrawal from Lebanon after the car bombing of the U.S. Embassy and then the U.S. Marine Corps barracks in Beirut.

The U.S. Convoy Effort and the *Bridgeton* Incident

In any case, Iran gradually shifted from attempts to capitalize on any U.S.-Iraqi tensions and attempts to embarrass the Reagan Administration with a slow war of nerves, to a war of nerves designed to push the U.S. Congress into canceling U.S. plans to escort Kuwait's tankers and even into withdrawing U.S. naval forces from the Gulf.

Iran began slowly. Iranian Revolutionary Guard boats fired on a Norwegian tanker, the 219,387-ton *Golar Robin*. They hit the crew's quarters and set the ship afire.[46] Guards units then attempted to seize the offshore terminal near Faw which involved some 40 small craft armed with 106-mm recoilless guns, machine guns, and rocket launchers. A 272,000 ton VLCC (very large cargo carrier), the *Primrose*, was hit by a mine in roughly the same area as the *Chuykov* on May 16. Guards units attacked a small 2.6-ton cargo vessel, the *Rashidah*, on May 22, and the liquefied propane gas (LPG) carrier *Nyhammer* on May 24. A speed boat attacked the *Nyhammer* without warning while it was on route to Ras Tanura. The Iranian boat fired two rockets, which missed the vessel, and then left.

The most Iran did that affected U.S. interests during May and early June was to challenge a U.S. merchant ship, the *Patriot*, to identify itself when it entered the Gulf on its way to Bahrain. The Iranian destroyer turned away immediately when the merchant ship's escort, the U.S. destroyer *Coynigham*, came to its aid. No major attack took place on Gulf shipping until June 11, when an unidentified warplane attacked the 126,000-ton Greek tanker *Ethnic* near Kuwait.[47]

Then, on June 19/20, Iraq made its first major air strikes in the tanker war since the attack on the *Stark*. Iraq hit one of the Iranian shuttle tankers, the *Tenacity*, with an Exocet missile. Iraq also attacked the western jetty at Kharg Island. These attacks came after Iraq had halted its attacks on Gulf targets for nearly a month. Iraq had clearly been afraid of losing Western support for the UN cease-fire effort, but it also reacted to the fact that Iran was exporting at its OPEC oil quota of 2.3 million barrels a day, and insurance premiums on Gulf tanker traffic had dropped.

While it is unclear whether Iran responded directly to these Iraqi attacks, Iran began active minelaying operations in the northern Gulf. Some of these mines reached Kuwait's port of Ahmadi. This caused enough concern for U.S. officials to announce that Saudi Arabia had agreed to allow its four minesweepers to help clear mines and to use its mine-sweeping helicopters and their sleds to help clear the mines in Kuwait harbor. Further, the U.S. announced that Saudi Arabia would allow the U.S. Air Force (USAF) to use Saudi Arabia's E-3A AWACS to expand surveillance coverage over the Gulf. The planes were to have Saudi pilots with U.S. crews.

On June 25, Iraq attacked a Turkish tanker with rocket fire near Iran's main loading terminal at Kharg Island. Then, on June 27, Iran attacked two Scandinavian tankers moving to and from Kuwait about 120 miles south of Ahmadi and 60 miles east of Saudi Arabia. Iraq replied on June 29 with its sixth attack in ten days, and an Iranian gun boat hit a Kuwaiti tanker on June 30.

As June ended, the U.S. rejected an Iranian proposal for a partial cease-fire that would only have affected the Gulf while preventing Iraq from shipping through the Gulf and allowing the land war to go on. The U.S. continued to press for an expansion of UN Resolution 582, which had resulted in a general call for a cease-fire in 1986, that would put real pressure on Iran to actually halt its role in the conflict. Iran replied by staging naval maneuvers, and both Iran's Prime Minister and Hassan Ali, the commander of the naval branch of the Guards, used the occasion to warn that the U.S. would get a "bitter and unforgettable lesson" if it challenged Iran in the Gulf.[48]

This jockeying for position made it increasingly clear that Iran was unlikely to back down in the face of the U.S. escort effort and that the U.S. faced a serious threat from mines, terrorism, suicide attacks, and small-craft raids. As for the overall intensity of the tanker war, some 53 vessels were damaged in the first 5 1/2 months of 1987. That total compared with 107 attacks in 1986, the highest number of attacks in any year since the beginning of the war. The tanker war had produced a total of 226 deaths between 1981 and 1986. It had killed 47 so far in 1987, some 37 of them aboard the USS *Stark*. The total insurance claims paid since the beginning of the war totaled roughly $1.5 billion. That figure, however, included 110 vessels paid out as total losses, and all but 17 of these ships had been trapped in the Shatt al-Arab at the start of the war.[49]

More Low-Level Attacks in the North

While Iran concentrated on its war of nerves in the Gulf during the late spring of 1987, it continued its land attacks. It launched a major artillery barrage against Basra on May 14. It continued to launch small actions along the border and to support Kurdish rebel forces in their attacks in the north. Iran claimed in mid-June that pro-Iranian Kurdish forces had killed 260 Iraqis and wounded 400 more in the previous two weeks of fighting and that PUK forces had held the town of Taqtaq, about 35 miles north of Kirkuk, for ten hours.

While such claims were probably exaggerated, U.S. experts estimated that some 35,000 to 50,000 Iraqi troops had to be kept in the region to deal with roughly 20,000 part-time PUK and KDP Kurdish guerrillas. These Kurdish forces were also felt to be causing a continuing series of low-level military clashes in the Arbil, Zahko, and Dahok regions, and some Iraqi-sponsored Kurdish paramilitary units were reported to have gone over to the PUK intact. These same experts felt that Iraqi forces had suffered at least 2,000 casualties in recent months as the result of the growing Kurdish presence and that the Kurdish forces now controlled a liberated zone of some 2,000 to 5,000 square kilometers of rough terrain in the north, had killed several thousand Iraqi troops and security forces, and were well armed with Soviet automatic weapons, mortars, and machine guns.[50]

Meanwhile, Iraq continued to strengthen its land defenses and created new defenses in-depth along much of the southern border. Where many Iraqi positions had previously consisted of one line of earthen fortifications, bunkers, and dug-in tanks, the Iraqis began to create several lines. Long artificial barriers about 15 feet high were placed in parallel about 200 to 800 yards apart. This allowed Iraqi forces to retreat quickly to a new defensive position without giving up ground and to deal better with the kind of human-wave attacks that could saturate part of a position.[51]

Iran responded by trying to drain Fish Lake and the rest of the water barriers in front of Basra. It also built up a large earthen berm in the lake on the eastern side and seemed to be preparing for another attack on Basra. Further, Iran launched two small attacks on June 17 and 18, 1987. The first attack was another joint attack with Kurdish rebels in the north. It took place near Arbil and seems to have been little more than a local clash. The offensive in the south took place a day later and was a three-pronged attack in the Misan sector. While Iraq reported that the attack was crushed, it seems to have scored some limited gains.

Iran launched another assault in the north on June 20, 1987. It claimed on June 22 that it had scored gains in the area around Mawat, in the northern Kurdish highlands about eight miles from the border, and that it had captured Mawat, 15 other villages, and 24 square miles of Iranian territory.[52] Iraq, however, claimed on June 27, 1987, that the attack was beaten back and that Iraq had recaptured all of the territory involved. While the details remain unclear, Iran does not seem to have made any significant gains.[53]

The Impact of New UN Peace Efforts

Ironically, the main impact of these Iranian offensives may have been to aid Iraq since they helped lead outside nations to agree to a new and far stronger UN cease-fire resolution. On July 20, 1987, the UN Security Council finally agreed to UN Resolution 598. The resolution expressed the usual concern with the cost and risk of war. It also, however, deplored attacks on civilian targets and the use of chemical warfare and

- demanded that "Iran and Iraq observe an immediate cease-fire, discontinue all military actions, on land, at sea, and in the air, and withdraw all forces to the internationally recognized boundaries without delay";
- requested the Secretary-General to dispatch a team of UN observers to verify, confirm, and observe the cease-fire;
- urged the immediate repatriation of prisoners of war the moment hostilities ceased;
- called on other nations to avoid escalating the conflict;
- requested the Secretary General to "explore, in consultation with Iran and Iraq, the question of entrusting an impartial body with inquiring into responsibility for the conflict and to report to the Secretary General as soon as possible";
- requested the Secretary General to assign a team of experts to

study the question of reconstruction and to report to the Secretary-
General;

- requested the Secretary General "to examine in consultation with
  Iran and Iraq and with the other states in the region, measures to
  enhance the security and stability of the region";
- decided to "meet again as necessary to consider further steps to
  ensure compliance."

There is little question that this UN action favored Iraq and
reflected the extent to which Iran's continuing offensives and strident
attacks on other states had begun to alienate much of the membership
of the UN. Iraq had pressed hard for such action for several years. The
text of Resolution 598 also effectively called for immediate Iranian
withdrawal from all the territory Iran occupied in Iraq and immediate
repatriation of prisoners of war. At the time the resolution was passed,
this language meant Iran had to make major concessions with little in
return except for the possibility that internationally recognized
boundaries meant Iran would retain the rights to the Shatt al-Arab it
had obtained in the Algiers Accord of 1975.

Resolution 598 did mention study of the question of guilt for the war
and vaguely referenced the possibility of aid in reconstruction, but the
timing of the resolution meant such action would only occur after Iran
had given up all of the negotiating leverage it had in terms of Iraqi
territory and prisoners of war. Further, the UN passed the resolution
at a time when the US and many other states were pressing hard for an
arms embargo as part of "further steps to enforce compliance" that
would have applied to any side that did not agree to Resolution 598,
but which would have effectively deprived Iran of the arms it needed
to continue its offensives.

It is not surprising, therefore, that the new UN resolution had little
more immediate impact on Iran than the much vaguer resolution that
the UN had passed the year before. Iran's response was to denounce the
UN for tilting toward Iraq and to demand that the issue of war guilt be
decided upon before any formal cease-fire was agreed to. It continued to
stress its demands for a partial cease-fire that would only apply to the
war in the Gulf, and it stepped up its attacks on the U.S. It also
attempted to strengthen its ties to the USSR in a largely successful
effort to make sure the Security Council would not agree to an arms
embargo. Further, Iran immediately held covert negotiations with the
PRC to try to ensure its flow of arms from that country and that the
PRC would not provide any substantive support for a UN arms embargo,
regardless of what it might say in public.

The net result was that UN Resolution 598 succeeded in giving the

UN peace effort a formal status and international profile that it had never had before but that the resolution also made the UN part of the complex war of negotiations that Iran and Iraq were conducting to try to obtain external support for their own positions in the war. In fact, the UN became an extension of war by other means.

The longer term impact of the UN resolution was very different. During the year that followed, Iran and Iraq constantly struggled for influence within the UN, with Iraq gaining the overall advantage because of its far more flexible diplomacy and willingness to deal with other nations. The U.S. led an effort to use UN sanctions to help bring an end to the fighting, but it was unsuccessful in finding any way to obtain Security Council agreement on an arms embargo. Instead, the U.S. and USSR became involved in a complex diplomatic duel over any applications of UN sanctions. The USSR generally rejected an arms embargo and sanctions and attempted to use this position to win support in Iran and convince the southern Gulf states that it was the only power that both sides would trust to negotiate a cease-fire. At the same time, the Secretary-General was thrust into the position of having to try to find some form of agreement between Iraq and Iran that would produce a more balanced cease-fire. While Resolution 598 did offer a diplomatic context in which peace could be achieved, it was the fighting and not negotiations that continued to decide the outcome of the war.

The UN resolution also did little to persuade "other states to exercise the utmost restraint and to refrain from any act which may lead to further escalation and widening of the conflict, and thus to facilitate the implementation of the present resolution." A complex mix of different causes began to broaden the role of outside powers only days after the passage of Resolution 598.

The U.S. Reflagging Effort Begins to Operate

The first U.S. flags went up on two Kuwaiti tankers on July 21, 1987, and the convoy effort—by then codenamed Operation Earnest Will—was under way. The U.S. had had nearly four months to prepare, but the resulting task force still had a complex mix of strengths and weaknesses. The U.S. faced a complex array of potential friends and enemies, shown in Table 9.3, but it had to rely primarily on its own forces.

The main strength of the U.S. force that accompanied the first convoys was that it consisted of a relatively large force to convoy only two tankers. The U.S. had four frigates, three cruisers, and a destroyer in the area around the Gulf and the Straits of Hormuz. These ships

TABLE 9.3 Naval Forces in the Gulf and the Gulf of Oman: July 1987

Country	Cruisers	Destroyers	Frigates	Corvettes	FAC	Patrol	Amphibious	Mine
U.S.[a]	2	1	4	—	—	—	—	—
Iran[b]	—	3	4	2	8	7	8	2
Iraq[c]	—	—	2	12	15	11	7	5
Britain	—	1	1	—	—	—	—	—
France	—	2	—	—	—	—	—	—
USSR	—	—	1	—	—	—	—	2
Kuwait	—	—	—	—	8	50	13	—
Saudi Arabia	—	—	4	4	12	46	15	4
Bahrain	—	—	—	—	—	4	—	—
Qatar	—	—	—	—	3	6	—	—
UAE	—	—	—	—	6	9	—	—
Oman	—	—	—	—	8	9	7	—

[a] The U.S. had an additional command ship in the Gulf and a carrier group with the *Constellation* and its escorts in the Indian Ocean. A battleship was in transit to the area.
[b] Does not reflect wartime damage or losses. Does not include naval Guards units.
[c] Does not reflect wartime damage or losses and includes ships trapped in port.

SOURCES: Adapted from the IISS, *Military Balance, 1987–1988* (London: International Institute for Strategic Studies, 1987), and *New York Times*, July 12, 1987, p. E-3.

had gone through three rehearsals since the last elements of the escort force had arrived in early July, and the escort plan had reached the size of an 80-page document. The U.S. also had a carrier task force, including the carrier *Constellation*, in the Indian Ocean. The battleship *Missouri*, two more cruisers, and a helicopter carrier were in transit to the region.

The convoy plan called for three to four U.S. ships to escort each of the two tanker convoys, while the cruisers stood buy to provide a defense against air attack. U.S. A-6 and F/A-18 attack aircraft, EA-6B jamming aircraft, and F-14 fighter planes were to provide support from the U.S. carrier *Constellation* in the Arabian Sea. The tankers were then to have at least three escorts once they passed beyond the Straits, with USAF E-3A AWACS providing airborne surveillance.

The U.S. planned to provide convoys once every two weeks during July and August. This interval was intended to allow the task-force concept to be tested and to find out Iranian reactions. It also eased the burden of being on constant alert against suicide attacks or other means of irregular warfare. The destroyer *Fox* and cruiser *Kidd* were selected in part because their 76-mm guns provided considerable firepower against sudden raids by the Iranian Navy or shore targets. All of the U.S. combat ships were equipped with long-radar radars, data nets, and Phalanx terminal defense guns.

The U.S. force also, however, had several weaknesses. These included the lack of local naval and air bases in the Gulf, its inability to provide a cross-reinforcing defense of single ships operating outside the convoy to minimize the success of a saturation attack, and its lack of mine-warfare defenses. It was the latter weakness that Iran chose to exploit.

The U.S. lack of mine-warfare defenses was partly a matter of inadequate planning, and the initial operational plan the Joint Chiefs and U.S. Central Command (USCENTCOM) developed for the convoy made no provision for mine forces in spite of warnings from U.S. intelligence officials and the U.S. Navy.[54] The U.S. Navy, however, was not ready to carry out the mine-warfare mission. It relied on its European allies for most mine-warfare missions, and the U.S. had made little initial effort to get direct allied military support. The U.S. had only 21 30-year-old minesweepers (MSOs) in service.[55] All but three of these minesweepers were in the Naval Reserve Force. The three active ships were assigned research duty and were not ready to perform their mission. They were augmented only by seven active-duty 57-foot minesweeping boats (MSBs) and 23 Sea Stallion RH-53D helicopters, four of which were also allocated to the naval reserves.[56]

The U.S. thus faced a wide range of threats, only part of which it was prepared to deal with. Iran had access to a wide range of sources for its mines. It had both surface mines and bottom mines and at least some timed or interval mines that only became active after a fixed time period or after several ships or minesweepers passed by. While Iran's mine assets were uncertain, it seemed to have contact, magnetic, acoustic, bow wave, pressure, temperature, and possibly remote-controlled mines as well. Some were large metal mines and could easily be detected by sonar, but many were too small for easy detection and others were nonmagnetic.

Another problem consisted of the distance the convoy had to move, and the fact it was continuously vulnerable from the time it approached the Straits to the moment it entered port in Kuwait. The convey had to follow a route that included a 60-mile voyage from Dibba, outside the Gulf, to the Straits. With a convoy speed of 16 knots, this would take 8 hours. For the next 50 miles, the convoy would pass through the Straits and near Iran's 20-mile exclusion zone and its Silkworm missiles. It would then sail for another 90 miles to a point near Abu Nuayr off the coast of Abu Dhabi. This meant passing by Abu Musa and the Tunbs. There was then a 60-mile stretch to the UAE's Zaqqum oil channel, followed by a 60-mile voyage to Qatar's Halul Island. The convoy then had to sail 90 miles to the Shah Allum shoals and a point only a mile from Iranian waters. At this point the convoy had about 285 miles more of relatively open sailing from a position off the Ras Tanura beacon ship to Kuwait. During all of this time, Iran could chose its point and means of attack.[57]

Finally, the U.S. faced the problem that—in spite of efforts to keep the convoy's composition and schedule and the details of its strengths and weaknesses secret—it received a relentless exposure in the media. Its weakness, particularly in regard to mine warfare, were fully communicated to Iran. Iran could predict the path of the convoy and its timing; this meant that small craft might succeed in hitting a ship even if they did nothing more than drop a few contact mines at night.[58]

The first convoy sailed on schedule on July 22, 1987. The U.S. sent in four combat ships, including a guided-missile cruiser. The reflagged ships included the 414,266-ton supertanker *Bridgeton* and the 48,233-ton gas tanker *Gas Prince*.[59]

Unfortunately, the U.S. concentrated far too much on the missile threat near the Straits and far too little on the risk of other forms and areas of attack. This became brutally clear about 6:30 A.M. on July 24. The *Bridgeton* struck a mine at a position of 27°58' north and 49°50' east.

The *Bridgeton* was hit in its number 1 port cargo tank. The mine blew a large hole in its hull and flooded 4 of its 31 compartments. The convoy was forced to slow from a speed of 16 knots to 5, and its warships were forced to follow the damaged *Bridgeton*, which was the only ship large enough to survive another mine hit. The only action the warships could take was to turn on their sonars and put riflemen on the bow to try to shoot a mine if they saw it.

Iran succeeded in capitalizing on the greatest single vulnerability in the U.S. convoy system and did so without leaving a clear chain of hard evidence linking Iran or the Iranian government to the attack. Although it later turned out that Iran had laid three different minefields, and at least 60 mines, this activity had not been fully detected and had not been filmed.

The impact of the Iranian attack was further heightened by the fact that it came only hours after the U.S. government had publicly expressed the feeling that the most threatening part of the passage was over. The day before, Rear Admiral Harold Bernsen, commander of the Navy's Middle East Task Force, declared that "So far it has gone exactly as I thought it would—smoothly, without any confrontation on the part of Iran." The admiral then went on to declare that Iran had been weakened by seven years of war, and "The Iranian Air Force and Navy are not strong. It would not be in their best interest to utilize their forces in a direct confrontation."[60] It is interesting to note that after the *Bridgeton* was hit, Admiral Bernsen was forced to admit that no one had checked the convoy's route for mines, although intelligence sources had warned him and the convoy commander that mines might be present.[61]

The cumulative result of the *Bridgeton* incident was to give Iran a major initial propaganda victory. Prime Minister Mir Hossein Mousavi promptly called the attack "an irreparable blow on America's political and military prestige," although he was careful to say that the blow came by "invisible hands." Rafsanjani extended the threat to Kuwait and Saudi Arabia: "From now on, if our wells, installations, and centers are hit, we will make the installations and centers of Iraq's partners the targets of our attacks." Rafsanjani also announced a "new policy of retaliation." Khameini reiterated this threat on July 27 and called Kuwait "the only country in the region that openly supports Iraq in the war." He specifically threatened Kuwait with the fact Iranian surface-to-surface missiles could reach any target in Kuwait.[62]

The next day, more mines were sighted south of the area where the *Bridgeton* was hit, and seven more North Korean versions of Soviet mines were discovered on July 27. This made it even more apparent to the world that the U.S. had no immediate contingency plan to deal with the situation. This further strengthened Iran's victory and those within Iran who favored continuing the war. Khomeini stated on July 28 that there could be no end to the war as long as Saddam Hussein was in power.[63]

The U.S. took time to respond. It could not deploy its own mine-sweepers in less than 10 to 15 days and could not use its helicopters without deploying suitable support ships. As a result, the most the U.S. could do initially was to airlift eight RH-53Ds to Diego Garcia and prepare the the amphibious landing ship, USS *Guadalcanal*, to operate four of them in the Gulf.[64] The *Guadalcanal* was operating in the Indian Ocean and could be deployed relatively rapidly but then had to be equipped and organized for the mine-warfare mission. The most the U.S. could do to speed up the deployment of its minesweepers was to load another amphibious ship, the USS *Raleigh*, with four minesweepers. This still meant a nearly month-long voyage to the entrance of the Gulf.[65]

The U.S. also faced serious problems in finding the basing facilities it needed for the helicopters, special forces units, and other elements it wanted to deploy in the Gulf. Although Kuwait had hosted a small U.S. mine-clearing detachment and had allowed U.S. military aircraft to operate out of Kuwait on 17 occasions in the previous month, it remained reluctant to offer any formal base for a U.S. combat unit for the reasons discussed earlier.

Bahrain and Saudi Arabia were willing to provide virtually all the support the U.S. wanted but could not agree to the kind of formal basing arrangements some U.S. officials wanted. Both nations felt they needed to keep a low military profile at a time when U.S. domestic politics were forcing it to do everything in a spotlight, and the Secretary of Defense was seeking formal basing agreements.[66]

This led to a compromise where Kuwait agreed to charter two large barges that were to be moored in international waters in the Gulf, and Bahrain and Saudi Arabia agreed to provide the staging support for them. These barges avoided the problems inherent in any formal U.S. base on Saudi or Bahraini territory but gave the U.S. a facility where it could stage attack, reconnaissance, and mine-warfare helicopters, army and navy commando units, and deploy intelligence sensors and electronic warfare equipment. Both barges were defended by Stinger missiles and Phalanx anti-missile close-defense systems and were heavily sandbagged and compartmented to minimize the damage impact of a single missile or air attack.

The U.S. stationed one of these barges, a converted Brown and Root North Sea drilling platform, only about 20 miles from Iran's Farsi Island. The barge, now code-named "Hercules" paid off immediately in providing a constant watch over Iranian activity at Farsi Island. It was so successful that the U.S. immediately began to plan for another facility near the naval Guards speedboat base at Abu Musa.[67]

Saudi Arabia also agreed to expand the use of its four minesweepers, and these helped discover the presence of additional mines after the *Bridgeton* was hit. It could not, however, fully commit its small force to protecting shipping to Kuwait when it was equally vulnerable. It quietly agreed to provide ship and aircraft fuel and to provide emergency landing and fueling support for U.S. carrier aircraft. Bahrain also agreed to a de facto basing arrangement where the U.S.

leased some extremely large platforms normally used for offshore oil work and created the equivalent of small bases in the Gulf without formally operating from Gulf territory.

Iran quickly responded. On July 31, Iranian "pilgrims" staged a massive riot during the pilgrimage to Mecca. Cadres began to mobilize agitators among the 70,000 Iranian pilgrims in Mecca itself at roughly 2:00 P.M. They completed getting ready for a mass meeting at 4:30 P.M. This was typical of similar disturbances Iran had caused in the past, but these had stayed outside the Grand Mosque.

This time, the Iranians slowly began to advance on the Grand Mosque. At about 6:30 P.M., they reached the Saudi security line barring the entrance. The Iranians used sticks, knives, and stones and may have used a limited number of small arms. The Saudi security guards and National Guard replied with tear gas and riot-control devices. The incident was over by 7:00 P.M. , but the resulting panic and fighting in the crowded pilgrimage area left 402 dead and 649 injured, and its intensity is revealed by the fact that while 275 of those killed were Iranian, 85 were Saudi security officers, and 42 were of other nationalities. While Saudi Arabia denied it used firearms and claimed to have relied on tear gas, the evidence does indicate that at least some Saudi officers fired pistols and M-16s.[68]

Iran made false claims the next day that the Saudi police had opened fire without warning and that 650 Iranians were dead or missing and 4,500 were wounded.[69] Iran made these claims in spite of detailed Saudi TV coverage which showed that the riots had been started by organized Iranian mobs throwing rocks at the police and considerable evidence that organized Iranian teams had been instructed to start the riots, and infiltrators were equipped with pistols and explosives.[70]

July ended in a growing confrontation between Iran, its neighbors in the Gulf, Britain and France, and the U.S. Iran had succeeded in challenging the U.S., but there was little sign that the U.S. intended to back down, and Iran remained highly vulnerable. While it could still act with considerable freedom in low-level war, it was extremely vulnerable to U.S. attacks on, or embargo of, its oil exports and arms imports. Its apparent strength existed only to the extent that the U.S. chose not to retaliate against Iran's weaknesses and much of the U.S. restraint had taken place because the Reagan Administration felt it could not get Congressional support for such action without a clear Iranian pattern of aggression—a "smoking gun."

If any outside nation benefited from this escalation, it may have been the USSR. During both June and July, it continued to publicly support the Iraqi and Arab position. It openly sent more arms to Iraq and denounced Iran for continuing the fighting. At the same time, it sharply criticized the U.S. for escalating the conflict in the Gulf and indicated that it would not provide a military escort for its reflagged ships. It also rejected the U.S. escort plan and declared it would leave the Gulf if the U.S. did.

There was relatively little land fighting during this period, and Rafsanjani gave a strong indication at one of his June press conferences that Iran would reject further human-wave attacks because they produced excessive casualties and, instead, would concentrate on surprise attacks. Iran avoided any major call-ups or other deployments that could have signaled a major offensive and limited its attacks on Basra to artillery fire and skirmishes. Iran did, however, continue to try to improve its attack position in the south by partially draining Fish Lake and improving its attack routes, a series of moves that were ultimately to do Iraq more good than Iran.

Iran continued to increase its support of the Kurdish forces in the north. This, in turn, led Iraq to step up its program to destroy hostile Kurdish villages and relocate their population. This reached a level by July 1987 where more than 100 villages had been destroyed and tens of thousands of Kurds had been relocated. Iraq had clearly shifted from trying to negotiate with the Kurds to a classic pacification and suppression campaign. The growing seriousness of the situation is illustrated by the fact that Iraq now had over 35,000 combat troops committed full-time to the pacification effort, and the Kurdish guerrilla movement had grown to as many as 8,000–10,000 men.[71]

A constant series of small engagements took place elsewhere on the border, but open fighting between the two armies was relatively limited. In mid-July, Iraq attempted to counterattack Iranian positions in Majnoon. Iraq almost certainly used poison gas and made some minor gains but did not achieved any strategic result. Iraq also seems to have conducted a counterattack against Iranian positions in Faw in late July and on the border about 80 miles north of Baghdad on July 24. Once again, there were few indications that these attacks resulted in any strategic gains, although each may have produced over 2,000 killed.[72]

Iran Expands Its Mining Effort, and European Forces Join the U.S.

During August 1987, the war continued to lead to the steady escalation of tensions between Iran and the West. Virtually every week brought a new Iranian effort to strike at the U.S. by indirect means, as Iran exploited every means it could find of attacking shipping in the Gulf that would embarrass the U.S. and potentially force it to withdraw. At the same time, Iran continued to escalate its political and military pressure on Kuwait and Saudi Arabia. Iran continued its efforts to limit the effectiveness of the UN cease-fire initiative, although its military actions in the Gulf progressively alienated more European countries and led the PRC to increasingly distance itself from any overt ties to Iran. The U.S., in turn, steadily improved its military capabilities and showed a growing willingness to confront Iran.

The first step in this process of escalation occurred on August 4, when Iran noisily announced a naval exercise in the Gulf called Operation Martyrdom, which was carefully timed and located to interfere with U.S. escort operations. The exercise also showed off the naval Guards force, a remote-controlled speed boat filled with explosives, and the existence of a small submarine.

On August 8, two U.S. F-14s from the carrier *Constellation* encountered an Iranian F-4 which refused to be warned off and appeared to be closing on a U.S. Navy P-3C patrol plane. The Iranian fighter closed to within threatening range of the P-3C, in spite of the fact the F-14s were closing directly on the Iranian fighter and issued a steady series of warnings. One F-14A then fired an AIM-7F missile whose motor failed to ignite. It then fired an AIM-7M missile which appeared to track the target but which was fired at the limit of its minimum range. This allowed the Iranian pilot to maneuver and dodge the missile, which lacked the rapid turn rate required for dogfight conditions. Once the Iranian pilot turned back, the U.S. fighters did not pursue. The entire exchange took place on radar since visibility was less than 8 miles, and the closing ranges varied from 20 to 5 miles and ended below 10,000 feet. The E-3A AWACS provided the tracking data used to detect the Iranian intercept and vector the F-14A fighters.[73]

Meanwhile, the USS *Guadalcanal* entered the Gulf after stopping at Diego Garcia to pick up the RH-53D Sea Stallion helicopters that had been airlifted to the base. The ship not only gave the U.S. an improved mine-warfare capability, it brought Marine Stinger teams to provide point air defense and Bell AH-1T/UH-1N attack helicopters with TOW missiles. This gave the U.S. an enhanced capability to strike at Iranian small craft and naval Guards operations.

The battleship USS *Missouri* was also arriving in the area, along with another Aegis cruiser and the USS *Raleigh*, which was carrying four 65-foot patrol boats operated by U.S. Navy SEAL special forces units and armed with 20-mm and 40-mm cannon. Another Army surveillance unit with surveillance and counterattack helicopters was also on the way. The U.S. planned to build up to a level of 31 ships and vessels and more than 25,000 naval personnel by early September.

This compared with a height of 27 vessels during the Iranian hostage crisis.

On August 10, Iraq bombed Iranian oil installations for the first time in 25 days. Iraq claimed to have flown 110 sorties and to have hit the refinery in Tabriz and oil sites in central and southern Iran at Biki Hakima, Marun, Karanj, and Gach Saran. At the same time, a U.S.-operated, Panamanian registered, 117,200-ton tanker—the *Texaco Caribbean*—was hit by a mine off the coast of Fujayrah, about 80 miles south of the Straits and in the Gulf of Oman. This was the sixth tanker to have hit a mine in the last three months but the first to be hit outside the Gulf.[74]

The next day, five more mines were found off Fujayrah. They were all Soviet-made mines Iran had bought from North Korea and of the type used against the *Bridgeton*. This mining incident had a major impact because Iran had chosen to escalate its naval operations to cover a sanctuary area outside the Gulf where virtually all the tankers entering the area waited before transiting the Straits. While Rafsanjani responded by saying the mines were planted "by the U.S. or its allies, if not Iraq" and announced that the Iranian Navy had been sent to clear the mines, there was no doubt regarding what Iran had done.[75]

Whatever Iran's calculations may have been in conducting this mining effort, it badly underestimated the hostile reaction of the major European states. Britain announced it would send four 615-ton Hunt-class minesweepers to the Gulf to join the destroyer, two frigates, and supply ship it already had in the Armilla Patrol. Further, the British made it clear they would cooperate with the U.S. France announced that it would send three minesweepers and a support ship to protect the Gulf approaches and join the carrier *Clemenceau*, two destroyers, and a support ship, which had just reached waters outside the Gulf. This created the mix of forces shown in Table 9.4.

These announcements did not mean immediate minesweeping capability. British mine vessels took 5 weeks to reach the Gulf, and the French vessels 13 days. Still, Iran had succeeded in creating a de facto coalition between the U.S. and Europe. It also did little to intimidate Europe by then threatening Britain and France, by alluding to the 1983 truck bomb incident in Lebanon, and by warning that it was "ready to repeat the events in Lebanon, which resulted in their flight."[76] Further, Iran's hard line—and the unilateral actions of Britain and France—led Belgium, Italy, and the Netherlands to realize they could no longer wait for international action. Each began to actively consider contingency plans to send national mine warfare contingents and military assistance groups.

TABLE 9.4 Western Ships in the Gulf and the Gulf of Oman, or En Route, August 15, 1987[a]

U.S. Task Forces	French Forces	British Forces
Middle East Task Force	Carrier:	Destroyer:
	Clemenceau	Edinburgh
Command Ship:	Destroyers:	Frigates:
LaSalle	Duquesne	Andromeda
Cruisers:	Georges Leygues	Brazen
Fox	Suffren	Mine Hunters:
Reeves	Frigates:	Bicester
Worden	Commandant Bory	Brecon
Destroyer:	Portet	Brocklesby
Kidd	Victor Schoelcher	Diligence
Frigates:	Mine Hunters:	Hurworth
Crommelin	Cantho	Supply Ship:
Flatley	Gariliano	Brambleleaf
Jarret	Vinh Long	
Klakring	Tendership:	
Temporary Assignment	La Garonne	
	Tanker:	
Amphibious Assault:	La Meuse	
Guadalcanal	Support Ship:	
Carrier:	La Marnet	
Constellation		
Cruiser:		
Valley Forge		
Destroyer:		
Cochrane		
Frigates:		
Cook		
Quellet		
Ammunition Ship:		
Camden		
Supply Ship:		
Niagara Falls		
Battle Group		
Battleship:		
Missouri		
Cruisers:		
Bunker Hill		
Long Beach		
Destroyer:		
Hoel		
Frigate:		
Curts		
Transport Ship:		
Raleigh		
Support Ship:		
Kansas City		

[a]The USSR then had 1 depot ship, 3 minesweepers, and 3 trawlers stationed in the Gulf.

SOURCE: U.S. Navy.

The U.S. faced the problem, however, that its commitment was becoming increasingly open-ended. The U.S. was now involved in a duel with Iran where the use of low levels of military force tended to favor Iran. No matter what the U.S. did in reprisal to any given Iranian act, its effectiveness had to depend on Iran's fear of the U.S. using its superior strength to destroy a large part of Iran's military forces in the Gulf or escalating to block its oil exports and arms imports.

Limited U.S. strikes on naval Guards units or the loss of a few Iranian ships and aircraft could not have any real military effect on Iran, and the resulting martyrdom was likely to encourage Iran's forces rather than deter them. Further, the fact the U.S., Britain, and France had limited their escort activities to ships flying their own flags in carefully designated zones in the Gulf meant Iran could use its peripheral strategy to strike at other ships flying flags of convenience, use indirect tactics like mining, use small Guards units as sacrifice pawns, and strike by using the Guards and pro-Khomeini movements and proxies to commit acts of sabotage, terrorism, and hostage taking.

These same limited encounters forced the U.S. to keep military units in the area costing one to two million dollars a month, depending on the definition of the costs to be included.[77] Further, they confronted the Reagan Administration with the fact that even limited U.S. casualties could create enough opposition to the U.S. presence in the Gulf to shift the Senate toward support of the House in limiting the President's freedom of action.

Since the Iranians were well aware of these vulnerabilities, a cautious strategy of escalation and steadily growing pressure on Iran tended to favor Khomeini, even though Iran lacked the military capability to survive a U.S. attack on its naval and air forces and was extremely vulnerable to any higher level of escalation that threatened its trade in arms and oil. This situation created the kind of escalation ladder that was a recipe for trouble. Each side had strong incentives to test the other to its limits. At the same time, the situation was an invitation to the USSR to attempt to exploit U.S. and Iranian tensions.

The next step in the escalation of the tanker war came in the Gulf of Oman. While the Iranian Navy was completing a "minesweeping" effort off Fujayrah that involved six ships and six RH-53 helicopters inherited from the Shah, two Iranian patrol boats attacked a Liberian registered chemical tanker, the *Osco Sierra*, outside the Straits of Hormuz. This marked the first use of the naval Guards vessels in direct attacks outside the Gulf.

This escalation also came at a time when the UN Security Council was calling for new pressure on Iran to obey its cease-fire resolution, and Secretary General Javier Perez de Cuellar was trying to arrange another visit to Iran and Iraq. It may well have helped convince Saddam Hussein that no progress in a cease-fire was likely. He resumed his attacks on Iranian cities after August 10 and hit Tabriz and Gachsaran. Other raids hit targets like oil fields, petrochemical and cement plants, sugar factories, power stations, and an aluminum plant.[78]

The damaged *Bridgeton* left the Gulf on August 23, completing the fifth one-way convoy movement down the Gulf. That same day, Iraq threatened to shift from concentrating its attacks on land targets and to renew its attacks on Gulf shipping. It made it clear that its strategy was now dependent on two factors: exploiting the UN initiative and other external efforts to reach a comprehensive cease-fire, and attempting to use the oil market and strikes against Iran's oil facilities to enforce a peace. When its threats drew no response, Iraq took action. On August 30, it resumed air strikes in the Gulf after a 45-day pause. It hit Kharg Island and the Iranian oil terminals at Sirri and Lavan and set at least one storage tanker on fire. That same day, the fourth U.S. convoy heading toward Kuwait entered the Gulf.[79]

In theory, Iran should have been highly vulnerable to strikes on its power plants, refineries, and key oil facilities. By mid-1987, oil exports accounted for 90 percent of Iran's foreign exchange earnings, and 80 percent of Iran's oil was still being processed through Kharg Island. On paper, strikes against Kharg looked particularly attractive. Kharg Island, however, still retained substantial surplus export capability. It had originally been designed for a capacity of 6 MMBD. Iran also had about 250,000 BPD of direct export capability from the islands of Lavan and Sirri in the southern Gulf, and since its OPEC quota was only 2.4 MMBD and it could export less than 3 MMBD, Iran could meet its export needs from Kharg if it could service an average of about one 1.8 million barrel-capacity tanker a day.[80]

Many of Kharg's facilities were highly redundant and buried, and its main control facilities were in a hardened building. Its Sea Island terminal to the west and Kharg terminal to the east were also massive concrete structures which were relatively easy to repair. This meant Iraq had to maintain an almost constant series of large-scale air raids against the island to have any effect. While Iraq did have hundreds of fighter-attack aircraft, it had lost some 40–50 aircraft in the fighting early in the year. It now had only about 70–80 top quality pilots, all of whom could be critical in dealing with an Iranian offensive. Further, while Kharg did not have heavy missile defenses, it had enough defenses to cause substantial losses if Iraq tried to maintain a constant series of raids.

By mid-1987, Iran also was relatively well-buffered against temporary losses of Kharg's export capability and even domestic refinery output. It was only consuming about 250,000 BPD domestically and had a fleet of storage tankers near Larak that acted as a massive reserve. Six supertankers maintained a reserve of about 19 million barrels worth of crude oil, and another 11 tankers maintained a reserve of product. This gave Iran about 7 days of reserves in the event it temporarily lost exports from Kharg.

Iraq insisted on continuing to use Exocet missiles, most of which it fired without ever closing to visual range. These missiles simply were not heavy enough for tanker killing. Many of the tankers in the Gulf were nearly 1,000 feet long and less vulnerable than most warships. Their steel hulls were 22–26 mm thick and capable of resisting most machine gun bullets. Rockets and missiles could penetrate them easily, but the explosion of any small missile like the Maverick, Exocet, Harpoon, or Sea Killer tended to be muffled by crude oil, and the oil rarely caught fire even exposed to a warhead explosion. Empty tankers had to flush their compartments with the exhaust from their engines to eliminate oxygen and the fire hazards from oil vapor as part of their standard operations. The ships also had up to 17 compartments, and only one was likely to flood as the result of the kind of missiles Iran was using.

Even the liquid-gas tankers were built with double hulls, and the inner pressure hull had to be separated from the outer hull by a distance of two feet. This separation reduced the lethality of small missiles. Similarly, the steering gear and engine rooms of most tankers were difficult to hit and there was no way Iraqi aircraft could attack them without overflying the tanker and guiding optical missiles to a specific point on the ship. Only gasoline tankers—which were relatively rare in the Gulf—were acutely vulnerable to air attack.[81]

As a result, Iraq rarely succeeded in actually destroying one of Iran's 18 shuttle tankers or even knocking one out for a sustained period of time. Since Iran only needed about 10 tankers to run its shuttle, this gave it a substantial reserve. Iraqi fighters would unquestionably have been far more lethal if they had dropped a mix of conventional bombs and napalm on the tankers, used laser-guided bombs, or using laser-guided cluster bombs with anti-armor and incendiary minelets. Heavy bombs would also have succeeded in killing the foreign tanker crews and rapidly discouraged further charters. Once again, however, Iraq lacked the sophistication to analyze the need for such attacks and execute them.[82]

This was part of the reason that Iraq attacked inland oil facilities, refineries, and power plants whenever it wanted to put pressure on Iran without disturbing other nations. These targets were less politically provocative to the West and GCC states than strikes in the Gulf, were easier to hit, and struck at both Iran's export capability and its ability to operate its economy in the face of Iran's cold winters. These attacks still, however, required sustained and highly accurate bombing by large numbers of aircraft to have a significant effect.

A more sophisticated Air Force could probably have accomplished this without major losses, but Iraq not only lacked pilot numbers, it had little operational research capability except for some support provided by France and limited battle-management and advanced-reconnaissance capability. Although Iraq had first hit targets near Larak on November 25, 1986, it did not renew such attacks until after it started its new bombing activity on August 10, 1987, and does not seem to have scored any major hits until October 5, 1987, when it still failed to sink any tanker or set one on fire.[83]

As for the overall pattern of the war in the Gulf, tensions had declined after Iran ceased its pressure on Basra and during the period that the UN cease-fire negotiations offered Iraq a potential alternative. Saddam Hussein had declared a unilateral cease-fire on attacks on Gulf targets after the UN Security Council agreed to its cease-fire resolution on July 20, 1987. Most of the tankers and cargo vessels moving through the Gulf in August did not have military escorts. Six out of every seven tankers moved on its own, plus dozens of cargo vessels and hundreds of dhows and small coastal vessels. Kuwait received 70 to 80 tankers per month, the vast majority of which traveled without incident. While the number of ships hit in the war had risen to 325, the total casualties were still only about 320, or less than one per attack on a ship. While the volume of trade was far below its 1984 level, this was due more to the fall in oil prices than the war.

Ironically, Iran had probably suffered almost as much from its attacks on shipping as Iraq. Some 35 to 40 ships were calling at ports in the Gulf of Oman and off-loading cargo to move by road to the UAE. Although Iran had mined the area, much of this traffic went to Iran. It had been heavily dependent on transshipping through Khor Fakkan since 1985, and the total flow of shipping had increased during 1986. While the number of cargo ships going to Dubai's ports at Port Rashid and Jebel Ali had dropped from 3,229 in 1983 to 2,888 in 1986, the number of dhows and small coastal vessels calling at these ports had risen from 6,366 in 1984 to 10,008 in 1986.[84]

The tanker war became far more serious, however, during late August and the first part of September. Saddam Hussein's unilateral cease-fire on attacks on Gulf shipping expired on August 29. Once it was clear that Iran would not accept some form of the UN cease-fire, Iraq sharply stepped up its strikes on Gulf targets in addition to the strikes on economic and urban targets that it had resumed on August 10. Iraq kept up its air raids on Gulf targets for four straight days, from August 30 to September 1, 1987. It hit Iranian tankers, oil facilities in the Gulf, and Iranian land-based oil facilities and factories. Iran replied on September 1 by having the naval Guards attack a Kuwaiti freighter with machine-gun fire and rockets. Iran was careful, however, to pick a target that was not reflagged and which was then about 350 miles from the nearest U.S. convoy.

Iraq and Iran exchanged another round of threats, and Iran stated that it would retaliate on a blow-for-blow basis and charged that Iraq was using its fighters to conduct extensive attacks on cities for the first time since a limited unofficial cease-fire on such attacks in February 1986. The next day, Iran hit 2 tankers carrying Arab oil. This triggered a round of Iranian and Iraqi attacks that hit 7 ships in one 24-hour period. Iraq now claimed to have hit 11 naval targets in 5 days, plus 2 power plants and a communications facility. Counting Iranian attacks, 20 ships were hit in the 6 days between August 27 and September 3, 1987. This was the most intense series of attacks in the history of the tanker war, and Lloyds raised its war risk premium by 50 percent.

The patterns in such strikes are interesting and reflect the importance of the UN cease-fire effort. The air war had been relatively quiet during April to mid-August. Iraq carried out 5 strikes on shipping during April, 1987, and Iran carried out none. Iraq carried out 7 air strikes on urban and economic targets, and Iran carried out none. Iraq carried out 6 strikes on shipping during May 1987, and Iran carried out 8. Iraq carried out 5 air strikes on urban and economic targets, and Iran carried out 2. Iraq carried out 1 strike on shipping during May 1987, and Iran carried out 1. Iraq carried out 1 air strike on urban and economic targets, and Iran carried out none. Iraq carried out 5 strikes on shipping during July 1987, and Iran carried out 4. Iraq carried out 6 air strikes on urban and economic targets, and Iran carried out none. Iraq carried out no strikes on shipping during August 1987, and Iran carried out 3. Iraq carried out 2 air strikes on urban and economic targets during August 1–15, and Iran carried out none.

During August 16–31, however, the breakdown of the cease-fire negotiations created a pattern of challenge and response that was to last for the rest of the year and well into 1988. Iraq escalated the moment it felt there was no chance of a cease-fire, that the situation was threatening to stabilize without a cease-fire, when it was under military pressure, or when it felt this would increase the impact of

Western military pressure on Iran. Iran either retaliated or escalated whenever it felt this would be to its advantage:[85]

- During August 16–31, Iraq carried out 13 air strikes on urban and economic targets, and Iran carried out 7.
- Iraq carried out 22 strikes on shipping during September 1–15, 1987, and Iran carried out 10. Iraq carried out 35 air strikes on urban and economic targets, and Iran carried out 8.
- Iraq carried out 19 strikes on shipping during September 16–30, 1987, and Iran carried out 7. Iraq carried out 19 air strikes on urban and economic targets, and Iran carried out 3.
- Iraq carried out 15 strikes on shipping during October 1–15, 1987, and Iran carried out 8. Iraq carried out 12 air strikes on urban and economic targets, and Iran carried out 6.
- Iraq carried out 19 air strikes on urban and economic targets , and Iran carried out three. Iraq carried out 9 strikes on shipping during October 16–31, 1987, and Iran carried out 1. Iraq carried out 4 air strikes on urban and economic targets, and Iran carried out 8, four with Scud.
- Iraq carried out 18 strikes on shipping during November 1–15, 1987, and Iran carried out 3. Iraq carried out 14 air strikes on urban and economic targets, and Iran carried out 9—one with Scud.
- Iraq carried out 12 strikes on shipping during November 16–30, 1987, and Iran carried out 7. Iraq carried out 10 air strikes on urban and economic targets, and Iran carried out 2—both with Scud.
- Iraq carried out 8 strikes on shipping during December 1–15, 1987, and Iran carried out 5. Iraq carried out 7 strikes on urban and economic targets, and Iran carried out 2.
- Iraq carried out 9 strikes on shipping during December 16–31, 1987, and Iran carried out 10. Iraq carried out 1 air strike on urban and economic targets, and Iran carried none. (This decrease in attacks may have been in response to the Gulf summit meeting on December 29, 1987.)

Other events then heightened the tensions in the Gulf in early September 1987. On September 3, Iranian speedboats attacked an Italian container ship and wounded two Italians in the crew. This led to a meeting of the Italian Cabinet on September 4, and Italy changed its position from seeking a UN peace force to one of sending Italian warships to join the U.S., British, and French warships in the Gulf. Italy was then receiving 40 percent of its oil from the Gulf.

That same day, Iran fired a Silkworm missile at Kuwait from a site on the far southern tip of the Faw Peninsula. The missile fell on an uninhabited strip of coastline, but it was two miles from one of Kuwait's main oil terminals, and two tankers were loading at the time. This initially made it uncertain as to whether the missile's terminal guidance system failed to acquire either of the two tankers, or Iran had merely intended the firing as a threat. Iran denied responsibility for the firing, but then fired another missile on September 4 and a third on September 5. The second missile hit near Mina Abdullah, 30 miles to the south of Kuwait City. This showed Iran could bracket the entire country. The third hit near Failaka Island, 13 miles from Kuwait's northern coast.

Kuwait protested the missile firings to the UN, complained to the permanent members of the Security Council, and expelled five of Iran's seven diplomats in Kuwait. This led Iran to charge that the U.S. had pressured Kuwait to expel the diplomats but that Kuwait would have to take the consequences. It also again called for the U.S. to leave the Gulf.[86] The GCC states responded by calling a meeting of their foreign ministers on September 12, 1987, although it was clear that there was little the southern Gulf states could do.

The U.S. rebuked Iran for its attacks but concentrated on attacking the Iranian delay in accepting the UN cease-fire proposal. The Secretary General's mission reached Tehran on September 11, 1987. When talks with the Iranians began the next day, both sides were claiming the other had violated the cease-fire. Iran said Iraq had killed 13 civilians. Baghdad said Iran had shelled eight Iraqi cities and towns in the last 48 hours, and naval Guards attacked a Cypriot supertanker carrying Saudi oil with rockets.

When the Secretary General arrived in Tehran, he found a very uncertain reception. Further, when the Secretary General reached Baghdad, both sides again charged the other with renewing the war. Iraq claimed Iran had shelled Basra and stared an offensive in the central sector, which it repulsed.[87] Tehran accused Iraq of shelling three Iranian cities. Saddam Hussein then met with the Secretary General and accused Iran of having started the war. Foreign Minister Tariq Aziz charged that Iran was only stalling and demanded that the UN impose sanctions and an arms embargo. The most that Perez de Cuellar could do on his return to New York, on September 16, was to tell the Security Council that Iran had offered to halt military action but would only honor a formal cease-fire after an international commission established Iraq's guilt in starting the war.

Iraq began a new series of air strikes on Iranian oil facilities and ships the same day the Secretary General returned to New York, and Iran shelled Basra, stepped up its naval challenges of Gulf shipping, and made limited gains by seizing several important hill positions on the central front. By September 19, Iran and Iraq were both attacking each other's inland oil facilities, and the war was continuing to escalate.[88]

Meanwhile, the European role in the Gulf continued to grow. (See Table 9.5 for a summary of the West's naval forces in the Gulf.) The French and British decision to send warships to the Gulf on August 11, 1987, was followed by growing British pressure on Belgium, Italy, and the Netherlands to take a more active role. As a result, a special meeting on cooperative action in the Gulf took place in the Western European Union (WEU) on August 20. This meeting failed, however, to produce any tangible result other than a call for freedom of navigation. The FRG could not agree on any positive course of action; Italy persisted in pushing for some form of UN initiative; and Britain and France had already moved beyond the point where they felt they could subordinate their freedom of action to a committee.

The Netherlands, which chaired the WEU and had tried to catalyze a common WEU effort in the Gulf then gave up and decided to act on its own. It turned to Britain for assistance, and Britain agreed to provide air cover and logistic support for a Dutch minesweeping effort in the Gulf. On September 7, 1987, the Netherlands announced that it would send two minesweepers to the region. Belgium, which had long worked closely with the Netherlands and Britain in planning the naval defense of the Gulf, followed the Dutch lead. It announced it would send two of its minesweepers to the Gulf, as well as a support ship. Belgium also agreed to a joint command with the Netherlands, with a Belgian officer in charge of the naval units on the scene and a Dutch officer in command of the overall task force effort.

The Belgian and Dutch ships sailed as a flotilla in late September but then demonstrated that the U.S. was not the only nation that could run into problems in deploying its mine forces. The Belgian minesweepers were ex–U.S. World War II ships of the Avenger class. One, the *Breydel*, was 30 years old and broke down in the Mediterranean. This meant the task force could not arrive by its scheduled date of November 1. The flotilla also ran into problems because it had no base in the Gulf and no air cover. The best that it could do was to rely on France to provide support from Djibouti and to use the Belgian support ship—the *Zinnia*—as a supply shuttle. The British agreed to provide air cover, but only as a third priority, after British warships and merchant ships. The Belgian-Dutch force was armed only with 20-mm guns, and this led the Netherlands to reinforce them with Stingers operated by Dutch Marines.[89]

As has been discussed earlier, Italy had decided to enter the Gulf on September 8, after an Iranian strike on an Italian tanker. This strike

TABLE 9.5 Western Ships in the Gulf and the Gulf of Oman, or En Route, September 20, 1987[a,b]

U.S. Task Forces[c,d]	French Forces[c]	British Forces[c]
Middle East Task Force	Carrier:	Destroyer:
	Clemenceau (1,338)	*Edinburgh* (253)
Command Ship:	Destroyers:	Frigates:
LaSalle (499)	*Duquesne* (355)	*Andromeda* (224)
Cruisers:	*Georges Leygues*	*Brazen* (175)
William H. Standley (513)	Frigates:	*Suffren* (355)
Reeves (513)	*Commandant Bory* (167)	Mine Hunters:
Destroyer:	*Portet* (167)	*Bicester*
Kidd (346)	*Victor Schoelcher* (167)	*Brecon*
Frigates:	Mine Hunters:	*Brocklesby*
Crommelin (200)	*Cantho*	*Hurworth*
Rentz (200)	*Loire*	Repair Ship:
Flatley (200)	*Vinh Long*	*Diligence*
Jarret (200)	Tendership:	Mine Support Vessel:
Klakring (200)	*La Garonne*	*Abdiel*
Transport Ship:	Tanker:	Supply Ship:
Raleigh (429)	*La Meuse*	*Brambleleaf* (42)
Amphibious Assault:	Support Ship:	MPA:
Guadalcanal (754)	*La Marne*	*Nimrods*
	Mine Support Ship:	
	Loire	
Other Temporary Assignments		
	Italian Forces	*Belgian Forces*
Carrier:		
Ranger	Frigates:	Minesweepers:
Cruiser:	*Scirocco*	*Breydel*
Valley Forge	*Gregala*	*F. Bovesse*
Destroyer:	*Perseo*	Support Ship:
Arcadia	Mine Vessel:	*Zinnia*
Frigates:	*Vieste*	
Cook	*Milazzo*	*Netherlands Forces*
Quellet	*Sapri*	
Ammunition Ship:	Supply Ship:	Minesweepers:
Camden	*Vesuvio*	*Hellevoetsluis*
Supply Ship:	Salvage Vessel:	*Maassluis*
Niagara Falls	*Anteo*	
Battle Group		
Battleship:		
Missouri		
Cruisers:		
Bunker Hill		
Long Beach		
Destroyer:		
Hoel		

(continues)

TABLE 9.5 *(continued)*

U.S. Task Forces	French Forces	British Forces

Battle Group (continued)

Frigate:
  Curts
Support Ship:
  Kansas City
Mine Vessels in Transit:
  Enhance
  Esteem
  Fearless
  Inflict
  Illusive
Mine Tow Ships:
  Barber County
  Grapple

---

[a]The Soviet Indian Ocean Squadron was commanded by a Vice Admiral, using the *Ladny*, a Krivak 1 class frigate. The Soviets had a total of a Sovremenny or Udaloly class destroyer, two frigates, three Natya-class minesweepers, one Urga-class submarine depot ship, an unstated number of submarines, and three AGI trawler, or intelligence-gathering vessels, in the region.

[b]Figures in parentheses are crew numbers and provide a rough indication of ship size.

[c]The aircraft complements of the ships in the Gulf included 1 ASW helicopter for the *William H. Standley*; 2 ASW helicopters for each U.S. frigate; 8 MSW helicopters, 4 attack helicopters, 2 transport helicopters, and 4 utility helicopters for the *Guadalcanal*; 6 MSC, 4 special-warfare boats, and 2 FPB for the *Raleigh*; 20 FBA, 10 AWX, and 10 ASW aircraft for the *Clemenceau*.

[d]U.S. forces were supplemented by E-3A and tanker aircraft in Saudi Arabia, cargo and support ships at Diego Garcia, P-3 aircraft in Masirah in Oman, and 150 support personnel at Jufair in Bahrain.

SOURCE: U.S. Navy.

gave the Italian Cabinet an excuse to act, and it announced the dispatch of eight ships, including three Lerci-class minesweepers, one Lupo-class frigate, and two Maestrale-class frigates. The ships set sail on September 15, 1987.[90]

As for the forces already in the Gulf, the French task force remained part of the French Indian Ocean Command (ALINDIEN) based at Mayotte in La Reunion. It included the *Clemenceau*, a 32,700-ton carrier with 38 aircraft and recently modernized air defenses, including Thomson CSF EDIR defense systems. The escorts included two guided-missile destroyers, a corvette, and three multi-role frigates. There were two replenishment ships under way and a 2,320-ton repair ship. The French force was reinforced by three minesweepers which began operations in the Gulf of Oman on September 11.[91] By late October, the French force had found nine M-08 mines in the area off the ports of Fujayrah and Khor Fakkan. Two were surfaced by sweeping, and seven were detected at depths of two to seven meters by sonar. The French frigate *Dupleix* had detected and destroyed two more mines off Qatar. That brought the total number of mines found since the beginning of the U.S. reflagging effort to 80.[92]

The British Armilla Patrol included the HMS *Andromeda*, a Batch 3 Leander-class frigate with Sea Wolf short-range air defense systems. It was supported by the destroyer *Edinburgh*, a Type-42 air defense ship, and the *Brazen*, a Type-22 Batch 1 anti-submarine warfare frigate. The British mine force had reached the Gulf of Oman on September 15. It included the 1,375-ton tender *Abdiel*, which carried spare minesweeping gear and cables and acted as a command ship, and three minesweepers from 1 and 4 MCM, which carried lightweight wire sweeps, mine hunting sonars, Barricade anti-missile decoys, and ROVs.[93] Fleet support was provided by the 40,200-ton replenishment tanker *Brambleleaf*, the stores ship *Regent*, and the repair ship *Diligence*, which provided repair, fire fighting, and diving facilities.

The U.S. was now deployed for a major war. A new carrier task force with the carrier USS *Ranger* had arrived to replace the task force led by the *Constellation*, so that the forces in the Indian Ocean continued to included a carrier wing of 87 aircraft. The *Valley Forge* acted as an air-cover control ship, coordination center with the Saudi Air Force, and escort for the *Constellation*. The *Cochrane* provided air-defense cover, and two Knox-class frigates—the *Cook* and *Quellet*—provided ASW cover and surface defenses with RGM-84 Harpoon missiles. The 53,600-ton support ship *Camden* provided fuel and munitions, a 16,070-ton Mars-class ship provided combat stores, and the *Niagra Falls* provided spares and aircraft repair parts and equipment. A second carrier group was rotating into the area led by the carrier *Ranger*.

The U.S. Naval Surface Group Western Pacific included a battery of 32 Tomahawk cruise missiles with both anti-ship and land-attack versions. The *Missouri* was escorted by an upgraded Aegis ship, the *Bunker Hill*, and the cruiser *Long Beach*—the first nuclear-powered warship—with Tomahawk and Harpoon missiles. The air defense for the surface group came from the *Hoel*, and the *Curts* provided anti-submarine defense. The supply ship *Kansas City* provided oil, fuel, ammunition, and provisions.

The Middle East Task Force in the Gulf continued to include the command ship *La Salle* but was reinforced by the amphibious assault ship USS *Raleigh*, which was equipped with a well dock. The *Raleigh* had carried four MSB5-class minesweeping boats, and four SEAL Seafox light special warfare craft, to the Gulf. The cargo ship *St. Louis* had arrived on August 27, with two more MSB5s and two Seafoxes.[94] The *Guadalcanal* had off-loaded its 700-man Marine unit and carried eight RH-53D Sea Stallion minesweeping helicopters. The force also included four AH-1T Sea Cobra attack helicopters, four UH-1N utility helicopters, and two CH-46C Sea Knight medium transport helicopters.

There were five missile-armed hydrofoil ships—the *Hercules, Taurus, Aquila, Aries,* and *Gemini* —with 76-mm guns and Harpoon missiles. A U.S. Army Special Forces units provided four MH-6A surveillance and counter-attack helicopters.

The convoys of the reflagged Kuwaiti shuttle tankers were escorted by Destroyer Squadron 14. This included the guided-missile destroyer *Kidd*. The squadron also included the guided missile cruiser *Fox*, and guided-missile frigates *Reid, Crommelin, Jarret,* and *Hawes*. These four frigates had 76-mm guns, and LAMPS 1 SH-2F or LAMPS III SH-60B helicopters. The force was supported by an area defense force including the frigates *Flatley* and *Klakring* and the guided-missile cruisers *Worden* and *Reeves*.

In short, there was a total of 11 U.S. ships, with about 4,500 crew members, actually in Gulf waters. This raised the Pentagon's estimate of the cost of the U.S. reflagging exercise to the Navy alone to $200 million a year.[95] The total number of Western ships scheduled for operation in the area rose to 35 U.S. and 35 allied vessels. Europe was sending a total of one aircraft carrier, three destroyers, 10 frigates, and five large and five small support ships. Europe was also sending a substantial minesweeping capability of fourteen modern vessels for the region.[96] The FRG also agreed to send its ships south to replace some of the ships other European nations had moved out of the Mediterranean. The FRG sent the destroyer *Moelders*, frigate *Niedersachsen*, and support ship *Frieburg*, all of which had arrived in the Mediterranean by mid-October.[97]

Iraq continued to sporadically strike at targets in the Gulf throughout the rest of September, but it was Iran that set the pace. On September 20, an Iranian speed boat attacked a Saudi tanker in the Straits. On September 21, Iran attacked a British flag tanker, the *Gentle Breeze*, and set it afire, killing a crewman. This led the British government to react by expelling all of the personnel in the Iranian Logistic Support Center in London that had been purchasing arms and to bring its full weight into the effort to halt arms sales to Iran.

The *Iran Ajr* Incident

Later that day, a more dramatic development occurred. After the *Bridgeton* had hit a mine, the U.S. publicly and privately stated to Iran on several occasions that its rules of engagement would lead it to strike without warning at any Iranian ship caught laying mines, or preparing to lay mines, in international waters. At the direction of the Chairman of the Joint Chiefs, Admiral William Crowe, the U.S. then dispatched a U.S. Army special forces unit to the Gulf from Task Force 160—the "wings of Delta Force"—at Fort Campbell, Kentucky.[98] In early September, Crowe visited Rear Admiral Harold Bernsen on the USS *La Salle*, and they worked out a plan to track and intercept any Iranian vessels that continued to lay mines.

The U.S. used its intelligence satellites, SR-71 reconnaissance aircraft, and the tactical intelligence-gathering assets it had deployed in the Gulf—including E-3As, P-3Cs, and specially equipped helicopters such as silenced OH-6As—to track Iranian minelaying efforts from the loading of the ships in port to the actual minelaying. The U.S. then picked out one of the Iranian vessels—an Iranian Navy LST called the *Iran Ajr*—and tracked it from the time it left port. It watched while the Iranian ship reached a point about 50 miles northeast of Bahrain and north of Qatar and laid at least six mines. The Iranian ship seems to have felt it was safe in doing this because it was operating at night. The U.S., however, had deployed the *Guadalcanal* and *Jarret* to the area and was using OH-6 light attack helicopters from the U.S. Army Special Operations Command which were equipped with night-vision devices, including forward-looking infrared (FLIR) equipment. They also had passive light-intensification devices and could track every movement on the Iranian ship.

Two of these helicopters, based on the frigate *Jarret*, flew at 200 feet to a point about 500 meters from the *Iran Ajr*. They watched the ship, and when they visually confirmed that it was still laying mines, they asked for permission to attack. Bernsen approved, and the helicopters attacked the Iranian vessel with their 7.62-mm machine guns and 2.75-inch rockets. They immediately disabled the ship and killed five crewmen. U.S. Navy SEAL teams from the *Guadalcanal* then used small boats to seize the ship and took 26 prisoners, one of whom later died from wounds. A day later, the U.S. blew up and sank the Iranian vessel.

This American strike exposed Iran's action in a way that publicly confirmed its guilt for all the past minelaying efforts. Iran could no longer make vague references to an invisible hand or blame the minelaying on an American plot. Further, the U.S. attack came while Khameini was at the UN. All he could do was to claim the ship was a merchant ship and describe the minelaying charge as "a pack of lies." Given the fact the U.S. found 10 fully armed Soviet-made M-08 mines on the ship along with charts showing where it had laid mines in the past day, filmed the captured crewmen discussing their minelaying activities, and recovered mines where the charts indicated they had been laid, the result was to sharply embarrass Khameini. This embarrassment was so acute that some experts questioned whether the incident was a deliberate attempt to embarrass Khameini and the Iranian moderates. In fact, the actual minelaying was part of a continuing effort by Iran and was not part of a special effort that could have been deployed to be caught. In fact, Rafsanjani was almost certainly correct when he later charged that the U.S. had timed the attack to divert attention from Khameini.[99]

In any case, the U.S. attack immediately gained a great deal of U.S. and foreign support. This support enabled Reagan to take a hard-line on maintaining the U.S. presence in the Gulf. At the same time, the Reagan Administration had shown it could and would hit Iran. This had a powerful impact in correcting the U.S. reputation for military errors and in reassuring both its European and Gulf allies that the U.S. would stay in the Gulf. The incident also seems to have helped make the PRC openly state in the UN that it would support an arms embargo if Iran did not move toward a cease-fire.

Further, it was clear that the Iranian actions could not simply be blamed on members of the Guards. A regular Iranian naval vessel was involved, and the documents found on the ship clearly indicated it was acting on the basis of formal orders from a relatively high level. Khameini tacitly admitted this when he took a much more moderate line a few days later. He stressed that Iran had no desire to go to war with the U.S. and stated that Iran had not closed the door to negotiations.

The USSR was the only major power which reacted to the U.S. attack by taking a stand favorable to Iran. Iran, however, did not get uncritical support from the USSR. Soviet spokesmen were careful not to imply that Iran had any justification for mining the Gulf. The Soviet Union was still concerned with Arab opinion. While both the U.S. and USSR had agreed to defer an arms embargo and continue diplomacy, even the USSR did not rule out the idea of an embargo in the near future.[100]

At the same time, Kurdish independence movements were causing increasing trouble for Iraq and Turkey. Once Iran halted its spring offensives in the South, it steadily increased its aid to anti-Iraqi

Kurds. The Ba'athist elite did a notably bad job of trying to win over those Kurdish factions that were willing to compromise. Baghdad reacted to each new attack by the Kurdish rebels by taking an increasingly harder line. While reports may be exaggerated, some 500 villages had been razed by late 1987, and 100,000 to 200,000 Kurds had been displaced.

This relocation effort was poorly managed, poorly funded, and ruthlessly discriminatory. The government tightened its fist around the rest of the Kurds it could reach and control after every new internal security problem, even when totally nonrelated movements like Al Daawa were to blame. When Al Daawa fired on a diplomatic reception in Baquba, about 50 miles north of Baghdad, on September 7, and killed 50 to 100 people, the result not only was interrogations and summary hangings in the area where the incident occurred, but new roundups of suspected Kurds.

The man immediately in charge of the effort to suppress the Kurds, Saddam Hussein's cousin Ali Hassan al-Majid, required more and more troops and began to drain manpower from Iraq's 5th Corps. While Major General Talia Khalil Douri, the 5th Corps Commander, denied the incidents and blamed Iran, this led the government to use the Iraqi Air Force to begin to bomb Kurdish villages. These attacks had the almost inevitable result of creating at least two new guerrillas for every one that was killed or imprisoned. For the first time, the KDP and similar movements really began to threaten control of the country-side and to give Iran's slow advances in the north strategic meaning.

Iran had internal problems of its own. The various opposition movements had little impact on the government, but the People's Mujahideen, led by Masoud Rajavi, was capable of occasional challenges to Khomeini. The Mujahideen were receiving massive Iraqi funding and had built up paramilitary forces in Iran called the National Liberation Army or NLA, but these had more visibility than effectiveness and could only carry out the occasional bombing and small raids. These raids were enough to lead the Guards units in western Iran to create special anti-NLA forces in late October 1987, but they did not present a significant threat to local security, even in the areas where they occurred.

The NLA does seem to have been more successful in a series of attacks in west Azerbaijan, Ilam, and Khuzistan provinces in late November, when it claimed to have inflicted 3,680 casualties and captured 467. Nevertheless, the Mujahideen's total claims for 100 clashes between January 1 and December 1, 1987, amounted to only 8,400 casualties and 845 prisoners. Further, it remained virtually impossible to determine what Rajavi really stood for and how many of his

Marxist and anti-Western roots he retained. The Royalist and middle class exile factions seemed even more powerless. They could not even mount effective meetings or media campaigns.[101]

The most interesting change in Iran's power structure was the steady growth of the role of the Revolutionary Guard. Even before the U.S. entered the Gulf, the Guard seemed to be winning most of its political battles, and the regular military seemed to increasingly be relegated to roles like artillery support, naval and air patrols, and other missions requiring technical expertise. By this time, the Guard had built up to at least 350,000 men and was getting most of the new weapons systems obtained from China, such as the Silkworm missile.

The naval elements of the Guards now had around 20,000 men and were substantially larger than Iran's 14,500-man Navy. They were responsible for the attacks on the Kuwait and Saudi embassies and had priority in establishing military factories and supply facilities. It was also clear that the two top men in the Guard—Minister Mohsen Rafiqdust and Commander Moshen Rezai—were gaining in power. What was far less certain was whether this increase in power was confined to military influence or policy-level and civil decision making as well.[102] Meanwhile, the Western forces in the Gulf had built up to the levels shown in Table 9.5.

At the beginning of October 1987, a pattern had been established where the war involved three parallel struggles. The first struggle was the escalating confrontation between Iran and the U.S., Western Europe, and Iran. The second struggle was a continuing political battle over the UN peace initiative, with the U.S. increasingly pressing for an arms embargo, the USSR seeking to strengthen its developing ties to Iran without alienating the Arab world, and Iran in the ambiguous position of either seeking concessions or simply using such demands to delay UN action. The third struggle was the continuing series of exchanges and low-level border conflicts taking place between Iraq and Iran.

The first and second of these struggles were highly interactive. During August 31 to October 1, Iran launched a new set of gunboat attacks. Iranian ships hit three tankers and often seemed to deliberately pass near western and Soviet naval forces. Iraq responded in kind, and this raised the number of attacks on Gulf ships to 375. It is interesting to note, however, that this struggle did comparatively little to alter each side's oil production. As Table 9.6 shows, both sides were able to sustain comparatively high monthly production rates.

These production levels were possible because several important factors limited the intensity of the oil war.

TABLE 9.6 Iranian and Iraqi Oil Production: October 1986–February 1988

Month	Output in MMBD	
	Iran	Iraq
1986		
October	1.5	1.8
November	1.6	1.6
December	1.9	1.7
1987		
January	2.2	1.7
February	1.7	1.7
March	2.1	1.7
April	2.2	1.9
May	2.6	1.9
June	2.4	2.0
July	2.5	2.0
August	2.7	2.2
September	2.1	2.3
October	2.4	2.5
November	2.2	2.6
December	2.2	2.6
1988		
January	2.0	2.4
February	2.0	2.5

SOURCE: Adapted from William L. Randol and Ellen Macready, *Petroleum Monitor*, vol. 7, no. 3, March 1988, pp. 16–17.

- Both sides conducted a limited war in the sense that they never tried to commit all their forces to halting their opponents oil shipments. Iraq had to be careful of provoking its allies in the southern Gulf into reducing their financial support because of Iran's threat to their oil exports and of losing Western and outside support for a cease-fire. It also risked provoking Iran into an all-out offensive and making any peace settlement impossible. Iran was even more constrained by the risk of dragging the West fully into the war, or at least into suppressing the Guards and Iranian Navy. Further, Iran was extremely vulnerable to Western embargos of its oil exports.
- Both sides had limited military means. Iran lacked the air power to strike at Iran's oil production facilities and pipelines. It could not openly compete with the Western naval forces in the Gulf. Iraq could not risk the airpower losses necessary to sustain

full-scale attacks on Iran's oil facilities and lacked the sensors and effective forces necessary to interdict Iranian shipping through the Gulf. Both sides lacked the kind of missile types and numbers necessary to destroy and sink large numbers of tankers and the C^{3}I/BM systems necessary to manage a large-scale efficient war against the number of ships moving to and from the opposing country.

- Both sides had had more than half a decade to build up their capability to repair limited damage to their oil-exporting capabilities. Iraq had the support of Turkey in protecting its pipelines through that country, and Iran had built up a considerable shuttle fleet and large number of tankers to act as a floating reserve.

One of the more important lessons of the war, however, is that there was nothing inevitable about this state of affairs. Both Iran and Iraq suddenly escalated toward something approaching an all-out oil war for short periods. Both would have been far more willing to escalate if they had had modern maritime patrol aircraft, longer-range and higher-payload aircraft and missiles, and better C^{3}I/BM systems. Both sides are in the process of acquiring such weapons, and future conflicts in the region and in the rest of the Third World will be far more capable of doing sudden and intensive damage to critical economic facilities and activities.

The third struggle was more quiet, although Iran claimed that it had begun a major buildup. Iran stated that it had begun to mass 10 to 20 Guards divisions of roughly 10,000 men each opposite Basra. It announced that as many as 120 volunteer battalions, or roughly 48,000 men, had been sent to the front in the last few days. It also said that another 85 battalions, or as many as 34,000 men, had been sent to the south to protect against the U.S. threat.

The Iraqi Air Force responded by stepping up its strikes at troop concentrations in the southern and central sectors of the 1,174-kilometer front and reinforced the 3rd and 7th armies. This, however, was largely precautionary. Iran seemed unlikely to attack before the beginning of the rainy season in late October or early November.[103]

At the same time, Iran gave some important signals that it might not be considering another frontal attack on Basra and that it intended to be more careful about its land attacks. Mohsen Rezai, the commander of the Revolutionary Guards, stated in September that Iran's two great advantages in the war were martyrdom and "innovation and creativity . . . in the tactics we used against the whole world."[104] The Supreme Defense Council seems to have been continuing the debate over how to react to Iran's massive losses at Basra, and on November 12, Khomeini announced what seemed to be a new strategy: "A stage has been reached where, with the continuation of operations and repeated blows, we should deprive the enemy of respite and bring closer the inevitable . . . defeat." Rafsanjani went on the next day to say that the war was entering a "totally new phase" and that Iran would rely on "numerous and consecutive" attacks to drain Iraq's military strength without allowing it to recover. Similarly, Khameini referred to the need for "continuous operations."[105]

The problem with these ideas was that they called for a major superiority in manpower to compensate for Iraq's superiority in weapons and supply. As became clearer in 1988, Iran was actually experiencing growing mobilization problems. They also called for a high degree of military experience and professionalism, but the Mullahs continued to favor revolutionary fervor over the professional advice of both the regular forces and Pasdaran and to allow divisions and conflicts in the operations of the regular army and Pasdaran units. Finally, these ideas called for consistency of policy, and they were not really innovations, but, rather, the repetition of ideas that Iranian leaders had raised repeatedly after every major reversal from 1983 onwards.

As for the cease-fire effort, the differing positions of the two sides effectively blocked effective UN action and pushed the U.S. and Iran toward further confrontation. On October 1, more mines were spotted off Farsi Island to the north of Bahrain, and a British minesweeper was dispatched to sweep the area. On October 2, intelligence sources discovered that Iran was planning a substantial strike on Ras al Khafji—a large Saudi-Kuwaiti oil field and processing complex with a capacity of 300,000 BPD near the Saudi-Kuwaiti border and about 110 miles from Kharg. It was this field which was used to produce the oil Saudi Arabia and Kuwait marketed for Iraq.

After consultation with the U.S., the Saudis put F-15 and Tornado aircraft on alert and began to move ships toward the area. They also warned Tehran they had learned of the plan. Tehran, however, decided to go on with the attack, at least to the point of forcing a Saudi reaction and demonstrating its resolve. On October 3, 48 to 60 Iranian speed boats assembled near Kharg Island. They then moved toward the Khafji oil field. U.S. E-3A aircraft detected the move and notified the U.S. commander of the Middle East Task Force and the key command centers in Saudi Arabia. The Saudis responded immediately by sending ships and F-15 and Tornado aircraft toward the Iranian force, and the U.S. task force—including the command ship *LaSalle*—sailed in the same direction. When the Iranian force detected these moves, it turned away.[106]

On October 5, Iraq launched a new series of long-range air strikes and struck at tankers loading near Larak, Iran's transloading point for its tanker shuttle. These attacks included a successful hit on the *Seawise Giant*, a 564,739-ton ship which was the largest ship afloat. While reports differed, up to four tankers may have been damaged during this raid. This brought the total number of Iraqi raids on Gulf shipping since late August up to 21, and Iraq stepped up its air attacks to the point where it was flying some 50 sorties a day during October 5–8.[107]

Iran, in turn, launched new Scud strikes on Baghdad for the first time since mid-February and continued to strike at Gulf shipping. Both the Guards and regular Iranian Navy were increasingly aggressive. Guards ships often attacked targets near Western warships. For example, they hit a Pakistani oil tanker only three to four miles from the French warship *Georges Leygues*. An Iranian destroyer moved within a mile of the U.S. destroyer USS *Kidd* and locked its fire control radar on the *Kidd*. The U.S. ship immediately warned the Iranian ship three times to cease illuminating and finally warned it to halt immediately or it would fire. The Iranian ship immediately halted and turned away.[108]

Iran hit a number of Japanese ships, and Japan again warned its ships not to enter the Gulf, although it was getting more than 50 percent of its oil from Gulf states. On October 7, 1987, Japan did announce that it would finance a precision navigation system to assist ships of all nations in avoiding mines. Prime Minister Nakasone also indicated that Japan might make a major increase in financing its share of the Western military presence in the area. Nevertheless, Japan conspicuously avoided taking sides and making any military commitment, and they had little effect on Iran. On October 8, Guards units set a 9,400-ton Japanese-owned ship under Panamanian registry, the *Tomoe-8*, afire about 60 miles east of Jubail. This came only one week after Japan had again allowed its ships to enter the Gulf.[109]

On October 8, another direct clash took place between U.S. and Iranian forces. A force of one Iranian corvette and three speedboats moved toward the *Hercules*, one of the barges that U.S. forces were using as a base near Farsi Island.[110] When the U.S. sent helicopters toward the Iranian force, which was moving directly toward the U.S. base, the Iranian ships fired on the U.S. helicopters. The force included three U.S. MH-6 night surveillance/attack helicopters. The aircraft were then about 15 miles southwest of Farsi Island and three miles outside Iran's 12-mile limit.[111] The U.S. army helicopters immediately returned the Iranian's fire. They attacked the Iranian force of four ships and sank one Boghammer speed boat and damaged two Boston-Whaler–type boats. An Iranian corvette either escaped or was not attacked.

Eight Iranians were killed or died later, and six were taken prisoner by SEAL units using Mark III Sea Specter patrol boats. An inspection of the damaged boats revealed that at least one had carried U.S.-made Stinger missiles of the kind being given to the Afghan Freedom Fighters. The Afghans later claimed these were part of six Stingers that Iranians had stolen from a group near the border in April, but U.S. experts felt they might well have been sold. The Iranians claimed they were part of another secret sale by McFarlane in 1986 and that many more had been delivered.

As for Iraq, Iraqi jets continued the tanker war. They hit a Greek-owned ship and killed one crewman that same day. This raised the total number of ships hit by both sides to nine in one week, with at least seven crewman killed and four missing. Iraq then continued to pound away at Iran's shuttle and storage tankers in the Gulf, although at high cost and usually with marginal success. By some U.S. estimates, Iraq was spending nearly $40 million a day on the war but doing little to interfere with the fact Iran was getting $20 million a day from its oil exports. Since October 1, Iraq had made 12 confirmed raids on Iranian tankers, some of which had reached as far down the Gulf as Larak. While it did hit several tankers, only one was destroyed. It also lost at least one Mirage fighter, and each raid generally used at least two Exocet missiles, which were reported to have cost as much as $1.3 million each. Since the damage rarely cost more than $500,000, and the chartered tankers still only cost Iran twice the normal daily rate, it was clear that Iraq was not winning on cost grounds, much less strategic ones. (See Table 9.7 for an analysis of tankers attacked by Iran and Iraq.)

Both Iraq and Iran continued to exchange artillery and missile attacks. By sheer bad luck, one of these attacks had an unusually bloody effect. On October 12, Iran fired its third Soviet-made Scud B missile in a week into Baghdad in a resumption of the war of the cities. This time the missile hit a school just as 650 children were preparing to enter classes. It killed 29 children and 3 adults, and Iraq claimed that it wounded nearly 200 people.

October 14 was less intense, but it showed that even a typical day was now anything but calm. Iran fired on Basra, and an Iranian gunboat machine-gunned a Saudi tanker off Dubai. Italy announced that it blamed Iran for the fact pro-Iranian Kurds had taken three Italians in Iraq prisoner and were demanding the withdrawal of Italian forces for their release. Kuwait announced that the PRC had agreed to reflag Kuwaiti tankers and would deploy forces to the Gulf.

TABLE 9.7 Targets in the Tanker War as of October 12, 1987

Year/Country	By Iran	By Iraq	Total
Total Attacks by Source			
1981	0	5	5
1982	0	22	22
1983	0	16	16
1984	53	18	71
1985	33	14	47
1986	66	45	101
1987	62	61	123
Target by National Flag of Ship Involved			
Australia	0	1	1
Bahamas	1	2	3
Belgium	1	0	1
China	1	0	1
Cyprus	9	33	43
FRG	1	4	5
France	5	0	5
Greece	10	22	32
India	4	4	8
Iran	0	48	48
Italy	1	1	2
Japan	9	0	9
Kuwait	11	0	11
Liberia	24	36	60
Malta	1	11	13
Netherlands	0	2	2
North Korea	0	1	1
Norway	4	1	5
Pakistan	2	0	2
Panama	18	28	46
Philippines	3	0	3
Qatar	2	1	3
Saudi Arabia	9	2	11
Singapore	1	5	6
South Korea	3	3	6
Spain	3	0	3
Sri Lanka	1	0	1
Turkey	2	8	10
UAE	1	0	1
U.S.	1	0	1
USSR	2	0	2
Yugoslavia	1	0	1
Unknown	2	42	44

(continues)

TABLE 9.7   *(continued)*

Flag of Target	1984	1985	1986	1987
Iranian Target by National Flag of Ship Involved,				
Including Mine and Silkworm Strikes				
Bahamas	—	—	—	2
Belgium	—	1	—	—
Cyprus	—	1	3	5
Denmark	—	—	—	2
France	—	—	4	1
FRG	—	2	—	—
Greece	—	1	5	9
India	2	—	—	2
Italy	—	—	—	1
Japan	—	—	1	5
Kuwait	4	2	2	4
Liberia	3	2	9	18
Maldives	—	—	—	2
Netherlands	—	—	2	4
Pakistan	1	—	—	1
Panama	4	2	5	10
Philippines	—	—	—	1
PRC	—	—	—	1
Qatar	—	—	1	1
Romania	—	—	—	2
Saudi Arabia	1	1	3	5
Singapore	—	—	—	2
South Korea	—	1	1	2
Soviet Union	—	—	—	2
Spain	1	—	—	2
UAE	—	—	1	1
United Kingdom	1	1	1	2
United States	—	—	—	2
Total	17	14	41	89

SOURCES: Adapted from the *Washington Post*, October 13, 1987, p.1, and information provided by the Center for Defense Information and the U.S. Navy.

Iran's Silkworm Attacks on Kuwait

On October 15, Iran added yet another new level of escalation to the war in the Gulf. It again fired a Silkworm missile at Kuwait from Faw, 40 miles to the north. This time, however, it hit a U.S.-owned tanker with Liberian registry. The tanker was the 275,932-ton *Sungari*, which was anchored in the Shuaiba Anchorage in Kuwaiti waters. The strike caused serious damage, but no injuries. It also showed that Kuwait had failed to reposition its Hawk defenses to Failaka Island, which was south of Bubiyan and provided an ideal location to defend Kuwait's port. The most Kuwaiti forces on Failaka could do was to fire a few ineffective short-range SA-7 manportable missiles.

Western intelligence exports estimated that Iran had a total of 50 to 70 Silkworm missiles and 12 launchers. According to some reports, the missile attacks were carried out by the 26th (Salman) Missile Brigade, which was located near Salman. The brigade, and a newly formed 36th Assef Brigade, were stationed in Faw and were under the command of Derakhshan—an aide of Rafsanjani. They were affiliated with the Guards Corps 1st Naval Region under the command of an officer named Sotoodeh. Another brigade remained in the Sirrik region, about 50 kilometers south of the town of Minhab in Iran's southern coastal province of Hormozgan, on the eastern side of the Straits of Hormuz. The 36th Brigade had been stationed at Sirrik originally, but had moved through Shiraz by truck.

The U.S. did not react to this missile attack. It stated that the attack was against Kuwait and not against a U.S.-flagged ship. This again reflected the decision by the Reagan Administration to avoid any commitment to defend Kuwaiti territory.[112] Most importantly, the U.S. did not want to create a further barrier to the UN cease-fire effort and had previously been told by Kuwait that it would be responsible for any defense of its territory.

Iran, however, proceeded to force the Reagan Administration's hand. On October 16, Iran fired another Silkworm missile into a tanker. This time, however, it was a U.S.-flagged Kuwaiti tanker, the *Sea Island City*. The missile hit the tanker about seven miles east of the Mina al Ahmadi port and two miles south of the oil terminal at Kuwait's sea island. It blinded the American captain, wounded the American radio officer, and wounded 17 other members of the crew, eight seriously. To make this worse, the French minesweeping force found four more submerged mines in the lower Gulf that same day.

While it was uncertain that Iran had deliberately chosen a U.S. flag target for its Silkworm strike, the U.S. stated it would retaliate because it was an attack on a U.S. flag vessel, and the U.S. would protect such vessels anywhere in the world. On October 18, President Reagan announced that the U.S. had chosen its option and would act. On October 19, the U.S. retaliated with a carefully limited attack. Its choice of target came only after prolonged debate and a full meeting of the National Security Planning Group (NSPG) under deputy national security advisor, Colin L. Powell. The U.S. had difficulty in attacking the Silkworm sites at Faw for several reasons. The Iranians were well aware of the vulnerability of their missiles. They normally kept them dispersed, set up the missiles at their sites at night, fired them near dawn, and immediately dispersed. They were so far up the Gulf that trying to hit the missiles while they were at the launch sites presented operational problems for U.S. carrier aircraft. There was a risk that U.S. aircraft might fly more than 600 miles into an area with large numbers of land-based SHORADS and hit nothing but the ramps and bunkers in the built-up site.

Further, the Iranian launch site was at the extreme southern tip of the Faw Peninsula. A U.S. strike on any target in Faw had the disadvantage that it would appear to aid Iraq. As a result, it was likely to do the most damage to the UN peace effort and further undermine the neutral status of the U.S. It also risked making an open-ended commitment to Kuwait that the U.S. not only was not ready to make, but which required bases in Kuwait or Saudi Arabia that the U.S. did not have.

These factors help explain why the Reagan Administration decided on a visible show of force in the Gulf. Four U.S. warships—the destroyers *Kidd, Leftwich, Young,* and *Hoel*—moved to within visible distance of Iran's Rustam offshore oil platform in the lower Gulf, about 120 miles east of Bahrain. They had air cover from two F-14s and an E-2C and were supported by the guided-missile cruiser *Standley* and the frigate *Thatch*. This oil platform had produced oil from the small Rashadat oil field of about 18,000 barrels a day, but oil production had halted about two years earlier. Further, Iraqi aircraft had heavily damaged the platform in November 1986 and knocked out the bridge between its two main units. It was now being used by Iranian forces, and these forces had fired on a U.S. helicopter on October 8.

The U.S. warships radioed to warn the naval Guards on the platform and allowed them to evacuate. They then fired some 1,065 rounds into the platform with their Mark-45 l guns.[113] This gunfire set the platform afire, and SEAL teams then seized the two halves of the platform and blew it up. In the process, the SEAL teams saw Iranian troops evacuating from a second platform. They investigated and found that this platform was also being used as a base, and they used explosives to largely destroy it. The SEALs who took the platforms found that both were armed and used for weapons storage and were equipped with radars or other surveillance equipment which the Iranians used to track tankers and other ships in the Gulf. The entire incident took about 85 minutes, and the only Iranian response was to launch an F-4, which turned back the moment its radar acquired a picture of the size of the U.S. forces in the area.[114]

While Secretary Weinberger ended his announcement of the U.S. attack by stating that "we now consider this matter closed," the U.S.

attack scarcely acted as a definitive deterrent to further Iranian action, and it left a number of U.S. planners unsatisfied. They felt the response was so limited that it did not act as a real deterrent. In fact, the Chairman of the Joint Chiefs and other U.S. military planners had strongly urged an attack on Farsi Island or an Iranian combat ship. Virtually all U.S. policymakers and planners wanted to avoid a level of escalation that would block any hope of the UN cease-fire proposal succeeding and commit the U.S. to a full-scale war at sea. At the same time, many felt such a limited U.S. response would actually encourage further Iranian action.

As for foreign reactions, the British, French, and West German governments sent messages of support, although the French statement expressed some fear of further escalation, and the Belgian, Dutch, and Italian governments were silent. Most of the smaller Gulf states made cautious statements. Saudi Arabia and Jordan expressed their support, but Crown Prince Abdullah ibn Abdul Aziz of Saudi Arabia—who was visiting Washington—made it clear that he wished the U.S. had attacked the Silkworm sites as well.

Kuwait issued a statement reiterating that it would not offer the U.S. bases but that Iran had committed repeated aggressive acts and had been repeatedly warned to stop its attacks before the U.S. reaction.[115] The USSR, however, continued to distance itself from U.S. policy. The Soviets kept their military presence in the Gulf down to one frigate and half a dozen minesweepers and supply ships. They called for restraint on all anti-ship attacks by both Iran and Iraq and continued to demand the withdrawal of all foreign fleets and reliance on diplomatic solutions. At the same time, the USSR continued to expand relations with Iran and to sell arms to Iran as well as Iraq.

Iran's first response to the U.S. strike was to issue a mix of new threats against the U.S. and to briefly shell northern Kuwait. While the twelfth U.S. convoy up the Gulf left without incident, Iran accused the U.S. of causing $500 million in damage and cutting Iran's oil production by 25,000 barrels a day. Iran also, however, held emergency consultations with Moscow, and the Soviet press denounced the attack as "military adventurism." Iran had clearly begun to realize its actions earlier in the year had pointlessly alienated a number of useful foreign governments. It was particularly careful to increase its courting of the USSR. It suddenly dropped all attacks on the USSR from the usual Friday diatribes against foreign nations and suddenly resumed Aeroflot flights to Tehran.

Iran, however, was still committed to military action. On October 22, Iran fired another Silkworm missile at Kuwait's Sea Island, an oil-loading facility nine miles out in the Gulf from the Ahmadi oil complex. This third Iranian Silkworm strike again raised questions about Iranian targeting, since the Silkworm missile either had to be fired into the harbor area and allowed to home on the largest target it could find or had to be retargeted by some observer within line-of-sight of the target. This made it difficult to be certain whether Iran was chosing specific targets or simply firing into an area where it knew the missile would find a target. The ships normally near Sea Island had now been moved away, however, and its 100-foot height made it by far the largest radar blip in the area. This made it easy for Iran to chose a target outside the direct coverage of the U.S. reflagging agreement without any difficulty.

The strike also had a much more significant effect than the previous strikes against tankers because the missile fragmented when it hit Sea Island and did extensive damage, although only one loading arm was seriously hit. The Sea Island terminal is a 2,500-foot-long pier which was the only facility in water deep enough so Kuwait could easily load supertankers of up to 500,000 tons. It provides some 33 percent of Kuwait's oil export flow and can handle a peak of 80 percent. It was then handling roughly 200,000 barrels of crude oil per day of Kuwait's average production of about 600,000 barrels. Kuwait's two other terminals were in shallower channels better suited to tankers of 150,000 tons.

The Sea Island terminal was not loading any tankers when it was hit, but the oil lines to it were pressurized, and the missile started a major oil fire in its overflow tanks and sent up a smoke column over 300 feet in height. The fire was out by early in the afternoon, but enough damage was done to force Kuwait to jury-rig alternative loading facilities and close the island. Kuwait's exports of roughly 600,000 barrels a day of petroleum products were not affected, but the Sea Island had to be closed until late November.[116]

The U.S. did not respond militarily to the new Iranian attack. It again took the position that it had no obligation to defend Kuwait.[117] The U.S. did, however, quietly help Kuwait plan the redeployment of part of the its 12,000-man army to help secure the island of Bubiyan and prevent any quick Iranian amphibious attack that might seize this strategic location between the Faw Peninsula and the Kuwaiti mainland. The U.S. reached an arrangement with Kuwait to deploy a large barge off the coast of Kuwait similar to the ones it had off the coasts of Bahrain and Saudi Arabia.

This allowed both the U.S. and Kuwait to avoid the problems inherent in any formal U.S. base on Kuwaiti territory but gave the U.S. a facility where it could stage attack, reconnaissance, and mine-warfare helicopters, army and navy commando units, and deploy intelligence sensors and electronic warfare equipment.[118] Finally, the U.S. also speeded up its effort to assist Kuwait in setting up decoys and other countermeasures to the Silkworm and in re-siting its Hawk missiles to Failaka to provide coverage against the Silkworm. In fact, the new Iranian strike on Kuwait led to a scramble throughout the rest of the southern Gulf for air-defense systems, as each GCC country sought to try to improve the defense of its own oil facilities. Bahrain asked the U.S. to speed up action on its request for 70 Stingers and 14 launchers, and the UAE quietly revived previous requests for the sale of Stingers and other U.S. air-defense equipment.[119]

During the rest of October, Iran was careful to avoid direct provocation of the U.S., and the thirteenth U.S. convoy through the Gulf arrived in Kuwait without incident. Iran seemed to be waiting to see if the U.S. would take the initiative and suspended most of its naval activity in the Gulf. Iran did, however, claim on October 24 that three of its fighters had flown within 10 miles of a U.S. warship in spite of warnings not to do so. Iran did, however, continue to use terrorism. A Pan American World Airways office in Kuwait was bombed on October 24. Pro-Iranian groups in Lebanon—such as the Islamic Jihad—revived the threat of terrorism during late October. They exhibited photos of the damage to the U.S. Embassy and Marine Corps barracks in Beirut, showed new films of the hostages, they still kept, threatened to take new hostages, and threatened to send suicide volunteers to the Gulf.

Iraq, however, continued to fight its tanker and oil wars. Iraq used its air power to demonstrate that it would not accept any form of partial cease-fire that only affected the tanker war. At the same time, it pursued a shift in its air strategy that it had begun in late August. It attempted to hit Iran's refinery system and power plants with sufficient force to make it difficult for Iran to provide fuel and power during the winter. This strategy had the potential advantage that it could cripple Iran's economy more quickly than an embargo on oil exports and that Iraq could reduce the number of its attacks in the Gulf and the resulting pressure from other states to halt them. During late October, Iraqi jets hit the Agha Jari oil field in southwest Iran, a refinery in Shiraz, and Iran's shuttle tankers. While Iraq also claimed a hit on a supertanker, it seems to have hit a hulk that was moored near the tankers as a decoy. Iraq claimed that these strikes were in response for the 134 killed and 2,036 wounded that resulted from the four Scud strikes Iran had launched against Baghdad in October.

Iran responded to Iraq's attacks by charging that Iraq was bombing civilian targets, and Iranian radio warned that the rulers of Baghdad should anticipate the "deadly response of the combatants of Islam as long as they continue their wicked acts." It warned all Iraqi civilians living near economic and military targets to abandon their homes and seek refuge in the holy cities of Najaf, Karbala, Kadhimain, and Samarra. Iran, however, could only carry out a few symbolic air raids and fire occasional Scud missiles. For example, Iran fired a total of five Scud missiles at Baghdad between October 4 and October 31. While each attack produced casualties, the volume of fire was so sporadic and the targets were so random that they almost unquestionably did more to increase popular hostility to Iran than to deter Iraq's use of its air power.[120]

Iraq had effectiveness problems of its own. It began to make an increasing number of claims to have damaged Iranian ships that later proved false. For example, Iraq claimed to have hit three Iranian tankers on October 28, 1987. In reality, however, no successful Iraqi attack on shipping took place between October 21 and November 4, when Iraqi jets hit the *Taftan*, a 290,000-dwt (dead weight ton) VLCC that was part of the National Iranian Tanker Company's shuttle fleet and which was loading at Kharg.[121]

Iran did not attack any ship moving in the Gulf between October 21 and November 6, 1987. It then, however, resumed its pattern of choosing the kind of indirect and peripheral targets in the Gulf that could embarrass the West but which would not provide a major Western response. It started to hit ships that were not flying U.S., British, French, Dutch, Italian, or Belgian flags. Iran seemed to be shifting to a lower-level war of attrition with the West in which it hoped that it could keep up constant low-level pressure on Gulf shipping while forcing the U.S. and its allies to maintain massive military deployments they would lack a reason to use.

On November 6, 1987, Iran's naval Pasdaran forces carried out a speed boat attack from Abu Musa that fired rocket-propelled grenades at a U.S.-operated tanker. This ship was the 105,484-dwt *Grand Wisdom*, which was sailing about 20 miles west of the main UAE port of Jebel Ali.[122] This attack came without warning and was the first attack against a foreign tanker since one of Iran's Silkworm missiles hit the *Sea Island City* on October 16. The Iranian attack on the *Grand Wisdom* seems to have involved the careful choice of a target that would affect the U.S. but which would avoid the consequences of attacking a ship flying under the U.S. flag. Further, it seems to have been carefully timed to embarrass the U.S. The Iranians hit the *Grand Wisdom* when it was near the guided missile cruiser USS *Rentz*. The *Rentz* had an attack helicopter on board but could take no action other than shadow the crippled *Grand Wisdom* as it sailed back to Jebel Ali.[123]

Both sides kept up their attacks on shipping during the second week in November, and Iraq continued to claim far more hits than it actually scored. Iraq claimed it hit eleven ships during this period but seems to have hit no more than three. On November 11, two Iranian gunboats hit a Japanese tanker. It was then sailing within 15 miles of the 17th U.S. convoy through the Gulf and was near a French warship escorting two French tankers. The gunboats also struck at a point when the USS *Missouri* and the cruiser *Bunker Hill* had entered the Gulf for the first time in order to escort the 12-ship U.S. convoy as it sailed through the "Silkworm envelope" at the Straits. A Soviet merchant ship reported an unconfirmed sighting of mines in the same general area. The Iranians had again showed that the Western rules of engagement could not protect freedom of navigation in the Gulf, although the U.S. did quietly add Bahrain-flagged tankers to one of its convoys for the first time.[124]

Further, Iraqi and Iranian attacks occurred during November 12–15, 1987, although it is important to note that each side hit less than one ship per day. Iraq, for example, claimed to have hit 15 ships between November 9 and November 15 but only damaged three. Both sides also attacked civilian targets. Iran bombarded Basra, and Iraq bombed the district capital of Kamyaran, about 50 miles east of the border. Iraq kept up its attacks on Iran's oil facilities and claimed to have attacked three Iranian oil fields—at Abed al-Khan, Marun, and Kaj Saran—on November 14, 1987. On November 16, however, Iranian speedboats attacked three tankers in one day. They hit the U.S.-managed Liberian tanker *Lucy* near the Straits of Hormuz. They also hit a U.S.-owned ship under the Bahamanian flag, the *Esso Freeport*. It marked the first time in the war that Iran had hit a ship owned directly by a major U.S. oil company like Exxon. Finally, they hit a small Greek-owned tanker, the *Filikon L.*

The air and sea wars continued to follow a similar pattern for the rest of the month. Iraq claimed Iran had attacked a hospital on November 19 and two major generating complexes at the Reza Shah and El-Diz dams on November 29. Both Iraq and Iran hit a ship nearly every three to four days, although Iraq claimed a total of 21 successful attacks during the 12 days between November 8 and November 20 and only actually scored four.[125] U.S. minesweepers found thirteen mines in the waters near Farsi Island during November 20–25, and U.K. mine forces found five more mines northeast of Bahrain, although it was unclear whether these were new or old Iranian mine deployments.

Iran's attacks on shipping during November affected only a small proportion of the shipping to and from Kuwait. Nevertheless, they did have some effect. Insurance rates continued to rise, and Kuwait decided on November 26 to keep the now repaired *Bridgeton* out of its tanker shuttle. The 401,382-ton ship was the only one of the 11 reflagged vessels that carried crude oil; the others carried gasoline, liquid natural gas (LNG), and refined products. This meant that U.S. convoys would only escort smaller tankers carrying product and that the only ship carrying crude oil was dropped from the convoy system. Even though Iran did not hit U.S. ships, it did succeed in forcing the U.S. convoy effort to lag far behind schedule. By the end of November, the U.S. had only completed 18 one-way convoys, or less than 5 a month. This compared with an original goal of 10 per month.

Further, the U.S. still faced a mine-warfare problem. MSOs deployed from the U.S. joined the MSCs and helicopters already in the Gulf in early November and became a fully operational mine-sweeping unit by mid-November. British, Dutch, and Italian units also operated independently in the area.[126] Nevertheless, Iran still had the remnants of 3 mine fields with 60 mines in the Gulf. While many of the mines had been swept and Iranian minelaying activity had halted or been sharply curtailed, there were reports that Iran was building new mines and might be getting more modern influence mines from Libya.[127]

The only direct military incident between the U.S. and Iran during this period occurred on November 22, when Iran claimed that it had fired on four U.S. helicopters. This latter claim was made by Commodore Mohammed Hussein Malekzadegan but seems to have been little more than part of a propaganda campaign in which Iran was using the U.S. threat to try to boost internal morale. It occurred a day after Hussein Alaie, a commander of the naval Guards, announced that no political solution to the U.S. presence in the Gulf was possible and that Iran had drawn up plans to destroy the U.S. fleet.[128]

These events left the U.S. with the alternatives of expanding its military presence, seeking immediate UN Security Council action on sanctions, or waiting and trying to mobilize added support for military and economic sanctions on a bilateral basis. The U.S. chose the latter option but had little success.

The military action in December 1987 concentrated on the tanker war. Iraq hit occasional land targets, including Iran's dams and refineries, and continued to strike at the Iranian tanker shuttle. As a result, roughly 60 percent of all the attacks on shipping during 1987 took place in the last four months of the year and after the failure of the temporary UN cease-fire on August 29. These attacks reached their peak in December. Twenty-one attacks occurred in November, but 34 occurred in December.[129]

Iran increasingly targeted its strikes against Kuwait and Saudi Arabia. Seventy-three of the 80 attacks Iran conducted on Gulf shipping in 1987 were enroute to and from Kuwait and Saudi Arabia. Iran averaged 3–6 attacks on shipping enroute to and from Kuwait during each month of the year and steadily increased its attacks enroute to and from Saudi Arabia at the end of the year. The cumulative total of Iranian attacks on shipping to Saudi Arabia was only 1 in February, 3 through March and April, and 7 through June and August. It reached 16 in September, 22 in October, 26 in November, and 38 in December.[130] These attacks did not affect oil flows from Saudi Arabia, but they did briefly threaten crude-oil exports from Kuwait. The U.S. convoy effort provided security for Kuwait's exports of product and liquid natural gas, but most crude oil shipments operated outside the convoys.

The attacks also forced tanker captains in the Gulf to try measures such as joining the tail end of Western convoys, maintaining radio silence, and even simulating convoys on radar by moving in convoy-like lines at night. These measures may have helped reassure the tanker captain and crew, but they had little real impact on vulnerability because of the constant Iranian patrols in the Gulf.

These Iranian attacks peaked shortly before Christmas. While the Guards conducted most attacks, the regular Iranian Navy sent out its frigates, and Iranian forces carried out three major attacks on crude-oil tankers enroute to Kuwait between December 18 and 23. Iranian frigates shelled a Norwegian tanker on the 18th and a Liberian tanker on the 22nd. The next day, naval Guards forces attacked another Norwegian tanker. These attacks did not injure the crews, but they did make all three ships unfit to carry crude oil. They were serious enough to force Kuwait to renew its use of the *Bridgeton* to ship crude oil and to include it in the U.S. convoy effort.

The exact sequence of events which halted this escalation is uncertain, but the U.S. seems to have quietly threatened Iran, and Syria seems to have put pressure on Iran to halt its attacks. Iraq also carried out an unusually long-range air strike on the Iranian tanker shuttle near Larak on December 22 and showed it could hit four of the supertankers which had been deployed there as oil storage ships. The 564,739-ton *Seawise Giant*, the world's largest tanker, was one of Iraq's targets.[131] Regardless of the cause, Iran avoided Western-escorted ships throughout the rest of the winter of 1987–1988 and rapidly reduced the intensity of its attacks. As a result, Kuwait was able to increase its crude-oil exports from around 970,000 barrels per day during the first two quarters of the year to 1.2 million barrels per day during most of the winter.[132] Further, Lloyd's reduced its war-risk premium from 0.75 percent to 0.45 percent in February 1988.[133]

As for the overall pattern of the tanker war, one estimate is shown in Table 9.8. Other sources indicate that there were a total of 80 Iranian attacks and 83 Iraqi attacks on shipping during 1987. These attacks raised the total number of attacks since 1984 to 180 Iranian attacks and 215 Iraqi attacks. It is important to note, however, that most of these attacks had only limited lethality. At the end of 1987, Iran had only destroyed or heavily damaged a total 16 ships since the beginning of 1984, and Iraq had only destroyed 49 and heavily damaged 9. While Iraq increased its total number of attacks on shipping from 65 in 1986 to 83 in 1987, Iranian oil exports through the Gulf were 40 percent higher in 1987 than in 1986, demonstrating that oil prices and the oil glut were more important than the tanker war. In fact, both Iran and Iraq steadily increased their oil exports throughout the second half of 1987.[134]

The mine war virtually faded from the world's headlines in late 1987. The mix of U.S. and allied mine-warfare forces in the Gulf not only had at least temporarily checked the Iranian mine threat, they allowed the U.S. to withdraw some of its smaller mine vessels and mine-warfare helicopters. Further, British, Dutch, and Belgian minesweepers were able to withdraw from the central Gulf. While some 80 mines had been detected and neutralized since the beginning of 1987, British ships had recently found only 4 mines laid earlier in the year, and the Belgian and Dutch ships had not found any.[135]

As for the missile war, Iran fired another Silkworm missile at Kuwait on December 6, 1987. This missile was aimed at the Mina al-Ahmadi terminal, but this time it failed to hit its target. The U.S. had helped Kuwait develop nearly a dozen barges with large reflector targets that decoyed the Silkworms away from nearby tankers and oil facilities.[136] One of these barges was about a mile from the terminal, and the missile veered away and struck the barge.[137] This Iranian attack may have been a response to the fact the U.S. had leaked that it had Kuwait's agreement to charter a Kuwaiti-owned barge to use as a third sensor, electronic warfare, special forces, and helicopter base. The U.S. also informed the press it would deploy this barge just inside Kuwaiti waters or just outside the waters of the Neutral Zone.[138] The fact Kuwait was willing to permit this and to provide a Kuwaiti barge for charter led to immediate Iranian threats against Kuwait and the U.S.[139] Iran was careful to limit its actions, however, and did not repeat its Silkworm attacks during the rest of 1987 and during the first two months of 1988.

The U.S. had less reason to be happy with other developments in the missile war. There were new reports that the PRC had sold Iran additional Silkworms and new types of anti-ship missiles, such as the

TABLE 9.8 The Pattern of Iranian and Iraqi Attacks in the Tanker War: 1984–1987

Year	Air-Launched Systems			Helicopter-Launched Missiles	Missiles from Ships	Rockets Grenades Gunfire from Ships	Mines	Unknown	Total Attacks
	Missiles	Rockets	Bombs						
1984									
Iraq	35	—	—	—	—	—	2	16	53
Iran	(18)	—	—	—	—	—	—	—	18
Total	52	—	—	—	—	—	—	16	71
1985									
Iraq	32	—	1	—	—	—	—	—	33
Iran	(10)	—	—	3	—	—	—	1	14
Total	(42)	—	—	3	—	—	—	1	47
1986									
Iraq	52	4	1	1	—	—	—	8	66
Iran	(9)	—	—	26	4	1	—	5	45
Total	(65)	—	1	27	4	1	—	13	110
1987 (to October 12, 1987)									
Iraq	57	—	3	—	—	—	—	2	62
Iran	—	—	—	1	14	34	8	5	62
Total	57	—	3	1	14	34	8	7	124
Total: 1984 to 1987									
Iraq	176	4	5	1	—	—	2	26	214
Iran	(37)	—	—	30	18	35	8	11	139
Total	(217)	—	5	31	18	35	10	37	353

SOURCES: Adapted from Bruce McCartan, "The Tanker War," *Armed Forces Journal*, November 1987, pp. 74–76, and reporting by Lloyd's and Exxon.

Chinese version of the Soviet Styx, the Chao PTG.[140] There were also reports that the PRC sold Iran up to 100 of the latest sea-skimming versions of missiles, such as C-601 and C-801.

Even so, the U.S. often had more reason to fear Iraq on a day-to-day basis than Iran. Iraq continued its often erratic air sorties in the Gulf and bombed a Saudi island by mistake. It flew Mirage F-1 attack sorties in the direction of U.S. combat ships. Further, it tried to launch its own purchases of Silkworm missiles from its Soviet and PRC-made bombers. Iraqi Tu-16s first approached a U.S. combat ship and had to be warned away. They then hit a tanker on the way to a Saudi port. In mid-February, an Iraqi bomber launched Silkworm missiles that flew within eight miles of a U.S. convoy. Oddly enough, Iraq did not use the bombers to extend its attack range down to Lavan, perhaps because it felt the bombers were too vulnerable to Iran's remaining fighters.[141]

The situation remained potentially explosive. Nevertheless, the U.S. was sufficiently confident by the beginning of January 1988 to begin cutting its naval deployments in the Gulf and the Indian Ocean. U.S. combatant strength, which had risen from 6 ships in January and February, to 13 in March through June, and then up to 24 in September through November, dropped to 22 in December. The U.S. rotated-in smaller ships to replace the *Guadalcanal* and several other vessels and began to adjust its forces to withdraw the battle group with the battleship *Iowa* from the region.

By the end of February, the total U.S. force had dropped from a peak of 39 ships of all types to only 25. The U.S. also sent back the rest of the 8 RH-53D Sea Stallion minesweeping helicopters it had deployed in August. These reductions did not produce any immediate Iranian response. The U.S. completed its 40th convoy without incident, and no deliberate Iranian attack on any Western-escorted convoy occurred through mid-March.[142]

Further, the U.S. consolidated the command of its forces in the Gulf so that command of land, air, and naval forces were all centered in a single officer based on the flagship of the Middle East Task Force off Bahrain. Under the previous system, one officer had commanded most operations actually in the Gulf while another, based on the battleship *Iowa*—hundreds of miles outside the Gulf—commanded most naval forces. Creating a single command in the Gulf also created one chain of command, reporting through USCENTCOM, to the Chairman of the Joint Chiefs in Washington.[143] At the same time, the U.S. announced that it was altering its rules of engagement to allow U.S. Navy ships to come to the aid of any NATO allied warship that asked for assistance. This formalized an arrangement that had tacitly existed since the beginning of Western deployments in the Gulf.[144]

The net result of nearly six months of war at sea was to create a relatively stable pattern of Western intervention, where Iran could challenge the U.S. and other Western forces, but only at the cost of immediate U.S. retaliation of a kind that presented little real risk to the U.S. While Iran could always strike at individual ships, it could not hope to use its Navy, the naval branch of the Guards, or its Silkworms to achieve any major results. In spite of the problems inherent in reflagging and mistakes at the beginning of the convoy effort, the U.S. had largely achieved its objectives. Iran, in contrast, had achieved a remarkable degree of isolation from its southern Gulf neighbors and the West with no perceptible benefits. It also had made it far harder for its purchasing agents to obtain arms, ammunition, and spares from the West and had created a situation where its own flow of oil exports was virtually a free-fire zone for Iraq, but every action it took increased the tilt of outside nations toward Iraq. Like the war on the land, Iran's leadership had done a great deal to defeat itself.

Notes

1. Iran's stocks of Harpoon may have been limited to seven missiles for its Kaman-class fast attack craft. Iran's stocks of surface-to-air missiles were so low that it tried to convert some of its standard ship-to-ship missiles to an air-to-surface role. Larry Dickerson, "Iranian Power Projection in the Gulf," *World Weapons Review*, August 12, 1987, p. 7.

2. *New York Times*, January 20, 1987, p. A-1; *Philadelphia Inquirer*, January 21, 1987, p. 5A; *Observer*, January 25, 1987; *Washington Times*, February 5, 1987, p. 7A; *Baltimore Sun*, March 1, 1987, p. 24. Many of these attacks took place outside Iranian waters and off the shore of the UAE. Little effort seems to have been made to identify the targets. The *Wu Jiang*, for example, was a PRC-registered freighter with no cargo of military value.

3. Iran's Sea Killers could be deployed in both a helicopter-launched and a deck-mounted configuration. The deck mount was a five round trainable launcher which could be integrated with the existing X-band radars, conical scan radars, and shipboard computers on many small combat ships.

The helicopter-fired version could be mounted on any medium-lift helicopter, although it was originally configured for use with the Agusta/Sikorsky SH-3D and AB-212. The heliborne system includes an MM/APQ-706 tracking radar, a missile control console, guidance computer, command link, optical tracker with joystick, pilot display, and Sea Killer/Marte missile.

The heliborne system weighs 865–1,165 kilograms, with 300–600 kilograms for one to two missiles, 400 kilograms for the launch console, 143 kilograms for the radar, and 22 kilograms for the optical sight. The missile can be fired directly from a helicopter flying at medium altitude or the helicopter can acquire the target on its radar, pop down to fly under a ship's radar, and then pop up to fire the missile. General Dynamics, *The World's Missile Systems— 1982*, Pomona, General Dynamics, 1982, pp. 233–234; Bill Gunston, *Modern Airborne Missiles*, New York, ARCO, 1983, pp. 110–111.

4. *Washington Times*, February 5, 1987, p. 7A.

5. *Baltimore Sun*, March 29, 1987, p. 1A.

6. The Armilla Patrol was set up in 1980 with four combat ships but was reduced to two in 1982, when Britain had to establish a permanent presence in the South Atlantic. A Type-42 destroyer was normally assigned to provide medium-range air defense, and a Type-22 or Leander-class frigate with Sea Wolf was assigned to provide an anti-missile capability. Only ships under the British flag or more than 505 beneficially owned are eligible for British protection, but Britain lets other ships join its convoys. Technically, the British warships accompany cargo ships rather than escort them, which implies wartime conditions. *Jane's Defence Weekly*, May 2, 1987, p. 824; *Christian Science Monitor*, January 21, 1987, p. 1; *Washington Post*, January 28, 1987, p. A-1.

7. *Washington Post*, March 24, 1987, p. A-25, and August 23, 1987, p. 12.

8. According to some Western sources, Iran had decided to buy the system in early 1986. In January, the Minister in charge of the Guards Corps, Mohsen Rafiqdoust, sent a team headed by an Iranian official named Riazi to the PRC. Riazi is associated with Rafsanjani and seems to have signed a $400 million contract for the Silkworm and HQ2J missiles. The first set of missiles arrived at Bandar Abbas in March 1986. In June, 52 regular navy officers and NCOs and 50 naval Guards personnel were secretly sent to China for training in the use of the Silkworm. Upon their return, one cadre established a training center at the Navy missile depot at Bandar Abbas in the First Naval Region. A second cadre formed two additional missile brigades which were later sent to the Faw Peninsula. Also see *Jane's Defence Weekly*, June 6, 1987, p. 1113, and *New York Times*, June 16, 1987, p. A-11.

9. Adapted from unclassified data provided by General Dynamics and *Jane's Defence Weekly*, June 6, 1987, p. 1113.

10. Free-floating mines were becoming a growing problem in the Gulf during this period. The Qatari and other navies were routinely destroying such mines with naval gunfire. *Jane's Defence Weekly*, May 2, 1987, p. 824; *Washington Post*, March 24, 1987, p. A-25.

11. Reports surfaced at this time that the changes in Iran's strike capabilities were not confined solely to anti-ship capabilities. There were reports that China was transferring enough technology to allow Iran to begin assembling or coproducing its own surface-to-surface missile or a Chinese variant of the FROG and Scud missiles. While such missiles could not threaten shipping, they could give Iran another way of offsetting Iraq's advantage in the air. While the FROG variant had a range of only about 40 miles, it could reach Basra. The Scud variant had a range of up to 180 miles and gave Iran the potential ability to fire at large area targets in Kuwait and the southern Gulf states. *Baltimore Sun*, March 29, 1987, p. 1A.

12. Caspar W. Weinberger, *A Report to Congress on Security Arrangements in the Gulf*, Department of Defense, June 15, 1987, p. 5.

13. Kuwait's conservative production policy has led to a decline in production and deficit spending. It earned $12.28 billion from oil exports in 1984, $10.46 billion in 1985, and $6.38 billion in 1986. It has the capacity, however, to produce nearly 3 million barrels per day. Its Fund for the Future has $40 billion in holdings and receives 10 percent of state revenues each year. It holds money in trust for Kuwait until the year 2001 and is one of the largest single foreign investors in the West. It owns such major Western oil firms as Santa Fe International and has major refining and other downstream investments, as well as a large tanker fleet. Only about 10 percent of Kuwait's income is now tied to crude in comparison with downstream products. *Washington Post*, July 5, 1987, p. A-1; *Christian Science Monitor*, July 10, 1987, p. 9; *Wall Street Journal*, June 25, 1987, p.1, July 23, 1987, p. 26.

14. *Washington Post*, August 28, 1987, p. A-16.

15. Kuwait denies providing any direct military support to Iraq. *Washington Times*, June 22, 1987, p. A-6.

16. This later became public when Secretary of the Navy James H. Webb sent a highly critical memo to Secretary of Defense Weinberger in July 1987 expressing his concern that the U.S. was being drawn into a morass and was building up a massive force without a clear assessment of the risks, limits to the forces involved, or ability to predict the course of the war. *Philadelphia Inquirer*, September 6, 1987, p. 9A.

17. *New York Times*, June 16, 1987, p. A-11.

18. *Washington Times*, April 14, 1987, p. 6A; *Washington Post*, May 5, 1987, p. A-1, and May 14, 1987, p. A-27; *Chicago Tribune*, April 18, 1987, p. Q-8; *Economist*, April 18, 1987, p. 39.

19. These claims were made by Colonel Behzad Moezi during Mujahideen-e-Khalq sponsored meetings with the press. He also claimed (a) that Iran had shot down 55 of its own planes because of the lack of functioning IFF and radar systems, including a Falcon jet transport which he said was shot down by a U.S.-supplied Hawk missile in early February, (b) that only 30–40 percent of Iran's C-130 transports were flyable and that several had crashed because of poor maintenance, (c) that two-thirds of the overall mix of 65 fighters Iran had operational were not 100 percent functional, (d) that all RF-4Es were shot down or lost, (e) that 1–2 of Iran's remaining P-3Cs out of a prewar total of 6 had serious computer and sensor problems, (f) that only 6–10 F-14s were still operational, (g) that only four tankers were still operational, (h) that over 180 pilots had defected and many with their aircraft, (i) that too few specialists remained to keep Iran's planes flying, and (j) that pilots were briefed on their missions only an hour or so before attacks to keep them from having time to plan defections. *Washington Times*, February 12, 1987, p. 6A, and *Aviation Week*, February 23, 1987, p. 25.

20. *Washington Times*, February 20, 1987, p. 8A; *Washington Post*, February 24, 1987, p. A-1; *Washington Post*, February 19, 1987, p. A-23.

21. The Chinese version of the SA-2 is an obsolete missile which was first deployed in 1958. It is lethal only against fighters flying at medium to high altitudes which do not use their radar warning receivers effectively enough to allow them to maneuver and dodge the missile. It is a radar-guided system

using the Fan Song Radar and a computer-aided command link. The missile has a maximum effective range of about 30 kilometers, a slant range of 50 kilometers, and a ceiling of around 5,500 meters. It is a large complex system requiring a well-prepared ground sight. The missile alone weighs 2,300 kilograms.

The Robot 70, or RBS70, is a portable air-defense system which is carried in three man-portable packs and which can be assembled in less than two minutes. One pack contains the stand, the second the sight and laser transmitter units, and the third the missile. The missile is 1.32 meters long and 106 centimeters in diameter. It weighs 13 kilograms and has a small, high-explosive fragmentation warhead with a proximity fuse. It has a maximum range of five kilometers and a maximum altitude of 3,000 meters. It is normally a laser beam rider, but it has been installed in both Land Rovers and APCs using search radars. General Dynamics, *The World's Missile Systems—1982*, Pomona, General Dynamics, 1982, pp. 85 and 187. The President of Bofors resigned on March 6, 1987, as a result of the sale after two years of investigation. *Washington Post*, March 7, 1987, p. A-24.

22. The land-based radars for the Silkworm have a maximum range of about 42 kilometers. The longer ranges assume remote designation by ship or aircraft-mounted radar. *Jane's Defence Weekly*, March 28, 1987, p. 532.

23. *Washington Times*, April 24, 1987, p. 12A.

24. *Jane's Defence Weekly*, May 9, 1987, p. 864.

25. *Washington Times*, April 29, 1987, p. 6A.

26. *Washington Post*, May 10, 1987, p. A-19.

27. *Washington Post*, April 16, 1987, p. A-24.

28. *Washington Times*, April 20, 1987, p. 6A.

29. *Washington Post*, April 21, 1987, p. A-21.

30. *Washington Times*, April 24, 1987, p. 12A.

31. The operational status of these missiles is uncertain, and stocks as low as seven missiles have been reported by some sources.

32. Estimates of the number of mines involved are extremely uncertain and often confuse large holdings of land mines with holdings of naval mines. The core of Iranian naval-mine holdings probably consisted of roughly 1,000 moored contact mines made by the USSR in the early 1900s, reconditioned, and then sold to Iran by North Korea.

33. Some estimates went as high as 80.

34. *Jane's Defence Weekly*, July 4, 1987, p. 1417; *Chicago Tribune*, July 12, 1987, p. 1; *Washington Post*, July 26, 1987, p. A-25; *World Weapons Review*, August 12, 1987, p. 7.

35. These assessments are based on various editions of the IISS *Military Balance*; the Jaffe Center's *Middle East Military Balance*; and *Jane's Defence Weekly*, July 11, 1987, p. 15.

36. *Chicago Tribune*, July 8, 1987, p. I-1; *Baltimore Sun*, July 7, 1987; *U.S. News and World Report*, July 6, 1987, p. 41.

37. The Naval Guards began significant anti-ship operations in November 1986 but did not become a major force in the tanker war until 1987. Naval Guards units conducted 17 known attacks on neutral ships between February

and late July 1987. *Washington Post,* April 30, 1987, p. 8A; *Jane's Defence Weekly,* May 23, 1987.

38. *Baltimore Sun,* May 6, 1987, p. 5A.

39. *New York Times,* May 9, 1987, p. 1; *Washington Post,* May 9, 1987, p. 1; *Washington Times,* May 9, 1987, p. 2A.

40. The outboard motors are made by Outboard Marine in Chicago and are painted olive drab. Although U.S. regulations prohibit the export of motors over 45 HP as military goods, they are said to range in power from 5 to 235 HP. While some of the small craft are used in the Gulf, they have even more value in the water barriers around Basra. *Philadelphia Inquirer,* May 15, 1987, p. 1E.

41. *Baltimore Sun,* May 14, 1987, p. 17A; *Washington Post,* May 14, 1987, p. A-32; *Jane's Defence Weekly,* May 16, 1987, p. 920.

42. The 272,000 VLCC *Primrose* was hit by a mine in a similar position about 34 miles east of Mina al Ahmadi as it left Kuwait on May 26, 1987. The mine was reported to have broken loose from the Shatt al-Arab waterway about 60 miles to the north and was about 10 miles west of the site where the *Chuykov* was hit. This shows the free-floating or breakaway mine theory was possible. At the same time, it was all too easy for Iranian Naval Guards units to put mines in the ship's path.

43. *Washington Post,* May 16, 1987.

44. *Washington Post,* May 25, p. A-1, and May 26, 1986, p. A-15; *Aviation Week,* May 25, 1987, pp. 23–25. One theory advanced immediately after the attack was that the "accident" was a deliberate Iraqi attempt to internationalize the war. Nothing about the Iraqi flight pattern or prior Iraqi activity supports this thesis.

45. Iraq did not allow the U.S. investigating team that visited Iraq to interview the pilot. It claimed that he had 1,300 hours of flying time, including 800 hours on Mirage fighters. The Iraqi ambassador to the U.S. later conceded that the Iraqi plane might have made a navigation error. *Washington Times,* July 17, 1987, p. A-1.

46. *Washington Times,* May 19, 1987, p. 8A; *Baltimore Sun,* May 19, 1987, p. 4A; *New York Times,* May 22, 1987, p. A-1.

47. *New York Times,* June 10, 1987; *Boston Globe,* June 12, 1987, p. 10.

48. *Washington Times,* June 24, 25, 27, and 29, 1987; *Washington Post,* June 24, 25, 27, and 29, 1987; *New York Times,* June 24, 25, 27, and 29, 1987; *Washington Times,* July 1, 1987, p. 1.

49. *Washington Post,* June 21, 1987, pp. A-1 and A-27.

50. Claims were made that the Kurds had a liberated zone of anywhere from 4,500 to 10,000 square miles. Their maximum gains at any period seem to have been about 4,500 square miles. *Los Angeles Times,* June 10, 1987, p. 12; *Baltimore Sun,* June 15, 1987, p. 5A; *Jane's Defence Weekly,* October 3, 1987, p. 797.

51. *New York Times,* June 8, 1987, p. A-1.

52. *Washington Times,* June 19, 1987, p. A-9; *Washington Post,* June 23, 1987, pp. A-13 and A-14.

53. *Baltimore Sun,* June 27, 1987, p. 2A.

54. The Pentagon released an unclassified version of the plan on June 16, 1987. It makes no reference to planning for the mine-warfare threat. *Baltimore Sun*, August 23, 1987, p. 2A.

55. *Washington Times*, August 3, 1987, p. 1.

56. To put these numbers in perspective, classified studies have indicated that it would take a minimum of 25 modern minesweepers to keep the Gulf ports open, assuming a 1,200-meter-wide channel is explored every 48 hours. *Jane's*, August 22, 1987, p. 296.

57. *U.S. News and World Report*, July 13, 1987, p. 39; *Washington Times*, July 2, 1987, p. A-1, and July 15, 1987; *Washington Post*, June 27, 1987, p. A-23, July 20, 1987, p. A-21, July 21, 1987, p. A-1; *Christian Science Monitor*, July 2, 1987, p. 11; *New York Times*, July 19, 1987, p. 12, July 21, 1987, p. A-8, and July 22, p. A-10; *Baltimore Sun*, July 1, 1987, pp. 1A and 2A, July 24, 1987, p. 2A; *Wall Street Journal*, July 1, 1987, p. 2, July 19, 1987, p. 12.

58. Free-floating or moored contact mines can be planted by dropping them over the side of any small ship with a crane. They also are difficult to destroy, since a direct hit on the tip of one of the mine's spiked contacts is necessary to make it explode.

59. *Chicago Tribune*, July 24, 1987, p. I-1; *Washington Post*, July 24, 1987, p. A-16.

60. *New York Times*, July 25, 1987, p. 1; *Washington Post*, July 25, 1987, p. A-1.

61. *Washington Post*, July 27, 1987, p. I-1, and August 2, 1987, p. A-23.

62. Kuwait is highly vulnerable to air and missile strikes. It has about 6–8 power and desalinization plants that are critical to economic operations and normal life and has only limited air-defense capability. There are three power plants near Doha and Shuwalkh and two more near Shuaiba. The desalinization plants are at Mina Ahmadi, Shuaiba, Mina Abdullah, and Mina Saud. Another power plant is under construction at Failakka Island. Kuwait also tends to layer liquid gas and oil processing and refining facilities, and the propane plant at the Ahmadi refinery is particularly vulnerable. A lucky hit could trigger a series of explosions that could cripple Kuwait's export capability. Iran's missiles, however, are too limited in number and accuracy to be used for surgical strikes, and its air attack capability is so limited it would take a major risk in committing its remaining active attack aircraft against even a small force like the Kuwaiti Air Force. A successful Iranian strike would require a massive amount of luck.

63. *Economist*, August 1, 1987, p. 38.

64. The *Guadalcanal* is an Iwo-Jima class amphibious assault ship which is designed for amphibious operations. It can operate four Sea Stallions simultaneously from its deck and can hold 11 of the helicopters. It is 602 feet long and has a 104-foot flight deck. In addition to the helicopters, it could also operate Harrier vertical and short takeoff and landing (VSTOL) fighters. It has air defense guns and regular guns, but no real missile defenses. Its maximum speed is 23 knots. It carries 47 officers and 562 crew and a landing force of 144 officers and 1,602 enlisted personnel. It was commissioned on July 20, 1963. *New York Times*, July 30, 1987, p. A-1, and *Washington Post*, July 30, 1987, p. A-1.

65. *Aviation Week*, August 3, 1987, pp. 25–26; *Washington Post*, August 4, 1987, p. A-1.

66. *Washington Post*, July 21, 1987, p. A-1; *USN&WR*, August 30, 1987, p. 30.

67. *Washington Post*, November 30, 1987, p. A-1, and December 2, 1987, p. A-33.

68. Any firing incidents were limited by the armament of the Saudi officers involved. Shuarah II, verse 197, of the Koran forbids any violence or even verbal abuse in the holy area, and Saudi policemen in the Mosque area are not allowed to carry pistols. In 1979, the Saudi leaders had to obtain a Fatwa to allow the use of force to put down insurgents that seized the Grand Mosque. Even the head of the Iranian Red Crescent, Dr. Vahid Dastjerdi, made much more modest claims during a press conference on August 16. He talked about pilgrims being stoned and gassed and killed underfoot or from poor medical care. Iran obviously was backtracking on claims about massed gunfire. He stated that there were 155,000 Iranians in Mecca, and 332 were killed and 40 to 50 missing. He again claimed 4,000 were hurt but described them as injured rather than as casualties. He made no effort to substantiate claims about large numbers of deaths from bullets, although he stated that all but 90 of the dead had been returned and made no effort to substantiate the unrealistically round number of 4,000. *Washington Times*, July 2, 1987, p. A-8, July 7, 1987, p. A-1, July 20, 1987, p. A-6; *Washington Post*, July 2, 1987, p. A-23, July 8, 1987, p. A-24, July 14, 1987, p. A-10, July 18, 1987, p. A-20, July 19, 1987, p. A-17, July 21, 1987, p. A-16, July 22, 1987, p. A-14, July 29, 1987, p. A-19, August 10, 1987, p. A-1, August 17, 1987, p. A-16; *Christian Science Monitor*, July 2, 1987, p. 11; *New York Times*, July 18, 1987, p. 1, July 19, 1987, p. 12, July 21, 1987, p. A-8, July 23, 1987, p. A-1, August 17, 1987, p. A-1; *Baltimore Sun*, July 4, 1987, p. A-1, July 19, 1987, p. 1A, July 24, 1987, p. 2A; *Wall Street Journal*, July 9, 1987, p. 24; *Philadelphia Inquirer*, July 3, 1987, p. 10A, August 11, 1987, p. 4A; *Los Angeles Times*, July 17, 1987, p. I–1; *Insight*, August 3, 1987, p. 30; *USN&WR*, August 17, 1987, p. 23.

69. These claims were never substantiated. Saudi Arabia returned most of the bodies involved. While some did have what appeared to be bullet wounds, these were only a relatively small number. No indications of large numbers of wounded were made public. Iran claimed that at least some Iranians were dead although Saudi Arabia had actually arrested them after the riot.

70. According to one report, the riots were triggered early. They were supposed to be led by Mahdi Karoubi and involve a tightly organized effort to use nearly 150,000 Shi'ite pilgrims and take over the Mosque. While such reports are uncertain, Khomeini did send a message on July 29, 1987, to the Iranian pilgrims in Mecca that stated, "If Moslems cannot denounce the enemies of God in their own home, where can they? . . . With confidence, I tell you . . . that Islam will eliminate all the great obstacles, internally as well as externally beyond its frontiers, and will conquer the principal bastion in the world." *Washington Post*, August 10, 1987, p. A-1.

71. *New York Times*, July 5, 1987, p. 11; *Wall Street Journal*, July 13, 1987, p. 18.

72. There was one minor incident between Iraq and Syria. Iraq shot down a

Syrian fighter that had blundered into Iraqi territory on July 28, 1987. *Washington Post,* July 26, 1987, p. A-25, and July 12, 1987, p. A-22.

73. The U.S. Navy was having a substantial quality control and reliability problem with virtually all of its radar-guided air-to-air missiles. It is not surprising, however, that the AIM-7M failed to achieve a hit. Radar-guided air combat generally requires large numbers of carefully orchestrated aircraft to achieve high kill rates. *Washington Post,* August 11, 1987, p. A-1, and August 12, p. A-20; *Aviation Week,* August 17, 1987, pp. 22–24; *New York Times,* August 11, 1987, p. 2.

74. *Washington Post,* August 12, 1987, p. A-1; *New York Times,* August 11, 1987, p. A-3.

75. *Washington Post,* August 14, 1987, p. A-29, September 20, 1987, p. A-25; *New York Times,* August 12 and 14, 1987, p. A-1; *Baltimore Sun,* August 14, 1987, p. 1A; *Economist,* August 22–28, 1987, pp. 42–43; *Wall Street Journal,* August 14, 1987, p. 11.

76. *Washington Post,* August 12, 1987, p. A-1, and August 13, 1987, p. A-29; *New York Times,* August 12, 1987, p. A-1; *Baltimore Sun,* August 13, 1987, p. 1A; *Economist,* August 22–28, 1987, pp. 42–43; *Washington Times,* August 14, 1987, p. A-9.

77. The costs can be calculated either as the total cost of the forces involved or as the incremental cost of the operation. On August 21, 1987, the Pentagon announced that roughly 10,000 of the U.S personnel in the Gulf would get danger pay of $110 a month. This alone raised the incremental costs by $1.1 million per month. Ironically, David J. Armor—the acting Assistant Secretary of Defense for Personnel who announced the raise in pay—had told the House Armed Services Committee only three weeks earlier that "the threat to U.S. warships in the Gulf is lower than the threat of terrorism ashore in many Middle Eastern countries. A general threat of terrorism has never been a basis for declaring imminent danger." *Washington Post,* August 27, 1987, p. A-21; *Wall Street Journal,* August 27, 1987, p. 22.

78. *Washington Post,* August 19, 1987, p. A-1, and August 20, 1987, p. A-1; *New York Times,* August 19, 1987, p. A-1.

79. *Washington Post,* August 29, 1987, p. A-18; *New York Times,* August 30, 1987, p. 14, August 31, 1987, p. A-1.

80. Iranian production levels are somewhat controversial. U.S. intelligence experts estimated that Iran produced 2.2 MMBD in January 1987, 1.7 MMBD in February, 2.1 MMBD in March, 2.2 MMBD in April, 2.6 MMBD in May, 2.4 MMBD in June, 2.5 MMBD in July, and 2.8 MMBD in August. These estimates, however, do not seem to include a careful effort to ensure that all domestic production and consumption are included in the total. Some commercial export estimates go as low as 1.1 MMBD, but it is difficult to find any supporting evidence.

81. Iran faced the same problems in attack tankers with light weapons and anti-tank guided missiles.

82. Statistical data are taken from the *Economist,* October 17, 1987, p. 51.

83. Larak is roughly 750 miles from Iraq.

84. *Economist,* October 17, 1987, p. 51.

85. This analysis is based on work by Gary Sick, the Center for Defense Analysis, and data furnished by the U.S. Navy. The reader should be aware that different sources provide substantially different estimates of the number and timing of the strikes on each side.

86. *New York Times*, September 4, 1987, p. A-1, September 5, 1987, p. 5, September 6, 1987, p. 3; *Washington Post*, September 4, 1987, p. A-1, September 5, 1987, p. A-1, September 7, 1987, p. A-23; *Washington Times*, September 7, 1987, p. A-2.

87. Basra was, in fact, being shelled daily from Iranian positions only nine miles away and had only about half of its normal population of 1.5 million.

88. *Washington Post*, September 12, 1987, pp. A-1 and A-17, September 13, 1987, p. A-25, September 14, 1987, p. A-25, September 16, 1987, pp. A-1 and A-24, September 20, 1987, p. A-25, September 21, 1987, p. A-20; *New York Times*, September 3, 1987, p. A-1, September 14, 1987, p. A-2, September 15, 1987, p. A-3, September 17, 1987, p. A-3, September 23, 1987, p. A-14; *Christian Science Monitor*, September 9, 1987, p. 1; *Washington Times*, September 7, 1987, p. A-1, September 16, 1987, p. A-8, September 21, 1987, p. A-10; *Baltimore Sun*, September 3, 1987, p. 2A; *Chicago Tribune*, September 17, 1987, p. I-5.

89. *Jane's Defence Weekly*, October 24, 1987, p. 938.

90. *Jane's Defence Weekly*, September 26, 1987, pp. 671–673.

91. The *Vinh Long* had sailed from Brest on August 17 but had to turn back because of engine problems. It was replaced with the *Orion*.

92. All were old Soviet-made M-08 contact mines which weigh 600 kilograms and have 115 kilograms of explosive. While Iran was reported to have modern influence mines, none were recovered.

93. The Barricade system was fitted to the Hunt-class MCMVs and *Abdiel* as a result of the attack on the *Stark*. It included chaff, flare, and other countermeasure rockets. It was fitted in 72 hours. Each Hunt was also armed with two Oerlikon-BMARC 20-mm cannons, a Bofors 40-mm dual purpose gun, and two 7.62-mm machine guns. The mine vessels were given Marconi satellite communications systems, passive "Replica" missile defenses consisting of electronic countermeasures that made the cross-section of the ship seem much larger than it was and created a false apparent location, and "Matilda" missile attack and electronic support measures (ESM) warning systems. Their sonars were modernized to include the EDO Alconbury 2059 sonar, which linked the standard sonar in the ship to a PAP-104 remotely operated vehicle. This extended the range and pinpointing capability of the ship's sonar system.

94. The Seafoxes are 11-meter, light, special-warfare boats which can go 32 knots and can carry four weapons, including machine guns, mortars, anti-tank weapons, grenade launchers, and 20-mm cannons.

95. *Washington Post*, September 5, 1987, p. A-29.

96. *Washington Post*, August 20, 1987, p. A-25, September 29, 1987, p. A-25; *Economist*, August 22, 1987, pp. 42–43, and September 26, 1987, p. 60; *Journal of Commerce*, September 17, 1987, p. 3B; *Philadelphia Inquirer*, September 16, 1987, p. 10; *Jane's Defence Weekly*, August 29, 1987, p. 361.

97. *Jane's Defence Weekly*, October 24, 1987, p. 941.

98. The group is nicknamed the "deathstalkers," and its motto is "Death waits in the dark."

99. *Aviation Week*, September 28, 1987, p. 32; *Time*, October 5, 1987, pp. 20–23; *Washington Post*, September 22, 1987, p. A-1, September 23, 1987, pp. A-26 and A-27, September 24, 1987, p. A-27; *New York Times*, September 22, 1987, p. A-1, September 23, 1987, p. A-14; *USN&WR*, October 5, 1987, pp. 26–28.

100. *New York Times*, September 24, 1987, p. A-13, October 1, 1987, p. A-1; *Washington Post*, September 24, 1987, p. A-1.

101. The NLA claimed to have conducted 94 operations in Iran between January and mid-October 1987 and to have killed or wounded 4,300 "Khomeini agents." Its largest claimed offensive was in the Marivan region on October 16, when it claimed to have caused over 400 casualties and taken 108 prisoners. The Khomeini regime, in turn, claimed to have arrested 1,000 Mujahideen agents at the border and captured 100 agents in Sistan-Baluchistan Province. Even if all the claims made on both sides were true, they added up to a token level of military activity. See various editions of *Iran Liberation*, especially No. 63, November 27, 1987, and the *Washington Post*, December 8, 1987, p. A-1.

102. *Insight*, September 4, 1987, p. 34; *Christian Science Monitor*, August 19, 1987, p. 2; *New York Times*, August 18, 1987, p. A-1, August 30, 1987, September 29, 1987, p. A-1; *Washington Post*, September 29, 1987, p. A-19; James Bruce, "IRGC-Iran's Shock Troops," *Jane's Defence Weekly*, October 24, 1987, pp. 960–961.

103. *Jane's Defence Weekly*, October 3, 1987, p. 712, and October 10, 1987, p. 792.

104. Tehran Radio, September 22, 1987.

105. Tehran Radio, November 12 and 13, 1989. For a political analysis of these developments, see Shahram Chubin and Charles Tripp, *Iran and Iraq at War*, Boulder, Westview, pp. 46–49.

106. *Washington Post*, October 4, 1987, p. A-1, October 5, 1987, p. A-21; *Philadelphia Inquirer*, October 4, 1987, p. 5A.

107. *Chicago Tribune*, October 6, 1987, p. I–1.

108. *Philadelphia Inquirer*, October 5, 1987, p. 3A; *Chicago Tribune*, October 5, 1987, p. I–5.

109. Ibid.

110. *Washington Post*, November 29, 1987, p. A-41.

111. This is unclear. Guards on an Iranian oil platform in the lower Gulf fired on another U.S. helicopter about 40 minutes later.

112. U.S. companies had 454 ships under the U.S. flag (363 active) and 429 merchant ships registered in other countries on July 1, 1987; 227 of the foreign flagged ships were registered in Liberia. These U.S.-owned ships flew the flags of 18 different nations. A ship with a foreign crew could cost $700,000 to operate versus $3.4 million for a ship under the U.S. flag, which required a 75 percent U.S. crew. The U.S. flag also meant stringent safety requirements and that 50 percent of any repairs done outside U.S. yards had to be paid in duty.

113. This exercise in overkill was supposed to demonstrate that the U.S. could have used far more power if it had wanted to. The guns involved were

radar-guided guns with track-while-scan capabilities coupled to a digital computer. They fire 5-in., 54-caliber ammunition at a rate of 16 to 20 rounds a minute. Each round cost $1,154 dollars, and the total exercise cost well over $1 million.

114. *Christian Science Monitor*, October 19, 1987, pp. 2 and 16; *New York Times*, October 21, 1987, p. A-10.

115. *New York Times*, October 21, 1987, p. A-10; *Washington Post*, October 21, 1987, p. A-27.

116. *New York Times*, October 20, 1987, p. A-1, October 23, 1987, p. A-1, October 24, 1987, p. 3; *Washington Post*, October 20, 1987, pp. A-1 and A-26, October 23, 1987, p. A-1; *Christian Science Monitor*, November 30, 1987, p. 9.

117. The U.S. also announced it would send five dolphins to the Gulf to improve its mine detection capability.

118. *Washington Post*, November 30, 1987, p. A-1, and December 2, 1987, p. A-33.

119. Senator Dennis DeConcini and Representative Mel Levine announced they would introduce legislation to block the sale of Stingers for one year because of the risk of transfer to Iran, which had been illustrated by the fact that Iran had gotten six systems from the Afghan Mujahideen.

120. *Washington Post*, October 31, 1987, p. A-2; *Washington Times*, October 8, 1987, p. I-6.

121. The attack on October 21 hit the *Khark 4*, a 284,000-dwt VLCC.

122. By this time, the oil platform at Rustam had been burning for 17 days.

123. *Washington Post*, November 7, 1987, p. A-16; *Washington Times*, November 7, 1987, p. I-6.

124. *Washington Post*, November 12, 1987, p. A-25.

125. *Washington Post*, November 17, 1987, p. A-22, November 18, 1987, p. A-29; *Chicago Tribune*, November 21, 1985, p. I-5; *Philadelphia Inquirer*, November 30, 1987, p. 13D.

126. The U.S. force ended up consisting of five, rather than six, Aggressive-class MSOs. Three arrived under their own power from the Atlantic fleet. Two more were towed from the West Coast of the U.S. by an amphibious landing ship. The third MSO developed engineering problems and had to return to base after service in Pearl Harbor. The MSOs coming from the East Coast did not enter the Gulf until late October. The Dutch force consisted of the *Hellevoetsluis* and *Maassluis*. It was operating with the British force in the Gulf of Oman and lower Gulf. It was then committed for 10 weeks. The Netherlands had still not finalized efforts to sell Kuwait two Alkmaar-class minehunters.

127. *Washington Post*, November 28, 1987, p. A-23.

128. *Philadelphia Inquirer*, November 22, 1987, p. 9A; *Chicago Tribune*, November 21, 1987, p. I-5; *Washington Times*, November 23, 1987, p. A-8.

129. *Baltimore Sun*, January 2, 1988.

130. Based on USCENTCOM briefing data.

131. *Washington Times*, December 23, 1987, p. A-8; *Philadelphia Inquirer*, December 23, 1987, p. 7A.

132. Department of Energy working data.

133. *New York Times,* February 4, 1988, p. D-18; *Economist,* January 30, 1988, p. 32.

134. Based on USCENTCOM briefing data.

135. *New York Times,* December 6, 1987, p. 11.

136. *Washington Post,* December 8, 1987, p. A-24.

137. *Philadelphia Inquirer,* December 8, 1987, p. 12C.

138. *Washington Post,* December 2, 1988, p. A-33; *Philadelphia Inquirer,* December 5, 1987, p. 3A.

139. *Philadelphia Inquirer,* December 5, 1987, p. 3A.

140. The U.S. did, however, seriously consider intercepting the ships carrying the weapons and turning them away. The basic design of the Styx SS-N-2 dates back to 1960. It is a 21-foot-long missile with a 350-pound warhead. The Chinese C-801 is a more refined version of the Styx that was deployed in 1984. It has sea-skimming capability. The U.S. put heavy pressure on the PRC not to sell this system to Iran.

141. Iraq did begin to fire such missiles successfully in early March. Iraqi Mirage F-1 pilots continued to fire blind at targets in the Gulf, many far from Iranian waters. During the last week of 1987, Iraq claimed to have hit four naval targets with Exocets. None were actually hit, but Iraq did hit a neutral Greek-owned freighter that sailed out of Kuwait at some point during the first week of 1988. An Iraqi Mirage F-1 also flew virtually the same kind of attack profile on the USS *Portland* on January 27, 1988, that had been flown against the USS *Stark.* This time, however, another U.S. warship obtained radio contact with the Iraqi pilot in time to warn it away. The USS *Chandler* came within seconds of firing on a similar type of attack on February 13, 1988. This led to another series of talks between Iraq and the U.S. designed to avoid such incidents. *Philadelphia Inquirer,* January 3, 1988, p. 20A; *Washington Post,* January 28, 1988, p. A-21, February 17, 1988, p. A-15; *New York Times,* February 14, 1988, p. 1; *Christian Science Monitor,* March 3, 1988, p. 10.

142. *Washington Times,* February 19, 1988, p. A-10; *Baltimore Sun,* February 17, 1988, p. 2A.

143. The new commander was Rear Admiral Anthony Less, who replaced Rear Admiral Harold Bernsen, commanding the forces in the Gulf, and Rear Admiral Dennis M. Brooks on the *Iowa.* The U.S. was particularly concerned with the risk of multiple lines of command because these had created serious problems during the invasion of Grenada. Reports of similar formal command changes among the European forces in the Gulf that put British, French, and Italian forces under a common command were false, although the coordination of mining and convoy efforts by all Western naval forces present in the area was steadily improving. *New York Times,* December 18, 1987, p. A-11; *Washington Post,* January 24, 1988, p. A-1.

144. *New York Times,* December 22, 1987, p. A-7.

10

IRAQI OFFENSIVES AND WESTERN INTERVENTION FORCE A CEASE-FIRE, SEPTEMBER 1987–MARCH 1989

The War Enters Its Final Phase

Nothing seemed less inevitable at the beginning of 1988 than an Iraqi victory. Iraq had fought good defensive battles at Basra and against most of Iran's later Karbala offensives, but Iran had scarcely abandoned its calls for final offensives and was calling for still more volunteers. Iran had retained the initiative in most of the battles in 1987, and Iraq usually had showed only limited capability to counterattack. Appearances, however, were deceiving. The course of the war was to change radically in the spring of 1988 and to result in a series of Iraqi victories that ended in forcing Iran to accept the same kind of terms for a cease-fire that it had rejected in 1982.

Three sets of factors shaped this new phase of the war. The first was a series of important changes in Iraq's armed forces and methods of warfare. The second was a change in Iran's ability to continue fighting because of the cumulative political and military impact of Iran's losses and mismanagement of the war. The third, less tangible, factor was the Western presence in the Gulf and Iran's growing diplomatic isolation.

Iraq Prepares for Offensive Operations

For all their shortcomings and mistakes in previous years, Iraq's forces had steadily improved in experience and professionalism. They suffered from little of the turbulence and internal political conflict that weakened Iranian forces and kept the Pasdaran and Iranian regular forces from benefiting from their experience. Iraq also steadily improved its land and air tactics. It benefited from outside advice from a wide range of sources, it had ready access to most of the weapons and forms of military technology it needed, and it was greatly helped by Western intervention in the Gulf, in large part because Iran's tactics resulted in its increasing diplomatic and strategic isolation, which steadily escalated the Western pressure against it.

As early as 1984, Iraq also realized that it might not be able to survive a defensive war of attrition. This was one of the critical factors that led Iraq into the tanker war, but it also led Iraq to reorganize its land and air forces. During the periods when Iran was not launching major offensives, Iraq began to pull selected combat units out of the front line and started to train and organize them as elite forces that could be used in counterattacks and as special forces.

These efforts made only limited progress during 1984 and 1985, in part because Iraq was under constant pressure from Iran and was still struggling to expand its total forces to match the expansion of Iran's Revolutionary Guards. By 1986, however, Iraq had built up to an Army of between 800,000 and 1,000,000 men.[1] It now had seven active corps and 50 divisions and roughly 77 division equivalents.[2] All of its corps now had excellent barrier defenses, and Iraq had completed a network of military roads that allowed far more rapid movement along interior lines than Iran could hope to manage even in defensive combat. Iraq had also steadily improved its combat helicopter forces and air units.

Iraq also began to slowly improve the command and control and overall battle management of its Air Force. It built new air bases in areas like Basra and Najaf and had at least 15 major operating bases with shelters and full-support facilities by 1988. Iraq also acquired more modern Soviet aircraft like the Su-22, Su-25, MiG-29, and MiG-25R, in addition to its Mirage F-1s.[3] Iraq slowly improved its reconnaissance systems. Iraq had some aircraft equipped with SLAR reconnaissance radars and had begun to use the French commercial satellite and U.S. LANDSAT to provide information like terrain imaging. It also retrained its helicopter forces to attack as more effective forward-reconnaissance units and as artillery spotters, correcting some of the problems it had previously had in using artillery at targets beyond visual range and in shifting fires rapidly in response to changes in the tactical situation. This latter development proved particularly effective during the fighting in the north.

Although the constant pressure of Iranian offensives limited Iraq's ability to fully develop these assets during 1986 and 1987 and to regroup and retrain its forces, Iraq did succeed in steadily expanding its elite Republican Guards and other forces it needed to launch successful counterattacks. There were only seven Republican Guards brigades at the start of 1986, but Iraq had at least 28 brigades by the beginning of 1988, with a total of 100,000 men.[4] These units were given extensive training in offensive operations, and mixed armor, mechanized, and special forces units.

The Republican Guards units were given the best available weapons. For example, they received Iraq's T-72s. They were given special treatment, like the supply of bottled water, and they were given large numbers of trucks to provide the logistical support for mobile and offensive operations. By late 1987, they were organized into six commands or divisional equivalents of three to four brigades each. These commands allowed tailoring of the force mix to support given types of operations, and they had independent artillery and helicopter units and sometimes had independent chemical corps support units.[5]

Iraq created similar elite naval infantry brigades that sometimes trained with the Republican Guards units, and it aggressively trained these forces for the two kinds of operations it generally had failed to conduct successfully during the period from 1983 to 1987: aggressive infiltration and assault operations and operations in wetlands and across water barriers. While Iraq's claims to have built training grounds with life-sized models of the area to be attacked cannot be confirmed, it is clear that Iraq began to conduct extensive training under trying weather and terrain conditions and practiced offensive operations of the kind it would need to counterattack at Faw, around Basra, and in mountainous terrain.

Iraq increasingly turned its chemical corps into an elite force. Although it had begun to use chemical weapons in 1983 and 1984, Iraq at first experienced severe problems in using its weapons effectively. Further, it found mustard gas to be too persistent to attack through. During 1985–1986, however, Iraq steadily improved its targeting and delivery means and ability to predict wind patterns. By mid-1987, Iraq also began to produce enough nerve gas to give it large stocks of highly lethal nonpersistent agents. Unlike mustard gas, Iraq could use nonpersistent nerve gases relatively near to its own troops and during the initial assault phase. This allowed Iraq to introduce a weapon that had a major impact both in inflicting casualties and in inflicting panic.[6]

Iraq also carried out intensive training exercises during much of 1987. It had withdrawn elite units for special combined-arms training in 1985 and 1986, but this kind of combined-arms training took on a far more serious character in the summer and fall of 1987. Iraqi armor and infantry were given special training in maneuver and combined-arms operations. The commanders at every level in carefully selected units—

including the Republican Guards—were allowed far more freedom of command in these exercises, and Iraq conducted corps-level exercises in fluid defense and counterattack tactics. Iraqi artillery units were given special training in concentrating and shifting fire and in providing fire at the call of forward air controllers (FACs) in the forward area rather than prepared fire. These measures scarcely restructured the entire Iraqi Army, but they did make a major improvement in a number of key Iraqi corps and divisions.

Iraq improved its tactical intelligence capabilities. It made better use of night-vision devices, improved its use of electronic warfare in the form of direction finding and radio intercepts, and improved its ability to use tactical radars to locate Iranian forces and artillery units. It also improved its use of helicopters and aircraft for reconnaissance and cut the number of bureaucratic barriers to the rapid transfer of information to field commanders.

While the exact nature of the changes involved is still unknown, Iraq also seems to have reorganized its Supreme Defense Council in 1986 and 1987 to give its field commanders and fighting officers a much stronger voice. These reorganizations seem to have been particularly important after the fighting in Basra in 1987, and they helped reduce the overcentralization of the Iraqi command structure and give professionalism more weight over politicization. One of the most obvious lessons of war is that politics kills effective command, as does over-centralization and management of the war that does not give combat commanders a major voice in decision making. It is a lesson that many nations ignore, but Iraq had learned it at least in part by the beginning of 1988.

Iraq had always had good logistics capabilities and mobility. Nevertheless, it continued to increase its numbers of tank transporters, and trucks during 1986–1987. Iraq raised its number of tank transporters from 1,000 to 1,500 and created a new road network to allow units to redeploy from the central to the southern front in 12 to 24 hours. To ensure that Iranian forces could not cut Basra off from Baghdad by thrusting through the north-south roads on the western bank of the Tigris, Iraq completed a new six-lane highway from Safwan on the Kuwaiti border, past Zubair and Nasiryah, and then north toward Baghdad. Given the fact that Iraq had still another road and a railway along the Euphrates, which were much further to the West, this mix of north-south lines of communication gave Iraq considerable insurance against an Iranian breakthrough. It also improved Iraq's ability to rapidly mass and sustain its forces in offensive operations.

These changes scarcely led to overnight shifts in Iraq's effectiveness but were part of a massive national effort that lasted for several years.

While their importance was overshadowed by Iran's constant offensive pressure during the first six months of 1987, it was already clear that some aspects of Iraqi performance were improving. Iraq's new elite forces showed increasing capability to act as a strategic reserve during Iran's offensives during early and mid-1987. Iran's growing problems in launching major offensives in the second half of 1987 then gave Iraq a vital breathing space which it used to fully organize its new forces and capabilities. By late 1987, Iraq reached the level of land and air strength where it finally had the forces it needed to conduct successful counteroffensives.

At the same time, Iraq also prepared for a massive change in the way it conducted the war against the cities. It obtained large numbers of long-range Scuds from the USSR, and the USSR provided substantial technical advice and actual support during their use in combat. Iraq also improved the mission planning and organization of its offensive air units. It continued to obtain more advanced weapons, like cluster bombs and air-to-surface missiles, and built up massive stocks of bombs loaded with nerve and mustard gas. This gave Iraq the capability to conduct both a major missile war and more effective interdiction and strategic bombing efforts.

Iran's Political and Strategic Mistakes

In contrast to Iraq, Iran had suffered significantly during the course of 1987. Iran's repeated offensives began to exhaust popular support for the war and Iran's ability to substitute ideological fervor for military professionalism and modern weapons. Even so, Iran pressed on with badly planned offensives that continued to emphasize popular warfare and revolutionary fervor at a time it was clear that it needed more military professionalism and that much of the previous popular support for the war had begun to decline. Iran's leaders lost touch with the feelings of its people and troops. Iran's leaders forgot a major lesson of war, much as did the leaders of the U.S. during the Vietnam conflict and the Soviet leadership during the war in Afghanistan. Regardless of the type of regime, any war dependent on large-scale mobilization and national sacrifice can only be sustained through continued popular support.

Equally important, Iran continued to make major strategic mistakes. It continued to provoke a series of naval encounters with U.S. and other Western naval forces that were to make it brutally clear to Iran that it could never succeed in forcing a partial cease-fire that ended the war at sea without accepting a cease-fire on the land. This helped increase Iran's growing diplomatic and strategic isolation.

These factors were to have a catalytic effect on Iran's ability to continue the war that went far beyond the tactical and strategic impact of the battles involved. In fact, the end of the Iran-Iraq War was to again demonstrate another important lesson of war: Few wars ever end in the destruction of the enemy's forces; they end when a combination of political and military factors destroys the enemy's ability to continue fighting.

Equally important, Iran continued to experience growing problems with chemical warfare. Iran did not make effective offensive use of gas weapons before 1987, and it then only seems to have been able to make limited use of gas during a few battles in the Fish Lake area and near Mehran. There were growing reports during early 1988 that Iran had begun to manufacture its own chemical weapons in significant amounts at its chemical weapons development facility near Shiraz. Nevertheless, Iran lagged badly behind Iraq in producing and using chemical weapons. Iran only seems to have made limited use of gas weapons in 1988, most notably at Halabjah. Even in 1988, it is unclear whether Iran could make enough phosgene, chlorine, hydrogen cyanide, or mustard gas to carry out any large-scale chemical warfare operations.

Iran did improve its chemical defense gear during 1986 and 1987. Iranian troops were extensively equipped with improved gas masks, protective clothing, decontamination kits, and atropine and amyl nitrate as antidotes to nerve gas. This equipment, however, only offered moderate protection against mustard and nerve gas, and even fully equipped troops suffered large numbers of casualties when they were exposed to Iraqi gas attacks. Iran also lacked the detectors, command-and-control system, and equipment to provide effective protection from nerve gas.

New Iranian Mobilization and Arms Procurement Efforts and an Emphasis on Campaigns in the North

The land war remained unusually quiet during the final months of 1987. Iran did continue to launch small offensives after its major attack on Basra. It conducted roughly a dozen small offensives along the border—with names like "Nasr," and "Najaf"—but these were generally limited attacks, and many did little more than try to seize a given ridge line or position in the mountains.

Iran was most successful in its attacks in the Kurdish sections in the north. It used its own forces, anti-Iraqi Kurdish forces, and a small unit of Iraqi prisoners of war that had agreed to fight Iraq. These forces did not dominate the countryside in the north, but they were able to occupy many villages at night. They often hit Iraqi convoys and closed roads during the day and sometimes were able to cut electric power to major cities like Kirkuk.

Iraq was forced to send some elements of its fourth division from the 7th Corps in the south into the area, but it did not have to commit major numbers of additional troops. Iraq, instead, relied heavily on bombing or bombarding Kurdish villages and on the ruthless relocation of the people in the villages under its control, while demolishing the homes and agricultural infrastructure that remained. This sometimes created more new enemies than such efforts eliminated, but Iraq was more irritated by the Kurds than threatened by them.

In the late fall, Iran again carried out its seasonal mobilization. It built up its artillery and ammunition supplies in the southern front north of Basra. Iranian radio and TV even talked of another final offensive. Iran issued reports of buildups of up to 200 battalions of Baseej, or 200,000–500,000 men.

In fact, however, the Iranian buildup seems to have only reached 60,000 to 100,000 men, allowing for rotations. This mobilization was not enough to fill out the force of roughly 20 Iranian combat formations, or "divisions," claimed to be in the southern sector. The impact of Iran's casualties during 1987 began to have a powerful effect on Iran's mobilization efforts. The total number of volunteers seems to have dropped from 80,000 in 1986 to 40,000 in 1987 and forced Iran to extend its conscription period from 24 to 28 months in early January 1988. According to some estimates, Iran only built up a force of 300,000 men, versus the 700,000 it mobilized for its push against Basra.[7]

Further, figures like Kamal Kazzari—a member of the Supreme Defense Council and its chief military spokesman—stated that Iran would make a series of major tactical thrusts, rather than carry out a single large offensive. These statements reflected the fact that Iran was actually shifting a substantial amount of its new manpower, and some of its most experienced units, to the north in late 1987. These shifts may partly have been a response to the rains, which were late, and allowed Iraq to use its armor effectively much later in the season. More probably, they were a response to the size of Iranian losses opposite Basra in early 1987 and to the reluctance to take more casualties in attacking a front whose defenses had been greatly improved.

Iran may also have been affected by Syrian and other pressure to avoid further attacks that would alienate the Arab world and by the fear such attacks would lead to Soviet and PRC support of a UN arms embargo. Finally, the move may have been the result of internal political divisions within the leadership around Khomeini, the desire to avoid any bloody defeat with Iranian elections coming up in the early spring, and from Iranian calculations that there was little real chance of victory. Further, a shift to campaigns in the north offered Iran some advantages because Iraq's pipelines at oil fields at Kirkuk could be approached through rough and mountainous terrain that denied Iraq the ability to take full advantage of its armor and the open killing grounds in front of its barrier defenses in the south.

Iran's new emphasis on the north did, however, ignore several important strategic considerations. One was that any major advance in the north had to be fought ridge-line by ridge-line and still offered Iraq the ability to make good defensive use of natural terrain and its vast superiority in helicopters and artillery. Second, Iraq's lines of communication into the north were far better than Iran's, and Iraq could redeploy reserves far more quickly to threatened areas than Iran could strengthen its offensive. Finally, and most important, Iran's redeployments to the north locked a very substantial amount of its army in mountain warfare at a time when Iran lacked any significant manpower advantage over Iraq.

The net result was to leave Iran's positions in the south under-strength and vulnerable at a time when Iraq was finally ready to exploit that vulnerability. Iraq maintained some 900,000 men all along the front versus around 600,000 full-time actives for Iran. It deployed up to 250,000 men in the south around Basra. It completed three rings of defensive positions around the city and completed a series of parallel north-south defensive lines to provide defense in depth all along the southern and central fronts.

In spite of its new emphasis on campaigns in the north, Iran seems to have tried to convince Iraq that it could still attack in the south. Iran carried out some of the seasonal shifts in equipment and supplies to the south it normally deployed before a massive offensive. Iran was also able to use Chinese, Austrian, and North Korean artillery deliveries to virtually double its artillery strength at the front and reduce its ratio of inferiority from roughly 3:1 to 2:1. It added some armor and built new roads to help it rapidly redeploy and reinforce during attacks. Nevertheless, it did not deploy the normal number of tents, trucks, and support equipment.

Iran's military problems during the course of 1988 do not seem to have been the result of a shortage of arms, although Iran was having growing problems in getting Western parts, ammunition, and replacement systems. Iran obtained roughly $1.5 billion worth of arms and got 60–70 percent of its arms from the PRC and North Korea, 20 percent more from Eastern Europe, and 20 percent from the rest of the world. During 1986 and 1987, Iran was able to obtain large numbers of new tanks, armored fighting vehicles like the BMP-1, and towed artillery. Iran also doubled its domestic artillery production during 1987 and was fully self-sufficient in small arms and small arms munitions. Its main problems were its dependence on foreign suppliers for fuses and propellents.

The PRC supplied some $600 million worth of arms in 1987, largely artillery, ammunition, and missiles. China also sold equipment for the manufacture of arms and missiles. It shipped another $200 million worth of arms in January 1988 and had agreements to provide $400 million more during the rest of 1988. North Korea sold another $400 million worth of arms in 1987, including artillery, fast patrol boats, and Soviet-designed Scud surface-to-surface missiles. New North Korean arms shipments, including Scud and Silkworm missiles, arrived in January 1988. The Warsaw Pact shipped some $350 million worth of arms, including a large number of troop carriers and some self-propelled artillery. None of these countries, however, seems to have delivered jet fighter aircraft, in spite of new rumors of sales by North Korea and the PRC.

Western supplies to Iran included some $150 million worth of ammunition and explosives from Spain and Portugal, at least some of which were actually made by France's Luchaire and the National Power and Explosive Company and sold with the same tacit knowledge of senior French defense and intelligence officials under a conservative government that had permitted them under a socialist one. These orders included up to 200,000 shells to be delivered during 1987–88, 200,000 detonators, 2,500 tons of TNT, and 650 tons of powder.

Japanese firms sold $100 million worth of trucks and spare parts to Iran, and private Swiss and West German firms continued to sell chemical warfare equipment. Iran's major Western supplier, however, was Brazil, which sometimes used Libya to act as a third party. This meant Iran was now experiencing far more serious difficulties in getting Western arms and parts, particularly critical aircraft parts like those for the F-5.[8]

The Fighting in the North in Late 1987

The only significant land action in the south during late 1987 occurred on December 20–21. Two Iranian brigades carried out a limited attack on the northern edge of the Hawizeh Marshes in the south-central front. Iran attacked along a river in the Fuka border area, near the border outpost of Zabaidat and east of the Iranian town of Misan (formerly Amara).

While both sides made the usual conflicting victory claims, Iran seems to have lost several thousand men and Iraq only several hundred. A brigade or division of Iranian troops seem to have tried to find a gap in Iraqi defenses and to have been caught up in a minefield. Iraqi was then able to use its advantage in artillery to inflict serious causalities. The experience was scarcely one that encouraged an Iranian attack on Basra.

The broader political and economic situation remained confused during early 1988. UN Secretary General Perez de Cuellar virtually gave up on his cease-fire negotiations with Iraq and Iran on December 10, 1987, and turned the issue over to the Security Council. Iraq remained unwilling to compromise on the timing of a cease-fire and withdrawal, and Iran insisted that Iraq be identified as the aggressor before the cease-fire. Getting the Security Council to act, however, presented two problems. The first was that it was unclear the PRC would agree to an arms embargo with or without Soviet support of such an embargo or that either the PRC or USSR would honor an embargo if they did agree to it.

The USSR continued to be torn between trying to court Iran and seeking some kind of formal Western agreement to a Soviet role in the Gulf as the price of its support of an embargo. It called for a United Nations flagged force in the Gulf as the price of support for an embargo, and the UN force concept was clearly designed to limit Western freedom of action. By the end of December, the Security Council could only agree on an announcement that it would move toward drafting and adoption of an arms embargo. On December 25, the permanent members of the Council agreed to start drafting a resolution early in 1988, but this agreement ignored the fact that several drafts already existed. Eight months after the UN had passed the original cease-fire resolution, there still was no formal agreement over enforcement.

The Fighting in 1988 Begins

The land and air war remained relatively quiet during the first months of 1988. Iran claimed to have raided Iraq's inactive Al Bakr and Al Amaya oil terminals in the Gulf, destroyed missile and radar sites, and killed at least 100 Iraqis. These claims, however, seem to have been exaggerated. Further, Iran claimed to have destroyed three Iraqi frigates, none of which was at sea in the Gulf at the time.[9]

Iran did launch a more serious offensive, the Bait al-Muqdas 2 attack on January 15, 1988. This attack took place in the Mawat border area on the northern front, east of Sulaimaniyeh. Iran had been fighting in this area since the spring of 1987 with mixed success. Iran claimed to have taken 42 square miles of new territory, including 11 heights and 29 peaks, to have killed or wounded some 3,500 Iraqi soldiers, and to have taken 750 prisoners. Iraq denied these Iranian victory claims, but Iran does seem to have scored some gains. While the area involved was sparsely populated and involved heights of 2,950 to 6,500 feet, it had some strategic value because it allowed Iran to improve its position in future attacks on the northern front and again strengthened its ability to supply anti-Iraqi Kurds.[10]

As for the air war, Iraq continued to strike both at ships and at targets like dams, bridges, and refineries throughout December, January, and March. Iran could do little about this, although it did experiment in trying to use its F-4s to fire Maverick missiles at ships in early January. It seems to have concluded that the Mavericks were now so old they had to be used before they became totally inoperable. In practice, however, the Maverick's small warhead and decaying guidance systems made them ineffective.

Iraq hit Kharg Island on February 7, 1988—for the first time since November 4, 1987—and continued to use bombing missions to probe Iran's air defenses. This led Iran to commit its F-14s to a rare ambush on February 9, 1988. The F-14s were armed with AIM-9 missiles and were able to close on two Iraqi Mirage F-1s when they turned north into Iranian waters at Farsi Island. At least one Mirage F-1 was shot down. While Iran had lost most of its air power, it still seemed to have about 20 F-4s, 20 F-5s, and 7–9 F-14s operational.[11]

The War of the Cities Turns into a Missile War

The most dramatic change in the air war, however, began in late February. Iraq carried out a major attack on the Rey oil refinery in Tehran on February 27, 1988. Iraq did not deliver an effective enough attack to knock out the refinery. Nevertheless, the raid did do serious damage and forced Iran to again start rationing petroleum products.

Iran replied to this Iraqi air raid by renewing the war of the cities and firing three Scud missiles at Baghdad. This was one of the largest number of missiles Iran fired at a single time during the war and was the first Iranian use of Scud missiles since November 8, 1987. It raised the total number of missiles targeted on Baghdad to between 21 and 37.[12] The Iranian firings were also significant because many experts believed that Iran was down to as few as 20–30 of the Scud missiles it had obtained from Libya and North Korea. The military effect, however, was negligible.

All three missiles struck in largely unpopulated regions south of Baghdad. Nevertheless, the new Iranian missile attack gave Iraq an excuse to sharply escalate the war. On February 29, Iraq launched five new long-range missiles that it called the Al Husayn and which seem to have been variants of the Scud-B or Scud-D.[13] It then repeated these attacks day after day, and it soon became clear that Iraq had been preparing its missile barrage for months.[14]

Iraq's new long-range missiles came as a surprise to both Iran and Western intelligence experts. They seem to have been modifications of regular Scud B missiles, which the Soviet Union calls the R-300 or R-17E. According to some experts, they used a lighter warhead and more of the missile's propellent, although some experts feel they used a strap-on booster that was made in Iraq with East German or North Korean assistance.[15] In any case, Iraq was able to give the Scud over twice its normal 300 kilometers, and some missiles did fly well over 500 kilometers. This was enough range for Iraq to reach Tehran and Qom from positions south of Baghdad.[16]

Iraq seems to have had several motives in starting this new phase of the missile war. The war of the cities helped publicize the seriousness of the war and to push the UN cease-fire effort forward. It was a means of striking at Iran which presented fewer political complications than attacks on Gulf shipping and which affected the Iranian people and their support of the war. Iraq was immediately successful in the former objective. The missile war achieved worldwide attention.

Iraq's attacks also may have been designed to divide the Soviet Union from Iran. If so, Iraq had some success. The Iranian government announced a few days later that it had discovered missile fragments showing the missiles Iraq had launched were Soviet and had been manufactured as recently as 1985 and 1986. They were probably part of a shipment of 300 Scud Bs that the USSR had delivered in 1986.[17] Iran publicly blamed the USSR for supplying the missiles Iraq was using.[18] The Iranian government allowed a carefully staged anti-Soviet riot to sack the Soviet Embassy in Tehran on March 6, and another riot attacked the consulate in Isfahan that same day.[19]

Estimates of the overall pattern of strikes involved differ, but Table 10.1 provides an estimate of the overall interaction between the tanker and missile wars between 1987 and 1988, based on Iraqi and Iranian claims. Many of these claims were exaggerated, particularly strikes on naval targets by Iraq and strikes on civil targets by Iran. Nevertheless, Table 10.1 is valid in indicating the intensity of the sudden rise in Iraqi missile attacks and attacks on urban targets. Other sources indicate that Iraq had hit Tehran some 33 times and Qom 3 times by March 6, 1988.

The variants of the Scuds that Iraq was using only seem to have had a 135–250 kilogram warhead and were scarcely "city killers," but they were audible over wide areas as they neared their target, made a loud

TABLE 10.1 Strikes Reported by Iran and Iraq Affecting the Tanker War and the War of the Cities in 1987 and 1988

Date		Shipping Attacks		Residential/Economic Attacks[1]			
				Iraq		Iran	
		Iraq[2]	Iran[3]	Total	Scud[4]	Total	Scud[5]
A. 1987							
Jan.	1–15	5	3	30	—	3	—
	16–31	2	2	18	—	15	3
Feb.	1–15	4	3	27	—	5	3
	16–28	5	3	8	—	5	5
Mar.	1–15	3	1	—	—	—	—
	16–31	5	3	4	—	—	—
Apr.	1–15	2	2	5	—	—	—
	16–30	3	3	2	—	—	—
May	1–15	4	4	4	—	1	—
	16–31	2	6	1	—	1	—
Jun.	1–15	—	1	—	—	—	—
	16–30	1	3	1	—	—	—
Jul.	1–15	5	3	6	—	—	—
	16–31	—	2	—	—	—	—
Aug.	1–15	—	2	2	—	—	—
	16–31	—	—	13	—	7	—
Sept.	1–15	22	10	35	—	8	—
	16–30	19	7	19	—	3	—
Oct.	1–15	15	8	12	—	6	—
	16–31	9	1	4	—	8	4
Nov.	1–15	18	3	14	—	9	1
	16–30	12	7	10	—	2	2
Dec.	1–15	8	5	7	—	2	—
	16–31	9	10	1	—	—	—
Total in 1987		153[6]	93	223	—	70	15

(continues)

TABLE 10.1 *(continued)*

| Date | Shipping Attacks | | Residential/Economic Attacks[1] | | | |
| | Iraq[2] | Iran[3] | Iraq | | Iran | |
			Total	Scud[4]	Total	Scud[5]
B. 1988						
Jan. 1–15	5	2	1	—	—	—
16–31	11	6	—	—	—	—
Feb. 1–15	13	5	3	—	—	—
16–29	—	—	5	—	3	—
Mar. 1–15	5	—	215	101	73	31
16–31	14	15	130	36	143	14
Apr. 1–15	2	1	78	40	96	11
16–30	2	5	33	26	63	5
May 1–15	12	—	2	—	—	—
16–31	2	5	2	—	—	—
Jun. 1–15	3	3	—	—	—	—
16–30	—	—	13	—	1	—
Jul. 1–15	5	5	3	—	—	—
16–31	—	—	4	—	—	—
Aug. 1–20[7]	—	1	5	—	—	—
Total in 1988	74	48	494	203	380	61

[1]Bombing and missile attacks as reported in daily war communiques and other sources.
[2]Attacks on maritime targets and off-shore oil terminals as reported in Iraqi daily war communiques.
[3]Iranian gunboat attacks on neutral shipping.
[4]Includes all long-range missiles.
[5]Includes Scud B missiles fired at Baghdad and other Iranian cities.
[6]Ninety-nine confirmed hits.
[7]From beginning of the month to the Iranian acceptance of a cease-fire and UN Resolution 598.

SOURCE: Adapted from a working paper by Gary Sick.

bang, blew out windows over a wide area, and produced nearly 60 killed and 130 wounded.[20] Iran, in turn, had fired 16 Scud missiles at Iraq, 12 of which were targeted at Baghdad. Iraq was able to fire an average of three Scuds a day, while Iran was at most firing one.

Iraq's success was due at least in part to Iran's failure to obtain resupply and to produce its own missiles. Iran did continue to fire its Oghabs and launched some 104 missiles in 1988.[21] The Oghab only had a range of 40 kilometers, however, and lacked the accuracy to hit anything other than large-area targets. While the Oghab did have a 70-kilogram warhead, Iran had no way to target it, and it was not particularly accurate or lethal. The most Iran could do was to launch the Oghabs at the Iraqi cities near the border. These targets included Basra, Abu al-Khasib, Al-Zuybar, Umm-Qasr, Mandali, Khanaqin, and Banmil, but the Oghab strikes had far less effect than artillery barrages.

Iran did obtain more Scud Bs from various sources.[22] During the 52 days of the war of the cities in 1988, Iran fired at least 77 more Scud missiles which it had obtained from North Korea. Sixty-one were fired at Baghdad, nine at Mosul, five at Kirkuk, one at Takrit, and one at Kuwait. Iran fired as many as five missiles on a single day, and once fired three missiles within 30 minutes. This still, however, worked out to an average of only about one missile a day, and Iran was down to only 10–20 Scuds when the war of the cities ended.[23]

Iran also began firing another missile of its own manufacture called the IRAN-130, although it failed to produce the IRAN-130 in any numbers. Some IRAN-130s were deployed to the Pasdaran, and the first such missiles were fired against Al-Amarah on March 19, 1988, and four more were fired against the city in April. These numbers were negligible, however, and it is unclear whether any of the IRAN-130s hit their targets or whether such hits had any tactical effect.

By March 10, Iraq claimed to have fired 47 missiles, all but five at Tehran, and Iran claimed to have fired 25 missiles at Baghdad and several at other Iraqi cities. Both sides also made use of their air power. Iraq hit as many as ten Iranian cities a day. Iran could do little more than launch a few token sorties, but Iran did renew heavy shelling of Basra. This helped lead Iran and Iraq to reach yet another short-lived cease-fire on attacks on the cities on March 11, but by then Iran had already lost 165 killed and 440 wounded.

The impact of Iraq's new missile and air strikes on Iran was far different than in the past. Where the Iranians had previously been able to adapt to the relatively limited and short-lived Iraqi bombing efforts, the constant pounding of missiles, and the growing fear that Iraq might use chemical weapons, had a major impact on Iranian morale. So did the rumors and reports that senior Iranian officials— including Khomeini—had left Tehran. According to some reports, nearly a million Iranians had fled Tehran by mid-March, and several million more had fled by late April.[24]

The Iraqi missile strikes did not do serious physical damage to any Iranian target and killed substantially less than an average of two dozen people a missile. The bombings were more lethal but still did not provide anything like the damage that occurred in Beirut during the Lebanese Civil War. It is unlikely, therefore, that the missiles and bombing alone would have had a severe impact on morale.

In practice, however, the Iraqi missile barrage acted in combination with a number of other variables, including a growing fear of chemical weapons, the impact of Iran's military casualties during the previous year, growing popular and military exhaustion with the conflict, Iran's inability to retaliate, reports of internal divisions within Iran's leadership, serious economic hardship and growing prices on the black market, the knowledge that Iran would no longer be threatened if it halted its offensives, and the fear of gas weapons.[25]

The war of the cities, however, scarcely pushed Iran's leaders toward trying to negotiate an immediate peace. In the diplomatic arena, Iran made new efforts to counter the Iraqi effort to push toward a cease-fire. It took new steps to try to block any efforts at a UN arms embargo, by claiming to accept the UN resolution in a way that was so ambiguous that it did not commit Iran to anything. The U.S., Britain, and France tried on March 5 to get Security Council support for an arms embargo, with a 30-to-60 day waiting period, but could not obtain either Soviet or Chinese support. The USSR then proposed a limited cease-fire on missiles, which Iraq angrily rejected. This again left the UN paralyzed, and the Secretary General could do little more than invite both sides to send their foreign ministers to New York for intensive consultations.[26]

As for the situation in the Gulf, there were no attacks reported on shipping between February 12 and March 6, one of the longest lulls since the beginning of Western intervention. On March 6, however, Iran naval Guards units fired on routine U.S. helicopter reconnaissance missions from both of their boats, as well as a naval oil platform. On March 8, Iraq hit the first Iranian ship since February 9, 1988. It previously had claimed 23 attacks since the beginning of 1988, but only 9 had been confirmed by shipping companies. Iraq now, however, began to hit Gulf targets regularly, and most of its strikes were confirmed by insurance groups or shipping agencies. Iraq also launched a major new raid on Kharg Island on March 19, burning two tankers and killing 46 sailors. Iran responded by launching a series of new Pasdaran attacks in the Gulf. Iran did little more than probe Kuwait's defenses. A minor clash took place between Kuwaiti troops on Bubiyan and Iranian gunboats on March 30, 1988.

New Land Battles in the North Begin in March

On March 13, the first reports began to surface of new land battles in the north. Iran had now carried out its redeployments and buildup in the north and began an attack on the northern front in the area of the Iraqi border towns of Halabjah, Khurmal, Kholmar, Dojaila, and Darbandkihan, just west of Nowsud in Iran and about 150 miles north of Baghdad.

Iran carried out major artillery barrages against the towns nearest the front lines, and a mix of Pasdaran forces, Kurdish rebels, and Iraqi rebels and ex-prisoners of war captured 7 border villages and 15 square miles of Sulaimaniyeh Province. Iraq claimed to have repulsed the attack and to have thrown back two attacking brigades and killed 1,000 Iranians. It was clear, however, that the Iranian attack had scored some gains. Further, the attack led to the breakdown of a temporary cease-fire in the missile war. The same day that Iran attacked in the north, Iraq fired 7 missiles at Tehran and used its aircraft to strike at 6 other Iranian cities.

Iran pressed on with the attack. Iranian forces struck at the southern edge of the most mountainous part of the border, near the Darbandikhan Lake or Reservoir. Iran's goal was to take enough territory in northern Iraq to be able to advance on Sulaimaniyah and to seize control of the Darbandikhan Reservoir. This reservoir was created by one of the largest dams in Iraq and fed hydroelectric power to much of northeast Iraq and Baghdad.

While Iran was forced to attack through mountains and use poor lines of communication, the attack offered Iran the possibility of opening an attack route into Iraq in an area where it could use terrain and Kurdish support to help offset Iraq's superior firepower, and it allowed Iran to achieve tactical surprise in a relatively lightly held area. As a result, Iran's attack produced substantial initial successes. Iraq kept most of its best forces in the south, both to prepare for its own offensives and because of its fear of another final offensive. It had only two divisions in the forward area, and these were of mixed quality. Iraq's forces also did not position themselves well for mountain warfare.

Iraq also made some important tactical mistakes. Its units withdrew from many of the heights and ridges in the area but then deployed forward to defend the towns at the border. Giving up the rough mountain terrain allowed the Iraqi forces to be outflanked, and several towns could not be held without defending the surrounding heights. Sending troops so far forward scattered the Iraqi defenders so that they could not concentrate against the main lines of attack. Iraq's forces had further problems in dealing with Kurdish infiltration behind their lines of communication and, according to some reports, Iran even managed to use speed boats to move its troops through part of the reservoir.

The end result of these mistakes was that Iraq lost much of its 43rd division, from 1,500 to 4,000 men, and large amounts of tanks, armored vehicles, artillery, support vehicles, and ammunition and spares from its 1st Corps. As in its Faw offensive in 1986, Iran found it could obtain substantial supplies when it overran Iraqi positions. Nevertheless, Iran could not advance fast enough to prevent Iraq from reinforcing along superior interior lines of communication. Iran could not sustain its gains or achieve a breakthrough that led to any major tactical or strategic advantage. Further, Iran locked many of its best troops into mountain positions in the north and failed to mobilize enough new forces to properly defend its southern front.

The Use of Chemical Weapons Escalates to the Level of Atrocity

More happened at Halabjah and Dojaila, however, than another Iranian mountain offensive. These towns were largely Kurdish, and their population had often supported the anti-Iraqi Kurds in the area. Iraq treated them as being little more than centers of treason and made heavy use of poison gas the minute its forces were forced to abandon the towns. Iraq also seems to have made extensive use of gas as a terror weapon. Rather than simply try to defeat Iran or punish the residents of Halabjah and Dojaila for their lack of support, Iraq used gas as a broad threat to the Kurds to stop challenging Iraqi control of the northeast. Kurdish forces had scored some important successes during the winter in spite of a bloody Iraqi campaign to control, relocate, and/or eliminate any Kurdish towns or population groups that showed any signs of support for the Kurdish rebels.

Kurdish forces had briefly occupied the Iraqi town of Kanimasi near the Turkish border in September, and Kurdish and Iranian forces had taken some 100 square miles of Iraqi territory in the area northeast of Kirkuk near Mawat, including some 29 heights and 6 villages on either side of the Little Zab River. Kurdish forces occupied the border town of Deirlouk in January 1988 and had conducted a massive raid on the Iraqi resort of Sari Rash, northeast of Arbil. Travel to the city of Rawanduz had become unsafe and more raids, ambushes, and assassinations occurred throughout northeastern Iraq. Jalal Talabani's Kurdish Patriotic Union of Kurdistan (PUK) had also began to cooperate more effectively with the Barzani clan's Kurdish Democratic Party (KDP). This cooperation may have been the result of negotiations which Rafsanjani had conducted in Iran in late 1987.[27]

Iraq was still able to secure much of the area with a mix of its regular troops, Kurdish security forces that still supported the government, and local militias. Iraq had to redeploy some of its troops and paramilitary forces to the north, however, and had to put sandbagged fire bases along the major roads in the area and to mine Kurdish-rebel infiltration routes. The Kurdish guerrilla campaign was also a violent one, with ambushes, assassinations, and large numbers of civilian casualties. Like most such wars, it was a war of intimidation, and there were atrocities on both sides.

Most people outside the region, however, only understood that poison gas had been used against civilians. Iran rapidly gained a major propaganda advantage. It released horrifying TV films showing that up to 4,000 civilians had died of mustard gas and other agents, possibly including phosgene, nerve gas, and/or cyanide.[28] As a result, it made brutally clear that Iraq had made extensive use of gas warfare against women and children. While evidence later persuaded American experts that Iran had also fired gas shells into the town of Halabjah during the struggle for the town, it was Iraq that faced worldwide condemnation.[29]

This mix of a limited victory and a favorable foreign reaction may have deceived Iran into exaggerating the importance of its victories in the area. Khomeini made a rare public appearance on March 20 and said he would press on for "final victory." That same day, Iran claimed it fired 13 missiles at Iraq.

Iran then resumed its offensives northeast of the Kurdish town of Sayyid Sadiq. Iraq had deployed some 7,200 troops (four battalions) from its 7th Army Corps in the south and counterattacked, but it was repulsed by roughly 30,000 Iranian attackers. Iran then advanced up to 16 kilometers through the Rishan Mountains and captured Sayyid Sadiq. The seriousness of this fighting is illustrated by the fact Iraq claimed it flew some 224 combat sorties per day. Iraq also lost up to 3 planes per day, although Iran may also have lost some of its few remaining F-5s.

Once again, however, the end result of Iran's victories was that they forced Iran to commit more troops from the south to the north, caused Iran more casualties, and did not produce any major breakthrough that Iran could exploit. As the fighting went on, Iraq was also able to bring more and more of its superiority in air power and firepower to bear. It reestablished its defensive lines by early April and gradually began to push the Iranian forces back. While it is impossible to determine how much use it made of poison gas, it seems to have recaptured Sayyid Sadiq, which according to some reports Iraq then evacuated and leveled.

Iraq retook Iranian positions around Qara Dagh, about 20 miles west of Lake Darbandikhan. Iran was conspicuously silent about Iraqi claims to have recaptured most of their losses and to have inflicted serious losses on the Iranian positions. While the exact details are unclear, the Iraqi front in the northern and central fronts seem to have become much more secure by the first week in April. As had been the case in several previous offensives, Iran lacked the technology and firepower to continue its advances or even hold most of its gains once Iraq adjusted for its initial tactical mistakes.[30]

New Developments in the War of the Cities

Iraq also continued its missile strikes and the war of the cities. It announced on March 22 that it had fired 106 missiles against Iranian cities. Iraq fired 10 missiles a day against Iranian targets. On March 27, 1988, Iran claimed that Iraq had started to use a new and heavier missile. This started new speculation about possible Iraqi use of the SS-12, although the missile involved was almost certainly a Scud with a still smaller warhead or a heavy air-to-surface missile launched from Iraq's Soviet-made Tu-16 bombers.

Iraq launched missiles at targets like Qom as well as Tehran and conducted major air raids at 4 Iranian cities. These missile attacks and bombing sorties were still relatively ineffectual on an individual basis, and only about 18 percent of the strikes hit a target. Nevertheless, Iraqi missiles and aircraft had now hit some 37 cities, and Iraq scored many hits on a cumulative basis. Iraq also no longer gave Iran time to recover from the Iraqi air attacks on its refineries and petroleum distribution points.

By April 7, 1988, Iraq had raised its total missile attacks on Iranian cities to 140. Iran had replied with some 65 Scud attacks, but virtually all missed their target or failed to do significant damage, and Iran seemed to have used up most of its missiles.[31] Iran was forced to use a few of its remaining aircraft to launch an air raid on Baghdad on April 7, 1988. This raid had little effect, however, and one Iranian aircraft seems to have been shot down.[32]

Iran's propaganda about Iraq's use of poison gas at Halabjah and continuing reports from the front of the further Iraqi use of gas also increasingly backfired against Iran. The fear of Iraqi gas attacks rose steadily among both the population of Iranian cities and among Iranian troops at the front. It was clear that the fear of gas warfare was having a significant effect on Iranian recruiting and the flow of volunteers and on the popular support for the war.

Iraq Retakes Faw

It was at this point that Iraq began a series of land offensives that reversed the course of the war. Iraq suddenly shifted from defense to launching major counteroffensives. There was only limited visible warning of this shift. While Iraq had made no great secret about the advanced-training counteroffensive combat described earlier, it had conducted similar training since 1984, and it drew only limited Iranian attention.

During early 1988, Iraq supported new attacks on Iran by the People's Mujahideen National Liberation Army on a 14-mile front near Shush. At the same time, Iraq begin to build up its forces in the south. This Iraqi build-up, however, initially appeared to Iran to be a routine strengthening of its defensive positions. While Iranian aircraft took the unusual step of beginning to attack Iraqi concentrations south of Basra on March 26, 1988, Iran does not seem to have taken the risk of an Iraqi counterattack seriously. Iraq had conducted a major deception operation for nearly a month before the attack began. It had kept moving troops around the country, generally giving the impression that it was deploying its forces north.

When the Iraqi attack did come, it was one of the largest Iraqi offensives since 1980. Iraqi forces had trained for months near Lake Habaniyah and Al Hara. Iraq had reinforced its 7th Corps and redeployed much of its Republican Guard and newly trained attack forces. It had built up large stockpiles of artillery and chemical weapons and about two weeks before the attack had quietly deployed massive stocks of ammunition. Iraq also waited until April 17, the first day of Ramadan and the beginning of the annual month of fasting. This was a period when Iran was rotating its troops and had left positions like Faw undermanned. Some reports also indicate that the Iranian garrison at Faw had slowly been reduced from a peak of 30,000 men to only 5,000 to 8,000 in preparation for a rotation of its troops.[33]

Most reports indicate that the garrison was manned with relatively low-grade older troops and volunteers and that its commanders were slow to react. Further, the Iranian defensive positions were surprisingly badly developed. They lacked depth and were not particularly well sheltered or reinforced with tank barriers. The only major sheltered area was the central Iranian command post in the town of Faw.[34] Many defensive facilities had been left unfinished, and there seems to have been little training or preparation for gas warfare.

Iraq's "Blessed Ramadan" offensive was carefully timed to achieve almost complete tactical surprise. At the moment the attack started, most of the Iranian defenders were celebrating the last evening before the Ramadan fasting with a feast.[35] Iraq built up for its attack at night without alarming them and then began to advance at 5:00 A.M. Forces from the 7th Corps, under the command of Major General Maher Rashid, advanced down the bank of the Shatt al-Arab waterway. Iraq also conducted two amphibious attacks to flank Iran's main defenses and made extensive use of gas weapons.

Republican Guard forces, including many of the elite units that had received advanced combined-operations training during 1986 and 1987, pushed south down the center of Faw some 21 miles southeast from positions between Zubair and Umm Qasr, with Iraq holding a superior force ratio of roughly 6:1. Third Corps forces attacked down the other side of Faw, and special forces attacked through the marshy tidal flats, or Great Salt Lake, west of Faw. Iraq used nonpersistent nerve gas to help smash through Iran's defensive lines, took advantage of relatively dry terrain conditions and good weather, and quickly made major gains.

At the same time, Iraqi forces launched successful amphibious attacks on the western side of the peninsula from Umm Qasr. These forces fought their way through minefields and barbed wire, as well as complex water barriers, with considerable success, although they took significant casualties. Iraqi artillery was also effective and clearly benefited from its improved training in 1987. Iraqi artillery moved more quickly, was more responsive to commanders in the forward area, and did a much better job of shifting and concentrating fires.

Although Iraqi forces took casualties in penetrating the minefields and other defenses around the now virtually destroyed town of Faw, particularly the 7th Corps forces, the Iranian forces never recovered from the initial assault and could not regroup.[36] Many Iranian forces put up only a brief defense, and the local commanders showed little ability to rally their troops. Few units showed any sign of the willingness to die that had characterized Iranian forces in previous campaigns. The Iranian defenders began to pour back across the Shatt, but Iraqi fighters also knocked out two of the three pontoon bridges across the Shatt al-Arab from Iran to Faw. This still allowed Iranian troops to retreat but forced them to retreat in disarray and without their equipment. Iraq claimed that its air force flew 318 fighter and gunship attacks in support of the offensive on the first day.

Only 35 hours after the beginning of the attack, Iraq's flag again flew above Faw. Iraq also captured virtually all of the major combat equipment, armor, artillery, and stocks on the Faw Peninsula. This further weakened Iran's forces in the south.

Iran's dismay over the course of the attack is indicated by the fact that on the 18th, it charged Kuwait with allowing Iraq to launch part of its attack from Bubiyan and claimed that U.S. helicopter gunships supported Iraq. At the same time, rumors surfaced that both Rafsanjani, and Mohammed Rezai, the commander of the Pasdaran, had been sent to the Faw area to save the situation and that Khomeini refused to see them on their return.[37]

The only immediate political result of Iran's defeat, however, was that Brigadier General Esmael Shorabi, the Chief of Staff of the Armed Forces, was replaced with Brigadier General Ali Shahbazi. Shorabi was reassigned to the largely symbolic post of "military consultant" to the Supreme Defense Council. When he was swearing in Shahbazi, President Khameini stated that "the Pasdaran and the army must work closely together to coordinate their operations in every area. At present, more than any other time, the army is in need of sincere efforts." The change in command gave every appearance that the Mullahs were blaming the military for problems that they had created.[38]

New Naval Conflicts Between the U.S. and Iran

The naval fighting in the Gulf reached a new peak at virtually the same time that Iraq reconquered Faw. Iran first escalated tension in the Gulf by supporting pro-Iranian terrorists in seizing a Kuwaiti B-747 airliner while on a flight from Bangkok to Kuwait on April 5. The hijackers took advantage of the almost nonexistent security at Bangkok airport and were able to take over 100 hostages. They immediately demanded that Kuwait free the 17 pro-Iranian terrorists it had convicted of acts of sabotage and began a cycle of killing and intimidation that took the aircraft from Tehran, to Larnaca in Cyprus, and finally to Algeria. Iran may well have allowed added hijackers to board the aircraft while it was in Tehran and seems to have given them grenades and machine guns in addition to the pistols they used to seize the aircraft. The hijackers also showed some indications of advanced training, since they quickly revealed an expert knowledge of both the layout of the aircraft and its technical details.[39]

On Thursday, April 13, 1988, Iran took a far more serious step. Small ships of the Iranian Revolutionary Guard laid a new minefield in the Gulf. The next day, the U.S. frigate *Samuel B. Roberts* hit one of the mines as it was returning to Bahrain after completing the twenty-fifth convoy of 1988.[40] The *Roberts* was one of 25 U.S. ships still operating in the Gulf, and the mine explosion lifted the ship's stern 15 feet and blew a massive 22-foot hole. Ten American sailors were wounded, and the engine was flooded.[41]

Like the attack on the USS *Stark*, the explosion illustrated the critical importance of modern damage-control and fire-fighting capabilities. The explosion not only ripped a hole in the ship, it broke its keel, ripped the ship's engines from their mounts, and sent a fireball 150 feet up its stack. Fuel lines ruptured and major fires broke out. There were no fatalities because the engine room was fully automated and no crew were present.

The crew did, however, face a series of massive problems. It had to lace the ship together with steel wire to keep it from breaking up and had to reinforce the compartments with wood timbers to prevent flooding. Steel plates had to be welded over massive cracks in the deck house. The ship was surrounded by mines and providing assistance was difficult.

At the same time, the *Samuel B. Roberts* had important advantages over the *Stark*. The crew was able to save the ship because it was fully deployed at battle stations. It had won an award for best performance for advanced damage-control training before its deployment that was partly the result of the lessons from the *Stark*. The Gulf was calm when the mine explosion took place, and all fire-fighting equipment was dispersed and operational.

The U.S. rapidly discovered firm evidence that Iran had deliberately placed the mines in the convoy channel. The U.S. recovered several of the mines; they were Iranian-made copies of the Soviet M-08 mine. The divers who inspected them found Iranian serial numbers and clear evidence that the mines had been newly planted. European minesweepers later found a number of other mines and that there was more than one new field.[42]

On April 14, the National Security Planning Group (NSPG) met at the White House and considered several options. It eventually decided on a strike at three Iranian oil platforms in the Gulf, all of which were used by the Iranian naval Guards. The NSPG chose this option because it avoided any strike on Iranian land targets, was far from the fighting in the upper Gulf, and demonstrated Iran's acute vulnerability to any interruption to its oil exports. President Reagan approved the drafting of contingency plans the same day and then approved the suggested strike plan at a meeting at 8:30 P.M. on April 17. The President briefed the leaders of Congress at 9:00 A.M. on April 18. It is important to note that the U.S. did not know that Iraq planned to attack Faw the same day.

Early in the morning, the U.S. set up an extensive air screen over the

Gulf using aircraft from the carrier *Enterprise*. This air screen included E-2C Hawkeyes in addition to the regular E-3A patrols. It also included F-14A on combat air patrol. The E-3As performed both long-range warning functions and attack coordination for A-6Es armed with Harpoon missiles, laser-guided weapons, and Mark 20 Rockeye cluster bombs. A-7E light attack aircraft were on standby alert.[43]

At 9:01 A.M. on April 18, the U.S. gave Iran's Saasan oil platform several minutes warning. The 20–40 Guards on the platform abandoned it, leaving four ZSU-23 anti-aircraft guns and several SA-7s. At 9:17 A.M., U.S. Naval Forces shelled the platform, and then blew it up with explosives. The U.S. used three ships in the attack: the *Merrill*, *Lynde McCormack*, and the *Trenton*. The *Trenton* was an amphibious ship which carried a 400-man Marine Corps unit which included AH-1T, UH-1N, and CH-46 helicopters. It was part of the Contingency Marine Air Ground Task Force (CM) 2-88. The Marines boarded the platform at 10:39 A.M. and blew up the remaining installations.[44]

At 9:32 A.M., three additional ships, the *Simpson*, *Bagley*, and *Wainwright*, gave a similar warning to Iran's Nasr oil platform off Sirri Island. Iranian forces started firing ZSU-23-4 anti-aircraft guns at the U.S. ships. The *Wainwright* fired several shells in return, and the Iranians abandoned the platform. The U.S. ships then shelled and destroyed the Nasr oil platform by 10:25 A.M. The two oil platforms were roughly 100 miles apart.[45]

The Iranian Navy ship *Joshan*, carrying Harpoon and Sea Cat missiles, closed within 10 miles of the USS *Wainwright* and the American ships around the Nasr oil platform at 1:01 P.M. The *Wainwright* warned it to remain clear or come under fire at 1:15 P.M. The *Joshan* then fired what seems to have been a Sea Cat at the *Wainwright*. The *Wainwright* fired chaff to counter the missile, and moments later, the U.S. ships replied with four missiles and hit the *Joshan*, which sank less than an hour later. At 1:52 P.M. the *Wainwright* fired two missiles at two Iranian F-4s closing on the ship after they fired a missile and may have damaged one aircraft. Iranians in a Boghammar speedboat then fired on a helicopter from the *Simpson*. The only other Iranian aircraft in the area on that day were a P-3 and a C-130, which took no aggressive action.

These attacks led the U.S. to break off the attack on a third oil platform because it was obvious that the fighting might escalate to further naval conflict, and the U.S. did not want to raise the threshold of conflict. Nevertheless, Iran took several other steps to escalate during the morning and early afternoon. At 12:15 P.M., three Iranian speedboats fired on a helicopter from the USS *Simpson* and then on the American tug *Willi Tide*, a U.S.-registered supply boat off the coast of the UAE. An Iranian vessel then attacked the 113,000-ton British flag tanker, *York Marine,* and at 2:26 P.M. it attacked the *Scan Bay,* a U.S.-operated oil platform in the Mubarak oil field, about 15 miles off the coast of Abu Dhabi.[46]

At 2:23 P.M., U.S. A-6 jets spotted three Iranian Boghammar speedboats attacking the Mubarak oil platform. The resulting command sequence provides an important lesson in the importance of satellite communications. The A-6s radioed the carrier *Enterprise,* which radioed the commander of the Middle East Task Force aboard the *Coronado* in the Gulf. He then radioed the commander of USCENTCOM in Tampa, Florida, who contacted the Secretary of Defense and the Joint Chiefs in the National Military Command Center in the Pentagon. The Chairman of the Joint Chiefs contacted the President's National Security Advisor, who asked the President for permission to attack the ships. The President approved, and the A-6s used laser-guided bombs to sink one and disable another. The fate of the third was unknown. The entire command sequence from the A-6 to Presidential approval was conducted in near real time using global secure communications. The transmittal of the President's approval to the lead A-6 pilot came less than three minutes after his original request.

The U.S. then intercepted communications that two Iranian frigates had been ordered to attack the U.S. force. The Iranian frigates kept closing on the U.S. force, and the U.S. warned them away at 3:59 P.M. At 4:00 P.M., the Iranian frigate *Shahand,* which had long been one of the ships firing at cargo carriers in the Gulf, appeared south of Qeshm Island in the Strait of Hormuz. At 4:21 P.M., the *Shahand* fired on three Navy A-6 attack fighters and the U.S. ships in the area. Between 4:34 and 4:43 P.M., the U.S. aircraft fired laser-guided Skipper 2 bombs, and the frigate USS *Strauss* fired a Harpoon missile.[47] By 5:06 P.M., the *Shahand* was dead in the water and afire. The Iranian frigate sank that night.

At 6:18 P.M., the Iranian frigate *Sabalan* fired a missile at the U.S. frigate *Jack Williams* and a second missile at U.S. Navy attack jets in the area. Both missiles missed, but a U.S. A-6 attacked the *Sabalan* with laser-guided bombs and seriously damaged it. Although the *Sabalan* was notorious for its strikes on Gulf shipping, Secretary of Defense Carlucci halted further strikes, and at 8:00 P.M., the U.S. allowed the ship to be taken under tow by two Iranian tugs and to limp home to Bandar Abbas. By the time the smoke cleared, the U.S. had scored a major victory, and its only loss was one Marine Cobra attack helicopter from the *Trenton* and its crew of two, who seem to have been lost because of an accident.

Iran had lost a great deal of its operational naval strength. Its destroyers were largely inoperable, and its other two frigates were in the process of a refit. U.S. weapons and countermeasures all functioned exceptionally well. There was, however, one major uncertainty as to what happened during the missile exchanges. The USS *Jack Williams* reported that it had been attacked by five Silkworm missiles and had turned to fire chaff and optimize its ECM coverage each time. Department of Defense officials stated only that they had no evidence that Silkworm missiles were fired. Witnesses, including members of the press, saw all five missiles, but it was not possible to confirm whether they had been fired from the mobile Silkworm sites near the Straits of Hormuz.

Iran's motive for taking on the U.S. Navy and losing nearly half of its operational major ships can only be guessed at. It is impossible to know if the Iranian government fully approved the new minelaying, although it later became apparent that it was a major Iranian effort. New mines continued to be found, and the U.S. was still finding more as late as April 22.

Iran's mining of the Gulf and willingness to commit its ships may have been related to Iraq's war of the cities, the halt of its offensive in Kurdistan, and Iraq's increasing use of poison gas. These actions caused Iran's leadership to take progressively harder-line positions regarding the continuation of the war. Khomeini received a strong majority in the first round of the Iranian election of a new Majlis on April 8, 1988. The elections also bolstered Rafsanjani and Mousavi, and the Majlis gained a number of new hardliners. For example, Hojatolislam Mehdi Karrubi came in second in the voting. He was a strong advocate of exporting the revolution and had been the main cause of the previous year's uprising in Mecca.[48]

Iran may also have misunderstood the nature of U.S. naval and air power. Commanders may have executed standard contingency orders without fully reassessing the situation. Iran may have been reacting to its defeat at Faw and some perception of U.S. and Iraqi collusion. Iran may have felt that such a clash would deter the USSR from agreeing to any arms embargo or build up sympathy in the Third World. Finally, Iran may have hoped that even one successful strike would cause major damage and that a large-scale clash would force the U.S. to trigger the War Powers Act.[49]

If so, Iran must have been rapidly disillusioned: The Congress gave President Reagan almost universal support. The main Congressional response in terms of the War Powers Act was for several leading Democratic members of the Senate to suggest that it should be modified to remove the automatic withdrawal provisions and to create an act that would remove any incentive for foreign blackmail or escalation and help create a true consensus behind U.S. action without tying the President's hands.

The Soviet press did attack the U.S. actions in the Gulf as "banditry," and the PRC announced that it could not support sanctions on arms sales as part of UN Security Council Resolution 598, but the Western European nations largely supported the U.S. and demanded a halt to Iranian minelaying. Prime Minister Margaret Thatcher called the attack, "entirely justified." After consultation and a meeting within the Western European Union (WEU), the Europeans supported the U.S. action and returned their minesweepers into the area where the mines had been laid. The European ships had been withdrawn when the U.S. notified Belgium, Britain, France, Italy, and the Netherlands that it was about to commence combat operations in the area. The minesweepers found eight newly laid mines the next day.[50]

The regional reaction was more complex. Rafsanjani declared on April 19, that, "Time is not on our side anymore. The world—I mean the anti-Islamic powers—has decided to make a serious effort to save Saddam Hussein and tie our hands." Iran also fired a Silkworm missile into the desert near Kuwait City on April 20 from new positions inside Iran. It seems to have done this to show it could still cover the area after its loss of Faw.[51]

The Gulf states largely supported the U.S. action but also expressed their dismay at the fact the U.S. had not provided protection for all merchant ships and oil facilities. The U.S. reacted to these complaints on April 21 by declaring that it would now come to the aid of any ship or target under attack at the time and place of its own choosing and effectively warned Iran that there were no safe targets in the region. The U.S. also quietly stepped up its cooperation with its European allies in the Gulf, and they resumed more active minesweeping activity.

This increased Western involvement and its victories at Faw seem to have helped persuade Iraq that it could halt the war of the cities. Iraq declared a unilateral cease-fire on April 21, 1988, supposedly at the urging of the People's Mujahideen.[52] By that time, Iraq had fired between 190 and 200 missiles, and Iran had fired nearly 50. Roughly 100 of the Iraqi missiles had landed in Tehran and virtually all had hit near population targets. Even so, it is unlikely that all the missile attacks on Iran between February 29 and April 21 killed more than 2,000 people and that all the missile attacks on Iraq killed more than 100.[53]

The U.S. clash with Iran also helped influence the actions of the southern Gulf states. Saudi Arabia took the step of breaking relations with Iran on April 25, 1988. Kuwait had long urged that Saudi Arabia take a stronger stand, and the combination of U.S. resolve and Iranian hostility evidently led the Saudis to calculate that they no longer had anything to gain from preserving relations. The Saudis went further and announced that they had acquired CSS-2 class intermediate-range ballistic missiles (IRBMs) from the PRC with ranges of 1,600 miles, that these had been specially modified with conventional warheads, and that they were targeted on Iran. The Saudi Airlines office in Kuwait was bombed one day later.[54]

Iraq Retakes Salamcheh and the Area Around Basra

There was comparatively little major fighting during most of the rest of April and through the first three weeks of May. Iran did, however, hold a major naval exercise called Zolfaqar-3.[55] According to Iran, some 50 ships were involved, including destroyers, frigates, minesweepers, anti-submarine, amphibious, and logistic ships. The Navy was supported by air, Army, naval Guard, and marine units, and the 55th Shiraz Airborne Brigade. The exercise was obviously intended as a show of strength, although it was not particularly convincing. By this time, Iran's three WWII-vintage destroyers— the UK-built *Damavand* and U.S.-built *Babr* and *Palang*—had been out of operation for more than a year because of problems with spares and their missile systems. While Iran put on a display involving dividing, transit of mineswept channels, F-4 flights, and other naval activities, it did little to convince anyone that Iran still had a Navy that could put up any kind of resistance to the Western forces in the Gulf.[56]

Iraq kept up its strategic bombing against economic targets and its attacks on Iranian shipping. Iraq also used the period to deploy a large part of its forces for an attack on the Iranian forces opposite Basra. Iraq had begun to drain much of Fish Lake earlier in the year, and Iranian attempts at counterflooding in the area were not successful.[57] This dried out the area near the Iranian positions opposite Basra and allowed Iraq to make far more effective use of its armor in attacking the Iranian positions in the area.

Iraq strengthened its Third Corps forces around Basra to the point where it deployed 105,000 to 135,000 men. These units included many of the new Republic Guards units and elite elements Iraq had given special counterattack and mobility training. While it is unclear that Iraq built life-size models, as some Iraqi officers later claimed, they conducted extensive sand tray modeling and trained with mock-ups of some areas. Iraq also again conducted a deception operation and tried to convince Iran that it might be preparing to attack at Majnoon. It also built up massive ammunition reserves.

In late May, Iraq built up its armor, Republican Guard, and naval infantry forces in the forward area. It established attack routes for its forces to use in moving through its defenses, which had now been strengthened to the point where Iraq had established concentric rings of earthen berms, concrete bunkers, and 30-foot high mounds with observation and artillery points throughout the forward area. Iraq also concentrated enough artillery in the area where it planned to attack to give it overwhelming superiority in firepower.

At 9:30 A.M. on the morning of May 25, Iraq's Republican Guards and 3rd Corps forces attacked along a 15-mile corridor to the east and southeast of Basra.[58] The Iraqis were supported by one of the most intense artillery barrages in history and again made heavy use of nerve gas during the initial attack phase. They took advantage of the fact that the ground had now dried out extensively, as well as Iraq's massive superiority in armor. The attacking Iraqi forces showed the same professionalism in the speed with which they attacked and in their use of combined arms that they had first exhibited in retaking Faw.

The Iraqi forces hit Iran at the southern edge of Fish Lake, about six miles south of Basra, and launched another small attack to the north. At the time they attacked, they had built up a local superiority in the battle area of nearly three or four to one. They drove across the Jassem River on the eastern bank of the Shatt al-Arab waterway and cleared a 15-mile corridor to the east and southeast.

The Iranian defenses in the area involved a well-designed mix of trenches, sand-mound fortifications, barbed wire, tank snares, and mine fields. The Iranians also initially fought well. Iraq took significant casualties in penetrating the Iranian defenses, even though it had attempted to flank some of the best-defended positions, and many Iranian dead were found later beside their guns. Iraq also had to fight off at least one Iranian counterattack, which succeeded in taking some Iraqi POWs. Iraqi attack helicopters were called in for emergency close-support missions, and at least one Iraqi armored unit ran into major problems when it advanced without proper infantry support.

Iraq continued to send in armor, however, and made effective use of its artillery, often using helicopters as spotters for targeting purposes. As the Iraqi attack gathered momentum after the Iranian counterattack, the combination of Iraqi mass and the use of chemical weapons finally broke the Iranian resistance. Nearly five Iranian divisions began a rapid retreat. Some Iranian troops abandoned their artillery and forward machine gun and other fire posts after expending only a relatively small part of their ammunition. Many Iranian defenses and gun emplacements were later found to be filled with unused ammunition, grenades, bullets, gas masks, personal effects, and small rockets.[59]

There is no way to determine how much of the Iranian retreat was driven by the Iraqi use of gas, panic, or loss of morale. The Iranian forces were driven out of their forward positions within five hours of the second major Iraqi wave of attacks, however, and quickly fell back toward Ahwaz and Khorramshahr, often commandeering private cars and passenger buses. Many of the retreating Iranian troops did not even remove their personal effects, and reporters who examined the battlefield after the Iraqi attack found little evidence of either an orderly withdrawal or high casualties. Iran took between six-to-eight times more casualties than Iraq and at least 350 Iranians surrendered without significant resistance. Iraq also captured significant numbers of artillery weapons, a number of other armored vehicles, and as many as 90 tanks, many of them abandoned without any sign of combat damage.[60]

After a total of ten hours of combat, the Iraqi flag was flying over the desert border town of Salamcheh, some 15 miles east of Basra. Iran's gains of 1987, which it had achieved at a cost of 50,000 dead, had been lost in a single day. Tehran Radio could do little more than announce a "withdrawal."

It was clear that Iran had suffered its second major defeat of the year, and there was little that Iran could do in response. It had already lost at least 10 percent of its major combat equipment, and while it could get replacements for some of the 150 artillery pieces, it could not obtain armor. According to some sources, recruiting also dropped off by nearly 70 percent.[61] The defeat also led Khomeini to issue an appeal to the Iranian troops. On May 28, he told them their losses did not matter because when they "began treading in this holy path, they have lost nothing to be worried about, nor have they suffered any loss of which they should repent." He also made it clear that the war would continue: "The fate of the Iraq-imposed war will be determined on the battlefronts, not at a negotiating table."[62]

Iraq also scored gains in the north during this period. It did not launch a single major offensive but conducted a series of attacks throughout the Kurdish areas that Iran had taken in 1987 and 1988. Iraq scored a series of small victories and drove the Iranian forces back, along with the supporters of Barzani and Talabani. In some cases, it took Kurdish villages and bases it had not occupied since 1986.

The Uncertain Situation in June 1988

At the beginning of June 1988, there still were few signs that Iran's defeats on the land and in the Gulf were pushing it toward a cease-fire. While Iran obviously lacked the public support for the war that had existed in early 1987, its new elections for the Majlis had increased the power of pro-war radicals, and Khomeini seemed no closer to agreeing to a cease-fire than in 1987. This seems to have led senior Iraqi officials, like Defense Minister Adnan Khairallah, to threaten to go on the offensive and seize the cities Iran was using as staging areas near the border. Iraq also threatened to keep up its missile and air attacks on Iran's cities and oil targets until it forced an end to the war.

The war in the Gulf was equally uncertain. Western ships found more than 13 newly laid mines. Iran had hit 31 tankers since the beginning of 1988, versus 20 for Iraq. This compared with 92 Iranian attacks and 87 Iraqi attacks in all of 1987. There were 30 U.S. ships still in the Gulf, including the carrier *Enterprise*. Britain had one destroyer, two frigates, four minesweepers, and two auxiliary vessels. Belgium had two minesweepers and one auxiliary ship. France had one destroyer, one frigate, and one minesweeper. Italy had three frigates, three minesweepers, and two auxiliary ships. The Netherlands had two minesweepers.

Iran also received new Silkworm missiles from the PRC or similar Styx missiles from North Korea. Iran also expanded its new Silkworm sites along the Gulf, including building a new set of cement platforms, storage sheds, concrete bunkers that could hold four missiles, and support facilities at Kuhestak, a town near the Straits of Hormuz. It was clear that Iran had not abandoned its effort to threaten Gulf shipping and that it might complete a sheltered launch facility near the Straits by the fall of 1988.

The U.S. responded by deploying the USS *Vincennes*, an AEGIS cruiser with countermeasures and weapons systems designed to defeat the Silkworm, to the area just inside the mouth of the Gulf. It also seems to have deployed a specially modified form of the Tomahawk sea-launched cruise missile, with a penetrating warhead that could be used to strike at sheltered missiles. Further, the U.S. improved its airborne electronic countermeasure capabilities and deployed improved electronic warfare aircraft to its carriers.[63]

As for the UN peace effort, it was still unclear whether the new fighting would move both sides toward a cease-fire or would make Security Council Resolution 598 as ineffective as resolutions like 435 (Nambia) and 242 (Arab-Israeli). Secretary General Javier Perez de

Cuellar began a new cease-fire initiative in late May and asked both Iran and Iraq to send representatives for intense new negotiations in early June. Neither side, however, responded with great initial enthusiasm. Iraq demanded that Iran's leadership publicly accept all the terms of 598 before it would agree to even a temporary cease-fire. Iran showed increased signs of internal political and social stress, but its leaders remained silent. The USSR and China continued to stand aside from any effort to enforce sanctions.

Iran's losses near Basra did, however, lead it to make new changes in its high command. On June 2, Khomeini formally announced that Rafsanjani had been appointed the commander in chief of all Iranian forces. This was in theory at the urging of President Khameini, the head of the Supreme Defense Council. It is hard to tell exactly what motives were involved. Rafsanjani had actually occupied the same position on a de facto basis for several months. Rafsanjani had long had the title of Khomeini's representative on the Supreme Defense Council and had certainly played a powerful role in the redeployment of Iranian forces to the north and other shifts in Iran's military position that had contributed to the loss of Iran's positions at Faw and around Basra. Like the earlier replacement of Brigadier Ismael Sohrabi with Col. Ali Sahbazi after Iran's loss of Faw, Rafsanjani's appointment seems to have been more a political act to assure absolute revolutionary loyalty than the result of an effort to make major changes in the leadership and organization of Iran's forces.

Some sources did indicate at the time that the shift was intended to prepare Iran for some form of compromise and that Iran had dropped its goal of insisting on an Islamic republic in Iraq and would accept a pro-Western replacement for Saddam Hussein. They also indicated that Rafsanjani wanted to concentrate on the internal revolution in Iran and to end the war.[64] This explanation seems doubtful. Rafsanjani immediately expressed his support for the war and stated that there would be "no compromise, no submission, and no backing down." Tehran Radio also announced on June 5, 1988, that thousands of new 18-year-old volunteers had left for the front.[65]

Other senior leaders around Khomeini also issued messages that indicate that Rafsanjani may have received the appointment largely to cope with the rising popular concern over Iran's defeats. Mehdi Karrubi, a member of the Majlis and head of the Martyrs Foundation, called for an investigation of the recent defeats. The Ayatollah Montazari called for Rafsanjani to unify and reorganize the armed forces and stated that their disorganization had "made the war most costly."[66] In short, Rafsanjani's appointment seems to have done little more than strengthen the leadership's commitment to the war and the existing bias toward revolutionary orthodoxy at the expense of military professionalism.[67]

There was growing reason for Iran's leadership to be concerned about Iran's internal politics and popular support for the war. Protests against the war had become more frequent, and protest rallies had been put down by troops at Komeinyshahr and Isfahan. The same day that Rafsanjani was appointed, ex-Prime Minister Mehdi Barzargan attacked Khomeini for continuing the war. In an open letter, he stated, "Since 1986, you have not stopped proclaiming victory, and now you are calling upon the population to resist until victory. Isn't that an admission of failure on your behalf? . . . You have denounced the policy of the U.S., and they are now installed solidly at our gates in the Persian Gulf. You have spoken of the failure of Iraq, and the crumbling of its regime, but thanks to your misguided policies, Iraq has fortified itself, its economy has not collapsed, and it is we who are on the edge of bankruptcy." Almost immediately, 40 of Barzargan's top supporters were arrested.[68]

This mix of pressures seems to have led Iran's leadership to attempt to show that it could still conduct a major offensive. On June 13, 1988, it launched an attack on the Iraqi Third Army positions in the Salamoheh area east of Basra. A force of at least 20,000–25,000 Revolutionary Guards, in formations of as many as 50 battalions, attacked before dawn in two thrusts in the area around Salamcheh. The Pasdaran forces seem to have penetrated the initial minefields and barbed wire, but Iraq did not lose all its forward defenses. Iran quickly claimed to have killed or wounded 19,000 Iraqis and to have taken some 2,100 prisoners.[69]

The fighting unquestionably was intense. Iraq reported that it flew nearly 300 fighter ground-attack sorties and another 650 helicopter gunship sorties during the three-day battle. At the height of the Iranian advanced, Iranian forces seem to have penetrated up to 10 kilometers inside of Iraq. The Third Army had some 40,000 troops and 11 brigades in the area, however, and rapidly redeployed its reserves. Iraq continued to counterattack with chemical bombs and shells. After about 19 hours of intense fighting, the Iranian forces were driven back. While they took significant numbers of Iraqi prisoners, they also suffered heavy losses and took several thousand casualties. If the battle was somehow supposed to be a symbol of Rafsanjani's new military leadership, it succeeded to the extent that it showed Iran could still attack Iraq. At the same time, it cost Iran more losses and did little to show that Iran was improving its military capabilities.[70]

Iraq also continued to make slow but significant progress in recapturing its territory in the north. This seems to have led Iran to attempt to organize the anti-Iraqi Kurds into a 50,000-man army, and the Revolutionary Guards Minister Mohsen Rafiqdoust, and Commander of the Guards Corps Mohsen Rezai, offered to provide the necessary arms. This had little military effect, and Iraq continued to retake a number of heights. On June 14, for example, Iraq recovered five heights in the area around Sulaymaniyeh. Iraq's victories in the south had allowed it to reinforce its positions in the north and to deploy more helicopter gunships and artillery. Iran had lost the initiative in the area and could not regain it.[71]

Iraq's Offensives at Mehran and Majnoon

The diplomatic struggle in June was complicated by a number of contradictory trends. No progress occurred in moving toward an arms embargo in the UN, although the Secretary General did quietly continue to encourage movement toward a cease-fire. The USSR continued to quietly support Iraq with more arms while occasionally calling for U.S. forces to leave the Gulf. Iran showed signs that it was trying to reestablish good relations with Britain and France, but moved slowly on key issues like hostages. Iran also declared on June 15 that no Iranian pilgrims would be permitted to go to Saudi Arabia for the Haj.

While Iraq continued to seek U.S. support, its Foreign Minister Tariq Aziz cancelled a meeting with Secretary Shultz when he learned a U.S. State Department official had met with Talabani. Iran and Iraq also squabbled noisily over oil quotas in a meeting of OPEC, and Iraq, Iran, and Saudi Arabia kept up the propaganda attacks that had begun the previous year.

Iraq, however, was concentrating on the land war and not on diplomacy. In mid-June, it deployed large amounts of armor and substantial forces from its Chemical Corps to the area near Mehran, which by now was little more than an abandoned mass of rubble and dead palm trees. On June 18, it launched a new offensive it called "Forty Stars."[72] A combination of Iraqi forces and Mujahideen e-Khalq forces, which had been trained and supported in Iraq, attacked the Iranian positions in the area.[73] Supported by the use of nerve gas and some 530 sorties of fighters and helicopter gunships, the attacking forces captured the city and took several positions in the heights near Mehran.

In part of the battle, the Mujahideen e-Khalq came close to wiping out an entire Iranian Pasdaran division and was able to take most of its equipment intact.[74] All in all, the Iranian regular forces seem to have lacked the supplies and support to fight effectively because so many resources had earlier been shifted to the Pasdaran forces in the North. Iran suffered at least 3,000–5,000 casualties and lost more major equipment.[75] The advancing Iraqi forces captured virtually all of the major Iranian equipment in the area—roughly two divisions' worth—and took the Iranian logistic depots intact, including a large number of Toyota trucks.

The Iraqi forces withdrew from the area after three days but left the Mujahideen e-Khalq, or National Liberation Army forces, in the area. At this point, Iran had only limited forces left in the area between the front and Kermanshah. Iran was forced to rush what reserves it could to the area, although it had few surplus forces left and even less major combat equipment.[76]

Iran's response to this victory was to claim that it had scored a major victory of its own by repulsing an Iraqi attack on Iranian positions at three points in the area near Mawat and an Iraqi border town in Sulamanlyah, about 200 miles northeast of Baghdad. Iraq does seem to have taken some minor reverses, but Iraq continued to make gains in the north. The same day Iraq attacked Mehran, it claimed to have taken 13 peaks, and Iraq claimed to have captured 25 peaks since March. Iraq also seems to have shot down at least one Iranian F-5 during this fighting.[77]

Iraq also launched a new set of strategic bombing attacks on Iranian oil targets. Iraqi fighter bombers launched their heaviest attacks in two months on June 23. They set 10 oil installations on fire, including 6 crude oil production units in Ahwaz, two pumping stations in Bibi Hakemeh, and other facilities at Kaj Saran. These were the first major raids on Iranian economic targets since the truce in the war of the cities on April 19. Iraq had then reserved the right to hit economic targets, but the only other major raid after April 19 was a strike on the power station at Neka, northeast of Tehran, on May 25. Iraq kept up these raids during late June and early July and hit an Iranian natural gas plant and offshore oil facility on June 31.[78]

Iraq's key activity during June, however, was to prepare for an attack on the remaining Iranian positions in Majnoon and to the rear of the Majnoon Islands. Once again, Iraq built up a massive set of attack forces supported by artillery and other support forces. It also built mock-ups of the area and used them to train forces for the assault. It prepared for both a frontal assault on the remaining Iranian positions in the northern island and a massive armored assault around the marsh areas to strike at the Iranian rear.

Iraq attacked on June 25 in its fourth major offensive of 1988. The offensive was called the "On God We Rely (Trust)" offensive, and it attacked both the Iranian forces in the islands and in the positions around them. The Iraqi forces assaulting the Iranian positions in the Majnoon islands attacked at 3:30 A.M. and consisted largely of infantry in small boats and specially trained Republican Guards units equipped with amphibious armored vehicles. These assaults seem to have preceded by at least some use of chemical weapons, and the Iraqi forces were supported by literally hundreds of artillery weapons and tanks that had been carefully positioned on built-up positions in the marsh to provide direct fire.

Iraq followed up its initial assaults by quickly using bridging equipment and bulldozers to establish access to the territory it won. The Iranian forces in the islands had little ability to reply to this kind of military sledge hammer, and Iraq's superiority in firepower is indicated by the fact Iraq felt safe enough to allow Saddam Hussein to appear on Iraqi TV leading a charge against the Iranian forces. The Iranian forces put up only a token defense, and their resistance had totally collapsed about eight hours after the beginning of the Iraqi attack.

Iraqi forces from the Republican Guards and Third Army, equipped with several thousand armored weapons, then attacked across the border. According to some U.S. estimates, the Iraqis had nearly 2,000 tanks and 600 artillery pieces in the area versus less than 60 Iranian tanks and a few artillery pieces. This gave Iraq a superiority in major weapons of roughly 20:1.[79]

The Iraqi assault forces were supported by massive reserves and the forces of Iraq's Chemical Corps. Some reports also indicate that a brigade of Iraqi paratroops were dropped in the rear of the Iranian forces, which would have been the first use of airborne troops since the start of the war.[80] The Guards attacked to the north and Third Army forces to the South. Iraq quickly enveloped the Iranian positions in both Majnoon and the Hawizeh Marshes and drove some 30 kilometers into Iran with only token opposition.

Iran suffered thousands of casualties, and many Iranians surrendered to Iraq.[81] Iran also claimed that 60 soldiers had been killed and 4,000 injured by attacks with nerve and cyanide gas. These claims were almost certainly true, and Iraq no longer even made a pretense that it did not use such weapons. On July 1, Tariq Aziz, the Iraqi Foreign Minister, acknowledged that Iraq had used chemical weapons. He also went on to claim that "Iran started its use. We were victims many times since the early beginning of the conflict." While the charge Iran had used gas first was almost certainly untrue, Tariq Aziz dealt with Western criticism as follows: "There are different views on this matter from different angles. You are living on a civilized continent. You are living on a peaceful continent."[82]

Once again, Iraq took virtually all of the supplies and equipment of the Iranian forces. Further, it may have inflicted major losses on the

Iranian Air Force when Iran committed up to 35 of its planes in trying to halt the Iraqi advance. Iraqi fighters and helicopter gunships seem to have flown over 400 sorties, and Iran was simply overwhelmed. Further, on the same day that Iraq took Majnoon, it claimed to have taken a total of 40 heights in the north since it had begun its counteroffensives there in March.[83]

Saddam Hussein celebrated these victories by stating that "today's battle was the last and hardest link in the chain. Final victory is very near, if God wills." Tehran Radio, in contrast, appealed for more troops to come to the front and said the nation "must give priority to sending trained fighters to the front and to place all our capacities in the service of the war effort."[84]

Iran responded by claiming that it had won a compensating victory in the north. It stated on June 28 that it had defeated Iraqi attacks in the Shakh-Shemiran heights and in the area near Darbandiknan and that Iraq had lost 70 percent of three army brigades and two battalions and thousands of casualties. In fact, Iraq seems to have used chemical weapons in both assaults, to have taken the entire Mawat (Awat) basin area, to have taken four positions along the Shehabi Ridge, and to have scored minor advances with limited casualties. Iran no longer had any of the offensive capabilities in the north that it had shown during its advances on the Darbandikhan area in March.[85]

It also seems clear that these new Iraqi victories raised additional concerns on the part of Iran's leadership about the reliability of Iran's armed forces and the splits between the Pasdaran and regular forces. The Ayatollah Montazari called, on June 30, for merger of the regular forces and Pasdaran: "The issue of the armed forces and revolutionary guards is now the issue of the day. . . . This difficulty should be solved in a sensible way by creating a single, powerful military organization, under whatever name, to prevent this duplication. We should solve this problem once and for all." This was good advice in theory, but it was impossible to implement in the middle of a series of major defeats. The most that Iran could do was to establish a new command headquarters that combined the regular forces, all the branches of the Pasdaran, the Baseej, Kurdish irregulars, and units of Iranian-based Iraqi opponents of Saddam Hussein. Rafsanjani announced the creation of this command on July 2, and it was far too little, far too late.[86]

A New Clash Between the U.S. and Iran
and the Shooting Down of Iran Air Flight 655 [87]

These new Iranian defeats seem to have led the naval branch of the Guards to initiate a new series of attacks on shipping in the Gulf. The first attack came near the Straits of Hormuz on July 2, when Iranian gunboats fired on a Danish freighter. These attacks halted when the USS *Montgomery* arrived on the scene and fired a warning shot.[88] The second Iranian attack came the next day and was to have far more tragic consequences.

On the morning of July 3, 1988, the USS *Elmer Montgomery* was patroling the northern portion of the Straits of Hormuz. At 0330 Zulu time, the *Montgomery* observed seven small Iranian gunboats approaching a Pakistani merchant vessel.[89] The small boats had manned machine-gun mounts and rocket launchers. Shortly thereafter, the *Montgomery* observed 13 Iranian gunboats breaking up into three groups. Each group had 3 to 4 gunboats, and they took position off the *Montgomery*'s port quarter.

At 0411Z, the *Montgomery* heard the gunboats challenging merchant ships in the area, It then heard 5 to 7 explosions coming from the north. At 0412Z, the AEGIS cruiser USS *Vincennes* was directed to proceed north to the area of the *Montgomery* and investigate. The *Vincennes*'s Lamps Mark III helicopter, which was already on patrol, was directed to observe the gunboat activity. Meanwhile, the *Vincennes* continued to observe an Iranian P-3 patrolling to the north.

At approximately 0615Z, the *Vincennes*'s helicopter was fired upon by one of the small boats. The *Vincennes* then took tactical command of the *Montgomery*, and both ships closed on the location of the firing at high speed. As the two U.S. ships closed on the area, two Iranian gunboats turned toward the U.S. ships. They continued to close, and the *Vincennes* was given permission to fire. This surface action continued during the entire time between the take off of Iran Air 655 and its downing. Another U.S. ship, the USS *Sides*, was transiting from east to west through the Straits of Hormuz and was about 18 miles to the east at this time.

The *Vincennes* was now about one mile west of the centerline of the civilian air path from the joint civil-military airport at Bandar Abbas to Dubai. Iran Air 655 took off at 0647Z as part of a routinely scheduled international airline flight to Dubai. At approximately 0647Z, and while still engaged with Iranian gunboats, the *Vincennes*'s AN/SPY1A radar detected Iran Air 655 at a bearing of 025 degrees, 47 nautical miles. The size of the aircraft could not be identified by the digital radar processing on the *Vincennes*, which does not show a "blip" in proportion to target size. It was simply assigned the digital identification code TN 4131.

The aircraft continued to close on the *Vincennes*, which was right on the flight path, with a constant bearing and decreasing range. It was at this point that the IDS, or identification supervisor, on the

Vincennes checked the airline guide to see if the aircraft could be commercial. Iran Air 655 was 27 minutes late, however, and the IDS incorrectly concluded that the aircraft could not be flight 655. At 0649Z, the *Vincennes* issued warnings on the Military Air Distress (MAD) frequency of 243 mhz. At 0650, it began warnings on the International Air Distress frequency (IAD) of 121.5 mhz. The airliner was then about 40 nautical miles from the *Vincennes*.

The *Vincennes* began to issue continuous MAD and IAD warnings when the airliner closed to within 30 miles of the *Vincennes*. The ship issued a total of five warnings on MAD and four on IAD. At this point, the ship experienced a foul bore in mount 51, and full rudder was applied to unmask the after-gun mount in the midst of an ongoing surface action. This further increased tension in the CIC. The *Vincennes's* warnings to Iran Air 655 continued, but there was no response.

At 0653Z, with the aircraft at a range of 15 to 16 nautical miles from the *Vincennes*, and 3.35 nautical miles to the west of the centerline of the air corridor, the USS *Sides* gave the last IAD warning to the aircraft. At 0654Z, the commanding officer of the *Vincennes* turned the firing key. The U.S. missile intercepted Iran Air 655 at a range of eight miles, and the aircraft crashed about 6.5 miles east of Hengham Island. Some 290 people from six different nations died in the crash.

This tragedy led to a storm of controversy, including false reporting from the *Vincennes*, based on the false beliefs of the officers inside its combat information center that had been generated by their interaction and tensions during the intercept. The personnel inside the CIC translated various oral reports to believe that they had a firm indication the aircraft had an F-14 identification of friend and foe (IFF) signal, that it was descending rather than climbing, and that it was off the standard flight path. As is discussed in detail in Chapter 14, this misleading information was not provided by the ships' sensors. The Iranian aircraft was on a normal commercial air-flight plan profile, was transmitting the commercial Mode III IFF signal common to such air flights, and was in continuous ascent from its takeoff at Bandar Abbas to the point where it was shot down.

The situation was made even worse when several Iranian officials charged that the U.S. had deliberately shot the plane down, and some U.S. commentators began to charge that Iran had somehow deliberately martyred the plane. In fact, however, the tragedy was the result of an unfortunate mix of combat conditions, sheer chance, and human error.

The *Vincennes* not only was shooting at Iranian gunboats; there were other gunboats in the area as well. The *Vincennes'* commander also had to consider the fact that Iran had conducted some 88 ship attacks in 1987, and 72 percent of these occurred in the shipping routes between the UAE and Abu Musa. All the Iranian ship attacks from November 1987 to April 1988 had been conducted in the southern Gulf, and nearly 50 percent were conducted at night. During the U.S. clash with Iran in April, the USS *Wainwright* had also encountered an aircraft that failed to respond to repeated warnings. The missile hit and damaged the aircraft, which turned out to be an Iranian F-4.

Although the F-14 is not normally used to deliver ordnance against ships, it can do so if it closes to a range of about two miles. The use of the F-14 was credible because of intelligence warnings that such modifications might take place and the fact Iran had had to conserve other air assets since August 1986, although most of the 187 attacks Iran had made of shipping between March 1984 and October 1986 were made by aircraft using iron bombs and Maverick missiles.[90]

The situation was further complicated by the fact that F-14s had recently been transferred to Bandar Abbas, and the Iranian Air Force had changed its operating patterns at Bandar Abbas significantly during the month prior to July 3, 1988. Iraqi F-14s had also flown 6 patrol missions out of Bandar Abbas in June and had already flown 2 in July. Iranian F-14s were observed flying at air speeds of 250 to 400 knots while climbing to station and at 500–550 knots during air intercepts.

The U.S. command in the Gulf had issued warnings about more aggressive behavior on June 18. It also had warned on June 30 and July 1 that the U.S. should anticipate more aggressive Iranian attacks on ships because of Iraq's gains on the ground and Iraqi air attacks on shuttle tankers. These warnings were accurate. The problem of tracking the commercial air liners in the area was also extremely complex. There are 18 air corridors across the Gulf covering 50 percent of its navigable waters. A total of 12 of these routes cross the southern Gulf and Straits of Hormuz area. Seven go to the Dubai/Sharjah terminal control area and five to the Abu Dhabi terminal control area. At least 1,775 commercial airline flights passed through the Oman control center area during the week ending July 13, 1988.

This made it almost impossible to track all of the civil air flights going over the combat area and forced commanders to rely on radio warnings. These, however, presented problems because they interfered with air traffic control. For example, when the USS *Halyburton* warned away British Airways flight 147 on June 8, 1988, the airliner immediately came into a near-miss situation with another airliner, and Dubai's air traffic control filed a formal protest.

The U.S. Navy inquiry into the shooting down of Iran Air 655 found that all of these circumstances combined with human error. The tapes recording all the data registered by the ships sensors and consoles showed that the operators misread the speed and altitude provided to them and showed the aircraft descending from 7,800 feet and flying at 445 knots. At least four members of the CIC crew had this impression, although it was not justified from the data provided. Similarly, the Identification Supervisor (IDS) made an error in reading IFF data that was not a result of sensor information. The commanding officer of the *Vincennes* had only three minutes and forty seconds of time to make up his mind, from the first identification of the aircraft to the point he had to fire; it is scarcely surprising that he acted as he did.

At the same time, Iran had to bear a considerable amount of the blame as well as the U.S. Even given the pilot workload during takeoff, the pilot of Iran Air 655 should have monitored the IAD warning frequencies. Similarly, Bandar Abbas, Approach Control, and Tehran Center either did not monitor or ignored the IAD warnings. Iran also allowed an airliner to fly at low altitude in close proximity to hostilities that had been underway for several hours. While it is unclear that the IRGC gunboats were in communication all of the time, they were certainly in communication with the military base at Bandar Abbas and had ample time to warn Iranian civil aircraft.[91]

The initial Iranian reaction, however, was to put all the blame on the U.S. and to attempt to use the incident to revive support for the war. Khomeini issued a statement that "we must all be prepared for a real war and go to the war fronts and fight against America and its lackeys." Khameini and Montazari denounced the U.S., and Tehran Radio stated that "the criminal United States should know that the unlawfully shed blood in the disaster will be avenged in the same blood-spattered sky over the Persian Gulf."[92]

This reaction was softened the next day when Rafsanjani cautioned against extreme reactions. While he stated that the incident was probably a "calculated plot," he obviously wanted to avoid any provocation of the U.S. that would lead to still more trouble in the Gulf. Tension was also eased somewhat when President Reagan expressed his regrets and indicated that the U.S. was considering compensation. The tragedy also failed to produce the kind of mass support for the war that Khomeini may have expected. If anything, it tended to bring home to the Iranian leadership and people the extent of their isolation and of their inability to break out of the vise created by the Western presence in the Gulf and Iraq's growing military success.

Iraq's Offensives on the Central Front
Force Iran to Accept a Cease-Fire

Iraq kept up its pressure on Iran. By the time the fighting at Majnoon was over, Iraq's land offensives had driven Iran out of virtually all of its significant gains since 1982, and it was clear that Iran's troops no longer had the will to resist. Iraq had not only inflicted a massive set of defeats, it had taken vast amounts of equipment and supplies, and the mere threat of gas sometimes panicked Iranian forces.

On July 12, Iraqi forces shelled the Iranian positions around the Zubaidat border area of Iran, a group of oil fields east of Al Amarah. These were some of the last positions on Iraqi territory, and the shelling was soon followed by a new Iraqi attack with a force of about five divisions. At 7:30 A.M., Republican Guards forces and forces from Iraq's 4th Corps advanced on the Iranian positions. It is unclear whether Iraq used gas, but the Iranian defenses quickly collapsed. Within a matter of hours, Iraq was in control of virtually all of the Iranian positions on its territory and took roughly 2,500 Iranian prisoners.

The Iranian regular army seems to have depended on logistic support from the Pasdaran and did not receive the reinforcement and support it expected. Further, the Iraqi forces then advanced almost unopposed some 40 kilometers into Iran and took Dehloran and some 1,500 square miles of Iranian territory. While Iraq withdrew from these gains after several days, it had proved that Iran was now virtually defenseless.[93]

The same day, two U.S. Army helicopters exchanged fire with two Iranian gunboats in the Gulf about 25 miles west of Farsi Island, but the only result was to force the gunboats to break off their attack on a tanker called the *Universal Monarch*. In spite of their losses, the naval Guard kept up occasional raids, striking at another tanker on July 15. Iraq, in turn, bombed two oil-pumping stations near Dezful.

A few days later, Iran's growing weakness received yet another public demonstration. On July 13, Iraq threatened Iran with an invasion of southern Iran if Iranian forces did not evacuate Halabjah and its remaining positions in Kurdistan. After its recent defeats, Iran was virtually defenseless in the south. It was down to less than 200 tanks and light tanks versus thousands of Iraqi tanks and still more thousands of other Iraqi armored vehicles.

In fact, Iraq had captured so much equipment that it was able to put on an incredible show on the outskirts of Baghdad. Iraq set up a large compound filled with captured Iranian equipment. This compound held tens of thousands of abandoned Iranian assault rifles, over 570 tanks, over 130 BMP-1 and Scorpion MICVs, well over 300 more armored personnel carriers, over 320 towed artillery weapons, roughly 45 self-propelled artillery weapons, well over 300 anti-aircraft guns, and many machine guns. Virtually all of this equipment was intact and functional, and much of it looked brand new. Rather than include all of Iraq's gains, it included the equipment that could either be used immediately or be easily reconditioned. Iraqi sources claimed that since March, Iraq had captured a total of 1,298 tanks, 155 armored infantry fighting vehicles, 512 heavy artillery weapons, 6,196 mortars, 5,550 recoilless rifles and light guns, 8,050 rocket-propelled grenades, 60,694 rifles, 322 pistols, 6,156 telecommunications devices, 501 items of heavy engineering equipment, 454 trucks, 1,600 light vehicles and trailers, 16,863 items of chemical defense gear, and 16,863 caskets.[94]

Tehran replied within hours that it would withdraw. Rafsanjani announced on July 14 that all Iranian forces would pull back from the occupied Iraqi territory north of Haj Omran, which Iran had first occupied in 1986. The town, which was about 80 miles north of Sulaimaniyeh, was the last major piece of territory Iran held on Iraqi soil.[95]

On July 18, on the twentieth anniversary of Ba'ath rule, Saddam Hussein again called for peace negotiations, stating that Iraq had no ambitions to take Iranian territory. He also warned, however, that Iraq would not give Iran time to rebuild its forces and would continue to strike against economic targets. This time, Iran had to listen. Iraq's victories, the growing pool of Iranian losses, the fear of chemical weapons and of the renewal of the war of the cities, the threat of Western naval power, and diplomatic isolation, finally drove Iran to formally request the UN to implement Resolution 598.

On July 17, 1988, President Khameini of Iran sent UN Secretary-General Javier Perez de Cueller a letter requesting a cease-fire. The letter blamed Iraq for starting the war and the U.S. for killing 290 innocent civilians in shooting down the Airbus, but it also went on to state that "we have decided to officially declare that the Islamic Republic of Iran—because of the importance it attaches to saving the lives of human beings and the establishment of justice and regional and international peace and security—accepts UN resolution 598."[96]

According to one press report, the decision to accept the cease-fire only occurred after an eight-hour meeting that Khomeini called with nearly 40 of his top officials. Khomeini was supposedly ill, and his son Ahmad presided over the meeting. Khomeini supposedly agreed to the cease-fire only because Mohsen Rezai, the commander of the Pasdaran, had said the war could only be won after five more years of conflict, and Iran would have to fight a defensive war until 1993. Supposedly, Iran could then only go on the offensive because it increased the Pasdaran by 700 percent and the regular army by 250 percent.[97]

In any case, the Iranian regime not only had been defeated on the battlefield, it was nearly bankrupt. Iran had used up most of its foreign exchange reserves, its industry was in near collapse, its currency threatened to become worthless, and its markets were in a state of near collapse. Regardless of the views of individual personalities in the Iranian leadership, it must have been clear to virtually all of Iran's leaders that Iran not only faced the threat of far more serious Iraqi military action but sufficient unpopularity to make it impossible to go on with the revolution.[98]

Iraq did not accept the initial Iranian cease-fire proposal, however, and stated that Iran's acceptance was far too ambiguous, that Khomeini had not publicly indicated that he would agree to a cease-fire, and that Iraq would not tolerate an Iranian mobilization. On July 18, Iraq also made its views known with something more forceful than words. It launched a major series of strategic bombing raids at industrial plants at Bandar-e-Khomeini and Ahwaz and struck again at Iran's nuclear reactor project at Bushehr. Iran replied with small air raids on targets near Faw and Kirkuk but lacked the air and missile forces to make any serious response to the Iraqi raids.[99]

Iran was forced, after boycotting it for seven years, to appeal to the UN Security Council. Then, on July 20, Khomeini made a statement indicating that he too accepted the cease-fire. Excerpts from his speech over Tehran Radio made his reluctance very clear but at the same time responded to some of the Iraqi demands.

> Taking this decision was more deadly than taking poison. I submitted myself to God's will and drank this drink for his satisfaction. . . . I had promised to fight to the last drop of my blood and to my last breath. . . . We formally announce that our objective is not to have a new tactic for continuation of the war. . . . To me it would have been more bearable to accept death and martyrdom. . . . (But, I had to accept the advice of) all the high-ranking military experts.

Khomeini went on to threaten the U.S. and stated, "I hereby warn the American and European military forces to leave the Persian Gulf before it is too late, and you are drowned in the quagmires of death." He also warned that the war might not be over. "Accepting the resolution does not mean the question of war has been solved. By declaring this decision, we have blunted the propaganda weapon of the world devourers against us. But one cannot forecast this course of events indefinitely."[100]

Iraq still, however, did not agree to a cease-fire. It now demanded face-to-face talks on all aspects of a peace settlement with Iran. It also became clear that there would be problems over the issue of prisoners of war. The Red Cross estimated that there were only 49,285 prisoners in 15 Iranian camps and 12,747 prisoners in 10 Iraqi camps. Both sides felt the number in the other's camps was much larger, and at least 4,000 Iraqi prisoners were unaccounted for.[101] At the same time, the UN struggled to ready a peacekeeping mission to patrol the cease-fire line with 250 men under the control of Lt. General Martin Vadset of Norway.

The end result was three weeks of rough negotiating punctuated by small military clashes. Iraq allowed an armored column of the Mujahideen e-Khalq (National Liberation Army) to strike some 60 miles into Iran. This drive seems to have been a test by both Saddam Hussein and the leader of the Mujahideen Massoud Rajavi to see whether the Mujahideen could start a popular uprising in Iran.

The Mujahideen were initially given support by Iraqi armor and air and Iraqi logistic support. They advanced toward Kermanshah (Bakhtaran) and drove some 90 miles into the country—the deepest penetration of Iranian territory of the war. Iran then seems to have trapped the Mujahideen force in a mountainous area near Islamabad and Karand on July 29, to have inflicted several thousand casualties, and to have executed its prisoners.[102] The incident also sparked a massive wave of new arrests of suspected Mujahideen sympathizers in Iran, and several thousand more may have been killed.[103]

Iran also claimed on July 31 that it had recaptured three towns in western Iraq—Oasr e-Shirin, Sar-e Pol-e Zahab, and Shirin.[104] Iraq replied that it had simply withdrawn its forces from the towns after accomplishing its objectives in disrupting Iran's supply capabilities and ability to help the Kurds. On August 3, Iranian gunboats fired on a Norwegian freighter, while Iran charged that Iraq had bombed its civilians with chemical weapons and injured 2,700 in two days.[105]

Finally, on August 6, 1988, nearly a decade of agony ended. The Secretary General of the UN, the U.S., most European states, and pro-Iraqi nations like Saudi Arabia had all put pressure on Iraq to accept a cease-fire. At the same time, the Secretary General was able to persuade Iran to agree to face-to-face talks shortly after the cease-fire. As a result, Saddam Hussein announced that he was ready "for a cease-fire on the condition that Iran announces clearly, unequivocally, and formally its acceptance to enter into direct negotiations with Iraq immediately after a cease-fire takes place."[106] After another day of negotiations, Iran accepted these terms

On August 8, 1988, the fighting came to a formal end. The Security

Council of the UN met and announced a cease-fire effective at dawn on August 20, 1988, but Iraq and Iran simultaneously announced an immediate halt to all fighting. It also was announced that Iranian and Iraqi representatives would meet face-to-face under the auspices of the Secretary General on August 25, 1988. U.S. Secretary of Defense Frank Carlucci announced that the U.S. would soon be able to cut its military presence in the Gulf. Finally, the UN announced that its observer force had been expanded to 350 men and would be called the United Nations Iran-Iraq Military Observer Group (UNIMOG) and would include an air unit to provide fixed wing aircraft and helicopters.[107] Ironically, the same day, the USS *Vincennes* saved five Iranian fishermen who had been drifting in a dinghy in the Gulf for more than a week.

"Cold Peace": The Aftermath to the Cease-Fire

In the months that followed, the UN was able to implement most of the terms of the cease-fire with little more than the usual claims about minor incidents at the front, overflights, and shelling during the initial days before the UN peacekeeping force was put in place.

The first Iranian and Iraqi peace talks began on schedule on August 24, 1988. While the UN cease-fire talks made little progress toward a final peace during the rest of 1988 and early 1989, they also did not break up, and the issues between Iran and Iraq finally boiled down to squabbles over key points along the border and control of the Shatt al-Arab—issues that bore a striking resemblance to those that had divided both countries before the Algiers Accord in 1975.

Iraq, perhaps in search of some material gain for eight years of war, insisted on total control of all waters in the Shatt and threatened in September to create a massive new canal from Basra to Umm Qasr if it did not receive its demands.[108] Iran insisted on the terms of the Algiers Accord. The prisoner of war issue remained deadlocked. Some 70,000 Iraqi POWs and 45,000 Iranian POWs were held hostage to the settlement of the debate over control of the Shatt, and even an attempt to exchange 1,500 sick and disabled POWs broke down on November 22, 1988.

The UNIMOG force did, however, steadily establish its land, air, and naval presence and even an air corridor for its aircraft to fly between Baghdad and Tehran. It also was able to function almost immediately after the formal cease-fire date, although the Iranian and Iraqi forces were only 50 meters apart, and there were hundreds of petty complaints over minor incidents.

Iran did not challenge shipping outside the exclusion zone after the cease-fire. The naval branch of the Guards conducted only limited patrols, and the regular navy carried out only routine patrols and limited minesweeping activity. When the Iranian Navy did conduct an exercise in the northern Gulf in November, it was conspicuously careful to avoid any provocation. The Iraqi Air Force halted all flights into the Gulf after the cease-fire, and the Iranians limited air activity to routine patrols and training.

A "cold peace" set in that was only slightly short of "cold war." Both Iran and Iraq continued to produce well over 2 MMBD. Iran removed its flotilla of 20–25 naval Guards speedboats from Abu Musa in October.[109] It opened Kharg Island to all oil shippers without incident on October 25 and steadily reduced its shuttle operations. It announced that it planned to end all shuttle operations in 1989 and that the resulting saving might be up to $300 million a year. It began studies of rebuilding its refinery at Abadan and a serious debate of what the revolution finally had to mean in terms of an actual civil economy and political system.

Iraq started a massive rebuilding effort in Basra and allowed consumer goods to come back into the country. It resumed shipping from its port at Umm Qasr.[110] It began to load 18,000-ton tankers from a secret pipeline it had built to Umm Qasr in 1985 and began to try shuttle operations to move from Al Faw.[111] It also began to examine ways to deploy the single-point mooring buoys it had bought to start shipping from the Gulf during the time the war was still in progress. Commercial shipping insurance rates dropped to something approaching their prewar levels, although the actual volume of shipping was still restricted because of the oil glut.

Both Iraq and Iran continued to play their respective diplomatic games, but Iran almost immediately showed an interest in rebuilding its diplomatic relations with Bahrain, Kuwait, and Saudi Arabia. Kuwait soon restored its relations to the Ambassadorial level, and then Bahrain. Saudi Arabia offered to restore relations with Iran in early October and then halted all media attacks on Iran.

Iran also began to court various European countries. It reestablished relations with Britain on October 1, 1988, and announced that it had abandoned the policy of using hostages. Iran still, however, seemed deeply divided over improving its ties to the West. While it immediately sought access to Western markets, its leaders could not agree on solving past hostage and diplomatic problems in ways that allowed it to quickly improve its relations with Britain and France.

The Western naval presence in the Gulf gradually ceased escort operations, and most minesweeping activity came to an end. A few drifting mines were found after the cease-fire but no signs of new minesweeping activity were seen. The Belgian and Italian minesweeping forces left the Gulf well before the end of 1988, and British, French, and Dutch forces sharply reduced the scope of their operations.

France replaced the carrier task force led by the *Clemenceau* with a small task force of two frigates, a destroyer, three minesweepers, a replenishment ship and six support ships in October 1988.[112] The British Armilla Patrol ceased protecting ships in the Gulf in October 1988, having participated in a total of 1,026 transits since it had started actively protecting ships in the Gulf, with 405 transits in 1987 and 621 in 1988. Britain did, however, leave three frigates in the Gulf.[113] The U.S. shifted from escorting ships to accompanying them on September 25 and then simply to monitoring their movements. It also slowly reduced the number and size of the warships it had in the area.[114] By January of 1989, the U.S. reached the point where it had reduced its strength in the Gulf to 14 ships, of which only six were destroyers and frigates. This was the lowest force level since July 1987. In February, Kuwait deflagged 6 of the 11 tankers that had originally been reflagged.[115]

The only fighting that continued was an immediate Iraqi effort to drive all pro-Talabani and Barzani Kurds out of Iraq and to relocate their sympathizers far from the border area. This Iraqi attack on the Kurds followed a new wave of Kurdish bombings in Baghdad and Irbil, and the Iraqi government acted with considerable ruthlessness and with the additional use of poison gas. Large numbers of Kurds were forcibly located to new settlements, which often had minimal facilities at best. Some 60,000 Iraqi troops and large numbers of helicopter gunships moved into the border area, and virtually all anti-Iraqi Kurds suspected of fighting for the Iranians or against Iraq were executed as traitors whenever they were captured.

By the end of August, the Iraqis had shattered the Kurdish resistance and had driven tens of thousands of Kurds into Turkey and Iran. Iraq also had stepped up its use of gas warfare, although the full extent of Iraq's use of gas was impossible to determine.[116] Up to 15 villages were hit with gas attacks after August 24 and heavy fighting took place against the Kurdish positions around Zaho, Dahok, Mosul, and Irbil. While at least 400 Iraqi soldiers died during the fighting in the final week of August, Iraq claimed on September 3 that it had driven virtually all organized Kurdish forces out of a "liberated zone" that once had included some 4,500 square miles of Iraqi territory.[117] Iraq also, however, avoided any provocation of Iran.[118] It did not cross the border in hot pursuit, and it reduced the activity of the Mujahideen e-Khalq's National Liberation Army to that of a small contingency force. Although it still claimed to have 10,000–15,000 troops, it ceased to conduct any operations.[119]

Both sides also seemed to pay more attention to internal affairs than rearming. While Saddam Hussein did charge that Iranian forces were massing on the border in January 1989, nothing came of the charge, and both sides agreed to resume their peace talks. Iran did claim in April 1988 that it had fired a new surface-to-surface missile with a range of 800 kilometers called the El-Abbas, and Saddam Hussein claimed that he had developed a new "super weapon" on September 28. Nevertheless, Iraq seems to have sharply reduced its orders for military imports and found itself involved in a major contract dispute with Italy over payment for the warships it had had on order since the start of the war.[120]

Iran showed few signs of receiving major arms deliveries, other than new artillery and possibly more Silkworm missiles.[121] There were reports in January 1989 that Iran had concluded that it needed a minimum of 2,500 tanks, 2,000 artillery pieces, tens of thousands of mortars and anti-tank rocket launchers, and vast amounts of engineering equipment if it were to compete with Iraq and that this would cost some $15 to $25 billion.[122]

Iran simply did not have the money or a clear source of such arms, and it concentrated more on trying to solve its political problems, including the divisions within its military command. On September 20, the Majlis dismissed Mohsen Rafiqdust as Minister in charge of the Revolutionary Guards and replaced him with Ali Shamkhani, the deputy IRGC commander of ground forces.

While Khomeini assured the Pasdaran commanders on September 17 that "you are needed in time of peace, as you are in time of war," Rafsanjani had told an assembly of hundreds of Guard commanders only two days earlier that they must now enforce discipline: "Up to now, you have not had the opportunity to learn military training and discipline. But from now on you must pay attention to hierarchy and to orders."

In October, Defense Minister Brigadier General Hussein Jalali stated that "the Army and the Revolutionary Guards Corps must be strengthened. This does not mean reinforcement for an offensive but rather the prevention of possible aggression for defense."[123] Iran also announced that the Revolutionary Guards had been reorganized into a far more orthodox order of battle. They had been converted from 8–10 divisions and a host of independent brigades, into a force of 21 Infantry divisions, 15 independent infantry brigades, 21 air-defense brigades, 3 engineering divisions, and 42 artillery and chemical defense brigades, with independent air and naval wings. While there was still talk of popular warfare and an army of 20 million, it seemed the Mullahs were finally learning the importance of military professionalism, although Iran's religious leaders conspicuously avoided any blame for what in many cases were their own personal mistakes.[124]

While it was far too soon to predict a stable cease-fire or any kind of agreed peace, by the spring of 1989, the Iran-Iraq War had at least paused. It also had paused with few changes in the basic conditions both sides faced when the war began. The ambitions of two competing autocrats and more than eight years of war had done nothing to alter the basic balance of power in the Gulf, to give one side a triumph over the other, or even to resolve the centuries-long squabble over control of the border area and the Shatt al-Arab. In spite of all their ideological ambitions and claims, the war left both Khomeini's Islamic fundamentalism and Saddam Hussein's Ba'ath Socialism weaker in terms of both domestic and foreign influence than when the war had begun. Few wars in modern history had done less to further the ambitions of the leaders that started them at so high a cost to their peoples.

Notes

1. The total manpower, including the Popular Army, was over 1.3 million men. Some 500,000 of this total was Popular Army forces, but not all of the Popular Army forces were active at the same time. Some performed internal surveillance and fund-raising work. Shahram Chubin and Charles Tripp, *Iran and Iraq at War*, Boulder, Westview, p. 93.

2. The corps areas from north to south were: V, I, II, I Guards, IV Corps, VI Corps, III Corps, and VII Corps. Saddam Hussein claimed to have deployed 50 divisions along the front after the battle of Majnoon in June. *Jane's Defence Weekly*, July 9, 1988, p. 14.

3. There are unconfirmed reports Iraq had some SU-24 long-range fighter bombers.

4. Some sources indicate the Republican Guards had 33 brigades by August 1988.

5. Based on interviews in Iraq in November 1987.

6. Based upon interviews in Iraq; the statement of the Honorable William H. Webster, Director, CIA, before the Committee on Governmental Affairs, U.S. Senate, February 10, 1989; testimony of W. Seth Carus, Fellow, Washington Institute for Near East Policy, before the Committee on Governmental Affairs, U.S. Senate, February 10, 1989; W. Seth Carus, "Chemical Weapons in the Middle East," *Policy Focus*, Washington Institute for Near East Policy, December 1988; *Washington Post*, December 10, 1987, p. A-13, December 17, 1988, p. A-46, December 25, 1987, p. A-1, December 26, 1987, p. A-25, December 29, 1987, p. A-12, January 15, 1988, p. A-25, February 10, 1988, p. A-32, February 21, 1988, p. A-1; *Washington Times*, December 8, 1987, p. C–5, January 6, 1988, p. A-8, February 12, 1988, p. A-8; *Philadelphia Inquirer*, December 18, 1987, p. 18C, January 22, 1988, p. 1-A; *New York Times*,

December 4, 1987, p. A-13, December 14, 1987, p. D-10, December 17, 1987, p. D-1, January 18, 1988, p. A-6, February 21, 1988, p. E-23; *Los Angeles Times,* January 20, 1988, p. I-5; *Wall Street Journal,* January 29, 1988.

7. James Bruce, "Mobilization a Problem for Iranian Leaders," *Jane's Defence Weekly,* April 2, 1988, p. 634.

8. Statement of the Honorable William H. Webster, Director, CIA, before the Committee on Governmental Affairs, U.S. Senate, February 10, 1989; testimony of W. Seth Carus, Fellow, Washington Institute for Near East Policy, before the Committee on Governmental Affairs, U.S. Senate, February 10, 1989; W. Seth Carus, "Chemical Weapons in the Middle East," *Policy Focus,* Washington Institute for Near East Policy, December 1988; *Washington Post,* December 10, 1987, p. A-13, December 17, 1988, p. A-46, December 25, 1987, p. A-1, December 26, 1987, p. A-25, December 29, 1987, p. A-12, January 15, 1988, p. A-25, February 10, 1988, p. A-32, February 21, 1988, p. A-1; *Washington Times,* December 8, 1987, p. C-5, January 6, 1988, p. A-8, February 12, 1988, p. A-8; *Philadelphia Inquirer,* December 18, 1987, p. 18C, January 22, 1988, p. 1–A; *New York Times,* December 4, 1987, p. A-13, December 14, 1987, p. D-10, December 17, 1987, p. D-1, January 18, 1988, p. A-6, February 21, 1988, p. E-23; *Los Angeles Times,* January 20, 1988, p. I-5; *Wall Street Journal,* January 29, 1988.

9. *New York Times,* January 10, 1988, p. A-3.

10. *Washington Times,* January 19, 1988, p. A-8; *Philadelphia Inquirer,* January 18, 1988, p. 8A.

11. *Philadelphia Inquirer,* February 10, 1988, p. 26.

12. Figures differ sharply. Some Iranian rockets which could not have hit Baghdad seem to be counted as failed missile strikes on the city in some source material.

13. *Economist,* March 5, 1988, p. 44; *New York Times,* March 2, 1988, p. A-1, March 4, 1988, p. A-8, March 12, 1988, p. A-3, May 1, 1988, p. 18; *Washington Post,* March 2, 1988, p. A-16; *Baltimore Sun,* March 6, 1988, p. 2-A. Iraq was believed to have about 50 Scud missiles before it began this series of attacks, but the number of attacks that followed rapidly showed its holdings were far larger. On March 8, 1988, Rafsanjani claimed Iran had evidence that the missiles were standard Scud Bs which used reduced warhead weight. *Washington Times,* March 1, 1988, p. 3; and *Washington Post,* March 9, 1988, p. A-19.

14. *Economist,* March 5, 1988, p. 44; *New York Times,* March 2, 1988, p. A-1, March 4, 1988, p. A-8, March 12, 1988, p. A-3, May 1, 1988, p. 18; *Washington Post,* March 2, 1988, p. A-16; *Baltimore Sun,* March 6, 1988, p. 2-A.

15. *New York Times,* March 6, 1988, p. 1; *Economist,* March 26, 1988, p. 34.

16. Baghdad has 23 percent of Iraq's population and is only 80 miles from the border. Tehran is about 290 miles from the front lines.

17. Steven Zagola, "Ballistic Missiles in the Third World," *International Defense Review,* pp. 1423–1426.

18. On March 10, 1988, Soviet officials denied that the Scuds given to Iraq could hit Tehran.

19. A popular poster in Tehran showed three flags. A U.S. flag largely burnt

away, an Israeli flag half burnt away, and a Soviet flag with limited burn damage. Another poster showed a Pasdaran holding what could only be a U.S.-made Stinger missile and shooting down a U.S. minesweeping helicopter.

20. There are some indications that the modified Scud or Al-Husayn missile was test-fired in 1987. Iraq announced it had completed such a missile in August 1987, and that it had a range of 650 kilometers. Expert first-hand observers estimated the explosive force as being roughly the same as that of a 500-pound bomb. The missiles impacted either in direct flight or in a pattern where the missile seemed to halt its rocket engine and the warhead/missile would fall. According to some observers, the warhead sometimes appeared to separate from the missile. This separation is characteristic of the Scud B. The warhead separates during the terminal dive to avoid the axial sway of a larger missile body, and this also allows the warhead to hit at speeds in excess of Mach 1.5. The impact would often come a few seconds after the warhead penetrated the earth, and the explosive force would rise in a V-shaped cone. This often sheared the side off buildings rather than vector the maximum force from the side.

21. The following details of the Iranian missile program are taken from W. Seth Carus and Joseph S. Bermudez, "Iran's Growing Missile Forces," *Jane's Defence Weekly*, July 23, 1988, pp. 126–131, November 19, 1988, pp. 1252–1253, and February 11, 1989, p. 219.

22. *Jane's Defence Weekly*, June 20, 1987, p. 1289.

23. Some estimates of Iranian Scud firings during 1988 go as high as 231 missiles. See Steven Zaloga, "Ballistic Missiles in the Third World," *International Defense Review*, 11/1988, pp. 1423–1437.

24. Based on discussions with Iranians present in the city at the time, Australian intelligence officers, and Robin Wright.

25. No missiles with chemical warheads were launched during the conflict, although Iraq did make extensive use of bombs, canisters, mortars, and 130-mm and 155-mm artillery shells (from a UN working paper).

26. *New York Times*, March 6, 1988 p. 1; *Economist*, March 26, 1988, p. 34.

27. Some cooperation began in 1986 after the failure of talks between Talabani and the government. The KPUK normally is strongest in the area around Sulaimaniyah and the KDP is strongest to the north and west. The Barzani clan is now headed by Massoud Barzani, the son of the former leader, Mustafa Barzani. See Patrick E. Tyler's excellent analysis in the *Washington Post*, February 19, 1988, p. A-15.

28. Some reports indicate that Iraqi bombers dropped cyanide gas in 100-liter containers that vaporized on impact. An Iraqi general captured in the fighting, Brigadier Nather Hussein Mustafa, claimed on Iranian TV on March 24, 1988, that he saw clouds of gas arise over Halabjah. Two other captured Iraqi officers confirmed this. The casualty figures are very controversial. So are data on the population of the towns involved. Halabjah is said to have had a population of up to 70,000, but nearly half the population seems to have fled after an uprising against the Iraqi military authorities failed in May 1987. Dojaila has a population of around 20,000.

29. It is easy to underestimate the importance of the moral sanctions

against the use of gas. In the 35 years between the end of World War I and the end of the Korean War, there were only two confirmed uses of lethal gas— Italian use of mustard gas against the Ethiopians during 1935–36 and Japanese use of gas against the Chinese during 1937–1942. *Washington Post*, March 24, 1988, p. A-37; *Economist*, April 2, 1988, pp. 35–37.

30. *New York Times*, April 21, 1988, p. 8, April 3, 1988, p. 9; *Washington Post*, April 8, 1988, p. A-23.

31. Iraq had fired 160 missiles by April 18, 1988.

32. *Washington Post*, March 28, 1988, p. A-17, April 15, 1988, p. A-26; *Washington Times*, March 29, 1988, p. A-8.

33. *Washington Post*, May 3, 1988, pp. A-20 and A-23; *Economist*, April 23, 1988, p. 42.

34. This center had a communications cable under the Shatt to a microwave relay tower and direct command links to Tehran.

35. *Philadelphia Inquirer*, June 5, 1988, p. 20A.

36. Experts differ over how much the Iraqi use of gas influenced the near panic on the part of some Iranian defenders.

37. *Washington Post*, April 18, 1988, p. A-17, April 19, 1988, p. A-22.

38. Shahbazi was born in Qom. He entered staff college at 22 and was a junior officer at the time of the revolution. He had very close links to the Pasdaran and was considered a complete Khomeini loyalist. *Jane's Defence Weekly*, May 21, 1988, p. 995.

39. *New York Times*, April 14, 1988, pp. 1 and 14.

40. The *Samuel B. Roberts* was an Oliver Hazard Perry-class guided-missile frigate. It was 453 feet long, displaced 3,740 tons at full load, and had a crew of 225. It was armed with SAMs, SSMs, a 76-mm gun, torpedoes, and a close in weapons system (CIWS). It has active sonar on the hull and towed array sonars.

41. The *Roberts* was towed to Bahrain by the USS *Wainwright* and arrived on April 16. Three of the ten wounded were seriously injured.

42. The U.S. had found 44 mines in the Gulf, 16 of them in 1988. The most recent mine detection was on April 9, 1988. All of the previous mines were encrusted with marine growth and showed signs of having torn away from their moorings. *New York Times*, April 15, 1988, p. 3.

43. *Aviation Week*, April 25, 1988, pp. 20–24.

44. The *Merrill* was a destroyer, the *Lynde McCormack* was a destroyer, and the *Trenton* was an amphibious transport. The *Simpson* was a guided-missile frigate, the *Bagley* was a frigate, and the *Wainwright* was a guided-missile cruiser. The *Joshan* was a 154-foot Combattante II-class French attack boat with Harpoon missiles and a complement of 21. The *Sahand* and *Sabalan* were Vosper-5 class British frigates commissioned in 1972. They were part of a force of four such vessels, with a complement of 125 and a length of 310 feet. The Boghammars were 43-foot-long speed boats. The Harpoon missile was introduced in 1977 and upgraded in the early 1980s. Only the U.S. Navy had the improved version. It has a range of over 50 nautical miles.

45. Sources differ as to whether the two platforms were then producing 30,000 or 150,000 barrels per day (BPD).

46. The field was operated by the Crescent Petroleum Company and was owned by Sharjah, one of the most pro-Iranian members of the UAE.

47. The Skipper 2 is a 1,000-pound bomb modified with a Shrike missile motor for greater stand-off capability.

48. The war on the cities had done comparatively little physical damage, but many people had fled the cities. Iran forced them back by issuing ration books only to those who both returned and voted.

49. At this point in time, Iran still had three destroyers, but they were at best capable of limited service, if any. It had two frigates, two corvettes, eight fast-attack craft, 10–12 Hovercraft, 1 minesweeper, 40–50 speed boats, and 70 or more small fast motorcraft. The U.S. forces in the area had a total of 29 ships, with 21 in the Gulf and a carrier battle group outside it. The ships in the area included the command ship *Coronado*; the guided-missile cruiser *Wainwright*; the guided-missile destroyers *McCormack* and *Strauss*; two guided-missile frigates, including the *Simpson*; two frigates, including the *Bagley*; two destroyers, including the *Merrit*; the amphibious landing ship *Trenton*; six minesweepers; and one support ship. The carrier *Enterprise* was in support outside the Gulf. These ships were due for rotation, with the carrier *Forrestal* and its task force replacing the *Enterprise*, and five of the frigates being rotated. This gave the U.S. the option of nearly doubling its effective force.

50. The *Washington Post*, April 19, 1988, pp. A-1 and A-22–23; April 20, 1988, p. A-28; April 21, 1988, p. A-26, April 22, 1988, pp. A-1 and A-18; *New York Times*, April 19, 1988, pp. 1 and 11, April 21, p. 4; *Baltimore Sun*, April 19, 1988, p. 1, and April 21, 1988, p. 4.

51. *Washington Post*, April 21, 1988, p. A-25.

52. Iran admitted to 1,509 killed in the missile war on this date, but foreign observers in Tehran said the figure was closer to 3,000. There were growing rumors of divisions within the Iranian leadership, and Iran was said to be down to $3–4 billion in reserves, although it claimed $5.5 billion.

53. Discussions with Gary Sick and Dr. Abdullah Toucan; *Economist*, March 5, 1988, p. 44; *New York Times*, March 2, 1988, p. A-1, March 4, 1988, p. A-8, March 12, 1988, p. A-3, May 1, 1988, p. 18; *Washington Post*, March 2, 1988, p. A-16; *Baltimore Sun*, March 6, 1988, p. 2-A.

54. *Washington Post*, April 26, 1988, p. A-21; *Christian Science Monitor*, April 28, 1988, p. 10.

55. *Jane's Defence Weekly*, June 4, 1988, p. 1091.

56. The UK-built destroyer was a 3,360-ton ship built in 1945. It was believed to be out of commission. The two U.S.-built ships were 3,320-ton Sumner-class vessels.

57. It is not clear how serious Iran was. It did create water barrier defenses for Ahwaz after the cease-fire.

58. Saddam Hussein and Defense Minister Adnan Khairullah were at the front during the entire battle.

59. *Washington Post*, May 30, 1988, p. A-23.

60. The author inspected much of the equipment involved. See the *Washington Post*, May 30, 1988, p. A-23.

61. These were Iranian sources critical of the regime and cannot be regarded as reliable.

62. *Philadelphia Inquirer*, May 29, 1988, p. 2; *Washington Times*, June 21, 1988, p. A-8.

63. The details of the countermeasure effort are secret. It is public, however, that the U.S. improved the countermeasure capability of its EA-6Bs around this time. (See Chapter 14 for more details.) *Washington Post*, June 2, 1988, p. A-32, and July 1, 1988, p. A-1; *Washington Times*, June 3, 1988, p. A-1, and June 21, 1988, p. A-8.

64. For example, see the *Washington Times*, June 9, 1988, p. A-7.

65. *Philadelphia Inquirer*, June 6, 1988, p. 14A; *New York Times*, June 5, 1988, p. 6.

66. *Washington Times*, June 7, 1988, p. A-9.

67. According to some reports, Montazari was trying to manipulate Rafsanjani into getting the blame for the war and called upon him to "devote all his time" to unifying the Guards and regular army. *Washington Post*, June 3, 1988, p. A-21; *New York Times*, June 5, 1988, p. 6, and June 19, 1988, p. 11.

68. *New York Times*, June 3, 1988, p. A-3, and June 6, 1988, p. A-1; *Christian Science Monitor*, June 3, 1988, p. 9.

69. *Jane's Defence Weekly*, June 25, 1988, p. 1268.

70. *New York Times*, June 14, 1988, p. 5, and June 15, 1988, p. A-15; *Washington Post*, June 15, 1988, p. A-27; and *Washington Times*, June 15, 1988, p. A-7.

71. *Washington Times*, June 15, 1988, p. A-7.

72. *Jane's Defence Weekly*, July 2, 1988, p. 1352.

73. The "National Liberation Army" had been formed on June 20, 1987, and was said to total 20,000 men.

74. *New York Times*, June 20, 1988, p. A-8.

75. Some Iraqi estimates indicate that there were 8,000 Iranians killed and wounded and 1,500 Iranian POWs and that 32 Iranian battalions were routed during the battle.

76. *New York Times*, June 20, 1988, p. A-8; and *Washington Post*, June 21, 1988, p. A-16.

77. *New York Times*, June 20, 1988, p. A-8; *Philadelphia Inquirer*, June 23, 1988, p. 5A; and *Washington Post*, June 21, 1988, p. A-16.

78. *Washington Times*, June 24, 1988, p. A-7; and *Washington Post*, July 1, 1988, p. A-17.

79. *Jane's Defence Weekly*, July 2, 1988, p. 1352.

80. *Jane's Defence Weekly*, July 9, 1988, p. 14. U.S. experts in Baghdad could not confirm any such reports.

81. Iraq claimed after it took Dehloran in the final phase of this offensive that it had taken 5,150 POWs and that it had inflicted 28,000 killed and wounded on Iran. *Jane's Defence Weekly*, July 23, 1988, p. 120.

82. *New York Times*, July 2, 1988, p. A-3.

83. *New York Times*, June 26, 1988, p. A-22; *Jane's Defence Weekly*, July 2, 1988, p. 1352; *Philadelphia Inquirer*, June 26, 1988, p. 3A; *USN&WR*, June 27, 1988, p. 12; and *Washington Post*, June 26, 1988, p. A-22.

84. *Washington Times,* June 27, 1988, p. A-8, and June 28, 1988, p. A-9.

85. *New York Times,* June 26, 1988, p. A-13; and *Washington Post,* July 1, 1988, p. A-17.

86. *Jane's Defence Weekly,* July 16, 1988, p. 75.

87. The technical and military issues surrounding the shooting down of Iran Air 655 are discussed in depth in Chapter 14.

88. *Washington Post,* July 3, 1988, p. A-25.

89. Local time was three hours ahead.

90. The Maverick has a range of 0.5 to 13 nautical miles. It is TV-guided, and the pilot must track the missile and control it until it hits the target. The F-14 cannot deliver the Maverick.

91. According to some reports, Iran had shot down two of its own aircraft because of IFF problems—an F-4 and a Falcon jet. *Washington Times,* July 11, 1988, p. A-1.

92. *New York Times,* July 5, 1988, p. A-9.

93. *Christian Science Monitor,* July 13, 1988, p. 7; *Washington Post,* July 18, 1988, p. A-9.

94. Anthony H. Cordesman visited the area for several hours in November 1988. These statistics were provided by Iraqi officers and were confirmed by the author and U.S. experts on the scene.

95. *Washington Post,* July 15, 1988, p. A-18.

96. Text as printed in the London *Times,* July 19, 1988.

97. *Washington Post,* January 17, 1989, p. D-23.

98. Press reports at the time were filled with the usual reports of splits within the senior Iranian leadership and with reports that Rafsanjani had moved for a cease-fire as a moderate or had been forced into it by Montazari and others.

99. *New York Times,* July 20, 1988, p. A-1; *Washington Post,* July 20, 1988, p. A-1.

100. *New York Times,* July 21, 1988, p. A-1.

101. *Washington Times,* July 22, 1988, p. 9.

102. *Philadelphia Inquirer,* August 6, 1988, p. 8A.

103. The Mujahideen acknowledged the loss of 1,000 troops. Tehran claimed 1,734. Some sources feel the true number was closer to 2,500. *Washington Post,* August 24, 1988, p. A-1.

104. *Washington Post,* August 1, 1988, p. A-15.

105. *Washington Post,* August 5, 1988, p. A-30.

106. *Washington Post,* August 7, 1988, p. A-1.

107. *Washington Times,* August 9, 1988, p. A-1; *Washington Post,* August 9, 1988, p. A-1.

108. While technically feasible, such a canal would cost at least $14 billion. There is a small 25-foot-deep canal from Basra to Khor Zubair, but such a canal would have to be a main shipping channel at least 35 feet deep and would still present the problem that Umm Qasr is not a full ocean-going port and only exists on the Khor Abdullah, whose main channel goes through Kuwaiti waters. The Shatt, however, was now filled with mines and had not been properly dredged in nearly a decade.

109. *Jane's Defence Weekly,* November 5, 1988, p. 1113.

110. Any estimates of Iraq's exact economic position are uncertain. Iraq's public debt was estimated at $70 to $85 billion. Its citizens, however, were estimated to hold up to $60 billion abroad. Iraq had deferred some $50 billion in development projects between 1981 and 1988, and many—including steel, aluminum, fertilizer, and cement plants—restarted work shortly after the cease-fire. It announced plans to build a north-south pipeline and to reopen Faw at some point in 1989 or 1990. Estimates of its future export capacity rose to 5 MMBD. Iraq's current oil earnings, however, were only about $12 to $14 billion a year, and it was forced to spend at least $5 billion to keep its military forces going and another $2 to $4 billion on debt service.

111. Although the channel had been quietly widened before the war was over, it still could not allow economically viable ships to pass. Tankers of 18,000 tons are too small to be of any economic impact. *New York Times*, August 22, 1988, p. D-10.

112. *Armed Forces Journal*, November 1988, p. 40.

113. *Proceedings*, February, 1989, p. 120; *Jane's Defence Weekly*, November 26, 1988, p. 1321.

114. There was a minor squabble within the U.S. over the command of the forces in the Gulf. They had been under a land commander because the area was part of USCENTCOM, and the U.S. Navy argued that the forces involved were actually naval forces and needed a naval commander who could work with the naval forces outside the Gulf. The cease-fire made the issue somewhat academic, and a U.S. Army General, Lt. General H. Norman Schwarzkopf, replaced Marine General George B. Crist on November 23, 1989.

115. *Washington Times*, January 16, 1989, p. A-5; and *Philadelphia Inquirer*, February 12, 1989, p. 21A.

116. The U.S. officially accused Iraq of using poison gas against the Kurds on September 9, 1988. It then leaked the fact it had intercepted radio messages from the Iraqi Air Force relating to the use of gas. *New York Times*, September 15, 1989, p. A-12.

117. *New York Times*, September 1, 1988, p. A-1, September 4, 1988, p. 18; *Washington Post*, September 9, 1988, p. A-1.

118. Iran also avoided any provocation of Iraq. It waited until October 15 to indicate that it would accept up to 100,000 Kurdish refugees in the spring of 1989 and indicated that they would not be allowed to organize military forces.

119. *Washington Post*, August 24, 1988, p. A-1.

120. Only three of the ships Iraq had ordered from Italy had been delivered—two corvettes and the supply ship *Agnadeen*. The remaining eight vessels—four Lupo-class frigates and four Esmereldas-class corvettes—remained at La Spezia as a result of the Italian embargo on arms deliveries. Foreign Minister Tariq Aziz and Trade Minister Mahdi Saleh visited Italy on January 24–26, 1989, to try to resolve a dispute over release of the ships and payment. Iraq claimed it had already paid some 600 billion Lira ($440 million) of the total cost of 3.6 trillion Lira. *Jane's Defence Weekly*, February 11, 1989, p. 205, and *Washington Post*, September 29, 1988, p. A-35.

121. *Los Angeles Times*, February 14, 1989, p. 7.

122. Such reports were leaked by the National Liberation Army and are uncertain. *Jane's Defence Weekly*, February 4, 1989, p. 167.

123. *Washington Times*, October 5, 1988, p. A-9.

124. *Jane's Defence Weekly*, October 1, 1988, p. 749, and October 8, 1988, p. 859.

11

C³I AND BATTLE MANAGEMENT: A REVIEW

The Problems of High Command

It is obvious from the preceding history of the Iran-Iraq War that the relative effectiveness of Iranian and Iraqi armed forces was heavily affected by problems in their high command. These points have already been discussed at length, but they are critical to any understanding of why both sides had such severe difficulties in realizing their military potential. It also is easy to forget the problem of high command and to blame subordinate commanders, troops, and equipment, or strategy and tactics. One of the key lessons of the Iran-Iraq War, however, is that the armed forces of autocratic states are ultimately no more effective than their autocrats.

It may be years, if ever, before the details of the actions taken by the Iranian and Iraqi high command become public. The details that are now available are so filled with rumor, often generated by the opponents of the regime involved, that it is impossible to establish the facts. There is ample literature, for example, that criticizes Rafsanjani for constantly imposing his own ideas and beliefs on the conduct of the war. Similarly, there is ample literature criticizing Saddam Hussein for overcentralizing authority and for politicizing his command structure. The problem is in establishing the truth, particularly in states where so little outside knowledge exists about the actions and decisions of subordinate commanders and where rumors about senior officials are infinitely easier to acquire than the facts.

What is clear, regardless of the personalities involved, is that both nations confronted their military with serious problems in acting on a basis of their military judgments and that both states created major barriers to improving the professionalism of the military forces. It can be argued that this is true of all states and systems of government and that the Western democracies have often had major problems in their high command that seriously degraded the performance of their forces. Iran and Iraq, however, unquestionably created unusual problems and ones that had unusual effects.

In the case of Iran, the ability of its senior Mullahs to take power over the state and armed forces meant that military decisions were shaped throughout the war on the basis of a belief in some form of divine mandate, in the primacy of revolutionary forces over military professionalism, and in the effectiveness of revolutionary fervor and human-wave tactics over organization and technology. In the end, this resulted in casualties and a lack of military effectiveness that were key factors in Iran's defeats in 1988 and in forcing it to accept a cease-fire.

In the case of Iraq, it took nearly a decade to fully realize that the Iraqi Army and other armed forces had to be reorganized on a professional basis and that the force structure, command system, and training had to be reorganized to create a force capable of effective maneuver warfare. It is to Iraq's credit that it did eventually learn these lessons and develop far more effective forces. At the same time, even shortly before the cease-fire, Iraq's largely ineffective People's Army was still forcibly drafting men in the streets of Baghdad, and Saddam Hussein or his senior colleagues were interfering in command decisions that should have been left to local commanders.

The key lesson from this experience is that the effectiveness of Third World forces, like that of any other force, must be judged on the basis of a careful review of the nature of its high command. Assuming that the strength of armies is a function of their size, equipment, training, and the skill of their professional military is simply unrealistic in the case of states where civil leaders interfere directly and constantly in all levels of military activity. This is particularly true in the case of highly ideological or authoritarian states, where the armed forces are assumed to require constant ideological supervision and/or are a threat to the regime. It is also particularly true of the many states whose leadership and armed forces have no real prior experience in large-scale warfare. Under these conditions, leadership elites are likely to seriously undermine the effectiveness of their forces and to seriously degrade the entire process of command at virtually every level.

Threat Assessment Technologies and Warning and Surveillance Systems[1]

The major problems in Iran and Iraq's ability to develop effective and objective intelligence have already been discussed in detail in the initial chapters of this book. They were more political than technical, but it is important to note that neither side began the war with advanced technical intelligence assets, and neither could do more than acquire a few scattered improvements to its capabilities before the cease-fire.

Neither Iraq nor Iran made effective use of SIGINT, and little use was made of ELINT until Iraq improved its performance during the last year of the war. While both sides had communications with commercial-quality encryption and some decryption gear, it is unclear to what extent use was made of secure communications and how well either side could decrypt such communications, even at the end of the war. Further, extensive use was made of land lines, directional microwaves, and personal conferences, and this would often have made intercepts extremely difficult.

Iraq seems to have received some intelligence data based upon such sources from third countries but had few capabilities of its own. PHOTINT was limited largely to fighter reconnaissance aircraft, using fair-weather daylight photography, during most of the war. The data obtained were slowly processed and poorly interpreted, and the evidence was then often subordinated to ideological considerations. Iraq does, however, seem to have improved its reconnaissance capability after 1986 and to have gradually produced less politicized targeting and damage-assessment data.

Both sides had developed remotely piloted vehicles (RPVs) by 1987 and may have used these systems successfully during some phases of their operations in 1987–1988. Iraq seems to have found such systems to be an important way of providing survivable real-time reconnaissance over the battlefield of a kind that its fighter-reconnaissance aircraft could not provide because of their vulnerability, lack of real-time sensor/data links, and limited endurance. While neither side seems to have used such systems in great numbers, and at least the early Iraqi systems had serious sensor coverage and data-link problems, both sides exhibited improved systems after the cease-fire and felt that RPVs had great potential value.

Although numerous air control, warning radars, naval radars, battlefield radars, and night-vision devices were available, the Iran-Iraq War was also very much a "visual-range war." It was fought by two sides who have bought large numbers of sophisticated weapons without the proper targeting, threat and damage assessment, and warning and surveillance systems to use them. Further, the intelligence system of both sides has been heavily ideological and politicized, and much of the HUMINT it produced remained worthless from the start of the conflict to the cease-fire.

The Intelligence Problem

It should be noted, however, that the mix of urban, marsh, rough desert, and mountain terrain where the war was fought and the heavy emphasis on night movement and dug-in positional warfare present a challenge to the intelligence assets of any Western state. It is extremely difficult for even sophisticated Western systems to accurately assess infantry movements and to assess the intentions and timing of forces constantly poised for the attack.

There is no question that sensors like SAR, SLAR, FLIR, electro-optics, and added night-vision devices could have provided warning against many of the attacks conducted during the war. There also are far more sophisticated data-processing assets than are available to Iran and Iraq. These could help improve the performance of Western forces under similar circumstances. The history of the war has also shown that both sides could benefit from RPVs and ELINT aircraft and by unattended ground sensors, just as Israel used many of these systems and technologies successfully in June 1982.

Nevertheless, many Western sensor systems depend on predictable patterns of deployment, on movements of major combat vehicles and aircraft, and on the ability to intercept and analyze comparatively objective and apolitical military communications. If the intelligence target has a command structure that lies to itself, consists of many scattered elements with limited coordination, and acts without prior plans or signals of intent, intelligence coverage is difficult. This is particularly true in the case of trying to detect and predict low level actions or escalation and the point at which long-standing infantry buildups turn to actual attacks.

Sensor technology cannot triumph over the self-inflicted wounds of ideology and self-delusion. Technical intelligence assets are heavily dependent on the accuracy of data transmitted through the C³ net, on the ability to monitor land forces by tracking the movement of armor and heavy equipment, and on predictable unit effectiveness. None of these collection conditions are present in the case of Iran, and it is unclear than any Western state has yet combined the intelligence, hardware, and software into systems or subsystems suited for the conditions encountered in the Iran-Iraq War, conditions which may be typical of those in other Gulf or low-level conflicts.

Air Defense Sensors

Neither Iraq nor Iran was able to make effective use of the air warning and surveillance systems they built up before the war. The Iranian radar network—which mixed FPS-88 radars and Marconi S-330

Surveillance Radars with a semi-automated air defense system called
"Seek Sentry"—was constructed during the Shah's regime.

The full Iranian system was never completed because of the
revolution. Long-range FPS-100 and FPS-113 radars were deployed on
mountaintops, and TPS-43 and ADS-4 sites were scattered throughout
Iran. Individual sites have been active, but they do not seem to have
been operational as a unified system or to have played a significant
role in guiding air intercepts. Iran could not correct this situation during
the war because of its lack of access to supply of advanced equipment
from the U.S. or any other source.

The improved Hawk anti-aircraft missiles which were linked to
the Iranian radar network also seem to have had relatively little
early warning or central control. While some hits must have occurred
against Iraqi aircraft, there is still no confirmed instance of an Iranian
Hawk missile hitting an Iraqi aircraft.[2]

The ineffectiveness of Iran's Hawks and other sophisticated ground-
based air defenses may have a great deal to do with the over-
complexity of the original design for the Seek Sentry/Peace Ruby C^3
system. When the Shah was in power, he purchased the most
prestigious (and often the most complex) weapons of the American
arsenal. The improved Hawk was one of those systems. A 1976 U.S.
Senate Subcommittee report went so far as to doubt the ability of the
Imperial Iranian Air Force to effectively operate the Hawk prior to
the mid-1980s. Yet, the Hawk missile is a "wooden round," which does
not require regular maintenance, and Iran's problems in using the system
with its own radar are unclear. Technology transfer should not have
presented this serious a problem, although the combined impact of the
revolution and the subsequent withdrawal of foreign technical support
may largely have deprived Iran of the benefits of technology transfer.[3]

The Iraqi early warning and SAM network was equally ineffective
throughout the entire war, despite the fact that Iraq had a 10,000-man
air-defense force, at least ten major radar sites, hundreds of radars, and
SA-2, SA-3, and SA-6 missiles when the war began. However, the
Iraqi system was not netted and integrated effectively; training and
readiness were dismal. The management of sensor and C^3I links to
aircraft and missiles was poor, and the system left major gaps in low-
altitude coverage.

In 1978 and 1980, low-flying Iranian aircraft continually penetrated
into Iraqi airspace without incurring serious losses from the more than
3,000 major SAMs incorporated into the Iraqi air defense network.
Iraq's SA-2s and SA-3s never seem to have been effective. As a result,
these Iranian aircraft inflicted enough damage on Iraqi air bases and
infrastructure to force the Iraqis to pull back their air units and to

deploy large numbers of mobile SA-6 missiles to provide additional protection to various Iraqi facilities and Basra. Iran's ability to launch large numbers of air strikes was soon cut severely by maintenance and support problems, but Iraq never succeeded in establishing effective 24-hour air control and warning coverage of even the front along the Iranian-Iraqi border. This required Iraq to acquire and deploy large numbers of French short-range surveillance radars—and lighter missiles like the SA-8, SA-9, Crotale, and Roland—to act as point defenses and fillers.[4]

The Iranians do seem to have begun the war with an effective IFF system, but Iraq either lacked an effective ground-based IFF capability or relied on "corridor" tactics, where its own aircraft could fly along a narrow corridor and all other aircraft are shot down. The Iraqis tried to avoid the problem of aircraft IFF by intercepting hostile aircraft as far away from defended targets as possible. All Iranian aircraft that penetrated the Iraqi fighter screen were then subjected to attack by ground-based defenses. This forward-fighter screen system was intended to eliminate the problem of identifying whether a plane was hostile or friendly. The Iraqis, however, found this tactic to be unsuccessful. Their ground-based radars could not provide the appropriate amount of early warning necessary to engage their fighters or even properly employ their SAMs in point defense. Throughout the war, they were unable to detect Iranian fighters flying at low altitudes.[5]

The IFF/detection problem was further complicated throughout the war by the close proximity of many Iraqi targets to the front. Iraq lacked the technology to compensate for its lack of strategic depth. Data transfer from ground controlled intercept (GCI) sites was poor. The various export models of the MiG-21 and MiG-23 available to Iraq had no real look-up or look-down capability and lacked the radar range and air-to-air armament to use GCI data effectively. The French Mirage F-1 reduced some of these problems in terms of aircraft capability, but Iraq remains unhappy about the quality of its Soviet-supplied AC&W and GCI equipment and has actively sought more advanced West European and improved Soviet equipment since the cease-fire.

The Need for an AWACS and Satellite Capability

Terrain was a critical factor in determining the effectiveness of various sensors and command-and-control systems. Both sides suffered badly from the lack of airborne sensors or AEW or AWACS aircraft, although Iran exploited terrain masking effectively to prevent radar coverage.

Iranian pilots displayed considerable initiative and managed to use terrain masking effectively on their approach to Iraqi targets. This pilot initiative was the result of a decision on the part of the Iranian leadership to release a number of previously incarcerated Air Force officers.

In contrast, the Iraqi Air Force initially flew textbook medium-altitude approaches and used comparatively high-altitude, weapons-delivery profiles and tried to bypass Iranian SAM defenses. This greatly aided Iranian air intercepts and helped give Iran the ability to win air superiority during the time Iran could keep its Air Force highly operational.

Iraq did develop a relatively low-cost airborne early warning aircraft at some point in the mid-1980s, which it called the Baghdad 1. This aircraft was a Soviet IL-76 Candid, equipped with a modified Thompson CSF Tiger radar. This radar is built under license in Iraq and is called the SDA-G. This aircraft could provide warning and coverage of Iranian high- and medium-altitude air movements over a limited area. The aircraft, however, had limited sensor range, could not cover targets flying at very low altitudes, and lacked any advanced airborne identification, intelligence, and control features.

The lesson regarding the potential value of an AWACS-type aircraft and satellite coverage is obvious. The U.S. had the advantage of having only AWACS and maritime patrol aircraft that could sustain regular coverage in the area. The U.S. monopoly of AWACS capabilities, supported by U.S. Navy shipborne radars, gave the U.S. a degree of coverage of air and naval movements in the Gulf that often proved to be of critical value in monitoring Iranian and Iraqi movement.

Airborne coverage was particularly important. The rough terrain of the area blocks or limits the coverage of surface-based radar, and thermal ducting in the Gulf reflects of alters radar returns. The U.S. ability to provide airborne radar and night-vision coverage of the Gulf with its E-3As, E-2Cs, ships, and other platforms was valuable from 1980 on and proved critical to the success of U.S. operations during 1987 and 1988. It is interesting to note that U.S. willingness to share the results of such data was also often of critical value to the West European countries operating in the Gulf in 1987 and 1988. The need for an AWACS coverage is a critical lesson of the war, but maritime patrol and AEW-aircraft also proved to be of great value.

The West and the USSR enjoyed a near-monopoly of satellite coverage, although both Iran and Iraq bought some commercial satellite data from France toward the end of the war. While the details involved remain classified, press accounts make it clear that intelligence satellites often gave the U.S. excellent intelligence coverage of all of Iran and Iraq.

Effective and Secure C^3I

Neither Iran nor Iraq had particularly effective or secure communications. Both also lacked advanced communications intelligence collection and decryption capability. European sources indicate that both nations had field radios that could use commercial-quality secure communications in some areas by the later years of the war but that they generally had poor communications security and discipline. This is likely to be a major vulnerability in many Third World states, although the extent of this vulnerability may be offset by the use of land lines and the emphasis on face-to-face meetings and conferences.

Iraqi and Iranian communications also presented another problem. Long before the war, Iraq and Iran had established a history of using their C^3I systems to "lie to please" at every command level. In Iran's case, this "command, control, and communicate by lie" was compounded by the disruption caused by the revolution.

The command structure of the Iranian Army was a near shambles when the war broke out. Iran then suffered from severe uncertainties regarding the chain of command and from orders and policies coming from conflicting centers of power within the government.

During 1979 and 1980, Iran failed to expand and improve its C^3I system in proportion to the vast expansion in its land-force manpower. Communications equipment was lacking and a clear C^3I system was often lacking. Soldiers sometimes vetoed the appointment of officers or had unpopular leaders removed from office. Revolutionary councils were formed, and these councils further hindered the chain of command.[6] The new revolutionary guards served as a parallel army with a separate command structure. In addition, the guards lacked modern communications equipment proportionate to their strength and were often unresponsive to the Iranian Army and Air Force during joint operations.[7]

The power struggle between Iranian President Bani-Sadr and the Mullahs in Tehran was particularly serious during the first two years of the war and created splits within the Iranian command structure that played havoc with the Iranian chain of command until the cease-fire. Bani-Sadr aligned himself with the regular military and tried to capitalize on the pro-military feelings the public displayed following the Iraqi invasion. As a result, Bani-Sadr served as a highly visible commander-in-chief, who, in the minds of many clerics, functioned to isolate the army from the influence of the Islamic revolution.

The cleric-dominated Supreme Defense Council responded by emphasizing revolutionary and popular volunteer forces and by appointing permanent representatives, or religious commissars, to supervise regular forces. These individuals limited the influence of Bani-Sadr and served to exacerbate Iran's chain of command problems until his ouster.[8]

Bani-Sadr's political defeat and exile in the summer of 1981 reduced these command problems within the Iranian military, although it left a parallel religious and military chain of command in place with Mullahs "guarding the revolution" in every regular army, navy, and air force unit. Further, Khomeini continued to show his distrust or fear of anti-revolutionary activity in the regular forces and again strengthened the Revolutionary Guards relative to the regular army in 1986.

Although Tehran announced the formation of a joint military command under the commanders of the Army and the Revolutionary Guard as early as 1982, such a command never really developed, and the situation was made worse by constant interference by the senior Mullahs. Repeated efforts were also made to integrate the Revolutionary Guard and the Army C^3I systems. These efforts included the provision of guard officers to command army units and Army commanders to command guard units. The more experienced commanders of both the Revolutionary Guards and the regular forces also increased their role in planning and executing Iran's offensives after the defeat of the revolutionary and Islamic offensives in early 1984.

Tensions remained, however, and reports of clashes between clerics, officers of the regular forces, and officers of the Revolutionary Guards continued through 1988. While it is impossible to accurately trace the details of all the disputes involved, it is clear that when armed forces are even partially divided against each other and then against the state, they lose a great deal of their effectiveness.[9]

The Iraqis also had a confused and heavily politicized military chain of command at the beginning of the war. Iraq's chief problem was gross overcentralization of command, mixed with high levels of politicization and incompetence at all levels of command. At the early stages of the fighting, junior officers and NCOs were so rigidly controlled that they were unwilling to advance without orders or to maneuver around a strong point once they had been ordered to advance. This often caused Iraq to fail to exploit its tactical advantages and take many more casualties than necessary. At the same time, higher level officers often refused to report bad news and exaggerated their successes.

These problems in Iraq's chain of command caused Iraq to make some extremely costly blunders throughout the war. They were particularly damaging at the start of the war and at Faw in 1986. According to several sources, the Iraqis twice entered and abandoned Susangerd at the start of their offensive and then gave up critical positions near Dezful during their initial offensive because they lacked clear orders and responsive command. The Iraqis also appear to have entered the conflict with only radio relay communications equipment to provide them with C^3 over a longer range. This radio relay system required a series of line-of-sight relay stations and broke down when Iraq had to deploy deep into Iran. A better system would have allowed Iraq to operate over a wider area using less C^3 equipment and requiring fewer personnel.[10]

It is doubtful, however, that Iraq's lack of advanced C^3I technology influenced the outcome of the fighting during either the start of the war or at any time up to the cease-fire. Iraq's key C^3I problems were political: Iraq had put its prewar emphasis on political control to prevent coups and simply was unready to use C^3I technology effectively.[11]

Like Iran, Iraq's C^3 capabilities also improved after the beginning of the war. By 1988, the Iraqi C^3 system had far better radio and land-line links and more flexibility at the major and mid-level command level. However, the fighting in 1986 and 1987 showed that Iraq's C^3I system could still be a system of lies. Iraq's command structure also often still proved that it remains too inflexible for effective counterattacks, combined arms, and combined operations.

These lessons regarding Iranian and Iraqi C^3I present both risks and opportunities to the West. The risks are the potential breakdown of, or weaknesses in, the C^3I organization, technology, and training of friendly local forces, and in their potential lack of interoperability with Western forces, particularly at the larger-unit or higher-command level. Opportunities will occur for the West to exploit these weaknesses in threat forces and to give friendly local forces an edge through suitable technology transfer tailored to the needs of a given friendly state. Such transfers could range from ensuring the availability of suitable radio and command equipment to the transfer of a major air and maritime C^3I system like the "Peace Shield" system the U.S. is selling Saudi Arabia.

It is also likely that sophisticated Western forces like USCENTCOM can exploit the technical advantages they will gain from superior C^3I organization and technology and could use a combination of electronic warfare, targeting, and strike systems that massively degrade the C^3I assets in Third World forces. The experience of Iraq and Iran indicates such strikes might cripple many Third World air forces and critically weaken their regular armies, particularly if they hit at both military and civil C³ links.

Notes

1. This analysis does not deal with the U.S. and Soviet problems in developing adequate satellite coverage of the region. The USSR, for example, was forced to reschedule its satellite coverage during the more intense periods of tension between Iran and the West. In November and December 1987, it was forced to alter the orbit of its Kosmos 1983 PHOTINT satellite to lower it to an altitude of only 170 kilometers over the battlefield between Iraq and Iran. Similarly, it altered the orbit of Kosmos 1985 in a way that implied it either had night coverage of the battlefield or was covering U.S. activity at Diego Garcia. *Jane's Defence Weekly*, December 19, 1987, p. 1400.

2. See Jim Bussert, "Iran-Iraq War Turns Strategic," *Defense Electronics*, September 1984, pp. 136–139. Reports in late 1986 did indicate, however, that Iran had used Hawks to kill several Iraqi fighters during attacks on Kharg Island.

3. U.S. Senate Committee on Foreign Relations, Subcommittee on Foreign Assistance, *U.S. Military Sales to Iran*, Washington: U.S. Government Printing Office, 1986.

4. Colin Legum, et al., *Middle East Contemporary Survey*, Vol. IV, New York: Holmes and Meier, 1981, p. 41.

5. See Bussert, op. cit., and Nick Cook, "Iran-Iraq: The Air War," *IDR*, November 1984, pp. 1605–1607.

6. William F. Hickman, *Ravaged and Reborn: The Iranian Army*, Washington, D.C., Brookings Institution, 1982, pp. 10–11.

7. Edgar O'Ballance, "The Iran-Iraq War," *Islamic World Defense*, vol. 1, Autumn 1981, p. 16.

8. Reports in 1986 also indicated that the regular army high command had been changed to strengthen the Pasdaran and that the Guards were to be given most of the new equipment purchased from the PRC, including F-6 and F-7 fighters. Hickman, op. cit., pp. 22–24. Also see "Iraq's Hussein Confirms New 80-Mile War Front," *Washington Star*, December 26, 1980, p. A-9, and William Branigan, "War Becomes Political Boon for Bani-Sadr," *Washington Post*, October 13, 1980, p. 61.

9. Hickman, op. cit., p. 31.

10. See "The Gulf War: Continuing Stalemate," *Armed Forces*, vol. 4, no. 8, August 1985, pp. 290–293; Bussert, op. cit.; Cook, op. cit.; and William O. Staudenmaier, "Iran-Iraq (1980–?)," *Lessons of Recent Wars*, Lexington, KY, 1985, pp. 211–239.

11. Interviews conducted by Anthony H. Cordesman in Iraq.

12

COMBINED ARMS
AND THE LAND WAR

The Land War

The Iran-Iraq War presents far more lessons about the problems of technology transfer and converting Third World armies to effective mechanized forces that are capable of combined-arms operations than it does about weapons and technology. Neither Iran nor Iraq was ever able to exploit its land weapons to their full potential. In fact, both had serious problems in conducting effective offensive maneuvers during most of the war and in achieving more than mediocre results with combined arms.

While Iran was hurt by its lack of easy access to modern arms and resupply for its Western-made equipment, the major problems on both sides were the lack of organization and training for modern war. This helps explain why force ratios had so little real impact on the outcome of the battle. The issue was rarely the total number of forces engaged; it was, rather, the comparative effectiveness of those force elements which could be directly engaged in combat. It also helps explain why Iran's human-wave tactics could be effective in many instances against a massive Iraqi superiority in firepower.

The general problems each army faced have been described in the historical analysis of the war, along with the problems Iran had in developing effective forces in the face of constant interference by its senior Mullahs and the problems that Iraq faced because of the initial politicization of its armed forces and the overcentralized command authority under Saddam Hussein. While a detailed analysis of the key aspects of land performance does provide some additional insights, it is important to stress that the most important insights are into the strengths and limitations of Third World armies and not into the relative effectiveness of their weapons.

Combined Arms

Neither Iran nor Iraq began the conflict with any real mastery of the operational art of war, and neither side developed a consistent capability to carry out combined-arms operations effectively, although Iraq made major improvements in 1987 and 1988. Both sides also learned that sheer mass is not an effective substitute for combined operations. Iran learned this in the case of its human-wave attacks. Iraq learned it in terms of its use of defensive firepower.

Both sides lost large numbers of tanks and armored vehicles during the first years of the war because they forced their armor to fight without proper support from artillery and infantry, or because they used them inflexibly in static defensive roles and as direct-fire artillery. These problems were especially serious at the beginning of the war. One of the major reasons that the Iraqi offensive bogged down in 1979–1980 was that Iraq attempted to use armor/mechanized units without dismounted infantry in terrain and built-up areas that clearly called for dismounted support. As the war progressed, the Iraqis made better use of infantry support for their armored vehicles but failed to develop independent foot infantry and an efficient counterattack capability.

The Iranians, on the other hand, had to assume an infantry-heavy offensive strategy, since much of their armor was not operational or was properly manned at the start of the war, and they were usually unable to replace or repair damaged and destroyed weapons. Iran gradually trained its infantry to fight alone, or with nothing more than limited artillery support, in marsh or mountain terrain, but Iranian infantry was not able to sustain offensive thrusts without armor or more artillery. Iran often achieved limited advances, even against well-prepared Iraqi defenses, but failed to achieve decisive results. During 1986–1988, Iran also learned, at great cost, that it could not achieve a decisive exploitation of its initial gains without more armor, more mobility, and better logistics support.

Both sides relied on artillery as well as infantry. Iran has proved superior in target acquisition and shifting fires, and Iraq has been superior in massing artillery and achieving high rates of fire. Both sides, however, failed to develop the kind of coordinated fire that would make their artillery fully effective in supporting combined operations, although Iraq again greatly improved its performance during 1986–1988. Their command chain often led to long delays in requests for the approval of artillery support. They did not make good use of forward artillery spotters and lacked more sophisticated forms of target acquisition. Even the Iranians have been slow to shift fires, and both sides found it difficult to cross-reinforce from one unit to another.

Neither side effectively blended armor, infantry, artillery, and helicopters, although both have occasionally made effective use of helicopters. Most branches of the land forces also only cooperated effectively when they fought from well-established static defenses or during the initial assault phase of an offensive. Interbranch coordination often broke down when a battle became fluid. Once again, this offers risks and opportunities for the West. There is an obvious need to transfer the skill and mix of technology necessary to help friendly Third World forces conduct combined operations, and it may well be possible to exploit serious weaknesses in the combined-arms capabilities of hostile nations.

Both Iran and Iraq do, however, deserve to be given credit for considerable technical capabilities. Regardless of their problems in integrating combined arms, each nation produced a wide range of highly specialized modifications of foreign and domestic equipment that was specially modified to suit local combat conditions. These modifications included the development of multiple rocket launchers, special-purpose bombs, modifications of tanks and other artillery vehicles, artillery modifications, and a host of specialized developments in combat engineering and logistic equipment. While the details of such modifications go beyond the scope of this book, they illustrate an important priority for Western technical analysis. Many such developments may be useful to Western forces, both in modifying their current equipment and in setting priorities for future designs.

Infantry in the Iran-Iraq War

The Iran-Iraq War provides additional support for the thesis that infantry can still have decisive impact in modern warfare in the Third World. The primary fighting throughout the war was infantry dominated until the Iraqi offensives of 1988. Infantry attacks accounted for most of the changes in the course of the war since its first few months, and most offensive maneuver was infantry maneuver, rather than mechanized, although Iraq often used mechanized maneuver defensively to shift its forces.

Iraq's Problems with Infantry

Iraq was not prepared for effective infantry combat when the war began. In accordance with Soviet doctrine, the Iraqis placed great stress on the use of tanks and mechanized units during the first stages of the war. The initial Iraqi invasion involved brigades and support elements from four armored divisions and two mechanized divisions. These forces thrust into the Khuzistan region without the support of large nonmechanized infantry units. However, the presence of a large number of water barriers and strong defenses in urban areas provided poor conditions for tank and mechanized warfare. This, coupled to the C^3I problems described earlier, delayed the Iraqi advance in the critical early days of the war.

The resulting losses and delays quickly led the Iraqis to reevaluate the need for dismounted infantry troops to support their armor. Iraqi troops, including elite Presidential units, had to rapidly learn urban warfare and open-area infantry tactics, and this took time. The lack of sufficient trained infantry to take built-up areas was particularly critical in the area around Khorramshahr and Abadan.

The Iraqis made a massive effort to create new infantry units after their initial reverses in 1980. Reserve forces were mobilized, and hundreds of thousands of "Peoples Army" militia were called up throughout 1981, eventually reaching a total strength of 400,000 to 650,000. These troops were organized into 1,000-man infantry brigades, but the initial level of leadership and training for the new People's Army units was poor.[1] The Iraqis were clearly aware of this problem, and many such units were used as a garrison troop assigned to rear-area duties or to secure what were thought to be low-priority areas.

This helped free more experienced Iraqi troops for duty at the front, but as Iran increased its own weight of infantry, Iraq had to send poor quality People's Army units to man its frontline defense positions. This helped lead to several Iraqi defeats in 1981 and 1982 and led to broad criticism of the Iraqi infantry as ineffective and lacking in courage. Such critics often relied on exaggerated reports of executions or desertions, however, or exaggerated the meaning of the harsh warnings about desertion broadcast over Iraqi radio and television.

After the first few months of the fighting, Iraq only experienced problems with its infantry force when it was forced to rely on its newly-formed volunteer units to bear the weight of a main Iranian thrust. These People's Army units were usually led by senior members of the Ba'ath rather than professional officers. They were not properly organized, led, or equipped for intense combat and began to surrender or collapse without being defeated in detail. Their failures helped permit many of the Iranian breakthroughs after early 1981, and they were also the source of many of Iran's prisoners of war. After this period, the People's Army units were given proven combat leaders and became far more effective.

Iraq had fairly effective defensive infantry forces after 1982–1983 but only really began to train large numbers to support counteroffensives in 1984, and this training only began to be fully effective in 1986–1987. It was only in 1988 that Iraq showed it had properly developed its infantry into an aggressive combat arm. In prior years, it tended to rely on complex static defenses and rarely patrolled aggressively in the mountains, marshes, and rough terrain. This may have been intended to minimize casualties, but it often allowed Iranian infantry to infiltrate and penetrate Iraqi positions. Iraq also tended to remain road-bound and failed to patrol rough country using the larger infantry units necessary to secure such territory.

This Iraqi experience provides important lessons for any force designed to fight in low-level war, particularly forces which cannot be tailored to a given terrain or contingency. Infantry must have the training, firepower, and sensors to operate aggressively and as a maneuver force in rough terrain, in mountain areas, and in built-up areas. Barrier defenses are a way of minimizing the need for manpower but not the need for aggressive action.

Iran's Early Emphasis on Infantry

In contrast to Iraq, Iran began the war with fewer tanks and artillery pieces than Iraq (see Figure 12.1), and this disadvantage grew throughout the war (see Figure 12.2) because the Iranians failed to find adequate sources of resupply. This lack of resupply and sustainability reinforced Iran's ideological emphasis on popular warfare and helped lead it to try to use its larger manpower base to create superior numbers of infantry as a substitute for weapons numbers and technology. (See Table 12.1.)

The Iranians were able to obtain the weapons needed to equip lightly mechanized infantry troops. Heckler and Koch 7.62-mm G3 rifles are produced in Iran and were available for use by the army and the Revolutionary Guards. So were large stocks of Soviet-style weapons obtained from North Korea, Czechoslovakia, the PRC, and Libya.[2] According to Iranian Minister of Defense Mohammad Salimi, the Iranians had three production lines for heavy and light ammunition and two lines for mortar production that were in operation since early in the war. Salimi also claimed Iran has the production facilities to repair Katusha and RPG-7 systems, as well as make anti-personnel grenades. These reports seem to be correct, and Iran was probably capable of meeting at least half its needs for small and light arms and ammunition. It also could produce and recondition artillery, multiple rocket launchers, and armored personnel carriers.[3]

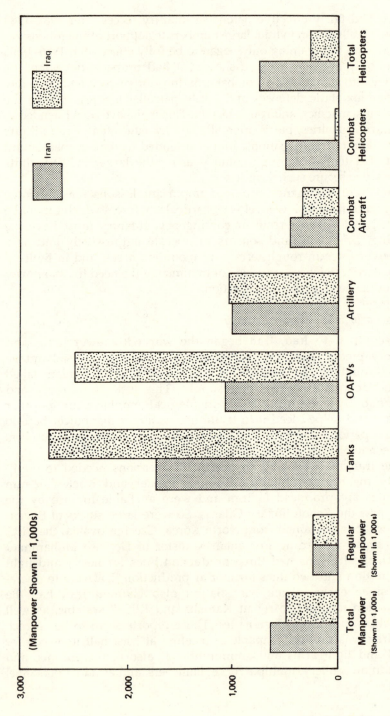

FIGURE 12.1 Relative Force Strengths: 1980. Adapted from IISS, *Military Balance, 1980–81* (London: International Institute for Strategic Studies).

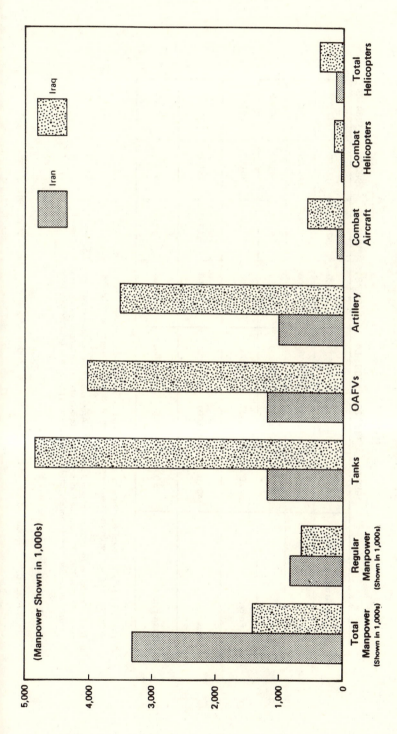

FIGURE 12.2 Relative Force Strengths: 1985. Adapted from IISS, *Military Balance, 1984–85* (London: International Institute for Strategic Studies).

TABLE 12.1 Armed Forces Personnel Strength [a]

	IRAN[b]			IRAQ			
	1980-81	1981-82	1983-84	1980-81	1981-82	1983-84	1984-85
Regular Armed Forces	240,000	195,000	555,000	242,000	252,000	517,000	642,500
Army:	150,000	150,000	250,000	200,000	210,000	475,000	600,000
Navy:	20,000	10,000	20,000	4,250	4,250	4,250	4,500
Air Force:	70,000	35,000	35,000	38,000	38,000	38,000	38,000
Reserves[c]	400,000	400,000	350,000	250,000	250,000	75,000	75,000
Paramilitary	75,000	75,000	2,505,000	79,800	79,900	454,800	660,000

a) The IISS data reflect massive definitional and consistency problems and must be used with caution. In general, the "high" estimate should be seen as the most realistic in any year after 1980-81.

b) The Iranian figures for total manning and the Regular Army should include at least 200,000 - 250,000 more men after 1980-81 from the Popular Army. The data on paramilitary forces are grossly exaggerated. Virtually all are Basidj or Hezbollahi part-time forces serving purely in internal security roles.

c) Most reserves have been active full-time since 1980.

SOURCE: Adapted from various editions of IISS, *Military Balance* (London: International Institute for Strategic Studies).

The Steady Improvement in the Effectiveness of
Pasdaran Infantry Forces

In spite of considerable turbulence because of the revolution, the forward command elements of both the regular Iranian infantry and the Revolutionary Guards did well in combat against the advancing Iraqi Army during the initial stages of the war. Their success was partly due to Iraq's failure to exploit its maneuver capabilities, partly due to Iran's ability to draw upon the equipment stocks built-up under the Shah, and partly due to efficient use of water barriers, rough terrain, and built-up areas. These natural barriers allowed Iranian infantry to operate effectively even though they operated as a mix of such diverse elements as regular troops, naval cadets, the Revolutionary Guards, and the then largely untrained Baseej militia (Popular Mobilization Army).[4]

As has been discussed earlier, the infantry in Revolutionary Guard units gradually became as well trained as regular army units and dominated most Iranian offensive action. They were also responsible for a variety of internal security actions and received far more trust from the regime than the Army throughout the war. It is interesting to note that Khomeini's first civilian Minister of Defense went so far as to state that the Army had been created by Satan (the Shah) to defend the interests of imperialism and Zionism.[5]

Although the regular army and the Revolutionary Guards supposedly acquired a joint command in 1982 and additional senior command elements were combined in 1986, no full integration ever took place. Problems in terms of joint operations and command coordination again emerged during 1987 and in the fighting in 1988. The Pasdaran, or Revolutionary Guards, also became a major political force. They acquired their own Ministry as well as their own separate budget, recruiting system, intelligence service, and public information office. This, incidentally, is another reason why intelligence assessment of Third World forces must focus heavily on the degree of politicization in individual major combat units and on the political, ethnic, and cultural differences among given units and forces.

The Strengths and Weaknesses of
Iran's Infantry Tactics

After Iraq shifted to a defensive posture in early 1981, Iran used its revolutionary forces to launch infantry-dominated offensives which succeeded in regaining considerable territory. These Iranian assaults also were usually conducted with only limited amounts of tank and artillery support. They succeeded, however, because of Iraq's slow-moving and road-bound response and because of (a) Iran's battle-trained leadership, (b) Iran's use of massive initial night attacks that saturated Iraqi defenses and penetrated to the rear, (c) Iran's heavy use of human-wave attacks, and (d) the regular army's ability to provide substantial firepower support at first light. Iraq usually reacted so slowly that the combined Iranian forces were able to seize key waterways, road junctions, and built-up areas and block Iraqi escape or reinforcement. This again highlights the need for night-warfare capability to deal with the problems of locating and killing large attack-infantry forces and for the ability to counter infantry infiltration and flanking efforts in all types of terrain.

Iran showed less skill once it began to invade Iraq. Many officers, NCOs, and experienced soldiers were casualties, and Iran's religious leaders failed to understand the cause of previous victories. As was discussed earlier, the Iranian offensives of 1982–1984 were character-ized by the use of large numbers of infantry and poorly prepared troops using human-wave tactics to overwhelm Iraqi defenses.

While there were exceptions, the preceding chapters have shown that far too many Iranian attacks were conducted without adequate tactical planning, logistical back-up, heavy weapons, or air support. As a result, Iran lost more of its seasoned troops and Revolutionary Guards during the fall 1982 offensive and many of its brigades were reduced to two and three battalions in strength. Losses among the elite Guard units were especially heavy. The new revolutionary command also lacked the professionalism to time their massed infantry assaults properly. In addition, they were easier for Iraq to ambush than regular forces.

Iran's infantry also had problems in dealing with special-forces missions. Iran did very well in assault and patrol functions but never developed effective long-range penetration and special-forces groups. Iraq was able to maintain a relatively stable rear area at minimal cost except in the north after 1986 when the Kurds provided the equivalent of special forces. It is important to note that in future wars, other Third World states may be far more aggressive in trying to compensate for their lack of armor and mobility by inserting special forces into rear areas.[6]

The reestablishment of firm, well-positioned Iraqi defenses along Iraq's borders was a key factor in limiting Iran's capability. The Iraqis also gained new motivation because they were defending their own territory and could now make good defensive use of their infantry to defend a single set of fixed lines. As a result, the breakthrough tactics of the Iranian land forces and infantry became steadily less effective during 1983 and 1984.

The Limits to Human-Wave Tactics

The changes in Iraqi defenses also meant that Iran faced serious problems in making use of its human-wave tactics. As has been discussed earlier, these tactics can produce lower total casualties than other forms of attacks on well-dug-in positions if they are properly executed. The use of volunteers to charge machine guns or walk over mine fields may sound appalling. However, this tactic can make sound military sense as a means of countering fewer but better-equipped forces as long as (a) it is not pushed too hard; (b) it takes advantage of night or some other form of tactical surprise; (c) successful penetrations are exploited; (d) attacks are halted if they do not succeed; and (e) the fighting has meaningful and achievable objectives. Such tactics could pose grave problems for USCENTCOM or other Western operations in the Third World.

Iran, however, was so caught up in giving its offensives the character of a "mini-jihad" that it failed to properly organize and control its human-wave attacks and then failed to exploit its initial successes. Rather than erode Iraqi forces in a series of carefully calculated blows, Iran attempted massive breakthroughs designed to achieve deep penetrations and rigidly pushed its attacks forward over broad areas rather than concentrating on exploiting local successes. Iran also failed to halt its attacks after limited gains and assumed that the righteousness of its cause could substitute for adequate logistics and an effective C^3 structure. As a result, Iran suffered serious casualties during the Wal-Fajr 4 fighting. While the total dead probably did not reach the 15,000 claimed by Iraq, it may well have approached 10,000.

The Implications of Mass Infantry Assaults for Western Power Projection

This Iranian disaster does, however, provide another warning to the West. It is far from clear that any Western state is prepared to engage in a Third World conflict which would approach such casualties, even on the enemy side. The fighting in 1985 through 1987 made the risks of engaging major Third World infantry forces even clearer. Iran's steadily improving tactics and more realistic command goals allowed it to threaten Iraqi forces, although Iraq had far superior weapons, good fixed defenses, air superiority, and a massive edge in armor and artillery. The West has generally been fortunate in being able to treat wars in the Third World as low-level wars, although Korea and Vietnam were brutal exceptions. The Iran-Iraq War shows that infantry-dominated conflicts can escalate to very high levels indeed. (See Figure 12.3.) Further, it indicated that extensive infantry combat

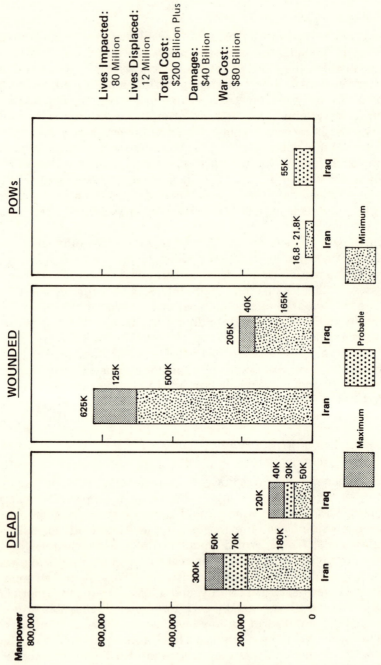

FIGURE 12.3 The Iran-Iraq War: The Thermometer of Death in Mid-1984. Adapted from working estimates by U.S. officials.

can take place long after a nation loses many of its high-technology weapons and assets.

At the same time, it is unlikely that any Third World state can win set-piece battles by trying to achieve decisive results with infantry-dominated forces in a combined-arms world. Infantry forces not only have a limited rate and span of advance, they rapidly become dispersed and lose concentration. Unless they are supported by armored personnel carriers and armor, they tend to lose momentum even when they are successful, and an armored opponent has time to concentrate his forces and recover from even a serious breakthrough.

This is especially true when the infantry is supported by towed or relatively static artillery and lacks rotary-wing and fixed-wing airpower. This gave Iraq the time to concentrate immense amounts of firepower, and while this was often inefficient by Western standards, it was effective in dealing with Iran.

Finally, these lessons reinforce the need for technology which can (a) provide improved area and direct-fire lethality against infantry attacks, even in the complex mix of built-up areas, wet terrain, and mountains common in the Iran-Iraq War; (b) allow Western and friendly local forces to have ample warning and combat capability against infiltrating and night-infantry attacks; and (c) allow Western forces to bring superior offensive and defensive technology to bear at the infantry and squad level, as well as in the heavier weapons now emphasized in most Western forces.

Tanks, Armored Vehicles, and Helicopters

Tank warfare had an important impact on the fighting from the beginning of the Iran-Iraq War but never in terms of the kind of maneuver warfare common in European and the Arab-Israeli conflicts.

Iranian Armor

Iran began the war with numerical inferiority. It started the war with only 1,700 main battle tanks and 250 light tanks. It was able to correct this situation. As of 1984, this number had been reduced to around 1,000 to 1,150 tanks. Iran procured or captured about 1,000 T-54s and T-55s, 260 T-59s and some T-72s during 1984–1988, but it also took substantial losses. In early 1988, Iran had less than 750 operational Western tanks, even counting large numbers which were not in operation. These included a maximum of 300 Chieftain Mark-3/5, 250 M-60s, and 200 M-47/48s. Many had limited or no operability due to shortfalls in spare parts and a lack of trained maintenance personnel and major workshop capability.

Iran also lost much of the rest of its armored mobility, attack helicopters, and helicopter lift. It began the war with about 250 Scorpion fighting vehicles, with Soviet BMPs just entering service in large numbers, with about 325 M-113s and about 500 Soviet-made BTR-40s, BTR-50s, and BTR-60s. Iran's only recent source of Western-made infantry fighting vehicles seems to be EE-9 and EE-11 Brazilian light-armored vehicles and BMP-1 Soviet-made APCs/AFVs. Attrition has, therefore, limited the numbers of infantry fighting vehicles that Iran was able to field.

As of late 1985, Iran had only about 700–950 operational APCs. Although Iran built up its strength during 1985–1988, it still only had roughly 130 EE-9s, 180 BMP-1s, 500 BTR-50 and BTR-60, and 250 M-113s by early 1988. These armored vehicles had to be scattered among Army units with twice the mobilization manpower of the forces Iran had under the Shah.

Similarly, Iran's Army had 205 AH-1J, 295 Bell 214A, 50 AB-205A, 20 AB-206, and 90 CH-47 helicopters in early 1980 and 40 Cessna 185, 6 Cessna 310, 10 0-2A, 2 F-27, 5 Shrike Commander, and 2 Falcon fixed-wing aircraft. Iran rapidly found that it could not repair or maintain much of its force. By February 1981, less than one-third of its rotary- and fixed-wing aircraft were operational, and in spite of major efforts to improve the situation and acquire parts on the black market, Iran was down to less than one-fifth of its prewar holdings by early 1988, and much of that force was not operational.[7]

Iraqi Armor

In contrast, Iraq steadily built up its tanks, other armor, and helicopter strength. In 1979, the Iraqis had about 2,500 older T-55 and T-62 model Soviet tanks. They also had a few (probably less than 100) more advanced T-72 tanks. Even during the opening stages of the war, Saddam Hussein was aware that these Soviet tank types were individually inferior to those used by the Iranians. In October 1980, he said: "Their (Iran's) cannons are greater in number, their tanks more advanced, their navy can reach long distance targets, and they have better arms."[8]

Iraq had roughly 2,750 tanks in late 1980. In early 1988, it had more than 4,500 Soviet T-54s, 55s, 62s, and 72s, some 1,500 Chinese T-59s and T-69-IIs, 60 Romanian M-77s, and some captured Iranian Chieftains. Iraq had about 2,500 other armored vehicles in late 1980. As of late 1985, Iraq had about 3,000 AFVs, including such advanced systems as the EE-9, EE-3, FUG-70, MOWAG version of Roland, ERC, BMP, BDRM-Z, and the VC-TH with HOT. It had about 5,100 such systems in early 1988, including roughly 1,000 new models of the Soviet BMP armored fighting vehicle.[9]

Iraq still kept most of its helicopters in its Air Force at the beginning of the war, which created major problems because of a lack of effective coordination between the Air Force and forward-deployed army units. In mid-1980, it had 35 Mi-4s, 15 Mi-6s, 78 Mi-8s, 18-34 Mi-24s, 47 Alloutte IIIs, 10 Super Frelons, 40 Gazelles, 3 Pumas, and 7 Wessex Mk-52s.

In early 1988, it had a strong Army Aviation Corps with 150–200 armed helicopters, including 40–80 Mi-24s with Swatter, 50–70 SA-342 Gazelles with HOT, 30 SA-316Bs with AS-12s, 56 BO-105 with AS-11, and 10 SA-321 Super Frelons with AM-38 Exocet. It also had 26 Hughes 530F, 30 Hughes 500D, and 30 Hughes 300C with light armament. It had 10 Mi-6 Hook heavy transport helicopters and 100 Mi-8, 20 Mi-4, and 10 SA-330 Puma medium-transport helicopters.

Armored Tactics and Lessons

Comparative tank technology and numbers of armored weapons never had anything like the impact on the fighting one might normally expect. Iranian and Iraqi tanks were rarely used effectively. For example, the initial Iraqi armored advance on Abadan was extremely slow. Tanks moved into hull-down positions prepared by Iraqi engineers. They then waited while the area to their immediate front was saturated by artillery. Only after such saturation fire was finished did the Iraqi tanks move forward. While these tactics had proved effective against inadequately armed Kurdish guerrillas in the late 1970s, they represented a critical mistake in fighting a more formidable adversary such as Iran.

Iraqi armor moved too slowly until Iraq's 1988 offensives, and Iraq failed to use its armor to engage in aggressive strikes against Iranian lines of supply and communication. The Iraqi use of tanks as mobile artillery also created severe problems with tank barrels, which rapidly wore out under constant use. Iraq was still exhibiting this problem during its defense of Faw in 1986 and defense of Basra in 1987.

Iraqi armor also did poorly in the intensive urban fighting that followed its initial invasion of Iran. Iran tenaciously defended sheltered urban positions, like Khorramshahr, Abadan, Ahwaz, Dezful, and Susangerd, using rocket launchers and anti-tank guided missiles (ATGMs). The Iraqis were totally unprepared for urban warfare, and this led to major Iraqi losses. These losses included both armored and infantry troops, but Iraq experienced its most serious problems in trying to use tanks in urban areas. Iraq could not exploit its armor at short ranges or provide protection against rocket-propelled grenade (RPG) and ATGM fire.

Iraq's Soviet-built T-55 and T-62 tanks were, however, reported to be surprisingly survivable against Iranian helicopter gunships during the period when Iran was still able to employ its helicopters in large numbers. Iraq mounted 12.5-mm machine guns on its tanks to fend off hostile helicopters. These tank-mounted guns have relatively long range, and they helped prevent Iranian helicopters from operating within lethal missile range after the Iraqis learned to organize cooperative and anti-helicopter fire. The Iraqis also claim that they occasionally used the main guns of their tanks to destroy Iranian attack helicopters.[10]

The Iraqis did suffer serious armor losses when Iranian helicopters flew nap-of-the-earth and pop-up attacks, but these attacks were rare after the first few months of the fighting. At least part of Iran's problems in using attack helicopters seem to have been caused by the disruption of its C[3]I system and command structure and a tendency to employ small-unit tactics without a clear overall knowledge of the battlefield.

Turning back to armor, the Iranians gradually deployed nearly all of their functioning heavy armor during the first year of the war. As the war progressed, Iranian units could not obtain resupply of their tanks and other armored fighting vehicles (OAFVs) or effectively recover and repair their armor. Iranian armored forces continued to dwindle in size, and their attrition rate was compounded by a number of Iranian blunders.

One example of these blunders occurred in the first major Iranian counteroffensive of the war, in which three under-strength Iranian tank regiments from the regular army attacked Iraqi troops at Susangerd on January 5, 1981, without infantry support and were soundly defeated. The tank units were part of the regular army, under the command of then President Bani-Sadr, and this lack of infantry support seems to have resulted from Iranian internal politics. The available infantry were units of the Revolutionary Guards, which were not under Bani-Sadr's command. Bani-Sadr either deliberately tried to demonstrate the strength of the regular army by sending unsupported tanks forward, or Iran's religious leadership withheld the Pasdaran infantry.

Bani-Sadr also overlooked the fact that his ground of attack was a sea of mud that critically inhibited Iranian ability to conduct resupply. Further, Iranian armor failed to maneuver quickly when it entered the "killing zone," which had been created by well-dug-in Iraqi tanks and infantry. As a result, Iraqi forces were able to surround the Iranian forces on three sides and to force the Iranians to abandon many of their armored vehicles because they could neither refuel nor resupply them.

This tank fire fight was typical of many armored battles in the Iran-Iraq War—and of Third World armored battles in general—in its lack of accuracy, maneuver, and long-range fire. Several reports agree that in spite of the fact that both sides usually fired at ranges under 1,000 meters, and that the firing was often limited and heavy and goes on for some time, losses were normally limited. Many of the Iranian losses in the January 5, 1981, battle occurred because of Iranian inability to maneuver and to resupply in the mud. Iranian armor was not so much defeated by fire as stuck and then abandoned. It is also clear that Iraq showed no ability to exploit its victory and counterattack. Israel has regularly exploited such weaknesses in Arab forces, and they provide an important lesson regarding the vulnerability of armor in Third World threats and allies.

Iran did better after Bani-Sadr's ouster in June 1981. It used its remaining tanks and supporting armor more flexibly than Iraq during the campaigns that drove Iraq out of most of Iran. These battles were infantry-dominated campaigns, however, and other armored fighting vehicles (AFVs) and helicopters did as much to support the Iranian offensives as tanks. Iran also took heavy tank losses during 1983 and 1985 that it could not replace. As a result, Iran tended to use tanks largely as artillery or to support infantry rather than in independent maneuver actions.

Iran did manage to obtain the North Korean and Chinese T-59 and Soviet tanks listed earlier and some modern T-62s and T-72s from Libya or Syria.[11] Iran did not demonstrate the ability to use these tanks effectively in maneuver warfare but found that they generally performed as well as Western types in support roles. While they lacked the fire-control systems to achieve a similar first-round kill probability or to fire on the move, their guns lasted longer, and direct-fire sighting was simpler than operating the sophisticated sight and fire-control systems needed for tank versus tank combat.

Tank warfare in the Gulf rarely took advantage of the more advanced features of modern tanks, including fire-control and range-finding equipment. Numbers generally proved more important in combat than quality, and appraisals of the value of given technical features were often contradictory. For example, the Iranians expressed a preference for the M-60 when they needed mobility but for the Chieftain when sheer weight of armor was critical.

If one judges by Iraq's actions, however, some technical lessons did emerge from the war. Iraq went to considerable trouble to try to improve the fire-control systems in some of its Soviet-made tanks with modifications of the Soviet fire-control system used on the T-72 (which was upgraded with Western range finders and computers), although it is uncertain that it had much success. Iraq found improved firepower to be important in dealing with Iranian targets like the Chieftain tank and hard targets. It upgraded some of its T-55s to use the Soviet 2A46 D-81M 125-mm tank guns used on the T-72.

Iraq also seems to have experimented with improved protection and to have added composite applique armor to some of its T-55s and other tanks. It is unclear, however, how many such modifications it actually deployed and how effective they were. Iraq added mine ploughs to some of its T-72s and mine rollers to some T-55s to allow armor to spearhead attacks through Iranian minefields. These systems seem to have been used on a number of occasions with at least moderate effectiveness.

Other Armored Vehicles

The patterns in the fighting involving OAFVs were somewhat similar to those in tanks. Iraq fielded a large number of infantry-fighting vehicles at the beginning of the war, but it failed to properly maneuver and had to either dismount its infantry or take heavy losses.[12] Iran did little better in using its AFVs, and its inability to obtain a significant number of new tanks was matched by its inability to obtain infantry fighting vehicles. In fact, neither side fought or maneuvered its AFVs much better than it fought its tanks.[13]

Both sides did try to increase the firepower of their other armored vehicles throughout the war by adding more machine guns and anti-tank guided missiles and converting some OAFVs to fire mortars. They made increased use of OAFVs for logistic and support purposes and as command vehicles and ambulances to compensate for their opponents improving artillery capabilities. Further, Iraq attempted to improve the armor of its BMP-1, which it found to be too vulnerable to Iranian RPGs and anti-tank missiles. At least some BMP-1s were given much heavier 35–40-mm bow plates and side skirts with rubber-on-steel. The numbers involved are uncertain, however, as is the value of such modifications in combat.

As a result, the main lessons that emerge from Iran and Iraq's experiences with armor have little to do with the technology, armament, or design details of individual vehicles. They are more consistent with the lessons from Arab behavior in the recent conflicts between Israel and its neighbors and with the weaknesses in Iranian and Iraqi combined arms discussed earlier. The limited ability of Third World states to drive, service, and operate armored vehicles in peacetime does not mean such states do not have the ability to operate armor effectively at the maneuver level, although armor often gives Third World forces far more effectiveness in holding prepared defensive positions that cannot easily be outflanked or bypassed.

The problem for the West is to (a) provide friendly local forces with the training and technology necessary to support large scale maneuvers and (b) persuade them to invest in training, recovery, and sustaining capability, rather than tank and armor numbers or the latest glitter factor in tank technology. Western forces also need to stress maneuver and avoid direct encounters with positioned Third World armor.

The Impact of Attack Helicopters on Armor

Iran never achieved the tactical results the Shah had sought in creating a massive force of attack helicopters. By the time the war began, Iran had already lost much of its operational capability, and the remaining capability declined steadily during the first years of the war. Iran often used helicopters effectively in small numbers but never as a major force.

Iraq was able to increase and sustain its helicopter strength but was never able to fully overcome severe problems in using its helicopters as an extension of its armor and land-force strike capabilities. It tended to use helicopters for more than the most narrow tactical purposes, often deploying them like forward artillery at the battle front or forward edge of the battle area (FEBA) and firing at advancing Iranian troops.

Iraq rarely used helicopters to strike deep or to insert troops into the rear. Like Iran, it would not usually risk deep helicopter attack strikes into the defended rear areas behind troops. Iraqi forces also indicate that they had serious problems with target acquisition. Pop-up tactics often worked against armor, but they do not seem to work well against dug-in or scattered infantry heavily equipped with automatic weapons and manportable surface-to-air missiles.

As a result, Iraqi pilots often found it difficult to acquire enough targets to merit risking the helicopter in combat and to survive long enough to acquire and attack other targets in the rear. Their problems were compounded by an inability to fly and fight at night and to easily acquire and kill targets in mountain areas, marsh areas, and built-up areas. The need for helicopters to have effective night-combat capability—and to be able to search out and kill infantry targets under a wide range of very demanding conditions—is another major lesson of the war.

This indicates a similar emphasis on training and sustainability will be essential wherever Third World forces use helicopters. Tactics and systems which are heavily optimized against maneuvering armor may fail to meet the real-world tactical needs of war in the Third World. Emphasis will also be needed on survivability, the use of helicopters to support war in unusual terrain and built-up areas, the ability to acquire and kill dug-in or well-positioned infantry, overall command and control in using helicopters, use of helicopters against infiltrating infantry, and use of helicopters in support of special forces.

Given the deployment problems that USCENTCOM and other Western forces face in massing heavy armor, the best substitutes for mass would seem to be combat helicopters and the use of smart submunitions that aircraft and MRLS can use in killing enemy tanks without direct fire. At the same time, sensor systems like SAR, SLAR, and FLIR, and area munitions, may need to be modified to locate and kill dug-in tanks, armor, and infantry rather than maneuvering forces of the kind more likely to be encountered in a NATO–Warsaw Pact conflict.

Precision-Guided Weapons and Specialized Land Munitions

Precision-guided munitions (PGMs) played an important part in the Iran-Iraq War from its beginning, although many of the systems used were comparatively old, and the war was not a major test of tactics or technology. The experience of both sides confirmed the fact that anti-tank guided weapons can play a major role both in countering armor and in dealing with a wide range of strong points and hard targets.

Iran's Use of ATGMs

Iran had to make heavy use of ATGMs to conserve its armor and air resources. The Iranians were able to use large numbers of U.S. PGMs, TOWs (BGM-71A) and Dragons (M-47), and French ENTACS, SS-11s, and SS-12s. It used weapons purchased by the Shah, obtained new ones from the world arms market, and obtained more TOWs as the result of covert U.S. arms sales.

Iran made particularly heavy use of TOW ATGMs during the first year and a half of the war, many of which were fired by crews from vehicles and from Cobra helicopters. It used them offensively against Iraqi bunkers, mountain defense positions, urban targets, and dug-in tanks. TOW units were often infiltrated forward in attacks or in mountain warfare. When Iran was able to obtain arms covertly from the U.S. during 1985–1986, it gave heavy priority to the obtaining of TOWs. Iran seems to have used such weapons against both Iraqi tanks and hard points during its attack on Faw in 1986 and its counterattack in Mehran later that same year.

Iranian ground troops also used Dragon missiles and, occasionally,

ENTACs and SS-11s. Both the TOW and Dragon missiles were effective in helping to halt Iraqi tanks, but Iran rarely achieved more than a 0.1 hit probability. It needed 3 to 4 times more missiles per TOW launcher than it had bought under the Shah and shortages rapidly developed. Part of these problems may have resulted from training and operating problems, but many resulted from the fact that Iran found that it was often forced to use large numbers of missiles under conditions where it was not possible to wait for a target opportunity with a high probability of kill.

Like Egypt in the Sinai in 1973, high rates of fire were more important to halting maneuver than high rates of kill. This is an important lesson for the West, which may have to employ such weapons against a major Soviet superiority in armor and in terrain that often shields tanks and other armored targets.

After 1982, Iran's lack of missiles and the slower pace of a more static war led to lower rates of fire and more precise targeting. In fact, at least 50 percent of the ATGM targets on both sides were static or dug-in tanks or hard points rather than maneuvering armor. This made warhead size and range critical performance factors in many tactical situations.

Shortages forced Iran to diminish its use of TOW and Dragon and led Iran to obtain Sagger and other Soviet-made anti-armor missiles and rocket launchers from North Korea, the PRC, Syria, and Libya. They also led Iran to place heavy emphasis on getting more TOW missiles in its black market purchases and covert purchases from the U.S. Iran seems to have used the TOWs it obtained from the U.S. during its counterattack at Mehran in 1986 and attack on Basra in 1987.

Iraq's Use of ATGMs

Like Iran, Iraq never claimed high kill probabilities from any type of ATGM. Iraq fired 6 to 8 Milan and HOT missiles per vehicle hit, and Iraq only scored about one hit per 20 to 30 Sagger or SS-11 missiles fired, although this may be more a function of tactics and training than technology. Further, the Iraqis would like ATGMs with more capability against infantry targets and bunkers and note that they would like advanced manportable mortars and grenade launchers. The need to provide forward infantry troops with heavier and longer-range firepower is a major lesson of the war.

Some additional insights regarding ATGMs emerged from the Iraqi side.

- Far more weapons are fired for effect than with a real hope of a hit or kill. About three to four times as many ATGMs and rocket launchers are fired for harassment as are fired with a good hope of a kill.

- Many weapons must be fired from within buildings or relatively closed defensive positions.
- AFVs are too vulnerable for use in firing ATGMs. Dismounted and concealed infantry weapons are far more desirable.
- ATGMs must be usable at ranges as short as 100 meters in the open and at very short ranges in cities and urban areas.
- As many ATGMs and rocket launchers have been fired at static defensive, mountain, and urban positions as at armor. These are the primary hard-target kill weapon of land forces.
- Effective night vision has generally been lacking in the ATGMs available to Iraq but would be highly desirable, particularly if an area warhead, as well as anti-armor, were available.
- Weapons with simple sighting, tracking, and fire control are essential. The complex method of tracking both the missile and target used in most Soviet missiles greatly reduces effectiveness.
- Both launcher and missile numbers are critical. ATGMs and rocket launchers must be provided throughout the force and to rear-area and support forces.
- Rocket launchers remain a critical weapon in spite of ATGMs. It would be highly desirable to have a range of anti-infantry rounds available for such systems to supplement light mortars and machine guns.

Rocket Launchers

Ordinary rocket launchers have also played an important anti-armor and infantry-support role. The RPG-7 was employed by both sides and was effective in close combat against the treads or other vulnerable areas of all of the tank types engaged. According to the Iranian Minister of Defense, the manufacture and repair of RPG-7s is now being carried out on a large scale by Iranian workers. By this he may mean that used launchers are being refitted to fire new grenades. Iran may, however, be able to produce RPGs, just as it presently produces heavy and light ammunition and its own mortars.

Given combat conditions and the quality of the data available from interviews and written sources, it is not possible to draw detailed comparative lessons about the effectiveness of specific types of precision-guided land weapons or any other type of anti-tank weapons. Neither side has been realistic enough about its claims to indicate relative kill capabilities and effectiveness. It is clear, however, that both sides prefer third-generation Western guidance systems (sight-on-target-only) to the awkward and complex first- and second-generation guidance systems (sight on both missile and target to track) of Soviet ATGMs.

Tube Artillery and Multiple Rocket Launchers

Neither Iran nor Iraq had the command structure, training, targeting, artillery sensors, fire control, and C³ capabilities to conduct effective point fire, counter-battery fire, on-call fire, or the "switched fire" of modern military forces, although Iraq again made major improvements in its capabilities during 1986–1988. Both sides of the Iran-Iraq War have made area bombardment their normal method of using artillery and have relied on maps, line-of-sight, or presurveyed fire for most of their target acquisition.

Iraq's Use of Artillery

The Iraqis used mass artillery fire ever since the intensive urban fighting in Khuzistan's major cities. Prior to sending their infantry into these areas, they made hour or even day-long efforts to soften up urban defenses with long-range artillery. The results were not impressive in this fighting since the resulting rubble often provided a more formidable defense than urban structures, and few Iranians were killed. Mass barrages were generally equally unimpressive in other fighting, with the exception of fire against exposed mass-infantry attacks.

Iraq also tried to use artillery warfare against urban targets to force the Iranians to make concessions and then to try to force them into agreeing to a cease-fire. It was in this context that Saddam Hussein warned the Iranians that his country would "sledgehammer your heads until you recognize our rights."[14] This type of "sledge hammering" was sometimes directed at military targets but largely included economic targets and population centers, which were targets that did not require precision bombardment.

Iraqi artillery, for example, helped destroy the oil refinery at Abadan during the initial part of the war. The Iraqis used their long-range artillery pieces (such as the 130-mm guns) to fire sporadically into urban centers and rear areas. This was done to disrupt military operations or civilian work rather than to inflict casualties. In describing the use of artillery at the Gzuyl sector (northeast of Basra) during 1984, one journalistic source reported hundreds of thousands of dollars worth of ammunition being used per hour. Artillery was fired as frequently as every two seconds.[15]

During 1984–1988, however, Iraq became increasingly more effective in developing the capability to deliver massive amounts of fire on advancing Iranian forces, in developing some counterbattery capability, and in shifting fires. Iraq also steadily increased its forces of self-propelled artillery and its ability to use artillery movement in support of armor and infantry. While Iraq never achieved the level of combined-arms capability common to most Western and Soviet-bloc forces, it was able to substantially improve its performance, and this was an important contribution to its victories in 1988.

Iran's Use of Artillery

Iran made extensive use of artillery but was much slower to organize the mass fire it needed to be effective. In describing early fighting in Susangerd, for example, the Iranian PARS news agency stated that the Iraqi success in attacking the city was due to Iran's own "lack of artillery support."[16] This lack of artillery support for Iranian units in the early part of the war was more a matter of organization than resources and may have been the result of heavy purges in the technical services of the army (including the artillery).[17]

The Iranians used massed firepower against targets like Basra and Iraqi defenses in much the same way as Iraq, although they could never approach Iraq's strength in numbers. They never relied upon sophisticated target acquisition, although this was partly continuation of the policies of the Shah's military. A senior British officer who was in overall command of a number of troops, including an Iranian brigade during the Dhofar campaign, went so far as to criticize what he called "a tendency to apply massive resources" without bothering to find a target in terms of artillery.[18]

Iran's most useful tube artillery weapons for such fire have been the 130-mm M-46 gun, 175-mm M-107 gun, and 203-mm M-110 howitzers. Iran also favored the 130-mm gun but has used the Soviet 122-mm D-74 gun and 152-mm and 155-mm gun-howitzers as well.

Lessons and Technical Issues

In spite of various news releases, both Iraqi and Iranian officers in the field realized they often failed to use massed artillery to achieve serious casualties. However, both the Iranians and Iraqis found the disruptive effect of random and mass artillery shelling to be useful. They often fired at civilian facilities and rear areas for political or shock effect and with little interest in inflicting casualties.

The "blind fire" techniques both sides used during most of the war proved to have significant limitations. The most important limitation was that both sides' artillery arms were often unresponsive to the real-time needs of the maneuver elements. While there has often been massive preassault fire, artillery rarely furnished effective direct or creeping barrage artillery support for maneuver units as they have advanced. Most preplanned fire ignored detailed terrain and maneuver considerations, and most artillery kills were achieved against exposed infantry attacking in mass during daylight when independent artillery units could target on a line-of-sight basis. Artillery was not used effectively to deal with unexpected problems or fluid battlefield situations, although Iraq made far more effective use of rapidly deployed self-propelled artillery to deal with Iranian attacks.

Iran and Iraq found that self-propelled artillery offered considerable advantages in shifting their target coverage and in allowing each side to mass its artillery fire. Both countries tried to create their own self-propelled artillery weapons, although both had limited success before the cease-fire took place. This is a further illustration of the fact that towed artillery weapons present time-of-reaction problems, even in relatively static conflicts.

Other interesting Iraqi efforts included the development of a six-wheeled 210-mm gun to try to outmatch the range and lethality of the M-107 175-mm guns in Iranian forces. This weapon is called the Al-Faw, weighs 48 tons, and is said to use a French-developed gun with a maximum range of 57,340 meters. Iraq is reported to have begun development of a radar-guided version of this 210-mm gun for coastal defense purposes.

Iraq also added hydraulic jacks to the Soviet D-30 122-mm gun to reduce its deployment times and converted Soviet 130-mm guns to use Western 155-mm barrels so that each gun could fire projectiles with more individual lethality while retaining a maximum range of roughly 37,000 meters.

Both sides found every kilometer of artillery range to be of great value in reaching such targets. Both sides preferred to use multiple rocker launchers for such missions when the proper combination of launchers, range, and ammunition was available. Iraq had had good access to high volumes of MRL fire since the war began, but Iran was slow to acquire the number of MRLs it needed and experienced erratic and limited ammunition supply as late as 1987.[19]

Iraq made heavy use of the Soviet BM-21 122-mm, ASTOS II 127-mm, BM-13/BM-16 132-mm, and BM-14 140-mm multiple rocket launchers, and Iran used PRC and North Korean Type-63s and BM-21s.[20] The 122-mm multiple rocket launcher has proved to be a particularly effective weapon. One observer, describing the Iraqi side of the front in November 1982, stated: "Rows and rows of tanks and mobile rocket launchers face east, dug in behind earth ramparts." This use of MRLs is in agreement with Iraqi doctrine which stresses the use of artillery against area rather than point targets. Iran gave high priority to acquiring BM-21 122-mm multiple rocket launchers. Both sides made extensive use of mortars, largely in direct support of infantry or forward-barrier positions.

Since the cease-fire, both Iran and Iraq have exhibited a number of domestically produced multiple rocket launchers and short-range battlefield rockets. It is unclear how many of these systems were actually used and deployed, but it is clear that both countries felt that this was a cheap way to acquire more firepower. Iraq has also exhibited a four-barreled 120-mm mortar that can be carried on an APC or towed. It claims this weapon has a range of about 10 kilometers and offers some of the firepower capabilities of a multiple rocket launcher.

Both Iraq and Iran complained about artillery and MRL fusing failures against wet and marsh terrain and against hard or rocky areas and of failures in Soviet-designed proximity fuses. Iraq also complained about the failure of Soviet artillery fire-control and targeting systems and aggressively sought European technology. It is impossible to determine whether these failures are the result of technology, training, tactics, or handling. Western studies of Soviet fusing do indicate, however, that the Soviet munitions exported into the region had relatively unsophisticated fusing. At the same time, even the U.S. Army has been slow to procure the kind of reliable, variable sensor and setting fusing necessary to achieve high lethality under these combat conditions.

Iraq also attempted to improve the lethality of its multiple rocket launchers by developing a 12 or 16 tube, computer-controlled launcher that fired rounds with a cluster-bomb warhead. This warhead had a diameter of 262-mm and a proximity fuse that released 200 bomblets about 150 meters above the target. This weapon was called the Ababil (a Koranic firebird). It was used during the latter stages of the war, but its effectiveness is unknown.[21]

It is clear that both sides would greatly benefit from the ability to properly target their systems and accurately deliver surge fire in near real time. Reliance on barrages, area fire, and fire for effect is the product of inadequate technology, as well as inadequate training and doctrine. Both sides also recognize that the use of tanks as direct-fire artillery is wasteful but cannot solve the C^3I/BM problem of bringing in artillery fire on a friendly position. These needs have obvious implications for Western and friendly local forces.

Mines and Barriers

More intensive use has been made of barriers and barrier munitions in the Iran-Iraq War than any of the other conflicts examined in this study. The Iranians were the first combatants to make extensive use of mines and barriers since they were initially on the defensive. They made particularly good use of deliberate flooding in the south to channel the Iraqis along a few routes of advance in the low-lying areas and forced Iraq into a massive engineering effort to create new roads and lines of communications. The Iranians also used water barriers to disrupt and delay the Iraqi advance on Abadan.

Iraq initially concentrated on building forward barriers to defend its gains and reduce the need to deploy forces to defend its lines. It did not, however, build major fixed defenses until 1981–1982. It concentrated on building up a limited number of improved roads. This made Iraqi forces vulnerable when Iran recaptured any given road link and reduced Iraq's ability to retreat.

Iraq did make massive use of flooding, water barriers, fixed-barrier defenses and mines, however, when Iran forced Iraq to go on the defensive. By the time Iraq was forced to pull back to its border with Iran, it fully realized the risk of defeat by the advancing Iranian troops. This led Iraq to create fortifications linked by a vast network of roads along its entire front. Iraq steadily improved this system after 1982 and made progressively greater use of dikes, damns, and flooding to create water barriers.

Iran's lack of technology for breaching Iraq's extensive mine and barrier defenses may have helped save Iraq during the most successful phase of Iran's offensives. The effects of Iran's shortage of armor and insufficient artillery were made far worse when Iranian infantry had to penetrate barrier defenses. Iraq also used earth barriers and artificial ridges to reduce the vulnerability of its rear areas to air attack during 1981 and 1982. These barriers were heavily defended with anti-aircraft (AA) guns and limited low-altitude attack capability against key targets, although their effectiveness has not been fully tested because they were only completed after Iranian operational air strength declined.

The Iranians seem to have been uninterested in technological solutions for defeating these barriers and land mines and are reported to have used troops to detonate mines by jumping upon them or using sticks to facilitate their explosion. There are major problems with many of these stories, however, and some can clearly be dismissed as Iraqi war propaganda.

The Iranians did, however, steadily improve their infiltration capability after 1984. While the Iranians often used human-wave tactics, they were usually careful to scout out lines of advances, to take advantage of weaknesses in the Iraqi positions, and to use the cover of terrain or night to try to penetrate Iraqi lines. Iranian patrols often spent weeks scouting out minefields at night and to use sappers to penetrate the fields at night ahead of attacking troops. The Iranians exhibited an outstanding ability to use engineering equipment to cross water barriers and assault mountain defenses in 1985 and 1986.

It is unclear that advanced technology would have been successful in stopping these Iranian tactics. As the PRC demonstrated in Korea and the Viet Cong in Vietnam, there is nothing inherently wasteful about using human-wave tactics to attack prepared positions as long as the initial losses are minimized by careful planning and tactical surprise. In any case, the West may well face similar problems with both enemy minefields, barrier defenses, and mass assaults. It must be able to both create its own barriers and penetrate those of others.

Mines and barriers have been as important as Iraq's superior weapons strength to maintaining Iraq's defense. Iraq also steadily improved its use of defensive lines and barriers as time went on. Iraq steadily expanded the length of its defenses along the front. It also created extensive concrete tank and anti-personnel barriers at the first defense line to improve on its former earth mound defenses.[22] Iraq created several lines of barrier defenses around key objectives like Basra as early as 1984, but it generally had relied on one strong line backed by extensive rear-area logistic and firepower support. Iraq's defeat in Faw in 1986 then led it to shift to defenses with several parallel road lines and with high capacity lines further in the rear. It also further improved an already high inventory of tanker transporters. After the Iranian attack on Basra in 1987, Iraq shifted from strong initial forward defense barriers to the extensive use of defense in depth. All of these improvements had a significant effect in allowing Iraq to counter Iran's human-wave assaults.

It is important to note, however, that each side's barrier defenses were only effective to the extent they were actively defended. They did not act as force multipliers or as substitutes for troops and active defenses. Iran demonstrated on many occasions since 1984 that it could rapidly infiltrate and penetrate strong barriers when they are lightly held and defended—a problem the Soviets experienced in Afghanistan, the Argentines in the Falklands, and Iran itself during its defense of Faw in 1988. This is an important lesson for the West, since many advocates of barrier defenses see these as force multipliers rather than as a limited extension of the capability of forces in being.

All-Weather and Night-Target Acquisition Systems

All-weather and night-target acquisition systems were not available to either side during much of the war but would have been important assets. This was particularly true in the case of Iraq, since a combination of temperatures up to 120° F during the dry season and Iran's lack of heavy equipment helped lead Iran to start large numbers of night battles. The Iranians developed night-attack capabilities using tactics and techniques dating back to World War I. They relied on scouts, patrols, careful preparation, special training, and complex attack plans and schedules. They made little use of advanced technology.

The Iraqis recognized the importance of night warfare early in the war, but it appears there was little they could do to quickly improve their capabilities. Some Iraqi officers claim that the Soviets failed to provide them with advanced night-vision or fire-control systems. Iraq, however, did not have the proper organization and communications equipment at the start of the war to use forward observers to call for artillery fire on point targets. Iraqi forces also had little prewar training for daytime artillery direction and virtually no training for night combat.[23]

Night-vision aids were slowly introduced into Iraqi and Iranian forces, but target acquisition remained a problem for both sides. They had no long-range or BVR ("beyond visual range") capability other than a limited number of recce aircraft, using day and IR photos, and a few artillery-locating radars. Neither source of data could provide adequate and timely information.

The Iraqi deployment of night-vision systems was also somewhat strange because Iraq issued many of its initial deliveries of night-vision systems to security units in cities and in the rear, although there was no real threat in that area. Iraq stepped up deliveries of night vision devices to the front in 1986 and 1987, but even in 1988, there were reports of shortfalls and a failure to provide anything like the number of night-vision devices and sights that were needed at the forward-combat unit level.

Both Iraq and Iran made slow progress in improving their fire-control and night and all-weather capability to use artillery. Both sides had artillery radars and counterbattery targeting aids, but Iran never seems to have been able to use them effectively. It relied largely on line-of-sight and classic visual counterbattery techniques and area fire, particularly as it became steadily more dependent on slow-moving static Soviet-bloc and PRC-made towed artillery.

The accuracy of each side's artillery fire increased after 1982, but this often was due to the stationary nature of the war. Iraqi and Iranian forces did not improve their targeting technology but made better efforts to survey the battlefield, to put in aiming stakes, and to plot their barrages in advance to cover possible avenues of approach. In addition, the Iraqis showed increasing ability to integrate artillery support into its overall defensive planning and to begin using forward observers to call in fire. There is no question that both sides would have been far more effective in using their artillery if they could have combined modern fire-direction technology with more advanced targeting systems.

Logistics and Logistic Systems

Iraq seems to have carefully considered the logistic implications of a war with Iraq well before the fighting actually started. Ammunition, water, gasoline, oil, and lubricants sites were constructed throughout the corps areas where they would be most needed. The Iraqis also did their best to maintain a logistic pipeline that would give commanders freedom of action once the war was underway.

When the Iraqis were in Iran, they constructed a paved highway from the southern sector through Ahwaz, then north to Dezful. After they went on the defensive, miles of lateral roads were built behind the front in Meisan province, and then throughout much of the central and southern front. Many lateral roads were also improved. These roads were built in order to enable combat reserves to move quickly into position to deal with any Iranian threat.[24] Another line of up to six-lane highways, later in the year, were rushed into completion. This seemed to be in response to the the Iranian victory at Faw in 1986 and the siege of Basra in 1987.

The Iraqis made logistic oversupply a key operational principle. They operated on the Soviet system of "supply push" rather than the U.S. system of "demand pull." Iraqi forces at the front were given massive ammunition stocks and war reserves. For example, Iraqi guns fired over 400 rounds per day in checking Iran's break out of Faw in early 1986. While the data are uncertain, Iraq routinely seems to expend about one U.S. Army "week" of munitions per weapon per day when it is in intense combat. Put differently, Iraq expended about as much ammunition per gun per week in early 1986 and 1987 as NATO countries have per gun in their entire inventory.[25]

The Iraqis also used tank transporters to move their armor to the front and used them to eliminate many noncombat-related maintenance problems. The improvement of this aspect of Iraqi capabilities was quite dramatic. The Iraqis expanded their inventories from about 200 tank transporters in 1973 to approximately 1,200 in 1984 and 1,700 in 1988. They also possess a large number of transports for AFVs.

The large and ponderous Iranian logistical system the U.S. constructed under the Shah perished with the departure of the thousands of American advisors who operated this multibillion dollar operation. Contrary to many reports, it was never really computerized and was run largely by U.S. and U.S.-trained technicians who were more concerned with storing supplies than the possibility they might have to be used. Iran had computers and computer-coded supplies in its logistical system but no records or software to locate many items. As a result, logistic supply had to be carried out at a rudimentary level once the war began. This was particularly ineffective in supplying complex spare parts for aircraft, tanks, and vehicles.

Iran's logistical problems grew steadily after the start of the war. This was partly due to a lack of transport vehicles for rough terrain but largely due to shortages in war material. The general shortages which permeated the country also had an impact on the frontline troops. Shortages of gasoline and motor oil sometimes led to a paralysis of resupply efforts, since the vehicles designated to bring supplies to the front were affected by these shortages.

One of the most notable problems associated with Iran's logistic and support effort was the large number of Iranian tanks abandoned by their crews during the first part of the war and in 1988. Many of these tanks had no real damage but were left behind because of an Iranian inability to resupply them or deal with minor repair problems. The tanks were subsequently seized by the Iraqis who presented about 50 of them to Jordan in early 1981. Others were retained by the Iraqis, who received training in the use of Western technology from Jordan.[26]

Another Iranian logistical problem that was apparent since the early stages of the war involved the British-made Chieftain tank. The Shah acquired 800 of these main battle tanks, and they formed the key component of the Iranian armor corps. At one point, Iran had more of these British-made tanks than did Britain. The Chieftains sent to Iran, however, have proved to have underpowered engines for rough terrain in warfare, inadequate filtering and cooling, and complex electric-current and gun-drive systems without hydraulic back-up. The Chieftains are particularly susceptible to overuse and breakdown. They require a very high degree of maintenance time, which is further complicated by Iran's lack of spare parts. The U.S. M-60 has also experienced rapid engine wear and major track-life problems in Iranian hands but has proved easier to service and repair than the Chieftain.[27]

Iran's resupply problem was partly solved by the massive PRC, North Korean, and other arms deliveries described earlier, but Iran's ability to keep its Western-made systems going got steadily worse. Iran had to buy in small lots of mixed quality. It had no real system for allocating parts and munitions to meet key needs and often delivered spares in small or random lots. Parts were often distributed by item rather than in the mixes needed. Ammunition was oversupplied and wasted in one area and undersupplied in another. While reports are uncertain, Iranian stocks may have sometimes dropped so low that Iran seems to have had critical problems with ammunition supply.[28]

Some aspects of Iran's experience in logistics and technology transfer bear an unfortunate resemblance to that of South Vietnam, which could not operate the complex logistic system it inherited from the U.S. This argues for a Western emphasis on giving friendly Third World states simpler, low-technology logistics systems and for Iraq's emphasis on large numbers of well-distributed stockpiles, rather than centralized systems.

Such an emphasis should aid friendly states to cope with the Soviet emphasis on supplying its clients with massive weapons stockpiles, should aid Western forces in joint operations with friendly local forces, and would minimize the need to devote scarce strategic mobility assets and limited Western munitions reserves to emergency resupply of a Third World state.

Notes

1. These units normally had characteristic two- and three-digit designations.

2. Robert Hutchinson, "Gulf War of Attrition," *Jane's Defence Weekly*, January 24, 1984, p. 108.

3. Tehran *Ettela'at*, "Interview with Mohammad Salimi, Minister of Defense," *JPRS-Near East/South Asia Report*, December 6, 1983. IISS, *The Military Balance, 1985–86*, London, International Institute for Strategic Studies, pp. 74–75. Anthony H. Cordesman, "Arms Sales to Iran: Rumor and Reality," *Middle East Executive Reports*, vol. 9, no. 2, February 1986, pp. 8–10.

4. The Basij were established in 1979 as a military support for the regime.

5. William F. Hickman, *Ravaged and Reborn: The Iranian Army*, Washington, D.C., The Brookings Institution, 1982, p. 12.

6. Part of Iran's problem was the inability to give such units the covert mobility they needed and a failure to realize that it needed full-time professional forces with special training. It sometimes sent Pasdaran forces on such missions, but it seems to have relied on ideological fervor and experience in regular combat to give them training and effectiveness.

7. These estimates are based on various editions of the IISS, *Military Balance*; Aharon Levran and Zeev Eytan, *The Middle East Military Balance, 1986*, Boulder, Westview, 1987, pp. 236–258; Thaif Deen, "Iran—Meeting Its Arms Requirements," *Jane's Defence Weekly*, November 28, 1987, pp. 1276–1277; Anthony R. Tucker, "Armies of the Gulf War," *Armed Forces*, July 1987, pp. 319–323; James Bruce, "Iran Building Up Its Own Arms Industry," *Jane's Defence Weekly*, June 20, 1987, p. 1302; Shahram Chubin, "Hedging in the Gulf," *International Defense Review*, 6/1987, pp. 731–736; "The Arming and Disarming of Iran's Revolution," *Economist*, September 19, 1987, pp. 49–50.

8. "Iraq Covets Opponent's Weaponry," *Middle East Economic Digest*, October 24, 1980, p. 7.

9. See the relevant country chapters or sections of the IISS, *Military Balance, 1987–1988*, and Levran and Eytan, op. cit.; Deen, op. cit.; Tucker, "The Arming and Disarming of Iran's Revolution," *Economist*, September 19, 1987, pp. 49–50.

10. "Iraqi Tank Guns Stop Missile Helicopters," *Aviation Week and Space Technology*, November 24, 1980, p. 66.

11. Drew Middleton, "Gulf War: Threats to Oil Signal a Shift," *New York Times*, November 3, 1983, p. A-12; Levran and Eytan, op. cit.; Deen, op. cit.; Bruce, op. cit.; Chubin, op. cit.; "The Arming and Disarming of Iran's Revolution," op. cit.

12. *War in the Gulf: A Staff Report Prepared for the Committee on Foreign Relations*, Washington, D.C., Committee on Foreign Relations, U.S. Senate, August 1984, p. 12; IISS, op. cit.

13. Like the Iraqis, the Iranians often resorted to the tactic of using tanks as mobile artillery rather than risking these systems in open combat. Cited in *Newsweek*, July 26, 1982, p. 31.

14. "Iraqi Leader Vows to 'Sledgehammer' Iran," *Washington Post*, March 8, 1981, p. A-25.

15. "Iran vs. Iraq: Bloodbath Without End," *U.S. News and World Report*, March 6, 1984.

16. Loren Jenkins, "Iraqis Press Major Battle in Gulf War," *Washington Post*, November 17, 1980, p. 1.

17. Drew Middleton, "Iran Said to Prepare for Decisive Push," *New York Times*, October 11, 1982, p. 3.

18. Major General K. Perkins, CB MBE DFC, "The Death of an Army: A Short Analysis of the Imperial Iranian Armed Forces," *RUSI*, June 1980, p. 23.

19. Deen, op. cit.; Tucker, op. cit.; Bruce, op. cit.; Chubin, op. cit.; "The Arming and Disarming of Iran's Revolution," op. cit.

20. Levran and Eytan, op. cit.; Tucker, op. cit.; "The Arming and Disarming of Iran's Revolution," op. cit.

21. *Jane's Defence Weekly*, October 29, 1988, p. 1045.

22. *Philadelphia Inquirer*, December 25, 1985, p. 7-D.

23. Anthony H. Cordesman, "Lessons of the Iran-Iraq War: Tactics, Technology, and Training," *Armed Forces Journal International*, June 1982, p. 78.

24. Drew Middleton, "On a Still Front, Iraq Lies in Wait for Iranian Military Machine," *New York Times*, November 19, 1982, p. A-1.

25. Colin Legum et al., *Middle East Contemporary Survey*, Vol. IV, New York, Holmes & Meier, 1981, p. 42.

26. Edward Cody, "Jordan Suspends Request for Tanks After Gift of Booty," *Washington Post*, February 24, 1981, p. 14.

27. See "Shah's Armory, a Legacy of Confusion," *Middle East Economic Digest*, October 24, 1980, p. 7.

28. Bernard Givertzman, "Iraq Said to Hold Advantage in War," *New York Times*, August 28, 1984, p. A-1.

13

THE AIR AND MISSILE WARS AND WEAPONS OF MASS DESTRUCTION

The Air and Missile Wars

The Iran-Iraq War involved the use of a wide range of air-defense, air, helicopter, and missile systems. It also was the first war in modern times to involve the extensive use of chemical weapons. Unlike the Arab-Israeli conflicts of 1973 and 1982, however, Iran and Iraq often lacked the strategic and tactical sophistication to make effective use of the technology they obtained, to integrate it into an effective combat force, and to exercise effective command and control.

The key lessons and issues raised by the war may be summarized as follows.

- Air power had an important impact upon the war, but it never had the major strategic or tactical impact that the number and quality of the weapons on each side should have permitted.
- Neither Iran nor Iraq were able to make effective use of their air control and warning and C^3I assets and medium or heavy surface-to-air missiles. Both were forced to rely on shorter-range systems, in part because of design problems and a lack of low-altitude coverage, but largely because of problems in technology transfer.
- Both Iran and Iraq made heavy use of anti-aircraft guns for point defense, area coverage, and as anti-infantry weapons. This follows a broad pattern in Third World forces and deserves careful study in the West.
- Both Iran and Iraq made heavy use of manportable and light surface-to-air weapons. Iraq, in particular, came to rely more on light surface-to-air missiles than medium or heavy systems, in large part because the lighter systems were easier to operate and

did not require integration into a complex air-control, warning, and battle-management system.

- Air-to-air combat was heavily influenced by technology, but the primary factor, again, was technology transfer and particularly each side's access to outside support and resupply.
- A variety of factors sharply limited the ability of fixed-wing aircraft to provide effective close air support, although helicopters were somewhat more successful. The main limiting factors were the target mix, widespread proliferation of area and point defense anti-aircraft weapons, problems in technology transfer, and problems in command-and-control and battle management.
- Efforts at interdiction of land forces and strategic bombing had mixed success. The interdiction mission presented many of the same problems as flying close air support. The strategic mission presented problems in range/payload capability, but the key problems were political and the result of a failure to commit sufficient resources to specific targets with the mass and consistency necessary to be effective.
- The use of surface-to-surface missiles was largely ineffective until the last year of the war, when Iraq successfully used mass missile attacks to seriously undermine Iranian morale and popular support for the war. The success of these missile attacks was, however, highly dependent on their interaction with other political and military factors.
- Iraq's use of chemical warfare became a critical instrument of war in the final year of the war in both military and political terms. This sets important precedents for the future.
- Neither side used nuclear weapons, but both sides made active efforts to obtain them.

In broad terms, the Iran-Iraq War did lead to the use of military technology in air and air-to-ground combat in ways that may set important precedents for the future. By and large, however, the main lessons of the air war are lessons in the limits of technology transfer and in the critical importance of assessing the degree to which friendly and threat forces in the Third World can actually use the weapons they obtain.

Command, Control, and Communications, Battle Management, and Air Control and Warning

The broad problems in Iran and Iraq's C^3I/BM and AC&W systems have already been discussed in Chapter 11. The Iranian systems were never effectively integrated before the fall of the Shah. The operation of individual elements of Iran's capability were then badly disrupted by the Revolution, and Iran lost access to the kind of Western equipment and software that might have allowed it to make major improvements in its systems. Iran had to rely on point defense and occasional use of its F-14s as a mini-AWACS. There is no question that Iran would have been better able to deal with the Iraqi air threat with an effective $C^3I/BM/AC\&W$ system.

Iraqi air C^3 was characterized by overcentralization and rigid planning, from the beginning of the war to the cease-fire. This often led to serious Iraqi mistakes or problems in Iraqi capability. Iraqi aircraft often flew rigidly preplanned missions that originated at high levels of command and too long of a period to plan. Iraq tended to ignore both the immediate needs of the tactical situation and to respond to targets of opportunity. A prime example occurred at the beginning of the war when unsheltered Iranian aircraft and helicopters on the ground were ignored by Iraqi fighter bombers that were unsuccessfully attempting to crater runways in Iran. If more Iranian combat aircraft had been eliminated at the outset of the war, this might have provided Iraq with a significant psychological edge over the Iranians in the combat that followed.[1]

The exact reasons that the Iraqi air control and warning and C^3I system performed so badly are unclear. Iraq does not seem to have had a high degree of readiness and technical proficiency when the war began, however, and seems to have had a system that was heavily overoptimized around medium to high altitude defense and had poor integration and data-transfer rates. This system could not deal with low-flying aircraft and seems to have been copied from a Soviet model with little operational value in dealing with threats like the modern fighter bombers of Iran and Israel. While Iraq attempted to improve its system throughout the war, Iran was still able to penetrate it with low flying F-4 sorties in 1988.

Iraq did better in structuring its offensive operations and in gradually improving the quality of its reconnaissance efforts, mission planning, damage assessment, and ability to respond to the tactical needs of land commanders on a timely basis. Iraq was often remarkably slow to learn from experience, however, and even at the cease-fire, it seemed unable to use its strategic and interdiction bombing capabilities with anything like the effectiveness its assets should have allowed.

Like the Arab-Israeli and Falklands conflicts, this experience indicates that superior C^3I and AC&W technology and organization can be a key asset for Western and friendly local forces in future low-level wars and that the West should seek to exploit its technical lead as much as possible. This exploitation will be particularly important because of the West's matching lead in IFF, ESSM, and EW.

There is no question, however, that part of the problem both nations faced was a lack of modern command-and-control and battle management systems. Iran or Iraq's capabilities would have been radically different if either side had had the E-3A AWACS and the E-2C in U.S. forces. Similarly, Iran and Iraq would also have benefited from a forward area C^3I/BM system to control their helicopters and from a targeting platform using ESSM, SAR, SLAR, FLIR, or electro-optics to locate targets beyond visual range, to provide warning of ground-based air defenses, and to ensure against surprise on the ground.

The lack of these assets—with the limited exception of Iran's ability to use the F-14A as a "mini" AWACS, and its P-3C maritime patrol aircraft to locate naval targets—was a critical factor in depriving both sides of the ability to make proper use of their vast investment in air power. Given Israel's success with the E-2C and Britain's crucial problems with the lack of such assets in the Falklands, there can be little doubt about the value of such airborne systems in low-level wars, provided that the sensors, software, and training are suitable to the region and type of conflict. The history of the tanker war and Iran's attempts to put pressure on the southern Gulf states also demonstrated the value of the U.S. sale of the E-3A and Peace Shield package to Saudi Arabia, a lesson that has broader implications for the West. The West not only can exploit the lack of such assets in threat forces, it can benefit from equipping friendly forces with such assets.

Surface-to-Air Missiles

The most effective ground-based air defenses during the Iran-Iraq War were anti-aircraft (AA) guns and short-range air-defense systems (SHORADS). Although both sides deployed large numbers of medium and heavy surface-to-air missiles (SAM), neither achieved great effectiveness in their use.

Iraq relied largely on SA-2 and SA-3 heavy and SA-6 medium surface-to-air missiles at the start of the war and kept these systems active throughout the conflict. It had roughly 120 SA-2 launchers, 150 SA-3 launchers, 25–60 SA-6 launchers at the time of the 1988 cease-fire. In practice, however, Iran soon came to rely on a mix of AA guns with SA-7, SA-8, and SA-9 missiles, and eventually the SA-14. Iraq also acquired 30 Crotale missile fire units from France in 1981 and built this force up to 60 Roland fire units by the end of the war.[2]

Few details are available on Iraq's problems in using its SA-2 and SA-3 surface-to-air missile systems during the war, but it is clear that Iraq found it difficult to integrate warning into its missile command and control system and to use its SA-2 or SA-3 missiles effectively. Iraq seems to have begun the war without clear operational doctrine and realistic technical understanding of the SA-2, SA-3, and SA-6. Even senior Iraqis privately admit that the top command levels of Iraq's ground-based air defenses were a political sinecure at the start of the war.

The Iraqi medium and heavy SAM units were also deployed for a medium- to high-altitude threat that proved largely nonexistent. Iraq adopted Soviet deployment and fire techniques and relied on the Soviet "book" without adaptation of the overall SAM system to Iraqi needs. Iraq maintained low, if not appalling, training and readiness standards in comparison with similar powers like Egypt and Syria. It also failed to test the weaknesses in Iran's C^3I/BM system and deployment pattern.

It is hard to tell how much Iraq improved its medium and heavy SAM capabilities between the start of the war and the 1988 cease-fire. Iranian air attacks were so infrequent after the early 1980s that it is difficult to make precise judgments. Even in 1988, however, it was clear that Iraq was unable to keep its SA-2 and SA-3 missile defenses on continuous alert without burning out some of its electronics and seriously degrading the operational capabilities of its missiles. Iraq was still experiencing systems-integration problems. Iraq seemed to be able to use its Crotales, Rolands, and SA-6s only on a target of opportunity or individual fire unit basis. The Iraqi SAM system never operated as an integrated or netted entity. As a result, some Israeli experts came to regard Iraqi ability to manage the command and control and electronic warfare aspects of their Soviet supplied surface-to-air missile systems as far inferior to those of Syria.

Iran began the war with comparatively good Hawk surface-to-air missile defenses, although these were organized largely for the defense of fixed military facilities, and its force structure emphasized fighter air defense and the use of aircraft like the F-14A. Iran was unable to use its Hawk's effectively during any period of the war, however, and could not even mount an effective point defense of its key oil facilities. This Iranian failure to use its Hawk defenses effectively may have been heavily affected by the turmoil and disruption following the Shah's fall. Iran seems to have suffered severely from the disorganization and purges that followed the revolution, from a lack of spare parts, and from a lack of foreign technical support. Iran did make its Hawk defenses more effective during the period when it had covert access to U.S. parts and arms, and this indicates that Iran was heavily affected by maintenance and supply problems.

Like Iraq, Iran had continuing problems in integrating its surface-to-air missile defenses into any kind of net. After the first months of the conflict, Iraq generally used its SAMs largely in a point-defense mode and placed primary reliance on the SA-6 and shorter-range systems. Although there are only a few confirmed instances of Iranian Hawk kills of Iraqi aircraft, the Iraqis still regarded the Hawk as far more effective than their Soviet missiles. They also excused some of the problems in the performance of their Air Force during parts of 1986 and 1987 on the ground that Iran was getting extensive resupply of its Hawk missiles. There are reports that Iraq began in 1986 to actively attack or suppress Iranian Hawks with Mirage F-1s using Matra Armat anti-radiation missiles, but the truth of such reports is unclear.[3]

Iran also used Short Tigercat SAMs and Oerlikon cannons controlled by Super Fledermaus radars to defend its air bases, but their performance is unclear. Iran did make good use of some 300 RBS-70 missiles it obtained from Sweden, but it could only obtain limited resupply. Iran's primary surface-to-air missile was the SA-7, and Iran used it for both the area defense of its forces and key point targets like oil facilities. The Iranians began to rely on the SA-7 for area defense during their winter 1982 offensives. From this point on, Iranian forces used large numbers of SA-7s in conjunction with curtain fire from automatic weapons and anti-aircraft guns to limit Iraq's ability to exploit its air superiority. While most such missiles were fired to degrade Iraqi sorties and to force aircraft to fly high or break off their attacks, Iran did find that Soviet-bloc supplied SA-7s, or SA-7s it could assemble with Soviet parts, outperformed Asian and other copies of the SA-7 and had a much lower misfire rate.

All in all, the Iranian and Iraqi experience with medium and heavy surface-to-air missiles highlights the problems and opportunities raised by the transfer of high-technology systems to Third World states. It is a further indication that most Third World states will be far less effective in operating modern SAMs than Egypt was during its Canal War of 1970 and that suppression of heavy SAMs may pose less of a problem in dealing with Third World forces than the suppression of SHORADS. Since many weaknesses in SAM operations can be monitored passively with ESSM and ELINT platforms, or probed with RPVs and decoys, the West is in an excellent position to characterize and exploit them. At the same time, it highlights the need to support SAM transfers to friendly states with proper planning and training.

It is important to note, however, that manportable surface-to-air missiles proved to be effective on both sides. Even though the vast majority of the missiles fired did not hit a target (it is unlikely that one kill was obtained per 20–30 missiles fired), the widespread proliferation of such missiles had a major impact in degrading the effectiveness of fighters and helicopters by forcing them to fly high, limited their ability to fly over target areas long enough to spot and kill targets effectively, and curtailing the conditions under which they could operate with a high degree of survivability.

It is interesting to note, however, that the Iraqis were surprisingly ineffective in their efforts to use flares or balloons to help their fighters and helicopters counter the SA-7. These countermeasures were readily available to Iraq, which was well aware that the Israeli use of such countermeasures meant that the SA-7 gave the Israelis little trouble during their Peace for Galilee operation in Lebanon. It seems likely that if the Iraqis had made the same kind of extensive use of flares and thermal balloons as the Israelis, the SA-7 would have been much less effective.[4]

The Iraqis did make an interesting attempt to adapt the SA-7 for use with helicopters. In order to do this, they mounted the SA-7 on the HOT missile pylons of the Gazelle attack helicopter. They did this because the Gazelle helicopters had little defense against Iran's Cobra helicopters during the first part of the war. The extent to which the Iraqis pressed forward with this experiment is not known, although there do not seem to be any Iranian reports of losses to such missiles.

Anti-Aircraft Artillery

Both sides found that the widespread proliferation of AA guns severely inhibited the other side's ability to use aircraft and helicopters effectively in interdiction and close air support missions. As was the case with manportable surface-to-air missiles, both sides found that the key to effective air defense was the ability to degrade the effectiveness of its opponent's air-to-ground operations and not the number of aircraft that ground-based air defenses killed.

Both sides also found that anti-aircraft weapons made effective anti-personnel weapons and deployed significant numbers in the forward edge of the battle area. Anti-aircraft machine guns proved to be a particularly effective means for providing fixed defenses with very high rates of fire and effective killing power at long ranges. The weapons could also be dug in or employed outside the effective range of enemy rocket launchers and machine guns. This made suppression very difficult and further enhanced the effectiveness of barrier defenses.

Iraq's anti-aircraft guns included a mix of Soviet AA machine guns, 23-mm AA guns, ZSU-23-4 radar-guided AA guns, M-1939 and twin 37-mm AA guns, ZSU-52-2 and other 57-mm AA guns, and 85-mm, 100-mm, and 130-mm AA guns.[5] The Iraqis made extensive use of unguided AA guns and heavy AA machine guns against both air targets and Iranian infantry. They claimed to have used Soviet-built radar-guided ZSU-23-4 anti-aircraft guns effectively against Iranian aircraft and helicopters, but they seem to have had serious problems in maintaining and operating the complex ZSU-23-4 guidance system, at least at the start of the war.

The overall importance of anti-aircraft guns is shown by the fact that Iraq increased its inventory of anti-aircraft weapons from roughly 1,200 weapons in 1980 to 4,000 weapons in 1985. Iraq seems to have kept its numbers of anti-aircraft weapons relatively constant after 1985, although it steadily increased the number of AA guns it used against Iranian infantry and bought more short range surface-to-air missiles.

Iraq's ability to deploy large numbers of AA weapons over a wide area was of considerable value to Iraq's air defense early in the war because Iraq could not utilize its air-defense warning system and surface-to-air missiles effectively and had to turn to point defense. AA guns and machine guns were deployed to cover virtually every important target and to provide area defense in some urban and industrial areas. The radar-guided ZSU-23-4 and other 23-mm AA guns were widely used to protect various stationary targets, such as bridges, from low-level attack.[6]

The ZSU-23-4 was also used to defend combat forces and was reported to have been especially effective in combat with Iran's armed helicopters, including Iran's Cobra gunships armed with TOW missiles.[7] At least some Iraqi officers feel that a mix of ZSU-23-4s and tanks using their machine guns in anti-helicopter fire provided enough protection against helicopter attacks to force Iran to sharply curtail its attack-helicopter operations. This Iraqi experience, however, may be more of a reflection of the steady decline in Iran's number of operational fighters and helicopters and in Iranian C^3 capability and training levels rather than the effectiveness of such defenses. The survivability problems that Iranian helicopters experienced after 1982 were compounded by serious shortages in spare parts and maintenance skills, poor command and control and mission planning, having to fly over relatively open terrain, and against extensive Iraqi barrier positions with dug-in AA guns and other automatic weapons with certain fire capability. Further, the Iraqis deployed large numbers of unguided AA guns and machine guns in the same areas where they used the ZSU-23-4 and missiles. A limited number of interviews indicate that unguided weapons may have produced a substantial number of the total kills. There is no way to be sure how much of the impact of AA weapons came from guided, aimed, and/or curtain fire.

The Iranians had about 1,800 23-mm, 35-mm, 40-mm, 57-mm and 85-mm towed AA guns and machine guns when the war began, and roughly 100 ZSU-23-4 and ZSU-57-2 self-propelled AA guns. They had about 2,200 air defense guns in 1985 and raised this total to around 2,800 in 1988. As was the case in Iraq, the Iranian ZSU-23-4 had radar guidance. All other weapons had to be aimed by hand.[8]

Like the Iraqis, the Iranians claim that AA guns were often effective against attack helicopters. This claim is important because the Iraqis were consistently able to deploy large numbers of armed helicopters from the beginning of the war to the 1988 cease-fire. Once again, however, it is not possible to get any precise estimates of kills or of the relative impact of guided, aimed, and curtain fire. Furthermore, Iraqi helicopter losses did decline steadily as Iraqi pilots learned to use nap-of-the-earth and pop-up helicopter tactics and to avoid dense concentrations of well-positioned Iranian troops.

No data are available on either side's losses of fixed-wing aircraft to anti-aircraft guns or on losses per sortie flown by type of sortie. It also is difficult to draw any conclusions about the overall vulnerability of helicopters to AA guns from the war. There again are no reliable data on the losses on either side. Iraqi helicopter pilots did avoid defended Iranian areas where possible, but this was part of a broad caution in committing air resources. Further, the Iraqis faced that same problem as Iran in trying to operate helicopters in areas where the target held the high ground and helicopter approaches could often be seen several kilometers away.

The problem of helicopter survivability in desert warfare in relatively open terrain and/or when the target forces occupy well-established defensive positions is one which needs more attention from U.S. and other Western planners as dependence on the helicopter and helicopter-mounted anti-tank guided missile (ATGM) systems increases. Much of the data on the estimated survivability and effectiveness of attack helicopters have been based on attacks on mobile or exposed armored forces exercises and simulations conducted in rough or wooded terrain or where the enemy is assumed to be "buttoned down" in armor, rather than dispersed in well-dug-in defensive positions. While both Iran and Iraq did find helicopters to be relatively survivable against AA guns in rough or mountainous terrain, more study is needed of their vulnerability in open deserts or flat, open marshes.

Air Strength and Capabilities

The history of the air war involved several phases which did not always coincide with those in the ground war. These phases included (1) an initial surprise attack by Iraq in September 1980, followed by a short period of intense air combat and ground-attack operations, with Iran then winning air superiority in late March 1981; (2) a stalemate from April 1981 to September 1983, with the ground forces settling into static defenses, Iran failing to obtain spare parts for its aircraft, and the gradual loss of Iranian air-defense capability; (3) the period from September 1983 to mid-1985 when Iraq acquired air superiority and steadily increased its effectiveness in attack missions; (4) Iraq's shift after mid-1985 to strategic bombing in an effort to cut off Iranian oil exports; (5) Iraq's shift to aggressive and more effective close air support and interdiction missions after Iraq's defeat at Faw in early 1986; and (6) the resumption of the war of the cities in August 1987, followed by the missile war of 1988.

The general course of the air war between Iraq and Iran was shaped by several factors:

- an initial Iraqi misconception of Iranian weaknesses, coupled to incompetent initial-attack planning and delusions about Iraqi offensive and defensive capabilities which helped inspire an attack by technically inferior Iraqi Air Forces;
- an Iranian Air Force which showed surprising determination and ability, especially in the ground-attack role, and a high level of technical competence resulting from the American training effort in that country;
- a high rate of attrition in Iranian Air Forces due to parts shortages and service problems, especially after the major Iranian offensives of 1982, which eventually gave Iraq air superiority;
- an Iraqi shift to reliance on Western-supplied aircraft and munitions for both air-defense and critical-attack missions; and
- Iranian efforts, so far unsuccessful, to substitute North Korean versions of Chinese and Soviet fighters for U.S. aircraft.

When the war began, Iraq's combat air strength was inferior to that of Iran. Iran had 445 fighter aircraft to Iraq's 372, and Iran generally had far superior aircraft. Only about 200 of the Iranian aircraft are believed to have been operational when the war started, however, and

Iran's operational air strength soon dropped to about 80 serviceable aircraft while Iraq kept up a strength of over 500.

The force strengths, technologies, and trends on each side have been discussed earlier, and the trends by type during the period in which Iran still had sufficient strength to engage in air-to-air combat are shown in Figure 13.1. Earlier data, made available in October 1985, indicated Iran had only about 23 to 35 operational R-4s, 5 to 14 F-14s, and 40 to 45 F-5s. Iraq had over 500 combat aircraft, with 44 to 50 Mirage F-1EQ/EBs, 150–200 MiG-21s, 48 MiG 23BMs, 75 Su-7s, 50 Su-20s, 25 to 30 MiG-25s, and 40 MiG-19s.[9] The mission range capabilities of the fighters used in the Iran-Iraq War and other fighting in the Middle East are shown in Table 13.1.[10]

Iraqi Aircraft

The Iraqi Air Force had 38,000 men when the war began, including some 10,000 air-defense personnel. Its main combat aircraft consisted of a bomber squadron with 12 Tu-22s and a light-bomber squadron with 10 IL-28s. It had 12 fighter ground attack (FGA) squadrons, with 4/80 MiG-23B, 3/40 Su-7B, 4/60 Su-20/22, and 1/15 Hunter FB-59/FR-10. Its fighter strength included five squadrons with 115 MiG-21s, plus a training squadron with 40 MiG-19s. It also had a number of armed helicopters, including 41 MiG-24s.

During the period from 1980 to 1988, Iraq stressed quality over quantity, although its combat air strength increased from 332 aircraft in 1980 to around 500 in 1988. At the time the cease-fire was agreed to in 1988, Iraq had 40,000 men, including some 10,000 air-defense personnel. Its main combat aircraft then consisted of two bomber squadrons with 8 Tu-16s and 12 Tu-22s. It had 11 FGA squadrons. These include 1/10–15 Su-25s, 4/40 MiG-23BM, 3 with Su-7Bs and Su-20/22, 2/20 Mirage F-1EQE equipped with Exocet, and 2/23 Mirage F-1EQ-220. Its fighter strength included five squadrons with 1/25 MiG-25s, 1/25 MiG-29s, 200 MiG-21s, 30 Mirage F-1EQs, 40 MiG-29s, and 115 MiG-21s. It had a small reconnaissance squadron with five MiG-25Rs. Its armed helicopters were assigned to the Army and included 40–60 MiG-24s, 50 SA-342 Gazelles (some with HOT), 10 SA-321 Super Frelons (some with Exocet), 30 SA-316B with AS-12s, and 44 MBB BO-105s with SS-11s.[11]

The Iraqis have 8–12 Tu-22 Blinder and 7–10 Tu-16 Badger Bombers. These are variously reported to have come from the USSR, Egypt, and the PRC. Iraq now has Chinese Silkworm missiles for their bombers and may also have longer-range Soviet AS-3 or AS-4 air-to-surface missiles. These missiles have a warhead of 1,000 kilograms and are much more effective in sinking tankers and large ships than smaller

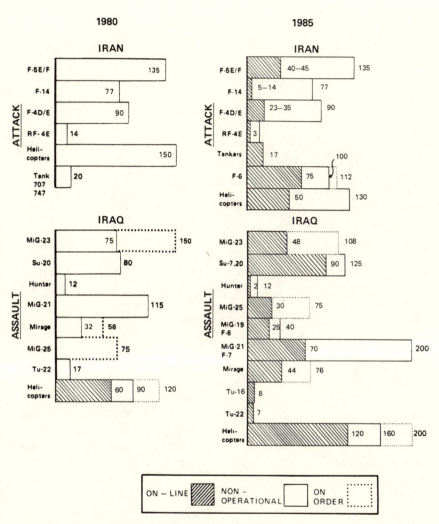

FIGURE 13.1 The Shift in Iranian-Iraqi Air Strength: 1980–1985. Adapted from IISS, *Military Balance,* various editions (London: International Institute for Strategic Studies), and from Jim Bussert, "Iran-Iraq War Turns Strategic," *Defense Electronics,* September 1984, p. 146.

TABLE 13.1 Comparative Combat Radius of Aircraft

Aircraft Type	Weapons Load (lbs.)	Dash Intercept	Combat Air Patrol	Ground Attack Hi-Lo-Hi Normal	Ground Attack Hi-Lo-Hi Refueled	Lo-Lo-Lo
A-4N	--	--	--	385	--	240
A-6E	6,000	--	--	700	950	--
A-7D/E	4,000	--	--	550	650	--
A-10	3,000	--	--	400	500	250
B-52G	60,000	--	--	8,406	12,000	7,800
F-104A	--	228	--	--	--	--
F-4E	4,000	429	683	275	400	257
F-5A	--	170	186	--	485	--
F-15C/D	8,000	--	729	750	950	450
F-15E	8,000	--	729	750	950	450
F-16A/B	5,000	--	675	530	--	350
F-16C	5,000	--	640	565	--	345
F-20A	--	385	570	450	--	122
F-18A	--	--	400	--	--	--
F-111	6,000	--	--	1,100	--	800
IL-28	--	--	--	600	--	--
Kfir	--	200	280	512	--	238
Kfir 2C	--	288	310	700	--	351
Kfir 7C	--	419	476	640	--	--
Lavi	--	270	500	637	--	281
Lightning Mk. 2	--	225	--	--	--	--
MiG-17	--	--	--	220	--	80
MiG-19	--	150	250	250	--	130
MiG-21F	--	260	325	--	--	--
MiG-21MF	--	140	220	357	--	120
MiG-21SMT	--	184	237	434	--	150
MiG-23S (Flogger B)	4,000	550	700	525	--	296
MiG-27 (Flogger D)	4,000	380	758	580	--	310
MiG-23MS (Flogger E)	--	550	700	560	--	296
MiG-23BM (Flogger F)	--	--	--	--	--	--
MiG-25A	--	593	1,079	1,187	--	391
MiG-29	8,820	415	500	438	--	385
MiG-31	--	680	1,200	1,200	--	580
Mirage IIIE	--	156	218	325	--	160
Mirage V	--	173	258	350	--	218
Mirage F-1C/BQ	--	365	581	593	--	348
Mirage F-1EQ	--	375	590	600	--	360
Mirage 2000	--	--	500+	600+	--	420
Su-7B	--	--	--	200	--	140

(continues)

TABLE 13.1 *(continued)*

Aircraft Type	Weapons Load (lbs.)	Dash Intercept	Combat Air Patrol	Ground Attack Hi-Lo-Hi Normal	Refueled	Lo-Lo-Lo
Su-17	6,000	--	--	330	--	190
Su-20	--	--	--	340	--	195
Su-24	4,000	--	--	970	--	200
Su-25	--	--	--	300	--	200
Su-27 (Flanker)	8 X AA-X-10	590	715	--	--	--
Super Etendard	--	--	--	403	--	256
Tornado	6,000	--	500 +	863	--	400
Tu-16	--	--	--	2,400 - 2,890	--	1,900
Tu-22	--	--	--	1,500 - 1,900	--	700
Tu-26	22,000	--	--	1,900 - 3,420	--	900

The header spans: *Radius of Action (nautical miles)* covers Dash Intercept, Combat Air Patrol, and Ground Attack. *Ground Attack* covers Hi-Lo-Hi and Lo-Lo-Lo. *Normal Refueled* sits under Hi-Lo-Hi.

SOURCES: Adapted from varoius editions of *Jane's All the World's Aircraft* and from the ARCO-Salamander Illustrated Guide series.

missiles like Exocet. They also are faster. The Silkworm and AS-4 have maximum air-launched ranges of around 460 kilometers. Iraq has made use of these bombers throughout the war. Neither aircraft proved particularly important, however, since the Tu-22 lacked the payload and accuracy to be much more effective in conventional missions than a modern fighter bomber, and the Tu-16 was so vulnerable that it rarely could be used for deep-penetration missions.

Iraq's main combat aircraft at the start of the war were the Su-7 and Su-20, the MiG-23B (and M), and various export versions of the MiG-21. The Iraqis had some 40 MiG-19s and up to several hundred MiG-21s.[12] The least sophisticated aircraft was the Soviet-made MiG-19s. The MiG-19 was the first Soviet supersonic fighter and was mass produced as a successor to the MiG-15 and MiG-17. Iraq has the newer version of the MiG-19, which includes a large central air brake and a more powerful engine, the RD-9. All MiG-19s can carry the K-13A missile, or AA-2 Atoll, and its underwing pylons can carry two 176-gallon drop tanks and two 551-pound weapons or dispensers.

The MiG-19 was never a lead aircraft in Iraqi air operations, but the MiG-21 continued to perform ground-attack and air-defense operations throughout the war. The MiG-21 was Iraq's primary air-defense fighter when the war began and was provided to Iraq in the standard export version. This aircraft is a moderately effective medium to high altitude day fighter with a mediocre radar and avionics. The Iraqis indicate that their versions of the MiG-21 lack adequate radar range, look-up capability, gun computers, and missile fire controls. They are blind in the look-down or low-altitude combat mode, and the pilot must rely on visual sighting and fire control. This means the fighter has little or no low-altitude or beyond-visual-range search and kill capability except when he is vectored precisely to a target by external radars. Even then, the MiG-21 lacks modern gun sights and an effective air-to-air missile system for dogfighting against a low-flying attacker.

The MiG-23 has some times been described as a miniaturized F-4, but this description is incorrect. The MiG-23 can perform the same general spectrum of roles but has grossly inferior avionics. The export model of the MiG-23 is referred to as the "Flogger E" by NATO and has the same high-Mach airframe and systems as the MiG-23 fighter but uses the inferior "Spin Scan" radar instead of the latter's "High Lark" nose radar. It lacks effective look-up and look-down capability, uses the inadequate Sirena-2 radar-warning radar, has mediocre fire control avionics, and can only use the AA-2 air-to-air missile rather than the AA-7 and AA-8 used on Soviet versions of the MiG-23.

The same basic airframe is used for a dedicated air-to-ground aircraft (Flogger D and F), as well as for an interceptor/air-superiority fighter. Although the MiG-23B was designed primarily for the strike role, later Soviet versions have emphasized the handling and maneuverability features necessary for effective air combat. The attack version, however, is simpler, capable of carrying more ordnance, and designed to operate effectively at low levels. The R-29B afterburning turbofan in Soviet MiG-23s produces 25,350 lbs. of thrust. This does not give the MiG-23 performance approaching modern Western fighters, but it reflects a considerable improvement in Soviet fighter capabilities.[13]

The Flogger E normally uses the less powerful R-27 engine instead of the R-29B, has a less capable ARK-9 radio compass instead of the ARK-15, has inferior navigation and attack munitions delivery aids, and does not have a laser. Nevertheless, Iraq had to use its MiG-23s in the air-defense role before it obtained the Mirage F-1.[14]

The Iraqis are believed to have asked for improved MiG-23Bs early in the war and to have begun discussing purchase of the export versions of the MiG-29, Su-25, and Su-22T in 1984 or 1985. The Iraqis evidently received 25 sanitized versions of the MiG-29 Fulcrum in May 1987, but it did not play a major role in the fighting. The aircraft rapidly proved to be fuel hungry and difficult to maintain. It was also delivered without the advanced look-down/shoot-down radars and computers which are standard on Soviet models of the MiG-29, and the Iraqi version can only be used in day fighter roles. The Soviets evidently supplied the MiG-29s in this condition in spite of Iraqi demands for the Soviet-version aircraft. They refused Iraq deliveries of more advanced versions of the MiG-23 and MiG-27, possibly on the grounds they already had a $10 billion arms debt to the USSR.

Iraq is also reported to have received at least 10 Su-25 attack aircraft. This aircraft is an armored close support aircraft similar to the Northrop A-9. There are some reports it has been effective in a limited number of close air support missions, but no real details are available.[15]

Some reports have suggested that Iraq's Soviet-made aircraft, like their Soviet counterparts, contain onboard anti-jamming ECM gear, in contrast to the Western emphasis on specialized jammer planes. There is little evidence, however, of internal ECM capability onboard any Iraq MiGs or Sukhois, and the Iraqis have bought external ECM pods in the West. Iraq does seem to have improved its ECM and countermeasure capabilities in 1987 and 1988, but reliable details are not available.

The primary air-to-air missile utilized by Iraqi Soviet-made aircraft is still the AA-2 Atoll, which is carried by MiG-21, MiG-19/CH F-6, and Iraq's more modern Soviet-made aircraft. The AA-22 is an old infrared (IR) homing missile, which is thought to be a copy of the Raytheon-Ford Sidewinder. It has proved to be an unreliable "tail chase" missile with limited range and maneuver capability in the 1973 Arab-Israeli conflict, in the 1982 fighting in Lebanon, and in the Iran-Iraq War.[16] Iraq is, however, steadily expanding its use of more modern air-to-air missiles like the Soviet-made AA-6, AA-7, and AA-8 and the French-made R-530 and R-550 Magic. Some Iraqis feel these changes distinctly improved Iraq's air-to-air combat capability by the mid-1980s.

In spite of the acquisition of newer types of Soviet fighters, the key shift in Iraq's air capabilities after the start of the war was the acquisition of two types of French aircraft: the Super Etendard and Mirage F-1. The Dassault Breguet Super Etendard was received on loan to deliver Exocet air-to-ship missiles while France was producing Mirage F-1EQ5s which were specially equipped to fire Exocet missiles. It was returned to France once the Mirage F-1EQ5 was delivered.

The Super Etendard was an obsolescent naval light strike fighter capable of high-supersonic speed. Intended as a replacement for the Etendard IVA carrier-based aircraft, it is powered by a SNECMA Atar 8K-50 single shaft turbojet. Its maximum speed is 745 miles per hour at low altitudes. This aircraft is able to refuel in flight. Its armament includes two 30-mm DEFA cannon. The Super Etendard has a nominal HI-LO-HI radius of 403 miles, or 650 km. This makes it a comparatively short-legged fighter. Nevertheless, it was the primary delivery system for Iraq's Exocet active radar-homing anti-ship missile until mid-1985. The Super Etendard carried the Exocet under the starboard wing, with the drop tanks slung under the port wing. Magic air-to-air missiles are optional.

The Exocet is 4.69 meters long, 350 mm in diameter, and weighs 655 kilograms at launch. The Exocet has a limited range of 31 to 43.5 miles, depending on launch altitude. It is a sea-skimmer fed with target data before launch with inertial mid-course correction. It flies at Mach 0.93 at about 2.5 meters altitude and switches an EMD Adac X-band monopulse active radar seeker to home in on its target.

The Exocet has a 165-kilogram Serat hexolite/steel block warhead. This penetrates armor at angles up to 70° and has proximity and delay fuses. It explodes after penetrating the hull. The resulting fire inside oil tankers has not generally been sufficient to sink a large tanker, but it has worked well against smaller ships and warships. The Exocet has been in service with the Super Etendard since 1978, and the aircraft normally carries one to two missiles on wing pylons. The Exocet has been in service with the Mirage F-1EQ5 since 1985.

The Dassault Mirage F-1 has become Iraq's lead fighter and replaced its Super Etendards. By 1988, Iraq had six squadrons of Mirage F-1s. Two were air-defense squadrons equipped with 30 Mirage F-1EQs. Four were attack squadrons equipped with a mix of 70 Mirage F-1EQ5s and Mirage F-1EQ200s.

The Mirage F-1 is a relatively modern multi-role aircraft with a relatively large payload, easy handling at low altitudes, and a high rate of climb. Dassault-Breguet claims that the Mirage F-1 has a higher maximum speed (Mach 2.2 rather than Mach 2) than the Mirage III, three times the endurance at high Mach numbers, and three times the patrol time before and after an interception. It also claims the Mirage F-1 has twice the tactical range at sea level, a 30 percent shorter take-off run at greater maximum weight, 25 percent lower approach speed, and improved maneuverability at both subsonic and supersonic speeds.[17] In addition, the Mirage F-1 holds 40 percent more fuel capacity than its predecessor, which is achieved by eliminating bladder-type tanks and replacing them with the integral full space type. The Mirage F-1 can also use short unpaved runways.

The Mirage F-1 is powered by one 15,870-pound SNEMCA Atar 9K50 afterburning turbojet. It is armed with two 30-mm DEFA 553 cannon with 125 rounds per gun. In the interceptor role, it normally carries two R550 Magic IR air-to-air missiles for short-range combat and one Super 530F radar homing air-to-air missile, and carries up to 4,000 kg (8,000 pounds) of ordnance in the attack role. Iraq made heavy use of its

Mirage F-1s in the attack role. It equipped some with Thompson CSF laser designators. It also used French AS-30 laser-guided bombs, modified Soviet X29L laser-guided missiles with ranges up to 12–15 kilometers, Armatts, and at least three types of cluster bombs.

Iraq currently has Mirage F-1EQ, F-1EQ-200, and F-1EQ5 aircraft. There is also a dual-seat trainer. The basic version of the Mirage F-1EQ has the more advanced avionics required by the all-weather role but does not have high radar range, an advanced avionics computer, or a true look-down capability. Some of the Mirage F-1s have been stripped of their air-defense avionics to provide increased range, have extra fuel tanks, and can carry the AM-39 Exocet.

As has been touched upon earlier, the Iraqis added the Super 550 and 530 missiles to their air-to-air missile inventory. The Super 530 is a modern follow-on to the R530 and has a nominal maximum range of 35 km. It uses SARH with an EMD Super AD-26 radar matched to the Cyrano IV radar in the Mirage F-1. It has speeds of up to Mach 3 and can hit targets up to 10,000 km higher or lower than the launch aircraft. It is equivalent to the best U.S.-made, radar-guided types and is one of the most lethal air-to-air missiles in service in the Third World. Both missiles are a more sophisticated version of the Matra Magic and have longer ranges.

The Magic missile, or R-550, is an improved version of the Sidewinder with a 140° attack hemisphere, head-on attack capability, high "G" launch and maneuver capability, a 0.32 to 10 km range, and advanced IR seeker. It has also reportedly achieved kills fired from Iraqi MiG-21s and proved far superior to the standard Soviet-supplied infrared missile, the Atoll. The Mirage F-1s are reported to have shot down several Iranian aircraft with the Matra Magic 1 missiles and to have scored kills even at very low altitudes.

Iraqi Air Force officers feel the Mirage F-1 is hard to maintain but is far superior to their Soviet-made fighters. They regard the avionics as far more effective in both the air-to-air and air-to-ground modes and regard French air-to-air missiles and air-to-ground weapons as far more lethal.

The Iraqi Air Force also made steady improvements in its ground attack weapons and equipment in the latter years of the war. These improvements included fitting both its Mirage F-1EQs and some of its MiG-23BN fighters with Dassault in-flight refueling systems for long-range operations.

Iraq also modified its Mirage F1EQ-5s to deliver a variety of precision-guided weapons, both to provide some stand-off capability from Iran's AA guns and shorter range surface-to-air missiles and to improve the accuracy of its fighter strikes. The first of these modifications was to add the French Thompson CSF Atlas laser-designator pod. This allowed the fighter to deliver the Aerospatiale AS-30L laser-guided missile at ranges up to 10 kilometers.

Iraq later modified the fighters to deliver the Soviet-made AS-14 (also known as the "716," X-29L, or "Kedge"). These missiles normally have a range of only 6–8 kilometers with Soviet laser-designator pods but could hit targets at ranges up to 12–15 kilometers with the Thompson Atlas designator. They did not prove to be particularly reliable, but Iraq found that it could get a reasonable hit probability if it launched two missiles at once. The AS-14 can also be launched by some of Iraq's Floggers.

In addition, Iraq obtained some TV-guided weapons, and an IR-guided bomb called the Saquar, which Iraq claimed had a range of up to 8 kilometers. The TV-guided weapons evidently consisted of 1,000-pound bombs fitted with a large guidance section and controllable fins. It is unclear that they were fully operational before the cease-fire.

This mix of weapons undoubtedly helped improve Iraq's survivability and lethality, but it is difficult to determine what the effectiveness of such weapons was. As has been described earlier in the history of the war, there were a number of instances where such systems could explain a sudden increase in mission effectiveness. At the same time, there were many instances when Iraq failed to hit targets with great precision as late as the Iranian offensives against Basra in 1987. While Iraq did improve the accuracy of its rear-area attacks in the mid-1980s, there also is only limited evidence that it could obtain anything like the accuracy with precision-guided weapons achieved by the U.S. or Israeli Air Forces.

This lack of data makes it difficult to draw any detailed lessons about the use of such weapons. It is clear, however, that both sides would have benefited from the use of "smart weapons" with enough range to allow aircraft to remain outside the range of AA guns and short-range SAMs, particularly if these were relatively simple to target and operate.

Iraq also went to considerable trouble to improve the fusing of its bombs and their lethality. It developed a range of cluster bombs and submunitions, evidently drawing in part on technology which it bought in Chile and which had been stolen from the U.S. Iraq seems to have had cluster bombs ranging from 500 to over 2,000 pounds. There are reports that Iraq also had fuel-air explosives and special heavyweight bombs for delivery by its Tupolev Tu-16 bombers. One bomb is reported to have weighed some 9,000 kilograms, with 4,000 kilograms of TNT, and impact, proximity, and airburst fuses.

Once again, it is not possible to trace any clear correlation between

Iraq's acquisition and use of such weapons and an increase in mission effectiveness. It is clear, however, that cluster and fuel-air explosive weapons have lethal areas up to ten times greater than a conventional bomb with the same weight. They may well, therefore, have helped account for some of the increased effectiveness of the Iraq Air Force later in the war. As for the heavyweight bombs, these seem to have greatly improved the effectiveness of bomber strikes against relatively hard rear-area targets when they hit, but the overall accuracy of such strikes improved only from low to moderate by the time of the cease-fire.

Iranian Aircraft

The Iranian Air Force was equipped with late-model U.S. weaponry under the Shah's regime. It began the war with the best mix of fighter capabilities and munitions of any Gulf air force and any Third World air force except Israel. The Iranian Air Force had 70,000 men when the war began. Its main aircraft included the F-4, F-5, and F-14. It had 10 fighter ground attack (FGA) squadrons with 188 F-4D/F and eight squadrons with 166 F-5E/Fs. It had four interceptor squadrons with 77 F-14As, and one reconnaissance squadron with 14 RF-4Es. It had 205 AH1J attack helicopters in the Army and 6 P-3F Orions in the Navy.

During the period from 1980 to 1988, Iran was unable to support its air strength at anything like the level it had reached under the Shah. Its combat air strength decreased from 445 aircraft in the Air Force alone in 1980 to only about 68–90 in 1988. At the time the cease-fire was agreed to in 1988, the Air Force also had only 35,000 men. Its main combat aircraft then consisted of 20–35 F-4D/Es, 30–45 operational F-5E/Fs, 10–14 F-14s, and 3 RF-4E. Army attack helicopter assets had declined to the point where less than 50 helicopters seem to have been operational. The Navy seemed to have 2 PF-3s still operational.[18]

The F-14 Tomcat was Iran's most advanced aircraft when the war began. It is a highly sophisticated, variable sweep-wing aircraft. It has an advanced AWG-9 air-defense radar, which utilizes the Phoenix missile in the air-to-air role for long-range defense. It has exceptional look-down/shoot-down capability, long-range radar surveillance capability, and can simultaneously attack several air targets.

The F-14A is a long-range aircraft and can fly combat air patrol (CAP) missions at radii up to 764 miles (1,167 km) and intercept missions up to 2,000 miles (3,200 km). It utilizes two 20,900-lb. thrust, Pratt & Whitney TF 30-412A afterburning turbofans. Initial climb rate is 30,000 feet per minute. Maximum speed is 1,564 miles per hour at height and 910 miles per hour at sea level. The F-14 uses one 20-mm M61-A1 multi-barrel cannon in fuselage and carries four Aim 7 Sparrows and four or eight Aim Sidewinders or up to six Aim-54 Phoenixes and two Aim-9s. The maximum external weapon load for the F-14 is 14,500 pounds.

According to most sources, the Phoenix missile systems and/or guidance avionics in the Iranian F-14As were sabotaged when the war began and have not been operational since. The Phoenix systems are reported to have been sabotaged by Iranian Air Force personnel friendly to the U.S. shortly after the Shah's fall, although some sources report they were sabotaged by Iranian revolutionaries to prevent Air Force operations. This meant Iran could not make optimal use of its best fighter or use an advanced all-weather, air-to-air missile with good shoot-down capability and a range up to 124 miles (200 km).

The F-14As could, however, still operate their AN/AWG-9 radar. This radar has a range of well over 100 nautical miles, and can track 24 targets with sufficient look-down capability to act as a mini-AWACS. They also could still fire Aim-7 and Aim-9 missiles. This allowed Iran to achieve a kill against an Iraqi Mirage fighter using the Aim-9 as late as the spring of 1988.

The Iranians used the F-14 both as a recce and air combat aircraft but have found this sophisticated aircraft to be difficult to keep in operational readiness without good maintenance crews and spare parts. Only three to ten still appear to be in full service. They are now used largely as airborne warning and control platforms and as reconnaissance fighters.[19]

The McDonnell Douglas F-4 is a high-payload attack aircraft with relatively long ranges of between 250 and 420 miles. The F-4E version carries an internal 20-mm M-61 multi-barrel, and the same gun can be carried in an external centerline pod. The F-4 carries centerline and wing tanks for bombs or other missiles and carries up to 16,000 lb (7,257 kg). It can climb at 28,000 feet per minute. It has a maximum speed of 1,500 miles per hour at height. Its maximum range on internal fuel is about 1,750 miles.[20]

The F-4, however, is an aging design and a complex aircraft that is extremely difficult to maintain, particularly in terms of avionics. The Iranians were not able to maintain the complex systems of the F-4E, even though they have cannibalized many aircraft. Indeed, it is doubtful that most of Iran's surviving F-4s can now fire radar-guided missiles like the Aim-7 Sparrow, although reports have surfaced that Iran received APQ-120 parts that allowed it to resume firing its Aim-7Es as part of its covert arms transfers from the U.S. It is also uncertain whether or not all of the F-4s have the avionics capabilities to use the Aim-9 Sidewinder.

The Iranian F-5E is a short-range, low payload, minimal avionics aircraft. It has an optimal range of 150 to 250 miles. The F-5E has a maximum speed at altitude of 1,060 miles per hour and an initial climb rate of 31,000 feet per minute. It is armed with two 20-mm M-39A2 cannon, each with 280 rounds in the nose, and Aim Sidewinders. The "E" version of the F-5 can carry 7,000 pounds in military loads. Although the F-5E is limited in range, it is still an effective and highly capable fighter. It also cannot be discounted as a possible vehicle for one-way suicide attacks. The F-5 has a low small radar profile.

Air-to-Air Combat

Air combat in the Iran-Iraq War was dominated largely by problems in command and policy, parts shortages, and personnel problems, rather than by aircraft numbers, technology, and tactics.[21] Both Iraq and Iran generally sought to conserve their aircraft and refused battle whenever possible. Iraq emerged with air superiority largely because of Iranian maintenance and resupply problems and not because of combat performance.

Fighter-against-fighter combat was only common during the first phase of the war. Iran's air force was the more successful force during this phase, but this was as much due to Iraqi incompetence and the lower performance of the sensors, avionics, and missiles on Iraqi fighters as to Iranian ability. In retrospect, there is little doubt that the Iraqis misjudged Iran's ability to fly air combat missions in spite of the revolution and overestimated their own effectiveness. Iraqi planners also overestimated their own level of air combat training, the performance capabilities of their aircraft, the operational readiness of Iraq's best squadrons, their reconnaissance assets, and their command-and-control capabilities.

In the first phase of the war, the Iranians had the fuel and endurance to win most air encounters by either killing with their first shot of an Aim-9 or forcing Iraqi fighters to withdraw. They also seem to have had a distinct edge in training, although one observer of air combat between the two sides is reported to have commented, "They can fly, but either they can't shoot or they can't aim." Iran has since lost that edge. It has suffered from repeated purges, and it has conducted only minimal training since 1979.

Most of the air-to-air combat seen by outside observers tended to be inconclusive. Engagements that should have taken less than two minutes have lasted as long as five. In most air-to-air combats, the successful pursuer either succeeded with his first missile or was not able to keep his opponent from breaking off and escaping. This may reflect the fact that air combat tends to spiral down to altitudes where neither side was properly trained to fight, but it may also reflect the fact that many of the IR missiles held by both sides were relatively ineffective in anything other than tail-chase firing at medium to high altitudes.

Iraq, however, steadily improved its training during the course of the war and made increasingly effective use of its new French aircraft and missiles. After 1982, it had the edge in most of the few encounters that took place, although its kill capability per encounter remained low. It still is unclear how much Iraq really improved versus how much Iran degenerated in operational readiness.

Iran lost most of its few air-to-air encounters after 1983 unless it used carefully planned ambush tactics against Iraqi attackers flying predictable paths of attack. Iran not only lost its technical edge over Iraq, the entire Iranian Air Force probably could not generate more than 30–60 sorties per day under surge conditions after 1983. Iran also lost one F-4 or F-5 on January 17–18, 1985, under conditions suggesting the Iranian aircraft had serious missile or radar problems. This indicates Iran has committed fighters to air combat with at least some inoperable avionics. Iran has reported growing reliability and survivability problems with all of its U.S.-made missiles and smart ordnance since 1984.[22]

Iraq, in contrast, was able to generate fairly high sortie rates from 1983 onwards, increasing from a maximum of 65 sorties per day, early in the war, to levels of 150 per day in 1984 and over 250 in 1986–1988, with claims of peaks as high as 600. Iraq had little reason to devote much of this sortie-generation capability to air defense after the early 1980s, but it did demonstrate that it could generate a high number of air-defense sorties with well-armed and fully operational aircraft. It is also interesting to note that Iraq claimed in late 1988 that its pilots had flown a total of 400,000 sorties of all types during the war.[23]

This pattern of combat reinforces the lesson of the Arab-Israeli conflicts that the West supplies, supports, and trains air forces which can be far more effective, relative to Soviet-bloc and PRC-equipped Third World forces, than their force numbers indicate. It reinforces the doubts regarding the capability of Soviet export fighters raised in past wars, as well as doubts about the dogfight capability of Soviet air-to-air missiles, cannon, and avionics.

At the same time, the Iraqis join with the Egyptians, Syrians, and Jordanians in noting the following problems in the support and training they received from the USSR.

- The USSR provided poor air combat training and little training in air operations. There was no real aggressor squadron training and no use of the advanced simulators common in the West and available to nations like Saudi Arabia. Iraq had to turn to France and India for assistance in this area.
- The USSR did not provide detailed operational data on its fighters and missiles, as distinguished from technical data, which, in turn, the Iraqis lacked the background to interpret.
- There was little Soviet effort to go beyond classic ground controlled intercept (GCI) training and doctrine and to deal with more fluid types of air defense.
- The USSR failed to provide adequate training and capability in electronic warfare and countermeasures and in low altitude combat. Training rarely dealt with combat below 5,000 feet.

Iraq has since gotten enough aid in all these areas from France, India, Egypt, and Jordan to adopt a "high-low" concept which mixes Soviet mass with Western quality. It is far too soon to tell how well Iraq will succeed with this concept, but it is interesting to note that Libya and Syria have also actively sought Western air-to-air missiles and aid in avionics and electronic warfare upgrades. They too are pressuring the USSR to improve its equipment and support.

It is also interesting that Iraq's experience has combined with the impact of Arab defeats in previous wars with Israel, and with the lessons of the Falklands conflict, to make many Third World nations refuse to buy any fighters and missiles which are not in first-line service in the U.S. and Western Europe. This may be a wise decision, given the far more advanced air-combat avionics and weapons on such fighters. It is clear from the Iran-Iraq War, however, that such technology must, however, be combined with suitable training and doctrine in order to be effective.

Close Air Support

Both Iran and Iraq generally proved unable to use fixed-wing air power effectively to provide close air support of their military forces. (See Figure 13.2 for the locations of their air bases and air-defense centers.) The Iranian Air Force was marginally better able than Iraq in carrying out attack missions at the start of the war, but numerous observers confirm the fact that the Iraqi Army could still operate with near indifference to the risk of Iranian air attacks against anything other than large, fixed-area targets. This may have been because Iran was conserving aircraft and flew very low sortie rates. Only about 18 to

FIGURE 13.2 Main Iranian and Iraqi Air Bases and Air-Defense Centers. Adapted from *Defense Electronics*, September 1984, p. 140.

50 percent of Iran's attack aircraft were fully operational at the outset of the war in 1979, and there are some indications that the avionics associated with attack missions failed earlier than those used in air-to-air combat. In any case, Iran rarely seemed able to locate and hit Iraqi forces effectively, even in the first few months of the war.

It is difficult to estimate what Iran's F-4s and F-5s could have accomplished if the Iranian Air Force had not been disrupted by revolution and had been able to keep its attack avionics and munitions operational. Iran's lack of a sophisticated C^3I/BM system and reliance on reconnaissance assets with near real-time processing capability would unquestionably have limited its effectiveness.

Iraq also faced the problem that the use of conventional iron bombs and rockets from high-speed jet aircraft that lacked sophisticated targeting and delivery aids does have low lethality, even against exposed armor, and even less lethality against dug-in forces, regardless of pilot skill and willingness to take risks. Iran had no fighter aircraft with anything approaching modern attack avionics or heads-up displays, although its F-4D/Es were relatively advanced for their time.

Iran lacked sophisticated area ordnance suited to close support against dispersed or well-sheltered infantry targets from the start of the war to the cease-fire, and there are no indications it was able to use the Maverick with any effectiveness against Iraqi armor. It is unclear whether this was the result of command-and-support problems or the technical and operational problems the Maverick creates in finding a target, exposing the aircraft to SHORAD fire, and guiding it to a small, moving, ground target in the face of terrain problems, light problems, dust, etc.[24]

It is also important to note that even the highly trained and well-equipped Israeli Air Force had low lethality against such targets in 1973, and most Western air forces have found that advanced attack avionics are absolutely critical to both achieve high kills per sortie and surviving ground-based air defenses. Nevertheless, individual Iranian squadrons and pilots did show during the early weeks of the war that their U.S. training was far more effective in attack missions against fixed or area targets than the Soviet training provided Iraq.

Unfortunately for Iran, it never had the opportunity to restructure its air force to correct its initial deficiencies. After Iran's July 1982 offensive against Basra, Iraq was able to operate up 400 first-line fighters in various forces of close air support and interdiction missiles versus fewer than 80 operational F-4s and F-5s for Iran. Many of the Iranian aircraft that were operational lacked fully operational avionics and had to be held in reserve. As a result, Iraq was able to use its growing fighter and helicopter force with only token opposition. Iran was forced to rely largely on anti-aircraft guns and surface-to-air missiles to deprive Iraq of its advantage in local air superiority.[25] This rapid decline in Iran's offensive and defensive air capabilities furnishes an important lesson in the importance of reliability, serviceability, adequate parts stocks, and forward-area maintenance technology. Iran lost its ability to field an effective air force in spite of what seemed to be massive prewar purchases of parts, munitions, and service facilities.

The exact reasons for Iraq's continued problems in making its average air-to-ground sortie effective during most of the war are uncertain. It is clear, however, that Iraq suffered from problems in command, training, technology, and tactics. The Iraqi command system did not favor armed reconnaissance and was slow to react to target opportunities until comparatively late in the conflict. Field commanders often lacked the authority to get a rapid response from on-call air support, and requests could be delayed for hours or even a day. There is also little evidence that Iraqi pilots got intensive mission pre-briefs or that the command system normally provided feedback on mission effectiveness, based on the effective use of reconnaissance aircraft or drones, until late in the war. It is surprising, for example, that Iraq has made comparatively little use of RPVs.

Iraq faced real tactical problems in that Iran conducted most movements and initial assaults at night and rarely presented attractive targets for close air support. Iranian forces were normally well dug-in and dispersed, and even in many assaults, the main targets were infantry, and fighters could only get a comparatively limited number of kills of low-value targets per sortie at the risk of exposing very expensive aircraft. Iran also often made good use of bad weather and had many well-dispersed anti-aircraft weapons and SA-7s. These problems might have been solvable with more aggressive use of area munitions, like cluster bombs, and by acquiring improved night combat capabilities, but the basic problem Iraq faced throughout the war was that it was generally only worth risking aircraft in close air support missions when Iran threatened a major breakthrough.

Iraq's technical problems were far more severe than those of Iran at the start of the war, although they were reduced with time. Iraq's Mirage F-1s were its most advanced attack aircraft, but they did not have fully modern attack avionics by Western standards, particularly in terms of computer capability and advanced heads-up display capabilities. Iraq's export versions of Soviet fighters all had much less sophisticated attack capabilities, although its Su-20/Su-22s had relatively good navigation and basic weapons-delivery capabilities.

Iraq also lacked the kind of advanced simulators and computerized training ranges that fully allow the pilot to exploit his aircraft's capability. These devices can be critical in Third World states which depend heavily on foreign training or advisors because pilot skills need constant refreshing once the pilot receives combat training, particularly because the pilot rarely has the time or visibility of target to appraise his own effectiveness.[26] It is also important to note that Iraq had truly massive amounts of artillery along the front during most battles and that the incremental kill capability of attack fighters was often limited. Unlike Western forces, Iraq was organized for mass barrages. It, therefore, had less priority to risk planes in close air support missions.

Once again, it is clear that most Western air forces would have an edge in such missions over their Third World counterparts. The value of this edge, however, could be seriously limited by the inability to bear the probable losses of flying close air support sorties in an environment with so many short-range air defenses and where the target mix is so poor. Given the fact that even the cheapest Maverick missile costs well over $50,000 and launching it involves at least some risk to a fighter that may cost well over $20 million, it is also unclear that such missions can ever be particularly cost-effective. They may prove necessary under crisis conditions—and the West has more effective area and hard-target ordnance available than were available to Iraq or Iran—but it seems unlikely that close air support can ever act as a practical force multiplier against large ground-force targets that are not dependent on a few high-value weapons like main battle tanks.

Interdiction and Air-Suppression Campaign

Neither Iran nor Iraq showed great capability to hit small to medium-sized interdiction targets, like bridges, although Iraq's performance improved from early 1987 to the cease-fire. Both sides also had trouble locating and attacking rear-area targets, such as large daytime movements of armor, even when these movements were unaccompanied by any air defense. In the case of Iran, this was heavily influenced by problems in aircraft numbers, although there is little evidence that Iran ever made particularly effective use of its RF-4Es to locate rear-area targets or was able to manage effective interdiction campaigns when it did commit its aircraft.

Iraq did slowly improve its effectiveness in interdiction missions during the war but was still unable to hit key targets, such as defended bridges, in 1987. While Iraq did improve its use of reconnaissance and armed reconnaissance from late 1986 onwards and was substantially more effective by late 1987 than at the start of the war, it was surprisingly ineffective in organizing the kind of campaign that could pound steadily at meaningful targets in the rear of Iranian forces and locate and kill targets of opportunity during the relatively short times they are exposed. This may partly have been due to the proliferation of Iranian short-range air defenses, but much of the problem seems to have stemmed from a desire to conserve air assets, even at the cost of effectiveness, and from a failure to understand that far larger numbers of aircraft were required to receive decisive results. There also is no question that the photo and other capabilities provided by Iraq's MiG-25R reconnaissance fighters fell far short of the sensors and avionics needed for targeting and air battle management.

Both nations had severe problems in using air strikes on enemy bases and facilities to suppress the other side's air forces. Iraq attacked ten Iranian airfields and air facilities during the first day of the war and did virtually no damage. In fact, Iraq did not achieve sufficient shock value to impose more than minor delays on Iranian Air Force operations.

Iran, in contrast, was able to hit at least two Iraqi air fields on the first day of combat. These attacks seem to have had sufficient shock effect to force mass dispersals to Jordan that Iraq had not planned for when the war began. A few Arab experts, however, explain Iraq's forced dispersal of its aircraft as the result of the fact that it had comparatively few main operating bases, that most were near Iran, and that although Iraqi aircraft were sheltered, most bases had large numbers of soft facilities. They believe it was the asymmetries in basing posture, rather than Iran's superior effectiveness, that forced Iraq to disperse.[27]

While some Iraqi have since charged that the cause of their failure to hit Iranian air fields effectively was defective Soviet-made bombs, there can be little doubt that when the Iraqis first attacked Iran in 1980, they suffered from the kind of "delusional blindness" that affected the Arabs in 1967 and the Israelis just prior to October 1973. The Iraqi Air Force lacked the intelligence and operational capability to objectively evaluate its effectiveness against any type of target and the survivability of the enemy. As a result, the Iraqi Air Force was forced to make realistic preparations for the air battle after the war was well underway.

There are several important lessons inherent in this experience.

- First, one cannot assume that Third World airpower will be committed realistically or with a professional understanding of the results.
- Second, forces with more sophisticated training, reconnaissance capability, attack aircraft and munitions, and command structures may be far more effective relative to Third World air forces than their numbers indicate.
- Third, it is critical to assess both friendly and unfriendly Third World air forces in terms of soft capabilities, such as exercise performance, training, command capability, and the other factors that shape readiness. Air strength alone, particularly as measured in terms of number of aircraft, may be virtually meaningless as an indication of real-world combat capability.
- Fourth, most Western air forces should have the aircraft, sensors and avionics, reconnaissance capabilities, and stand-off munitions to be far more effective in interdiction missions than most of their Third World counterparts. The practical problem will be to determine which missions have the most tactical or strategic effect, something that may be far from easy to judge given the different art of war and value judgements used by many Third World forces.

Strategic Operations

Both sides made use of strategic bombing against economic targets. Iran conducted most of its effort during the first year of the war. Iraq conducted a major strategic bombing effort against oil and economic targets, and the war ended in a cease-fire after a major strategic bombing effort against civilian targets.

Iranian Strategic Bombing Operations
Against Economic Targets

The Iranians lost much of their strategic bombing capability after 1981 but generally had the edge in the early stages of the war.[28] Iran launched some relatively accurate and well-planned attacks. It exhibited good air-strike planning in attacking Iraqi power plants and demonstrated considerable coordination in several attacks. This coordination was particularly striking in an attack launched on Iraq's H-3 oil field complex and air base at al-Walid where Tu-22 and IL-28 bombers are based. This target is over 800 km from the nearest Iranian air base at Reza'iyeh. Iran retains some of this refueling and long-range strike capability.[29]

While the evidence is contradictory, informed Western and Arab observers agree on the following points relating to Iran's initial superiority in strategic bombing missions.

- First, Iranian proficiency and accuracy in delivering conventional attack ordnance, like rockets and bombs, owes a great deal to the fact that something like 100 U.S.-trained Iranian pilots were freed from jail in the first days of the war.
- Second, Iranian missions were better planned and indicated far better use of maps and recce capabilities and pilot briefings.
- Third, Iran made effective use of the Maverick on at least some occasions, including strikes on Basra.
- Fourth, the superior range/payload of most Iranian fighter bombers proved critical against area targets. Iran's ability to deliver two-to-three times as many bombs or rockets per plane per sortie made up for much of the Iranian Air Force's lack of accuracy in using such munitions and had telling effect on dispersed targets, like refineries, tank farms, and petrochemical plants.

Iraqi Strategic Bombing Operations
Against Economic Targets

Iran and Iraq did show early in the war that they could hit storage tanks, large facilities, and area targets. Discussions with some of the

Iraqi experts involved—and confirmed by Arab, Western, and Japanese observers—indicate, however, that air power had a much greater effect in forcing both nations to temporarily shut down operations than in doing lasting and unrepairable physical damage. While each side occasionally did lasting damage to the other's refineries and chemical facilities, this was not true in most cases, even when the press has reported major damage. The psychological impact of burning oil tanks and petrochemical plants tended to disguise the fact that most of the key equipment emerges intact and that the key military result was to force a temporary shutdown of operations.

Iraq had a virtual monopoly on strategic bombing after 1982 but rarely achieved more significant strategic effects. This can be partly explained by the fact that many key Iranian targets were barely within range of Iraq's fighter-bombers when they flew demanding flight profiles and were difficult for Iraq to attack. The key factors limiting the effectiveness of Iraqi strikes, however, seem to have been a mixture of political restraint to minimize the risk of more land attacks on Iraq, Iraq's exaggeration of the impact of limited attacks and failure to accurately appraise the limits to its success, and Iraq's desire to reduce aircraft losses. There is little doubt that if Iraq had repeatedly attacked in the numbers required against key targets like power plants, refineries, water facilities, and less protected oil facilities, it could have had a far more decisive effect.

Even so, it is difficult to determine why Iraq could not knock out Kharg Island and destroy all the loading jetties, knock out Iran's refineries, or knock out its power plants. Iraq had the resources to keep any one of these critical sets of targets from functioning if it concentrated its forces and could do so with acceptable losses. The problem was that it either failed to understand the need to focus its strategic bombing and concentrate sufficient forces or failed to do so for political reasons.

Iranian and Iraqi Strategic Bombing Operations Against Urban Targets

In spite of occasional large-scale raids, Iran and Iraq generally limited their strikes on each other's population centers until the war of the cities in 1988, which was heavily influenced by the use of long-range surface-to-surface missiles, and which will be discussed shortly. Iraq did use aircraft extensively in the war of the cities, however, and made use of cluster bombs, napalm, and possibly some fuel air explosives.

Iraq also conducted high-altitude strikes with Tu-22 bombers. At least one of these strikes produced extensive damage to Iranian auto and steel plants near Tehran.[30] Iraq's use of chemical agents also suggest that far more lethal strikes could be delivered by attack aircraft.[31] Once again, the Iran-Iraq War only hints at the potential lethality of future strategic bombing efforts.

The Overall Impact of Iranian and Iraqi Attacks in the Oil War

If one looks at the overall outcome of the oil war rather than simply strategic bombing against land targets, Iran's major successes consisted of land and amphibious attacks on Iraq's oil-loading facilities in the Gulf and its political efforts in persuading Syria to cut off Iraqi oil exports through Syria. Iran, however, was unable to do anything to prevent Syria from finding alternative ways to export Iraqi oil through Turkey, Saudi Arabia, Kuwait, and Jordan. Iran never had the strategic bombing capability to prevent Iraq from creating new pipelines and new ways to export. (See Figure 13.3.)

Similarly, Iraq's massive effort to attack Iranian oil facilities and Iranian and other tankers was only marginally effective in reducing the flow of Iranian exports. As Figure 13.4 shows, the only points in the war where the combination of Iraqi air strikes against tankers, oil facilities, and Kharg Island may have produced a significant drop in Iranian exports were August–November 1986, February 1987, and the period after August 1987. These dips in production never, however, resulted in a critical, sustained drop in export capability.[32]

Part of the reason for Iraq's lack of effectiveness in cutting Iraq's oil exports seems to be that Iraq flew comparatively limited numbers of sorties and lacked the willingness to take aircraft losses and quality of mission planning necessary to achieve high lethality per sorties. Similarly, Iraq lacked the maritime reconnaissance assets and high payload missiles to properly locate and kill high-value tanker targets rather than damage them.

The data in Figure 13.4 do suggest, however, that Iraq's mix of attacks on Iran's oil-export capability may have become more effective in late 1987 than in early 1986 and that it might have been more decisive if the war had continued. It is also important to point out that Iraq did force Iran to use a tanker shuttle, massively discount its oil, and spend hundreds of millions of dollars on repairing oil facilities and obtaining new tankers.

If the outcome of Iraq's strategic bombing efforts is measured in terms of competitive strategy, virtually all experts agree that it cost Iran far more to try to deal with the results of Iraq's attacks than it cost Iraq to make its attacks. Further, the constant threat that Iraq might escalate to large numbers of sorties, as it did in late 1987, acted as a constant

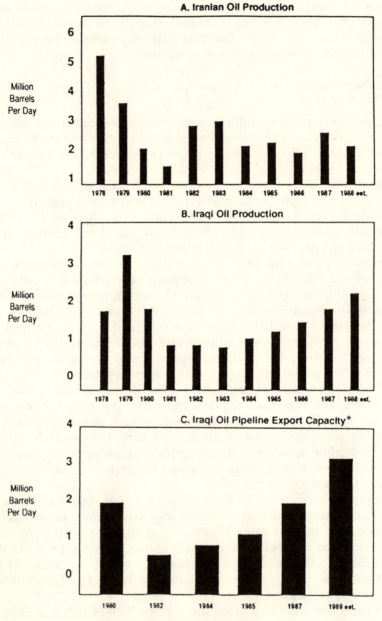

*Does not include prewar or postwar export volumes through facilities on the Gulf.

FIGURE 13.3 Relative Oil Production of Iran and Iraq from 1978 to 1988, and Expansion of Iraqi Pipeline Capability. Adapted from work by Cambridge Energy Research Associates and Jim Plaicke.

pressure on Iran's leadership. Finally, it is unlikely that any future strategic air attacks on major oil or economic targets will be conducted without the use of more sophisticated targeting equipment and attack capabilities, and the Iran-Iraq War may not provide a clear picture of the future threat that local air power can pose to Gulf oil-export capabilities.

This risk strategic bombing poses to key oil complexes like Ras Tanura (with its over-concentrated mix of oil and liquid gas facilities), and the other central oil-export facilities in the Gulf, cannot be judged by the Iran-Iraq War. Future conflicts may well involve the capability to selectively attack key point targets, such as the sensitive equipment involved in refineries and oil extraction with high lethality.

Air Reconnaissance and Identification
of Friend or Foe

Many of the problems in the reconnaissance and IFF capabilities of each side have already been discussed in Chapter 11. It is important to note, however, that Iran had an important advantage in maritime reconnaissance, and Iranian air reconnaissance over the Gulf was an important feature of the war from its start to the cease-fire.[33] Iran used its F-4s as well as two-to-three operational P-3F Orion surveillance and anti-submarine warfare (ASW) aircraft. While the P-3Fs soon lost operational radar capability, they still gave Iran an important advantage in locating Iraqi naval targets and gave Iran an advantage in targeting reprisal strikes on tankers operating east of Qatar as the war escalated after mid-1983.

Iraq had no maritime patrol aircraft and continued to experience serious problems in locating naval targets and tankers. This provides a lesson regarding the importance of airborne sensor systems. At the same time, Iran has had nothing approaching the U.S. E-3A and E-2C, and this has left it without effective air and naval battle management in dealing with the U.S. and other Western forces in the Gulf.

The previous analysis of close air support and air-interdiction operations also shows that both Iran and Iraq would have benefited from a forward area C^3I/BM system to control their helicopters and from a targeting platform using ESSM, SAR, SLAR, FLIR, or electro-optics to locate targets beyond visual range, to provide warning of ground-based air defenses, and to ensure against surprise on the ground. The lack of all these assets—with the limited exception of Iran's ability to use the F-14A as a mini-AWACS and its P-3C maritime patrol aircraft to locate naval targets—was a critical factor in

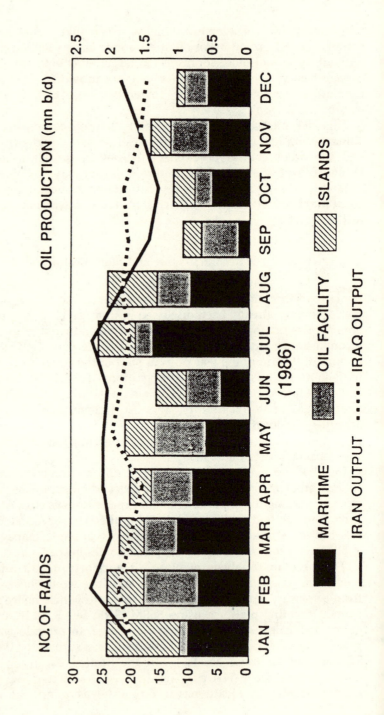

NO. OF RAIDS

OIL PRODUCTION (mn b/d)

(1986)

MARITIME   OIL FACILITY   ISLANDS

IRAN OUTPUT   ..... IRAQ OUTPUT

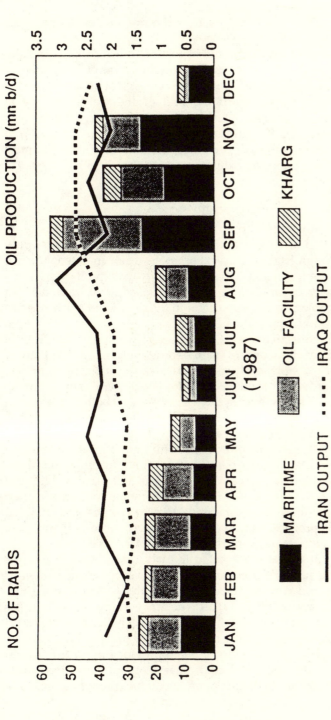

FIGURE 13.4 Impact of Iraqi Airforce Strikes on Iranian Oil Production: 1986, 1987. Adapted from work by Abdullah Toucan.

depriving both sides of the ability to make proper use of their vast investment in air power.

It also seems fairly clear from the history of the war that both sides could have benefited from the use of remotely piloted vehicles or RPVs. Iraq did become increasingly more successful at using helicopters to find artillery targets toward the end of the war, but only at considerable risk to the helicopter. It also seems to have made some preliminary use of RPVs, although no details are available. Iraq displayed four RPVs—the Al Yamama, Marakeb 1000, and Sahreb I and II—at the Baghdad trade exhibition in October 1988.[34]

Helicopters

Both sides developed the ability to use their helicopters successfully as gunships, troop carriers, and emergency supply transports, although Iran quickly experienced major maintenance and supply-parts problems and never was able to exploit the Shah's massive purchases of attack and transport helicopters. Iran and Iraq also found helicopters to be more useful in the close air support mission than fixed-wing fighters.

In spite of the effectiveness of enemy curtain fire and SHORADS, Iranian and Iraqi helicopters were sometimes of great tactical importance. For example, early in the war, Iranian helicopters helped limit the Iraqi advance around Mehran. They were critical to the Iranian supply of Abadan during the Iraqi siege, and both Iran and Iraq increasingly substituted helicopters for fighter close-air support since the start of the March 1982 offensive.

Since 1982–1983, Iraq was often successful in using helicopters as a substitute for fighters in support of its ground forces in daylight, perhaps because the Air Force command was still far too rigid and unresponsive to the needs of Army field commanders. While Iraqi helicopter pilots often stayed behind their own lines and avoided flying high-risk profiles, they were consistently more responsive in flying close air support missions than the Iraqi Air Force.

Iraq's Army Air Corps was created in early 1981 in response to the lack of Air Force support. It began with the Mi-24 attack helicopter as its main weapon and now has Super Frelons with AM-38 Exocets, HOT-armed Gazelles, and MBB BO-105s. The Iraqi Army Air Corps has learned to fly low, use pop-up tactics, and to make better use of forward observers. It also has occasionally made good use of its 48 Mi-24s, firing Soviet UB-32 rockets, and machine guns to provide on-call fire against Iranian human-wave assaults. Iraqi military communiques frequently stress the ability of combat helicopters to conduct sorties against well dug-in Iranian opposition. The Mi-24 acts as mobile artillery for the Army, with its UB-32 rockets and nose-mounted machine guns.[35]

The HOT-armed Gazelle helicopter fulfills the anti-tank role, and it reportedly has had considerable success against a wide variety of targets, from Chieftain tanks to coastal patrol craft. On the other hand, the Gazelle's IFF is reportedly poor, requiring visual identification on the battlefield. There is no information available on the efficacy of the HOT-armed B0-105 helicopters.

Iran's use of Cobra helicopters is also reported to have become steadily more effective in close support missions after early 1981 and to have stressed the use of nap-of-the earth tactics to surprise Iraqi troops.[36] This suggests that the Iranians learned how to avoid being targeted by Iraqi anti-aircraft weapons, such as tanks and the ZSU-23-4, which were reported very effective in the early months of the war. Iran's operations were badly hurt, however, by its lack of operational helicopter strength. Iran could have made far more extensive use of helicopters in supplying its Faw offensive in 1986 and in mountain fighting in 1984–1988. Both the Iranians and Iraqis have found helicopters critical in moving across water barriers, in small tactical troop movements in mountain areas, and to fly around terrain barriers.[37]

There seems to be a consensus on both sides that combat helicopters are survivable when they are used with proper tactics and regard for terrain and can play a critical role in making up for the lack of proper planning, armored maneuver capability, and combat support in emergencies.

Iranian and Iraqi helicopters also played an active role in transport and support missions. Iranian helicopters have provided an effective system for resupply in several instances during the Gulf War. The partial envelopment of Abadan Island during the early stages of the war could, for example, have led to an earlier Iranian defeat had the Iranians not resupplied their forces by using boats and helicopters.

Neither side ever used a large number of helicopters in a large heliborne offensive. If they had, such forces might have provided the means to bypass the slow-moving, dug-in defenses on both sides. As in Afghanistan, it should have been possible for Iraq and Iran to use helicopters to seek out and kill targets that jet fighters cannot find and to operate in mountainous and built-up terrain where helicopters can locate and maneuver around light AA guns and man-portable missiles that fighters cannot spot and thus overfly.

Both sides unquestionably could have used helicopters even more effectively if they had had (a) the ability to mass them for more decisive tactical impact, (b) a suitable C³I system for combined operations, (c) better beyond visible range targeting and intelligence, and (d) an adequate forward air control system. The need for such assets in every aspect of maneuver and air war is one of the major lessons of the conflict. This lesson, however, must be tempered with the fact such systems can only be effective if the USSR can develop the proper training and technical support capability.

Combined Operations

Combined operations in the Iran-Iraq War were marred by repeated failures of coordination and execution between services and branches within a service. The command problems that have already been noted in Iran were especially troublesome in any attempt to implement air/land operations. The Iranians managed to improve their combined operations after 1980, but only after repeated battlefield setbacks in which ground and air forces fought without meaningful coordination and after the partial consolidation of clerical power in Tehran. The impact of these improvements was then blunted by the attrition of Iranian aircraft and armor and by the constant interference in military operations of senior Mullahs in the leadership around Khomeini. While Iran failed to use combined operations effectively in most campaigns after its invasion of Faw in 1986, this seems to owe more to the political interference of figures like Rafsanjani than to a lack of professionalism on the part of the regular Iranian military and experienced Pasdaran commanders.

Iraqi combined operations should have had more initial success than those of Iran, since Iraq's command structure had not been ravaged by revolutionary turmoil, (although it had been repeatedly purged). Nevertheless, Iraqi combined operations experienced problems throughout most of the fighting and only became reasonably effective in 1988.

Many of the problems in Iraqi air/land operations appear to have two causes. The first cause was the separation of the command of land and air forces. This badly slowed both the tempo and focus of the air units participating in combined operations and sometimes led to reaction times that robbed airpower of much of its effectiveness. Further, these problems were compounded by a command-level emphasis on preserving aircraft, even at the cost of effectiveness.

The second cause stemmed from the tactical, training, and technical problems affecting Iraqi pilots. Many of these problems have already been discussed earlier, but it is also important to note that Iraqi pilots tended to bomb the Iranians from high altitudes, which is far less effective than low-level attacks.

Other causes of the problems in Iraqi air/land operations may have been caused by policies under which commanders, who repeatedly lost aircraft in combat, were punished, even if they inflicted significant damage on the enemy. This may also have helped make Iraqi air commanders claim to have inflicted absurd levels of damage on the Iranians, while failing to commit large numbers of aircraft.

Iraq did gradually make significant progress in dealing with these command-and-coordination problems in its land-air operations. The Iraqi leadership removed control of the attack helicopters from the Air Force and placed them under the jurisdiction of the Army. It then replaced the commander of the Air Force, and finally, beginning in 1987, created the kind of command structure that allowed the Air Force to respond far more quickly to the needs of field commanders. Nevertheless, the problems in developing suitable C^3 technology, training, and organization for combined operations were obvious in the actions of both sides and seem typical of Third World forces. Once again, this stresses the lesson that such forces must be judged by a careful analysis of all the major qualitative factors shaping their effectiveness and not just in terms of force strength as measured by unit numbers, manpower, or equipment.

Surface-to-Surface Rockets and Missiles

Surface-to-surface rockets and missiles were used sporadically from the first day of the war onwards, but they did not play a major role until the end of the war. While they could penetrate to targets more safely than aircraft, the missiles available to Iran and Iraq had severe limitations in accuracy and range/payload, and neither side had any ability to target the missiles accurately. Nevertheless, both sides used 750–900 long-range rockets and missiles during the course of the war.

Iraq had FROG missiles when the war started, and Iraq began the use of surface-to-surface rockets during the Iran-Iraq War by firing FROG-7s during the first weeks of the conflict. It soon found, however, that these rockets had little military effect. They lacked the lift to carry an effective conventional warhead, and Iraq lacked any means of effective beyond visual range (BVR) targeting. A good example of such ineffectiveness occurred early in the war when Iraq fired four FROG-7 surface-to-surface rockets in an attempt to disorganize some of the staging areas of the Iranian Army near Dezful and Ahwaz. The rockets exploded without any significant effect.

The reasons why are easy to understand. The FROG-7, which is also called the R65A or Luna, was designed for nuclear attack and has only limited effectiveness as a conventional weapon. It has a single-stage, solid-propellent rocket motor. It was first exhibited in 1967. It is 9.0 meters long, 61 centimeters in diameter, and weighs 5,727 kilograms. There is no guidance system other than a spin-stabilized ballistic trajectory. If any trajectory correction is made after launch, it will begin during boost. After boost, the trajectory is ballistic.

The FROG's warhead weight is 455 kilograms, and its maximum range is 60 kilometers. The FROG-7 can also carry a nuclear or chemical warhead. It is normally mounted upon, and launched from, a wheeled erector launcher called the ZIL-135. The main nozzle is surrounded by a ring of much smaller nozzles, and the system is far superior in reliability and accuracy to early FROGs.[38]

The FROG's lack of weapons accuracy, lethality, and targeting capability soon forced Iraq to fire them at cities and large economic targets rather than military targets or assembly areas. Iraq started such firings during the first months of the war, but the resulting fire was also inaccurate and often missed even city-sized targets or exploded without effect when the target was beyond visual range. For example, the small town of Andimeshk was hit by FROG rockets early in the war, despite the fact that it had no military or economic value. The missile did hit the town, but it was almost certainly a rocket that was meant for Dezful and had failed to strike its target.[39]

According to one estimate, Iraq fired 10 FROGs in 1980, 54 in 1981, 1 in 1982, and 2 in 1984, for a total of 64 missiles.[40] Even so, Iraq's FROG-7 operators continued to have serious problems in finding a meaningful use for the missile until the 1988 cease-fire, and the FROG never proved to be an effective conventional weapon.

The missile that did have an impact on the war was a variant of the Scud B. The Scud B first became operational in 1967. It is a Soviet design, and the Soviet Union designates the system as the R-17E or R-300E. The Scud B has a range of 290–300 kilometers with its normal conventional payload. The missile is 11.25 meters long, 85 centimeters in diameter, and weighs 6,300 kilograms. It has a single-stage, storable-liquid rocket engine and is usually deployed on the MAZ-543 eight wheel transporter-erector-launcher (TEL).

The Scud is far more sophisticated than the FROG-7. It is a true guided missile. It has a strapdown inertial guidance using three gyros to correct its ballistic trajectory and uses internal graphite jet vane steering. It has a warhead that detaches from the missile body during the final fall toward target. This provides added stability and allows the warhead to hit at a velocity above Mach 1.5. The Scud C is a larger missile and has more range. It is 12.2 meter longs, is one meter in diameter, weighs 10,000 kilograms, and has a range of 450 kilometers. The Scud D (SS-1e) was designed to deliver submunition busses and is more accurate than previous Scuds. It entered Soviet service in the early 1980s.

Iraq had limited holdings of Scud missiles when the war began and a Scud regiment with nine launchers. It was not until October 1982, however, that Iraq could make this unit combat effective. Experts disagree over how many Scuds Iraq fired during the war. According to some sources, Iraq began to fire regular Scud Bs on October 27, 1982, and fired a total of 3 missiles in 1982, 33 in 1983, 25 in 1984, 82 in 1985, none in 1986, 25 in 1987, and 193 in 1988. According to some U.S. experts, however, Iraq fired 8 Scuds without any effect in 1980 and then fired 3–8 annually in 1981–1983. Iraq fired no Scuds in 1984, 15 in 1985, none in 1986, 15 in 1987, and 189 in 1988. Iraq began to use Scud largely to conduct sporadic terror attacks on urban areas or military concentrations, and its strikes seem to have been designed largely to try to put political pressure on Iran. Most of the time, Iraq used its Scud missiles against Iranian population centers to the rear of the battlefield.[41] Typical targets were cities relatively near the border, like Dezful, Ahwaz, Khorramabad, and Borujerd (190 kilometers from the Iran-Iraq border).[42]

Iran acquired its Scuds later in the war—first from Libya and then from North Korea. It deployed these units with a special Khatam ol-Anbya force attached to the air element of the Pasdaran and fired its first Scuds in March 1985. It fired as many as 14 Scuds in 1985, 8 in 1986, 18 in 1987, and 77 in 1988. Iran's missile attacks were more effective from the start than Iraq's attacks. This was largely a matter of geography. All of Iraq's major cities were comparatively close to its border with Iran, but Tehran and most of Iran's major cities that had not already been targets in the war were outside the range of Iraqi Scud attacks. Iran's missiles, in contrast, could hit key cities like Baghdad.

Iran could never exploit its range advantage, however, because it lacked the number of missiles needed to sustain frequent attacks, because Iraq had vastly superior air resources it could use as a substitute, and because most Iranian missiles struck outside Baghdad. The optimal theoretical accuracy of the Scud is in excess of a kilometer at long ranges, and its practical accuracy, taking siting and other factors into account, was often closer to five kilometers.

It is scarcely surprising, therefore, that many of the Iranian Scuds fired at Baghdad hit in the outskirts of the city. Further, even the missiles that did hit inside the city often hit in open spaces, while hits on buildings rarely produced high casualties. Iran never hit any of its proclaimed major targets, which included the Iraqi Ministry of Defense and Iraqi oil facilities. In fact, the net impact of using Scud missiles against urban targets was roughly similar to randomly lobbing a 500-pound bomb into a city every few days or weeks. The Scud strikes usually did little more than produce a loud bang, smash windows, and kill a few innocent civilians. The most lethal attacks on both sides seem to have occurred when missiles hit targets like a school or a large funeral by sheer accident.

Until 1988, the net impact of Iranian and Iraqi missile strikes on the opposite side's public opinion and morale was limited, relatively short-lived, and often ambiguous. The side doing the firing was able to propagandize the firing as lethal retaliation against the enemy. The side receiving the fire, however, experienced only brief periods of panic at worse, which then often quickly changed into anger and demands for reprisals, as the civilians in the target area realized they could survive the enemy's attacks. Since each Scud missile cost around $500,000–$1,000,000, such attacks were also extremely expensive. Nevertheless, both Iran and Iraq attempted to improve their ability to use long-range missiles by acquiring much larger numbers of missiles and/or building their own.

Iran tried desperately to obtain large numbers of Scud missiles from Libya, North Korea, and Syria and to create its own missile-manufacturing capabilities. It sought to buy additional Scud Bs, to manufacture them in Iran, to develop its own systems, and to obtain alternative systems like the PRC-made M-9. It succeeded in producing its own version of a Chinese Type-83 artillery rocket, which it called the Oghab, and tried to develop its own long-range rocket, called the Iran-130.[43] Iran claimed during the course of 1985–1988 that it had over 100 factories manufacturing some sort of part or equipment for missiles and rockets, with major production facilities at Sirjan and a launch facility at Rafsanjan.

Iran was only successful in the case of the Oghab. It started producing this system in 1985 and immediately began to use it in combat. It seems to have made about 325 Oghab rockets and to have fired roughly 260–270 rockets out of this total. This allowed Iran to fire nearly 250 in 1988. The Oghabs only have a range of 40 kilometers, however, and they lack the range and/or accuracy to hit more economic or urban targets. The Oghabs also only have a 70–300 kilogram warhead, and their CEP (circular error of probability) is in excess of 1,000 meters.[44]

Iran had no way to target the Oghab. The most Iran could do was to launch the Oghabs at the Iraqi cities near the border. These targets included Basra, Abu al-Khasib, Al-Zuybar, Umm-Qasr, Mandali, Khanaqin, and Banmil, but the Oghab strikes generally had far less effect than artillery barrages.[45]

Experts disagree on the number of Scuds that Iran fired, as well as on the number fired by Iraq. According to some sources, Iran obtained additional Scud missiles from Libya or Syria in 1986, but it was still only able to fire a total of 18–22 missiles in 1987. Iran then turned to North Korea, and in June, 1987, North Korea agreed to ship 100 more Scuds as part of a $500-million arms package. These missiles were delivered to Iran in early 1988. Iran also seems to have sought Scuds from the PRC but to have been unable to obtain them.

Some sources indicate that during the 52 days of the war of the cities in 1988, Iran fired at least 77 Scud missiles. Sixty-one were fired at Baghdad, nine at Mosul, five at Kirkuk, one at Takrit, and one at Kuwait. Iran fired as many as five missiles on a single day and once fired three missiles within 30 minutes. This still, however, worked out to an average of only about one missile a day, and Iran was down to only 10–20 Scuds when the war of the cities ended.[46] Some U.S. experts feel there is firm evidence that Iran began to fire Scuds only in 1985 and fired 13–15 missiles in 1985, 8–10 in 1986, 15–17 in 1987, and 48–52 in 1988.

This situation might have been very different if Iran had ever made good on its claims to be able to produce the Scud. The Minister in charge of the Pasdaran, Mohsen Rafiqdust, started making such claims in November 1987. Iran also claimed in April 1988 that it was working on a missile with a 320-kilometer range and claimed that 80 percent of the Scuds it fired were produced in Iran. In fact, however, this was pure propaganda. Iran never succeeded in firing an Iranian-made Scud missile.

Iran also failed to develop and produce the IRAN-130 in any numbers. The full details of this system remain unclear, but it seems to have been an attempt to use commercially available components and a simple inertial guidance system to build a missile that could reach ranges of anywhere from 130 to 200 kilometers. In practice, the missile proved highly unreliable until the August 1988 cease-fire and reached a maximum range of about 120 kilometers, with very poor reliability and accuracy. Some IRAN-130s were deployed to the regular Pasdaran, however, and the first such missiles were fired against Al-Amarah on March 19, 1988, and four more were fired against the city in April. It is unclear that these strikes hit their targets or had any tactical effect.

It was Iraq that eventually was successful in finding the long-range missiles it needed, although it took nearly half a decade to obtain them. Iraq tried actively from 1982 onwards to acquire longer-range missiles. Various Iraqi statements made in early 1983, for example, suggested that the Soviet Union might be willing to supply newer Soviet missiles with longer ranges, like the SS-12, to the Iraqis. No new missile capabilities materialized, however, until February 29,

1988, when Iraq launched five new extended-range missiles that it called the Al Husayn.[47]

These missiles were variants of the Scud-B, Scud-C, or Scud-D.[48] It is unclear when Iraq obtained these missiles, but they seem to have been based on 300 Scuds that the USSR delivered to Iran in 1986. Iraq announced it had tested a missile with a range of about 400 miles, or 650 kilometers, in August 1987. These reports were initially dismissed as propaganda, but Iraq was almost certainly telling the truth. Iraq could have gotten the added range in several ways. It could have taken a standard Scud and modified it by (a) cutting its payload from 400 to 200 kilograms, (b) altering it to burn all the propellant at the cost of reliability, or (c) doing both.[49] Iraq also could have used strap-on boosters. There are reports of weld marks and other alterations on fragments of the Scuds recovered in Iran. It is still unclear which option was really involved, however, and the precise range capabilities of the Iraqi Scuds are unknown because the Iraqis regularly moved the missile launch sites during this phase of their attack. What did immediately become clear was that the Iraqi Scuds could reach Tehran and Qom from positions south of Baghdad.[50]

Estimates of the overall pattern of Scud strikes both sides made during the decisive phase of the war of the cities differ significantly according to source, but Table 13.2 provides an estimate of the overall interaction between the strategic bombing and missile wars between 1987 and 1988 based on Iraqi and Iranian claims. These claims are often exaggerated, but the data in Table 13.2 are almost certainly valid in indicating the general size of the sudden rise in Iraqi missile attacks and in the total number of air and missile attacks on urban targets.[51]

Iraq fired an average of nearly three Scuds a day, and the impact of Iraq's missile and air strikes on Iran was far greater in 1988 than in the past. Where the Iranians had previously been able to adapt to the relatively limited and short-lived Iraqi bombing efforts, the constant pounding of missiles interacted with a growing fear that Iraq might use chemical weapons, and this had a major impact on Iranian morale. So did the rumors and reports that senior Iranian officials—including Khomeini—had left Tehran. According to some reports, nearly a million Iranians had fled Tehran by mid-March and several million more had fled by late April.[52]

It is important to stress, however, that the Iraqi missile strikes alone would probably have had relatively little serious impact if they had not interacted with a number of other factors. The Scud strikes were audible over wide areas as they neared their target, made a loud bang, and blew out windows over a wide area. Nevertheless, the Scud strikes did not do serious physical damage to any Iranian target

TABLE 13.2 Strikes Reported by Iran and Iraq Affecting the War of the Cities in 1987 and 1988

		Residential/Economic Attacks[1]			
		Iraq		Iran	
Date		Total Bombing	Scud[2] & Missile	Total Bombing	Scud[3] & Missile
A. 1987					
Jan.	1–15	30	—	3	—
	16–31	18	—	15	3
Feb.	1–15	27	—	5	3
	16–28	8	—	5	5
Mar.	1–15	—	—	—	—
	16–31	4	—	—	—
Apr.	1–15	5	—	—	—
	16–30	2	—	—	—
May	1–15	4	—	1	—
	16–31	1	—	1	—
Jun.	1–15	—	—	—	—
	16–30	1	—	—	—
Jul.	1–15	6	—	—	—
	16–31	—	—	—	—
Aug.	1–15	2	—	—	—
	16–31	13	—	7	—
Sept.	1–15	35	—	8	—
	16–30	19	—	3	—
Oct.	1–15	12	—	6	—
	16–31	4	—	8	4
Nov.	1–15	14	—	9	1
	16–30	10	—	2	2
Dec.	1–15	7	—	2	—
	16–31	1	—	—	—
Total in 1987		223	—	70	15

(continues)

TABLE 13.2 (continued)

	Residential/Economic Attacks[1]			
	Iraq		Iran	
Date	Total Bombing	Scud[2] & Missile	Total Bombing	Scud[3] & Missile
B. 1988				
Jan. 1–15	1	—	—	—
16–31	—	—	—	—
Feb. 1–15	3	—	—	—
16–29	5	—	3	—
Mar. 1–15	215	101	73	31
16–31	130	36	143	14
Apr. 1–15	78	40	96	11
16–30	33	26	63	5
May 1–15	2	—	—	—
16–31	2	—	—	—
Jun. 1–15	—	—	—	—
16–30	13	—	1	—
Jul. 1–15	3	—	—	—
16–31	4	—	—	—
Aug. 1–20[4]	5	—	—	—
Total in 1988	494	203	380	61

[1]Bombing and missile attacks as reported in daily war communiques and other sources.
[2]Includes all long-range missiles but not Oghabs or any Iran-130s that failed to hit economic or civil targets.
[3]Includes Scud B missiles fired at Baghdad and other Iranian cities.
[4]From beginning of the month to the Iranian acceptance of a cease-fire and UN Resolution 598.

SOURCES: Adapted from work provided to the author by Gary Sick and from W. Seth Carus and Joseph S. Bermudez, "Iran's Growing Missile Forces," Jane's Defence Weekly, July 23, 1988.

and killed substantially fewer than an average of two dozen people a missile. The variants of the Scuds that Iraq was using only seem to have had a 130–250 kilogram warhead and were scarcely "city killers."[53]

What gave the Iraqi missile barrage a radical new strategic impact was that it occurred in combination with (a) the growing fear of chemical weapons, (b) the impact of Iraq's air raids, (c) the effect on morale of Iran's military casualties during the previous year, (d) growing popular and military exhaustion with the conflict, (e) Iran's inability to retaliate, (f) rumors of internal divisions within Iran's leadership, (g) serious economic hardship and growing prices on the black market, and (h) the knowledge that Iran would no longer be threatened if it halted its offensives.[54] This experience reinforces a lesson from many previous conflicts. The effect of strategic bombardment with conventional weapons on the course of a war is likely to be determined far more by its effect in catalyzing public opinion and in shaping the overall political conditions affecting the war than by the size of the casualties or actual damage that is inflicted by the weapons involved.

It is also important to realize that such bombardments may well have limited effects in the future unless they interact with a wide range of other factors. Table 13.3 shows the range and lethality of a wide range of current surface-to-surface systems and indicates that missiles can deliver far less range/payload capability than most Third World fighter bombers. Further, it should be clear from Table 13.3 that the long-range missiles now available to Third World states lack the combination of accuracy and payload to be highly lethal as long as they use high-explosive warheads. This is especially true because the velocity and vector of most such missiles produces less damage effect than an explosion by a similar amount of high explosive (HE) in a regular free-fall bomb.

Conventionally armed ballistic missiles without terminal homing-guided systems cannot even damage military targets as large as airfields except through sheer luck, since they have so little probability of hitting a meaningful target. They have less than a 0.3 Pk per round against a building-sized target when fired into a crowded city. Such missiles may have technical glamor, but they are no substitute for aircraft, multiple rocket launchers, and artillery in inflicting damage.

This situation is only likely to change when user countries acquire chemical or biological warheads or when cruise missiles with advanced guidance systems reach the Third World. Even missiles with chemical and biological warheads, however, may be more terror weapons than weapons of mass destruction. It takes tons of even lethal nerve gases to produce large amounts of casualties. To put this into perspective, under optimal weather and delivery conditions, it takes about 21 tons of phosgene to achieve 50 percent lethality over a one

TABLE 13.3 Comparative Range and Lethality of Surface-to-Surface Missiles

Source Country	Type	IOC	Range (Km)	Warhead Payload (Kg)	Nominal CEP at Range (Meters) Engineering	Operational	Warhead
USSR	SS-1b/ Scud A	1957	130	900	900	1,800	HE, N, CB
USSR	SS-1c/ Scud B	1965	290	900	900	1,600	HE, N, CB
USSR	Scud C	?	450	550	900	2,200	HE, N, CB
USSR	FROG-7	1965	60–70	455	400	900	HE, N, CB
USSR	SS-21	1978	8–120	1318–1557	300	900	HE, N, CB
USSR	SS-23	1980	500	350	350	900	HE, N, CB
USSR	SS-12	1969	800	300	750	3,000	Nuclear
USSR	SS-22	1979	900	300	300	700	Nuclear
USSR	Sepal SS-C-1b	1962	450	—	—	900	Nuclear
US	BGM-109G GLCM	1983	2,500	—	20	100	Nuclear
US	MGM-31A/B Pershing 1A	1962	160–720	350	400	800	Nuclear
US	Pershing II	1984	160–1,770	—	40	180	Nuclear
US	MGM-52 Lance	1972	110	250	150–400	400–900	HE, N
France	Pluton	1974	10–120	—	150–300	300–500	Nuclear
Argentina	Alacran/ Condor II	?	600–800	600–1000	—	—	?
PRC	CSS-2 DF-3	1970	2,700	1,800	800	2,000	HE, N
PRC	CSS-2 DF-3 (Saudi)	1987	2,400–3,000	2,200	800	2,000	HE, N
PRC	CSS-1 DF-2	1970	1,200	1,100	700	1,800	HE, N
PRC	M-9	198?	200–600	2,200	400	700	N, CB
PRC	M-11	1988	650–850	500–1,000	—	—	HE, C, B?
Iran	IRAN-130	1987	130–200	—	—	—	HE
Iran	Scud R-300/ R-17E	1985	320	—	—	—	HE, C?
Iraq	Scud C/D/ R-300/R-17E Variant Al Huseyn	1988	650	135–250	900	2,500	HE, C, B?
Iraq	Scud C/D Variant/ al Abbas	?	650–850	500–1,000	—	—	HE, C, B?
Israel	Jericho I	?	200–480	250	—	—	Nuclear
	Jericho II	?	490–750	450–680	—	—	Nuclear
	Jericho III	?	800–1,450	750	—	—	Nuclear

(continues)

TABLE 13.3 *(continued)*

Source Country	Type	IOC	Range (Km)	Warhead Payload (Kg)	Nominal CEP at Range (Meters) Engineering	Operational	Warhead
USSR	BM-21						
	122mm MRL	1964	20.5	40 X 17	400	900	HE, CW
USSR	M-1972						
	122mm MRL	1972	20.5	40 X	400	900	HE, CW
USSR	BM-14/16						
	140mm MRL	1952	9.8	40 X	300	800	HE, CW
PRC	T-63						
	107mm MRL		8.1	12 X 15	200	600	HE
PRC	140mm MRL		10	19 X 24	300	1,200	HE
US	MLRS						
	115mm MRL	1981	30+	12 X 40	50	200	HE
Iran	Oghab	1986	40	—	—	—	HE
Iran	Shanin 2	1988	70	180	—	—	HE
USSR	M-46						
	130mm Gun	1954	27.2	74	—	—	HE, CW
USSR	2S5						
	152mm Gun	1980	27	96	—	—	HE,CW
US	M-107						
	175mm Gun	1962	32.7	147	70	150	HE, CW
US	M-109A1						
	155mm How	1966	18–30	95	70	120	Nuc, HE, CW
US	M-110						
	203mm How	1962	21.3	170	70	120	Nuc, HE, CW

SOURCES: Adapted from various editions of the *IISS Military Balance*, London, International Institute for Strategic Studies; *Jane's Weapons Systems*; and working papers by General Dynamics.

square kilometer area, four tons of mustard gas, two tons of Tabun, 0.5 tons of Sarin, or 0.25 tons of VK.[55] Under most real-world conditions, far larger amounts are required, and the actual number of deaths is far smaller.[56]

Biological warheads can be far more lethal but are extremely difficult to engineer and require large and well-planned testing efforts to produce predictable and effective results. Cruise missiles are the only missile systems which have the accuracy required to be lethal against strategic targets with conventional warheads at long ranges. Even these systems, however, require mapping and targeting capabilities that are far beyond the capabilities of most Third World nations, and they are unlikely to reach the Third World arms market until the middle to late 1990s.

No one can sensibly dismiss the risks inherent in weapons systems capable of killing thousands of people. It is far from clear, however, that long-range surface-to-surface missiles are an effective way of delivering "cheap nuclear weapons."[57] In most cases, high-payload, long-range fighter bombers with advanced avionics will offer a far more predictable and effective way to deliver the large payloads required under the highly specialized delivery conditions necessary to be effective. Until Third World states acquire either effective biological warheads for their missiles or actual nuclear weapons, the effectiveness of missiles is likely to depend more on their political impact than their actual ability to inflict casualties or physical damage.

Chemical/Biological Weapons and Defensive Systems[58]

Both Iraq and Iran used poison gas a number of times during the fighting. While most such uses did not have a decisive impact on a battle, Iraq unquestionably became steadily more competent in using gas weapons. As a result, Iraq's use of gas warfare began to have a major impact on the war in terms of both casualties and damage to Iranian military and popular morale. The details of these uses of chemical weapons have been discussed in earlier chapters. It is important to note, however, that the use of chemical weapons during the Iran-Iraq War also provides an important lesson in the risks inherent in the proliferation of weapons of mass destruction.

Iraq's Chemical and Biological Weapons Efforts

Both Iraq and Iran signed the Geneva Protocols of 1925, which prohibit the use of poison gas, and both signed the Biological Warfare Convention of 1972, which bans the development, production, and deployment or stockpiling of biological weapons. Iraq, however, has been actively interested in biological weapons since the 1960s and sought chemical weapons from Egypt and the USSR following Egypt's use of chemical weapons in the Yemens.

It is not possible to precisely date when Iraq acquired chemical weapons, but it seems to have begun to seriously examine acquiring such weapons in the 1960s and to have decided to create its own production facilities following the October War in 1973. There are some indications that it acquired small numbers of chemical weapons from the USSR at this time and that it may have had assistance from Egypt in developing suitable production and storage techniques in the period before the Camp David Accords.[59] There are some indications that Iraq may have used poison gas shells or bombs against the Kurds during its campaigns of 1973–1975.[60]

Iraq seems to have begun the construction of its own chemical weapons plants in the mid-1970s in response to reports that both Egyptian and Israeli forces were equipped with chemical weapons at the time of the October War and the threat posed by Iran and its Kurdish rebels.[61] (See Table 13.4.)

Iraq seems to have weaponized mustard gas for use by mortars and artillery long before the Iran-Iraq War and to have had shells for at least 120-mm mortars and 130-mm artillery.

One of Iraq's first steps in acquiring a large-scale domestic production capacity was to turn to the Pfaudler Company of Rochester, New York, for assistance in creating a major "pesticide"-blending complex.[62] Pfaudler is a large producer of corrosion-resistant, glass-lined steel vessels, of the kind suitable for producing large amounts of toxic chemicals. Iraq approached the Pfaudler Company in 1975 and asked about purchasing a relatively small production facility.

Once the company's representatives reached Baghdad, however, it became clear that Iraq sought to create a massive facility. It rejected the safety concerns of the Pfaudler experts and asked for plans that meant rushing ahead without a pilot plant. It also became clear that Iraq wanted to blend organophosphate pesticides, which have a very uncertain value for agricultural purposes and which are commonly recognized as precursors for the production of nerve gas.[63]

The Iraqi production goals called for the handling of 600 metric tons per year of Amiton, 300 metric tons of Demiton, 150 tons of Paraoxon, and 150 tons of Parathon. All of these agents are extremely toxic.[64] Amiton and Paraoxon are the most toxic agents, followed by Parathion and then Demeton. Even in 1974, all four were relatively outdated agents for agricultural purposes and had been largely abandoned for safety reasons.[65]

During 1975–1976, Pfaudler sought to persuade the Iraqis to proceed on a pilot-plant basis. Iraq finally rejected this approach in mid-1976 and insisted on completion of a massive plant. The Iraqi negotiators also changed from the Ministry of Agriculture to the Ministry of Industry. The resulting impasse gradually led Iraq to break off negotiations.

Iraq then turned to Imperial Chemical Industries, PLC (ICI), with virtually the same proposal. Unlike Pfaudler, ICI was familiar with a British government list of items whose export was controlled because they could be used to produce gas weapons and immediately recognized that Iraq was seeking the precursors for nerve gas. ICI refused to negotiate further.

This refusal did not discourage Iraq, however, which turned to West German, Swiss, Dutch, Belgian, and Italian firms and seems to have

TABLE 13.4 Claims of Uses of Chemical Warfare

User/Area	Gas	Delivery Means	Effects/Casualties	Date
Iraq Susangerd	CS	Artillery	Limited	June 1982
Iraq Mandali and Basra	CS/Mustard	Artillery/ Mortars	Unclear	July 1982
Iraq Southern front	Mustard	Unknown	Used against forces massing for human wave attacks. Effect unknown.	December 1982
Iraq Haj Omran/ Piranshahr/ Mt. Kordeman	Mustard	Aircraft Helicopters	25–100 casualties	August 1983
Iraq Panjwin	Mustard	Helicopters/ Artillery	Heavy casualties Significant impact on battle	October– November 1983
Iraq Majnoon Islands	Mustard/CS	Aircraft	Heavy casualties Significant impact on battle	February– March 1984
Iraq Basrah	Nerve/ Mustard	Artillery	Limited	March 1984
Iraq Hawizeh Marshes	Nerve/ Mustard	Aircraft/ Artillery	Heavy casualties Significant impact on battle	March 1985
Iraq al-Faw	Nerve/ Mustard	Aircraft Artillery	Heavy casualties Significant impact on battle	February 1986
Iraq Khorramshahr	Mustard	Bombs	Disrupt buildup against Basra	January– February 1987
Iraq and Iran* Basra	Nerve/ Mustard	Aircraft Artillery	Heavy casualties Significant impact on battle	February– April 1987
Iraq Khorramshahr	Mustard	Bombs	Disrupt buildup against Basra	April 1987
Iran Mehran	Mustard/ Cyanogen	Artillery	Limited	July 1987
Iraq Sardasht	Mustard	Bombs	650–3,500 Kurdish civilians	June– July 1987

(continues)

TABLE 13.4 *(continued)*

User/Area	Gas	Delivery Means	Effects/Casualties	Date
Iraq Somar	Mustard	Bombs	Disrupt buildup against Basra	October 1987
Iraq and Iran Halabjah	Mustard/ Cyanogen	Aircraft Artillery	Up to 5,000 Kurdish civilians	March 1988
Iraq al-Faw, East of Basra	Nerve/ Mustard	Aircraft Artillery	Heavy casualties Significant impact on battle	April 1988
Iraq Mehran	Nerve/ Mustard	Aircraft Artillery	Heavy casualties Significant impact on battle	May 1988
Iraq Majnoon, Dehloran, Hawizeh	Nerve/ Mustard	Aircraft Artillery	Heavy casualties Significant impact on battle	June– July 1988
Iraq Kurdistan	Nerve/ Mustard	Aircraft	Terrorize Kurdish rebels and population	August 1988

*Iran may have used gas artillery shells during this battle.

SOURCES: Estimate based on various editions of the SIPRI Yearbook; Edgar O'Ballance, *The Gulf War*, London, Brassey's, 1988; W. Seth Carus, "Chemical Weapons in the Middle East," *Policy Focus*, Research Memorandum, no. 9, December 1988; JCSS, *Military Balance in the Middle East, 1987–1988*, Boulder, Westview, 1988.

obtained most of the components it needed.[66] While the precise source of its equipment is unclear, Iraq later seems to have received enough support to build a special "pesticide" plant from Pilot Plant, a unit of Karl Kolb, which is a major West German laboratory equipment supplier and three other pilot facilities. The Kolb plant had some of the special equipment necessary to make Sarin, but not special pumps.[67]

Iraq also is believed to have purchased technical assistance from a West German firm called Fritz Werner.[68] It received heavy-duty pumps and chemicals from Water Engineering Trading G.m.b.H of Hamburg which sold some $11 million worth of equipment and tons of chemicals, including trichloride, a nerve gas precursor and equipment from Quast, which provided reactor vessels, centrifuges, and piping line with Hastalloy.[69]

It is unclear how far these efforts had gotten when the war began, although at least one major pesticide plant was being operated by the Iraqi State Ministry of Pesticide Production in 1980–1981, some mustard gas was probably in production at Samarra, and two small pilot plants with the capacity to produce around 30–50 tons of nerve gas per year were completing construction at Samarra.[70] These two plants, however, were only able to produce nerve agents using fairly advanced and specialized feedstock. Finally, Iraq may have obtained additional production equipment for the manufacture of plastics which could produce massive amounts of hydrogen cyanide as a byproduct. This equipment seems to have been modified for the production of cyanide gas.

In short, Iraq does not seem to have had large stockpiles of weapons when the war began or to have given gas warfare high priority while it was still on the offensive. Iraq does seem to have had enough CS gas and mustard gas to use some form of gas in the battles around Basra and Mandali in 1982, but it evidently did not have the feedstock and the ability to increase production capacity needed for the large-scale use of gas in warfare.

It was only after Iraq was forced on the defensive and suffered major defeats that it seems to have begun to treat gas warfare as a possible solution to its military problems. In 1982, Iraq made major new efforts to acquire technology and feedstock overseas. For example, the Iraqi State Ministry of Pesticide Production turned to a unit of Phillips Petroleum Company in Tessenderloo, Belgium, to obtain 500 metric tons of a chemical called thiodiglycol.[71] Thiodiglycol is not suited for the production of nerve agents, but it can be easily combined with hydrochloric acid to produce mustard gas. About one ton of the chemical is required to produce one ton of mustard.[72]

Mustard gas offered Iraq significant military advantages. While mustard gas is 10 to 100 times less lethal than the simpler nerve agents in terms of direct exposure, it is easier to produce and handle and to deliver in actual practice. Mustard gas is also more effective when it is delivered against infantry or exposed humans in other facilities. It is more persistent, and the casualties consume large amounts of medical services and support. Lethality is not the only issue. Limited exposures to mustard gas can result in blindness or blistering for periods of 4 to 6 weeks. Mustard gas thus offered Iraq special advantages in dealing with Iranian infantry, which often spent considerable time in static, exposed locations and which had relatively poor rear-area medical facilities.

Phillips states it did not react to the order because it was placed by KBS Holland B.V., a Dutch trading firm. It was only after the trading firm began to ship its initial order in July 1983 that Phillips learned that the actual customer was in Iraq and Phillips then paid little attention because the customer was said to be a large "agricultural" organization. In early 1984, when the State Ministry of Pesticide Production placed a second order for 500 tons, Phillips grew suspicious and cancelled the order. Phillips then notified the Belgian government, which reacted by cancelling Phillips' license to produce the chemical.[73] By this time, Iraq already had enough feedstock for nearly 500 tons of gas, and Iraq began construction of the special refinery and other facilities necessary to make its own thiodiglycol out of more commonly available chemicals. Iraq's industrial complex at Al Fallujah seems to have been able to make thiodiglycol, as well as the precursors for nerve gas, before the cease-fire.

Iraq also acquired the equipment and feedstock to make nerve gas. By sheer coincidence, U.S. customs stopped another State Ministry of Pesticide Production order for 74 barrels of potassium fluoride, another precursor of Sarin nerve gas, in February 1984. The order was placed by Al-Haddad Enterprises Incorporated, owned by Sahib al-Haddad, a naturalized Iraqi citizen. The shipment was not then illegal because potassium fluoride was not yet controlled, and there is no clear way of determining how many other shipments occurred in the U.S. or other countries. However, at least one Dutch firm—Melchemie Holland B.V.—has since been convicted of export violations for selling phosphorous oxychloride, another precursor of nerve gas. Iraqi agents also bought large amounts of equipment from a West German firm in Drereich, equipment that Iraq seems to have claimed would be used to make organophosphate fertilizer but which could be used in the manufacture of nerve gas.[74]

These efforts paid off relatively quickly. A major Iraqi research center for chemical weapons was completed at Salman Pak.[75] The facilities necessary to produce mustard gas and Tabun and Sarin nerve agents were established at Iraq's Samarra chemical complex, which houses one of the insecticide plants obtained from the West.[76] The Samarra facility was heavily sheltered and occupied 26 square kilometers in an area about 100 kilometers north of Baghdad. It was defended by troops and SA-2 missiles. Iraq established another major plant near Karbala and at least one more gas warfare complex at Fallujah, 65 kilometers west of Baghdad.[77]

By 1983, Iraqi production of mustard gas was sufficient for Iraq to begin to deliver small amounts with artillery, fighters, and Mi-8 helicopters. It is unclear exactly when Iraq developed bombs using chemical agents, but Iraq seems to have used 250-kilogram bombs it bought from Spain and to have begun to use Fitter aircraft to deliver such bombs. This mustard gas was exceptionally pure, which indicates that Iraq was still producing batches under laboratory conditions rather than mass producing mustard gas in tons. This mustard gas seems to have been produced at the Iraqi chemical weapons facility at Samarra.[78]

Iraq seems to have begun to produce significant amounts of nonpersistent nerve gas Tabun or GA in 1984 and to have put Sarin or GB into full-scale production in 1986. Its main production facility seems to have been at Samarra, although the complex at Al Fallujah may have produced the actual gas as well as the precursors. Iraq seems to have at least experimented with hydrogen cyanide, cyanogen chloride, and Lewisite.

By late 1985, Iraq could produce about 10 tons a month of all types of gases. This seems to have expanded to a capacity of over 50 tons per month by late 1986.[79] In early 1988, Iraq could produce over 70 tons of mustard gas a month and six tons each of Tabun and Sarin.[80]

By mid-1989, Iraq had at least five major plants for chemical agent research and production.[81] Iraq also seemed to be actively working on the production of biological weapons and on developing a way to deliver gas and biological weapons with surface-to-surface missiles. Some sources feel that Salman Pak is the Iraqi center for the development and production of biological weapons, as well as the development of chemical weapons. There is no reliable way to determine what biological weapons Iraq was developing and whether actual production was under way. Logical biological weapons included Botulin toxin, anthrax, tularemia, and equine encephalitis. Iraq also seemed to be producing VX, a persistent nerve gas.[82]

Iran's Chemical and Biological Weapons Efforts

Iran became serious about chemical warfare much later than Iraq, but it is hardly surprising that Iraq's attacks led Iran into a crash effort to develop its own chemical agents and to purchase massive stocks of chemical defense gear.

The purchase of defense gear was relatively easy, and Iran purchased large stocks of chemical defense gear from the mid-1980s onwards. Iran also obtained large stocks on nonlethal CS gas, although it quickly found such agents had very limited military impact since they could be used effectively only in closed areas or very small open-air areas.

Acquiring poisonous chemical agents was more difficult. Iran did not have any internal capacity to manufacture poisonous chemical agents when Iraq launched its attacks with such weapons.[83] While Iran seems to have made limited use of chemical mortar and artillery rounds as early as 1985—and possibly as early as 1984—these rounds were almost certainly captured from Iraq.[84]

Iran seems to have begun a crash effort to acquire an internal production capability in 1983–1984. Iran sought aid from European firms like Lurgi to produce large "pesticide" plants and began to try to obtain the needed feedstock from a wide range of sources, relying heavily on its Embassy in Bonn to manage the necessary deals. While Lurgi did not provide the pesticide plant Iran sought, Iran obtained substantial support from other European firms and feedstocks from a wide range of Western sources.[85]

These efforts began to pay off in 1986–1987.[86] Iran began to produce enough lethal agents to load its own weapons.[87] The director of the CIA and informed observers in the Gulf have made it clear that Iran could produce blood agents like hydrogen cyanide, phosgene gas, and/or chlorine gas.[88] These gas agents were loaded into bombs and artillery shells and were used sporadically in 1987 and 1988.

By the time of the cease-fire, Iran was beginning to produce significant amounts of mustard gas and nerve gas. It is interesting to note that debates took place in the Majlis in late 1988 over the safety of Pasdaran gas plants located near Iranian towns and that Rafsanjani described chemical weapons as follows:

> Chemical and biological weapons are the poor man's atomic bombs and can easily be produced. We should at least consider them for our defense. Although the use of such weapons is inhuman, the war taught us that international laws are only scraps of paper.[89]

By mid-1989, it was clear that Iran had established a significant chemical weapons production capability and was seeking to obtain and/or manufacture surface-to-surface missiles that could be used for both chemical and nuclear strikes. There also were some indications that Iran was actively working on biological weapons. Rumors of such biological weapons activity surfaced as early as 1982, along with reports that Iran was working on mycotoxins—a simple biological agent that requires limited laboratory facilities. It is doubtful, however, that Iran had a major biological warfare research effort before the late 1980s.[90]

The Use of Chemical and Biological Weapons in the Iran-Iraq War

There is no evidence of large-scale use of lethal chemical synthetics and/or biological agents during the initial stages of the Gulf War, although Iran claimed Iraq used chemical weapons in the Susangerd area during the first six weeks of the war.[91] These Iranian claims are uncertain and may reflect Iranian propaganda or a botched Iraqi attempt to use lethal chemical or biological agents. (See Table 13.5).

Iraq first began to make significant use of chemical warfare against Iran when Iraq was put on the defensive. Beginning in 1982, Iraq began to use tear gas and nonlethal agents, and a broadcast over Baghdad's Voice of the Masses Radio stated in a reference to the Iranians that there was "a certain insecticide for every kind of insect."[92] Iraq made extensive use of lethal chemical weapons in July 1983 (Wal-Fajr 2).[93] In December 1982, Iraq began to use mustard gas to deal with human-wave and night attacks.

Iraq again warned Iran that it might make extensive use of poison gas in September 1983. The Iraqi high command issued a statement that it "was armed with modern weapons that (would) be used for the first time in war . . . not used in previous attacks for humanitarian reasons . . . if you execute the orders of Khomeini's regime . . . your death will be certain because this time we will use a weapon that will destroy any moving creature on the fronts."[94]

The warning was soon followed by further attacks. Iraq made extensive use of lethal chemical weapons in October 1983 (Panjwin offensive).[95] Chemical warfare seems to have been used extensively on August 9 near Piranshahr and then around Panjwin in late October and early November 1983.[96] Two Iranian soldiers wounded by mustard agents during this campaign were sent to Vienna where they died. Two members of a second group of wounded soldiers were sent to Stockholm for medical treatment and also died. Further Iranian charges were made that Iraq used chemical weapons during the March 1984 offensive which led to the Iranian seizure of Majnoon Island.[97] These charges stated Iraq had killed some 1,700 Iranian troops and used GD and GB nerve agents, as well as mustard gas. Many of the Iranian allegations about the Iraqi use of lethal synthetic gases during the following months also related directly to the fighting on the islands.[98]

Iraq does not seem to have made extensive use of chemical agents between March 1984 and Iran's Faw offensive in early 1986. It did, however, sporadically use chemical weapons when its forces came under intense military pressure.

Iran attempted to deal with this situation by mobilizing world opinion. After Iran's protests failed to arouse a significant world reaction, it flew chemical warfare casualties to London. A UN team then flew to Iran and found several bombs for dispersing chemical agents with Spanish markings. These weapons were later found to have contained mustard gas. Other investigations after the 1984 attacks confirmed a high probability that Iraq was using a nerve gas agent called Tabun.[99] These conclusions were validated by a second UN

TABLE 13.5 Major Chemical Agents That May Have Been Used During the Iran-Iraq War

CONTROL AGENTS: Agents which produce temporary irritating or disabling effects when in contact with the eyes or inhaled. They can cause serious illness or death when used in confined spaces.

Tear: Cause flow of tears and irritation of upper respiratory tract and skin. Can cause nausea and vomiting:
Chlororacetophenone (CN)
O-Chlorobenzyl-malononitrile (CS)
Vomiting: Cause irritation, coughing, severe headache, tightness in chest, nausea, vomiting:
Adamsite (DM)

INCAPACITATING AGENTS: Agents which cause short-term illness, psychoactive effects (delirium and hallucinations). Can be absorbed through inhalation or skin contact:

BZ

BLISTER AGENTS: Agents that destroy skin and tissue, cause blindness upon contact with the eyes, and which can result in fatal respiratory damage. Can be absorbed through inhalation or skin contact. Some have delayed and some have immediate action:

Sulfur Mustard (H or HD)
Nitrogen Mustard (HN)
Lewisite (L)
Phosgene Oxime (CX)

CHOKING AGENTS: Agents that cause the blood vessels in the lungs to hemorrhage and fluid to build up until the victim chokes or drowns in his own fluids. Can be absorbed through inhalation. Immediate to delayed action:

Phosgene (CG)

BLOOD AGENTS: Interfere with use of oxygen at the cellular level. CK also irritates the lungs and eyes. Rapid action:

Hydrogen Cyanide (AC)
Cyanogen Chloride (CK)

NERVE AGENTS: Agents that quickly disrupt the nervous system by binding to enzymes critical to nerve functions, causing convulsions and/or paralysis and often resulting in death. Can be absorbed through inhalation or skin contact:

Tabun (GA)
Sarin (GB)—nearly as volatile as water and delivered by air
Soman (GD)
GF
VK—a persistent agent roughly as heavy as fuel oil

SOURCES: Adapted from Matthew Meselson and Julian Perry Robinson, "Chemical Warfare and Chemical Disarmament, "*Scientific American*, vol. 242, no. 4, April 1980, pp. 38-47, and unpublished testimony to the Special Investigations Subcommittee of the Government Operations Committee, U.S. Senate, by David Goldberg, Foreign Science and Technology Center, U.S. Army Intelligence Center, February 9, 1989.

investigation in 1986, and it later became apparent that Iraq also had chlorine gas agents and that Iraq had a major chemical weapons production complex.

Iran's efforts to make a propaganda issue out of Iraq's use of gas may have had some temporary success. Iraq made little use of chemical agents between 1984 and the Iranian offensive in Faw in 1986. There are, however, alternative explanations. While this pause in Iraq's use of gas may have been because of the hostile reaction in the West and the Third World, it may also have been because Iraq lacked the organization and dispensers to use gas safely. There are indications that unfavorable winds caused Iraqi deaths at Haji Omran in August 1983, at Majnoon in March 1984, and near Fish Lake in 1987. Iran also seems to have become more cautious after the U.S. formally condemned Iraqi use of chemical weapons in March 1984.

Changes in the training of the Iraqi Chemical Corps also indicate that Iraq was attempting to become more selective in its use of mustard gas and to attack Iranian rear areas with more care. Further, Iraq was clearly converting its forces to be able to use nonpersistent nerve gases against attacking Iranian troops or in its own attacks on Iranian positions.

In any case, Iraq resumed extensive use of gas warfare in its defense of Faw in 1986 and also used gas in its defense of Basra in 1987. Iraq found that mustard and nerve gas were effective in defending against attacking Iranian troops in the north during their attacks on Iraq in 1987 and in the early months of 1988. Chemical weapons offered a potential solution to the problem of mountain or rough-terrain warfare, and in many cases, it allowed Iraq to secure a mountainous area with relatively few troops. Iraq was particularly ready to use gas against those Iraqi Kurds fighting on the side of Iran, a group which the government regarded as nothing but traitors.

Iraq made massive use of chemical weapons during its recapture of Faw in early 1988 and in its assaults to recover its positions outside Basra. By April 1988, Iran claimed that the new round of attacks had raised the total number of casualties from chemical weapons since the start of the war to around 25,600, with some 260 dead. These claims may well be legitimate. Although Iran now had extensive defensive equipment, it did not organize or train to use it effectively. Many Iranians died, for example, because they did not shave often enough to allow their gas masks to make a tight seal.[100]

During the final months before the cease-fire, Iraq used chemical weapons in its attacks on Iranian positions in Mehran, the Majnoon Islands, the Hawizeh Marshes, and Dehloran.[101] By the time the war ended in a cease-fire, the Iraqi use of chemical weapons seems to have produced around 45,000 casualties, although there is no way to calculate the seriousness of these casualties or the number of dead.

More controversially, anti-Iraqi Kurdish factions charged that Iraq began to make extensive use of gas against noncombatant Kurdish villages and areas early in 1987. According to such reports, there were some 15 such attacks between April 15, 1987, and February 26, 1988. Three of these attacks are claimed to have produced 100 or more casualties: attacks on Arbil, Kanibard, Zeenau, Balookawa, Shaikwassan, the Derasheer mountains, and the Sawseewaken areas on April 16, 1987; attacks on the Dahok/Amadia area on May 6, 1987; and attacks on the Sulaymania/Sergaloo, Yakhsamar, Haledan, Gweezeela area on February 25, 1987.[102]

While these charges cannot be confirmed, the worst single use of gas against civilians occurred when both Iraq and Iran used gas during an Iranian attack on the Kurdish town of Halabjah on February 26, 1988. Up to 5,000 Kurdish civilians were killed in the fighting.

Iraq seems to have begun the attack by bombing the town with mustard gas that produced a burning white cloud after its troops had been driven out of the area. Some of the gas victims seem to have fled toward Iraq rather than Iran, and this may have confused Iranian forces into thinking they were Iraqi troops. Iran seems to have fired hydrogen cyanide gas into the area with artillery shells. The cyanide fired by Iran may have done much of the actual killing and may have accounted for many of the casualties that Iran blamed on Iraq when it showed the results of the attacks on its state television network.[103]

In spite of the hostile outside reaction to Halabjah, Iraq seems to have begun a major new offensive against its own Kurds on August 25, 1988, and seems to have made considerable use of gas warfare as part of an effort to depopulate hostile areas. While the exact scale of Iraq's use of gas is uncertain, some 65,000 Kurds fled to Turkey, and many of the refugees gave convincing reports of the use of gas warfare. These attacks only halted after a new wave of world protests tended to isolate Iraq from its supporters and after extensive diplomatic pressure from the U.S.[104]

As for other Iranian uses of chemical weapons, Iran seems to have made its first use of chemical weapons in 1984 or 1985, using mortars and artillery to deliver gas rounds. Some of these rounds may initially have been captured from Iraq. While reports are controversial, Iran seems to have made more extensive use of chemical weapons in the area near Fish Lake during the fighting around Basra in early 1987, and again during the battle to retake Mehran.

The exact nature of the chemical agents available to Iran during the war is unknown. In early 1988, however, Iran seems to have been able to produce mustard, phosgene, and hydrogen cyanide gas and was actively working on the production of nerve gas.[105]

If the Iran-Iraq War should resume at anything like the level of conflict that existed before the cease-fire, it seems likely that there will be further use of gas and possibly of biological agents as well. It is important to note, however, that neither Iran nor Iraq has yet demonstrated an effective capability to deliver gas and chemical weapons by missile.

As for the overall impact of chemical weapons, it is clear that Iraq had substantially greater success in using such weapons after 1987. While 45,000 casualties from gas was a relatively minor part of the well over one million military and civilian casualties that resulted from the war, chemical weapons also seem to have had a critical effect on Iranian military and civilian morale in the Iraqi counteroffensives and "war of the cities" in 1988. Sheer killing power also is not the issue. Troops that feel they are defenseless may well break and run after limited losses. Populations which fear chemical attacks may well cease to support a conflict. These are lessons that many developing nations have already taken to heart, and further uses of chemical weapons, and possibly biological weapons, now seem all too likely.

Nuclear Weapons

Neither Iraq nor Iran seem likely to acquire nuclear weapons in the near future, but both sides have been actively trying to acquire them for over a decade. Given their use of chemical weapons, it is possible that if either side had had such weapons, they would have used them.

Iraq's Nuclear Weapons Effort

Iraq began its efforts no later than the early 1970s. The Osirak reactor that Iraq purchased from France in 1976 was unusually large and had special features for irradiating uranium which allowed it to be used to produce significant amounts of plutonium, enough to produce a bomb over a several year period. In 1981, when Israel attacked and destroyed the reactor, Iraq was negotiating to buy a heavy-water power reactor from Italy and a sizable reprocessing facility whose purpose was almost certainly plutonium production.

Earlier, in 1980 and 1981, Iraq had brought large amounts of natural uranium from Brazil, Portugal, Niger, and Italy. Iraq also placed an order in early 1980 for 25,000 depleted uranium fuel pins from a West German firm called NUKEM. They were sized for irradiation in the

Osirak reactor and had no other real purpose than to produce about ten to twelve kilograms of weapons-grade plutonium. While the reactor was under IAEA (International Atomic Energy Agency) inspection and French technicians were to remain until 1981, Iraq seemed to be following the bomb development plan Sweden had used in the early 1960s and was developing an open ability to handle plutonium technology while stockpiling for weapons purposes. Iraq also seems to have tried to buy plutonium illegally from Italian sources after the Israeli raid on Osirak.

Iraq has had little success since 1981 in either obtaining aid in building new reactors suitable for weapons purposes or obtaining fissile materials. Iraq continues to hold 12.5 kilograms of French-supplied highly enriched uranium and could theoretically make one nuclear weapon, but there is no indication it has done so.[106] It tried unsuccessfully to obtain 33.9 kilograms of plutonium from an Italian smuggling ring but could not find any substitute.[107]

It seems highly likely, however, that Iraq will continue to try to find a replacement for Osirak and try to expand its facility at Tuwaitha to create some capability to process uranium or plutonium. Iraq still has a 10-megawatt reactor, built by the Soviet Union, operating at Tuwaitha, but this is under tight Soviet control. Tuwaitha has also acquired massive new surface-to-air missile defenses since the Israeli attack.[108]

In the longer run, Iraq may be able to use larger power reactors. It is seeking to provide 10 percent of its power needs with nuclear power and contracted with the Soviet Union in 1984 to build a 440-megawatt plant at a cost of $2 billion. The plant is supposed to be built by the Soviet Atomenrgo group, but there is no current sign that Iraq has been able to get the USSR to start construction or Soviet support in building a new reactor Iraq could integrate into a weapons development cycle. Iraq is also evidently seeking Latin American support in building an uncontrolled reactor somewhere in northern Iraq. In the long run, Iraq is likely to succeed in obtaining at least some fissile material and in becoming a nuclear power.[109]

Iran's Nuclear Weapons Effort

Like Iraq, Iran has an extensive nuclear effort, and for all its rhetoric about popular warfare, the Khomeini regime seems to have revived the nuclear weapons program begun under the Shah. The Shah established the Atomic Energy Organization of Iran in 1974 and rapidly began to negotiate for nuclear power plants. By the time he fell in January 1979, he was attempting to purchase some 12 nuclear power plants from the FRG, France, and the U.S. Two 1,300-megawatt

German plants at Bushehr were 60 percent and 75 percent completed and work had begun on two 935-megawatt French plants at Darkhouin. Thousands of Iranians were training in nuclear technology in France, the FRG, India, the U.K., and the U.S. In addition, Iran had negotiated for long-term supplies of enriched fuel with France, the U.K., and the U.S, had bought a 10 percent share of EURODIF in 1975, and was negotiating to buy a share of COREDIF.[110]

Far less publicly, the Shah began a nuclear weapons research program, centered at the Tehran Research Center, whose operations were never affected by the Shah's fall. This research effort included a laser enrichment program, which began in 1975, and led to a complex and highly illegal effort to obtain laser separation technology from the U.S. This effort continued from 1976 until the Shah's fall, and three lasers operating in the critical 16 micron band were shipped to Iran in October 1978. At the same time, Iran worked on ways to obtain plutonium. It created a secret reprocessing research effort to use enriched uranium and set up a small nuclear weapons design team. In 1976, Iran also began to try to purchase 26.2 kilograms of highly enriched uranium. The application to the U.S. was still pending when the Shah fell.

The Khomeini government initially let the Shah's program slide but revived it in 1981. It kept a small 5-megawatt reactor working under IAEA safeguards at Tehran University. Iran revitalized its laser separation program in 1983 and held several conferences on the subject, including an international conference in September 1987. It opened a new nuclear research center in Isfahan in 1984 and sought French and Pakistani help for a new research reactor for this center.

The government began to restart work at the Bushehr in 1984, although the FRG officially refused to support the effort until the war ended. Iran got around this by obtaining Argentine support in completing the Bushehr 1 reactor, which is 75 percent finished. Reports surfaced in April 1987 that the Argentine nuclear power agency, CNEA, had signed an agreement with Iran. CNEA works closely with West Germany's Kraftwerke Union (KWU), which had the original contract for the reactor. The Spanish firm Impressarios Agupados may also be part of the consortium.[111] While the FRG firm Kraftwerk Union pulled out of the Bushehr project in September 1980, it was working on the reactor when Iraqi aircraft bombed it on November 17, 1987. Several Kraftwerk technicians were injured and one was killed.

Argentina also sold Iran enriched uranium for its small Tehran University reactor in May 1987. The five-megawatt university reactor uses a core with 93 percent enriched uranium, which is suitable for some forms of nuclear weapon. A CNEA team visited Iran in late 1987 and early 1988 and seems to have agreed to sell Iran the technology necessary to operate its reactor with 20 percent enriched uranium as a substitute for the highly enriched core. Argentina has not ratified the nuclear nonproliferation treaty (NPT), but Iran is an NPT signatory, and Argentina has agreed to IAEA safeguards. It is unclear what impact the Argentinian agreement with Iran will have on Iran's nuclear weapons program.

There are significant uranium deposits in the Sarghand region of Iran's Yazd Province, but Iran's enrichment plant at Pilcaniyeu has so far been unable to reach enrichment levels above 8 percent.[112] Iran has also suffered a major blow to its program because Iraq successfully and repeatedly bombed its reactor projects at Bushehr. Iraq first struck the reactor on March 4, 1985, and then launched major raids on November 17 and 19, 1987. This may have been in response to the fact that Iran had begun to move IAEA safeguard material to the area in February 1987.[113]

Given this background, it is unlikely that either Iraq or Iran will have any nuclear capability before the mid-1990s or a significant delivery capability until well after the year 2000. It is clear, however, that both nations are likely to continue their weapons efforts as well as efforts to improve their chemical weapons and develop biological weapons. Further, their difficulties in nuclear proliferation may well accelerate their chemical and biological efforts.

Notes

1. "Iranian/Iraqi Air Strikes Appear at 'Limited' Level," *Aviation Week and Space Technology*, October 6, 1980, p. 20.

2. Estimate based on the data in the IISS, *Military Balance, 1988–1989*, London, International Institute for Strategic Studies, pp. 102–103.

3. Iraq now has AN/TPS 43/59/63 and AN/TS9-73 radars and Fan Songs, Flat Face P-15, Spoon Rest P-12s, Low Blows, Straight Flush Missile/gun radars, and Squint Eye and Long Track early warning radars.

4. See IISS, *Military Balance, 1985–1986*, London, International Institute for Strategic Studies, pp. 74–77; Jim Bussert, "Iran-Iraq War Turns Strategic," *Defense Electronics*, September 1984, pp. 133–148.

5. IISS, *Military Balance, 1980–81 and 1985–86*, London, International Institute for Strategic Studies.

6. Clarence A. Robinson, Jr., "Iraq, Iran Acquiring Chinese-Built Fighters," *Aviation Week and Space Technology*, April 11, 1983, p. 18.

7. Iran had 150 Cobras and 300 other assault helicopters in 1980, and Iraq had about 120 assault helicopters.

8. These estimates are based on various editions of the IISS, *Military Balance*; Aharon Levran and Zeev Eytan, *The Middle East Military Balance,*

1986, Boulder, Westview, 1987, pp. 236–258; and Anthony R. Tucker, "Armies of the Gulf War," *Armed Forces,* July 1987, pp. 319–323.

9. IISS, *Military Balance, 1985–1986,* pp. 74–76.

10. See Anthony R. Tucker, "The Gulf Air War," *Armed Forces,* June 1987, pp. 270–271.

11. Strength estimates based on various editions of the IISS, *Military Balance.*

12. Iran had 12–15 Hawker Hunter aircraft when the war began. The Hunter is a vintage light fighter/fighter bomber. It has a maximum speed of 710 miles per hour at sea level and an initial climb rate of 5,500 feet per minute. Its range on internal fuel is about 490 miles. The Hunter is armed with four Aden cannons. The engine is a Rolls Royce-Avon single-shaft turbojet. It is no match for modern missile-armed fighters, but little information is available on the frequency of actual use or effectiveness of this aircraft. It is not thought to have played a significant role in the air war.

13. Chris Chant, *A Concise Guide to Military Aircraft of the World,* London, Temple Press, p. 150.

14. The Soviet Su-17/20 "Fitter C" includes SRD-5M "High Fix" radar, an ASP-5ND fire-control system, and comprehensive communications and IFF, circa 1977. Given the state of Iraqi Air Force communications, i.e., C^3 and IFF, it is unlikely that this kind of sophisticated equipment is operational on the Iraqi variant. See Bill Gunston, *Modern Soviet Air Force,* New York, ARCO, 1982, pp. 110–111, and Bussert, op. cit., pp. 137–138.

15. *Jane's Defence Weekly,* July 18, 1987, p. 70; IISS, *Military Balance, 1987–1988,* London, International Institute for Strategic Studies; Levran and Eytan, op. cit.

16. *Defense Electronics,* February 1981, p. 161.

17. Chant, op. cit., pp. 69–70.

18. Strength estimates based on various editions of the IISS, *Military Balance.*

19. Anthony H. Cordesman, "Policy Options and Regional Implications," *American-Arab Affairs,* no. 9, Summer 1984, p. 12.

20. Bill Gunston, *The Illustrated Encyclopedia of the World's Modern Military Aircraft,* New York, 1977, p. 27.

21. Nick Cook, "Iraq-Iran: The Air War," *International Defense Review,* November 11, 1984, p. 1605; and Jim Bussert, "Iran-Iraq War Turns Strategic," pp. 143–145.

22. Anthony H. Cordesman, *The Iran-Iraq War: 1984–1986,* Los Angeles, CA, Analytical Assessments Center, May 1986.

23. *Jane's Defence Weekly,* January 21, 1989, p. 81.

24. Anthony H. Cordesman, "The Iran-Iraq War: Attrition Now, Chaos Later," *Armed Forces Journal International,* May 1983, p. 41.

25. Anthony H. Cordesman, "Lessons: Part Two," *Chicago Tribune,* November 15, 1985, p. 40.

26. Ibid.

27. Jeffrey Ullrich, "Jordan May Give Iraqis Military Aid," *Washington Post,* October 13, 1980, p. A-3.

28. See Anthony R. Tucker, "The Gulf Air War," pp. 270–271.

29. Colonel William O. Staudenmaier, *A Strategic Analysis of the Gulf War*, December 9, 1981, p. 23.

30. Cordesman, "Lessons: Part Two"; *Economist*, November 2, 1985, p. 36.

31. See "Saudis Down Two Iranian Jets," *Los Angeles Times*, June 5, 1984, p. 1. However, subsequent reports corrected the number of kills to one.

32. Readers lacking in experience with oil export and Iraqi sortie claims should be very careful about taking such figures too seriously. These claims to some extent represent worst-case estimates of the effect of Iraqi attacks, and they ignore the fact that the oil glut and rapid declines in prices often did as much to influence demand for Iranian exports as Iraq's strikes did to influence the Iranian capability to export.

Other data on Iraqi and Iranian oil-export patterns during 1987 to 1988 also provide a very different picture of Iranian production levels at the end of the war. For example, the CIA and First Boston Corporation show the following data for export levels:

Iranian and Iraqi Average Monthly Oil Production in 1987 and 1988

Date	Iran	Iraq
1987		
May	2.6	1.9
June	2.5	2.0
July	2.5	2.0
August	2.7	2.2
September	2.1	2.3
October	2.4	2.5
November	2.2	2.6
December	2.2	2.6
1988		
January	2.0	2.4
February	1.9	2.5
March	2.0	2.5
April	2.2	2.7
May	2.2	2.6
June	2.2	2.7
July	2.3	2.8
August	2.3	2.6
September	2.4	2.7
October	2.4	2.7
November	2.5	2.7
OPEC January 1, 1989, Quota	2.64	—

(SOURCE: First Boston Corporation, *Petroleum Monitor*, October 1988, vol. 7, no. 10, pp. 16–17, and January 1989, vol. 8, no. 1, pp. 16–17.

33. Fred Hiatt, "Iran Sends Jets Over U.S. Ships in the Gulf," *Washington Post*, December 30, 1983, p. 420.

34. *Jane's Defence Weekly*, October 29, 1988, p. 1045.

35. For one example, see Baghdad Voice of the Masses, "Armed Forces

Command Communique No. 772," *FBIS (Middle East-North Africa)*, May 26, 1982, p. E-1; and Baghdad INA, "Army Battles Iranians to Control Khorramshahr," *FBIS (Middle East-North Africa)*, May 25, 1982, p. E-1.

36. Cook, op. cit., p. 1606.

37. Group Captain Bolton, "Military Lessons of the Iran-Iraq Conflict," *Minutes of the RUSI Conference on the Gulf War*, February 1986.

38. *The World's Missile Systems, Seventh Edition*, General Dynamics, Pomona Division, April 1982, pp. 65–66.

39. Scott James, "Does Western Technology Offset Larger Soviet Numbers?" *Defense Electronics*, February 1981.

40. Steven Zaloga, "Ballistic Missiles in the Third World," *International Defense Review*, 11/88, pp. 1423–1437.

41. "U.S. Reasserts Aim to Keep Oil Flowing from Gulf," *Washington Times*, February 22, 1984, p. A-1.

42. "Iraqis Fire Missiles on Iranian Cities," *Chicago Tribune*, February 25, 1984, p. 20.

43. The following details of the Iranian missile program are taken from W. Seth Carus and Joseph S. Bermudez, "Iran's Growing Missile Forces," *Jane's Defence Weekly*, July 23, 1988, pp. 126–131.

44. Iran publicly displayed the Oghab at a military show in Libreville in 1989. It is 230 mm in diameter, 4,820 mm long, and weighs 320 kilograms, with a 70-kilogram warhead. Iran also displayed another rocket called the Nazeat, which is 355 mm in diameter, 5,900 mm long, weighs 950 kilograms, and has a 180-kilogram warhead. *Jane's Defence Weekly*, February 11, 1989, p. 219.

45. *Jane's Defence Weekly*, June 20, 1987, p. 1289.

46. One source claims Iran fired 231 Scuds in 1988. This total seems much too high. See Steven Zaloga, op. cit.

47. Iraq was believed to have only about 50 Scud missiles before it began this series of attacks. On March 8, 1988, Rafsanjani claimed Iran had evidence that the missiles were standard Scud Bs which used reduced warhead weight. *Washington Times*, March 1, 1988, p. 3, and *Washington Post*, March 9, 1988, p. A-19; *Economist*, March 5, 1988, p. 44; *New York Times*, March 2, 1988, p. A-1, March 4, 1988, p. A-8, March 12, 1988, p. A-3, May 1, 1988, p. 18; *Washington Post*, March 2, 1988, p. A-16; *Baltimore Sun*, March 6, 1988, p. 2-A.

48. *Economist*, March 5, 1988, p. 44; *New York Times*, March 2, 1988, p. A-1, March 4, 1988, p. A-8, March 12, 1988, p. A-3, May 1, 1988, p. 18; *Washington Post*, March 2, 1988, p. A-16; *Baltimore Sun*, March 6, 1988, p. 2-A.

49. The USSR claimed that none of the Scuds it sold to Iraq had the range to reach Teheran. Iran claims to have recovered parts showing the Scuds used in the attacks were of recent Soviet manufacture. Some sources claim that Egypt, Italy, France, the Federal Republic of Germany (FRG), PRC, and/or USSR helped the Iraqis add boosters or modify the missiles to use more of their fuel and/or a smaller warhead.

50. Baghdad has 23 percent of Iraq's population and is only 80 miles from the border. Tehran is about 290 miles from the front lines.

51. Steven Zaloga provides the following estimate of missile firings during the course of the war:

| Year | Iraqi Firings | | Iranian Firings | |
	FROG-7	Scud	Oghab	Scud
1980	10	—	—	—
1981	54	—	—	—
1982	1	3	—	—
1983	—	33	—	—
1984	2	25	—	—
1985	—	82	14	—
1986	—	—	8	18
1987	—	25	18	61
1988	—	193	231	104
Total	67	361	271	174

(SOURCE: Adapted from Zaloga, op. cit. Zaloga seems to have inverted the Iranian Scud and Oghab columns in his original article.

52. Based on discussions with Iranians present in the city at the time, Australian intelligence officers, and Robin Wright.

53. The warhead may have been as small as 130 kilograms. Iraq announced in April 1988, however, that it had an improved missile called the al-Abbas with a maximum range of 850 kilometers and with a payload of 500–1,000 kilograms at a range of 650 kilometers. *Jane's Defence Weekly*, October 29, 1988, p. 1045.

54. No missiles with chemical warheads were launched during the conflict, although Iraq did make extensive use of bombs, canisters, mortars, and 130-mm and 155-mm artillery shells (UN working paper).

55. W. Seth Carus, "Chemical Weapons in the Middle East," *Policy Focus*, no. 9, Washington Institute for Near East Policy, December 1988, p. 7.

56. Some 60 pounds of mustard gas were required in World War I per casualty. Only 2 percent of the casualties died.

57. Most biological agents require extremely demanding dispersal conditions in terms of altitude, light and temperature conditions, wind patterns, and dispersal into some form of reentry. This requires the ability to deliver hundreds of liters of biological agents, specialized bombs, and extremely specialized missile warheads to allow proper delivery at the extreme velocities involved.

58. General references for this section include "Chemical and Biological Warfare," Hearing before the Committee on Foreign Relations, U.S. Senate, 91st Congress, April 30, 1969; Department of Political and Security Council Affairs, *Chemical and Bacteriological (Biological) Weapons and the Effects of Their Possible Use*, Report of the Secretary General, United Nations, New York, 1969; unpublished testimony of W. Seth Carus before the Committee on Governmental Affairs, U.S. Senate, February 9, 1989; W. Seth Carus, op. cit.; unpublished testimony of Mr. David Goldberg, Foreign Science and Technology Center, U.S. Army Intelligence Agency, before the Committee on Governmental Affairs, U.S. Senate, February 9, 1989; unpublished testimony of Dr. Barry J. Erlick, Senior Biological Warfare Analyst, U.S. Army, before the Committee on Governmental Affairs, U.S. Senate, February 9, 1989; unpublished testimony of Dr. Robert Mullen Cook-Deegan, Physicians for Human Rights, before the Committee on Governmental Affairs, U.S. Senate, February 9, 1989; Elisa D. Harris, "Chemical Weapons Proliferation in the

Developing World," *RUSI and Brassey's Defense Yearbook, 1989,* London, 1988, pp. 67–88; and "Winds of Death: Iraq's Use of Poison Gas Against Its Kurdish Population," Report of a Medical Mission to Turkish Kurdistan by Physicians for Human Rights, February 1989.

59. Based upon discussions with Israeli sources in January 1989.

60. Anthony H. Cordesman visited the area several times during this period. Reports of such use were provided by both Iranian and Israeli officials and were confirmed by a British expert.

61. Peter Dunn, "The Chemical War: Journey to Iran," *NBC Defense & Technology International,* pp. 28–37, and "Iran Keeps Chemical Options Open," pp. 12–14.

62. For a good discussion of the early Iraqi effort to acquire chemical weapons, see David Ignatius, "Iraq's 13-year Search for Deadly Chemicals," *Washington Post,* Outlook section, September 25, 1988.

63. The building block at the base of the organophosphorus industry is elemental phosphorus. Thus, at a minimum, a supply of phosphorus would be needed to make nerve agents such as the G agents, Tabun (GA), Sarin (GB), and Soman (GD), and the V agents, such as VX and Edemo (VM).

There is a very wide range of possible chemical precursors to the production of gas warfare. Ones which may have been sent to Iran and Iraq include Thiodiglycol and chloroethanol (mustard gas); dimethalmine, dimethalmine hydrochloride, and phosphorus oxychloride (Tabun or GA nerve gas); and dimethyl methylphosphonate, difluoro or methylphosphony, and potassium flouride (Sarin or GB nerve gas). For a good description of the technology of proliferation see Lois R. Ember, "Worldwide Spread of Chemical Arms Receiving Increased Attention," *C&EN,* April 14, 1988, pp. 8–16.

64. All are useful in the production of Tabun nerve gas. The corrosion resistant reactors, pipes, and pumps needed for processing these pesticides can be rapidly converted to nerve gas production. See Ignatius, op. cit.

65. Tabun and the more lethal Sarin nerve gases were discovered in Germany in 1936 as part of an effort to develop more advanced pesticides. They could not be used for this purpose because they proved to be as effective in killing people as insects. The Nazis produced some 12,000 tons of nerve gas in World War II but never used it because they believed that Britain and the U.S. were also aware of the technology. See John J. Fialka, "Fighting Dirty," *Wall Street Journal,* September 16, 1988, p. 1.

66. Based on work by Leonard Spector of the Carnegie Endowment for International Peace and from other working material.

67. *Christian Science Monitor,* December 12, 1988; and BBC Panorama, 1986.

68. *Christian Science Monitor,* April 13, 1988, p. 32.

69. Some thirteen West German firms are now under investigation by the West German government.

70. This is a small amount. About 15–20 tons of a nerve agent like Tabun are needed to cover a single square kilometer.

71. Fialka, op. cit.

72. Mustard gas can be made by three easy routes. The first is the reaction

of vinyl chloride (readily available or which can be made from ethylene or acetylene) and hydrogen sulfide. The second is the reaction of ethylene and sulfur monochloride. The third is reacting thiodiglycol with hydrogen chloride after making the thiodiglycol from ethylene oxide (from ethylene) and hydrogen sulfide. The sulfur and ethylene feedstocks can be drawn from a typical refinery, and hydrogen chloride or chlorine gas are simple to make from a source of chlorine, such as salt, seawater, or produced brines from petroleum operations.

73. Phillips has since claimed that it did not react to the first order for thiodiglycol because such orders were routine. A number of experts disagree, however, and feel that only limited amounts could have credibly been assumed to be used in printing, textiles, and automotive manufacturing. Fialka, op. cit.

74. Ibid.

75 *Jane's Defence Weekly*, January 9, 1988, p. 3; February 27, 1988, p. 336.

76. Unpublished "Statement of the Honorable William H. Webster, Director, Central Intelligence Agency, Before the Committee on Governmental Affairs, Hearings on Global Spread of Chemical and Biological Weapons," February 9, 1989.

77. Dunn, "The Chemical War: Journey to Iran," pp. 28–37, and Dunn, "Iran Keeps Chemical Options Open," pp. 12–14, *Jane's Defence Weekly*, January 9, 1988, p. 3, February 27, 1988, p. 336.

78. Seth Carus, *The Genie Unleashed: Iraq's Chemical and Biological Weapons Production*, Washington, D.C., Washington Institute Policy Papers, no. 14, 1989, p. 11.

79. "Iraq's Scare Tactic," *Newsweek*, August 2, 1982; *Washington Post*, April 5, 1988, p. A-1.

80. Ibid.; Carus, *The Genie Unleashed*, pp. 7–9.

81. Dunn, "The Chemical War: Journey to Iran," pp. 28–37, and Dunn, "Iran Keeps Chemical Options Open," pp. 12–14.

82. W. Seth Carus puts the production of Tabun and Sarin at 50 tons per year and of mustard gas at 720 tons per year. Carus, "Chemical Weapons in the Middle East," p. 4. Also see "Iraq's Scare Tactic"; *Washington Post*, April 5, 1988, p. A-1.

83. *Washington Times*, October 29, 1986, p. 9-A.

84. Ibid.

85. Iran was caught trying to buy 430 drums of thiodiglycol feedstock in April 1988 for a U.S. firm called Alcolac. *Baltimore Sun*, February 11, 1988, p. 6.

86. While rumors surfaced in November 1986 that Iran had bought nerve gas bombs and warheads from Libya—which had obtained such weapons from the USSR—these reports were almost certainly false. Iran does not seem to have used nerve gas at any time during the conflict.

87. *Washington Times*, October 29, 1986, p. 9-A.

88. Unpublished "Statement of the Honorable William H. Webster, Director, Central Intelligence Agency, Before the Committee on Governmental Affairs, Hearings on Global Spread of Chemical and Biological Weapons," February 9, 1989.

89. IRNA (English), October 19, 1988, as reported in FBIS, *Near East and South Asia*, October 19, 1988, pp. 55–56.

90. Such reports begin in the SIPRI yearbooks in 1982 and occur sporadically through the 1988 edition.

91. Loren Jenkins, "Iraqis Press Major Battle in Gulf War," *Washington Post*, November 17, 1980, p. 1, and *SIPRI Yearbook, 1985*, Philadelphia, Taylor and Francis, 1985, pp. 206–219. W. Andrew Terrill, "Chemical Weapons in the Gulf War," *Strategic Review*, Spring 1986, pp. 51–58.

92. "Iraq's Scare Tactic," *Newsweek*, August 2, 1982.

93. Jenkins, op. cit.; *SIPRI Yearbook, 1985*; Terrill, op. cit.

94. Shahram Chubin and Charles Tripp, *Iran and Iraq at War*, Boulder, Westview, 1988, p. 59; BBC, ME, April 14, 1983.

95. Jenkins, op. cit.; *SIPRI Yearbook, 1985*; Terrill, op. cit.

96. "In the Pipeline," *The Middle East*, December 1981, p. 72; "Iraqis Trained for Chemical Warfare," *Washington Post*, November 3, 1980, p. 313. The Iraqis may also have been favorably impressed by the effectiveness of tear gas in instilling panic in Iranian troops. An August 1984 report in *Newsweek* stated an entire Iranian division fled in panic when they were exposed to Iraqi tear gas. The Iranians had no idea what type of agent they were being exposed to and had no defenses against any kind of chemical agent.

97. "In the Pipeline," *The Middle East*, December, 1981; "Iraqis Trained for Chemical Warfare," p. 72; *Washington Post*, November 3, 1980.

98. Beginning in 1982, Iraqi agents bought extensive amounts of equipment from a West German manufacturer of equipment to make organophosphate pesticides. The manufacturer, located in Drereich, claims it had no way to know the Iraqis were buying extensive feedstock for nerve gas in other countries, including the U.S. There may now be five major chemical agent production plants in Iraq. See Gustav Anderson, "Analysis of Two Chemical Weapons Samples from the Iran-Iraq War," *NBC Defense and Technology International*, April 1986, pp. 62–66; Dunn, "The Chemical War: Journey to Iran," pp. 28–37; and Dunn, "Iran Keeps Chemical Options Open," pp. 12–14.

99. "Report of the Specialists Appointed to the Secretary General to Investigate the Allegations of the Islamic Republic of Iran Concerning the Use of Chemical Weapons, United Nations Security Council, Document S 16433, March 26, 1984. Also see the April 1986 edition of *NBC Defense & Technology International*.

100. Carus, "Chemical Weapons in the Middle East."

101. *Washington Times*, March 23, 1988, p. 1; *Toronto Globe and Mail*, March 24, 1988, p. 1; *Washington Post*, March 24, 1988, p. 1, and April 4, 1988, p. 24.

102. *Congressional Record*, U.S. Senate, September 9, 1988, p. S12135.

103. *Washington Times*, March 23, 1988, p. 1; *Toronto Globe and Mail*, March 24, 1988, p. 1; *Washington Post*, March 24, 1988, p. 1, and April 4, 1988, p. 24; *Wall Street Journal*, September 16, 1988, p. 1.

104. See Peter W. Galbraith and Christopher Van Hollen, Jr., "Chemical Weapons Use in Kurdistan: Iraq's Final Offensive," A Staff Report to the Senate Committee on Foreign Relations, September 21, 1988, and Physicians

for Human Rights, *Winds of Death: Iraq's Use of Poison Gas Against Its Kurdish Population*, February 1989.

105. Such reports begin in the SIPRI yearbooks in 1982 and occur sporadically through the 1988 edition.

106. It takes 15 to 25 kilograms to make one relatively simple nuclear weapon. More advanced weapons take substantially less.

107. Leonard S. Spector, *The New Nuclear Nations*, New York, Vintage, 1985, pp. 44–54.

108. James Bruce, "Iraq and Iran: Running the Nuclear Technology Race," *Jane's Defence Weekly*, December 5, 1988, p. 1307.

109. This analysis is based on the work of Leonard Spector of the Carnegie Endowment, and Steve Weissman and Herbert Krosney, *The Islamic Bomb*, New York, New York Times Books, 1981, pp. 94, 100, and 266–268; Jed C. Snyder, "The Road to Osiraq: Baghdad's Quest for the Bomb," *The Middle East Journal*, Autumn 1983; and Richard Burt, "U.S. Says Italy Sells Iraq Atomic Bomb Technology," *New York Times*, March 18, 1980, p. 1.

110. The bulk of this analysis is based on research by Leonard Spector of the Carnegie Endowment.

111. *Washington Times*, April 22, 1987, p. 6; *Economist*, Foreign Report, April 2, 1987, p. 7.

112. *Washington Post*, April 12, 1987, p. D-1; Bruce, op. cit.

113. Many of the details relating to Iraq and Iran are drawn from working papers provided by Leonard Spector of the Carnegie Endowment.

14

THE TANKER WAR AND THE LESSONS OF NAVAL COMBAT

The Tanker and Naval Wars

The Iran-Iraq War involved two complex forms of naval conflict: Iraq's attempts to weaken Iran by destroying its ability to use tankers to export oil and a U.S.-led Western naval presence in the Gulf that was intended to ensure the freedom of passage for tankers to Kuwait and the overall security of shipping to and from neutral Gulf countries. Both forms of conflict led to substantial escalation. Iran reacted to Iraq's tanker war by putting increasing military and political pressure on the southern Gulf states to halt their support of Iraq. The U.S. and Western European presence in the Gulf led to growing clashes with Iran that escalated steadily to the point where they were a major factor in Iran's decision to agree to a cease-fire.

The history of these two naval conflicts, and their overall impact on the war, has already been described in some detail. The naval fighting involved the use of a wide range of naval, air, missile, and mine warfare systems, however, and presents a number of interesting lessons regarding the use of these systems in naval warfare. It also provides important insights into the effect of strategic air attacks on naval shipping and the problems of conflict management and controlling escalation.

The key lessons and issues raised by the war may be summarized as follows.

- The tanker war was the most important aspect of the fighting at sea, but it never produced a major interruption in Iran's oil exports. Both for political and military reasons, Iraq never achieved the concentration of force necessary to severely reduce Iran's exports on a sustained basis and lacked the targeting assets and the ability to use sufficiently lethal weapons to achieve decisive results.

- Iran was able to create a tactical counterweight to Iraq's high-technology capability to strike at its tankers in the form of a relatively low-grade revolutionary force which was equipped largely with small boats and minecraft and which was able to strike at ships going to nations friendly to Iraq. The naval branch of the Revolutionary Guards was not successful largely because of U.S. intervention but illustrated that unconventional war can be a major naval threat.
- U.S. and other Western forces were largely successful in using power projection to help control and terminate the conflict in the Gulf. Nevertheless, they ran into serious problems in dealing with a number of major issues in low-level war. These ranged from serious problems in mine-warfare capability to problems in managing missile defense and the IFF problems inherent in dealing with a mix of friendly and hostile ships and aircraft operating in the same area.
- On a technical level, the experiences of the Iran-Iraq War were somewhat similar to those of the Falklands conflict in that they illustrated the need for more reliable and quick-reacting missile defenses and more emphasis on fire-fighting and damage control. They also indicated the need for mine-warfare capabilities suited for low-level conflict, for better identification of friend and foe systems, and for tailoring command-and-control systems and training to the special politico-military conditions inherent in a given low-level conflict.

Naval Operations and the Tanker War

The tanker war served as a primary catalyst in shaping the outcome of the Iran-Iraq War. It gave Iraq a means of striking at Iran at a time Iran was heavily on the offensive and Iraq had no other means of putting pressure on Iran. The resulting Iranian reaction was also a key factor leading the U.S. and its European allies to intervene in the Gulf. The tanker war, however, only acquired real importance in the fourth year of the war. While both sides struck at ships at the start of the conflict, the escalation to large-scale strikes on third country shipping began in 1984. After that time, the tanker war became a war where Iraq repeatedly attempted to use air strikes against tankers and oil facilities to force Iran to a settlement. Iran, in turn, attempted to respond with air and naval strikes on neutral ships and tankers moving to countries supporting Iraq. As a result, the tanker war involved the West in a growing series of naval encounters.

The history of this conflict has already been described in detail. It is also important to stress that most of the lessons from this aspect of the war were lessons in escalation and conflict management, rather than ones in tactics and technology. Nevertheless, several aspects of the tanker war merit special treatment.

The Beginning and Initial Impact of the Tanker War: 1980–1984

The beginnings of the tanker war provided some important insights into the process of escalation that helped shape the naval fighting. After 1985, the tanker war became so integrated into the overall structure of conflict in the Gulf that it is impossible to separate the naval fighting from the overall patterns in the fighting. The history of the tanker war from 1980 to 1984 is different, however, and provides an interesting example of how a seemingly minor aspect of a Third World conflict can suddenly change its strategic impact and meaning for the West.

The early history of the tanker war is summarized in Table 14.1. It is interesting to note that although Iraq experienced its most critical problems in terms of oil exports during the period from 1980-1984, it was comparatively slow to turn to the war at sea as a means of inflicting similar damage to Iran. This is partly explainable by the fact the Iranian Navy kept the Iraqi Navy in port during virtually all of the war and totally dominated the Gulf. It is also partly explainable by the difficulties Iraq faced in terms of the range and munitions capability of its fighter bombers and its reluctance to commit aircraft to missions where it ran a high risk of loss until Iran lost most of its air-defense capabilities.

The practical problem that Iraq had to solve was to find a way to use aircraft to strike deep into Iranian waters with a high degree of survivability. Iran's sea control denied Iraq other options, and it took some years before Iraq could acquire the mix of fighter bombers and air-to-ship missiles it felt it needed. It is also evident from Table 14.1 that even the acquisition of Exocet was not a substitute for sea control. While Iraq made extensive use of advanced technology weapons like the Exocet air-to-surface missile, Iran also scored a high hit rate per sortie using unguided air-to-air rockets.

To the extent that the lessons of the early phases of the tanker war can be separated from the later phases of the conflict, they may be summarized as follows.

- The tanker war escalated so slowly in large part because Iraq did not have a fully modern long-range fighter bomber with the kind of sensors and air-to-surface munitions available in an aircraft

TABLE 14.1 The Tanker War: A Partial Chronology

1980

7 October	Three foreign freighters were sunk and two others damaged by Iranian shells in the Iranian port of Khorramshahr during an exchange of fire with attacking Iraqi forces. At least 20 crewman killed.

1981

21 May	Iraqi aircraft slightly damage Panamanian bulk carrier *Louise I* outside northern Iranian port of Bandar-e-Khomeini.
19 October	Iraqi missile damaged Liberian bulk carrier *Al Tajdar* near Bandar-e-Khomeini. The Panamanian bulk carrier *Moira* was bombed and seriously damaged. Both were later repaired.
25 October	Iraqi missiles set the Indian bulk carrier *Rashi Vish Wamitra* on fire near Bandar-e-Khomeini, causing heavy damage.

1982

11 January	Two Iraqi missiles set fire to the Panamanian freighter *Success*, which was abandoned. Greek bulk carrier *Anabella* was damaged by a mine near Bandar-e-Khomeini.
14 February	The 16,000-ton Iranian tanker *Mokran* was seriously damaged by mines laid by the Iraqis near the northern Iranian port of Bandar Mahshahr.
30 May	The Turkish tanker *Atlas* was seriously damaged during an Iraqi bomb attack on Kharg Island.
6 June	The Greek 26,000-ton bulk carrier *Good Luck* was damaged by Iraqi missiles off Bandar-e-Khomeini. The crewmen were killed.
9 August	Iraqi missiles sank the 15,000-ton Greek freighter *Lition Bride* near Bandar-e-Khomeini and damaged the 16,000-ton South Korean bulk carrier *Sanbow Banner* beyond repair. Eight crewmen were missing and one was killed aboard *Sanbow Banner*.
4 September	The Turkish bulk carrier *Mar Transporter* was damaged beyond repair by a direct Iraqi missile hit on its engine room in waters near Bandar-e-Khomeini. It was sailing in a ten-ship convoy escorted by Iranian naval vessels.
11 September	The Greek freighter *Evangelia S.* struck an Iraqi mine at the entrance to Bandar-e-Khomeini harbor. It was grounded and abandoned.

(continues)

TABLE 14.1 *(continued)*

---

21 November	The Indian bulk carrier *Archana* was slightly damaged by an Iraqi missile attack near Iranian port of Bushehr.
18 December	Iraqi missiles set fire to the Greek tanker *Scapmount*. It was abandoned in the channel at Bandar-e-Khomeini.

1983

2 January	Iraqi aircraft set fire to Singapore freighter *Eastern* and the *Orient Horizon* of Liberia while in convoy from Bandar-e-Khomeini, forcing them to run aground.
15 May	Panamanian oil tanker *Pan Oceanic Sane* was set ablaze by an Iraqi missile attack and was abandoned in Bandar-e-Khomeini channel.
25 May	Iraqi aircraft slightly damaged the Panamanian supply ship *Seatrans-21*.
31 May	The Indian bulk carrier *Ati Priti* was seriously damaged by Iraqi missiles near Bandar-e-Khomeini.
31 October	The Greek freighter *Avra* was set ablaze by Iraqi missiles near Bandar-e-Khomeini as it sailed in a convoy escorted by Iranian naval vessels.
21 November	An Iraqi missile sank the 13,000-ton Greek bulk carrier *Antigoni* near Bandar-e-Khomeini as she sailed in a convoy escorted by Iranian naval vessels.
8 December	The 16,000-ton Greek bulk carrier *Iapetos* was attacked by Iraqi missiles off Bandar-e-Khomeini and abandoned; it was later repaired.

1984

1 February	A convoy of four Cypriot freighters—*Breeze, Neptune, Skaros,* and *City of Rio*—were attacked by Iraqi aircraft near Bandar-e-Khomeini. The *Breeze* and *Skaros* were set afire by missiles and lost. The *City of Rio* struck a mine and was grounded. The *Neptune* was set ablaze but was not extensively damaged.
16 February	Iraqi missiles extensively damaged the Liberian freighter *Al Tariq* in the Iranian port of Bushehr.
1 March	The Indian bulk carrier *Apj Ankiba* was sunk by an Iraqi missile in an attack on a 15-ship convoy sailing between Bushehr and Bandar-e-Khomeini. The 19,000-ton British bulk carrier *Charming* was set ablaze and grounded after an Iraqi missile hit its superstructure. The Turkish freighter *Sema-G* was set ablaze and abandoned.

(continues)

TABLE 14.1 *(continued)*

27 March	In its first operational use by the Iraqi Air Force, a Super Etendard jet fighter fired an Exocet missile at the 85,000-ton Greek tanker *Filikon L.*, carrying 80,000 tons of crude oil from Kuwait, south of Kharg Island. The Iraqi pilot apparently assumed the tanker was carrying Iranian oil. The missile tore a gash in the hull, slightly damaging the starboard side of the bow, slop tank, and number 4 tank but failed to detonate. Two hundred tons of oil leaked out. U.S. experts later defused the missile.
29 March	The 16,000-ton Greek freighter *Iapetos* was set afire by an Iraqi missile and abandoned at the head of the Gulf.
3 April	Iranian shelling set fire to the Indian freighter *Varuna*.
18 April	An Iraqi missile slightly damaged the 52,000-ton Panamanian tanker *Robert Star* while sailing in ballast to Kharg Island.
25 April	The 357,000-ton Saudi tanker *Safina-Al-Arab*, carrying 340,000 tons of Iranian crude, was seriously damaged by an Iraqi missile south of Kharg Island. This missile blew a 240-square-foot hole in the starboard side, bending the hull plates inward and causing an explosion and fire in the number 11 starboard tank which spread to numbers 9 and 10. The fire raged for two days and burnt 10,000 tons of oil. The ship was declared a total loss.
27 April	Iraqi missiles slightly damaged the 179,000-ton Liberian freighter *Sea Eagle* near Bandar-e-Khomeini.
7 May	The 118,000-ton Saudi tanker *Al-Ahood*, loaded with 114,000 tons of Iranian crude, was set ablaze by an Iraqi missile near Kharg Island. The fire took five days to extinguish and burned 34,000 tons of oil. The missile struck the accommodation section near the engine room and caused extensive damage. One crewman was lost.
13 May	An Iraqi missile slightly damaged the 69,000-ton Iranian tanker *Tabriz*, fully loaded with Iranian oil, south of Kharg Island.
13 May	In the first reported attack by an Iranian aircraft on commercial shipping, the 80,000-ton Kuwaiti tanker *Umm al-Casbah*, carrying 77,000 tons of Kuwaiti oil, was slightly damaged by Iranian rockets south of Kuwait. After being observed by a spotter plane, an Iranian F-4 jet fighter dove and fired two rockets. Both hit the deck.
14 May	The 30,000-ton Kuwaiti tanker *Bahrah*, sailing in ballast to Kuwait, was damaged by Iranian aircraft. Two F-4s fired five rockets at close range. Two hit the starboard side, blowing a massive hole. One rocket hit numbers 4 and 5 wing tanks which subsequently caught fire. Two crewmen were injured before the fire was extinguished eight hours later. The ship continued to Kuwait.

(continues)

TABLE 14.1 *(continued)*

---

14 May	An Iraqi missile set fire to the 62,000-ton Panamanian tanker *Esperanza II* while sailing in ballast to Kharg Island. The engine room and accommodation section were burned out.
16 May	An Iranian rocket attack damaged the 215,000-ton Saudi tanker *Yanbu Pride*, carrying 120,000 tons of Saudi crude, within Saudi territorial waters near the port of Jubail. Of the five rockets fired by the two F-4s, two hit the vessel and caused fire and explosions. The fire started in the starboard hold, but was quickly extinguished. Prior to the firing, the F-4s circled the tanker for identification.
18 May	An Iraqi missile sank the 17,000-ton Panamanian bulk carrier *Fidelity* near the Iranian port of Bushehr.
24 May	Iraqi missiles narrowly missed the *Arizona*, a fully loaded 140,000-ton Panamanian tanker, south of Kharg Island.
24 May	Two Iranian F-4s damaged the 29,000-ton Liberian tanker *Chemical Venture*, sailing in ballast in Saudi waters, near the port of Jubail. Iranian rockets hit the vessel in the middle of the superstructure, causing a fire in the accommodation section and the bridge. The fire was extinguished but the wheelhouse was burned out. Ten crewmen were injured.
25 May	The 19,000-ton Liberian bulk carrier *Savoy Dean* was hit by an Iraqi missile in the Gulf.
3 June	The 153,000-ton Turkish tanker *Buyuk Hun*, sailing to ballast to Kharg Island, was damaged by an Iraqi missile 50 miles south of the island. The missile hit the accommodation section, killing three crewmen. The tanker was towed away by an Iranian tugboat.
7 June	An Iraqi mine blew a hole below the waterline of the Liberian freighter *Dashaki* near the Straits of Hormuz. The ship had dropped off cargo at Bandar Abbas and was heading for Saudi Arabia.
10 June	An Iranian F-4 attacked the 295,000-ton Kuwaiti tanker *Kazimah*, sailing in ballast east of Qatar. The plane dropped bombs which missed, then proceeded to hit with rockets. The damage was slight and no injuries occurred.
24 June	The 152,000-ton Greek tanker *Alexander the Great*, fully loaded with Iranian oil, was slightly damaged by an Iraqi missile at Kharg Island. The missile penetrated an oil tank but failed to explode.
27 June	The Swiss-owned, Liberian-registered 260,000-ton Kuwaiti tanker *Tiburon*, loaded with 250,000 tons of Iranian oil, was damaged by an Iraqi missile southeast of Kharg Island. The missile hit the engine room,

(continues)

TABLE 14.1 *(continued)*

---

27 June *(continued)*	and 100-foot flames spread to the accommodation section. Fire and subsequent explosions destroyed the entire superstructure and caused the funnel to collapse. Two days after the attack, the ship was wallowing with only three feet of hull above the water. Salvage tugboats saved the oil by extinguishing the fire before it reached the tanks. Eight crewmen were killed and three seriously injured. The tanker was towed to Bahrain.
1 July	The 6,200-ton South Korean cargo vessel *Wonju-Ho* was damaged by an Iraqi missile while on her way to Bandar-e-Khomeini. The 13,000-ton Greek freighter *Alexander-Dyo* was heavily damaged by an Iraqi missile during the same attack. Two crewmen were killed and four injured.
5 July	Iranian jets damaged the Japanese-owned, Liberian-registered supertanker *Primrose*. It was hit by two rockets but continued at full speed.
10 July	In an apparent case of mistaken identification, an Iranian F-4 attacked the 133,000-ton British tanker *British Renown* while sailing to pick up crude from the tanker *Tiburon*, which had been struck by an Iraqi missile on 27 June. Following the appearance of a spotter plane, an F-4 fired two rockets at the tanker. One bounced off the deck and another hit its oil-loading equipment, igniting a small fire which was quickly extinguished. The attack took place in international waters 70 miles northwest of Bahrain.
7 August	An Iraqi missile slightly damaged the 123,000-ton Greek tanker *Friendship L.*, fully loaded with Iranian oil, 30 miles south of Kharg Island. The missile pierced an oil tank and caused a minor fire, which spread to the engine room and accommodation section but was quickly extinguished.
15 August	An Iranian jet fired two rockets at the 89,000-ton Pakistani tanker *Johar*, but missed. The tanker was attacked while sailing to Saudi Arabia to load oil.
18 August	The 47,000-ton Panamanian tanker *Endeavor* was attacked by an Iranian jet 100 miles east of Bahrain with a full load of Kuwaiti oil. One rocket struck starboard side, starting a small fire on the deck and in the main tank, but was brought under control. The tanker continued on toward Dubai.
24 August	The 53,000-ton Cypriot tanker *Amethyst*, carrying 50,000 tons of Iranian crude, was damaged by an Iraqi missile south of Kharg Island. It was saved from sinking by tugboats, which brought the blaze under control. The fire spread from the engine room to the accommodation section and some oil tanks. One crewman was lost.

(continues)

TABLE 14.1 *(continued)*

27 August	The 21,000-ton Panamanian tanker *Cleo-1* was hit by an Iranian rocket 70 miles northeast of Qatar while on its way to Ras Tanura to load oil. Proceeded to Dubai.
11 September	The fully loaded, Liberian-registered, Norwegian-owned 251,000-ton tanker *St. Tobias* was slightly damaged by an Iraqi Exocet, 50 miles south of Kharg Island. The missile blew a 6-foot hole on the ship's starboard and started a fire that was quickly extinguished. The oil cargo remained intact, and the tanker continued to Abu Dhabi under its own power.
12 September	The 500-ton German supply ship *Seatrans 21*, which had been slightly damaged on 25 May, was sunk by an Iraqi missile 50 miles south of Kharg Island.
16 September	The Greek-owned, Liberian-registered tanker *Medheron*, 122,000 tons, was struck by Iranian rockets while on its way to Ras Tanura. The rockets were fired at close range following the appearance of a spotter plane. There was serious damage—the bridge and 30 percent of the crew quarters were destroyed, and three crewmen were injured. The incident occurred in the central Gulf, and the ship sailed to Bahrain for repairs. The 127,000-ton South Korean tanker *Royal Colombo* was hit by Iranian planes while on its way to Ras Tanura. Rockets ripped through the engine room and injured three crewmen. Damage was slight and the tanker proceeded to load oil at the Saudi terminal.
8 October	The Liberian-registered 258,000-ton tanker *World Knight* was struck by an Iraqi missile southwest of Kharg Island. Damage was heavy. The missile wrecked the engine room and set fire to the crew quarters. Seven crewmen were killed and five badly injured. Tanker was on its way to Kharg Island.
11 October	The Indian 21,000-ton tanker *Jag Pari* was struck by Iranian planes while on its way to Kuwait. Ship suffered minor damage and one crewman was wounded. Proceeded to Bahrain.
12 October	Fully loaded liquified Panamanian gas tanker *Gaz Fountain*, 24,000 tons, was damaged by three rockets fired from Iranian aircraft in the central Gulf after loading nearly 20,000 tons of pressurized propane and butane gas at Ras Tanura. The crew abandoned the ship; it was declared a total loss.
15 October	The fully loaded Iranian 219,000-ton tanker *Sivand* was hit by Iraqi missiles and set afire after leaving the Kharg Island oil terminal.
19 October	In southern Gulf, Iranian F-4 jet fighter fired rockets into a Panamanian-registered diving support ship, the 1,538-ton *Pacific Prospector*, east of Bahrain, setting it ablaze and killing two people.

(continues)

TABLE 14.1 *(continued)*

---

3 December
: The 386,000-ton Cypriot tanker *Minotaur* was damaged by an Iraqi missile while on its way to the Kharg Island oil terminal. The engine room was set ablaze, but the fire was under control five hours after the hit.

8 December
: An Iranian F-4 jet fighter rocketed a Kuwaiti supply boat in neutral waters off the exclusion zone imposed by Iraq around Kharg Island.

9 December
: An Iraqi warplane fired an Exocet missile at the Bahamian-registered, 163,000-ton tanker *B. T. Investor*, on the way to the Kharg Island oil terminal. The missile punched a hole in a port tank, just above the waterline. It failed to ignite a fire and caused negligible damage. No crewmen were hurt.

15 December
: The 241,000-ton Greek tanker *Ninemia* was heavily damaged by two Iraqi missiles while on its way to Kharg Island. The first missile set the tanker's engine room afire, killing two crewmen.

17 December
: The 21,000-ton Greek cargo ship *Aegis Cosmic* was hit in a port side cargo hold, apparently by an Iraqi missile, 85 miles north of Bahrain. The vessel was only slightly damaged. Crew suffered no casualties. Ship continued journey.

21 December
: The 53,000-ton Liberian-registered tanker *Magnolia* was hit by an Iraqi missile 31 miles south of Kharg Island, and two crewman were killed. The Norwegian supertanker *Thorshavet*, loaded with 230,000 tons of Iranian oil, was heavily damaged by an Iraqi missile during the same attack. Twenty-six crewmen abandoned ship.

25 December
: The fully loaded, 277,000-ton Indian tanker *Kanchenjunga* was hit by Iranian planes, setting fire to the vessel's bridge and control room and wounding crewmen. The fire was brought under control within a few hours. The rocket attack was carried out 70 miles northeast of Qatar after the tanker had taken on a full load of crude oil at Saudi Arabia's Ras Tanura terminal and was heading to India. The ship headed instead for Dubai for repairs.

26 December
: The 239,000-ton Spanish supertanker *Aragon* was damaged by two rockets fired from Iranian warplanes. The tanker, which was on its way to Ras Tanura to pick up a load of Saudi crude destined for Spain, continued the journey.

SOURCES: Adapted from Dr. Raphael Danziger, "The Gulf Tanker War," *Proceedings*, vol. III/5/987, May 1985, pp. 160–175, and Nigel Line, "Merchantmen in the Gulf Front Line," *Jane's Naval Review*, 1985, pp. 55–64.

like the Su-24, Tornado, and F-15E. Iraq experienced some of its initial problems in carrying out such strikes and in hitting ships near Kharg or further east because its nearest secure air base was at Nasiriya, about 150 miles northwest of the Gulf and 300 miles from Kharg Island. Iraq initially could only fire anti-ship missiles from Super Frelon helicopters with a maximum combat radius well under 200 miles. The five Super Etendards Iraq obtained in November 1983 had a maximum combat radius of well over 200 miles but still had range problems. Only the extended range Mirage F-1s Iraq began to receive in 1985 provided a combat radius of over 300 miles. Iraq then had to overcome its fear of combat losses, lack of a targeting system with long range and endurance, and lack of operational experience. The key lesson Iraq learned was the need for long-range target acquisition and attack capability, a lesson similar to the one learned by the Argentine Air Force in the Falklands.[1]

- Iraq asked for the loan for the Super Etendards as early as February 1983 and began immediate training in France. It took delivery on the planes in November 1983. Nevertheless, it could not make them operational until six months later. Iraq then seems to have lost at least one of the five Etendards to maintenance problems and pilot error. This again illustrates the problem developing nations face in rapidly absorbing purchases of advanced arms.

- The fighter radars on the Super Etendard did not allow the pilot to properly characterize targets. This led the Iraqis to waste missiles on peripheral targets where overflights or maritime reconnaissance aircraft would have led to better targeting. Iraq could not solve this problem with its Mirage F-1s, and it indicates a need for either some form of modern naval reconnaissance aircraft or for a "smart" radar and avionics on the fighters used to deliver air-to-ship missiles that can do far more to characterize the nature of naval targets.

- The Iraqis did use direct air strikes and air-dropped mines from their Mirage F-1s and MiG-23BMs early in the tanker war, but rarely hit moored ships with bombs and could not predict the targets with mines or ensure high lethality. They seem to have avoided direct rocket attacks by fighters for vulnerability and/or political reasons. There are few confirmed cases of Iraqi fighters striking at moving ships with rockets or bombs, although both the Mirage F-1 and MiG-23BM should be relatively effective against such targets with such ordnance. This is in sharp contrast to the U.S. ability to sink Iranian ships in 1988, using A-6s with laser-guided bombs. The importance of air ordnance that can cheaply and effectively kill commercial vessels is obvious.[2]

- Some reports claim that the Exocets launched through 1984 scored a very high ratio of hits: 52 out of the 53 missiles hit their targets, and only 2 out of 53 clearly failed to explode. Other sources indicate that the Exocets have experienced a number of detonation problems, similar to those fired in the Falklands, although it is difficult to tell whether the missiles' proximity and/or delay fuses failed or Iraqi arming and service crews should be blamed. This illustrates another lesson of war: the acute difficulty in getting reliable data on the actual performance of individual weapons systems.

- The Exocets and other small missiles generally failed to "kill" large merchant ships. They did, however, significant damage to 11 out of 17 tankers hit in 1984, which displaced over 50,000 tons, and slightly damaged 6. The Exocets were more effective against smaller vessels and against more complex or automated ships (the automated *Safina al-Arab* had to be written off because her machinery was too sophisticated to repair) and against ships where the hit happened to trigger a fire. Seven of the 33 small to medium-sized vessels were sunk, 19 were heavily damaged, and 7 received only slight damage.[3]

- Iraq was slow to turn to bombers using air-to-ship missiles. It waited until 1987 and then seems to have used the Chinese Silkworm. This illustrates the problem of predicting intentions rather than analyzing capability. Some reports indicate the Egyptians sold and delivered eight Badger-A and six Badger-G bombers to Iraq in 1982. Both types of aircraft had a free-fall bomb capability, but the Badger-G also had an air-to-surface missile launch capability. This capability was particularly important because there were rumors that AS-4 Kelt liquid-fueled missiles were included in the transaction and that Iraq sought to purchase AS-6s from the USSR. Later reports indicated that Iraq obtained AS-4s from the USSR or that it obtained air-launched Silkworm missiles from the PRC. What is clear is that Iraq was able to launch such missiles by 1987.

  The capabilities of these missiles are described in Table 14.2. The key systems include (a) the AS-2 Kipper, an obsolete Soviet anti-shipping missile; (b) the AS-4, a stand-off missile which is carried by Soviet Tu-22 Blinder bombers and could be used by Iraq's Tu-16s or Tu-22s; and (c) the AS-6 Kingfish, a precision-guided Mach 3 missile which has not been widely exported.

- While Iran never actually used suicide aircraft, there were

TABLE 14.2 Air-to-Ship Missiles Affecting the Gulf Conflict

Type	Exocet AM.39	Harpoon AGM-84A	Maverick AGM-65B/C	AS-2 Kipper	AS-4 Kitchen	AS-5 Kelt	AS-6 Kingfish	Sea Killer
■ Make	French	U.S.	U.S.	USSR	USSR	USSR	USSR	Italy
■ Launch weight (Kg)	655	526	210	4,500	5,900	300	5,000	300
■ Warhead weight (Kg)	365	227	37.6	1,000	1,000	1,000	1,000	70
■ Warhead type	Serat/ Hexolite Block	NWC	Shaped/ Blast Frag.	HE/N	HE/N	HE/N	HE/N	HE
■ Range (Km)								
•High atl. launch	70	92+	40	350	460	250	560	NA
•Low atl. launch	50	60	16	200	200+	180	250	6-25
•Launch w/ remote TA	—	92+	—	—	400+	—	500+	—
■ Guidance	a	a	TV/ Optical Homing	b	c	d	e	f
■ Flight profile	Dives to Skim	Dives to Skim	Optical to Target	Med. Alt. & Final Skim	Med. to Low Alt. & Skim	Med. to Low Alt.	Skim or Med. Alt. & Dive	Sea Skim
■ Fusing	Prox & Delay	Impact /Delay & Prox	Impact/ Prox.	Prox.	?	Prox.	Prox.	Contact & Prox.
■ Speed (Mach)								
•High alt.	0.85	1.2	1.2	1.2	3.5	1.2	3	NA
•Low alt.	0.7	0.75	1+	0.7	0.95+	0.85-0.95	0.95	0.9
■ Typical launch aircraft	Super Frelon/ Super Etendard/ Mirage F-1	P-3C/ F-15CD MSIP	F-5EII F-16	Tu-16 F-4F	Tu-22/ Tu-16	Tu-16 B/G	Tu-16 G/ Tu-22	Heli-copter

[a]Radar programmed with inertial mid-course correction, X-band radar terminal homing for Exocet, and advanced active radar homing for Harpoon.
[b]Simple autopilot midcourse correction with SARH.
[c]Inertial with midcourse correction and unknown homing system.
[d]AEM or SARH and IR with autopilot and midcourse correction.
[e]SARH/IR and ARM with autopilot and midcourse correction.
[f]Radar beam riding with radar altimeter, plus command if required. Backup optical guidance.

SOURCE: Adapted from General Dynamics, The World's Missile Systems, 7th ed., 1982; and various editions of Jane's Weapons Systems and Soviet Military Power, 1985.

recurrent unconfirmed reports of Iranian training efforts to use specially armed F-5s or F-7s in suicide attacks on warships. The chronology of the early days of the tanker war indicates that such attacks might have been a quite effective use of technology in a narrow cockpit, like the Straits of Hormuz or the Gulf, where ships normally have only 15 to 20 km of low altitude warning (less than five minutes flight time) because of terrain masking. Such attacks would now risk major U.S. reprisals, however, and could be detected by E-2C and E-3A aircraft.[4]

The Final Impact of the Tanker War: 1984–1988

Table 14.3 summarizes the overall impact of the tanker war from 1981–1988. It is clear from these data that Iraq stepped up its attacks as Iran shifted to a tanker shuttle. It is also clear that Iran stepped up its attacks as it began to use the Seakiller, naval Guards, and Silkworm. It is interesting to note, however, that in the four years of war that took place after 1984, the time when the tanker war first reached serious intensity, and the cease-fire in 1988, there was remarkably little decisive combat.

This is easy to understand in the case of Iran. There were no Iraqi targets, and when it put too much pressure on ships going to neutral ports, the West intervened. While Iran might have dominated the tanker war by using low-technology small craft and light weapons against ships going to nations friendly to Iraq and by forcing these nations to pressure Iraq to halt its strikes on tankers, the West never gave Iran the opportunity to find out.

What is harder to understand is why Iraq never committed enough aircraft to achieve decisive military results. Ships continued to sail to and from Iran and oil continued to be exported. Although Iran was forced into an expensive tanker shuttle between Kharg Island and transshipment points in the lower Gulf, it was always able to continue exporting oil.

Iraq's failure to achieve decisive results has a number of possible explanations. One is that Iraq was unable to achieve decisive results because it lacked the combination of maritime patrol aircraft or other sensors necessary to find its targets and long-range attack aircraft with munitions powerful enough to kill large commercial ships. Another explanation is that Iraq was forced to act with considerable political restraint and had to to conserve its military assets.

On a purely technical basis, Iraq's main problem seems to have been target acquisition, although it is surprising that it could not cover the waters around Kharg Island more effectively. On a political level, Iraq may have been worried about provoking Iran into massive new

TABLE 14.3 Patterns of Attacks in the Tanker War: 1981–1988

	Targets in the Tanker War		
Year/Country	By Iran	By Iraq	Total

Total Attacks by Source (Including Mines)

1981	0	5	5
1982	0	22	22
1983	0	16	16
1984	53	18	71
1985	33	14	47
1986	66	45	111
1987	91	88	179
1988	39	—	—

Target by National Flag of Ship Involved

Australia	0	1	1
Bahamas	1	2	3
Belgium	1	0	1
China	1	0	1
Cyprus	9	33	43
FRG	1	4	5
France	5	0	5
Greece	10	22	32
India	4	4	8
Iran	0	48	48
Italy	1	1	2
Japan	9	0	9
Kuwait	11	0	11
Liberia	24	36	60
Malta	1	11	13
Netherlands	0	2	2
North Korea	0	1	1
Norway	4	1	5
Pakistan	2	0	2
Panama	18	28	46
Philippines	3	0	3
Qatar	2	1	3
Saudi Arabia	9	2	11
Singapore	1	5	6
South Korea	3	3	6
Spain	3	0	3
Sri Lanka	1	0	1
Turkey	2	8	10

(continues)

TABLE 14.3 *(continued)*

Country	Targets in the Tanker War		
	By Iran	By Iraq	Total
UAE	1	0	1
U.S.	1	0	1
USSR	2	0	2
Yugoslavia	1	0	1
Unknown	2	42	44

	The Pattern of Attacks by Nature of Attack System								
				Helicopter-	Missiles	Rockets Grenades Gunfire			
	Air-Launched Systems			Launched	from	from			
Year	Missiles	Rockets	Bombs	Missiles	Ships	Ships	Mines	Unknown	Total Attacks
1984									
Iraq	35	—	—	—	—	—	2	16	53
Iran	(18)	—	—	—	—	—	—	—	18
Total	52	—	—	—	—	—	—	16	71
1985									
Iraq	32	—	1	—	—	—	—	—	33
Iran	(10)	—	—	3	—	—	—	1	14
Total	(42)	—	—	3	—	—	—	1	47
1986									
Iraq	52	4	1	1	—	—	—	8	66
Iran	(9)	—	—	26	4	1	—	5	45
Total	(65)	—	1	27	4	1	—	13	110
1987 (to October 12, 1987)									
Iraq	57	—	3	—	—	—	—	2	62
Iran	—	—	—	1	14	34	8	5	62
Total	57	—	3	1	14	34	8	7	124
Total: 1984 to 1987									
Iraq	176	4	5	1	—	—	2	26	214
Iran	(37)	—	—	30	18	35	8	11	139
Total	(217)	—	5	31	18	35	10	37	353

(continues)

TABLE 14.3 *(continued)*

Type	Casualties and Losses by Year				
	1984	1985	1986	1987	Total
Killed	34	7	34	41	116
Wounded	17	20	43	87	167
Missing	9	3	10	15+	37+
Total of Above	60	30	87	143+	320+
Attacks with No Reported Casualties	8	36	55	117	216
Attacks with No Casualty Data Reported	17	4	6	20	47

Type	Patterns by Type of Ship Attacked				
	1984	1985	1986	1987	Total
Oil Tanker/Product Carrier	21	35	78	125	259
Cargo/Freighter/Combination	11	9	1	31	52
Supply/Support	3	3	0	4	10
Tug	0	3	3	6	12
Other/Not Specified	2	0	2	3	7
Total	37	50	84	169	340

SOURCES: Adapted from Bruce McCartan, "The Tanker War," *Armed Forces Journal*, November 1987, pp. 74–76; reporting by Lloyd's and Exxon; *Washington Post*, October 13, 1987, p.1; Ronald O'Rourke, "The Tanker War," *Proceedings*, May 1988, pp. 31–32; and information provided by the Center for Defense Information. Data sources are not consistent.

land offensives and a backlash from friendly Gulf states who became caught up in Iran's attacks. One also cannot dismiss the fact that Iraq simply lacked the commanders and experienced pilots to conduct the kind of well-planned and continuous attacks it needed to make. Iraq did, for example, claim to have carried out far more strikes than it ever executed, and while these claims may have been propaganda, they may also reflect a considerable lack of realism and battle-management capability within the Iraqi Air Force.

Probable Improvements in Third World Threats to Commercial Shipping

In any case, it is unlikely that Third World states will suffer from the same technical limitations in the future as Iran did in the Iran-Iraq War. Third World navies and air forces seem likely to procure heavier anti-ship missiles with the larger warheads necessary to kill large cargo ships and tankers. The lessons of the Iran-Iraq War and the Falklands conflict also are likely to lead them to more use of laser-guided bombs and to deal with arms exporters for the design and purchase of cheap air- and ship-mounted stand-off weapons for such missions. Many Third World nations are very vulnerable to attacks on shipping to and from their ports, and it is easy to foresee cases where aircraft and small craft will be used to launch missiles or mines that are far more lethal against commercial vessels than the Exocet or the weapons on the vessels used by Iran's naval guards.

Many Third World states are already considering ways to improve their naval target acquisition and battle-management capabilities. Both the second half of the tanker war and the Falklands conflict have led many Third World states to consider buying maritime patrol aircraft for naval conflicts that will provide long periods of target coverage and complex battle management near a target area.

Recent wars have also shown the a need for smarter radars and better target-identification systems in order to characterize naval vessels and targets, although such systems are not currently available. It is also interesting to speculate, however, whether the Iran-Iraq War will lead more advanced states like the USSR to consider combining cruise missiles and satellite imaging for long-range kills against commercial ships. The most critical commercial targets in the Gulf would probably show up on modern satellites. While cruise missiles are comparatively slow flying, it might still be possible to use them against such large, slow-moving, and undefended targets at very long ranges and without committing surface ships to combat.

Protecting Commercial Shipping

It is unclear what commercial ships can do to improve their defenses against more sophisticated threats. They can, for example, mount light anti-ship missiles of their own; use chaff, reflectors, and decoys; and mount light surface-to-air missiles. These measures might help against low-level and unsophisticated attacks, but are unlikely to help against the far more sophisticated electronics on most combat ships and aircraft.[5] The only defenses such ships have against mines are their size and ability to survive a hit—a defense that may be even less effective against more sophisticated mines than the Soviet M-08.

It is clear, therefore, that the West will have to reconsider the way in which it plans to project naval power in the future. While Western navies will have a distinct technical and operational edge over most Third World navies, they also may find it far harder to take losses in political terms. There are also obvious problems in dealing with prolonged deployments in areas which divert forces from NATO or other commitments.

Further, the evolving air and missile threat in the Third World is such that only Britain, France, and the U.S. can really afford to protect their vessels. These three nations must be fully ready to equip their smaller ships and on-board aircraft and helicopters with enough defenses and countermeasures to deal with Third World threats.[6] At the same time, consideration should be given to designing small frigates or hydrofoil specifically for such missions. This could greatly cut deployment costs.[7] Similarly, the West should do everything possible to suitably equip friendly Third World navies as a substitute for Western power-projection forces.

The U.S. deployed two other systems to the Gulf in mid-1987 which may also provide important lessons for reducing the risk and cost of future naval power projection. One was an RPV with an endurance of five hours and a flight range of 110 miles. This aircraft was only 16 feet long and has day/night sensors. These RPVs cost about $400,000 each and are relatively expendable. They can perform close scouting missions against enemy naval forces and along defended coasts with minimum risk.[8]

The other U.S. system was the Tomahawk conventional cruise missile. The U.S. deployed these systems to the Gulf in early 1987. The Tomahawk is 21 feet long, 21 inches in diameter, has a wing span of 8 feet, 7 inches, and uses a turbofan engine in the 600-pound thrust class. It has a cruise speed of about 550 miles per hour and a land attack range of 1,550 miles. It has an anti-ship range of 275 miles. It can be launched from armored box launchers or vertical launch systems. The system moves to its target with great accuracy by following an exact computer simulation of the terrain or water areas it must pass over to reach its target. It can be set to fly low and pop-up to dive into a ship or to explode its warhead after penetrating.

The U.S. never used cruise missiles during the Gulf conflict, but it developed the necessary high resolution computerized mapping capability for strikes against Iran's fixed Silkworm sites, key oil facilities, and a wide range of other targets. They offered a high-technology solution to getting precision kills at very long ranges with virtually no risk of combat losses.[9]

Finally, long-range helicopters or new systems like the V-22 tilt-rotor aircraft also act as a means of expanding the coverage of ships. The U.S., Britain, and France all deployed armed helicopters to the Gulf. They all equipped their helicopters with advanced countermeasures, and it is interesting to note that Britain also equipped its Lynx helicopters to provide airborne jamming against the Silkworm and Stinger, using AN/ALQ-167 (V) electronic jammers and IR counter-measures. The minimum attack altitude of the Sea Skua missile on the Lynx also had to be lowered to one meter to attack the Iranian Boghammars.[10]

The Attack on the USS *Stark*
and Lessons for Surface Warfare[11]

Most of the naval encounters in the Gulf were so one-sided that they do not provide major lessons except for the fact that many new naval weapons systems worked as advertised and that the U.S. reliance on advanced weapons and electronics and carrier task-group-oriented combined operations can have great effectiveness in war. The lessons of the attack on the USS *Stark* are interesting, however, for what they say about the impact of human error, the vulnerability of modern ships, and naval fire fighting.

The Conditions That Led to the Attack

At approximately 9:12 on the evening of May 17, an Iraqi Mirage F-1EQ attacked the U.S. radar frigate, the USS *Stark*, about 85 miles northeast of Bahrain and 60 miles south of the Iranian exclusion zone. It fired two Exocet missiles, both of which hit the ship, and one of which exploded. While the Iraqi attack was unintentional, it sparked a whole series of debates over the U.S. role in the Gulf, U.S. defense capabilities, and U.S. relations with Saudi Arabia.

The *Stark* had left Manama in Bahrain at 8:10 A.M. after completing an eight day in-port upkeep period. It cleared restricted navigational waters at 12:30 P.M. and proceeded into its operating area west of the Iranian declared exclusion zone. It was participating in a two-day exercise with the USS *Coontz* and USS *La Salle*—which also were assigned to the Middle East Task Force—and with the USAF E-3A AWACS detachment, or Elf-1 force, based in Saudi Arabia.[12]

Early that evening, an Iraqi fighter took off from the Shaibah airfield near Baghdad. This was the third Iraqi sortie directed against shipping in a twelve-hour period. This time, however, the Iraqi Mirage flew an unusual night attack mission—1 of only 10 or 12 night air attacks up to that date.

The Iraqi fighter was tracked during virtually all of this mission by a USAF E-3A AWACS flying out Dhahran in Saudi Arabia. The E-3A first detected the Iraqi fighter at roughly 7:55 P.M.[13] It was subsequently identified as a Mirage F-1 by a joint U.S.-Saudi ground tracking station. It was then heading southeast on a course of about 155 degrees. The AWACS continued to report on the Mirage continuously from this time on.

About one hour later, the Mirage crossed the Late Detect Line, a line drawn at about 27 degrees, 30 minutes, across the middle of the Gulf. The Iraqi flight flew unusually close to the Saudi coast and then turned north toward Iran. This led to the Iraqi fighter being classified as a "critical class track" which is watched more carefully than usual. A "Force Tell" communication was issued to alert all U.S. ships in the Gulf and the commander of the Middle East Task Force on the USS *LaSalle*. The AWACS increased its reporting frequency, and these reports were sent directly through the Navy Tactical Data System (NTDS) to the nearest ship, the USS *Coontz*, and were relayed to the USS *Stark*.

By this time, the Iraqi Mirage was flying southeast at a speed of 200 MPH and an altitude of 1,000–3,000 feet. It was also about 15 miles from Saudi Arabia and close enough to allow the pilot to confirm his track using the lights on the shore. The pilot, however, was flying at an unusually slow speed and was coming far closer to Saudi Arabia than was normal. Saudi Arabia responded by sending up two Saudi Air Force F-15s, which remained near the AWACS throughout the rest of the Iraqi fighter's flight.[14]

The U.S. ships in the Gulf could not yet track the Iraqi Mirage. Although their AN/SPS-49 Air Search Radars have a maximum range of 200 miles, this range is highly dependent on weather conditions and target altitudes. The AWACS, however, was now providing an unedited real-time downlink to the *Coontz*, which relayed the track to the *Stark* at 8:10 P.M.

The *Stark's* Captain, G.R. Brindel, was advised of this track no later than 8:15 P.M., roughly one hour before the *Stark* was attacked and when the aircraft was still 200 miles away. He instructed the Tactical Action Officer (TAO), the senior officer in command of the CIC, to keep a close watch on the aircraft's progress. He then left for the bridge and arrived on it at 8:31 P.M.

At this time, the USS *Stark* was operating in an area along the Iranian exclusion zone called Radar Picket Station–South. At 8:24 P.M., it began a full-power run in preparation for the exercise to be held in a few days. The ship's engines were raised to full power and the speed was increased to 30 knots. The ship's engines, however, began to produce abnormal temperature readings, and ship speed was reduced to 15 knots, and the course was changed to 300 degrees (northwest).

These problems in preparing for the coming exercise may have contributed to some of the events that followed, although the *Stark* was kept in a state of Condition 3 readiness. This is the third of five different readiness states and requires all weapons and sensor stations to be manned and allows all weapons systems to be engaged in a short period of time. All consoles in its combat information center (CIC) were supposed to be fully manned and operational, although this does not seem to have been the case.[15]

The Iraqi fighter was first detected by the radars on the USS *Coontz* at 8:43 P.M. when it was about 120 nautical miles from the *Stark* and on a bearing of 285 degrees. As a result, the Captain of the *Stark* became concerned because his ship was not tracking the aircraft. He sent an order to the CIC at roughly 8:55 P.M. to shift the AN/SPS-49 air search radar to the 80-mile mode to attempt to acquire the Mirage. This command shifted the antenna to focus on aircraft lower on the horizon and closer to the ship. The change in radar mode worked, and the *Stark's* radar detected the aircraft at a distance of about 70 nautical miles (NMs) and a bearing of 260 degrees.

The Events That Made the Stark Vulnerable

The sequence of events that followed was critical to making the *Stark* vulnerable. Shortly before 9:00 P.M., the USAF E-3A in the area and the USS *Coontz* reported the fighter was at 26-36N/050-51E and on a new easterly course of 043 degrees and flying at 290 nautical miles per hour (NMPH) at an altitude of 3,000 feet. Moments later, the personnel on the CIC reported a surface contact, which later turned to out to be a misreading. At 9:02, an electronic warfare technician in the CIC detected an aircraft's radar emissions and correlated them to the Cyrano IV radar on the Mirage F-1.[16]

At virtually the same time, the watch supervisor on the USS *Stark* advised the TAO that the aircraft was approximately 43 miles from the ship. The maximum range of the Exocet is about 40 miles, and the watch supervisor asked the TAO if he should radio a standard warning to the aircraft. At 9:03, the TAO instructed him to wait. About one minute later, the watch supervisor advised the TAO that the Mirage was now on a course that had a closest point of approach (CPA) within four miles of the *Stark*. The TAO replied that he expected the aircraft would soon turn away from the ship.

At 9:03, the *Coontz* reported to all U.S. ships and the E-3A that the Iraqi aircraft was flying at 310 NMPH at 3,000 feet and was headed toward the *Stark*. At 9:04, at the request of the *LaSalle*, the *Stark* confirmed that it was monitoring the Iraqi flight and that no other surface ships were within 25 NM.

At 9:05, the Mirage F-1 turned directly toward the *Stark* and flew within 32.5 NM of the ship. This turn was not detected in the ship's CIC until 9:07, but the radar operator on the *Stark* detected the fact the ship was being illuminated by the fighter's Cyrano 4 radar in the search mode. At 9:06 P.M., the operator confirmed he was tracking the aircraft in response to a query by the AWACS. He also temporarily turned on the audio signal from the SLQ-32 so everyone in the CIC could hear when the ship was being searched or tracked by the fighter.

The Mirage F-1 then moved within 22.5 NM of the ship and fired its first Exocet missile.

At 9:07 P.M., the watch supervisor advised the TAO that the CPA had increased to 11 miles but that the Mirage was now only 15 miles from the ship. The TAO first asked a specialist in the CIC to man the weapons control officer console around 9:07. This was briefly delayed because the Executive Officer was sitting at the console.

At 9:08, the TAO ordered that a radio warning be given and ordered that the Captain be called to the bridge. The first warning was broadcast on 243.0 Mhz (a Guard frequency all aircraft in the Gulf were supposed to monitor). The warning said, "Unknown aircraft: This is the U.S. Navy warship on your 072 at 13 miles. Request you identify yourself, over." This wording departed radically from the orders governing the proper content of such messages and did not provide a formal warning to the aircraft.

The AN/SLQ-32 ESM radar on the *Stark* again detected that the ship was being illuminated by the Iraqi fighter's Cyrano 4 tracking radar at about 9:08 P.M. The radar operator asked the *Stark's* TAO for permission to arm the ship's two SRBOC chaff launchers on its port and starboard sides. Permission was given. The operator ran to the deck above, prepared the launchers, and returned some 30 seconds later.[17]

The Iraqi fighter made a sharp turn to the right and increased speed between 9:08 and 9:10 P.M. At approximately 9:08 P.M., the *Stark* issued a second warning, stating its position as being on a bearing of 076 degrees and at a distance of 11 NM. This message again did not follow the proper format for a warning. No reply came from the Iraqi fighter, and it is important to note that Iraqi tactics routinely involved firing at radar blips, rather than at targets confirmed by sight. Iraqi pilots also were not compelled to monitor international distress or Guard frequencies and often did not do so. Further, at least the second warning came after the launch of the first missile, and this may have been true of the first.

The *Stark* then detected a lock-on by the fighter's radar which lasted 5–7 seconds.[18] Between 9:08 and 9:09, the TAO finally began to take more active defensive measures. He called General Quarters and switched the ship's Phalanx close-in weapons system (CIWS) to the Anti-air Warfare Mode. This made its radar active and allowed it to perform all functions except firing. It would now search automatically for incoming missiles and lock-on its tracking radar but could not fire without an order.

The TAO also ordered the ship's Mark 92 fire control system—which guided its three-inch guns, standard missiles, and Harpoon missiles—to lock-on its tracking radar if it detected an incoming missile, and to notify the CIC it was ready to fire on order. The ship's radar operator could not comply, however, because the primary STIR radar was blocked by the ship's superstructure. The TAO then ordered that the secondary CAS radar be utilized, but this was too late to be effective.[19]

At 9:09 P.M., a lookout on the port side reported the first inbound missile.[20] Visibility was about 2,000 meters. The lookout did not originally recognize what he was seeing, but seconds before impact, he realized the flash and the bobbing blue fireball that followed near the horizon was a missile and started screaming "inbound missile." This warning came far too late to have any effect. The missile was closing at a speed of 600 miles per hour and was coming from a direction 10 to 15 degrees off the port bow. This was within a 30-degree blind spot where the ship's structure obscures the radar coverage of the Phalanx.[21]

Damage, Damage Control, and Fire Fighting

The *Stark* was hit about five seconds later. The first missile hit on the port side on the second deck. It did not explode but broke into two parts, spewing some 300 pounds of flammable propellent through a sleeping area where sailors were just settling down and then tore through the barber shop and post office and came to rest against the opposite hull. Power to the CIC was lost only momentarily and most of the crew did not realize the ship was hit.

The second missile, however, was spotted seconds later and detonated at 9:10, 20–30 seconds after the first hit and just as the Captain entered the CIC for the first time. It hit in the same general area in the crew quarters near the ship's Combat Information Center, ripped a 15-foot hole in the side of the ship, and exploded about five feet into the hull. This blew five men into the water, and 37 American seamen died and 11 others were seriously wounded. It shut off all power to the CIC, caused serious structural damage, compromised watertight integrity, and cut the main port water main used for fire fighting.

The explosion set the remainder of the first missile on fire and led to the burning of some 600 pounds of propellant from the two missiles in the berthing compartment. This caused a set of secondary fires which eventually forced the abandonment of the RICIR (Radar IFF CIC equipment room) and CIC, sometimes reached temperatures of 1,400 degrees, and produced blinding smoke throughout much of the ship. All radio capability was lost, and PRC (portable radio communications) radios from the aircrew survival vests had to be used to establish communications.

The crew had only partial training in using its oxygen breathing apparatus (OBA), and even though the ship had nearly twice its normal stocks of some fire-fighting equipment, mostly insufficient gear proved to be available for fire fighting. Many of the emergency escape breathing devices seem to have only functioned for a limited period. Even the OBAs often gave only 22 minutes of air versus the hour they were supposed to, and the need to change canisters in a smoke-free environment meant they sometimes allowed only 10-to-12 minutes for fire fighting. The crew also rapidly found it lacked the proper clothing and power-cutting devices for fire fighting and suitable emergency-pump capability.[22]

The *Stark* managed to restore fire main pressure at 9:38 but not in the ship's magazines. The crew could remove the threat of ammunition explosions only by throwing some supplies overboard and using hoses to cool the magazine. The ship maintained electrical power but stopped the engines and went to a maximum list of 16 degrees. At 11:30, a salvage tug arrived. It provided water cannons and a hose to cool the ships magazine.

The ship suffered major additional damage because it was not prepared to use its fire-fighting equipment. It was only able to limit casualties and go on fighting because supplies were brought in by helicopter and from other ships. It would almost certainly have sunk if it had not been for the aid of a commercial tugboat. The heat was so severe that radiation between bulkheads spread the fire, and it melted aluminum ladders and deformed the aluminum superstructure. Although the ship's power drive was not hit, the fires eventually forced it to halt. Even flooding the magazines was not enough because of the heat. If the water from the tugboat had not kept the missile storage compartments (which were in the path of the fire) flooded, the ship might have exploded.[23]

The Problem of Human Error

It is impossible to evaluate how well the ship might have done in different hands, but the *Stark's* defenses should have been formidable. The USS *Stark* was tracking the fighter when it fired on the ship, but it never turned on its fire-control radars. The only major questions were whether the ship's electronic warfare systems were able to detect the fact the ship was being illuminated by the tracking radar on the Iraqi Mirage F-1EQ and whether the radars should have detected the actual firing or separation of the missile. The evidence cited by the U.S. Navy indicates that if all the systems in the ship had been properly turned on and operated, it would have been able to defend itself.[24]

The USS *Stark's* defensive systems included Standard ship-to-air missiles, Phalanx automatic anti-missile radar-directed Gatling guns, automatic chaff dispensers, and electronic warfare equipment.[25] The ship also had turbine engines capable of rapidly accelerating it to 33 knots. All these maneuvers, however, could further confuse the missile's guidance system in combination with its other defenses.[26]

In practice, the previous series of command changes meant that none of the *Stark's* defenses were used—a fact which eventually led to a U.S. Navy report which blamed the incident on a collapse of command, and which resulted in the relief of the ship's Captain, executive officer, and tactical action officer (TAO).[27] The Captain and tactical action officer were reprimanded and allowed to resign from the navy. The executive officer was disciplined but allowed to stay in the service.[28]

The Iraqi attack was never really challenged because of human error. Its commanders did not treat their duty as a combat situation and did not maintain or establish proper watch manning and standing or weapons readiness. While the ship had tracked the incoming Iraqi fighter, the *Stark* had delayed any warning of the Iraqi aircraft.

Even though the *Stark's* Captain was first notified of the fact an Iraqi aircraft was operating in the area when the plane was still over 120 miles away, he did not continue to monitor its progress. He instead conducted a high-speed-run exercise and then left the bridge at 10:00 P.M.

Although the tactical weapons officer was asked if he should warn the Iraqi fighter it was closing on a U.S. ship when it was still 43 miles away, the TAO waited until the aircraft was within a range of 13 and then 11 miles to send a warning. The Captain was making a "head call" and was in his cabin when the missiles hit, and his two senior officers did not take measures to position the *Stark* to improve its defensive coverage or activate its defenses.[29]

The ship had never been turned in the proper direction toward the target. This meant the ship could not use its main fire-control radar antenna effectively. An automatic audio alarm to warn of incoming missiles had been turned off because a crewman found it distracting, and the crewman who should have visually detected a radar blip at missile launch was later reported to have been occupied with other duties. This makes it impossible to know whether the radars and electronic warfare systems on the ship detected the firing of the missile, but it seems likely that they did so.[30]

The *Stark* did not detect the fact the Iraqi Mirage had fired two Exocet missiles until a lookout on the deck saw one of the missiles coming. The ship then had only about five seconds of warning, and none of its automatic defenses were turned on. Further, the failure to re-position the ship blinded the radar on the Phalanx system, which is designed not to track in areas where it might lock-on the ship's superstructure.[31]

This sequence of human error is partly excusable. Part of the reason for the *Stark's* failure to react was that U.S. Navy ships in the Gulf routinely experienced Iraqi strikes against shipping in their area of operations. Even so, the USS *Stark's* officers should clearly have taken precautionary measures much earlier.[32]

The Role of the Iraqi Pilot

The Iraqi pilot was also clearly to blame. He had flown 15 previous missions in the Gulf and knew of the risk he might strike at friendly ships. It is true that the attacking Mirage F-1EQ aircraft was flying an unusual night mission and was carrying two Exocets, which were twice its rated capacity.

This represented a payload which would have produced constant buffeting of the fighter from aerodynamic drag, raised fuel consumption, and created high pilot fatigue.[33] Nevertheless, the pilot was grossly negligent. He later claimed to have been monitoring both major distress frequencies on 243.0 Mhz and 121.5 Mhz. This, however, was not standard Iraqi practice, and it is unlikely that he did so. He also claimed he never received any signal from the *Stark*, which is absurd, given his distance from the ship and the fact that a radio log confirms that such messages were sent.

Most importantly, the Iraqi pilot claimed that his navigation gear indicated the ship was 5–10 nautical miles inside the exclusion zone, not 10–15 nautical miles outside it. Nevertheless, the Iraqi pilot seems to have preserved radio silence and simply fired at the first target confirmed by his radar.[34] All the pilot's actions in flying both to and from his target indicate that he knew his position and knew he was firing outside the Iranian exclusion zone. If he had not known his position, he could not have flown the precise return course he used to get back to base. Finally, the Iraqi pilot only turned on his tracking radar seconds before he fired. This was only justifiable in a combat environment where he faced hostile ships with air defenses, which he did not. The Iraqi pilot made no real attempt to identify his target, even by radar.[35]

The Major Lessons of the Stark Incident

The major lessons from the attack on the USS *Stark* are familiar ones and may be summarized as follows.

- No commander in a war zone can afford to take the risk of dealing with attacks or intrusions as routine matters. Every possible attack must be dealt with as an attack, and all officers on a ship must act accordingly.

- Rules of engagement must encourage military defense, not political restraint. Battle orders must be issued for the specific conditions under which a ship operates and not simply in generic terms.
- Full combat readiness and placing every man on his duty station are as critical with modern ships as at any past time in naval combat. It is virtually impossible to defend a ship or deal with damage without having all men at their duty stations.
- IFF has become as important in the case of missiles as in the case of aircraft.
- Given the world arms market, no system can be assumed to be friendly.
- Defense systems must be much more tightly integrated and be less subject to constant operator attention. The CIC of a ship must be able to take integrated and decisive action from several points.
- Regardless of the exact cause of damage to the *Stark*, all Western missile electronic warfare systems need extensive review to see if they can reliably detect all Western-designed missiles and not simply Soviet or communist designs. Far too many Western naval missile defense systems are over optimized toward a limited number of threat missiles.
- Special emphasis needs to be placed on short-range defense. Many anti-ship missiles can only be detected at ranges of 22 miles or less. This requires the ability to quickly react and to use several defenses at the same time. Increasing emphasis is being placed on combined light-missile and rapid-fire gun defenses. Heavy emphasis is also being placed on new guidance systems which can deal with the IR and radar reflections, or clutter, inherent in tracking low-flying missiles.[36]
- Fire fighting and damage control are as important in naval combat as active defense. The U.S. Navy had had the advantage of learning from earlier carrier fires and from the damage done to British ships in the Falklands but immediately had to strengthen its fire-fighting capability as a result of what it learned from the damage to the *Stark*.[37]
- Damage-control training levels were high, and equipment had been added as a result of the British experience in the Falklands. Nevertheless, the U.S. Navy recommended a major increase in breathing aids, bulkhead-cutting equipment, night-vision devices with thermal sensors to detect small fires, added fire main jumping stations, emergency radios, larger deck scuttles to allow free movement of the crew, high-capacity, light, smoke-removal

equipment, topside deck drains to remove fire fighting water, improved fire-fighting uniforms, high-volume fire-suppression systems in critical electronics areas, and added pumps.

- While aluminum may not present a serious risk per se, many Western warships are designed with too much emphasis on defense and mission capability and too little emphasis on survival. Packing the maximum amount of electronics in a ship like the *Stark* compromises survival, and the cost-effectiveness may only exist if the ship never fights a serious war. This is particularly true because of the West's acute limitations in military shipyard capability. Under many conditions, a war would be over before significant repairs could take place.

The *Bridgeton* and the Mine War

The West feared an Iranian effort to mine the Gulf from the very start of the Iran-Iraq War. At the same time, it tended to focus on the threat to close the mouth of the Gulf and to ignore any other threat except the occasional risk of free mines. Mining the Straits of Hormuz seemed to be beyond the military capabilities of a nation like Iran. Oman controlled the shallow passage and Coin Islands in the Straits, and the deep water channel between the island of Jazye Larak in Iran and the rocks off Didamar in the south is nearly 20 miles wide and is an average of 60 meters deep, with a maximum depth of 89 meters.

Strong currents move through the Straits, and the two types of mines which are hardest to clear—pressure and acoustic—cannot be used below 40 to 50 meters. Magnetic contact mines could be deployed in either bottom or moored forms and horned-antenna contact mines could be bottom-moored. These mines, however, weigh roughly about a ton, and 2,000 to 3,000 would be needed to close the Straits, in a place where even limited mining activity would be quickly detected by the West. Mobile, unanchored, oscillating mines, drifting mines, and drag (chain) mines would also have to be laid in large numbers and would be detected. While Iraq cannot defend the Straits against mining or naval action, the West can, and the technology ensures considerable warning.

The U.S. in particular, however, forgot that a bottle can be broken in more places than its neck. As a result, it learned important lessons about mine warfare from its naval deployments in the Gulf, many of which were far from pleasant.

The Background to the Attack

The *Bridgeton* incident was the key to these lessons. If the Iraqi attack on the USS *Stark* challenged both the quality of U.S. anti-air and anti-missile defenses, the mining of the Bridgeton raised other issues. It again raised questions about the quality of American military planning and about the U.S. Navy's ability to fight low-level wars. Further, it exposed the weaknesses in the U.S. mine-warfare program and the potential dangers the U.S. faces in relying on its allies to perform specialized roles and missions.

It is clear that the U.S. should have been far more alert to the risk of mine warfare than it was before the *Bridgeton* was hit. Soviet ships had already hit mines on their way back and forth to Kuwait. U.S. defense spokesmen had stated early in the U.S. effort to reflag 11 Kuwaiti tankers that mines were one of the two greatest risks the U.S. faced. Further, the U.S. had been reminded of the reality of the threat only days before the *Bridgeton* hit a mine.

The U.S. announced on July 14, 1986, that it would begin to escort the reflagged Kuwaiti ships in one week. That same day, the U.S. indicated it had delayed its convoy activity because clearing the Iranian mines from Kuwait's main shipping channel was taking longer than had originally been anticipated, and the other channel was too close to Iranian waters to be safe. The U.S. announced at the same press conference that the *Bridgeton* (*Al Rekkah*) would be one of the first tankers to be escorted by the time the mines were cleared.[38] In response to follow-up questions, a U.S. official noted that none of the 9 U.S. warships in the Gulf was a minesweeper and that the U.S. had no MH-53 Sea Dragon minesweeping helicopters in the region, although five were ready to deploy.[39]

The U.S. stated later that a plan to send a 200-man detachment and mine-warfare helicopters to the Gulf was deferred because Kuwait planned to lease Dutch minesweepers and obtain Dutch technical assistance. This mine-clearing effort in Kuwait had a peculiarly international character. Some of the work was done by Soviet and Dutch experts and other work by Saudi minesweepers and an 18-man U.S. Navy Explosive Ordnance Disposal detachment. The mines turned out to be old Soviet MO-8 mines, which Iran had bought from North Korea, could be planted to a depth of 350 feet, and which had 250 pounds of explosive.[40]

The Strengths in the U.S. Convoy Effort

Part of the reason for the U.S. failure to plan for mine warfare seems to have been in the way the U.S. Navy focused on the Iranian threat and the resulting balance of strengths and weaknesses in the forces it deployed to protect its first convoy.

The main strength of the U.S. force that accompanied the first convoys was that it consisted of a relatively large force to convoy only two tankers. The U.S. had four frigates, three cruisers, and a destroyer in the area around the Gulf and the Straits of Hormuz. These ships had gone through three rehearsals since the last elements of the escort force had arrived in early July, and the escort plan had reached the size of an 80-page document. The U.S. also had a carrier task force, including the carrier *Constellation*, in the Indian Ocean. The battleship *Missouri*, two more cruisers, and a helicopter carrier were in transit to the region.

The convoy plan called for three to four U.S. ships to escort each of the two-tanker convoys, while the cruisers stood by to provide a defense against air attack. U.S. A-6 and F/A-18 attack aircraft, EA-6B jamming aircraft, and F-14 fighter planes were to provide support from the U.S. carrier *Constellation* in the Arabian Sea. The tankers were to have at least three escorts once they passed beyond the Straits, with USAF E-3A AWACS providing airborne surveillance.

The U.S. planned to provide convoys once every two weeks during July and August. This interval was intended to allow the task force concept to be tested and to find out Iranian reactions. It also eased the burden of being on constant alert against suicide attacks or other means of irregular warfare. The destroyer *Fox* and cruiser *Kidd* were selected in part because their 76-mm guns provided considerable firepower against sudden raids by the Iranian Navy or shore targets. All of the U.S. combat ships were equipped with long-radar radars, data nets, and Phalanx terminal defense guns.

The Inherent Weaknesses in U.S. Mine-Warfare Forces

The U.S. force also, however, had several weaknesses. These included the lack of local naval and air bases in the Gulf, its inability to provide a cross-reinforcing defense of single ships operating outside the convoy to minimize the success of a saturation attack, and its lack of mine-warfare defenses. It was the latter weakness that Iran chose to exploit.

The U.S. lack of mine-warfare defenses was partly a matter of inadequate planning. The initial operational plan the Joint Chiefs and USCENTCOM developed for the convoy made no provision for mine forces in spite of warnings from U.S. intelligence officials and the U.S. Navy.[41] The U.S. Navy, however, was not ready to carry out the mine-warfare mission. It relied on its European allies for most mine-warfare missions, and the U.S. made little initial effort to get direct allied military support. The U.S. had only 21 30-year-old minesweepers (MSOs) in service.[42] All but three of these minesweepers were in the Naval Reserve Force. The three active ships were assigned research duty and were not ready to perform their mission. They were augmented only by seven active-duty 57 foot minesweeping boats (MSBs) and 23 Sea Stallion RH-53D helicopters, four of which were also allocated to the naval reserves.[43]

The MSOs were 830-ton vessels with a maximum speed of 14 knots. They had sonars with mine-hunting capability but lacked the ability to simulate the magnetic or acoustic image of larger tankers to detonate modern influence mines. The MSBs were only 30-ton vessels which could often make only seven knots in the open sea. Only one of the MSBs had a sonar to prevent hunting before sweeping. None of the vessels had the electronics and sweeping equipment to be fully effective against modern acoustic and magnetic influence mines or sophisticated mines like the Soviet 99501 combination bottom and influence mines that Libya had used in mining the Red Sea approaches to the Suez Canal.[44]

The U.S. had begun a $1.5 billion program in the early 1980s to replace its 1950s-vintage minesweepers and to build 14 large wooden-hulled Avenger-class minesweepers and 17 small high-technology fiber glass coastal minesweepers. The Avenger-class ships were designed as fully modern 224-foot mine vessels with a size of 1,040 tons and SQQ-30 variable-depth mine detection/classification sonars, a Honeywell mine-neutralization vehicle, and acoustic and magnetic sweeps. The program ran into major coast overruns, however, and the cost rose from $100 million to $153 million. The ship also experienced degaussing, engine, and transmission problems, and the Peterson Builder construction effort also slipped two years in delivery, with the first ships scheduled to enter active service in 1988.[45]

The initial order of coastal minesweepers had to be canceled in 1986, in part because the fiberglass hulls peeled under the simulated shock of nearby mine explosions. The U.S. then had to order a new type of ship from Italy's Intermarine and Hercules Powder at a cost of $120 million. Work on the first of these MCC-51s was scheduled to begin in November 1987.[46]

The U.S. could use the SH-2 ASW helicopters on its frigates to spot mines visually, and these helped contribute to spotting and destroying 10 of the mines found off Kuwait. They were not, however, capable of detecting deep mines or of minesweeping. The Navy's only heliborne minesweeping assets were three squadrons with a total of 23 RH-53D Sea Dragon helicopters, which were based at Norfolk. These helicopters had serious structural reliability problems, were only usable in daylight and shallow water, and had relatively limited endurance.

New Sikorsky MH-53E AMCM minesweeping helicopters were supposed to replace them. These were designed to provide night operations capability, a major increase in range payload, a 50 percent increase in towing capability, improved hot-day performance, an on-station mission time of more than four hours, improved coverage for the AQS-14 towed sonar, and more effective use of dual acoustic and magnetic minesweeping sleds. They were lagging badly in delivery, however, and Sikorsky had been penalized for slow progress. Only 15 of 32 aircraft were actually on order, and those which had been delivered were still in a training or shakedown role and could not be deployed.[47]

In any case, helicopters have important limitations. To sweep mines, the helicopters either had to drag a V-shaped device with explosive cutters to break the mine's cable and let it rise to the surface or tow a sled along the surface and generate a strong electromagnetic current to detonate magnetic mines while giving off the sound of a ship's propeller to detonate acoustic mines.[48]

The Mark 104 sled uses a cavitating disk in a venturi tube to simulate the acoustic sound of a ship. The Mark 105 is a hydrofoil sled towed at about 25 knots about 135 meters behind the helicopter. It has a generator which supplies current to a twin electrode magnetic tail with creates a magnetic field like that of a ship. It can be refueled by the helicopter. The Mark 104 can be attached to one of the tails of the Mark 105 to sweep both magnetic and acoustic mines. The combined system is called the Mark 106 and was used with some success in the Gulf of Suez minesweeping effort in 1984. A system called the magnetic orange pipe is a magnetized pipe filled with styrofoam. Up to three can be used to sweep magnetic influence mines in shallow waters.[49]

The speed of sweep for mechanical mines is 10–12 knots, and the speed for acoustic magnetic mines is 22–25 knots. This means the helicopters were forced to chose between the kinds of mines to be swept, although mine operations often use a mix of mines. While helicopters are faster than ships, the weight of the sleds and deployment-time considerations reduces the helicopters mission time to two hours.[50]

Planning for Only Part of the Iranian Threat

The U.S. thus faced a wide range of threats, only part of which it was prepared to deal with. Iran had had access to a wide range of sources for its mines. It had both surface mines and bottom mines and at least some timed or interval mines that only became active after a fixed time period or after several ships or minesweepers passed by. While Iran's full mine assets were uncertain, it may have had contact, magnetic, acoustic, bow wave, pressure, and temperature mines, and possibly remote-controlled mines. Some were large metal mines and could easily be detected by sonar, but many were too small for easy detection, and others were nonmagnetic.

Another problem consisted of the distance the convoy had to move and the fact it was continuously vulnerable from the time it approached the Straits to the moment it entered port in Kuwait. The convey had to follow a route that included a 60-mile voyage from Dibba, outside the Gulf, to the Straits. With a convoy speed of 16 knots, this would take 8 hours. For the next 50 miles, the convoy passed through the Straits and near Iran's 20-mile exclusion zone and its Silkworm missiles. It then sailed for another 90 miles to a point near Abu Nuayr off the coast of Abu Dhabi. This meant passing by Abu Musa and the Tunbs.

There was then a 60-mile stretch to the UAE's Zaqqum oil channel, followed by a 60-mile voyage to Qatar's Halul Island. The convoy then had to sail 90 miles to the Shah Allum shoals and a point only a mile from Iranian waters. At this point, the convoy had about 285 miles more of relatively open sailing from a position off the Ras Tanura beacon ship to Kuwait. During all of this time, Iran could chose its point and means of attack.[51]

Finally, the U.S. faced the problem that—in spite of efforts to keep the convoy's composition and schedule and the details of its strengths and weaknesses secret—it received a relentless exposure in the media. Its weaknesses, in regard to mine warfare, were fully communicated to Iran. Iran could predict the path of the convoy and its timing. This meant that small craft might succeed in hitting a ship, even if they did nothing more than drop a few contact mines at night.[52]

Using Tankers to Protect the U.S. Navy

The first convoy sailed on schedule on July 22, 1987. The U.S. sent in four combat ships, including a guided-missile cruiser. The reflagged ships included the 414,266 ton supertanker *Bridgeton* and the 48,233 ton gas tanker *Gas Prince*. The convey transited the Straits safely, amid wide speculation that a week-long lull in the tanker war somehow meant Iran had decided not to attack. In fact, the most Iran did publicly was to send four of its F-4s near the convoy when it entered the Gulf and to announce new naval maneuvers which were code-named Operation Martyrdom.[53] The convoy reached the half-way point on July 23, when Iran declared it had a cargo of "prohibited goods."[54]

Unfortunately, the U.S. concentrated far too much on the missile threat near the Straits and far too little on the risk of other forms and areas of attack. This became brutally clear about 6:30 A.M. on July 24. The *Bridgeton* struck a mine at a position of 27°58' north and 49°50' east. This was a position roughly 18 miles from the Iranian naval Guards base on Farsi Island. It was about 80 miles southeast of the four mine hits reported between May 16 and June 19 in the approach channel to Mina al Ahmadi and about 50 miles north of the Juaymah departure channel. The *Bridgeton* was hit in its number 1 port cargo tank, and the mine blew a large hole in her hull and flooded 4 of her 31 compartments.

The convoy was forced to slow from a speed of 16 knots to 5, and its warships were forced to follow the damaged *Bridgeton*, which was the only ship large enough to survive another mine hit. The only action the warships could take was to turn on their sonars and put riflemen on the bow to try to shoot a mine if they saw it.

The Lessons of the Bridgeton Incident

In the months that followed the *Bridgeton* incident, the U.S. deployed its mine-warfare forces to the Gulf and acquired the aid of the Belgian, British, French, Italian, and Netherlands navies. The U.S. showed it can seek out and destroy Iranian mine vessels, and Iran dissipated any political advantages it gained by acts which catalyzed American public opinion to support the U.S. presence in the Gulf and alienated much of Western Europe.

At the same time, the *Bridgeton* incident was costly to the U.S. in political terms, and this cost could have been far higher if Iran had not made compensating mistakes. Like several other recent incidents when Western forces have engaged Third World states, the *Bridgeton* incident offers some important lessons and warnings.

- Virtually all of the European mine vessels sent to the Gulf ran into endurance and maintenance problems or required extensive preparation. The mine-warfare effort in the Gulf raised broad questions about the normal readiness of NATO mine forces that need to be addressed.
- Mine vessels operating in Third World contingencies may lack air- and missile-defense support and will need defenses of their own. For example, the U.K. had to provide extensive preparation for its four Hunt-class mine countermeasure vessels (MCMVs) and the mine support ship *Abdiel*. It added its Replica DLF-2 anti-missile decoy system to provide deck-launched passive broad band decoy capability. It added the MEL Matilda electronic support measure (ESM) system. This system provides generic warning of attack. The U.K. also added two additional Oerlikon-BMARC 20-mm cannon, the Barricade anti-missile decoy, and Marconi SCOT satellite communications systems. The mine-

hunting systems included the EDO Almondbury 2059 acoustic tracking sonar, which is combined with the Standard Type-193M mine-hunting sonar and PAP type remotely operated vehicle. The EDO precisely tracks the location of the PAP and other data from a hull-mounted sensor.[55]

- Both the U.S. and U.K. soon realized that they needed visual inspection systems to determine the exact nature of mines. Britain deployed a small remotely guided surface vessel called SACRAB for this purpose, and the U.S. acquired a small remotely guided submersible called the Super Sea Rover, carrying camera and sonars. These "robotic" systems offer a way of dealing with mines at minimum risk to personnel and ships.[56]

- By the time of the cease-fire, the Western minesweeping effort in the Gulf had found a total of 89 mines in seven different minefields.[57] These included 79 M-08 Soviet mines and 10 Iranian-made Myam mines, which were smaller contact mines. In addition, there were large numbers of floating mines. The total number of mines neutralized was 176, including 89 moored and 87 floating, and a total of 83 M-08s and 95 Myams.

  These figures clearly demonstrate that Third world states can and will take the risk of challenging Western powers, even superpowers. This is particularly true when the West either lacks any effective way of striking directly at their leadership elites or when those leadership elites have a deep anti-Western political or ideological commitment.

- None of the minesweepers that deployed to the Gulf would have been able to quickly and reliably sweep more modern non-magnetic or influence mines, particularly ones which could be set to operate at fixed intervals or become active only when approached by given sizes of ship.[58] If Iran had used the more sophisticated mines it was rumored to have bought from Libya, it might well have created a far more serious problem, and one that would have required weeks of additional sweeping and the virtual interdiction of all naval traffic out of Iran. In 1982, for example, when mines were discovered in the Red Sea, it took a British minesweeper six days to identify, disarm, and neutralize a sophisticated 1,500-lb. mine.[59] Far more sophisticated mine warfare threats are likely to occur in the future.

- No Western power can ever afford to dismiss the ability of Third World states to use every available weapon and technology. In fact, Third World states are forced to use unconventional means and weapons to challenge the broad Western superiority in military technology. Any force which is not tailored to respond to all known low-level threats from a given country is poorly planned and improperly equipped.

- Third World countries are fully aware of the major political vulnerabilities inherent in Western power projection and will make every effort to exploit them. This is particularly true when they feel Western political leaders are in a weak political position and may not be able to take casualties or cannot take embarrassing loses.
- U.S. power-projection forces must be capable of dealing with every threat. The U.S. may be able to leave the bulk of some military mission to its allies, but it cannot ever leave an entire mission in allied hands or disregard it in its focus on other kinds of war.
- Western task force commanders cannot rely on mass or technology as a substitute for military flexibility. As the British experience in the Falklands also demonstrates, any commander dealing with out-of-area operations must be fully prepared to use tactics and innovation and must be fully responsive to intelligence warnings.

In a broader sense, the West cannot afford to ignore the mine-warfare threat from Soviet forces or assume it will be limited to certain European waters, simply because the USSR is more likely to conduct missile, air, or submarine warfare. The USSR has just as much incentive to be unconventional as Iran.

The West also needs to consider the fact that the Third World is rapidly changing its military capabilities, and gunboating in any form is not a substitute for combined arms. In the last five years alone, Third World states have acquired 154 major surface combatants, 482 minor surface combatants, 26 submarines, and 99 missile attack boats. They have acquired some 2,844 supersonic combat aircraft, 597 subsonic combat aircraft, 1,656 military helicopters, and 24,684 surface-to-air missiles. Their armies have acquired some 13,800 main battle tanks, 16,700 major field artillery weapons, and 18,680 other armored vehicles.

The U.S. may have been exceptionally lucky in the fact that most of Iran's air force is not operational, and most of its ships lack operational missile systems and fully operational electronics. No Western force can count on such weaknesses in Third World opponents in the 1990s. In fact, the process of technology transfer and arms sales is now beginning to transfer some weapons to the Third World before they are fully deployed in the forces of the Western nations that make them.

The Lessons of the Convoy Effort

Experts are likely to debate for decades whether the U.S. convoy effort was entirely necessary. It can be argued that the Iranian and Iraqi threat to Gulf shipping was never serious enough to merit the U.S. commitment to the region. It can also be argued that by agreeing to reflagging the ships of Kuwait, the Gulf state most friendly to Iraq, the U.S. forced a confrontation with Iran that it might have avoided by simply declaring it would protect all ship outside the declared war zones.

If one only looks at the pattern of Iranian attacks, the statistics on the U.S. presence do seem to imply that the U.S. provoked Iran. From July 22, 1986 to July 1987—the year before the U.S. started the reflagging effort—Iran attacked 54 commercial vessels, and Iraq attacked 63, for a total of 117. In the year between July 23, 1987, and July 22, 1988, Iran hit 105 ships and Iraq hit 82. Accordingly, the Iranian strikes nearly doubled during the reflagging period.[60]

This focus on the number of Iranian attacks on shipping, however, ignores the overall pattern of military events in the region. While there is no question that the reflagging effort did coincide with an increase in Iranian attacks, it is important to understand that the Iranian's formally created the naval branch of the Guards in May 1986 and built them up to a force of 20,000 men and several hundred boats before the reflagging effort. They also gave the naval Guards Silkworm missiles. It is almost certain that Iran would have made even greater increases in the number of its ship attacks without the reflagging effort and would have been far more effective. It also is uncertain as to whether it would ever have agreed to a cease-fire in 1988 if it had not been for the U.S. presence in the Gulf.

Experts can also argue whether the U.S. really faced any serious threat that the USSR would expand its influence in the Gulf if the U.S. did not take action and whether the eventual U.S. confrontation with Iran did have a major impact in bringing the war to a close and in forcing Iran to accept a cease-fire.

The previous chapters have strongly suggested that Iran was acquiring sufficient naval capability to bring strong pressure on Kuwait and Saudi Arabia to halt their support of Iraq and would have used this capability. They suggest that while reflagging probably was not the best approach, it was a reasonable political risk. They suggest that the U.S. covert arms sales to Iran and withdrawal from Lebanon had left the U.S. in far too weak a position not to take action in the Gulf, and they suggest that the U.S. presence in the Gulf did have a major impact in forcing Iran to accept a cease-fire. It also is possible to support these points with countless quotes by Iranian leaders and many of the leaders in the southern Gulf. No one will ever be certain whether the Western presence in the Gulf was necessary in a purely game-theoretical sense, but it was certainly perceived as a major success by virtually every friendly leader in the region after the 1988 cease-fire.[61]

The Overall Performance of the U.S. Convoy Effort

Regardless of the broader policy issues, it is clear that the U.S. convoy effort was successful in protecting the ships it was deployed to protect. Iranian strikes against ships in the Gulf, including mines and Silkworm missiles, increased from 17 in 1984, to 14 in 1985, 41 in 1986, 89 in 1987, and 39 in 1988. During this time, Iranian strikes against Kuwaiti ships shifted from 4 in 1984, to 2 in 1985, 2 in 1986, 4 in 1987, and none in 1988.[62] The only U.S.-escorted ship hit during the convoy effort was the *Bridgeton*, although the U.S. escorted or accompanied 252 ships during the period from the sailing of the *Bridgeton* and *Gas Prince* on July 22–24, 1987, and the time the U.S. halted accompanying or escorting ships with the accompanying of the *Courier, Ranger*, and USS *Mars* on 13–15 December 1988. If one looks only at the direct impact of the U.S. convoy effort as part of Operation Ernest Will, the U.S. covered 177 ship transits by reflagged tankers, 57 by MSC ships, 14 by other U.S.-flagged ships, and 4 by foreign flag ships.

The broader impact, however, was far greater. As the previous chapters have shown, the U.S. presence catalyzed a general effort by West European and southern Gulf states to protect the flow of shipping through the Gulf. Regardless of the increase in the number of Iranian attacks, Iran had a negligible impact on the flow of shipping and only a minor impact on insurance rates. It is unlikely that any of these efforts, by either European states or southern Gulf states, would have taken place without Operation Ernest Will.

If there is any lesson that can be drawn from this experience, it is that there are unlikely to ever be cases in low-intensity combat where the conditions involved are so unambiguous that it is possible to prove the need for American intervention, avoid major uncertainties and problems, and avoid having to intervene under less than ideal conditions. Crises only tend to become unambiguous at the point they cease to be manageable with limited amounts of force, and national interests only become totally clear when they are threatened to the point where they may be seriously damaged. Regardless of the faults in the precise way the U.S. entered the Gulf and conducted its military operation, it is virtually certain that the U.S. was far more successful than it would have been if it (a) had waited long enough to see if Iran's actions in the Gulf would seriously threaten the flow of oil and southern Gulf support of Iraq, (b) let its influence and credibility continue to decline, and (c) failed to exert reasonable pressure to end the war on terms that left Iraq independent.

The Military Clashes During the U.S. Convoy Effort

There were six military clashes between U.S. and Iranian forces during the convoy effort. None of these efforts involved a serious test of U.S. military capabilities or weapons. The key message from a short chronology of the events involved does indicate, however, that the pattern of events followed an almost inevitable process of escalation, which only culminated when it became clear that no amount of pressure could force the U.S. to withdraw from the Gulf and when the U.S. had inflicted sufficient Iranian losses to force Iran to halt naval operations.

- *September 21, 1987: U.S. helicopters on a night surveillance patrol observe the Iranian ship* Iran Ajr *laying mines in international waters near the Bahrain Bell.* U.S. helicopters engage the *Iran Ajr* until the minelaying ceases. At daylight, U.S. forces board the ship, which has been abandoned by its crew. Nine operational mines are discovered, as well as evidence of the previous night's minelaying activity. The Iranian crew is rescued from life boats and is repatriated through a third country. There are no U.S. casualties or losses; the *Iran Ajr* is captured and scuttled.
- *October 8, 1987: U.S. helicopters on patrol near Farsi Island are fired upon by Iranian patrol boats.* U.S. helicopters return the fire. There are no U.S. losses or casualties. One Iranian Boghammer is sunk. Several Iranian Boston Whalers are damaged.
- *October 19, 1987: U.S. forces attack Iran's Rashadat oil platforms,* which are armed surveillance and patrol boat centers for the Iranian naval Guards, in response to a October 16, 1987 Iranian Silkworm attack against the U.S. flag tanker *Sea Isle City.* The U.S. uses gunfire and demolition charges. The Iranian personnel abandon the platforms in response to a prior U.S. warning. There are no U.S. casualties. The platforms are destroyed or neutralized.
- *April 14, 1988: USS* Samuel Roberts *strikes Iranian mine in central Gulf:* The *Roberts* is severely damaged and is transported to the U.S. by heavy lift ship for a major overhaul. There is no damage to Iranian units.

- *April 18, 1988: U.S. forces attack several Iranian oil platforms, known to be used as surveillance and attack-boat support bases, in response to the mining of the USS* Roberts. Iranian naval and air units respond against U.S. forces and strike at third-country oil platforms. The U.S. lost one AH-1 Cobra. Iran lost the Saan and Siri oil platforms. It lost the guided missile frigate *Sahand* to U.S. air and surface attack, and the guided missile patrol boat *Joshan* was lost to a surface action group. The guided missile frigate *Sabalan* was severely damaged. A Boghammer was lost and another damaged by U.S. air attack, and an Iranian F-4 was damaged by a U.S. surface-to-air missile.
- *July 3, 1988: Iranian small boats fire on U.S. helicopters while on routine patrol.* The USS *Vincennes* and USS *Montgomery* investigate and engage Iranian forces when they continue to close at high speed. The USS *Vincennes* shoots down an unidentified aircraft while simultaneously engaging an Iranian ship. U.S. forces suffer no losses. Iran loses two small boats and another is damaged. The aircraft later turns out to be Iran Air Flight 655, and 290 Iranian civilians are killed.

If there are lessons that can be drawn from this process of escalation, it is that the U.S. efforts to deal with Iranian pressure by "measured response" did generally contain Iran's ability to act without leading to broader conflict. It is important to note, however, that the U.S. operated under exceptionally favorable conditions. While Iran dictated the actual steps involved in escalating the conflict, it had fewer air assets, and its naval forces were largely ineffective. Iran was extremely vulnerable to attacks on its oil facilities and could not protect its military forces. It is uncertain that future contingencies will be as favorable to Western power projection, particularly given the quality and quantity of aircraft and missiles being sold to the Third World. In future cases, therefore, the West may have to respond with much more decisive levels of force to avoid becoming trapped into a similar process of escalation under far more dangerous conditions.

The Need for Allies

Although the previous history of the war has repeatedly made the point, it is also important to note that one of the key lessons of the convoy effort was that the U.S. could never have been successful without help from its local and West European allies. At the peak of the Western intervention in the Gulf, there were 40 Belgian, British, French, Italian, and Netherlands ships present, and even in November

1988, there were still 21 West European warships in the area. The British Armilla Patrol alone participated in a total of 1,026 transits after it started actively protecting ships in the Gulf in 1987, with 405 transits in 1987 and 621 between January and August 1988.[63]

Large as the U.S. military effort in the region was, the U.S. was also heavily dependent on Kuwait and Saudi Arabia for fuel, the use of air and naval facilities, the ability to base E-3A and P-3C aircraft, and staging the naval, marine, and army forces it deployed in the area.

Kuwait paid for the leasing charges on the barges the U.S. used in the Gulf and some nine million gallons of fuel a month. It permitted port calls and provided cooperation at a number of other levels. Saudi Arabia permitted the U.S. to base P-3s on Saudi territory and U.S. minesweepers to occasionally use Jubail. It provided E-3A and tanker support for the U.S. presence. The E-3As in the northern part of the AWACS orbit were Saudi E-3As with U.S. crews; the aircraft covering the southern part of the orbit were Saudi E-3As with Saudi crews. Saudi Arabia allowed U.S. barges to deploy in Saudi waters and U.S. carrier aircraft to refuel.

Similarly, Bahrain provided vital medevac and fire-fighting services in dealing with the attack on the USS *Stark* and repair services after it was hit. U.S. helicopter forces routinely staged out of Bahrain, and Bahrain allowed frequent port calls. At the peak of the U.S. buildup, one supply ship a week and five USAF C-141, DC-8, and DC-10 flights a day were off-loading in Bahrain.

The UAE allowed U.S. E-2s to refuel, allowed port visits, and allowed E-3As to overfly UAE territory. Dubai provided major repair services for the USS *Roberts*. Oman allowed the U.S. to base P-3s at Masirah and served as the "home port" for the carrier battle groups. It also allowed U.S. logistic support flights to use Muscat airport and the air field at Masirah.

While the exact extent of local cooperation with the U.S. is still secret, the U.S. commanders involved regarded such cooperation as being extraordinarily forthcoming and as absolutely vital to the success of their operations.

Similarly, the West European presence in the Gulf not only helped compensate for the lack of U.S. mine-warfare capability, it acted as a power influence in marshalling broad international support for the U.S. effort and in convincing Iran that no amount of escalation could drive the West from the Gulf. The issue was not simply one of ships— although the European contribution reduced U.S. force requirements by at least one-third in terms of ship numbers—it was one of political and strategic impact.

The Need for Innovation

Finally, it is worth pointing out that the U.S. faced much the same need for innovation that Britain did in projecting naval forces to the Falklands. Fleets designed for open war at sea or classic exercises in power projection are not ideal tools for every possible contingency in low-level war. This is particularly true in an area like the Gulf, where the U.S. was forced to operate in a very narrow area where Iran could strike with small craft and aircraft with very little warning and where so many complex political constraints applied to the operation.

While the U.S. was able to establish six different convoy routes through the Gulf, the waters in which it could operate were often very narrow, particularly in the area around Farsi Island. Iran's exclusion zone technically covered the main channel through the upper Gulf, and the 12-mile wide channel near Abu Musa in the Straits of Hormuz presented a similar challenge, as well as the risk of Silkworm attacks. The U.S. was forced to divide the Gulf into seven different zones and create a different mix of air and naval assets, strike systems, and countermeasures for each zone. The area also placed special demands on men and equipment. Temperatures outside the ships often reached 100–115 degrees, and temperatures inside often averaged 117 degrees. Sand was a constant problem, and the fine particles required special filters.

Defeating the Silkworm required the creation of a new mix of electronic warfare capabilities. The previous chapters have already described how the U.S. was forced to improvise to deal with the threat of the Iranian naval Guards and with the Silkworm. They have pointed out that the U.S. was forced to lease large oil barges from Brown and Root and use them as bases for its helicopters, sensors, and special forces. These two barges were called the *Winbrown 7* and *Hercules* and were stationed in international waters, some 40 miles from Farsi Island. Each held about 200 U.S. Army, U.S. Marine, and U.S. Navy personnel, including SEAL teams. They were commanded by a U.S. Navy officer, with a U.S. Army Lieutenant Colonel in charge of the helicopter force. The barges both flew the Panamanian flag and were surrounded by floating reflectors to help defend against enemy radars and missiles. While they were used as forward sensor posts and for special operations, they were routinely used to stage AH-58D Warrior helicopters for night-surveillance and attack missions and SEAL Mark III 20-meter patrol boats for day operations.[64]

The U.S. was also forced to improvise floating barges with radar reflectors to help protect Kuwait against Iranian Silkworm attacks.

This project involved mounting specially shaped metal sheets designed by U.S. Navy research laboratories on 20 barrages and effectively protected Kuwait against Silkworm attacks. In other efforts, the U.S. had to modify its jammers for the EA-6Bs used to help protect its ships against air and missile attacks and its LAMPS III SH-60B Sea Hawk helicopters to tailor their sensor mix and software to the missions required in the area.[65]

The U.S. also was forced to rapidly build up from a force of a command ship and four destroyers and frigates in the Gulf to a force of over 14 ships in the Gulf and 25 ships in the region, plus extensive additional special forces and air assets. While the full details of all the many innovations the U.S. was forced to do remain secret, some indication is provided simply by reviewing Table 14.4, which shows the changes the U.S. had to make in its forces during Operation Ernest Will. The obvious lesson inherent in the constant stream of changes in the U.S. force between June 1987 and May 1988 is that when one cannot predict the nature of combat, it is the ability to adapt to new conditions that will determine success.

The USS *Vincennes* and the Destruction of Iran Air Flight 655

The loss of Iran Air Flight 655 as part of the July 3, 1988, clash between U.S. and Iranian forces was a major tragedy, even in a war filled with so many similar tragedies. It killed nearly 300 innocent people and occurred largely because of human error. The operators of the ship-to-air missile defenses on the USS *Vincennes* interpreted radar data incorrectly and concluded that the air liner was actually a hostile fighter that was attacking the ship. The causes of these errors provide important lessons regarding the need to tailor any forces that are used in low-level conflicts to the particular conditions in the region and to political and civil, as well as military, risks.[66]

The Events That Led to Shooting Down Iran Air Flight 655

The sequence of events that led to the shooting down of Iran Air 655 is a case study in the complexity of modern combat, even in low-level conflicts. On the morning of July 3, 1988, the USS *Elmer Montgomery* was patrolling the northern portion of the Straits of Hormuz. At 0330 Zulu time, the *Montgomery* observed seven small Iranian gunboats approaching a Pakistani merchant vessel.[67] The small boats had manned machine-gun mounts and rocket launchers. Shortly thereafter, the *Montgomery* observed 13 Iranian gunboats breaking up into three

TABLE 14.4 Changes in U.S. Forces Committed to Operation Ernest Will: June 1987–May 1988

Date	Shift in Force Structure
1987	
2 June	Joint Chiefs of Staff (JCS) message to augment force in Gulf from 5 to 8 combatants.
1 July	Augmentation of combatants complete.
1 August	JCS messages to deploy additional army helicopters, USS *Guadalcanal* amphibious assault ship, and airborne mine countermeasures (AMCM). Four KC-10 tankers deployed to Diego Carcia.
5 August	Six army helicopters arrive.
8 August	Two ocean-going tugs from Kuwaiti oil company rigged for minesweeping.
10 August	Four patrol boat riverines (PBRs) arrive by C-5A.
14 August	*Guadalcanal* with AMCM and Marine Aviation Detachment plus two SEAL platoons, Contingency Marine Air Ground Task Force (CM) 2-88, and Marine special-purpose raid force arrive.
25 August	*Constellation* and *Ranger* carrier battle groups rotate in and out of region.
27 August	USS *St. Louis* arrives with two Mark III patrol boats and two Seafoxes.
30 August	USS *Missouri* battleship battle group arrives.
31 August	USS *Raleigh* arrives with four MSBs, four Mark III patrol boats, and two Seafoxes.
6 September	USS *St. Louis* departs.
2 October	Four additional Army helicopters arrive in Bahrain.
3 October	P-3C surveillance aircraft deploy to Saudi Arabia.
7 October	First of two Kuwaiti chartered barges commences operations under U.S. control.
9 October	USS *Mount Vernon* arrives with two Mark III patrol boats.
11 October	Mark II anti-swimmer system arrives in Bahrain for port security.
24 October	USS *Raleigh* departs with four coastal minesweepers.
30 October	Two ocean-going minesweepers (MSOs), USS *Esteem* and USS *Enhance*, arrive at Bahrain.
1 November	Two UH-60B helicopters arrive to augment Army helicopters.
2 November	Two additional PBRs arrive by C-5A.
5 November	Three MSOs—USS *Fearless*, USS *Inflict*, and USS *Illusive*—arrive at Bahrain.

(continues)

575

TABLE 14.4 *(continued)*

Date	Shift in Force Structure
15 November	USS *Guadalcanal* and USS *Okinawa* rotate in Gulf of Oman. *Guadalcanal* takes three RH-53 minesweeping helicopters with it when it returns to U.S.
18 November	*Ranger* and *Midway* carrier battle groups rotate in the Bay of Bengal.
25 November	USS *Missouri* battle group leaves area.
28 November	*Reef Point* deployed back to U.S. Pacific Command (PACOM).
7 December	The second of two Kuwaiti-chartered barges arrives in Gulf.
12 December	USS *Iowa* battleship battle group arrives in area.

1988

27 January	USS *Mount Vernon,* a landing-ship dock (LSD), rotates with USS *Portland* LSD. Three PBRs leave the area and two Mark III patrol boats are deployed.
12 February	USS *Iowa* battle group departs the area and is not replaced.
16 February	USS *Enterprise* carrier battle group rotates with USS *Midway* battle group.
23 February	USS *Trenton* (LPD-14) replaces the USS *Okinawa* (LPH-3) in the Gulf.
24 February	First two of eight OH-58D helicopters arrive in the Gulf to replace TF-160 helicopters. Two AH-6 and one MH-6 helicopter leave the Gulf the next day.
28 February	USS *Coronado* (AGF-11) replaces the USS *LaSalle* (AGF-3) in the Gulf and becomes the command ship of the Commander, Joint Task Force Middle East (CJTFME). Two Sea Fox boats redeploy with the USS *LaSalle.*
1 March	USS *Portland* (LSD 37), with two Sea Foxes, departs the Gulf, and the vessels are not replaced.
26 March	Second two of eight OH-58D helicopters arrive in the Gulf to replace TF-160 helicopters. Two AH-6 and one MH-6 helicopter leave the Gulf the next day.
16 April	USS *Roberts* hits mine.
4 May	USS *Stump* replaces the USS *Roberts.*
18 May	Two additional P-3Cs ordered to deploy to Daharan, Saudi Arabia.
20 May	USS *Forrestal* carrier battle group rotates with USS *Enterprise* battle group.
22 May	First AEGIS cruiser, USS *Vincennes,* arrives in Gulf.
25 May	Two additional P-3Cs arrive in Daharan, Saudi Arabia.
31 May	One additional PBR arrives in the Gulf.

SOURCE: Adapted from material provided by the U.S. Navy in February 1989.

groups. Each group had 3 to 4 gunboats, and they took position off the *Montgomery*'s port quarter.

At 0411Z, the *Montgomery* heard the gun boats challenging merchant ships in the area. It then heard 5 to 7 explosions coming from the north. At 0412Z, the AEGIS cruiser USS *Vincennes* was directed to proceed north to the area of the *Montgomery* and investigate. The *Vincennes*'s Lamps Mark III helicopter, which was already on patrol, was directed to observe the gunboat activity. Meanwhile, the *Vincennes* continued to observe an Iranian P-3 patrolling to the north.

At approximately 0615Z, the *Vincennes*'s helicopter was fired upon by one of the small boats. The *Vincennes* then took tactical command of the *Montgomery* and both ships closed on the location of the firing at high speed. As the two U.S. ships closed on the area, two Iranian gunboats turned toward the U.S. ships. They continued to close and the *Vincennes* was given permission to fire. This surface action continued during the entire time between the takeoff of Iran Air 655 and its downing. Another U.S. ship, the USS *Sides* was transiting from east to west through the Straits of Hormuz and was about 18 miles to the east at this time.

The *Vincennes* was now about one mile west of the centerline of the civilian air path from the joint civil-military airport at Bandar Abbas to Dubai. Iran Air 655 took off at 0647Z as part of a routinely scheduled international airline flight to Dubai. It began a normal climb out to 14,000 feet. It reached the Amber 59 air corridor, which was 20 miles wide (10 miles on either side of the centerline) and made a routine position report to Bandar Abbas at 0654Z. It was ascending through 12,000 feet at the time, with a speed of 380 knots. It was only about four miles off the centerline down the air corridor, but this was unusual because most aircraft flew the center line exactly. The Iran Air 655 never communicated with the air traffic control center at Dubai, and the center never picked it up on its radar. There was no readily detectable commercial air control traffic, and although there were no military electronic emissions, Iranian F-14s some times fly "cold nose," or without using military radars or avionics.

At approximately 0647Z, and while still engaged with Iranian gunboats, the *Vincennes*'s AN/SPY1A radar detected Iran Air 655 at a bearing of 025 degrees, 47 nautical missiles. The size of the aircraft could not be identified by the digital radar processing on the *Vincennes*, which does not show a blip in proportion to target size. It was simply assigned the digital identification code TN 4131.

At 0648Z, the USS *Sides* detected Iran Air 655, at a bearing of 355 degrees and a range of 32 miles. The aircraft continued to close on the *Vincennes*, which was right on the flight path, with a constant bearing and decreasing range. It was at this point that the IDS or identification supervisor on the *Vincennes* checked the airline guide to see if the aircraft could be commercial. Iran Air 655 was 27 minutes late, however, and the IDS incorrectly concluded that the aircraft could not be flight 655. At 0649Z, the *Vincennes* issued warnings of the Military Air Distress (MAD) frequency of 243 mhz. At 0650Z it began warnings of the International Air Distress Frequency (IAD) of 121.5 mhz. The airliner was them about 40 nautical miles from the *Vincennes*.

At 0650Z, several people in the *Vincennes* combat information center (CIC) heard a report of F-14 activity on internal voice circuits. The IDS also thought he had momentary indication of a Mode II-1100 IFF signal being detected, which he correlated with an F-14, although no such indication was later found in the data tapes. This identification as an F-14 was reported throughout the CIC on internal voice circuits, and the ship display assistant, hearing the identification, tagged the display signal with an F-14 symbol on the screens of the commanding officer, tactical action officer, and guided weapons officer.

The *Vincennes* began to issue continuous MAD and IAD warnings when the airliner closed to within 30 miles of the *Vincennes*. The ship issued a total of five warnings on MAD and four on IAD. At this point, the ship experienced a foul bore in mount 51, and full rudder was applied to unmask the after gun mount in the midst of an ongoing surface action. This further increased tension in the CIC.

At 0651Z, with the airliner as close as 28 nautical miles, the *Vincennes* informed the commander of the Joint Task Force Middle East (JTFME) that it had detected a closing Iranian F-14 and intended to engage at a range of 20 miles if the aircraft did not turn away. The commander concurred, but told the *Vincennes* to warn the airliner first. The combat information officer also warned the commanding officer that the aircraft could be a commercial airliner.

The *Vincennes's* warnings to Iran Air 655 continued, but there was no response. Although the aircraft reached the 20-mile point, the commanding officer of the *Vincennes* decided not to engage. The order was given to use the fire-control radar to illuminate the target, but there were no ESM indications. Due to an error in procedure, the illumination also did not occur until firing, although the impact was meaningless since the Iran Air flight had no military radar to detect the fact it was being illuminated.

At this point, the aircraft was ascending through 10,000 feet. Nevertheless, a false report circulated through the CIC that the aircraft was descending, although the aircraft continued to ascend until it was shot down. The individual responsible for this error could not be identified.

At 0653Z, with the aircraft at a range of 15-to-16 nautical miles from the *Vincennes* and 3.35 nautical miles to the west of the centerline of the air corridor, the USS *Sides* gave the last IAD warning to the aircraft. The aircraft was now climbing through 12,000 feet and had a speed of 382 knots.

At 0654Z, the commanding officer turned the firing key. The launch sequence took 14 seconds, and four seconds later two SM-2 Block II missiles left the firing rails. The missile intercepted Iran Air 655 at a range of eight miles from the *Vincennes*, at an altitude of 13,500 feet, and at a flight speed of 383 knots. The aircraft crashed about 6.5 miles east of Hengham Island. Some 290 people from six different nations died in the crash. At approximately the same time the aircraft was hit, an Iranian military aircraft took off from Bandar Abbas. Iranian F-4s were observed in the area some 30 minutes later.

The tragedy was compounded by several factors, including false reporting from the *Vincennes*, based on the false beliefs of the officers inside its combat information center that had been generated by their interaction and tensions during the intercept. The personnel inside the CIC translated various oral reports to believe that they had a firm indication that the aircraft had an F-14 IFF signal, that it was descending rather than climbing, and that it was off the standard flight path. In practice, this information was not provided by the ships' sensors, and the data from the tapes of the Vincennes's combat operations, as corroborated by the information of the USS *Sides* and independent intelligence sources, showed that the aircraft was on a normal commercial air flight plan profile, was squawking in the 6760 Mode III IFF common to such air flights, and was in continuous ascent from takeoff at Bandar Abbas until it was shot down.

The Combat Environment

The shooting down of a civilian airliner would have led to a storm of controversy under any circumstances, but the initial reports from the *Vincennes* and Iran were so contradictory that the end result was a host of conflicting media reports, defending or attacking the American position. These were rapidly followed by a host of equally misleading criticisms of the weapons systems, sensors, and battle management capabilities of the *Vincennes*, many of which failed to understand the digital nature of the radar on the *Vincennes* or which claimed the ship had IFF capabilities which simply did not exist.

These reports lost sight of the combat environment in which the *Vincennes* operated. They ignored the limited reaction times involved, the fact that the *Vincennes* was engaged in surface combat at the same time, that another Captain and ship were severely criticized when the USS *Stark* did not fire on a fighter on May 17, 1987, and that the sensors and battle-management systems on the *Vincennes* were designed to deal with complex air threats in a combat environment, and not to detect or identify civilian aircraft.

Little media attention also was paid to the overall pattern of combat activity in the area. The U.S. ships not only were shooting at Iranian gunboats, there were other gunboats in the area. They also were aware of patterns in Iran's behavior that led them to think the ship was at risk. Iran had conducted some 88 ship attacks in 1987, and 72 percent of these occurred in the shipping routes between the UAE and Abu Musa. All Iranian ship attacks from November 1987 to April 1988 with conducted in the southern Gulf, and nearly 50 percent were conducted at night. During the U.S. clash with Iran in April, the USS *Wainwright* had also encountered an aircraft that failed to respond to repeated warnings. The missile hit and damaged the aircraft, which turned out to be an Iranian F-4.

Although the F-14 is not normally used to deliver ordnance against ships, it can do so if it closes to a range of about two miles. The use of the F-14 was credible because of intelligence warnings that such modifications might take place and the fact Iran had had to conserve other air assets since August 1986, although most of the 187 attacks Iran had made of shipping between March 1984 and October 1986 were made by aircraft using iron bombs and Maverick missiles.[68]

The situation was further complicated by the fact that F-14s had been permanently transferred to Bandar Abbas, and the Iranian Air Force had changed its operating patterns at Bandar Abbas significantly during the month prior to July 3, 1988. Iraqi F-14s had flown six patrol missions out of Bandar Abbas in June and had already flown two in July. Iranian F-14s were observed flying at air speeds of 250 to 400 knots while climbing to station, and at 500–550 knots during air intercepts. Warnings were issued about more aggressive behavior on June 18, and the *Vincennes* had been warned specifically about the transfer of the F-14s, and again on June 30 and July 1, it was warned to anticipate more aggressive Iranian attacks on ships because of Iraq's gains on the ground and Iraqi air attacks on shuttle tankers. These warnings were accurate. A commercial ship—the *Karama Maersk*—had been attacked in the area by Iranian gunboats the day before.

The problem of tracking the commercial airliners in the area was also extremely complex. There are 18 air corridors across the Gulf, covering 50 percent of its navigable waters. A total of 12 of these routes cross the southern Gulf and Straits of Hormuz area. Seven go to the Dubai/Sharjah terminal control area and five to the Abud Dhabi terminal control area. At least 1,775 commercial airline flights passed through the Oman control center area during the week ending July 13, 1988.

While commercial aircraft did normally use the standard commercial IFF signals, Iranian combat aircraft used a variety of Mode I, II, and III IFF signals and often flew commercial air corridors. Iranian fighters also sometimes flew these corridors in carrying out attacks on ships, as did Iraq. Departures from commercial flight schedules were also common. Iran Air 655 was due to take off at 0620Z but actually took off AT 0647Z.

This made it almost impossible to track all the civil air flights going over the combat area and forced commanders to rely on radio warnings. These, however, presented problems because they interfered with air traffic control. For example, when the USS *Halyburton* warned away British Airways flight 147 on June 8, 1988, the airliner immediately came into a near-miss situation with another airliner, and Dubai's air traffic control filed a formal protest.

The U.S. Navy concluded after the incident that the *Vincennes* and other ships in the JTFME did not receive sufficient data on civil IFF procedures or airline schedules. The military naturally concentrated on the military threat. Even so, the *Vincennes* had no prior reason to worry about the problem. The U.S. force had issued 150 challenges during the month, from June 2 to July 2, and only 2 affected civil airliners. The other 148 affected military aircraft, and 125, or 83 percent, went to Iranian military aircraft. Seven were challenges to Iranian F-14s.

The Results of the Navy Inquiry

The shooting down of Iran Air 655 led to a rush to judgment that led to a flood of reports about technical malfunctions in the AEGIS air and missile-defense system on the *Vincennes*. These charges were generally based on early tests of the AEGIS system or mistakes based on press reports. None of the charges proved to be true when the tapes giving the exact history of the ship's sensors and data systems were examined in detail by a Navy inquiry.

For example, some reports claimed that the ship's crew should have known the size of the aircraft from the size of the radar "blip." Blips, or signals based on radar cross section amplitude, are not a reliable indication of aircraft size in analogue radars, and there are no blips in digital radar, only digitally processed readouts which are constant in size. Other reports claimed that the *Vincennes* had an operational system that could identify aircraft type and size from the radar readout. The actual technology involved refers to a secret airborne system still in early development and has never been deployed.

Charges were also made that the subsystems on the *Vincennes* were only suited for open-ocean operations. In fact, the subsystems were fully programmable and had been specially adjusted to deal with the short reaction times inherent in operating so close to the land. The AEGIS system is the only system in the world capable of such adjustment. Charges were also made that the system was so automated that it led to the mistaken identification and firing. In fact, there were men in the loop in every critical function, and it was their reaction under stress that led to errors in identifying the target. Finally, charges were made that Iran Air 655 should have been identified by an AWACS aircraft. The E-3As in the region were flying a northern orbit and could not cover the region with their sensors. An F-14 was dispatched from a U.S. carrier but could not reach the area in time to make any identification.

The U.S. Navy inquiry into the shooting down of Iran Air 655 produced very different findings. It found that the *Vincennes* had had good overall training and readiness and extensive special training for its mission in the Gulf. It found that its weapons sensors, battle-management systems, and weapons were functional. The anti-aircraft watch organization was properly manned and trained, and no anomalies were found in the operation of the AEGIS system or operator statements. One console was not operational, and one mount of the close in weapons system (CIWS) was down, but neither affected any aspect of the operation relating to Iran Air 655. There were difficulties in some aspects of internal communications, and these may have contributed to the misinformation that resulted from human stress.

A detailed examination of the tapes, recording all the data registered by the ship's sensors and consoles, clearly showed that the operators misread the speed and altitude provided to them and showed the aircraft descending from 7,800 feet and flying at 445 knots. At least four members of the CIC crew had this impression, although it was not justified from the data provided. Similarly, the identification supervisor (IDS) made an error in reading IFF data that was not a result of sensor information.

The end result was that a mix of the pressures of immediate combat and human error confronted the commanding officer, who had only three minutes and forty seconds of time from identification of the aircraft to the point he had to fire, with the following indicators:

- F-14s had recently been moved to Bandar Abbas.
- Iranian fighters had flown at the same time as the naval engagement on April 18.
- Any aircraft could be used in a suicide mission.

- The aircraft was not responding to verbal warnings over IAD or MAD.
- There had been warnings of an increased threat over the July 4th weekend.
- Increased hostile activity had been predicted for the 48 hours following a recent Iraqi victory.
- Iran Air 655 was not following the air corridor in the same manner as other commercial aircraft consistently followed: exactly on the centerline.
- The aircraft was reported to be flying at a lower altitude than commercial aircraft (COMAIR) was reported to fly in the past. It was reported to be descending and increasing in speed. The aircraft appeared to be maneuvering into an attack position.
- The aircraft was reported to have sent an IFF signal squawking in the Mode II common to the F-14.
- The F-14s were reported to have an anti-surface capability with Maverick and modified Sea Eagle missiles.

The end result was a mix of coincidence and human error that cost 260 lives. At the same time, however, Iran must also bear a considerable amount of blame. Even given the pilot workload during take-off, the Iranian pilot should have monitored the IAD warning frequencies. Similarly, Bandar Abbas, Approach Control, and Tehran Center either did not monitor or ignored the IAD warnings. Iran also allowed an airliner to fly at low altitude in close proximity to hostilities that had been underway for several hours. While it is unclear that the IRGC gunboats were in communication all of the time, they were certainly in communication with the military base at Bandar Abbas and had ample time to warn Iranian civil aircraft.

The Lessons of Shooting Down Iran Air 655

The key lessons of the shooting down of Iran Air 655 had nothing to do with military technology. The first lesson is that no mix of technology can control the risks and uncertainties of combat. This is particularly true in low-level conflicts which are highly political in nature and which involve opposing forces where there are no fixed patterns of conflict. Mistakes and problems are simply inevitable on both sides, and some will always involve innocent lives. It is clear that both the U.S. and Iran concentrated too much on the military situation and did not examine all of the risks to civilians in the proper depth. At the same time, the conflict in the Gulf involved so many possibilities that it is unclear any amount of prior thought or planning could have focused enough resources on this particular contingency to prevent it.

The second lesson, and one that has been driven grimly home by virtually all recent low-level wars, is that war cannot be managed to the point where it can avoid civilian losses or unpredictable tragedy. There is an acute danger in assuming that modern technology and communications can somehow create either perfect war or perfect conflict management. It is obvious from the Iran-Iraq War, the Falklands conflict, Israel's 1982 invasion of Lebanon, and the Soviet invasion of Afghanistan that such expectations are false to the point of absurdity. War kills, and it does not kill wisely or fairly. Nothing is ultimately more predictable than the fact that war will produce unpredictable losses. Any realistic intervention in a military situation must be based upon this reality.

Third, at a more technical level, the shooting down of Iran Air 655 showed that far more attention is needed to training under stress and to going beyond technical excellence to training crews to accept the actual stress of combat. Nothing is more human than to react to stress by imposing preconceptions or sudden misinterpretations on the actual evidence. This was a major recommendation of the U.S. Navy inquiry and one that has broad application to virtually every aspect of complex weapons-system training.

Fourth, wherever possible, nations should attempt to work out rules of engagement that offer the maximum possible protection to civilians. Little real effort was made to restructure flight paths and handle the problem of protecting civilian airliners until Iran Air 655 was shot down. The warning procedures, notification procedures, air control procedures, and flight patterns all increased the risk of such an event. While war may have no rules, particularly in highly politicized conflicts, it should be possible to negotiate a wide range of agreements, and special attention should be given to such negotiations the moment a conflict begins or seems likely.

Fifth, more attention needs to be given to the command-and-control and related subsystems at every level of military organization and technology to take account of the fact that low-level wars often do not involve an easy ability to identify friend or foe and may be subject to major political constraints. In the case of the *Vincennes*, for example, the displays, command, and communication procedures were heavily overoptimized for total war. A number of displays and command procedures have to be changed to establish better controls and checks to avoid shooting down an aircraft that blundered into a combat zone. It also would have been desirable to have computerized the civil air patterns in the area and to have added more radios to improve civil communications. The *Vincennes* had insufficient VHF radio capability to both issue warnings to an aircraft and survey the civil air traffic control facilities in the area at the same time. These radios were provided to U.S. warships in September 1988, but by this time, the war had already ended in a cease-fire.[69]

Notes

1. "Iraq: Those Reports of New Weapons," *Defense and Foreign Affairs Daily*, Vol. XIII, June 25, 1984, p. 24.

2. Rupert Pengelly, "Gulf War Intensifies," *International Defense Review*, 3/1987, pp. 279–280.

3. The hit effect of the Exocet was often impressive, given the comparatively small size of the missile. The AM 39 Exocet has a launch weight of 655 kg and a 165-kg warhead, with ability to trigger burning of its remaining fuel on impact. It normally penetrates before exploding or burning (which means oil will damp out many of its effects unless oxygen is present in the burn explosion area), but it lacks the power to burst most naval compartmentation. This indicates large warships like carriers would be far less vulnerable to such missiles.

4. Tony Banks, "Running the Gauntlet in the Gulf," *Jane's Defence Weekly*, August 1, 1987, p. 182; Larry R. Dickerson, "Iranian Power Projection in the Gulf," *World Weapons Review*, August 12, 1987, pp. 7–11; Pengelly, op. cit.; and U.S. State Department, "U.S. Policy in the Gulf," Special Report No. 166, July 1987.

5. Various companies made a small fortune selling devices like simple jammers, reflecting paint, reflectors, chaff, and decoys to tankers and cargo ships. These may have provided a morale boost but had little effectiveness against the missile systems used by Iraq and Iran. Most anti-ship missile systems can easily overcome such low-grade countermeasures.

6. The French and British both had to greatly improve the countermeasure defenses of their naval helicopters against small surface-to-air missiles when they deployed to the Gulf. *Jane's Defence Weekly*, April 9, 1988, p. 694, February 6, 1988, p. 205, and February 13, 1988, p. 269.

7. For an interesting analysis of the hydrofoil option, see Lt. Stephen Chapin, "Countering Guerrillas in the Gulf," *Proceedings*, January, 1988, pp. 66–69.

8. *New York Times*, December 20, 1987, p. 1.

9. *Washington Post*, January 20, 1988, p. A-18.

10. *Jane's Defence Weekly*, April 9, 1988, p. 694, February 6, 1988, p. 205, and February 13, 1988, p. 269.

11. Unless otherwise specified, the analysis in this section is based upon unclassified materials furnished by the U.S. Navy. The key source is Rear Admiral Grant Sharp, "Formal Investigation into the Circumstances Surrounding the Attack on the USS *Stark* (FFG 31) on 17 May 1987," Miami, Florida, U.S. Navy Cruiser-Destroyer Group Two, Ser00/S-C487, June 12, 1987.

12. During the days following the attack, rumors surfaced that there were two Mirages flying in such close formation that they appeared as one radar blip; that the planes had French, Egyptian, or Indian pilots; that the *Stark* was attacked with a laser-guided missile or bombs, and that the attack was a

deliberate Iraqi effort to bring the U.S. into the war. There is no current evidence to support any of these rumors.

13. *Aviation Week,* June 22, 1987, pp. 32–33.

14. The times used here are taken from the report of the House Armed Services Committee on the Iraqi missile attack on the USS *Stark,* "Report on the Staff Investigation into the Iraqi Attack on the USS *Stark*," issued on June 14, 1987, and from a chronology issued by the Department of Defense and presented by Rear Admiral David N. Rogers after he went on a fact-finding trip to the Middle East for the Joint Chiefs of Staff. Because of changes in the time zones in the Gulf, some reports use times one hour earlier.

15. Condition 1 is General Quarters, with all crewmen manning battle stations and all noncombat activities, such as mess operations, halted. Condition 2 is when a ship has been operating at Condition 1 for an extended period and critical operations like mess and repairs must be carried out. Condition 3 puts one-third of the crew at battle stations at all times. It is the normal wartime operating state. Condition 4 is used for routine sailing from port to assignment or in untroubled waters. Condition 5 is when a vessel is in port and only partly manned.

16. Iraq claims the course was 061 degrees. Ironically, an Iraqi fighter had flown a similar flight profile toward the USS *Coontz* only three days earlier. The *Coontz,* however, transmitted a message asking the Iraqi fighter for its identification and intentions while it was still 39 miles away. The ship also changed course to bring it broadside to the Mirage, mounted a Standard surface-to-air missile, armed the chaff launcher, and unmasked its radars. It never locked on its fire-control radar because the fighter's radar stayed in the surveillance mode. The Iraqi fighter came within 10 miles of the *Coontz,* but never turned on its fire-control radar, and went on to attack a tanker.

17. Other reports indicate that the *Stark* detected illumination by the search radar at 9:06 P.M., when the aircraft was 27 NM away and on a bearing of 269 degrees, and the *Stark* was then at 26.47.4N/051.53.8E.

18. Radars have two primary modes of operation: search and track. The radar pictures are displayed on a cathode ray tube screen and search radars cover a wide circular area, with displays somewhat similar to the weather patterns shown on TV. A tracking or fire-control radar emits a concentrated signal that follows or tracks a given object. When a radar switches from search to track, it is warning that the operator is considering firing his weapons. This is sometimes referred to as being "painted" or as "lock-on." Depending on the weapons system, its fire-control computer may need either a continuous or temporary track to fire the system.

Most modern weapons have terminal guidance to reduce or eliminate the need for continuous tracking. The Exocet has variable modes that allow terminal homing at ranges of 2, 4, or 6 miles from the target. The SLQ-32 on the *Stark* was programmed to detect the tracking radar on the missile. In theory, the radar operator on the *Stark* should have had both an audible and a visual alert that the Exocet missile was tracking the ship the moment its radar began terminal homing. In practice, he had turned off the audio alert because so many signals were coming in that he could not concentrate on his duties. He denies he had visual warning, but this may have been ignored in the confusion caused by so many activities in a complex signal environment. Further, the Iraqi Exocet may have been modified to turn on its tracking radar only at the last minute.

19. Repositioning the ship was critical for both optimal radar operation and to allow its close-in defenses to function. The STIR (separate track and illumination radar) has nearly twice the target track range of the CAS (combined antenna system). The CIWS cannot function if the superstructure of the ship is between it and the bridge. Failure to reposition the ship and take every alert measure as soon as possible creates far more activity in the CIS, which distracts all radar and early warning (EW) crew.

20. There are some differences in the reports because some ships had a nominal time one minute earlier or later than others. According to one report, the Iraqi fighter had fired one Exocet missile at 9:10:05 P.M. and a second at 9:10:30 P.M.

21. *New York Times,* June 4, 1987, p. A-9, and *Wall Street Journal,* p. 66.

22. The ship had only 30 OBAs and 400 air canisters when the attack occurred. It eventually needed 1,400 more canisters during the 18 hours required to fight the fire.

23. U.S. Navy reports issued in October 1987 valued the damage to the *Stark* at $142 million, with $77 million damage to the ship and $62 million in damage to government-furnished equipment. The Navy recommended that all new ships receive design changes to improve survival in missile attacks but noted that new U.S. ships like the DDG-51 already incorporated most of the lessons of the *Stark* attack because of information provided by Britain on its lessons from the Falklands conflict. The Navy also recommended more fire insulation for the bulkheads and undersides of decks, reductions in combustible materials (particularly electric cables), the use of diesel fuel for pumps, more smaller pumps, and improved fire-fighting equipment, including protective clothing and equipment for cutting through decks. One of the basic problems the U.S. advisory team faced was that the greatest single problem was electrical cables, and the solution required a conversion to next-generation optical fibers, which permitted both the use of fire-resistant cabling and a major saving in cable weight. *Jane's Defence Weekly,* October 24, 1987, p. 935; *Philadelphia Inquirer,* September 6, 1987, p. A-1; *Washington Post,* October 16, 1987, p. A-1.

24. The captain of the *Stark* later charged that the SPS-49 air-search and SPS-55 surface-search radars on the ship could not reliably detect a missile as small as the Exocet. This might have been true, but the *Stark* probably would have detected the missile if the Mark-92 CAS search/fire radar had been in the fire-control mode. He also charged that the SLQ-32 did not function. The SLQ-32 did have to be modified to improve its coverage of Exocet. Given the problems the operator had at the time, however, it seems just as likely that the operator did not notice, or react to, the warning. *Defense News,* November 23, 1987, p. 1, and *Navy Times,* October 26, 1987, p. 1.

25. The *Stark* did not, however, have the Block One version of the Phalanx. This uses an improved version of closed-loop spotting to simultaneously

measure both target and bullet location and constantly update the fire-control solution. It uses a six-barrel M61A1 Gatling gun with electrical train and elevation controls, and its improved ammunition feed system has over 50 percent more capacity than the original model. The radar is integrated into the system by a digital computer which controls a servo/gun mount. The radar operates in a standby mode, and the improved Block 1 version can attack high-elevation as well as low-altitude targets. There are well over 400 of the older Phalanx systems in service in 52 different navies.

26. The long range SPS-49 radar on the ship provides up to 200 miles of warning of aircraft movement. The Standard missile is a General Dynamics system with ample range to have attacked the fighter but was not used because it was not believed to be hostile. The AN/SLQ-32 electronic warfare and surveillance system is designed to detect and identify incoming radar-guided anti-ship missiles but does not seem to have warned of the attack or identified the missile. The Mark Sperry Mark-92 fire-control radar, which also directs the 76-mm Oto Melara radar-controlled gun, was supposed to detect the narrow-beam radar used when missiles were fired, but it may not have done so. The General Dynamic Phalanx gun system consists of a six-barrel radar-guided 20-mm Gatling gun that can fire 30,000 rounds per minute. Finally, the ship had a Tracor Super Rapid Blooming Chaff system with another automatic sensor and launch system, but this was not turned on.

27. *Washington Post*, June 20, 1987, p. A-1.

28. *Washington Times*, July 29, 1987, p A-6; and *Washington Post*, July 20, 1987, p. A-1, and October 16, 1987, p. A-1.

29. Three days earlier, the USS *Coontz* had a similar experience. It warned the Iraqi fighter at a range of 39 miles, turned the ship to improve its defensive position, and readied its chaff and terminal defense weapons.

30. At least the ergonomics of the system are highly questionable. The system produces only a short visual blip during the actual tracking of a missile. The operator not only had to watch the scope for this blip but had to communicate orally with the TAO. The ship's radars do, however, have a relatively slow scan rate and are designed for optimal detection of ships and aircraft rather than high-speed missiles.

31. The system had had some intermittent failures in late April, but there is no reason to assume it was not fully operational at the time of attack.

32. U.S. ships often were illuminated or painted by the radars of Iraqi aircraft. *Washington Post*, June 4, 1987; *Jane's Defence Weekly*, May 30, 1987, p. 1040; *New York Times*, June 4, 1987, p. A-9, and June 1, 1987, p. A-1.

33. *Washington Post*, June 2, 1987, p. A-11.

34. *Washington Post*, May 25, p. A-1, and May 26, 1986, p. A-15; *Aviation Week*, May 25, 1987, pp. 23–25. One theory advanced immediately after the attack was that the "accident" was a deliberate Iraqi attempt to internationalize the war. Nothing about the Iraqi flight pattern or prior Iraqi activity supports this thesis.

35. Iraq did not allow the U.S. investigating team that visited Iraq to interview the pilot. It claimed that he had 1,300 hours of flying time, including

800 hours on Mirage fighters. The Iraqi ambassador to the U.S. later conceded that the Iraqi plane might have made a navigation error. *Washington Times,* July 17, 1987, p. A-1.

36. Robert M. Greeley, "Falklands, Gulf War Spur Navy to Upgrade Short-Range Ship Defenses," *Aviation Week,* April 4, 1988, pp. 17–18.

37. For an excellent analysis of the detailed fire-fighting lessons involved, see James Kitfield, "Fire-Fighting: Have the Lessons Been Learned?" *Military Forum,* March 1988, pp. 22–37.

38. Ironically, the reflagging made a significant increase in the U.S. cargo fleet. The U.S. merchant marine was now half the size of the Soviet one. Although the U.S. calculated it would need some 373 vessels in a national emergency, with a deadweight tonnage of 19.4 million, it had less than 200 vessels with a capacity of 13.2 DWT and less than one-half of the tankers it required. U.S. shipyards were building less than 1 percent of world shipping, and the number of yards was expected to drop from 116 in 1982 to 65 in 1990. Furthermore, 45 of the tankers that did remain in U.S. service did so only because foreign flags were forbidden to move oil between Alaska and the U.S. This had some interesting implications for any war in the Gulf because U.S. ships had carried 80 percent of the military cargos in the Korean conflict and 16 million long tons of POL (petroleum, oil, and lubricants) and 65 percent of other cargo during the Vietnam conflict. Tankers were 30 percent of the ships Britain deployed to the Falklands.

39. This was not accurate. The force was not ready to deploy and was not airlifted to the Gulf until August 1, 1987.

40. Some of these mines later turned out to date back to 1908. *Washington Times,* July 2, 1987, p. A-1, and July 15, 1987; *Washington Post,* July 2, 1987, p. A-26; *Baltimore Sun,* June 27, 1987, p. 2A; *Christian Science Monitor,* July 2, 1987, p. 11; *New York Times,* July 2, 1987, p. A-2.

41. The Pentagon released an unclassified version of the plan on June 16, 1987. It makes no reference to planning for the mine-warfare threat. *Baltimore Sun,* August 23, 1987, p. 2A.

42. *Washington Times,* August 3, 1987, p. 1.

43. To put these numbers in perspective, classified studies have indicated that it would take a minimum of 25 modern minesweepers to keep the Gulf ports open, assuming a 1,200-meter wide channel is explored every 48 hours. *Jane's,* August 22, 1987, p. 296.

44. Department of Defense sources indicate that the USSR has only three ships designed specifically for minelaying operations but has 125 vessels which can lay mines, as well as aircraft and submarines. U.S. experts estimate that it has stocks of some 100,000 moored contact mines and 200,000 magnetic/acoustic fused mines. The Tango-class submarines, the oldest Soviet type in service, can carry 30 mines. The USSR has some 300 submarines with at least limited minelaying capability.

45. The Avenger program was funded in FY1986 at a cost of $256.6 million, with $297.3 million requested in FY1988. Ships are also being built by Marinette Marine. The MHC program was funded at $120.1 million in FY1986, but no money was requested in FY1987, and the House vetoed a request of $297.3

million in FY1988. The Administration plans to request $199 million in FY1989. *New York Times,* August 18, 1987, p. 6.

46. *New York Times,* July 29, 1987, p. A-1, and *Defense Technology Viewpoint,* August 31, 1987, p. 8.

47. The U.S. had an active strength of 21 RH-53D Sea Stallions. It took delivery on the first squadron of 12 on June 26, 1987, and had obtained three more by July 1, 1987. Its plans then called for 35 MH-53E Sea Dragons to be in service by 1990. See Scott Truver, "Airborne Mine Countermeasures in the U.S. Navy's Front Line," *International Defense Review,* 10/1987, pp. 1353–1359.

48. Helicopters are sometimes given credit for helping to sweep the mines from Haiphong Harbor in Vietnam. In fact, the U.S. sweeping operation only found one mine. The rest were rendered harmless by internal timing devices.

49. A new system called the AN/ALQ-166 will be deployed in the late 1980s combining advanced features for both acoustic and magnetic minesweeping and allowing multiple refueling and use by multiple helicopters without being returned to base.

50. *Washington Post,* August 2, 1987, p. A22; *Aviation Week,* August 3, 1987, pp. 25–26.

51. *U.S. News and World Report,* July 13, 1987, p. 39; *Washington Times,* July 2, 1987, p. A-1, and July 15, 1987; *Washington Post,* June 27, 1987, p. A-23, July 20, 1987, p. A-21, July 21, 1987, p. A-1; *Christian Science Monitor,* July 2, 1987, p. 11; *New York Times,* July 19, 1987, p. 12, July 21, 1987, p. A-8, and July 22, p. A-10; *Baltimore Sun,* July 1, 1987, pp. 1A and 2A, July 24, 1987, p. 2A; *Wall Street Journal,* July 1, 1987, p. 2, July 19, 1987, p. 12.

52. Free-floating or moored contact mines can be planted by dropping them over the side of any small ship with a crane. They are difficult to destroy, since a direct hit on the tip of one of the mine's spiked contacts is necessary to make it explode.

53. *Chicago Tribune,* July 24, 1987, p. I–1.

54. *Washington Post,* July 24, 1987, p. A-16.

55. *Jane's Defence Weekly,* September 18, 1987, p. 586.

56. *New York Times,* December 10, 1987, p. A-11; *Defense News,* April 4, 1988, p. 8.

57. Two fields were in the lower Gulf, with the rest strung out over the convoy routes. The mines were often poorly moored and had no safety devices.

58. The U.S. and U.K. are working to improve methods and software to detect influence mines. The state of current progress is classified.

59. James D. Hessman, "Mine Warfare: The Lessons Not Learned," *Sea Power,* October, 1988, pp. 37–45.

60. These statistics are based on work by the Center for Defense Information.

61. Anthony H. Cordesman talked at length with senior officials of Bahrain, Kuwait, and Saudi Arabia during a November 1988 trip to the Gulf. All felt the U.S. intervention was both necessary and successful. The same points were made in very different ways by senior Iraqi and Iranian officials.

62. The data involved were provided by the U.S. Navy and differ slightly

from the statistical summary presented earlier, which was prepared using commercial databases.

63. *Washington Times*, January 16, 1989, p. A-5, and *Philadelphia Inquirer*, February 12, 1989, p. 21A.

64. *Jane's Defence Weekly*, August 13, 1988, p. 243.

65. See David Harvey, "Lamps III," *Defense Science*, August 1988, pp. 28–30; and Bruce Henderson, "Interim Jammer Helps Make Prowler Effective in Gulf," *Aviation Week*, October 24, 1988, pp. 48–57.

66. Most of the analysis of the shooting down of Iran Air Flight 655 is based upon the *Investigation Report* by Rear Admiral William M. Fogarty, USN, which was submitted to the Department of Defense on July 28, 1988. Use is also made of extensive supporting material provided by the U.S. Navy. Other sources include "A300 Downing Clouds Aegis Capabilities," *Aviation Week*, July 11, 1988, pp. 16–22; Julian S. Lake, "The Recurring Nightmare," *Defense Science*, September, 1988, pp. 13–17; *Time*, August 29, 1988, p. 30; the *Economist*, July 9, 1988, pp. 9, 23, and 35; and Paul R. Jazka, "AEGIS System Still Gets High Marks," *Defense Electronics*, October 1988, pp. 48–60. Use was also made of reporting during the period by the *Washington Post* and *New York Times*.

67. Local time was three hours ahead.

68. The Maverick has a range of 0.5 to 13 nautical miles. It is TV-guided, and the pilot must track the missile and control it until it hits the target. The F-14 cannot deliver the Maverick.

69. *New York Times*, September 9, 1988, p. A-6.

15

CONCLUSION

The Major Lessons of the Iran-Iraq War

Any study of the lessons of war runs the constant risk of oversimplifying one of man's most complex activities. The Iran-Iraq War was an exceptionally complex conflict, and one which can only be understood by a close examination of its history and of the many shifts that took place during the course of the war. There are, however, several lessons that do clearly stand out from the rest:

- *Few wars have successful outcomes that are not based on a clear grand strategy and which are not forced on one or more of their participants in ways that make war an unavoidable alternative.* The Iran-Iraq War is a classic demonstration of the cost of an inadequate grand strategy. The ambitions of two competing autocrats and more than eight years of war did nothing to give one side a triumph over the other or even to resolve the centuries-long squabble over control of the border area and the Shatt al-Arab. In spite of all their ideological ambitions and claims, the war left both Khomeini's Islamic fundamentalism and Saddam Hussein's Ba'ath Socialism weaker in terms of both domestic and foreign influence than when the war had begun. Few wars in modern history did less to further the ambitions of the leaders that started them at so high a cost to their peoples.
- *Force ratios are a remarkably uncertain measure of military strength, both in terms of battles and in terms of the strength and weakness of a nation.* Iraq learned the hard way that a state in the middle of a popular revolution is far less vulnerable than the size and readiness of its military forces may make it appear. Iran learned the hard way that it could never exploit its potential superiority in manpower. Both sides found that there was little real correlation between the forces and firepower they possessed at any given time and the actual outcome of battles. The reality

of war involves far more complex variables than war games or military plans which only examine force ratios.

- *Military professionalism remains a critical variable in war.* For all of Iran's revolutionary fervor, it could not overcome the fact that the very fervor destroyed its ability to conduct a war with the military professionalism it needed to win. Iraq, in contrast, solely acquired much of the professionalism it lacked at the start of the war, and this eventually enabled it to win. In Third World states, however, military professionalism is highly dependent on a realistic and objective approach to allowing professionalism to exist at all levels of command and on honestly and objectively dealing with the problem of technology transfer. Most such states will find this difficult or impossible, and this will sharply degrade both their professionalism and their military effectiveness.

- *All of the military forces in recent wars have found it very difficult to effectively use combined arms and combined operations. Most have found it very difficult to use maneuver warfare effectively in any form.* Both Iran and Iraq had to struggle with their weaknesses in these areas for nearly a decade. Iran actually lost capability as the control of its forces passed into the hands of senior political officials. Iraq gradually acquired the level of capability it needed to defeat Iran, although at great cost and without achieving the level of effectiveness common in Western and Soviet-bloc forces.

- *Sheer mass, whether in terms of weapons or manpower, is no substitute for effective organization and command and control.* Time and again, it was the effectiveness of organization and leadership, not numbers, that shaped the outcome of battles. At the same time, the ability to find ways of improving targeting, battle management, and damage assessment proved equally critical. Iraq benefitted greatly from acquiring superior technology to manage its firepower and maneuver capabilities and from being able to adopt superior tactics.

- *Infantry remains a critical aspect of modern war.* For all of Iraq's advantages in weapons numbers and quality, it could not ignore the impact of effective infantry forces. Particularly at the time it invaded Iran, Iraq suffered badly from ignoring the need to support its armor with infantry and to have the ability to deal with infantry in urban warfare. Regardless of the advances in armor, firepower, and airpower, infantry strength is often still the most important single factor in shaping the outcome of combat.

- *Airpower remains one of the most difficult aspects of modern war* to use effectively and an area where most military forces tend to sharply exaggerate the effectiveness of their forces. Both sides in the Iran-Iraq War found it difficult to use their airpower to do more than deny the other side its ability to use its airpower. The strategic bombing, interdiction, and close air support efforts of both sides had remarkably little overall impact on the battle, given the resources each side invested, particularly before the war. Iraq did slowly improve its capabilities, but it took nearly half a decade to make the Iraqi Air Force effective, and it still had grave shortcomings when the war ended. Iraq's experience is also far from unique. Virtually all of the air forces engaged in recent large-scale combat have tended to grossly exaggerate their capability to influence the land battle at the time the war began and their actual impact on the land battle as the war proceeded.

- Complex weapons systems like aircraft, helicopters, and surface-to-air missiles require far more extraordinary efforts at technology transfer than most buyer and supplier states seem to realize. This is particularly true of sustained combat. Neither side was ever able to make its air control and warning, air battle management, and surface-to-air missile command-and-control systems effective. Neither side was able to fully solve the problems of maintaining complex systems like modern fighters and heavy surface-to-air missiles. Iraq benefitted greatly, however, from access to external resupply as a substitute for internal capability and from a steady improvement in its internal maintenance and support capabilities as well. It seems clear that the strength and effectiveness of most Third World states that acquire complex and high-technology weapons systems will be a function of the quality of their technology-transfer effort and not a function of the quality or quantity of what they buy.

- Barrier defenses and combat engineering can be extremely important in shaping the outcome of combat. Many of the battles of the Iran-Iraq War were decided as much by the quality of the barriers and combat engineering efforts on both sides as any other aspect of their forces.

- Logistics and supply are critical factors in any conflict, and expenditure rates may be far higher than most forces now plan for. Iraq, for example, consistently expended far more ammunition per gun in battle than Western armies plan to fire. It also consistently benefitted from providing oversupply rather than trying to predict or service demand. At least in this respect, the Soviet doctrine of "supply push" that Iraq built upon in structuring its logistic and supply system seems consistently more effective than the U.S. doctrine of "demand pull."

• *Power projection in low-intensity combat remains one of the most critical and complex missions for Western forces.* It is clear that this requires a great deal of flexibility and improvisation and that even a power as large as the U.S. will often be dependent on regional allies and other Western states for its success. It also is clear that any Western power that is forced to project power into Third World conflicts is likely to have to send forces designed for other types of combat and other missions and send them into very uncertain political and military conditions.

Under these circumstances, it is critical to allow the forces deployed to act on the basis of military professionalism and to avoid overmanaging the forces at the political level or expect military forces to substitute for successful political goals and capability. The U.S. benefitted a great deal from luck in terms of allied support, in terms of having the time to use its professionalism to adapt to military conditions for which it was not ready when it entered the region, and in terms of Iran's self-destructive actions and willingness to isolate itself in the international community. As Vietnam and Lebanon have shown, however, luck is not always a substitute for competence.

The Future of Iran and Iraq

While this book is not a study of the future of the Gulf region, of its politics, or of the West's relations with the Gulf, it is obvious that the tensions between Iran and Iraq are likely to shape the region's security problems for decades to come. It is equally obvious that the West cannot decouple its military planning from the need to secure its sources of imported oil.

Regardless of what regime is in power in either country, it is virtually certain that Iraq and Iran will continue to drive the arms race in the region during the next decade, as they have since the late 1960s. Even the best peace between Iraq and Iran is unlikely to prevent a continuing political struggle between the two states and a continuing struggle for influence over the southern Gulf states.

Iraq is almost certain to try to consolidate its present military superiority over Iran, to try to become the dominant military power in the region, and to try to expand its influence over the southern Gulf states. While Iraq may not radically expand its army, it is almost certain to try to obtain the most modern air-defense and air-attack systems available. It will continue to attempt to buildup a long-range missile strike force, expand its chemical warfare capabilities, and develop at least some form of biological and/or nuclear weapons capabilities.

The U.S. defeat of Iran's navy—and Iran's nearly decade-long lack of ready access to parts, munitions, and weapons modernization—will soon transform the naval balance in the region. A full cease-fire will mean Iraq's modern major combat ships in Italy can transit to ports in Iraq. Iran will have little choice other than to seek to rebuild its naval power and former supremacy.

At the same time, Iraq will still face serious military problems. It cannot increase its limited strategic depth. It cannot secure the Shatt al-Arab against the growing threat of Iranian missiles or ensure Iraqi access to the Gulf. Iraq will lack naval bases and seaports that give it a secure ability to use the Gulf, even if it should somehow obtain access to Bubiyan or Waribah. While Iraq's pipelines to the West offer an alternative to the Gulf, they will become progressively more difficult to defend as Iran rearms with long-range strike systems.

These Iraqi problems raise several interesting issues for the future. One is whether Iraq understands the limitations to any minor territorial gains it made, either in its conflict with Iran or in dealing with Kuwait. Another is whether Iraq will chose to build on its greatly improved relations with the southern Gulf states or will return to its past political and strategic ambitions and attempt to dominate them. Iraq also faces the problem of deciding how to deal with its war debts and oil-export policy.

The way in which Iraq handles these decisions could lead to added military tensions throughout the region, although the most likely near-term prospect is that Iraq will seek to form a political block with the southern Gulf states, not threaten them. Iraq seems likely to solve many of its debt problems by transforming its regional debts into grants or un-repaid loans and is likely to be content with export parity with Iran and the preservation of reasonable levels of oil prices. It is the long-term impact of Iraq's military power that is far more uncertain.

Iran is more of a wild card. It is still in the grips of a revolution which is only now beginning to deal with the internal issues it ignored during the war and whose long-term outcome is still very unpredictable. For more than a decade, its military forces have suffered from a lack of ready access to Western and Soviet military exports, from the collapse of its advanced training system, from the failure to develop modern logistic and support capabilities, and from an ineffective and divided command system.

Iran's defeats in mid-1988 crippled its land forces and resulted in the loss of more than one-third to one-half of its major weapons. Iran now needs thousands of armored and artillery weapons and hundreds of modern combat aircraft. It will require time, and at least $15 to $25 billion worth of investment, to recover its past military power.

At the same time, Iran's future approach to military modernization is unclear. In spite of the fact that the Revolutionary Guards have lost much of their status as a result of their defeats in 1988, Iran's forces seem likely to remain divided into prerevolutionary regular forces and revolutionary forces. The future mission and organization of Iran's revolutionary and regular forces is highly unpredictable, however, and Iran still has to make hard choices as to how it will allocate resources between conventional military, popular warfare, and internal security elements.

Given the events of the last few years, it seems unlikely that any outcome of the struggle for the leadership of a post-Khomeini Iran will result in an attempt to produce Iranian forces which rely largely on popular warfare. If anything, the near collapse of Iran's Revolutionary Guards in the face of the Iraqi offensives of 1988 and Iran's losses to a high-technology U.S. Navy seem likely to push Iran in the direction of finding some reliable supplier of high-technology military equipment for both its revolutionary and regular forces, although Iran may well find some mix of PRC and European imports and domestic production to be an adequate substitute for dependence on either the West or the Soviet bloc.

Key Military and Strategic Uncertainties

There is no way to estimate how this complex mix of trends will shape the future structure of Iranian and Iraqi forces. It is clear, however, that these trends will lead to dramatic changes in the military forces of both countries, in the regional military balance, and in the risk inherent in any resumption of large-scale fighting.

There are several key factors that will help shape the future military trends in the Gulf.

- No one can predict how, and how fast, Iran will rearm. It is important to note, however, that Iran successfully operated about 450 modern combat aircraft at the time of the Shah's fall and retains the basing and infrastructure to support a first-line fighter force.
- In spite of the near collapse of its training and logistic program, the Iranian Army has extensive combat experience and has operated a force of about 1,700 main battle tanks, or four times the present strength of Saudi forces. Its current Army manning is close to 20 times that of Saudi Arabia. If Iran can acquire major new

sources of arms, sufficient sea or airlift, or the ability to drive through southern Iraq, it will be a serious threat to the southern Gulf states.

- The Iranian Navy has lost many of its most modern missile-equipped ships and most of the rest are largely inoperable.[1] It does, however, retain large numbers of smaller ships, Hovercraft, and landing ships. It has extensive numbers of anti-ship missiles and missile sites covering the Straits of Hormuz, Kuwait, and the Iraqi coast. It can be expected to rebuild its Navy and to steadily improve its anti-ship missile and mine-warfare capabilities. It will be a growing threat to Gulf shipping, with growing Gulf-wide coverage.[2]
- Iran's Air Force is now reduced to substantially less than 100 fully operational combat aircraft, none of which has been modernized for nearly a decade. Nevertheless, Iranian acquisition of several hundred modern Soviet fighters, or Mirage F-1/Mirage 2000 equivalents, would restore its air power. This would allow it to challenge the southern Gulf states, even if they were equipped only with the aircraft they are now requesting. The Saudi Air Force will be vulnerable to saturation by high-intensity bombing raids on key targets, and the other southern Gulf states lack the air and sea power to cover the eastern or lower Gulf.
- Iran was arming for its own missile war at the time Iraq successfully launched its massive missile attacks. It is virtually certain to acquire missiles capable of striking at all the oil and urban targets along the southern Gulf coast at some point in the 1990s.
- Iraq's trend towards political maturity and friendly relations with the southern Gulf states began in the mid 1970s and before the Iran-Iraq War. This trend has been reinforced by the painful lessons of that conflict, but there is no guarantee that the present Ba'ath regime will remain in power. There is still at least some risk that Iraq's considerable military forces could come under hostile or radical control in the 1990s.
- Iraq now has about one million men under arms, and some 4,500 tanks, 500 combat aircraft, and 150 armed helicopters. It has 8 Tu-22, 8 Tu-16, and 4 CH-6D bombers, some armed with AS-4 Kitchen and AS-5 Kelt air-to-surface missiles. It has 94 Mirage F-1s (some with Exocet and others with extended-range fuel tanks), 150 MiG-21/J-7s, 40 J-6s, 70 MiG-23BNs, 15 MiG-25s, 30 Su-7Bs and Su-20s, 25 MiG-29, and 30 Su-25 fighters. It has R-530, R-550 Magic, AA-6, AA-7, and AA-8 air-to-air missiles, and AS-30 Laser, Armat, and Exocet AM-39 air-to-surface weapons. It will replace at least 100 of its current fighters with advanced types, such as the

Mirage 2000, Su-24, and MiG-29, by the mid-1990s. This will not only give it massive land superiority over Kuwait and Saudi Arabia, but air superiority as well, unless Kuwait and Saudi Arabia can obtain the the modern fighters and air-defense systems they are now requesting.

- Iraq will soon take delivery on a significant number of new naval vessels, including four Italian missile-equipped *Lupo* frigates and four 650-ton corvettes.[3] Iraq already has a major air capability to strike at tankers and targets in the southern Gulf. By the early 1990s, it will have modern strike fighters equivalent to those in the French and Soviet Air Forces with a range of up to 800 miles and much heavier and more lethal surface-to-surface, air-to-ship, and air-to-surface missiles. Iraq also has vast supplies of modern land force armor, advanced munitions, and C^3I equipment on order. Like Iran, it is certain to steadily expand its land and air-strike capability against the southern Gulf states throughout the next decade.[4]

- Iraq and Iran emerged with a desperate need to maximize their oil exports. Both can increase their oil exports to around 4 MMBD, and Iraq will probably be able to build to levels around 6 MMBD. This raises the specter of major pressure on the southern Gulf states to cut their production. While such oil wars are not a direct military threat, they certainly are viewed as one of the most serious strategic threats the region and the West may face in the near future.

- Both Iran and Iraq are certain to expand their gas-warfare capabilities and to conduct covert efforts to develop nuclear weapons. This will eventually give them the ability to add highly lethal warheads and bombs to their long-range missile and air-strike capabilities.

Iraqi and Iranian Progress in Creating
Weapons of Mass Destruction

All of these trends may prove to be important, but the most dangerous trends may well prove to be the expansion of each side's capacity to use chemical weapons and other weapons of mass destruction. Both Iraq and Iran used poisoned gas in the Iran-Iraq War. While chemical warfare was only one of the factors that contributed to Iran's defeat, it became increasingly important to the outcome of the war. Iraq acquired sufficient amounts of chemical agents to make mass use of such weapons, and the threat of gas attacks had a powerful impact on the morale of both Iran's troops and civil population.

TABLE 15.1 Iranian and Iraqi Progress in Creating Weapons of Mass Destruction

IRAN

Delivery Systems
- Scud B (R-17E) missiles with 230 KM range.
- Possible order for PRC-made M-9 missile (175–375 mile range).
- Iranian-made IRAN-130 missile with 150+ KM range.
- Iranian Oghab rocket with 40+ KM range.
- F-4D/E fighter bombers.
- HY-2 Silkworm missiles.
- Multiple rocket launchers and tube artillery.

Chemical Weapons
- Production of nerve agents has started or is nearing completion.
- Stockpiles of cyanide and mustard gas weapons.
- Substantial assistance in some aspects of production may have been provided by Japanese companies.

Biological Weapons
- Extensive laboratory and research capability.
- Active research effort may have begun in 1987.

Nuclear Weapons
- Efforts made to revive nuclear weapons production plant begun under Shah.
- Significant West German and Argentine corporate support in some aspects of nuclear weapons effort.
- Stockpiles of uranium.

IRAQ

Delivery Systems
- Tu-16 and Tu-22 bombers.
- Acquiring MiG-29 fighters and Su-24 fighter-bombers.
- Mirage F-1, MiG-23BM, and Su-20 fighter attack aircraft.
- Extended-range Scuds and other missiles called Al Husayn (390 KM) and al-Abbas (540 KM). Some reports of ranges up to 800 kilometers.
- Possible cooperation with Egypt in paying for development and production of "Badar 2000" long-range missile. This is also reported to be a version of the Argentine Condor II or Alcran missile. Ranges have been reported from 480 to 900 kilometers or of the Brazilian SS-300 Avibras with a range of 300 kilometers.
- FROG 7 rockets with 40-kilometer range.
- Multiple rocket launchers and tube artillery.

Chemical Weapons
- Massive production facilities and stockpiles of mustard, nerve, and cyanide agents.

Biological Weapons
- Major research effort. Production may have begun of at least one highly lethal weapon.
- Laboratory capability to make biological agents.

Nuclear Weapons
- Stockpiles of uranium and limited holdings of enriched material.
- Significant nuclear weapons research effort.
- Seeking to rebuild reactor capability destroyed by Israel.
- Unauthenticated reports may be "cannibalizing" enriched material France originally provided for Osirak for use in nuclear weapons or using plutonium obtained by reactor irradiation to build a few weapons.

Neither Iraq nor Iran will ignore these trends in shaping their forces, and a future conflict could be far more serious than the fighting between 1980 and 1988. It seems highly unlikely, for example, that Iraq would risk an invasion of Iran instead of a massive strategic bombing effort or that it would fail to use chemical weapons and biological weapons, if it can develop them. Iran seems likely to make equal efforts to develop its own biological and chemical weapons and seems equally likely to use them if a future war escalates beyond limited border clashes.

The major weapons systems affecting each country's current and future capacity to deliver weapons of mass destruction are summarized in Table 15.1. It seems almost certain that both sides will try their best to improve these capabilities unless they are far more successful in agreeing on a peace than seems likely. This, in turn, may drive other nations in the region to follow in their footsteps and may ultimately confront the West with the problem of trying to intervene in such a conflict.

While it seems impossible to learn some lessons from history, one clear lesson that emerges out of both the Iran-Iraq War and the recent trends in the region is that everything possible must be done to contain the violence in the area and to fight the proliferation of weapons of mass destruction. Tomorrow's wars may be infinitely more dangerous to the West and infinitely more tragic for the peoples of the region.

Notes

1. During the battle with the U.S. on April 18, 1988, the Iranian Navy lost the frigate *Sahand* and the guided-missile patrol boat *Joshan*. The frigate *Sabalan* was severely damaged by a hit from a laser-guided bomb.

2. See the IISS, *Military Balance, 1980–81* and *1984–85* for details (London, International Institute for Strategic Studies).

3. See Aharon Levran and Zeev Eytan, *The Middle East Military Balance, 1986*, Jaffe Center for Strategic Studies, Tel Aviv University, 1985, and the IISS, *Military Balance, 1987–1989*, for details on Iraq's current force strength.

4. For an analysis of the threat to Gulf tankers, see Dr. Raphael Danziger, "The Persian Gulf Tanker War," *Proceedings of the Naval Institute*, May 1985, pp. 160–176, and Anthony H. Cordesman's article in the February 1988 edition of *Seapower* magazine.

SOURCES AND METHODS

No effort to describe a process as complex as war can ever hope to be complete. This is particularly true when much of the material on the conflicts under study is still classified and where so many of the sources available on the war are in conflict. It should also be obvious to the reader that this study of the Iran-Iraq War is affected by the inevitable limitations of dealing with unclassified material and that this both increases the uncertainty in much of the analysis and forces it to focus on those areas where the most information is available.

Sources

It was possible to visit Iraq on several different occasions during the war and to talk to Iraqi officials and officers at some length, both in Iraq and overseas. It was not possible for Anthony H. Cordesman to visit Iran after the revolution, although he lived in Iran during the time of the Shah. It was possible, however, to interview Iranian officers in exile in Europe and the U.S., as well as journalists and scholars who had traveled to Iran. It also was possible to interview a number of U.S. and European officials on a background basis and access was provided to official working papers in some cases.

Nevertheless, most of the sources used for the analysis of the Iran-Iraq War were unclassified material and media, including translations of radio broadcasts and news materials, articles, books, and similar materials. While both Iran and Iran provided a virtual flood of propaganda as inputs to these sources, most of the unclassified analysis of the war was done by Western military experts and usually on the basis of uncertain data and limited access to the battlefield or those who fought upon it.

This has meant that much of the analysis presented in this study is based on sources which are often in conflict. The combination of Iraqi and Iranian propaganda sometimes provided insights, but it generally added the fog of politics to the fog of war and extended the fighting on the battlefield into a war of lies in the media. Western reporting on the war was often remarkably good, but it often also had to be based on such limited access to either side that it relied heavily on speculation.

The analysis of the history of the Iran-Iraq War presented the inevitable problems of trying to analyze history in real time. While the use of computer data bases allowed the rapid cross-correlation and checking of media reporting, it became obvious that many reporters were simply repeating what they heard from other sources and that there was little follow-up effort to check the facts surrounding a given battle. As a result, the reporting on factors like force strengths, unit types and identities, tactics, and conflict outcomes is often contradictory; citing multiple sources simply compounds the problem.

Mapping and location names also presented a major problem. The authors used U.S. Army and U.S. Air Force detailed maps, commercial maps, and, in some cases, commercial satellite photos. In many cases, however, the place names and terrain descriptions used in the combat reporting by both sides, as well as by independent observers, presented major contradictions that could not be resolved from available maps. This made it impossible to confirm the details of given battles and to provide meaningful maps of those battles. This was particularly true in the case of battles in areas where the land is subject to seasonal or deliberate flooding and where major changes can take place in the size and nature of water barriers. Similarly, many battles in mountainous terrain involved the use of local names or approximate locations which made it difficult to trace the action.

Methods

Many of the reports and data on the Iran-Iraq War disagree. In many cases, figures and data were adjusted on a "best-guess" basis. In others, the original data provided by a given source were used without adjustment, even though this leads to some conflicts in dates, place names, force strengths, etc., within the material presented. The authors felt the reader would benefit more in these cases from being able to see the actual data provided by a given source, rather than see the result of the authors' effort to standardize all figures, names, and similar material.

A special effort was made to analyze only those lessons of war which seemed to be clearly justified by the data, regardless of the conflicts in the data, and to draw general conclusions which could be repeatedly validated. Even so, judgments have had to be made throughout this book as to which interpretation of a given lesson was right, and many of these judgments had to be based on confidential interviews which cannot be described by source.

As in the other two volumes in this series, it became all too clear that no one outside the actual commanders involved in a given battle can be certain as to which interpretation of many issues is right. At the same time, it also became clear that combat experience is highly impressionistic. Participants in war are scarcely objective observers of the details of tactics and technology. They operate on the basis of limited and constantly changing knowledge, and their priority is combat and command, not record keeping and analysis. While some data can be reconstituted after the fact, much cannot. Once again, this forces any analyst into making judgments and informed guesses on the basis of inadequate data and sharply conflicting viewpoints.

The authors of this book fully recognize these limitations, as they do similar problems in the previous volumes. The fog of peace is just as much a problem in understanding conflict as the fog of war and is just as unavoidable. In practice, therefore, the reader should be aware that any given lesson in this book requires careful analysis of other sources and should not be taken for granted. At the same time, we believe that the mix of interviews, data bases, and written sources upon which this book is based represent a valid starting point for what is ultimately an impossible process—understanding the overall nature of modern conflicts.

RESEARCH BIBLIOGRAPHY

Abdulghani, Jasim M., *Iraq and Iran: The Years of Crisis*, Baltimore, Johns Hopkins University, 1984.

Abir, Mordechai, "Saudi Security and Military Endeavor," *The Jerusalem Quarterly*, 33 (Fall 1984), pp. 79–94.

Akhavi, Shahrough, "Institutionalizing the New Order in Iran," *Current History*, vol. 86, February 1987, pp. 53–56 and 83–84.

Akins, James E., et al., *Oil and Security in the Arabian Gulf*, New York, St. Martin's Press, 1981.

Albert, Garret L., *The Iran-Iraq War and the Development of U.S. Responses Towards the Region*, Maxwell Air Force Base, Alabama, Air University Press, 1985.

Albrecht, Gerhard, *Weyer's Warships of the World 1984/85*, 57th ed., Annapolis, Md., Nautical & Aviation Publishing Co., 1983.

Allen, Calvin, *Oman: The Modernization of the Sultanate*, Boulder, Westview, 1986.

Allen, Robert C., "Regional Security in the Persian Gulf," *Military Review*, LXIII, 12 (December 1983), pp. 17–29.

Amin, S.H., "The Iran-Iraq War: Legal Implications," *Marine Policy*, vol. 6, no. 3, Glasgow, Marine Policy Institute, 1985.

Amirsadeghi, Hossein, ed., *The Security of the Persian Gulf*, New York, St. Martin's Press, 1981.

Anthony, John Duke, "The Gulf Cooperation Council," *Journal of South Asian and Middle Eastern Studies*, 5 (Summer 1982).

————, *Goals in the Gulf: America's Interests and the Gulf Cooperation Council*, Washington, D.C., National Council on US-Arab Relations, 1985.

ARAMCO *Yearbook* and *Facts and Figures*.

ARCO Series of Illustrated Guides, New York, Salamander Books, ARCO.

————, *The Israeli Air Force.*

————, *Military Helicopters.*

————, *The Modern Soviet Air Force.*

————, *The Modern Soviet Navy.*

————, *The Modern U.S. Air Force.*

————, *The Modern U.S. Navy.*

————, *Weapons of the Modern Soviet Ground Forces.*

Armed Forces Journal International, various editions.

Army, Department of, *1985 Weapon Systems*, Washington, D.C., Government Printing Office.

————, *Soviet Army Operations*, IAG-13-U-78, April 1978.

Army Armor Center, Threat Branch, *Organization and Equipment of the Soviet Army*, Fort Knox, Kentucky, January 1981.

Atkin, Muriel, "The Kremlin and Khomeini," *Washington Quarterly*, no. 4, Spring 1981, pp. 50–67.

Auer, Peter, ed., *Energy and the Developing Nations*, New York, Pergamon, 1981.

Aviation Week and Space Technology, "F-15C/D Display Nears Test Stage," February 20, 1985, pp. 77–81.

———, "Integrated Systems Evaluated on F-15," April 11, 1985, pp. 47–57.

———, "Mirage 2000 Fighter," June 24, 1985, pp. 38–39.

———, "Saudis, British Define Terms of Tornado Sale," September 30, 1985, p. 29.

Axelgard, Frederick W., "The Tanker War in the Gulf: Background and Repercussions," *Middle East Insight*, III, 6 (November–December 1984), pp. 26–33.

———, *Iraq in Transition: A Political, Economic, and Strategic Perspective*, Boulder, Westview, 1986.

———, "Iraq and the War with Iran," *Current History*, vol. 86, February 1987, pp. 57–60.

Ayoob, Mohammad, ed., *The Middle East in World Politics*, London, Croom Helm, 1981.

Azhary-El, M.S., ed., *The Iran-Iraq War: A Historical, Economic, and Political Analysis*, New York, St. Martin's and the Centre for Arab Gulf Studies, 1984.

Aziz, Tareq, *Iraq-Iran Conflict*, London, Third World Center, 1981.

Baker, A.D., III, ed., *Combat Fleets of the World 1986/87, Their Ships, Aircraft, and Armament*, Annapolis, Md., Naval Institute Press, 1986.

Bakhash, Shaul, "The Politics of Oil and Revolution in Iran," staff paper, Washington, D.C., Brookings Institution, 1982.

———, *The Reign of the Ayatollahs: Iran and Islamic Revolution*, New York, Basic Books, 1984.

Banks, Ferdinand, *The Political Economy of Oil*, Lexington, Mass., Lexington Books, 1980.

Bass, Gail, and Bonnie Jean Cordes, *Actions Against Non-Nuclear Energy Facilities: September 1981–September 1982*, Santa Monica, Calif., Rand Corporation, April 1983.

Batatu, Hanna, "Iraq's Underground Shi'a Movements: Characteristics, Causes and Prospects," *Middle East Journal*, XXXV, 4 (Autumn 1981), pp. 578–594.

Baylis, John, and Gerald Segal, eds., *Soviet Strategy*, Totowa, N.J., Allanheld, Osmun & Co., 1981.

Be'eri, Eliezer, *Army Officers in Arab Politics and Society*, New York, Praeger Publishers, 1970.

Benard, Cheryl, and Zalmay Khalilzad, *The Government of God: Iran's Islamic Republic*, New York, Columbia University, 1984.

Bernstam, Mikhail S., "Soviet Oil Woes," *Wall Street Journal*, January 10, 1986.

Bertram, Cristoph, ed., *Third World Conflict and International Security*, London, Macmillan, 1982.

Betts, Richard K., *Surprise Attack*, Washington, D.C., Brookings Institution, 1982.

Bhatia, Shyam, *Nuclear Rivals in the Middle East*, London, Routledge, 1988.

Bill, James A., *The Eagle and the Lion: The Tragedy of American-Iranian Relations*, New Haven, Yale, 1988.

Bishara, Ghassan, "The Political Repercussions of the Israeli Raid on the Iraqi Nuclear Reactor," *Journal of Palestine Studies*, Spring 1982, pp. 58–76.

Blake, G. H., and R. E. Lawless, *The Changing Middle Eastern City*, New York, Barnes and Noble, 1980.

Blechman, Barry M., and Stephan S. Kaplan, *Force Without War*, Washington, D.C., Brookings Institution, 1978.

Bloomfield, Lincoln, "Saudi Arabia Faces the 1980s: Saudi Security Problems and American Interests," *Fletcher Forum*, 5, no. 2, 1981.

Borowiec, Andrew, "Turks Seek Aid to Upgrade Army," *Washington Times*, May 16, 1986, p. 7.

Bradley, C. Paul, *Recent United States Policy in the Persian Gulf*, Hamden, Conn., Shoe String Press, 1982.

Brassey's Defense Yearbook (later *RUSI and Brassey's Defense Yearbook*), London, various years.

Brodman, John R., and Richard E. Hamilton, *A Comparison of Energy Projections to 1985*, International Energy Agency Monograph Series, Paris, OECD, January 1979.

Brossard, E.B., *Petroleum, Politics, and Power*, Boston, Allyn and Bacon, 1974.

Brown, Neville, "An 'Out-of-Area' Strategy?" *Navy International*, October 1982, pp. 1371–1373.

Brown, William, *Can OPEC Survive the Glut?* Croton-on-Hudson, N.Y., Hudson Institute, 1981.

Bussert, Jim, "Can The USSR Build and Support High Technology Fighters?" *Defense Electronics*, April 1985, pp. 121–130.

Campbell, John C., "The Middle East: House of Containment Built on Shifting Sands," *Foreign Affairs*, Fall 1981, pp. 593–628.

Carlsen, Robin Woodsworth, *The Imam and His Islamic Revolution*, New York, Snow Man Press, 1982.

Carroll, Jane, *Kuwait, 1980*, London, MEED, 1980.

Carus, W. Seth, "Chemical Weapons in the Middle East," *Policy Focus*, Washington Institute for Near East Policy, no. 9, December 1988.

Carver, Michael, *War Since 1945*, London, Weidenfeld and Nicholson, 1980.

Chalian, Gerald, *Guerrilla Strategies*, Berkeley, University of California Press, 1982.

Chicago Tribune, various editions.

Choucri, Nazli, *International Politics of Energy Interdependence*, Lexington, Mass., Lexington Books, 1976.

Christian Science Monitor, various editions.

Chubin, Shahram, "Gains for Soviet Policy in the Middle East," *International Security*, Spring 1982, pp. 122–173.

————, *Security in the Persian Gulf: The Role of Outside Powers*, London, International Institute for Strategic Studies, 1981.

————, ed., *Security in the Persian Gulf: Domestic Political Factors*, London, International Institute for Strategic Studies, 1980.

Chubin, Shahram, and Charles Tripp, *Iran and Iraq at War*, Boulder, Westview, 1988.

Cittadino, John, and Frank McLeskey, "C³I for the RDJTF," *Signal*, September 1981.

Clark, Wilson, and Jake Page, *Energy, Vulnerability, and War*, New York, W. W. Norton, 1981.

Clemens, Walter C., Jr., *The U.S.S.R. and Global Interdependence*, Washington, D.C., American Enterprise Institute Studies in Foreign Policy, 1978.

Collins, John M., and Clyde R. Mark, *Petroleum Imports from the Persian Gulf: Use of U.S. Armed Force to Ensure Supplies*, Issue Brief IB 79046, Washington, D.C., Library of Congress, Congressional Research Service, 1979.

Collins, Michael, "Riyadh: The Saudi Balance," *Washington Quarterly*, Winter 1981.

Conant, Melvin A., and Fern Racine Gold, *Access to Oil: The U.S. Relationship with Saudi Arabia and Iran*, Washington, D.C., Government Printing Office, 1977.

————, *The Oil Factor in U.S. Foreign Policy, 1980–1990*, Lexington, Mass., Lexington Books, 1982.

Congressional Budget Office, *Cost of Modernizing and Expanding the Navy's Carrier-Based Air Forces*, Washington, D.C., Congressional Budget Office, May 1982.

————, *Rapid Deployment Forces: Policy and Budgetary Implications*, Washington, D.C., Government Printing Office, 1981.

Congressional Presentation for Security Assistance Programs, vols. 1 and 2, Washington, D.C., U.S. State Department, Fiscal Year 1987.

Congressional Research Service, Library of Congress, *Soviet Policy and the United States Response in the Third World*, Washington, D.C., Government Printing Office, 1981.

Conine, Ernest, "Soviets Sit on Oil's Power Keg," *Los Angeles Times*, February 17, 1986.

CONOCO, *World Energy Outlook Through 2000*, April 1985.

Conway's All the World's Fighting Ships 1947–1982, London, Conway Maritime Press, 1983.

Cordesman, Anthony H., "After AWACS: Establishing Western Security Throughout Southwest Asia," *Armed Forces Journal*, December 1981, pp. 64–68.

————, *American Strategic Forces and Extended Deterrence*, Adelphi paper no. 175, London, International Institute for Strategic Studies, 1982.

————, "The Crisis in the Gulf: A Military Analysis," *American-Arab Affairs*, 9 (Summer 1984), pp. 8–15.

————, "Defense Planning in Saudi Arabia," in *Defense Planning in Less-*

Industrialized States, edited by Stephanie Neuman, Lexington, Mass., Lexington Books, 1984.

―――, "The Falklands Crisis: Emerging Lessons for Power Projection and Force Planning," *Armed Forces Journal*, September 1982, pp. 29–46.

―――, *Jordan and the Middle East Balance*, Washington, D.C., Middle East Institute, 1978.

―――, "Lessons of the Iran-Iraq War," *Armed Forces Journal*, April-June 1982, pp. 32–47, 68–85.

―――, "Oman: The Guardian of the Eastern Gulf," *Armed Forces Journal International*, June 1983.

―――, "The 'Oil Glut' and the Strategic Importance of the Gulf States," *Armed Forces Journal International*, October 1983.

―――, "Saudi Arabia, AWACS and America's Search for Strategic Stability," International Security Studies Program, Working Paper no. 26A, Washington, D.C., Wilson Center, 1981.

―――, "The Saudi Arms Sale: The True Risks, Benefits, and Costs," *Middle East Insight*, vol. 4, nos. 4 and 5, pp. 40–54.

―――, "U.S. Middle East Aid: Some Questions," *Defense and Foreign Affairs*, June 1986, pp. 15–18.

―――, *The Iran–Iraq War and U.S.-Iraq Relations: An Iraqi Perspective*, Washington, D.C., National Council on U.S.-Arab Relations, 1984.

―――, *Western Strategic Relations with Saudi Arabia*, London, Croom Helm, 1986.

―――, *The Iran-Iraq War and Western Security, 1984–1987*, Jane's, 1987.

―――, *The Arab-Israeli Military Balance and the Art of Operations*, Washington, D.C., University Press of America-AEI, 1987.

Cottam, Richard W., *Iran and the United States: A Cold War Case Study*, Pittsburgh, University of Pittsburgh, 1988.

Cottrell, Alvin J., and Robert J. Hanks, "The Strait of Hormuz: Strategic Chokepoint," in *Sea Power and Strategy in the Indian Ocean*, Beverly Hills, Calif., Sage Publications, 1981.

Cottrell, Alvin J., and Michael L. Moodie, *The United States and the Persian Gulf: Past Mistakes, Present Needs*, New York, National Strategy Information Center for Scholars, 1981.

Crist, George B., "Prepared Statement to the Defense Policy Panel," *Hearings on National Security Policy*, House Armed Services Committee, 100th Congress, 1st Session, GPO, 1987.

Croan, Melvin, "A New Afrika Korps," *Washington Quarterly*, no. 3 (Winter 1980), pp. 21–37.

Cummings, J. H., H. Askari, and M. Skinner, "Military Expenditures and Manpower Requirements in the Arabian Peninsula," *Arab Studies Quarterly* 2 (1980).

Danziger, Raphael, "The Persian Gulf Tanker War," *Proceedings of the Naval Institute*, May 1985, pp. 160–176.

Darius, Robert G., John W. Amos II, and Ralph H. Magnus, *Gulf Security into the 1980s: Perceptual and Strategic Dimensions*, Stanford, Hoover Institution Press, 1984.

Davis, Jacquelyn K., and Robert L. Pfaltzgraff, *Power Projection and the Long-Range Combat Aircraft,* Cambridge, Mass., Institute for Foreign Policy Analysis, June 1981.

Dawisha, Adeed I., *Saudi Arabia's Search for Security,* Adelphi Paper no. 158, London, International Institute for Strategic Studies, Winter 1979–1980.

————, "Iraq: The West's Opportunity," *Foreign Policy,* no. 41 (Winter 1980–81), pp. 134–154.

————, "Iraq and the Arab World: The Gulf War and After," *The World Today,* March 1981.

de Briganti, Giovanni, "Forces d'Action Rapide," *Armed Forces Journal,* October 1984, pp. 46–47.

Deese, David A., and Joseph Nye, eds., *Energy and Security,* Cambridge, Mass., Ballinger, 1981.

Defense and Foreign Affairs, various editions.

————, "France's Special Operations Forces," June 1985, pp. 32–33.

Defense News, various editions.

Defense Update, "Helicopter Special," no. 60, March 1985.

de Galard, Jean, "French Overseas Action: Supplementary Budget," *Jane's Defence Weekly,* December 14, 1985, p. 1281.

Dunn, Keith A., "Constraints on the U.S.S.R. in Southwest Asia: A Military Analysis," *Orbis,* 25, no. 3 (Fall 1981), pp. 607–629.

Dunn, Michael C., "Gulf Security: The States Look After Themselves," *Defense and Foreign Affairs,* June 1982.

Economist, various editions.

Economist Publications, London and New York.

————, "Growing Pains, The Gulf Cooperation Countries, A Survey," February 8, 1986.

————, "Oil Turns Manic Depressive," February 15, 1986, pp. 61–62.

Economist Intelligence Unit, Keith McLauchlan and George Joffe, *The Gulf War,* Special Report 176, London, Economist Publications, 1984.

————, *EIU Regional Review: The Middle East and North Africa, 1985,* London, Economist Publications, 1985.

————, *EIU Regional Review: The Middle East and North Africa, 1986,* London, Economist Publications, 1986.

————, Keith McLauchlan and George Joffe, *Iran and Iraq: The Next Five Years,* Special Report 1053, London, Economist Publications, 1987.

————, Keith McLauchlan, *Iran and Iraq: Building on the Stalemate,* Special Report 1164, London, Economist Publications, November 1988.

al-Ebraheem, Hassan Ali, *Kuwait and the Gulf: Small States and the International System,* Washington, D.C., Georgetown University, 1984.

El Mallakh, Ragaei, *Qatar: Energy and Development,* London, Croom Helm, 1985.

Epstein, Joshua M., "Soviet Vulnerabilities in Iran and the RDF Deterrent," *International Security,* vol. 6, no. 2 (Fall 1981), pp. 126–180.

————, *Strategy and Force Planning: The Case of the Persian Gulf,* Washington, D.C., Brookings Institution, 1987.

Eshel, David, *The U.S. Rapid Deployment Forces*, New York, Arco Publishing, Inc., 1985.

Farad, Abd al-Majid, ed., *Oil and Security in the Arabian Gulf*, London, Croom Helm, 1981.

al-Farsy, Foud, *Saudi Arabia: A Case Study in Development*, London, Stacey International, 1978.

Fatemi, Faramarz S., *The USSR in Iran*, New York, A.S. Barnes, 1980.

Feldman, Shai, "A Nuclear Middle East," *Survival*, 23, no. 3 (May–June 1981), pp. 107–116.

————, *Israeli Nuclear Deterrence, A Strategy for the 1980s*, New York, Columbia University Press, 1982.

Fesharaki, Feridun, and David T. Isaak, *OPEC, the Gulf, and the World Petroleum Market*, Boulder, Westview, 1983.

Feuchtwanger, E. J., and Peter Nailor, *The Soviet Union and the Third World*, London, Macmillan, 1981.

Fiecke, D., B. Kroqully, and D. Reich, "The Tornado Weapons System and Its Contemporaries," *International Defense Review*, no. 2/1977.

Financial Times, London and Frankfurt.

Fischer, Michael M. J., *Iran: From Religious Dispute to Revolution*, Cambridge, Mass., Harvard University Press, 1980.

Flavin, Christopher, *World Oil: Coping with the Dangers of Success*, Worldwatch Paper 66, Washington, D.C., Worldwatch Institute, 1985.

Forbis, William H., *The Fall of the Peacock Throne*, New York, McGraw-Hill, 1981.

Fricaud-Chagnaud, General, "La Force d'Action Rapide," July 2, 1986.

Fukuyama, Frances, *The Soviet Union and Iraq Since 1968*, Santa Monica, Calif., RAND, N-1524, AF., 1980.

Fuller, Graham, "War and Revolution in Iran," *Current History*, February 1989, pp. 81–84.

Furling, R.D.M., "Israel Lashes Out," *International Defense Review* (Geneva) 15, no. 8, 1982, pp. 1001–1003.

————, "Operational Aspects of the F-15 Eagle," *International Defense Review*, 3/1975, pp. 129–139.

Gabriel, Richard A., *Fighting Armies: Antagonists in the Middle East, A Combat Assessment*, Westport, Greenwood Press, 1983.

Gail, Bridget, "The West's Jugular Vein: Arab Oil," *Armed Forces Journal International*, 1978, p. 18.

Gawad, Atef, "How the Gulf Was Won: Oil and Islam in Soviet Foreign Policy," *American-Arab Affairs*, no. 22, Fall 1987, pp. 56–68.

Ghassan, Salameh, "Saudi Arabia: Development and Dependence," *Jerusalem Quarterly*, no. 16, Summer 1980, pp. 137–144.

Goldberg, Jacob, "How Stable Is Saudi Arabia?" *Washington Quarterly*, Spring 1982.

Gordon, Glia, "Gorbachev's Middle East Strategy," *Foreign Affairs*, vol. 66, no. 1, Fall 1987, pp. 41–57.

Gordon, Murry, ed., *Conflict in the Persian Gulf*, New York, Facts on File, 1981.

Griffith, William E., *The Middle East 1982: Politics, Revolutionary Islam, and American Policy*, Cambridge, Mass., M.I.T. Press, 1982.

————, "The Revival of Islamic Fundamentalism: The Case of Iran," *International Security*, 5, no. 4, Spring 1981, pp. 49–73.

Grimmett, Richard F., *Trends in Conventional Arms Transfers to the Third World by Major Supplier, 1980–1987*, Washington, D.C., CRS Report 88-352F, May 9, 1988.

————, *Trends in Conventional Arms Transfers to the Third World by Major Supplier, 1978–1985*, Washington, D.C., CRS Report 86-99F, May 9, 1986.

Grummon, Stephen R., *The Iran-Iraq War: Islam Embattled*, Washington Paper 92, Center for Strategic and International Studies, New York, Praeger Publishers, 1982.

Gulf Cooperation Council, *Cooperation Council for the Arab States of the Gulf, Information Handbook*, Riyadh, Bahr Al-Olum Press, 1982.

Gunston, Bill, *Modern Airborne Missiles*, New York, ARCO, 1983.

————, *Modern Soviet Air Force*, New York, ARCO, 1982.

Gunston, Bill, and Martin Streetly, "Su-24 Fencer C; Major Equipment Change," *Jane's Defence Weekly*, June 22, 1985, pp. 1226–1227.

Haffa, Robert P., Jr., *The Half War, Planning U.S. Deployment Forces to Meet a Limited Contingency, 1960–1983*, Boulder, Westview Press, 1984.

Halloran, Richard, "Poised for the Persian Gulf," *The New York Times Magazine*, April 1, 1984, pp. 38–40, 61.

Hameed, Mazher, *An American Imperative: The Defense of Saudi Arabia*, Washington, D.C., Middle East Assessments Group, 1981.

————, *Arabia Imperiled: The Security Imperatives of the Arab Gulf States*, Washington, D.C., Middle East Assessments Group, 1986.

Hanks, Robert, *The U.S. Military Presence in the Middle East: Problems and Prospects*, Cambridge, Mass., Institute for Foreign Policy Analysis, 1982.

Hardt, John P., "Soviet Energy: Production and Exports," Issue Brief no. 12B75059, Library of Congress, Washington, D.C., Congressional Research Service, 1979.

Hargraves, D., and S. Fromson, *World Index of Strategic Minerals*, New York, Facts on File, 1983.

Hartley, Keith, "Can Britain Afford a Rapid Deployment Force?" *RUSI Journal*, vol. 127, no. 1, March 1982, pp. 18–22.

Hauner, Milan, "The Soviet Eurasian Empire and the Indo Persian Corridor," *Problems of Communism*, vol. 36, January–February 1987, pp. 25–35.

Hawdon, David, ed., *Changing Structure of the World Oil Industry*, London, Croom Helm, 1985.

Hedley, Don, *World Energy: The Facts and the Future*, London, Euromonitor, 1981.

Heikal, Mohammed, *Iran: The Untold Story*, New York, Pantheon, 1982 (also published as *The Return of the Ayatollah*, London, Andre Deutsch, 1981).

Heller, Mark A., Dov Tamari, and Zeev Eytan, *The Middle East Military Balance*, Jaffe Center for Strategic Studies, Tel Aviv University, 1985.

Heller, Mark A., *The Iran-Iraq War: Implications for Third Parties*, Cambridge, Harvard University Center for International Affairs, 1984.

Helms, Christian Moss, *Iraq: Eastern Flank of the Arab World*, Washington, D.C., Brookings Institution, 1984.

Hetherton, Norris S., "Industrialization and Revolution in Iran: Force Progress or Unmet Expectation," *Middle East Journal*, 36, no. 3, Summer 1982, pp. 362–373.

Hickman, William F., *Ravaged and Reborn: The Iranian Army, 1982*, Staff paper, Washington, D.C., Brookings Institution, 1982.

Hiro, Dilip, *Iran Under the Ayatollahs*, London, Routledge and Kegan Paul, 1985.

Horwich, George, and Edward Mitchell, eds., *Policies for Coping with Oil Supply Disruptions*, Washington, D.C., American Enterprise Institute, 1982.

Hottinger, Arnold, "Arab Communism at Low Ebb," *Problems of Communism*, July–August 1981, pp. 17–32.

Howarth, H. M. F., "The Impact of the Iran-Iraq War on Military Requirements in the Gulf States," *International Defense Review*, 16, no. 10, 1983.

Howlett, Lt. General Sir Geoffrey, "NATO European Interests Worldwide— Britain's Military Contribution," *RUSI Journal*, vol. 130, no. 3, September 1985, pp. 3–10.

Hunter, Shireen, ed., *Political and Economic Trends in the Middle East*, The Center for Strategic and International Studies, Boulder, Westview Press, 1985.

———, *The Gulf Cooperation Council: Problems and Prospects*, Washington, D.C., CSIS, 1984.

———, "After the Ayatollah," *Foreign Policy*, Spring 1987, pp. 77–84.

Hurewitz, J. C., *Middle East Politics: The Military Dimension*, New York, Praeger Publishers, 1969.

International Defense Review, Geneva, Switzerland, various editions.

International Defense Review, Special Series, various editions.

International Energy Statistical Review, Washington, D.C., National Foreign Energy Assessment Center, CIA, various editions.

International Institute for Strategic Studies, *The Middle East and the International System*, Parts I and II, Adelphi Papers no. 114 and 115, London, 1975.

———, *The Military Balance*, London, various years.

International Journal of Middle East Studies, New York.

Isby, David C., *Weapons and Tactics of the Soviet Army*, New York, Jane's, 1981.

———, *Weapons and Tactics of the Soviet Army, Fully Revised Edition*, New York, Jane's, 1987.

Ismael, Tareq Y., *The Iran-Iraq Conflict*, Toronto, Canadian Institute of International Affairs, 1981.

———, *Iraq and Iran: Roots of Conflict*, Syracuse, N.Y., Syracuse University Press, 1982.

Ispahana, Mahnaz Zehra, "Alone Together: Regional Security Arrangements in Southern Africa and the Arabian Gulf," *International Security*, VIII, 4, Spring 1984, pp. 152–175.

Iungerich, Raphael, "The U.S. Rapid Deployment Force: What Is It? Can It Do Its Job?" *Armed Forces Journal*, October 1984, pp. 88–106.

Iungerich, Ralph, "U.S. Rapid Deployment Force—USCENTCOM—What Is It? Can It Do the Job?" *Armed Forces Journal International*, CXXII, 3, October 1984.

Jacobs, G., "Afghanistan Forces: How Many Soviets Are There?" *Jane's Defence Weekly*, June 22, 1985, pp. 1228–1233.

The Jaffe Center for Strategic Studies, *The Middle East Military Balance*, Tel Aviv, Tel Aviv University, various years.

Jane's, *All the World's Aircraft*, London, various years.

———, *Armour and Artillery*, London, various years.

———, *Aviation Annual*, London, various years.

———, *Combat Support Equipment*, London, various years.

———, *Defence Review*, London, various years.

———, *Fighting Ships*, London, various years.

———, *Infantry Weapons*, London, various years.

———, *Military Annual*, London, various years.

———, *Military Communications*, London, various years.

———, *Naval Annual*, London, various years.

———, *Naval Review*, London, various years.

———, *Weapons Systems*, London, various years.

Jenkins, Brian Michael, et al., "Nuclear Terrorism and Its Consequences," *Society*, 17, no. 5, July–August 1980, pp. 5–25.

Johnson, Major Maxwell Orme, U.S.M.C., *The Military as an Instrument of U.S. Policy in Southwest Asia: The Rapid Deployment Joint Task Force, 1979–1982*, Boulder, Westview, 1983.

———, "U.S. Strategic Operations in the Persian Gulf," *Proceedings of the Naval Institute*, February 1981.

Jones, Rodney W., *Nuclear Proliferation: Islam, the Bomb and South Asia*, Washington Paper no. 82, Center for Strategic and International Studies, Beverly Hills, Calif., Sage Publications, 1981.

———, ed., *Small Nuclear Forces and U.S. Security Policy*, Lexington, Mass., Lexington Books, 1984.

———, with Harald Muller, "Preventing a Nuclear Sarajevo: Proliferation in the Middle East and South Asia," *Arms Control Today*, January/February 1989, pp. 15–22.

Jordan, Amos, "Saudi Arabia: The Next Iran," *Parameters: The Journal of the Army War College*, 9, March 1984.

Jordan, John, *Modern Naval Aviation and Aircraft Carriers*, New York, Arco, 1983.

Joyner, Christopher C., and Shahqat Ali Shah, "The Reagan Policy of 'Strategic Consensus' in the Middle East," *Strategic Review*, Fall 1981, pp. 15–24.

Judge, John F., "Harpoon Missile Target's Ships and Cost," *Defense Electronics*, April 1985, pp. 92–98.

Kaplan, Stephen S., *Diplomacy of Power*, Washington, D.C., Brookings Institution, 1981.

Karsh, Efraim, *The Cautious Bear*, Boulder, Westview Press, 1985.

————, *Soviet Arms Transfers to the Middle East in the 1970s*, Tel Aviv, Tel Aviv University, 1983.

————, *The Iran-Iraq War: The Military Implications*, London, IISS Adelphi Paper no. 220, 1987.

Kassicieh, Suleiman, and Jamal Nasser, "Political Risks in the Gulf: The Impact of the Iran-Iraq War on Governments and Multinational Corporations," *California Management Review*, vol. 28, Winter 1986, pp. 69–86.

Katz, Mark, *Russia and Arabia: Soviet Foreign Policy and the Arabian Peninsula*, Baltimore, Johns Hopkins University, 1985.

Kazemi, Farhad, *Poverty and Revolution in Iran*, New York, New York University Press, 1980.

Keddie, Nikki R., *Roots of the Revolution: An Interpretive History of Modern Iran*, New Haven, Yale University Press, 1982.

Keegan, John, *World Armies*, New York, Facts on File, 1979.

————, *World Armies*, 2nd ed., London, Macmillan, 1983.

Kerr, Malcolm, and El Sayed Yassin, eds., *Rich and Poor States in the Middle East*, Boulder, Westview, 1982.

Kidron, Michael, and Dan Smith, *The War Atlas: Armed Conflict—Armed Peace*, New York, Simon and Schuster, 1983.

King, Ralph, *The Iran-Iraq War: The Political Implications*, London, IISS Adelphi Paper no. 219, 1987.

Klare, Michael T., *American Arms Supermarket*, Austin, Texas, University of Texas Press, 1984.

Korb, Edward L., ed., *The World's Missile Systems*, 7th ed., Pomona, Calif., General Dynamics, Pomona Division, 1982.

Kostiner, Joseph, "The Gulf States Under the Shadow of the Iran-Iraq War," *Conflict*, vol. 6, no. 4, 1986, pp. 371–384.

Kraft, Joseph, "Letter from Saudi Arabia," *New Yorker*, July 4, 1983.

Krapels, Edward N., ed., "International Oil Supplies and Stockpiling," Proceedings of a conference held in Hamburg, September 17–18, 1981, London, Economist Intelligence Unit, 1982.

Kupchan, Charles A., *The Persian Gulf and the West: The Dilemmas of Security*, Boston, Allen and Unwin, 1987.

Kurian, George, *Atlas of the Third World*, New York, Facts on File, 1983.

Kuwait, *Annual Statistical Abstract*, Kuwait City, Ministry of Planning, Central Statistical Office, various editions.

Kuwaiti News Service, *The Gulf Cooperation Council*, Digest no. 9, KUNA, Kuwait, ninth issue, 3rd ed., Kuwait, Kuwaiti Universal News Agency, December 1982.

Lachamade, Pierre, "The French Navy in the Year 2000," *Jane's Naval Review*, London, 1985, Jane's, pp. 79–90.

Laffin, John L., *The Dagger of Islam*, London, Sphere, 1979.

————, *The War Annual 1*, London, Brassey's, 1986.

Leites, Nathan, *Soviet Style in War*, New York, Crane, Russak & Co., 1982.

Leltenberg, Milton, and Gabriel Sheffer, eds., *Great Power Intervention in the Middle East*, New York, Pergamon Press, 1979.

Lenczowski, George, "The Soviet Union and the Persian Gulf: An Encircling Strategy," *International Journal*, 37, no. 2, 1982.

Leon, Dan, "Iran-Iraq: The End of an Era," *New Outlook*, vol. 31, September–October, 1988.

Library of Congress, "The Persian Gulf: Are We Committed?" Washington, D.C., 1981.

Lieber, Robert J., *The Oil Decade: Conflict and Cooperation in the West*, New York, University Press of America, 1986.

Liebov, Robert J., "Energy, Economics and Security in Alliance Perspective," *International Security*, Spring 1980, pp. 139–163.

Limbert, John W., *Iran: At War With History*, Boulder, Westview, 1987.

Litwak, Robert, ed., *Security in the Persian Gulf: Sources of Inter-State Conflict*, London, International Institute for Strategic Studies, 1981.

Livingston, Neil C., and Joseph D. Douglass, *CBW, The Poor Man's Atomic Bomb*, Cambridge, Institute for Foreign Policy Analysis, 1984.

Long, David E., "U.S.-Saudi Relations: A Foundation of Mutual Need," *American-Arab Affairs*, no. 4, Spring 1983, pp. 12–22.

———, *The United States and Saudi Arabia: Ambivalent Allies*, Boulder, Westview, 1985.

Long, David E., and Bernard Reich, *The Government and Politics of the Middle East and North Africa*, Boulder, Westview, 1980.

Los Angeles Times, various editions.

Lottam, Emanuel, "Arab Aid to Less Developed Countries," *Middle East Review*, 1979–1980, pp. 30–39.

Lutz, Colleen, ed., *U.S. Role in the Persian Gulf and the Middle East Peace Process*, Washington, D.C., U.S. Department of State, Bureau of Public Affairs, April 1988.

MacDonald, Charles G., "The U.S. and Gulf Conflict Scenarios," *Middle East Insight*, 3, no.1, May–July 1983, pp. 23–27.

McGuire, Michael, "Projection of Force by External Powers," in *The Indian Ocean: Perspectives for a Strategic Arena*, William L. Dowdy and Russel B. Trood, eds., Durham, Duke University Press, 1985.

Macksey, Kenneth, *Tank Facts and Feats*, New York, Two Continents Publishing Group, 1974.

McLaurin, R.D., "U.S. Strategy in the Middle East and the Arab Reaction," *Journal of East and West Studies*, XI, 2, Fall–Winter 1982.

———, and Lewis W. Snider, *Saudi Arabia's Air Defense Requirements in the 1980s: A Threat Analysis*, Alexandria, Va., Abbott Associates, 1979.

McNaugher, Thomas L., "Arms and Allies on the Arabian Peninsula," *Orbis*, vol. 28, no. 3, Fall 1984, pp. 486–526.

———, *Arms and Oil: U.S. Military Security Policy Toward the Persian Gulf*, Washington, D.C., Brookings Institution, 1985.

———, and Shireen Hunter, ed., *Gulf Cooperation Council: Problems and Prospects*, CSIS Significant Issues Series, VI, 15, 1984, pp. 6–9.

———, "Rapid Deployment and Basing in Southwest Asia," *Strategic Survey*, London, International Institute for Strategic Studies, April 1983, pp. 133–137.

————, "The Soviet Military Threat to the Gulf: The Operational Dimension," Working paper, Washington, D.C., Brookings Institution, 1982.

Maddy-Weitzman, Bruce, "Islam and Arabism: The Iraq-Iran War," *Washington Quarterly*, Autumn 1982.

Malik, Hafeez, ed., *International Security in Southwest Asia*, New York, Praeger, 1984.

Manetti, Lisa, *Iran and Iraq: Nations at War*, New York, Franklin Watts, 1986.

Mansur, Abdul Kasim (pseud.), "The Military Balance in the Persian Gulf: Who Will Guard the Gulf States from Their Guardians?" *Armed Forces Journal International*, November 1980.

Mansur, Abdul Kasim (pseud.), "The American Threat to Saudi Arabia," *Armed Forces Journal International*, September 1980, pp. 47–60.

Marcus, Jonathan, and Bruce George, "French Rapid Deployment Force," *Jane's Defence Weekly*, April 28, 1984, pp. 649–650.

Martin, Lenore G., *The Unstable Gulf: Threats from Within*, Lexington, Mass., D.C. Heath, 1984.

Masters, Charles D., "World Petroleum Resources—A Perspective," USGS Open File Report, pp. 185–248.

Masters, Charles D., David H. Root, and William D. Dietzman, "Distribution and Quantitative Assessment of World Crude-Oil Reserves and Resources," Washington, D.C., USGS, unpublished, 1983.

Meir, Shemuel, *Strategic Implications of the New Oil Reality*, Boulder, Westview Press, 1986, p. 55.

MERIP Reports, "The Arabian Peninsula Opposition Movements," February 1985, pp. 13–19.

Middle East, "Guarding Turkey's Eastern Flank," April 1986, pp. 9–10.

Middle East Economic Digest, London.

————, *Oman: A Practical Guide*, London, 1981.

————, *Saudi Arabia: A Practical Guide*, London, 1981.

————, *UAE: A Practical Guide*, London, 1981.

Middle East Economic Digest Special Report Series, *Bahrain*, London, September 1981 and September 1982.

————, *France and the Middle East*, May 1982.

————, *Oman*, November 1982.

————, *Qatar*, August 1981 and August 1982.

————, *UAE: Tenth Anniversary*, November 1981.

————, *UK and the Gulf*, December 1981.

————, *UAE*, London, MEED, 1982.

Middle East Insight, various editions.

Middle East Journal, Washington, D.C., Middle East Institute, various editions.

Middle East Review, 1985, World of Information, Saffron Walden, England, 1985.

————, *1986*, World of Information, Saffron Walden, England, 1986.

Mottahedeh, Roy Parviz, "Iran's Foreign Devils," *Foreign Policy*, no. 38, Spring 1980, pp. 19–34.

Mottale, Morris Mehrdad, *The Arms Buildup in the Persian Gulf*, New York, University Press of America, 1986.

Mylroie, Laurie, "Persian Gulf Peace," *The World and I*, vol. 3, October 1988, pp. 63–77.

———, "Iraq's Changing Role in the Persian Gulf," *Current History*, February 1989, pp. 66–73.

Naff, Thomas, ed., *Gulf Security and the Iran-Iraq War*, Washington, D.C., National Defense University Press, 1985.

Nakhleh, Emile A., *The Gulf Cooperation Council: Policies, Problems, and Prospects*, New York, Praegar, 1986.

———, ed., *The Role of the U.S. Navy in the Persian Gulf*, CNA 88-0535, Arlington, Va., Center for Naval Analysis, March 14, 1988.

Nation, Craig R., *Soviet Conceptualization of the Iranian Revolution*, Paper no. 402, The Carl Beck Papers in Russian and East European Studies, Pittsburgh, University of Pittsburgh, 1986.

National Foreign Assessment Center, *International Energy Statistical Review*, Washington, D.C., Photoduplication Service, Library of Congress, 1978–1986.

Natkiel, Richard, *Atlas of the 20th Century*, New York, Facts on File, 1982.

Navy, Department of, Office of the Chief of Naval Operations, *Understanding Soviet Naval Developments*, Washington, D.C., Government Printing Office, April 1985 .

"Nearby Observer," "The Afghan-Soviet War: Stalemate or Solution?" *Middle East Journal*, Spring 1982, pp. 151–164.

Neuman, Stephanie, *Defense Planning in Less-Industrialized States*, Lexington, Mass., Lexington Books, 1984.

Neumann, Robert G., and Shireen T. Hunter, "The Crisis in the Gulf: Reasons for Concern but Not Panic," *American-Arab Affairs*, 9, Summer 1984, pp. 16–21.

Newhouse, John, "The Diplomatic Round, Politics and Weapons Sales," *New Yorker*, June 9, 1986, pp. 46–69.

New York Times, various editions.

Nichols, Bill, and Les Aspin, eds., *National Security Policy Implications of U.S. Operations in the Persian Gulf*, Report of the Defense Policy Panel and the Investigations Subcommittee of the Committee on Armed Services, House of Representatives, 100th Congress, 1st Session, July 1987.

Nissman, David B., *The Soviet Union and Iranian Azerbaijan: The Use of Nationalism for Political Penetration*, Boulder, Westview, 1987.

Nonneman, Gerd, *Iraq, the Gulf States, and the War: A Changing Relationship*, London, Ithaca Press, 1986.

Novik, Nimrod, *Encounter with Reality: Reagan and the Middle East*, Boulder, Westview Press, 1985.

Noyes, James H., *The Clouded Lens*, Stanford, Calif., Hoover Institution, 1982.

Nugent, Jeffery B., and Theodore Thomas, eds., *Bahrain and the Gulf: Past Perspectives and Alternative Futures*, New York, St. Martin's, 1985.

O'Ballance, Edgar, "The Iran-Iraq War," *Marine Corps Gazette*, February 1982, pp. 44–49.

————, *The Gulf War*, London, Brassey's, 1988.

Ochsenwald, William, "Saudi Arabia and the Islamic Revival," *International Journal of Middle East Studies*, 13, no. 3, August 1981, pp. 271–286.

Odell, Peter R., and Kenneth E. Rosing, *The Future of Oil: A Simulation Study*, London, Nichols, 1980.

O'Dwyer-Russel, Simon, "Beyond the Falklands—The Role of Britain's Out of Area Joint Forces," *Jane's Defence Weekly*, January 11, 1986, pp. 26–27.

OECD/IEA, *Oil and Gas Statistics, 1985*, no. 4, Paris, 1986.

The Oil and Gas Journal, "Worldwide Report," December 31, 1984.

Olson, William J., "The Iran-Iraq War and the Future of the Persian Gulf," *Military Review*, LXIV, 2, March 1984, pp. 17–29.

————, "The Gulf War: Peace in Our Time," *Parameters*, vol. 16, Winter 1986, pp. 47–56.

————, ed., *U.S. Strategic Interests in the Gulf Region*, Boulder, Westview, 1987.

Oman and Its Renaissance, London, Stacey International, 1980.

Oman: A Practical Guide, London, MEED, 1982.

Oman, Sultanate of, *Oman in Ten Years*, Muscat, Ministry of Information, 1980.

————, *Second Five Year Plan*, 1981–85, Muscat Development Council, 1981.

Organization of Petroleum Exporting Countries, *Annual Report*, Vienna, various years.

Osama, Abdul Rhman, *The Dilemma of Development in the Arabian Peninsula*, London, Croom Helm, 1987.

Osbourne, Christine, *The Gulf States and Oman*, London, Croom Helm, 1977.

Page, Stephen, "The Soviet Union and the GCC States: A Search for Openings," *Arab-American Affairs*, Spring 1987, pp. 38–56.

Pagliano, Gary J., ed., "Insuring U.S. Interests in the Persian Gulf," Summary of the Workshop of the Congressional Research Service, Washington, D.C., CRS, October 6, 1987.

Pahlavi, Mohammed Reza, *The Shah's Story*, London, Michael Joseph, 1980.

Pajak, Roger F., *Nuclear Proliferation in the Middle East: Implications for the Superpowers*, Washington, D.C., National Defense University, 1982.

Paul, Jim, "Insurrection at Mecca," *MERIP Reports*, no. 86, October 1980.

Peck, Malcom C., *The United Arab Emirates: A Venture in Unity*, Boulder, Westview, 1986.

Perlmutter, Amos, Michael Handel, and Uri Bar-Joseph, *Two Minutes Over Baghdad*, London, Corgi, 1982.

Perry, Charles, *The West, Japan, and Cape Route Imports: The Oil and Non-Fuel Mineral Trades*, Cambridge, Mass., Institute for Foreign Policy Analysis, 1982.

Peterson, Eric, *The Gulf Cooperation Council, Search for Unity in a Dynamic Region*, Boulder, Westview, 1988.

Peterson, J. E., *Defending Arabia*, New York, St. Martin's, 1986.

————, "The GCC States After the Iran-Iraq War," *Arab-American Affairs*, no. 26, Fall 1988, pp. 96–106.

Petroleum Intelligence Weekly, New York.

Pierre, Andrew J., "Beyond the 'Plane Package': Arms and Politics in the Middle East," *International Security*, 3, no. 1, Summer 1978, pp. 148–161.

———, *The Global Politics of Arms Sales*, Princeton, N.J., Princeton University Press, 1982.

Pipes, Daniel, "Increasing Security in the Persian Gulf," *Orbis*, 26, Spring 1982.

Pikva, Otto von, *Armies of the Middle East*, New York, Mayflower Books, 1979.

Plascov, Avi, *Security in the Persian Gulf: Modernization, Political Development and Stability*, Aldershot, Gower, 1982.

Platt's Oil Price Handbook, New York.

Pradas, Col. Alfred B., *Trilateral Military Aid in the Middle East: The Yemen Program*, Washington, D.C., National Defense University, 1979.

Pridham, B.R., ed., *The Arab Gulf and the West*, New York, St. Martin's Press, 1985.

———, *Oman: Economic, Social, and Strategic Developments*, London, Croom Helm, 1987.

Pry, Peter, *Israel's Nuclear Arsenal*, Boulder, Westview Press, 1984.

Quandt, William B., "The Crisis in the Gulf: Policy Options and Regional Implications," *American-Arab Affairs*, 9, Summer 1984, pp. 1–7.

———, "Riyadh Between the Superpowers," *Foreign Policy*, no. 44, Fall 1981.

———, *Saudi Arabia in the 1980s: Foreign Policy, Security and Oil*, Washington, D.C., Brookings Institution, 1982.

———, *Saudi Arabia's Oil Policy: A Staff Paper*, Washington, D.C., Brookings Institution, 1982.

Ra'anan, Uri, *The USSR Arms the Third World*, Cambridge, Mass., M.I.T. Press, 1969.

Raj, Christopher, "The Iran-Iraq War and the Arab Response," *IDSA Journal*, vol. 16, January–March, 1984, pp. 232–239.

Ramazani, R.K., *Revolutionary Iran: Challenge and Response in the Middle East*, Baltimore, Johns Hopkins University, 1986.

———, "The Iran-Iraq War and the Persian Gulf Crisis," *Current History*, vol. 87, February 1988, pp. 64, 86–88.

Randol, William L., *Petroleum Monitor*, New York, First Boston Corporation, various editions.

Ransom, David M., Lt. Colonel Lawrence J. MacDonald, and W. Nathaniel Howell, "Atlantic Cooperation for Persian Gulf Security," *Essays on Strategy*, Washington, D.C., National Defense University, 1986.

Record, Jeffrey, *The Rapid Deployment Force*, Cambridge, Mass., Institute for Foreign Policy Analysis, 1981.

Roberts, Hugh, *An Urban Profile of the Middle East*, London, Croom Helm, 1979.

Robinson, Julian Perry, *Chemical Warfare Arms Control: A Framework for Considering Policy Alternatives*, London, Taylor and Francis, 1982.

Rosen, Barry, ed., *Iran Since the Revolution: Internal Dynamics, Regional Conflict, and the Superpowers*, New York, Columbia University, 1985.

Ross, Dennis, "Considering Soviet Threats to the Persian Gulf," *International Security*, 6, no. 2, Fall 1981.

————, "Soviet Views Toward the Gulf War," *Orbis*, XVIII, 3, Fall 1984, pp. 437–446.

Rouleau, Eric, "Khomeini's Iran," *Foreign Affairs*, Fall 1980, pp. 1–20.

————, "The War and the Struggle for the State," *MERIP Reports*, no. 98, July–August 1981, pp. 3–8.

Royal United Services Institute/Brassey's, *International Weapons Development*, 4th ed., London, Brassey's, 1981.

Rubin, Barry, *Paved with Good Intentions*, New York, Oxford University Press, 1980.

Rubinstein, *Soviet Policy Towards Turkey, Iran, and Afghanistan: The Dynamics of Influence*, New York, Praeger Publishers, 1982.

al-Rumaihi, Mohammed, "Arabian Gulf Security," *American Arab Affairs*, no. 23, Winter 1987–1988.

Rumaihi, Mohammed, *Beyond Oil: Unity and Development in the Gulf*, London, Al Saqi Books, 1986.

Russi, Pierre, *Iraq, the Land of the New River*, Paris, Les Editions, J.A., 1980.

Rustow, Dankwart, *Oil and Turmoil: America Faces OPEC and the Middle East*, New York, Norton, 1982.

Saboe, Cynthia, ed., *U.S. Policy in the Persian Gulf and Kuwait Reflagging*, Washington, D.C., U.S. Department of State, Bureau of Public Affairs, June 1987.

Safran, Nadav, *Saudi Arabia: The Ceaseless Quest for Security*, Cambridge, Mass., and London, Belknap Press of Harvard University Press, 1985.

Saikal, Amin, *The Rise and Fall of the Shah*, Princeton, N.J., Princeton University Press, 1980.

————, "Soviet Policy Towards Southeast Asia," *Annals of the American Academy of Political Sciences*, vol. 481, Spetember 1985, pp. 104–116.

Saivetz, Carol R., *The Soviet Union and the Gulf in the 1980s*, Boulder, Westview, 1986.

Salameh, Ghassane, "Checkmate in the Gulf War," *MERIP Reports*, XIV, 6/7, July–September 1984, pp. 15–21.

al-Salem, Faisal, "The United States and the Gulf: What Do the Arabs Want?" *Journal of South Asian and Middle Eastern Studies*, 6, Fall 1982.

Salvy, Robert, "Updating Older Combat Aircraft," *International Defense Review*, 12/1988, pp. 1587–1593.

Sandwick, John A., ed., *The Gulf Cooperation Council: Moderation and Stability in an Interdependent World*, Boulder, Westview, 1987.

Saudi Arabia, Kingdom of, *Annual Report of the Saudi Fund for Development, 1984–1985*, Saudi Arabia, 1985.

————, Ministry of Finance and National Economy, *Statistical Yearbook*, annual, Jidda, various years.

————, Saudi Arabian Monetary Agency, Research and Statistics Department, *Statistical Summary*, Riyadh, various years.

————, *Third Development Plan*, 1980–85, Riyadh, Ministry of Planning Press, 1980.

Schahgaldian, Nikola B., *The Iranian Military Under the Islamic Republic*, Santa Monica, Rand R-3473-USDP, 1987.

Schmid, Alex P., *Soviet Military Interventions Since 1945*, New Brunswick, N.J., Transaction, Inc., 1985.

Schmitt, Richard B., "U.S. Dependence on Oil, Gas Imports May Grow," *Wall Street Journal*, April 23, 1985.

Schrage, Daniel P., "Air Warfare: Helicopters and the Battlefield," *Journal of Defense and Diplomacy*, vol. 3, no. 5, pp. 17–20.

Schultz, James B., "New Strategies and Soviet Threats Spark EW Responses," *Defense Electronics*, February 1985, pp. 17–21.

Sciolino, Paulo, "Iran's Durable Revolution," *Foreign Affairs*, Spring 1983, pp. 893–920.

Segal, David, "The Iran-Iraq War: A Military Analysis," *Foreign Affairs*, Summer 1988, pp. 946–963.

Sella, Amon, *Soviet Political and Military Conduct in the Middle East*, London, Macmillan, 1981.

Senger, F.M. von, and Etterlin, *Tanks of the World 1983*, Annapolis, Md., Nautical & Aviation Publishing Co., 1983.

Sick, Gary G., *All Fall Down: America's Tragic Encounter with Iran*, New York, Random House, 1985.

———, and Alvin A. Rubinstein, ed., *The Great Game: Rivalry in the Persian Gulf and South Asia*, New York, Praeger, 1983.

———, "Iran's Quest for Superpower Status," *Foreign Affairs*, vol. 65, no. 4, Spring 1987, pp. 697–715.

Sigler, John H., "The Iran-Iraq Conflict: The Tragedy of Limited Conventional War," *International Journal*, vol. 41, Spring 1986, pp. 424–456.

Snyder, Jed C., and Samuel F. Wells, Jr., eds., *Limiting Nuclear Proliferation*, Cambridge, Mass., Ballinger Publishing Co., 1985.

———, *Defending the Fringe: NATO, the Mediterranean, and the Persian Gulf*, Boulder, Westview, 1987.

"Special Report, Middle East Aerospace: Saudi Arabia," *Aviation Week and Space Technology*, May 23, 1983.

Staudenmaier, William O., "Military Policy and Strategy in the Gulf War," *Parameters: The Journal of the Army War College*, June 12, 1982.

Steinberg, Gerald M., "Indigenous Arms Industries and Dependence: The Case of Israel," *Defense Analysis*, vol. 2, no. 4, December 1986, pp. 291–305.

Stempel, John D. *Inside the Iranian Revolution*, Bloomington, Indiana University Press, 1981.

Stewert, Richard A., "Soviet Military Intervention in Iran, 1920–46," *Parameters, Journal of the U.S. Army War College*, 11, no. 4, 1981, pp. 24–34.

SIPRI, *World Armaments and Disarmaments; SIPRI Yearbook 1985*, London, Taylor & Francis, 1985.

Stockholm International Peace Research Institute, *Tactical Nuclear Weapons: European Perspectives*, New York, Crane, Russak & Co., 1978.

———, *World Armaments and Disarmaments: SIPRI Yearbook*, various years (computer printout for 1982), London, Taylor & Francis, Ltd.

———, *The Problem of Chemical and Biological Warfare: A Study of the Historical, Technical, Military, Legal, and Political Aspects of CBW and Possible Disarmament Measures*, Stockholm, Almquist and Wiksell, 1975.

Stookey, Robert W., *The Arabian Peninsula: Zone of Ferment,* Stanford, Hoover Institution, 1984 .

Subramanian, Ram Rajan, "Nuclear Proliferation in South Asia," Canberra Paper on Strategy and Defense, no. 26, Australian National University, 1982.

Sullivan, William H., "Iran: The Road Not Taken," *Foreign Policy,* no. 40 (Fall 1980), 175–187.

————, *Mission to Iran,* London, W. W. Norton, 1981.

————, "A Survey of Saudi Arabia," *Economist,* February 13, 1982.

Sweetman, Bill, "New Soviet Combat Aircraft," *International Defense Review,* 1/1984, pp. 35–38.

Szaz, Z. Michael, ed., *The Impact of the Iranian Events upon Persian Gulf and U.S. Security,* Washington, D.C., American Foreign Policy Institute, 1979.

Szuprowicz, Bohdan O., *How to Avoid Strategic Materials Shortages,* New York, John Wiley, 1981.

Tahir-Kheli, Sharin, *U.S. Strategic Interests in Southwest Asia,* New York, Praeger, 1982.

Tahir-Kheli, Sharin, and Shaheen Ayubi, *The Iran-Iraq War: New Weapons, Old Conflicts,* New York, Praeger, 1983.

Tahir-Kheli, Sharin, and William O. Staudenmaier, "The Saudi-Pakistani Military Relationship: Implications for U.S. Policy," *Orbis,* Spring 1982, pp. 155–171.

Taylor, Alan, *The Arab Balance of Power,* Syracuse, N.Y., Syracuse University Press, 1982.

Thompson, W. Scott, "The Persian Gulf and the Correlation of Forces," *International Security,* Summer 1982, pp. 157–180.

Tillman, Seth, *The United States in the Middle East,* Bloomington, Indiana University Press, 1982.

Truver, Scott C., "Mines of August: An International Whodunit," *Proceedings of the U.S. Naval Institute,* May 1985, vol. III, 5/1987, pp. 94–118.

U.S. Arms Control and Disarmament Agency, *World Military Expenditures and Arms Transfers,* various editions, Washington, D.C., 1980.

U.S. Central Intelligence Agency, *Economic and Energy Indicators,* DOI, GIEEI, Washington, D.C., Government Printing Office, various years.

————, *Handbook of Economic Statistics,* various editions.

————, *International Energy Situation: Outlook to 1985,* 041–015-00084-5, Washington, D.C., Government Printing Office, 1977.

————, *International Energy Statistical Review,* NFAC, GI-IESR, Washington, D.C., Government Printing Office, various years.

————, *USSR Energy Atlas,* Washington, D.C., CIA, 1985.

————, *World Factbook,* Washington, D.C., Government Printing Office, various years.

U.S. Congress, House of Representatives, Committee on Appropriations, *Foreign Assistance and Related Programs Appropriations for 1982. Part 7: Proposed Airborne Warning and Control Systems (AWACS), F–15 Enhancement Equipment, and Sidewinder AIM 9L Missiles Sales to Saudi Arabia,* 97th Cong., 1st Sess., Hearings.

U.S. Congress, House of Representatives, Committee on Armed Services, *U.S.*

Military Forces to Protect "Reflagged" Kuwaiti Oil Tankers, Hearings, June 5, 11, and 16, 1987.

U.S. Congress, House of Representatives, Committee on Foreign Affairs, *Activities of the U.S. Corps of Engineers in Saudi Arabia,* 96th Cong., 1st Sess., 1979.

———, *Proposed Arms Sales for Countries in the Middle East,* 96th Cong., 1st Sess., 1979.

———, *Proposed Arms Transfers to the Yemen Arab Republic,* 96th Cong., 1st Sess., 1979.

———, *Saudi Arabia and the United States,* Congressional Research Service Report, 97th Cong., 1st Sess., 1981.

———, *Saudi Arabia and the United States: The New Context in an Evolving "Special Relationship,"* no. 81-494 0, Washington, D.C., Government Printing Office, 1981.

———, *U.S. Interests in, and Policies Toward, the Persian Gulf, 1980,* No. 68-1840, Washington, D.C., Congressional Printing Office, 1980.

———, *U.S. Security Interests in the Persian Gulf,* No. 73-354-0, Washington, D.C., Government Printing Office, 1981.

U.S. Congress, House of Representatives, Committee on Foreign Affairs and Joint Economic Committee, *U.S. Policy Toward the Persian Gulf,* 97th Cong., 1st Sess., 1975.

U.S. Congress, Senate, Committee on Armed Services, *Military and Technical Implications of the Proposed Sale of Air Defense Enhancements to Saudi Arabia. Report of the Hearings on the Military and Technical Implications of the Proposed Sale of Air Defense Enhancements to Saudi Arabia, Based upon Hearings Held Before the Committee in Accordance with Its Responsibilities Under Rule XXV (C) of the Standing Rules of the Senate,* 97th Cong., 1st Sess.

U.S. Congress, Senate, Committee on Energy and Natural Resources, *Geopolitics of Oil,* no. 96-119, Washington, D.C., Government Printing Office, 1980.

U.S. Congress, Senate, Committee on Foreign Relations, *Arms Sales Package to Saudi Arabia—Part 2,* 97th Cong., 1st Sess., 1981.

———, *Persian Gulf Situation,* 97th Cong., 1st Sess., 1981.

———, *The Proposed AWACS/F-15 Enhancement Sale to Saudi Arabia,* 97th Cong., 1st Sess., Staff Report, 1981.

———, *Saudi Arabia,* A Report by Senator Mike Mansfield, 94th Cong., 1st Sess., October 1975.

———, *U.S. Arms Sales Policy,* 94th Cong., 2nd Sess., 1976.

———, *War in the Gulf,* 98th Cong., 2nd Sess., Staff Report, 1984.

———, *War in the Persian Gulf, The U.S. Takes Sides,* Staff Report, November 1987.

U.S. Defense Security Assistance Agency, *Foreign Military Sales, Foreign Military Construction Sales and Military Assistance Facts,* Washington, D.C., Government Printing Office, various years.

U.S. Department of Defense, *Soviet Military Power,* Washington, D.C., Government Printing Office, various years.

————, *Foreign Military Sales, Foreign Military Construction Sales and Military Assistance Facts*, September 1984.

————, *Saudi Arms Sale Questions and Answers*, February 24, 1986.

U.S. Department of Energy, *Secretary of Energy Annual Report to the Congress*, DOE-S-0010(84), September 1984.

————, *Energy Projections to the Year 2000*, DOE/PE-0029/2, October 1983.

————, *Annual Reports to Congress*, Washington, D.C., Government Printing Office, various editions.

————, *Petroleum Supply Monthly*, various editions.

————, *World Energy Outlook Through 2000*, April 1985.

U.S. Energy Information Administration, *International Energy Annual*, Washington, D.C., DOE/EIA-02 (84).

————, *Impacts of World Oil Market Shocks on the U.S. Economy*, DOE/EIA-0411, July 1983.

————, *Monthly Energy Review*, Washington, D.C., Government Printing Office, various editions.

————, *International Energy Annual*, Washington, D.C., Government Printing Office, various editions.

U.S. Department of Energy, International Affairs, *International Energy Indicators*, DoE/IA-0010, Washington, D.C., Government Printing Office, various years.

U.S. Library of Congress, Congressional Research Service, Foreign Affairs and National Defense Division, *Western Vulnerability to a Disruption of Persian Gulf Oil Supplies: U.S. Interests and Options*, 1983.

U.S. News and World Report, various editions.

Van Hollen, Christopher, "Don't Engulf the Gulf," *Foreign Affairs*, Summer 1981, pp. 1064–1078.

Volman, Daniel, "Commanding the Center," *MERIP Reports*, XIV, 6/7 (July–September 1984), pp. 49–50.

Wall Street Journal, various editions.

Waltz, Kenneth N., "A Strategy for the Rapid Deployment Force," *International Security*, Spring 1981, pp. 49–73.

War Data, Special editions of the "Born in Battle" series, Jerusalem, Eshel-Dramit.

Washington Post, various editions.

Washington Times, various editions.

Weinburger, Caspar W., *A Report to Congress on Security Arrangements in the Persian Gulf*, Washington, D.C., Office of the Secretary of Defense, June 15, 1987.

Weissman, Steve, and Herbert Krosney, *The Islamic Bomb*, New York, Times Books, 1981.

Wenger, Martha, "The Central Command: Getting to the War on Time," *MERIP Reports*, XIV, 9 (Fall 1984), pp. 456–464.

Whelan, John, ed., *Saudi Arabia*, London, MEED, 1981.

White, B.T., *Wheeled Armoured Fighting Vehicles in Service*, Poole, Dorset, Blandford Press, 1983.

Wiley, Marshall W., "American Security Concerns in the Gulf," *Orbis*, XXVIII, 3 (Fall 1984), pp. 456–464.

Wittam, George H., "Political and Military Background to France's Intervention Capability," McLean, Va., National Institute for Public Policy, June 1982.

Wohlstetter, Albert, "Meeting the Threat in the Persian Gulf," *Survey*, XXV, 2 (Spring 1980), pp. 128–188.

Wolfe, Ronald G., ed., *The United States, Arabia, and the Gulf*, Washington, D.C., Georgetown University Center for Contemporary Arab Studies, 1980.

World of Information, *Middle East Review*, London, various years.

World Industry Information Service, *Energy Decade: A Statistical and Graphic Chronicle*, San Diego, Calif., 1982.

Wright, Robin, "A Reporter at Large (Iran)," *The New Yorker*, September 5, 1988, pp. 32–72.

Yodfat, Aryeh Y., *The Soviet Union and the Arabian Peninsula: Soviet Policy Towards the Persian Gulf and Arabia*, New York, St. Martin's, 1983.

Zabih, Sepehr, *The Iranian Military in Revolution and War*, London, Routledge, 1988.

————, *The Left in Contemporary Iran*, Stanford, Hoover Institution Press, 1986.

Zahri, Mehdi Massoud, *The Origins and Causes of the Iranian-Iraqi War*, Ann Arbor, University Microfilms International, 1984.

Zaloga, Steven, "Ballistic Missiles in the Third World," *International Defense Review*, 11/1988, pp. 1423–1437.

Zelniker, Shimshon, *The Superpowers and the Horn of Africa*, Center for Strategic Studies, Tel Aviv University, Paper no. 18, September 1982.

Zuhair, Ahmed Hafi, *Economic and Social Developments in Qatar*, London, F. Pinter, 1983.

Index

713 - 410/7 hrs
348 - 1358 Bucks Club / Bryan Elkins